Essay
Writing Skills
with
Readings

Sixth Canadian Edition

John Langan
Atlantic Cape Community College

Sharon Winstanley
Seneca College

Nancy Rishor
Sir Sandford Fleming College

Fred Wood
Sir Sandford Fleming College

McGraw-Hill
Ryerson
Connect. Learn. Succeed.

The McGraw·Hill Companies

McGraw-Hill Ryerson
Connect. Learn. Succeed.

Essay Writing Skills with Readings
Sixth Canadian Edition

Copyright © 2011, 2008, 2005, 2003, 2000, 1996 by McGraw-Hill Ryerson Limited, a Subsidiary of The McGraw-Hill Companies. Copyright © 2008, 2005, 2001, 1997, 1993 by The McGraw-Hill Companies. All rights reserved. No part of this publication may be reproduced or transmitted in any form or by any means, or stored in a data base or retrieval system, without the prior written permission of McGraw-Hill Ryerson Limited, or in the case of photocopying or other reprographic copying, a licence from The Canadian Copyright Licensing Agency (Access Copyright). For an Access Copyright licence, visit www.accesscopyright.ca or call toll-free to 1-800-893-5777.

ISBN-13: 978-0-07-000529-7
ISBN-10: 0-07-000529-X

1 2 3 4 5 6 7 8 9 10 TCP 1 9 8 7 6 5 4 3 2 1

Printed and bound in Canada

Care has been taken to trace ownership of copyright material contained in this text; however, the publisher will welcome any information that enables it to rectify any reference or credit for subsequent editions.

Vice-President and Editor-in-Chief: *Joanna Cotton*
Publisher: *Cara Yarzab*
Sponsoring Editor: *Karen Krahn*
Marketing Manager: *Margaret Janzen*
Developmental Editors: *Sara Braithwaite, Jennifer Cressman*
Editorial Associate: *Marina Seguin*
Manager, Editorial Services: *Margaret Henderson*
Supervising Editor: *Cathy Biribauer*
Copy Editor: *Gillian Scobie*
Proofreader: *Colleen Ste. Marie*
Production Coordinator: *Lena Keating*
Inside Design: *Peter Papayanakis*
Composition: *Laserwords Private Limited*
Cover Design: *Peter Papayanakis*
Cover Photo: *M Reel/Shutterstock*
Printer: *Transcontinental Printing Group*

Library and Archives Canada Cataloguing in Publication Data
Essay writing skills with readings/John Langan . . . [et al.]. — 6th Canadian ed.

Includes index.
Previous Canadian eds. written under title: College writing skills with readings / John Langan, Sharon Winstanley
ISBN 978-0-07-000529-7

1. English language—Rhetoric—Textbooks. 2. Essay—Authorship—Textbooks.
3. Report writing—Textbooks. 4. English language—Grammar—Textbooks. 5. College readers.
I. Langan, John, 1942- . College writing skills with readings.

PE1408.L27 2011   808'.0427   C2010-904855-5

Table of Contents

PART 2   PATTERNS OF ESSAY DEVELOPMENT

ADDITIONAL CHAPTERS ONLINE

Editing Tests

ESL Pointers

Manuscript Form

Readings Listed by Rhetorical Mode

Narration

Shame	*Dick Gregory*
Headlands	*Jonathan Bennett*
Lamb to the Slaughter	*Roald Dahl*

Description

What Is Poverty?	*Jo Goodwin Parker*
Headlands	*Jonathan Bennett*
Lamb to the Slaughter	*Roald Dahl*

Example

Here's to Your Health	*Joan Dunayer*
The Nobel Lecture	*Kofi Annan*
Just a Little Drop of Water	*Eve Tulbert*

Process

How to Make It in College, Now That You're Here	*Brian O'Keeney*
Lamb to the Slaughter	*Roald Dahl*
Just a Little Drop of Water	*Eve Tulbert*

Cause and Effect

Why Are Students Turned Off?	*Casey Banas*
Shame	*Dick Gregory*
The Nobel Lecture	*Kofi Annan*
Just a Little Drop of Water	*Eve Tulbert*

Comparison or Contrast

The Story of Mouseland	*As Told by Tommy Douglas in 1944*
Aboriginal Hot and Heavy	*Drew Hayden Taylor*

Definition

Shame	*Dick Gregory*
What Is Poverty?	*Jo Goodwin Parker*
Just a Little Drop of Water	*Eve Tulbert*

Division and Classification

How to Make It in College, Now that You're Here	*Brian O'Keeney*
Aboriginal Hot and Heavy	*Drew Hayden Taylor*

Argumentation

Why Are Students Turned Off?	*Casey Banas*
Here's to Your Health	*Joan Dunayer*
My Body Is My Own Business	*Naheed Mustafa*
What Is Poverty?	*Jo Goodwin Parker*
The Nobel Lecture	*Kofi Annan*
Just a Little Drop of Water	*Eve Tulbert*
Aboriginal Hot and Heavy	*Drew Hayden Taylor*

Permissions

Gregory, Dick, "Shame." Copyright 1964 by Dick Gregory Enterprises, Inc., from *Nigger: An Autobiography by Dick Gregory*. Used by permission of Dutton, a division of Putnam Group (USA) Inc.

Mustafa, Naheed, "My Body Is My Own Business." From *The Globe and Mail*, June 29, 1993 (A-26). Reprinted with permission of the author.

Dahl, Roald, "Lamb to the Slaughter." Taken from his book *Someone Like You* published by Penguin Books.

Anan, Kofi, The Nobel Peace Prize 2001, Nobel Lecture, Oslo, December 10, 2001. Courtesy of the United Nations and the Nobel Foundation.

Parker, Jo Goodwin, "What Is Poverty?" From *America's Other Children: Public Schools Outside Suburbs*, edited by George Henderson. Published 1971 by the University of Oklahoma Press.

Banas, Casey, "Why Are Students Turned Off?" From *The Chicago Tribune*, August 5, 1979. Copyright © 1979 by *The Chicago Tribune*. Used with permission.

Bennett, Jonathan, "Headlands." This piece also appeared in the book *AWOL: Tales for Travel Inspired Minds* by Jennifer Barclay and Amy Logan. Vintage Canada, © 2003. Reprinted with permission of the author.

Tulbert, Eve, "Just a Little Drop of Water." Reprinted with permission of the author.

Douglas, Tommy, "The Story of Mouseland," as told by Tommy Douglas. Courtesy of the Saskatchewan New Democratic Party.

Taylor, Drew Hayden, "Aboriginal Hot and Heavy." Reprinted with permission of the author.

Dunayer, Joan, "Here's To Your Health." Reprinted by permission of Townsend Press.

O'Keeney, Brian, "How to Make It in College, Now that You're Here." Reprinted by permission.

Preface

This sixth edition of *Essay Writing Skills with Readings* represents not only a revision of the fifth edition, but a significant "re-vision" and expansion of this book's mission and purview. While maintaining our fundamental core values of the four bases of effective writing (unity, support, coherence, and sentence skills), we have re-envisioned and re-created much of the book with an eye to today's first-year college and university students. We have listened to faculty and students from across Canada, and responded to their requests for more intensive information on creating effective thesis statements, for more detailed directive material to help students generate better support for their essays, for less restrictive approaches to essay length, and for even greater attention to the research process and styles of documentation. In re-envisioning *Essay Writing Skills with Readings,* we place increased emphasis on student writers' continuous attention to purpose and audience, on helping students with critical self-awareness, and on assisting them to master research skills through regular practice.

How This Book Is Organized

Part 1: Essay Writing, in a newly sequenced series of chapters, focuses first on the writing process itself and on the four bases of writing. **Part 2: Patterns of Essay Development** brings a new approach to the different rhetorical modes, taking students step by step through each mode, and showing how modes work together within an essay. **Part 3: Special Skills and Research** guides students through summary writing, through conducting effective research, and through writing and documenting a research paper. This section contains a new chapter presenting examples of both an MLA and an APA research essay with annotations. **Part 4: Handbook of Sentence Skills** serves as a concise and easy-to-use handbook, focusing specifically on the fourth base of the writing process. **Part 5: Reading for Writing** provides a variety of engaging, mainly contemporary readings that represent each of the rhetorical modes presented in Part 2. Accompanying each reading are questions and activities that reinforce and enhance, for students, the four bases of writing.

What's New in the Sixth Canadian Edition?

The sixth Canadian edition of *Essay Writing Skills with Readings* offers a significant range and number of changes designed with care to speak to the specific requirements of Canadian college and university students today. In response to extensive reviewer feedback, the following are the highlights of what is new in this edition:

- Part 1 has been redesigned and re-sequenced to take students through the writing process, from prewriting through proofreading, in a clear, concise, and direct fashion.

- Parts 1, 2, and 3, with the use of checklists and activities at each stage of the writing process, help students to evaluate their own progress and choices as they work on their essays.

- Beginning in Part 1, the PAT formula appears for the first time, and is carried through Parts 2 and 3. Students use a simple acronym (Purpose, Audience, Thesis) to help them clarify choices at each stage of the writing process.

- In this edition, new and highly detailed pedagogy on creating effective thesis statements appears for the first time. This is reinforced, chapter by chapter, in Part 2, for each pattern of development.

- Additionally, new emphasis is placed on the types and quality of support required by various types of essay; this new emphasis is also reinforced, chapter by chapter, in Part 2.

- This sixth edition presents new student-essay exemplars in Parts 1, 2, and 3 which cover a wide range of more mature, less personal topics, such as Canadian media history and ecological concerns. Many essays are based on prize-winning student essays from McGraw-Hill's writing contest.

- Modes are now shown as predominantly used in combination in all student essay models. Both pedagogy and exemplars throughout Parts 1 through 3 sustain this point.

- Model essays and pedagogy both now emphasize variability of essay length, depending on the number of supporting points for the thesis.

- Each chapter in Part 2 now presents two levels of student model essay exemplars: one "basic model" and one longer, more advanced essay with research citations.

- Parts 1, 2, and 3 now address the student reader directly with helpful, prescriptive pedagogy.

- Coverage of plagiarism has been updated and expanded to include listings of what constitutes plagiarism and how to avoid it.

- Research and its importance are given even more emphasis and more consistent coverage throughout this edition, beginning in Part 1, continuing with essay examples showing research citation in each chapter of Part 2, constituting most of Part 3, and featured in assignments in Part 5. Research is an essential skill at the postsecondary level, and this edition treats it as such. Chapters 18 and 19 have been revised to present research skills, the most current documentation information, and writing a research essay in the clearest, easiest-to-follow fashion. New to this edition, Chapter 20 presents two full examples of annotated research essays in both MLA and APA styles.

- OLC logos at the end of the chapters alert students and instructors to expanded coverage of topics, activities, and further assignments available online.

Part 1: Essay Writing

- Part 1 emphasizes the essential nature of knowing purpose and audience from Chapter 1's pedagogy and introduction of the PAT formula onward.

- Chapter sequence in Part 1 is reorganized and revised, with Chapter 5 now devoted to revision.

- Beginning with Part 1, essay length is now seen and exemplified as variable, with the number of body paragraphs dependent on supporting points and requirements of assignment.

- Chapter 1 is completely revised to straightforwardly address student audiences' questions about writing; i.e., "Who is your audience?" and "What is your point?"

- Chapter 2 has been revised to present prewriting first, followed by creating the thesis statement.

- Chapter 2 now presents significantly increased content on generating thesis statements, including thesis development questions, using the PAT formula, thesis try-outs and directional questions, revising the thesis, and writing thesis-planning sentences. Also new to this edition, in keeping with its emphasis on student self-evaluation, are student-focused pedagogy and activities on evaluating thesis statements.

- Chapter 3 has been revised to follow from developing the thesis to developing the outline and creating support. New content on outlining appears in this chapter.

- In Chapter 3, an important addition to this edition appears: major attention is given to support and supporting details. Forms of support are presented and analyzed, and students are presented with activities and checklists that help them to learn to critically evaluate and improve their choices of supporting material for various types of essays.

- Additionally, students and instructors will find new pedagogy and activities on developing topic sentences from supporting points.

- This edition's Chapter 4 now begins with drafting, then focuses on revising for coherence, with new content and new activities, to underline the importance of revising in the writing process.

- As part of revising, there is new material on parallel structure as a way of creating coherence.

- Chapter 4's sections on introductions and conclusions have been dramatically rewritten, relating approaches to and methods for openings and closings to the PAT formula, and inculcating the idea that there is no one "magic formula" but, rather, a set of variables dependent on purpose, audience, and essay content.

- New specialized content on creating titles, relative to an essay's mode, appears here for the first time.

- Chapter 5 continues to reinforce the essentiality of revising by shadowing a student's progress as he revises, then presenting detailed new revision checklists focused on three of the four bases for effective writing. Here again, the purpose is to continue to stress self-evaluation as part of the student-writer's skill-set.

- Along with the checklists come new student exemplars and continued reminders of the PAT formula.

- Finally, chapter 6 is now focused on editing and proofreading, as these follow naturally from revising.
- Many of the new exemplars demonstrate the use of research, and always present more mature subject-matter and fresh, relevant content.

Part 2: Patterns of Essay Development

- Each chapter within Part 2 now offers one student exemplar at a normative entry level, and one (usually longer) exemplar at a higher level (often including some research MLA and APA style—to show the range of first-year student essays).
- Nearly every chapter presents a new student essay model.
- Topics of exemplar models cover a wide range of interests, from the media to ecological and scientific concerns.
- Each chapter now contains mode-specific questions about exemplar essays. These questions also reinforce consistent use of multiple modes within an essay.
- For the first time, there is, in chapter 13, a student model of a literature-based essay in the comparison-contrast mode. This represents a significant addition and is supported by the addition of two new fiction selections in Part 5.
- Significantly, each chapter now assists students with new sections of mode-specific pedagogy that walk them through the stages of writing in that mode: (1) Writing a Thesis Statement, (2) What Is Your Purpose and Who Is Your Audience?, (3) What Is Your Point of View?, and (4) How Will You Support Your . . . . Essay?
- As well, each mode's new pedagogy describes how other modes are used as subsidiaries within essays.
- Chapters continue this edition's attention to the importance of research and its documentation with both the new exemplars and special explanatory notes.

Part 3: Special Skills and Research

- Part 3 now offers a most detailed and careful step-by-step approach to conducting and documenting research and writing a research essay, ideal guidance for first-year students.
- All research and documentation information is up-to-date, based on MLA 7 and APA 6.
- This part of the book follows through on the entire text's emphasis on research as essential to postsecondary education.
- Chapter 17 contains new material on cue words and phrases appropriate for summaries.
- Chapter 18 is devoted entirely to research skills, and presents new content on research notes.
- New and revised "Research Tip" boxes offer timely and concise information on research-related topics.

- In chapter 18, new, up-to-date information on plagiarism appears: what precisely constitutes plagiarism, and how to avoid plagiarizing.
- Chapter 19 is now "Writing and Documenting a Research Paper."
- Chapter 19's content has been revised and re-sequenced to show the process of creating the paper, with fresh material on writing a first draft and use of various modes as related to research papers.
- This chapter offers significant and useful new material on quotation and paraphrasing, the "when, why, and how," showing examples of MLA and APA style for each example.
- Methods of integrating source material, with examples using both MLA and APA styles, are given greater importance in this edition.
- Comprehensive and current information on MLA 7 for in-text citation and Works Cited pages is presented.
- Coverage of APA style is greatly increased, based on APA 6, including material on the DOI system for identifying digital objects.
- This edition offers most extensive listings of examples for MLA and APA documentation models.
- Chapter 20, "The Model Research Paper: MLA and APA Styles," is a completely new chapter covering page format for MLA and APA, and presenting complete annotated examples of an MLA and an APA research essay.

Part 4: Handbook of Sentence Skills

All examples in the Handbook of Sentence Skills have been updated, and many chapters now contain a pre- and post-test so students can assess their knowledge and determine what they need more practice with.

Part 5: Readings for Writing

Six new readings appear in this edition, so half the selections are fresh; they range from the contemporary to the classical in prose style, and two literary pieces are now represented. All readings, and especially the new selections, represent striking uses of the rhetorical modes to reinforce and extend the book's pedagogy. Part 5 again includes new writing assignments; these extend this new edition's points of emphasis by requiring third-person voice and, frequently, research.

Supplements and Services

Online Learning Centre: The OLC features learning, quizzing, and study tools as well as a passcode-protected Instructor's Resource Centre with downloadable supplements, including the complete Instructor's Manual and Microsoft® PowerPoint® slides. Additional textbook chapters on Editing Tests, ESL Pointers, and Manuscript Form are also available through the Online Learning Centre at **www.mcgrawhill.ca/olc/langan.**

- **Instructor's Manual:** Prepared by the author, Sharon Winstanley, Seneca College, the Instructor's Manual contains a wealth of teaching resources, including hints and tips for approaching the course, a model syllabus, and supplementary activities and tests.
- **Microsoft® PowerPoint® slides:** These slides offer instructional support in the classroom and provide a visual complement to lectures. These slides are comprehensive and can be adapted to meet the needs of any course.

Connect Catalyst: Access to Connect Catalyst is available to accompany each new copy of *Essay Writing Skills with Readings*. Available at **www.mcgrawhillcatalyst.ca**, Connect Catalyst offers course management and peer review tools, interactive tutorials, diagnostic tests, and thousands of electronic grammar exercises and activities.

iLearning Sales Specialist: Your **Integrated Learning Sales Specialist** is a McGraw-Hill Ryerson representative who has the experience, product knowledge, training, and support to help you assess and integrate any of the products, technology, and services listed below into your course for optimum teaching and learning performance. Whether helping your students to improve their grades or putting your entire course online, your *i*Learning Sales Specialist is there to help you do it. Contact your *i*Learning Sales Specialist today to learn how to maximize all of McGraw-Hill Ryerson's resources.

iServices Program: At McGraw-Hill Ryerson, we take great pride in developing high-quality learning resources while working hard to provide you with the tools necessary to utilize them. We want to help bring your teaching to life, and we do this by integrating technology, events, conferences, training, and other services. We call it *i*Services. For more information, visit **www.mcgrawhill.ca/olc/iservices**.

National Teaching and Learning Conference Series: The educational environment has changed tremendously in recent years and McGraw-Hill Ryerson continues to be committed to helping you acquire the skills you need to succeed in this new milieu. Our innovative National Teaching and Learning Conference Series brings faculty together from across Canada with 3M Teaching Excellence award winners to share teaching and learning best practices in a collaborative and stimulating environment. Preconference workshops on general topics, such as teaching large classes and technology integration, are also offered. We will also work with you at your own institution to customize workshops that best suit the needs of the faculty at your institution.

Acknowledgments

As with each edition, I am grateful for the continuing enthusiasm, support, and dedication of the editors at McGraw-Hill Ryerson. Each editor's desire for excellence is an inspiration, and each one's expertise teaches me invaluable lessons. They are "the voices at the other end of the line" who reassure me and offer fresh perspectives on familiar tasks. I would like to thank Karen Krahn, humanities sponsoring editor, for her help with this edition, and I am especially grateful to Sara Braithwaite, developmental editor extraordinaire, for her consistent helpfulness and support. I would also wish to thank Cathy Biribauer, supervising editor, and Gillian Scobie and Colleen Ste. Marie for their careful handling of the copy editing and proofreading, respectively.

My thanks always go to my students at Seneca@York. They inspire me, delight me, amuse me, and make me happy to teach them.

My gratitude as well goes to the students who allowed me to use their pieces as exemplars of various rhetorical modes: Anna Baltazar, Iman Bukhari, Hilary Dumas, Ryan Dyer, Carlton Ellis, Nicholas Hinsberger, Jumoke Isekeije, Joshua Jurcich, Hayden Kee, Dana Kinnaird, Catherine O'Rourke, L.G. Smith, Tracy Stewart.

Finally, I would like to thank the reviewers who provided helpful ideas and feedback for the sixth Canadian edition:

Janet Allwork, Douglas College
Trevor Arkell, Humber College
Nava Bobby, Memorial University
Lisette Bolly, Seneca College
Marilyn Boyle-Taylor, Seneca College at York
Bill Bunn, Mount Royal University
Tim Callin, Camosun College
Susan Daykin, Thompson Rivers University
Elizabeth Gooding, Kwantlen Polytechnic University
Annika Hannon, George Brown College
Dana Hansen, Humber College
Debbie Hlady, Camosun College
Karen Inglis, Kwantlen Polytechnic University
Peter Laurie, Sir Sandford Fleming College
Shannon MacRae, Niagara College
Alexis Muirhead, Mohawk College
Diana Patterson, Mount Royal University
Emilia Popova, Seneca College
Katrine Raymond, Mohawk College
Nancy Rishor, Sir Sandford Fleming College
Rhonda Sandberg, George Brown College
Janice Sargant, Algonquin College
Bronwen Welch, Camosun College
Angela Woollam, Algonquin College

SHARON WINSTANLEY
SENECA COLLEGE

I would like to thank Lisa Rahn, former humanities sponsoring editor at McGraw-Hill Ryerson, for giving me the opportunity to revise the Handbook of Sentence Skills, and Sara Braithwaite, developmental editor, for her keen attention to detail and positive encouragement throughout the process. My sincere thanks go out to my students at Fleming College who motivate me to bring fresh ideas and fun activities to the classroom. I am also grateful for my family: my husband Niklas Rishor for his ongoing support during my project, and my children, Connor and Charlotte, for their energy, inspiration, and good humour. I would finally like to thank the reviewers for their time and care in providing useful feedback for the sixth Canadian edition.

NANCY RISHOR
FLEMING COLLEGE

I would like to acknowledge and express my appreciation for both the opportunity and the support provided by Sara Braithwaite of McGraw-Hill Ryerson. I am indebted for her assistance, direction, and advice. I'd also like to acknowledge both my Trent University and Fleming College students for their insightful questions, comments, and active participation.

FRED WOOD
FLEMING COLLEGE

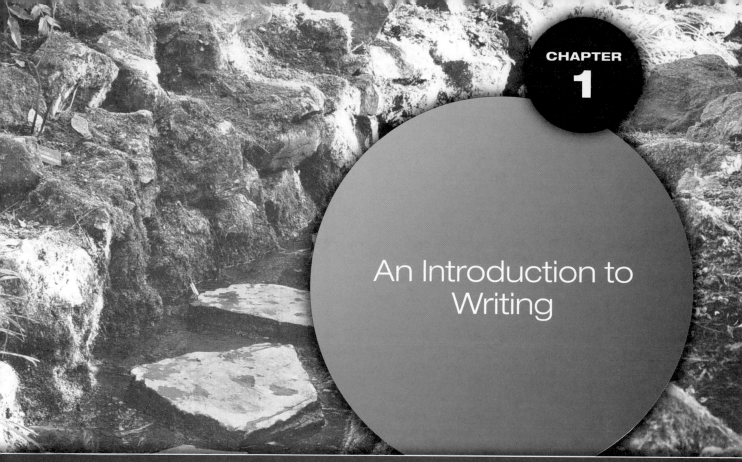

An Introduction to Writing

LEARNING OUTCOMES

Work through this chapter carefully so that you

- develop audience awareness and understand its impact on writing;

- consider the purposes for each writing project;

- can define *tone* as it relates to purpose and audience;

- can explain the importance, in essay writing, of the thesis;

- know the meaning of *voice* and how readers perceive different voices;

- identify the importance of essay writing;

- learn the structure and parts of the essay.

Canadian college and university students like you ask questions that shape each new edition of this book. You ask why writing is essential to career success. Sometimes you ask why writing seems so difficult. Often you ask how writing first-year essays relates to future career and academic writing. And very frequently you ask for workable guidelines for research.

This sixth Canadian edition of *Essay Writing Skills with Readings* can provide you with practical answers for your questions as it guides you, step by step, through a clear, logical approach to the writing process. When you work with this book, you will gain an understanding of why you take each step and you will learn to evaluate your progress as you go along. You will learn to adapt your essays to a variety of writing situations. As you do so, you will learn and practise solid research skills, essential in many future tasks.

Part 1 begins by asking you some questions. The answers to those questions take you directly into the basic principles that will help you write with greater confidence and clarity.

WHY DO YOU WRITE?

Each time you write, you write for a reason. For even the shortest casual message, you have a purpose that prompts you to communicate in text.

• • • • ACTIVITY 1

QUESTIONS

- What is the writer's purpose here? *texting*
- Could he or she have more than one purpose, and if so, what are they? *2 ; what*
- Which part(s) of the message display the writer's purpose(s)? *second one.*

People tend to plunge directly into writing without consciously thinking about their purpose. Then they wonder why what they have written seems so muddled or why the person reading it does not understand what they mean or what they want.

• • • • ACTIVITY 2

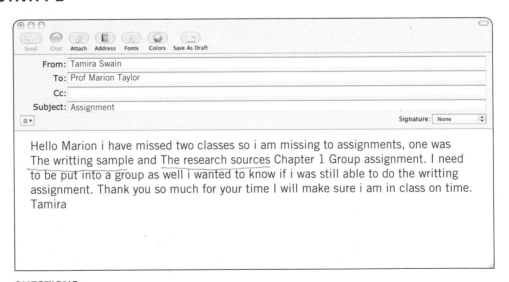

From: Tamira Swain
To: Prof Marion Taylor
Cc:
Subject: Assignment

Hello Marion i have missed two classes so i am missing to assignments, one was The writting sample and The research sources Chapter 1 Group assignment. I need to be put into a group as well i wanted to know if i was still able to do the writting assignment. Thank you so much for your time I will make sure i am in class on time. Tamira

QUESTIONS

- What is the writer's purpose in writing this email? *ask about her assignment*
- Is there one purpose or more than one? If there are other purposes, what are they?

- Is one of the purposes more important than the others? *Not really.*
- How could the writer express any of her purposes more clearly? *write it more specificly*
- How would you respond to this message if you were Tamira's instructor?

1 ....
2 ....

You are now ready to learn more about general and specific purposes for writing on page 9. Clarifying your purpose will always help you to choose what to write, how to structure your ideas, and keep you on track as you write.

WHO ARE YOU WRITING FOR?

Unless you are writing a private journal entry, you are writing for someone else: an audience. In fact, even your journal is a conversation with yourself—you are your audience. In college and university, you must learn to "profile" or analyze specific reading audiences every time you write.

• • • • • ACTIVITY

hey pete whatsup? i know im not doing the best in ur class. You havent seen me in awhile but id just like to say i really think ur a great professor anyway. Can i get the last 4 assignment sheets from u so i can hand them in before exams next week? I'll try to come by ur office sometime and thanks.

Tony

QUESTIONS

- Who is Tony's audience? *Professor*
- How would Pete, as an instructor, feel about Tony, based on the note here? *too friendly*
- What specific aspects of the message would cause Pete to feel this way? *used words too casual.*
- What is Tony's purpose here? How likely is he to achieve his goal? Why, specifically? *get assignments ahead.*
- What might Pete, as Tony's instructor, want from Tony in this situation? Why? *tell him write it more polite way.*
- How is Pete likely to respond to Tony when they meet in person? Why? *Professional way.*
- How would you describe the tone of this note? Why?
- How would you rewrite Tony's message? Explain the changes you would make, and how these relate to Pete's needs and interests.

Count the number of times *I* (or *i*) appears in Tony's note. Based on your total, who does the note seem to focus on? Does it take into account Pete's situation as an instructor hearing from an absentee student? No. In fact, Tony's voice, expressed constantly through all those *i*'s, hammers away at the reader, spotlighting Tony as the focus of his own writing. Each writer has a *voice,* often expressed in pronouns such as *I* and *we.* When you write about a topic in college and university, put your emphasis on your topic, not on your relationship with it. Your writing voice, therefore, is less personal from now on. Later in this chapter, on page 10, you will learn more about voice. Many writing assignments will require you to evaluate the effects of choosing one voice over another.

Begin your work on every essay by focusing on your audience. Who is this person? Your instructor is a typical educated adult, a stand-in for your future managers, professors, or supervisors. He or she wants to understand your ideas about your subject as easily as possible. To make yourself clearly understood, use standard English, the common language shared by you and your reader. Finally, the *tone* of your essay should be suitable for a college or university assignment. Tone describes your attitude toward your subject as expressed by the words you choose: simple or complex, slangy or formal.

Now ask yourself whether or not your audience can read your mind. Why? You know what is in your mind as you write, but have you explained it clearly so that your instructor can see where your ideas come from? For example, a student made this point about a short-story character: "Emily is a very disturbed woman." The student then moved on to discuss the town the character lived in, assuming that her professor would know what she meant by "a very disturbed woman," because he knew the short story well. But how could he have known what led her to make her point? How could he evaluate her understanding of the character? Never assume that your reader "knows what you mean"; explain and support each point you make.

Finally, give yourself the best chance for a good grade by giving your audience essays that respond accurately to the requirements of the assignment. If your instructor is confused because your essay does not relate to the topic, how is he or she likely to evaluate you? By misunderstanding or ignoring your instructor-audience, you risk losing goodwill as well as marks.

First-year essay assignments are previews of your future academic and professional writing challenges. Writing these essays is thus less about expressing yourself and more about meeting the requirements of your audience and your assignment.

TIP: Purpose and audience, further explained on page 10, are special focuses of each of the patterns of essay development in Part 2.

WHAT IS YOUR POINT?

The essay is a goal-driven writing format. It is a "try," an attempt to make your reader see the truth of your point as clearly as you do. Your point about your topic is your thesis, the "deal" you make with readers—that you will explain, illustrate, or clarify your point for them in the body of the essay.

EXAMPLE

Subject: Marketing [assigned subject]

Topic: Marketing to special-interest groups [subject narrowed down to one area of marketing by the student]

Thesis: Green marketing [topic further narrowed by student] reflects the people's desire to seem ecologically minded. [student's viewpoint on topic]

Once someone reads your thesis, he or she is in a state of tension, waiting to see how you will support and prove its value. Your thesis drives your essay, giving direction and momentum to it.

QUESTION

- In the example above, what do you, as a reader of this student's essay, want to know?

Of course, you already know how to make a point. You do it every day in conversation. You might say, "Bicycle lanes are a great idea," and someone might challenge your statement. If so, you answer by giving a reason why you feel that way. That is the extent of the support you offer for your point. Listeners do not expect more because they may already know what you think, or they may not want to challenge you. Also, conversations generally move quickly from subject to subject, so no one expects long explanations.

In an essay, though, the quality of your point and your support for it is crucial. First, your point is not a spontaneous thought or opinion, as it might be in a chat. Instead, you must think about your topic. You discover a viewpoint, as the student did in the example above. Now your readers will want to know why your viewpoint is a good one. They may or may not agree with you. Your job is to supply enough good support for your thesis to reward your readers for the time and concentration they have put into this "conversation" with you, so that when you "make your point," they are satisfied.

TIP: Narrowing a topic and creating an effective thesis are covered in depth in Chapter 3. Also, for each of the patterns of essay development in Part 2, there is a special section on writing a thesis.

> ### Three Keys for Starting Work on an Effective Essay: Work Out Your Purpose, Audience, and Thesis
>
> As you start any essay-writing assignment:
> - Determine your general and your more specific *Purpose*
> - Learn as much as possible about your *Audience*
> - Make a clear point so that you can later express it as a *Thesis*

WHY WRITE ESSAYS?

What is the ultimate transferable skill, the skill you will use in every position in your career? It is the ability to think clearly and solve problems. And preparing an essay teaches you how to learn and how to think more effectively—to solve problems. You will be assigned essays that ask you to explore and learn more about your subjects. You must read deeply and conduct research to stimulate your thinking and to find material relevant to your topic. Learning in college and university does not mean collecting and memorizing facts. To take a position on a topic and to explain or defend that position, you must understand and interact with information gained from reading and research. You learn a new way of learning. As you test the facts and ideas you find, you expand your ability to think. In fact, you are practising the essential skill of critical thinking, which is distancing yourself from those automatic "like/dislike, yes/no" responses to ideas. You repeat this thinking and problem-solving process, selecting, weighing, and testing information, each time you work on the argument and proof for an essay.

● ● ● ● ● ACTIVITY 1

You have been assigned the topic of funding for religion-based schools in your town or city. Now, consider your approach to this topic.

- What is your immediate response to the topic? Why?
- What are two other possible viewpoints on funding religion-based schools? Why is each one reasonable for some people?
- What is your viewpoint on this topic, now that you have considered it? Why?

What is the ultimate communication skill? It might be writing well enough to achieve your goals in life, or to persuade others to do as you wish.

● ● ● ● ● ACTIVITY 2

- How do you want writing to help you in your future?
- How would you define effective writing? Give examples of writing that works.

However you define effective writing, writing the academic essay for a specific purpose to a definite audience is the best training. If you want to write well enough to meet important goals in your life, you will always need to be able to state your point and assure your reader that what you say is fair and valuable. To engage your reader, you must create interest, then hold your reader's attention. You must know your audience. You must express yourself in words that help your reader to trust you as competent and well informed; you must choose the appropriate tone, as defined above. You must also choose words and language that suit your topic and your purpose, and supply the right level of detail for your audience. And finally, you must choose a pattern, a way of arranging your information that reveals your ideas in the most understandable and appealing way. If this list of "musts" seems intimidating, know that you are about to learn practical ways to meet each of these challenges as you work with this book through the process of writing the academic essay.

THE ESSAY: GETTING STARTED

You read essays in newspapers and on Web sites and blogs, perhaps without realizing they are essays. The four main types are the personal essay, the journalistic essay, the review, and the persuasive or argumentative essay. Each category has a different purpose and each uses slightly different structuring techniques. The structure is the freest in the personal essay; the writer's goal is to show readers his or her view of a topic, usually through personal anecdotes. Journalists make their point with a "lead," rather than a formal thesis, and focus on concrete events that support the point made in their lead. Reviewers evaluate works of art and media products; their viewpoint or judgment is their thesis and they base it on the aspects of a work that justify their view. Reviews generally contain a summary section as well, as you will see online at **www.mcgrawhill.ca/olc/langan** under "Writing a Review."

The academic essays you will write are mainly of the persuasive/argumentative type. In academic essays, you make a point and back it up with evidence to convince readers of its validity. Although these essays are carefully structured, they are flexible. Once you gain some expertise with essay writing, you can apply this skill to various subjects: to explore the effects of privatization on Canadian health care, to write a literary essay showing the importance of setting in "The Painted Door," or, as a science student, to explain how some chemical process works. In Part Two you will see that you can vary the method you use to support your point, depending on your purpose and topic. And although you will often see five-paragraph model essays, the number of body paragraphs in your essays depends on the number of points you need to support your thesis. Academic essays can be adjusted to suit topic and situation.

Ultimately, the academic essay is the foundation for business and technical memos and reports, research papers, analyses, and most of the writing formats you will work with in the classroom, the lab, or on a co-op placement.

Understanding Essay Structure

Julian Lopez is a Media Studies student and the author of the following essay. He first wrote an in-class paragraph about socializing with computers and later decided to develop his topic more fully. Reading his essay will help you understand the form of an essay as it develops from the first paragraph.

> The title attracts readers' attention and suggests the essay's topic.

Socializing Computers

1. Introductory Paragraph

> The opening sentence of the introductory paragraph, the attention-getter, works to intrigue readers and suggest the topic of the essay.

> The thesis statement, expressing the writer's topic and viewpoint on it, appears near the end of the introductory paragraph.

A curious scientist peers through the windows of student residences or apartments in Bowmanville, Moose Jaw, or Abbotsford to find out what young people are doing in their leisure time. What does she see? Chances are, a group, eighteen to twenty-five, amusing themselves in front of a computer screen. Their parents' generation enjoys solitary relationships with their computers, but the "iGeneration," who grew up with computers, interacts in groups with their technology. Today's youth has an ingenious new use for the computer, as the hub for group entertainment, social interaction, and group multitasking.

2. First Supporting Paragraph

> The topic sentence of the first body-paragraph presents the first supporting point of the thesis: "group entertainment."

> Supporting details for the first supporting point make up the rest of the first body-paragraph.

One asset the "social computer" brings to a gathering is its helpfulness with choosing entertainment. The computer helps people make decisions and reach compromises easily and quickly. Suppose some friends decide to watch a *Harry Potter* marathon. What happens when, an hour into the first movie, three out of five people get bored? No need for bad tempers or arguments because any number of entertainment options is only a few mouse-clicks away. Some may be happy to watch online cartoons or TV show episodes on YouTube, or everyone could just as happily enjoy an hour or two of gaming with Everquest or Halo. Friends can play or watch in twos or as a group, but any choice starts conversations and friendly competitions. People reach quick decisions and compromises when they control their choices and have lots to choose from.

3. Second Supporting Paragraph

> Topic sentence of the second body-paragraph, presenting the second supporting point of the thesis: "social interaction."

Another reason why the computer is a welcome guest is its ability, once it is happily online, to challenge and interact with others. It is made for a generation that enjoys testing itself and expects quick feedback. The Internet is ready to serve individuals and groups with personality and IQ tests, trivia sites, and

> **Supporting details for the second supporting point of the thesis.**

quizzes. Instead of gossiping, friends can see who knows more about the original cast of *DeGrassi Junior High* or torment each other with facts about quantum physics. Quizzes encourage interaction between people and the computer and between the people themselves. Friends challenge themselves, compare their results, and learn more about one another as part of an evening's fun.

4. Third Supporting Paragraph

> **Topic sentence of the third body-paragraph, presenting the third supporting point of the thesis: "group multitasking."**

Ultimately, though, the most interesting reason why computers are such regular guests is how similar they are to their owners. Computers and young people are both multitaskers; they are comfortable doing several things at a time. While listening to the latest Drake or Feist tunes, people program the evening's music, check out Facebook or Twitter, print movie or sports schedules, and chat with friends on IM. Other groups play games, chat with players on the other side of the world, and compare scores on another site. Such social multitasking allows everyone in the room to be sharing the same overall experience while individuals or pairs of people pursue interests of their own.

> **Supporting details for the third supporting point of the thesis.**

5. Concluding Paragraph

> **Concluding paragraph presents a summary of thesis' supporting points.**

Younger generations and computers adapted well to each other; they are constant companions. The computer offers passive entertainment or active participation, and always gets along well with its human friends. When it's time to play, the "social computer" is ready for any occasion. Perhaps humans and technology will live happily ever after.

> **Concluding paragraph ends with a final thought; here, a prediction.**

Introductory Paragraph

Open your introductory paragraph with a sentence or two, an attention-getter, that will attract your reader and reveal something about your essay's content. Then make the point you hope to prove about your topic (your thesis). In your thesis, you may sometimes include a plan of development, a list of your supporting points. Alternatively, you might only suggest a plan of development, or state it in a sentence separate from the thesis.

Body Paragraphs

Develop each of your thesis' supporting points in one body paragraph. In Julian's example, you see three body paragraphs, one for each of his supporting points, but there is no magic number of points needed to explain or prove a thesis. Beginning each internal paragraph with a topic sentence that supports and refers back to your thesis helps guide readers through your essay and reminds them of your purpose.

Concluding Paragraph

Round off your essay with a concluding paragraph in which you summarize what your essay has said, possibly by briefly restating the thesis. You will also wish to add a more general or "outward looking" final thought or two about the subject of the essay.

Understanding the Essay's Audience, Purpose, Voice, and Tone

"Socializing Computers" is a typical first-year essay. It is not perfect; no essay is. In fact, Julian saw it as a work in progress. He had started with an in-class paragraph assignment, then thought he had more to say.* Trying to expand on his theme led to the essay above.

As you think about Julian's essay, and about the essay assignments ahead of you, consider the **PAT** formula: PAT is an acronym, a word made up of the first letters of *Purpose, Audience,* and *Thesis.* Each time you begin an essay assignment, ask yourself, *What is my purpose? Who is my audience? What is my thesis?* You will see examples of the PAT formula throughout Parts 1 and 2 of this book.

Because academic essays are goal-driven writing formats, you should always make your purposes clear to yourself. *Purpose* is the first key concept in the PAT formula. Three main general purposes for writing are to entertain, to persuade, or to inform. If you write about electric cars, your general purpose may be to inform readers about them. However, you are likely to have a secondary purpose as well: as you explain to readers how efficient electric engines are, you are also likely to be persuading them that electric cars are preferable to gas-fuelled cars. You also work out a specific purpose as you develop your thesis. Your specific purpose might be to explain the beneficial effects of driving an electric car, and your thesis will suggest or state that. Working through Part 2 will give you opportunities to build your skills in determining general and specific purposes for essays.

ACTIVITY 1

- What do you think is the general purpose of Julian's essay?
- Are there secondary purposes as well as a general purpose? What are they?
- Does his thesis suggest a more specific purpose? What is it?

You want your readers to accept your essay's ideas and become involved in your thinking process. So apply the *Audience* part of the PAT formula. An academic essay's structure requires you to place your thesis in the opening paragraph. In doing so, you are making things easier for your readers. You are lessening the risk of annoying them by making them search or wait for your point. The academic essay's form follows its function—to engage readers quickly. Next, you owe any reader two things: a clear expression of ideas and error-free grammar and sentence structure. Any time readers have to struggle to understand what you write, they quickly lose interest, no matter how good your ideas are. Finally you can do more than you think to work out your audience's interest in and knowledge of your subject. The following activity will introduce you to this concept and you will learn more about it in Chapter 2.

ACTIVITY 2

- Who is the audience for Julian Lopez's essay?
- What do you think is the reader's interest-level in Julian's topic? Why?
- Does Julian try to catch his reader's interest? How and where?

*In fact, in its final form Julian's essay was a ten-paragraph research paper for his psychology course.

- How much do you think Julian's audience knows about his topic? Why?
- Does Julian assume that his audience understands him?
- Does he help his reader to understand his point and details? How?

Finally, Julian's thesis expresses at least one of his purposes, and his viewpoint on his topic, in a way that his audience will relate to.

• • • • ACTIVITY 3

- What is Julian's thesis?
- How does his thesis engage his possible audience(s)?

Your writing voice, as shown in your pronoun choice, helps to show readers your point of view. Your voice indicates what you want to emphasize and your *stance,* or where you stand in relation to your subject. Writing in the first-person voice as *I* immediately "red flags" your presence to your reader. *I* can be a "noisy" pronoun. Your *I* can make it seem that your connection to your subject is more important than the subject itself. Do not distract your reader from your ideas in an essay. Your subjective, personal voice suits journals, blogs, personal essays, or eye-witness reports, but it works against you in academic essays, where you want your readers to focus on the quality of your thinking, not you.

• • • • ACTIVITY 4

- Do you recall the student asking his instructor for assignments on page 3? How would you describe his voice? Why?
- What do you remember about his note?
- How would you describe Julian's voice in his essay? Why?
- What do you remember about his essay?

Julian does not write as *I;* instead, he is an invisible presence. He uses the transparent third-person point of view or voice, allowing you to concentrate on his points and supporting details. Practising with the third-person writing voice will help you develop a sense of which subjects, which audiences, and which writing tasks will benefit from that voice. Chapter 7 offers more extensive coverage of writing voices, and most of the chapters in Part Two challenge you to choose an appropriate voice.

As noted earlier, when you choose words to suit a writing situation and an audience, you create a tone. Tone is the way you "speak" to your audience. Some students mistakenly assume they should write essays in a stiff formal tone, as if formality and large, ornate words somehow compliment and flatter their instructor. If you were your instructor, would you rather read "the selection of nourishment in correct equilibrium is essential to well-being . . ." or "choosing well-balanced meals is needed for good health"? Choose clear, straightforward writing every time. Otherwise you miscalculate your audience's needs and miss your purpose in writing an essay: to make your ideas as accessible as possible. Julian's essay is lighthearted, but not jokey or juvenile. He does not use slang; he speaks to you in a clear, even tone. Speak clearly to your instructor, but avoid speaking too familiarly in print. Your instructor is not your close friend, who uses the same slang and speech patterns as you do; recall Tony's note to his instructor earlier in this chapter.

ACTIVITY 5

- Now that you know Julian's purpose, audience, and voice, choose two phrases or sentences from his essay that reflect a good choice of tone.
- How is each of your selections appropriate to his purpose and audience?

ACTIVITY 6

1. In a group of four, come up with a list of situations in which having a sense of humour is a good thing.

   Now, choose four of those situations, one per person, and have each person explain why a sense of humour is beneficial in his or her situation.

   Finally, as a group, try to come up with a few general overall "reasons why" that would cover all four situations chosen by the group.

   Write that "reason why" in a sentence or two. Your group now has a trial thesis. Compare your group's thesis with those of other groups in your class.

2. Next, assume you will write an essay based on your group's thesis for each of these audiences:
   - Your friends
   - Your instructor
   - Your manager or boss at your summer or part-time job

   Would you use the same four situations as examples to back up your thesis for each of these audiences? If not, work out some situations that would be good supporting examples for each group of readers.

   Which situations did you choose for each audience, and why? Did you have to come up with new situations for any audience, and why?

3. In general, which audience would be most interested in the essay you wrote for them? Why?

   Which audience would be least interested? Why?

4. Choose an overall purpose for writing an essay to each of these audiences. Will you write to inform, to persuade, or to entertain? Why?

FINAL THOUGHTS

As you finish this chapter, you may think, "Well, that's a lot of information, but what about the actual writing part? That's what I find so difficult." Do you believe that everyone else finds writing easier than you do, or that there is a "magic formula" for writing well? The fact is, writing is not a smooth one-way trip from beginning to end for anyone. It is a process; you proceed through it in stages. Writing involves discovering, then ordering what you think, and no one thinks in tidy packages. Moreover, writing well is a skill, not a trick. As with all skills, you develop competence with practice, with trying.

Following is a preview of four general steps that make up an effective plan for creating strong essays. The following chapters cover these steps, beginning with practical strategies for discovering what to write.

Four Steps for Effective Essay Writing

1. Discover your point, and advance a clear thesis statement.

2. Support your thesis with specific evidence.

3. Organize and connect your specific evidence.

4. Revise, edit, and proofread your essay.

CHECKLIST OF LEARNING OUTCOMES FOR CHAPTER 1

Be sure that you have understood and reached the learning outcomes for this chapter. Answer the following questions:

✓ What are three basic ways to make your work acceptable to your audience in college and university essays? Why do so?

✓ How will clarifying your purpose help you to be a better writer?

✓ What is tone? How do you create tone in writing? How does your tone relate to your audience?

✓ How do you state your point in an essay? What does a thesis do? How does your thesis relate to your audience?

✓ Define *voice* in writing. Which voice is preferable for essay writing and why?

✓ What is a "transferable skill"? Why is essay writing such an important skill?

✓ Describe the structure of an essay. What are its main parts?

The Writing Process: Prewriting and Creating a Thesis

LEARNING OUTCOMES

After reading this chapter and working through its activities, you will

- deepen your understanding of the writing process;
- be ready to use prewriting strategies to generate ideas;
- review the steps for creating an effective essay;
- narrow a subject into a topic appropriate for an essay;
- use forms of questioning to develop a thesis statement;
- write more effective thesis statements.

The stages you will go through in structured writing situations such as those you find in this book comprise your writing process. Beginning with this chapter, you will find a guide, a method for helping you to work through each stage of this process.

THINKING AND WRITING—STARTING THE PROCESS

Writing is not creating a perfectly formed essay on your first try—no one does that. You work your way through a series of stages as you write an essay. As you work, you will discover what you think. You find new avenues of thought, change direction, or even go backwards for a while.

While everyone's writing process is a bit different, following the sequence on the next page teaches you to separate the tasks involved and allows you to benefit from using the appropriate type of thinking for each task. Do not see this as a rigid pattern, but as a guideline to make your work easier. There are specific strategies to assist you with each stage.

The Stages of the Writing Process

1. **The Discovery Stage: Prewriting**

   Generate raw material, finding out what you have to say, using the creative, spontaneous parts of your mind as you explore your thoughts. Working on the ideas you generate with your prewriting will help you find a focus, a point to which your ideas relate.

2. **The Analyzing and Ordering Stage: Creating a Thesis and an Outline**

   Test the focus you have discovered, the point you would like to make, as you develop it into a trial thesis. Now analyze your purpose, what you want your essay to mean to your audience, and finalize your thesis. As you do so, you clarify your supporting points as well. With your thesis prepared, you are ready to use the ordering parts of your mind. Give the ideas from your prewriting a structured shape by creating an outline based on your thesis. When you outline, you form your essay's skeleton, and begin to see its full shape.

3. **The Writing Stage: Drafting**

   When you write your first draft, you develop your outline into full sentence form. You concentrate on your content, on expressing your ideas and support as clearly as possible. Do not yet worry about sentence structure or grammar; focus on your content. Be prepared to write at least two drafts.

4. **The Revising Stage: Polishing Ideas and Sentences**

   In the final stage, you have two tasks: revising your content and proofreading your writing. This stage is crucial to writing effectively for your purpose and audience; leave yourself enough time to do your ideas justice.

Explore and practise various forms of prewriting as you work through the following pages and through your semester. Find starting points for your writing process that work for you.

Later in this chapter, you will begin stage two of your writing process as you consider your purpose, your audience, and analyze how to state your thesis or point. The chapters of Part One will guide you through the rest of the writing process. In Chapter 3, you return to stage two, and begin, thesis in hand, to create an outline, a structure for your essay. You will also learn methods for developing effective support for your thesis. Once you have done so, you are prepared for stage three, drafting and refining your essay. Chapter 4 helps you to craft your essay so that it is coherent and well structured. Finally, Chapter 5 brings you to revising and proofreading your essay, preparing it for your reader.

STAGE 1: PREWRITING—EXPLORING YOUR IDEAS

When you use any prewriting strategy, you generate raw material and notes to lead you toward a topic-focus and a direction for your first draft. Make a conscious decision to work only on this idea-generating stage for the time being. Turn off your internal censor, the voice telling you that you might do something wrong. There are no mistakes at this stage, except not prewriting at all.

> As you begin, here are three common-sense tips. Neglecting any of these can undo even your best efforts.
>
> 1. Leave enough time to do a good job. You need a minimum of three days to work through the four stages of the writing process.
>
> 2. If you are unclear about any part of your assignment, speak to or email your instructor. Writing instructors appreciate your concern and are willing to help.
>
> 3. If you are concerned about language or sentence-structure problems, and you delay starting writing assignments because of this concern, ask your instructor about language or writing-skills assistance available from your college or university. As you begin working on these issues, you will find expressing yourself less intimidating.

Start Here: Narrow and Specify Your Topic

To generate ideas, you need a topic, a single idea you can explore in your essay. Even if you have been assigned a topic, you will still need to find a specific aspect that interests you. More often, you will be assigned a general subject; for example, "food banks." You could write a book (or several books) on that subject. For an essay, you could have real trouble developing a viewpoint on an idea as broad and as general as "food banks."

Even if you narrow it to "food banks in Canada," you would still have enough material for a book or lengthy report. What you need is a specific aspect, a well-defined subsection of that narrowed topic. "Faith-supported food banks in Calgary," for example, represents a third and fourth division of the subject: *food banks>food banks in Canada>food banks in Calgary>faith-supported food banks in Calgary*. College and university essays do not deal in vague generalities about large subjects; they look deeply into a single specific topic.

● ● ● ● ACTIVITY

Here are typical lists reflecting stages you might go through in moving from a general subject to a specific topic. Number the stages in each list from 1 to 4, with 1 indicating the most general stage or subject, and 4 marking the specific topic.

LIST A

_____Class sizes
_____Education
_____Lectures and tutorials
_____Small-group learning

LIST B

_____Bicycles
_____Dangers of bike riding
_____Transportation
_____Personal vehicles

LIST C

_____Retail companies
_____Supermarkets
_____Dealing with customers
_____Working in a supermarket

LIST D

_____Genetic studies
_____Genetically modified vegetables
_____Science
_____Biology

PREWRITING: FOUR TECHNIQUES

Here are four techniques that will encourage you to think about and develop a topic and get words on paper: (1) freewriting, (2) questioning, (3) making a list, and (4) diagramming. General prewriting can help you generate ideas and focused prewriting can help you to organize and refine your thoughts. Any of these techniques can be used in combination with another, as you will see in the following sections.

Technique 1: Freewriting

Freewriting is jotting down, in rough sentences or phrases, everything you can think of about a possible topic. Write non-stop for three to five minutes. Explore any idea and put down whatever pops into your head. If you get stuck for words, repeat yourself until more words come.

When you freewrite, your only goal is to get your mind running. You will find any writing task easier when you have something other than a blank page or screen to work from. Ideas and impressions become clearer after you put them on paper. These ideas, in turn, usually lead to other ideas and connections, and unexpected thoughts may even lead you to another possible focus. That's fine. Through continued practice, you will develop the habit of thinking as you write.

Now, put away the eraser or liquid paper, resist the urge to hit "delete," and start freewriting. Forget about spelling, grammar, and punctuation; let the inventive part of your mind run free.

Freewriting: A Student Model

During general freewriting, you discover that your specific topic emerges as the thing you are writing most about. Or, like Jed, the student writer below, you consciously decide on one idea that sparks a connection. Typically you use freewriting to generate ideas about a broad topic, then you use it in a more goal-directed way to explore your specific topic. You may also, after doing some reading about your topic, go directly to writing a rough draft of your essay: this is **directed freewriting,** about which you will read more below.

General Freewriting to Generate Ideas

Jed Gawrys, a General Arts and Sciences student, was assigned the general topic of values in society. Here is his freewriting, complete with errors:

Values are moral values? Whos supposed to show these values, celebrities? They don't have values that i can understand but socieity watches every move they make. Tiger Woods? What are values? How we treat other people or do unto others or something. Individual people can have values, can groups have values? What we put value on—that's it—turns into what media says is right***. Right now—street racing is like a crime but movies glamorize it like Fast & Furious. What's right here? Im stuck here no I've been watching Stanley Cup playoffs and everybody says hockey is violent. But teams have to win to suceed just like any business. So society says winning is good and it doesn't matter what it costs—that's a value but a wrong one. Stuck again and again and we don't want to think about poor people either. Like with sports we don't care about the losers and what will happen if we don't have health care in Canada anymore? We only care about success and what the media tells us is good like being wealthy and being a winner. Look at what hockey and basketball players earn, it doesn't make any sense.

Jed completed his first freewriting in class and showed it to his instructor: "I have some possibilities for topics here, but they seem kind of weak. The idea about media and society telling us something is good when it's not is interesting. And I keep coming up with connections to professional sports. But those aren't topics yet, are they?" Still trying to clarify his ideas about social values, he Googled the phrase. One of his notes appears below:

- values of groups of people shape what we accept—hockey players & violence
- set of values doesn't necessarily last forever—racism used to be accepted
- examples of moral values: equality, no discrimination, treating the poor and sick people—are these values society and media have?

URL: http://www.cencomfut.com/social_values.htm

If you feel, after trying any prewriting strategy, that you do not know enough about your topic, or would just like to try a different way to stimulate your thinking, do some reading. Try words related to your topic as keywords on a search engine, then make notes of any relevant ideas. Every time you make a note, write down the URL of the site where you found your information. If you have time, check the print resources in your school's library, and note the title of the book or article and the author's name. If you wish to add some research information to your essay, read Chapter 18 on quoting, paraphrasing, and citing your sources. Doing a little research is an excellent preparation for future academic and career writing.

Directed Freewriting: Discovery Drafts

Many writers, like Jed, prefer to write a very rough draft of their essay once they have a sense of their topic. They write this rough or discovery draft after doing some prewriting, and perhaps a little research. Directed freewriting does not mean that you skip a step in the writing process by not making an outline. You will make your outline after this draft. Writing a discovery draft is simply another, more structured type of freewriting, in which you are working toward turning your topic into a trial thesis.

Here is Jed's discovery draft, with spelling and sentence-structure errors corrected, based on his freewriting and his reading:

Professional sports show us how bad society's values can be. Competition has always been the core at the pro level—it's all based on winning because that's what brings in the money. What's the difference between hockey players trying to disable each other and corporations destroying their competition? Society says winning makes it all okay, no matter whom you hurt. Was it always this way—some values do change—racism isn't accepted anymore. People who were racists thought they were winning out over people they insulted. They were stronger because they could hurt other people. In North America the rich seem to discriminate against the poor now, but racial issues still cause a lot of violence in some places, and society and the media condemn this violence. They only accept violence when it makes them more powerful. Look at sports again—I read an article that said that in 2008 there were 664 fights in 1230 NHL games. Violence is okay if it sells tickets and makes the sports industry powerful. It's the same with movies. Who has any morals in this—powerful people?

Jed thought about this draft and decided that he had some kind of point. He liked the idea of how similar the negative values in professional sports were to those reflected in everyday society.

His instructor asked him who he thought his audience was: Jed felt it was adults like his instructor and probably his fellow students as well. "Everyone knows that pro sports has a twisted value system," he said. "And even people my age know that you don't always get paid for hard work and being a good person. Movies and the music industry show us that all the time. Who has any values now?"

Later in this chapter you will see how Jed developed this idea into thesis-planning sentences that defined his purpose and method of development for his essay.

Technique 2: Questioning

If you are a methodical individual who likes order and structure, questioning may offer you a comfortable method to work with. Freewriting gets around the ordering parts of your mind; questioning gives you a framework for inquiry. Its structure gives you a sense of direction and clarity, especially if you find unstructured approaches too "loose." Questioning can also help you through a temporary blank period, and show you different angles on your topic. This technique is particularly effective in writing situations where you have some knowledge of your subject, whether you have gained it through experience or research. Ask yourself as many questions as you can think of about your subject; your answers will be a series of different "takes" or focuses on it. Such questions include *Why? When? Where? Who?* and *How?*

Begin by dividing your page or screen into two columns: *Questions* and *Answers,* as you see on the following page. Leave enough space in the *Answers* column so that you can return to a particular response if more details come to you later. Next, ask yourself these preliminary questions: *What is my topic? What is my purpose? Who is my audience?* For the moment, just put down rough answers to the *purpose* and *audience* questions; you may adjust these as you work on your questioning. Then, write your answers for the rest of your question-and-answer series. If one question stops you, just go on to another.

Here are some questions that Tina, a student writer, might ask while developing an essay on the disadvantages of seeing movies in theatres:

Questioning: A Student Model

Questions	Answers
What is my topic and viewpoint?	I do not like seeing movies in theatres.
What is my purpose?	To explain why I dislike going to movie theatres—to justify myself?
Who is my audience?	People my age? Other movie fans who like or dislike going to the theatre?
Why don't I like to go to the theatre?	Just too many problems involved.
When is going to the movies a problem?	Could be any time—when movie is popular the theatre is too crowded, when traffic is bad the trip is a drag.
Where are problems with movie-going?	On the highway, in the parking lot, at the concession stand, in the theatre itself.
Who creates the problems?	I do by wanting to eat too much.
	The patrons do by creating disturbances.
	The theatre owners do by not having enough parking space and showing too many commercials.
How can I deal with the problem?	I can stay home, download movies, or watch them on DVD or cable TV.

Questioning as Second-Stage Prewriting

If you have done some general freewriting, but are still not sure about a focused topic for your paper, try questioning, using your freewriting as a reference. Look for key words or phrases in your freewriting, words you have returned to or that seem particularly connected to your topic. Use that word or phrase in your series of questions.

Questioning can give you a surer sense of purpose, or help you revise your purpose. For example, if you find more details accumulating under a *why* question than under a *how* question, your overall purpose could be to show causes of something (*Why* did something happen? *Why is something a good/bad idea?*) or to persuade readers, rather than to explain something to them. (*This is how something happens. This is how something became good or bad.*) As well, questioning may reveal more about audience-focus. If your points explain too much or too little for the audience you have in mind, or if information in your answers does not match your audience's needs, this is the ideal time to change your audience-focus or to work further on your prewriting if your audience is set out in your assignment.

- Questioning may reveal your main supporting points clearly as answers to one or more questions.
- Questioning can yield answers that may be rich sources of connected ideas—making some of your organizing and outlining a little easier.
- Questioning can show you directions for paragraphs within an essay; if you have many answers to *Why*, you may want to explore the causes of a subject.

● ● ● ● ● ACTIVITY

Practise questioning by writing down a series of questions about good or bad experiences. How many details can you accumulate in your answers in ten minutes? Don't waste time worrying about "mistakes"; the important thing here is your ideas.

Now, examine your answers. You are looking for a potential direction or focus, based on the questions that yielded the most responses.

Choose the question that generated the most answers and answer these questions: *What is my topic? Do I have a particular viewpoint on it? What would be my purpose in writing about my subject? Who would be my audience?*

For example, assume you asked yourself questions about the good experience of learning to ride horses, and the most fruitful question was *Why?* Your topic-focus is learning to ride; your viewpoint is that it is a valuable and/or healthful experience. Your purposes could be to inform and persuade in general, and more specifically, to explain to readers why riding is such an excellent activity. Your audiences would likely be your peers and instructor, and people who do not already ride horses.

Technique 3: List Making

List making is simply making point-form notes of ideas that relate to your subject. List as separate points as many ideas as you can about your topic. Avoid making sentences out of your points, and never worry about repeating yourself; your mind may be trying out a variation on some idea. Lists have more structure than freewriting, but less than questioning, so list making appeals to a variety of writers.

One risk you may find when you list ideas for the first time is this: because listing ideas is an ordering activity, you could be tempted to organize your ideas prematurely. If this happens, stop ordering and keep adding new items. Use listing for its value as an informal, clean-looking way of recording ideas on the page or screen.

After writing his directed draft, Jed wanted to see his ideas set out more clearly. He made the following list of his ideas:

List Making: A Student Model

- pro sports show how bad our values are
- people seem to approve of violence in sports—hockey
- winning sells tickets, so it's good (?)
- what about corporations "killing off" competing companies and firing people when they want to close factories somewhere?

- in business, you're in to win—the same as sports—all those motivational speakers!
- does the idea about racism or discrimination go next?
- racism is against the law here, but it's not gone in other places
- social values do change sometimes—that website
- there are all kinds of discrimination
- rich people are the winners and the celebrities and no matter what they do, they're "right"
- should I put *a* beside sports ideas and *b* beside society or business side?
- violence is bad—everybody knows that—people associate fighting with power though
- find out the number of fights in the NHL in 2010—from that site

One detail led to another and then another. By the time he had finished his list, he was ready to think about his thesis and group his points under trial topic headings.

List making works as a first or second stage of prewriting.

- List making after freewriting can stimulate you to think of more points and details.
- List making after freewriting or questioning displays your thoughts in a simple, uncluttered form, so you can evaluate them.
- List making is useful for writers who like to connect ideas graphically with lines and circles.

List Making as Second-Stage Prewriting

Second-stage list making is an excellent method for organizing ideas and creating a hierarchy or order of importance for your ideas. Number your points and ideas before outlining, or sort out points and related supporting details from your list.

If you work on the computer, you can move items around easily and copy, cut, and paste phrases into different positions. You can keep your document clean and tidy as you work, making the ordering process less confusing. Number your points in order of importance, or try bolding the main points and grouping related ideas beneath them in plain text. You can save any ideas about which you are uncertain at the bottom of the screen or in a separate document.

• • • • ACTIVITY

List a series of realistic goals, major or minor, that you would like to accomplish within the next year. Your goals can involve personal, academic, and career matters.

- Now, imagine you are listing your goals for your best friend to read—revise your list to reflect any changes.
- Next, revise your list to suit your instructor as your reading audience.
- Finally, adjust your list for a complete stranger, someone sitting next to you on a bus, to read.
- What changes did you make, and why, in each case?

Technique 4: Clustering

Clustering, or *diagramming* or *mapping,* is another strategy for generating ideas. People who enjoy thinking visually can use lines, boxes, arrows, and circles to show relationships among the ideas and details that occur to them. Clustering also prevents "sentence block" because you note points and details only in words and phrases.

State your subject in a few words in the centre of a blank sheet of paper. Then, as ideas and details come to you, put them in boxes or circles around the subject. As you find relationships between ideas and groups of ideas, draw lines to connect them to each other and to the subject. When you cluster to generate ideas, keep creating "word bubbles" and connecting them to each other. You will need to allow some time after completing your first stage to decide which ideas are more important than others. Clustering, like freewriting, shows relationships between ideas rather than their order of importance.

There is no right or wrong way of clustering; it is a way to think on paper about how various ideas and details relate to one another. Below is an example of clustering that Tina, the student writing about the disadvantages of movie-going, might have produced to develop her ideas *after* freewriting.

Clustering: A Student Model

When you use clustering to organize your first-stage prewriting, you will need to show the specific relationships between items in your diagram. Decide on a method for doing so. You may work vertically on the page, placing your main

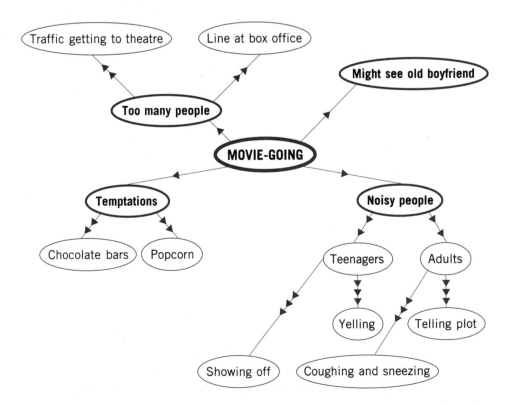

2: THE WRITING PROCESS: PREWRITING AND CREATING A THESIS   **23**

idea at the top and extending your supporting-point bubbles below it, followed by detail-bubbles beneath each. You could also, as Tina has done, work from the centre of the page outward, showing your levels of structure in different colours or degrees of boldness. In this case, the main-idea and supporting-point bubbles are in bold, and the relationship of details to supporting points is clearly visible.

Clustering as Second-Stage Prewriting

The pictorial aspect of clustering makes it useful for the second stage of prewriting. When you are trying to decide between main points and details, and show how these fit together, a cluster diagram with visual ordering cues will help you to see the overall shape and content of an essay.

- Second-stage clustering can reveal a paragraph's focus and the levels of details within, as Tina's "noisy people" set of clusters shows.
- Second-stage clustering can prepare you for outlining and drafting if you show different levels of links between points and details.

The only limitation of clustering is that your page can sometimes become too messy to follow. Avoid this by starting a clean second page where you can distinguish between possible supporting points and details. Refer back to the diagram of clustering for techniques to help you clarify levels of support and connections.

• • • • **ACTIVITY**

Use clustering to organize the list of year-ahead goals that you created for the previous activity (page 21).

There is only one guideline for prewriting: go with what works for you. When one technique is not working, simply stop and try another. Occasionally, you may use several techniques at once: you may cluster and sort through a list at the same time. Any technique that gets your ideas flowing is good.

Now look at the plan below. You are partway through your first step; you have a topic and some ideas in hand, and it is time to move on to creating a key part of your essay—your thesis statement.

Four Steps for Effective Essay Writing

1. **Discover your point, and advance a clear thesis statement.**
2. **Support your thesis with specific evidence.**
3. **Organize and connect your specific evidence.**
4. **Revise, edit, and proofread your essay.**

STAGE 2: CREATING A THESIS

Once your topic is focused and you have explored some related ideas, you are ready to work on the key element in your essay: your thesis statement. As you read in Chapter 1, essays are goal-driven writing formats. Your goal is to challenge your readers to see why you make the point you do about your topic. Your thesis statement is your challenge to readers.

A thesis statement is, in its simplest form, your topic and your viewpoint on your topic. After prewriting, you have limited your topic; now you must establish what you think about your topic and why: this is your viewpoint. Your viewpoint on your topic drives your essay.

Military service should be required in Canada.
Topic   *Viewpoint*

What is your first response to the statement above? It is probably *Why?* You react to a statement that is not a simple fact. An effective thesis is a point that needs to be argued: that Canada should have compulsory military service. In terms of argument, the thesis statement is a conclusion you come to after considering your topic, but it is your introduction to your argument for your readers.

Without the viewpoint or controlling concept (your attitude, limiting thought, or focus) this topic alone is just a fact; it has no force:

This essay is about military service (in Canada).

What is your response to this statement? Is it *So what?* There is no force here, no challenge to you as a reader: this sentence is a label, not a thesis statement. How then do you create a thesis statement that is interesting and worthwhile to readers?

Writing an Effective Thesis Begins with Asking Questions

I: Thesis Development Questions

You can ask yourself certain types of questions based on your prewriting that will help you form a trial or working thesis. If you worked through the activities on questioning on pages 18 and 20, you have already explored this method of defining a thesis. Recall the PAT concept from Chapter 1: you decide, based on responses from questioning, what your purpose, audience, topic, and viewpoint are.

Look at your prewriting and ask yourself the following questions:

What is my topic?

What do I want to do with my topic? (In other words, what is my purpose? To explain? To persuade? To define? To analyze?)

So what then is my viewpoint?

Who is my audience, aside from my instructor?

Why will my topic interest my audience?

What ideas are there in my prewriting that will help me with what I want to get across to my audience?

Answering these questions will usually lead you to a clear statement of topic and viewpoint, a trial thesis.

The responses below are those of the student author of the thesis statement about compulsory military service.

What is my topic? Serving in the Canadian Forces

What do I want to do with my topic? (What do I want to prove? What is my purpose?)

I think I want to tell people why it's a good thing for young people to join the Canadian Forces. No, I keep looking at the stuff I wrote down and it's more than that. Young people should serve in the Canadian Forces—that's it. That's really what I think; most of us have no direction and no idea of what's going on outside of our group of friends.

So what then is my viewpoint?

Young people should be required to serve in the Canadian Forces.

Who is my audience, aside from my instructor?

Other people my age, obviously—but also adults who think we're lazy and not interested in anything but ourselves—and also people who know anyone serving overseas.

Why will my topic interest my audience(s)?

I think generally because it's so different—Canadians don't think about going into the military. Especially people I'm in school with; they have probably never met anyone who's had anything to do with the Canadian Forces. It's kind of an informative essay, I think, as well as a persuasive one.

What ideas are there in my prewriting that will help me with what I want to get across to my audience(s)?

If I'm writing to students, they should know that the Forces pays up to half their tuition in college or university. They will learn discipline and teamwork . . . and learn a lot more about people and the world . . . I don't know if discipline and teamwork will convince students though—that would appeal more to parents and adults. Taking part in important events? Both should like that. Representing your country—I'm not sure who that's important to . . .

• • • • ACTIVITY

As you can see above, your topic and audience are interconnected. Start with broad topic #1 below. Now choose one of the audiences and develop and refine your topic into a working thesis for that audience. Repeat for audience number two, then follow the same pattern for topic #2.

For example, imagine that your broad topic is student loans. Your audiences include current students, prospective students, parents of students, college or university administrators, and bankers, among others. What are the concerns of these groups? Would current students be more concerned with lower interest rates? Would they think student loans are always a good idea? How would your answers affect your trial thesis?

1. *Topic:* body image

   Audiences: peers, fitness instructors

   Working Thesis:

2. *Topic:* time management

Audiences: your instructor, co-workers at your summer or part-time job

Working Thesis:

II: Thesis Try-Outs and Directional Questions: Refining Your Trial Thesis

Another way to discover your viewpoint for a working thesis is to work through a two-part process: try out various attitudes to and viewpoints on your topic, then determine the direction your essay might take.

Start by trying out a range of response-words and phrases that express your reactions to your topic. Assume your assigned topic is "money management." You have narrowed that topic to "credit cards," and finally focused on "credit cards for students." Now, looking over your prewriting, the viewpoint emerging is that credit cards for students have some good points. To clarify your response to your topic, try a pattern of positive responses like this:

Credit cards for students *are a good idea.*
Credit cards for students *are a good thing sometimes.*
Credit cards for students *help students to manage their money.*

Now, try reversing your responses to your topic:

Credit cards for students *cause more problems than they are worth.*
Credit cards for students *give them a false sense of maturity.*

Which of these statements comes the closest to your thoughts during prewriting and your thoughts right now? Which one sparks the most ideas?

Once you settle on the statement that best reflects your views, you have two parts of your working thesis. Now you will refine that statement into a thesis that shows the purpose and direction of your essay more clearly.

Directional Questions: Combine your subject and your viewpoint with as many question words and phrases as you can think of:

What is good about credit cards for students?
For whom are student credit cards a good thing?
When are credit cards for students a good idea?
Why are credit cards for students a good idea?
What are the benefits of credit cards for students?
What is relevant to whom about credit cards for students?

From among these directional questions, choose the question you want to answer, the challenge you find most interesting, or the problem you want to solve. Right now your prewriting need not determine which question you choose as the basis of your thesis. In fact, if you are most interested in a question unrelated to your prewriting, just use it as the springboard for some additional prewriting; your final essay will be better for the change. Using directional questions, you develop a more specific thesis, which you will find more satisfying to support, and which clearly indicates the direction of the argument you will pursue in your essay.

The box below reviews the stages in developing a thesis:

General/Broad Topic	Limited/Narrowed Topic	Working Thesis (Limited Topic + Viewpoint on It)
Families	Single parents	Single parents face continual challenges.
Money	Unemployment insurance	Collecting E. I. can be humiliating.
Food	Cooking	Learning to cook is not as much fun as FoodTV makes it look.
Recycling	Recycling boxes in school hallways	Students generally ignore the recycling boxes in the halls.

Revising Your Thesis

Types of Thesis Statements

So far, a thesis statement has been defined as a narrowed topic plus a viewpoint on it. The working thesis statements above are examples of that two-part definition. There are two main forms of thesis statement: simple and extended.

The Simple Thesis

Whether in trial or revised final form, the topic + viewpoint statement is called a simple thesis: for example, *Tornadoes are a real threat in Canada*. Depending on your instructor's preference, you may find a simple thesis suitable for some shorter essays, four to six paragraphs long. Because a simple thesis does not reveal how you will support it in your essay, you may find it useful if you wish to reveal your argument slowly to readers.

The Extended Thesis

In many cases, however, your instructor will require you to write an extended thesis statement: for example, *Tornadoes are a real threat in Canada: Canada experiences more tornadoes than any country except the U.S., and Canadians are not trained to prepare for tornadoes.* Here, you include your two supporting points in your thesis. This more detailed statement guides readers into your essay by telling them what to expect, and is essential for essays with multiple body paragraphs and for research essays.

● ● ● ● **ACTIVITY**

For each thesis statement below,

a. Identify the topic and the viewpoint;

b. Explain whether it is a simple or an extended thesis;

c. Change three simple thesis statements to extended statements.

1. The new building on our campus could be more functional if some changes were made.

2. Celebrities make poor role models because of the way they dress, talk, and behave.

3. Working as a security guard can be a stressful experience.

4. Canada's health care system is still superior to the U.S. system in terms of equity and efficiency.

5. Reality shows have changed television programming for the worse.

Writing Thesis-Planning Sentences

To make sure that you are clear about your ideas and your purpose, write a sentence or two stating exactly what you are planning for your essay as you finalize your thesis. Writing thesis-planning sentences will help to clarify your purpose, your support for your point, and even your method of developing your point. You can use these sentences as guides for outlining and drafting your essay. Use as many sentences as you like. This is excellent practice for writing longer, more complex essays and research papers. Follow the patterns below:

In this essay, I plan to (argue, defend, explain, demonstrate, analyze) that _____because of (1)_____ , (2)_____ , and (3)_____ .

Here is an example of the thesis-planning sentences written by Jed Gawrys, the student author of the freewriting and discovery draft earlier in this chapter:

In this essay, I plan to argue that the values that make professional sports so appealing to people are the same cruel and immoral values that rule North American society. Because of extreme competitiveness, violence, and forms of discrimination, our society has come to accept and even applaud destruction, cruelty, and harm to human life.

You can revise your thesis-planning sentences into a polished thesis, but for the moment you have statements to guide you.

● ● ● ● **ACTIVITY**

Complete the following extended thesis statements by adding a final supporting point that will parallel the others already provided. Parallel structure means that items or phrases in a list follow the same grammatical pattern. First, you might want to check the section on parallel structure in Chapter 6.

1. Being a successful vegetarian is difficult because cooking meals takes more effort, menu choices in restaurants are limited, and . . .

2. A good salesperson needs to like people, to be aggressive, to know the products, to dress appropriately, and . . .

3. Rather than blame themselves for failing courses, students blame the instructor, their course-load, and even . . .

4. Anyone who buys an old house and is planning to fix it up should be prepared to put in a lot of time, hard work, money, and . . .

5. Older cars may use too much gas and . . .

Evaluating Your Thesis for Effectiveness

As you revise your thesis, go through the following checklist to help you avoid common errors that can undermine your chances of writing an effective essay.

1. Does Your Thesis Contain a Clear Viewpoint?

The subject of this essay will be soccer fans.
Some Vancouver high schools could close as soon as this fall.
Video-gaming is the concern of this essay.

Do these sentences challenge you to think about their topics? If not, they are probably not thesis statements. They just announce their topics; they do not engage you on any level because they do not make any point about their topics. Below, each of those announcements has been revised so that it is a reasonable thesis statement:

Hooliganism, riots, and racism are extreme aspects of soccer fans' outrageous loyalty.
The possible closing of some Vancouver high schools is cause for concern.
Players develop useful skills from time spent on video-gaming.

• • • • **ACTIVITY**

Revise the following announcements so that they are simple or extended thesis statements.

1. Personal electronics that are popular with students is the subject of this essay.

2. This essay's concern is near-death experiences reported by accident victims.

3. A discussion of planning errors in the downtown area forms the core of this paper.

4. The topic to be considered is loneliness.

5. This essay will concern itself with career planning strategies.

2. Is Your Thesis Statement Too Broad or General for an Essay?

Disease has shaped human history.
Insects are fascinating creatures.
Since the beginning of time, men and women have been very different.

First, could you argue and accurately support any of these statements in a three- to four-page essay? Where would you begin with vast subjects such as *disease,* *insects,* and *the differences between men and women?* These are sweeping, often meaningless, claims that you cannot fulfill for your readers—your thesis must be a controlling concept that sets the limits of your argument. Do not promise more than you can deliver. Avoid beginning any thesis statement with phrases like, "All over the world . . . " or "People everywhere. . . . " The following sentences based on the topics above represent possible thesis statements.

> Plane travel has made local diseases global problems.
> Strength, organization, and communication make ants one of nature's most successful insects.
> Men and women are often treated very differently in entry-level positions.

● ● ● ● ACTIVITY

Revise the following vague or general thesis statements so that each makes a point that could be developed in a three- or four-page essay.

1. Life today makes everyone suspicious and unfriendly.

2. Contagious diseases are global problems.

3. The media distort every issue concerning young people.

4. Parenthood is the most important job there is.

5. Automotive exhaust fumes damage the environment everywhere.

3. Is Your Thesis Statement Too Narrow? Is It One That You Can Support In an Essay?

> There are speed bumps in the north end of Winnipeg.
> In March 2009, there was a moderate earthquake just outside of Leamington Ontario.
> The main road into town is lined with fast-food outlets.

Are you challenged by any of these statements? Can you think of ways to support any of them? These sentences, in fact, are simple statements of fact that do not present a viewpoint or require any support. They are often called "dead-end" statements. Remember, a thesis statement must be broad enough to require support in an essay. The following sentences, based on those above, represent successful thesis statements.

> Speed bumps in north Winnipeg fuel drivers' tempers, increase noise pollution, and add to greenhouse gases in the air.
> Towns in most parts of Ontario, like Leamington, are unprepared for earthquakes.
> Town councils should regulate the number of fast-food operations on entrance roads.

● ● ● ● ACTIVITY

Revise the following narrow or dead-end statements so that each makes a point that could be developed in a three- or four-page essay.

1. Volunteer positions are available at local retirement homes.

2. Film courses are always popular with students.

3. The bicycle lanes on campus are new this year.

4. The average karate student simulates competition fighting.

5. Libraries provide access to computers and study spaces.

4. Does My Thesis Statement Present More than One Idea?

> Waste prevention is the key to waste management; in developing countries, though, waste management creates jobs and community participation.
> Studying with others has several benefits, but it also has drawbacks and can be difficult to schedule.
> The "baby boom" generation has had many advantages, but it also faces many problems.

How many ideas are in each of these thesis statements? "One of the most serious problems affecting young people today is bullying . . ." is one topic and one view-point and ". . . it is time more kids learned the value of helping people" is another. The thesis statements above all present more than one idea; they point readers in two different directions. The point of an essay is to communicate a *single* main idea to readers. The following sentences, based on each of the examples above, represent more effective thesis statements.

> Community-based approaches to waste management can lead to waste prevention and productive use of waste.
> Studying with others requires careful planning as well as cooperation and discipline on everyone's part.
> The "baby boom" generation has enjoyed many advantages, including sheer numbers and wealth.

● ● ● ● **ACTIVITY**

Revise the following statements that contain more than one idea so that each becomes a thesis statement that advances a single main point.

1. Although infomercials are misleading, sometimes they are quite informative.

2. Movies with computer-generated backgrounds look spectacular, but they are not as appealing as those shot on location.

3. Owning a pet is a lot of work, and it can be good for reducing stress.

4. Wheelchair ramps are mandatory but they often change the appearance of entrance areas.

5. Shopping online is easy and fun, although it is not always secure.

After working through the following review activities, you will be prepared to move on to Chapter 3, completing the second and third stages of the writing process.

REVIEW ACTIVITIES

Review Activity: Prewriting

Below are examples of how the four prewriting techniques discussed in this chapter could be used to develop material for the topic "Problems of Combining Work and College or University."

1. Identify each technique by writing F (for freewriting), Q (for questioning), L (for list making), or C (for clustering) in the answer space.
2. Some of these examples demonstrate a second stage of prewriting. Which examples do so, and why?

_____	Never enough time Miss parties with people in my program Had to study (only two free hours a night) Gave up activities with friends No time to rewrite essays Can't stay at school one minute after I finish Friends don't call me to go out any more Sunday no longer relaxing day—have to study Missing sleep I need Marks aren't as good as they could be Can't just watch TV weeknights Really need the money Tired when I sit down to study at nine o'clock

_____	*What* are some of the problems of combining work and college?	Schoolwork suffers because I don't have enough time to study, rewrite essays, or do enough research. I've had to give up things I enjoy, like sleep and ball hockey. I don't have any time for RTV parties because I have to go to work as soon as my last class is over.
_____	*How* have these problems changed my life?	My marks are not as good as they were when I wasn't working. Some of my friends have stopped calling me. My relationship with a girl I liked fell apart because I couldn't spend time with her. I miss TV.
_____	*What* do I do in a typical day?	I get up at 7 to make an 8 a.m. class. I have classes till 1:30 two days, and those days, I drive to Sobeys where I work till 8. I drive home, shower, and by then it's around 9. So I only have a couple of hours those days to study—work on media assignments, read textbooks, write essays. The other two days, I finish classes at 5 and work till 9,

		so schoolwork's a write-off. I work all day Friday, and I just don't do schoolwork Friday night.
_____	*Why* do I keep up this schedule?	I can't pay tuition or buy books without working, and I need a diploma and airtime practice to try to get into radio. If I can make this work, I'll be doing what I've always wanted to do.

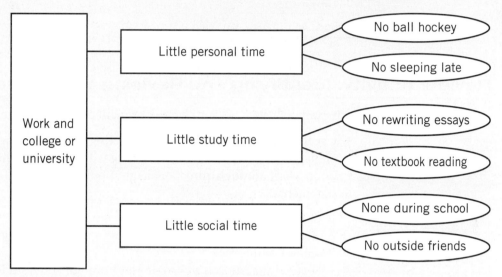

	It's hard working and going to school at the same time. I never realized how much I'd have to give up. I won't be quitting my job because I need every dollar just to stay in my program. And the people at Sobeys are pretty good. I've had to give up a lot more than I thought. We used to play ball hockey and touch football every Sunday. It was fun and we'd go for drinks afterwards. Sundays are now just catch-up time for assignments for my courses, and I don't know how I'll handle an internship when that comes up. I have to catch up because I don't get home until 8 some days and nearly 10 other days, and I work all day Friday and Saturday. So even two nights a week, I can't get to school work until after 9 p.m. I've been up since before 7 a.m. Sometimes I write an English essay in half an hour and don't even read it over. I feel that I'm missing out on a lot in university. The other day, people I like were sitting outside listening to music and talking after class. I would have given anything to stay and not to have to go to work. I almost called in sick. I used to get invited to parties. I don't much anymore. My friends know I never make it, so nobody bothers. I can't sleep late on weekends or watch TV during the week.

Group Review Activity: Narrowing Topics and Writing a Working Thesis

Following is a list of six general subjects. Form groups of four, and choose three of the subjects per group, then narrow each topic, and produce a working thesis statement for each. Compare your narrowed topics and thesis statements with other groups.

General Subject	Narrowed Topic
1. Music	
2. Inspiration	
3. Work	
4. Careers	
5. Travel	
6. Cooking	

Review Activity: Identifying and Revising Thesis Statements

Each example below presents a weak or ineffective thesis statement. For each one,

- Use the questions found in the "Evaluating Thesis Statements" section starting on page 29 to determine what is wrong with the statement,
- Then work through directional questions to create effective revised thesis statements.

1. Credit cards are a necessity everywhere in the world.
2. The use of service dogs in catastrophes and emergency situations is the subject of this essay.
3. Severe exhaustion is a chronic condition for some students.
4. Although many dishes in Armenian cooking, such as *meza* (appetizers) and *pilaf* are similar to those in other Middle Eastern cultures, Armenian cuisine offers unique items found nowhere else.
5. Dried sumac berries are used as a spice and a herbal medicine.

CHECKLIST OF LEARNING OUTCOMES FOR CHAPTER 2

Be sure that you have understood and met the learning outcomes for this chapter. Answer the following questions:

✓ Explain the stages of the writing process in your own words.

✓ What are the four prewriting strategies in this chapter? Which one would be most useful to you, and why?

✓ What steps are involved in creating an effective essay?

✓ Describe how you would modify a broad subject into a topic appropriate for an essay.

✓ Explain two methods of questioning you could use in developing a working thesis.

✓ What are four questions you should ask yourself as you revise your thesis?

Preparing Your Essay: Developing an Outline and Supporting Your Thesis

LEARNING OUTCOMES

After reading this chapter and working through its activities, you will

- be prepared to create a clear and useful outline;
- confirm the connection between your thesis and supporting points;
- develop specific details to expand on each of your essay's supporting points;

- develop enough details to expand on each of your essay's supporting points;
- evaluate the quality and credibility of your support;
- choose an effective order for your support.

You have now completed the first stage of your writing process, and begun stage two by crafting your thesis statement. The next step is organizing your essay's structure in an outline, then developing the points and details that support your argument.

DEVELOPING AN OUTLINE

Now that you have your thesis and supporting points you are at exactly the right point to construct an outline. You can now focus on your essay's structure and on the relationships between your ideas.

Do not avoid outlining and jump from a small amount of prewriting directly into drafting. It is a recipe for disaster. Essays are relatively formal structures, not casual, free-flowing strings of paragraphs that you can spin off from pure inspiration. As a final step before drafting, outlining will clear your mind and make writing drafts a more pleasant task.

Essay Outline Plan

You may wish to make an essay plan that runs down the page using a number and letter system,* indicating your paragraphs as described below:

Paragraph 1: Begin with your thesis statement at the top of the page or screen.

Paragraph 2: Write your first supporting point as a trial topic sentence, numbered with the Roman numeral *I,* directly under it.

- Indent and write your first detail for supporting point *I* directly below. Number the first detail with a capital *A.* If you have examples for your details, or "sub-details," indent again and note them beneath the detail with Arabic numbers. Continue with your details, numbering the second one with a capital *B,* and so on, for as many details as you have.

Paragraph 3: Write your second supporting point beneath your paragraph 1 space. Number it with the Roman numeral *II.*

- Indent and write your first detail for supporting point *II* directly below. Number the first detail with a capital *A.* Continue with your details, numbering the second one with a capital *B,* and so on.

Continue this pattern for as many supporting points/body paragraphs as you have.

Concluding paragraph: Thesis restatement.

Here is a partial example of such an essay plan, using Jed Gawrys' essay:

Paragraph 1. Thesis Statement: Key values in professional sports reflect society's acceptance of destruction and harm to human life.

Paragraph 2. Topic Sentence I (Supporting point I): Competitiveness is a key aspect of professional sports.

    A. Primary objective of teams is to win, at any cost.
       1. Because of money—how much players are paid, keeping coaches, ticket prices.
       2. This drives players to put winning above morality.
       3. Players are told to try to injure opposing star players.
       4. Players are scolded by coaches for not trying to hurt opponents.

    B. Our society is filled with people who want to get ahead, no matter the cost or whom they hurt.
       1. Corporations sell in volume at reduced prices, making it impossible for small competitors.
       2. Big corporations don't care if people lose jobs as a result.
       3. Name-calling and smear campaigns in elections by so-called responsible, moral politicians—in the name of winning.

*This is an MLA-style essay outline format. For further information on MLA style, turn to Chapter 19.

Paragraph 3. Topic Sentence II (Supporting point II): Another aspect of professional sports that is reflected in society's acceptance of destruction and harm to human life is violence.

A. Harming others is a way of life; not just in sports but also in our society.

　1. Football is based on tackling and harming other players.

Notice that Jed has partly filled in examples or "sub-details," using Arabic numerals. If you have multiple illustrations for any detail in your outline, follow this pattern. You will see Jed's drafts and revisions in Chapter 4.

Alternatively, you may want to use an outline diagram like the one Jed begins below. Use whichever style is more comfortable for you, and write either form of outline using sentences or phrases; just be consistent.

You will find a blank version of this outline diagram on the OLC at **www.mcgrahill.ca/olc/langan**; you can print copies from there. Save your first copy as "Outline." In Word, you can save this as a template, rather than a document. Every time you reach the outlining stage of an essay assignment, copy and paste the "Outline" template into a new document. Save this with an appropriate name.

Working onscreen allows you to easily add, delete, and move material around on your outline. Deletions do not clutter the screen, and you can save ideas at the foot of your document.

Here is Jed's opening paragraph and first body paragraph shown in an outline diagram:

Opening Paragraph: Introductory/Opening Material

Thesis Statement: Key values in professional sports reflect society's acceptance of destruction and harm to human life.

Supporting Points (if expanded thesis is used)

I.

II. The number of points depends on how many points support your thesis.

This pattern of paragraphs continues, depending on the number of supporting points you have for your thesis. Each supporting point has its own body paragraph.

Finally, do not worry about introductions or conclusions at this stage. Work on those next, when you draft and revise.

Body Paragraph: Supporting Point I. Competitiveness is a key aspect of professional sports.

Supporting Detail A. Primary objective of teams is to win, at any cost.

Sub-details/Examples

1. Because of money—how much players are paid, keeping coaches, ticket prices.

2. This drives players to put winning above morality.

3. Players are told to try to injure opposing star players.

4. Players are scolded by coaches for not trying to hurt opponents.

Supporting Detail B. Our society is filled with people who want to get ahead, no matter the cost or whom they hurt.

Sub-details/Examples

1. Corporations sell in volume at reduced prices, making it impossible for small competitors.

2. Big corporations don't care if people lose jobs as a result.

3. Name-calling and smear campaigns in elections by so-called responsible, moral politicians—in the name of winning.

• • • • ACTIVITY

1. Write a thesis statement based on the topic first-year students. Review pages 24–31 on thesis planning and directive questions, if necessary.

2. Generate three or four supporting points for your thesis.

3. Come up with a few details to expand on each supporting detail.

4. Now create an essay outline of either type.

DEVELOP AND ORDER YOUR SUPPORTING POINTS

Your Thesis, Supporting Points, and Details

After prewriting and revising your thesis by questioning, then creating an outline, you have a good sense of the ideas that support your topic and viewpoint. Now you will begin step two of your essay-writing checklist: support your thesis with specific evidence.

Developing Topic Sentences

Your supporting points will form the topic sentences for the body paragraphs in your essay. As you create your outline, turn each supporting-point word or phrase into a topic sentence.

Making Sure You Have Enough Supporting Details: Re-Generating and Sorting

Now is the time to develop and select suitable details to expand on for each supporting point, and then to decide on an appropriate order for them.

You have generated ideas in your prewriting; you may want to do some very focused "re-generating," or brainstorming, to create enough supporting details for each of your supporting points. You will have some material from your prewriting, but if there is not enough, here is a workable method for making the best use of your prewriting details and generating some new ones.

a. Listing and Regenerating:

1. Turn each of your supporting points into a trial topic sentence.
2. If you have two supporting points, make two columns with one topic sentence at the top of each. (If you have three or four, adjust the number of columns.)
3. Write one trial topic sentence at the top of each column.
4. Enter any details from your prewriting that would fit under any one of your topic sentences.
5. Now work on expanding those lists of supporting details, using any form of prewriting. Try to have roughly the same number of details under each topic sentence.

b. Sorting and Selecting:

1. Go over each list, checking for details that seem weak or unsuitable. Cross those out.
2. Choose your best details and number them, starting with #1 for the best.

Here is a sample of one such list made by Jed, the student author featured in the next section. He marked his new ideas with *n*.

Trial Topic Sentence:

The worst aspect of professional sports that is reflected in society is discrimination.

- ~~racial discrimination is illegal now~~
- all kinds of discrimination
- ~~discrimination against street people?~~
- #1 discriminating means choosy as well as prejudiced against something
- ~~society says it doesn't practise racial discrimination, but look at the 9/11 stuff that's still around~~
- # 4 discrimination in sports could be about glorifying star players
- # 4? look at Kobe Bryant or Tiger Woods—the media just forgets that they're not the best characters
- # 5—example—hockey stars aren't necessarily good people—they're athletes—Sean Avery—some are pretty crude
- #2—relates to glorifying success at any price [under topic sentence 1] ???
- # 6 if we're not discriminating against appearances—discriminating against anyone who isn't rich or successful—would anyone like Donald Trump?
- ~~people who are good who are successful?—any examples? Wayne Gretzky?~~
- bad idea and social values approve it—only real success is being the best *n*
- #4 in pro sports, they hide players who aren't stars—they don't play as much—is that discrimination? If it's all about money, it is. Examples of underused players? *n*

- whoever has the most money is the best—that's what our values tell us *n*
- is this why people like gangsters? *n*
- #3 does it depress people—can't live up to celebrities who make millions—Will Smith? *n*
- #8 no everyday heroes? *n*

● ● ● ● ● ACTIVITY

Here is a trial topic sentence from a student's essay about being competitive:

Having to compete makes some people fearful.

- Generate a list of details that would illustrate this point. Your details can be examples, short anecdotes, or any specific ideas that would make this point clear to readers.
- Cross out details that seem weak or unrelated.
- Number your five best details.

Making Your Supporting Details Specific

Just as a thesis must be developed with supporting points, those supporting points must be developed with specific details.

What Is a Supporting Detail?

Supporting details mean examples, precise descriptions of items, facts or statistics, quotations, or even brief anecdotes.

- Some *examples* are situations, people, character types, places, events, or objects that illustrate a supporting point; for example, Donald Trump in Jed's list above.
- *Descriptions* are careful word pictures of objects, situations, or beings that make ideas concrete to readers.
- *Facts* are items of information about things that exist or have existed—they can be confirmed by other sources; statistics are verifiable information that is represented numerically.
- *Quotations* are the exact words of some other person; that person must be credited, and the quotation must appear in double quotation marks. Refer to Chapter 19 for information on citing quotations in your essays.
- *Anecdotes* are short accounts of true incidents used to illustrate or provide evidence for a point.

What Is the Value of Specific Supporting Details?

First of all, specific details are *hooks;* they attract and excite your reader's interest. Second, details explain your points; they *show* your readers what your ideas mean, and offer the evidence needed for them to understand your supporting points' concepts.

Too often, body paragraphs in essays contain vague generalities rather than specific supporting details. Here is what one of the paragraphs in "Professional Sports and Society," the essay by Jed Gawrys, would have looked like if he had not used specific details to explain his main point.

The third and possibly most devastating aspect of professional sports that is reflected in our society is discrimination. Sports leagues are huge organizations but only a few players have a lot of playing time. Star players are the most skilled; their skills make their fortunes. They have only become successful because they are the players the public sees most often. Similarly there are "stars," people who are very successful in society. These people are not necessarily good or moral; they just seem good because they are so famous. The public often obsesses about these people; whereas they do not value or care about people who work hard jobs for very little money. These people are devalued and discriminated against, based on how unsuccessful, in society's terms, they are. Eventually this divides society up, creating different class-levels and stereotyped, wrong ideas about people.

Compare the paragraph above with the revision notes Jed made for his fourth paragraph in Chapter 5. In his revision paragraph, Jed notes where he needs to provide details, then examples to support those details or "sub-details." Jed illustrates his point about how much celebrities earn for so little time with the specific example of Will Smith, to be found online. Additionally, he gives contrasting details about the wages and hours of a garbage collector. These specific details and examples bring Jed's ideas to life and make them stick in the reader's mind. Reading audiences are hooked by specifics; they do not enjoy guessing what writers mean.

● ● ● ● ACTIVITY

Provide three specific details that logically support each of the following topic-sentence points. Your details can be drawn from your own experience, or they can be invented. State your details briefly in several words rather than in complete sentences.

Example Learning to cook every day for themselves is a challenge for students living on their own.

1. Shopping takes time and energy.
2. Cooking nutritious meals takes work.
3. It is tempting and expensive to order out.

1. Cell phones are essential to personal safety.

   _____

2. Independence has numerous challenges.

   _____

3. There are several ways in which students can earn extra cash.

   _____

Making Your Support Appropriate and Effective

Not all support is created equal. Supporting details vary in how reliable or convincing they are to readers; for example, suppose you write an essay on parole programs in local correctional facilities, and you support your view only with your own opinions and those of your friends. Are your readers likely to be convinced by your support? Will they see your paper as anything other than a subjective, somewhat narrow personal essay? What kinds of support would work here?

Supporting evidence must suit the essay-writing situation. Depending on the type of essay and the subject for which you are writing, different forms of supporting evidence will be appropriate. For personal essays or response papers in literature classes, your subjective reactions and experiences are relevant and useful. For other English or literary essays, you can base your support on an assigned piece of literature. In essays where you are asked to comment on aspects of cultural or ethical dilemmas, for either communications or social sciences subjects, you can present your own thoughts, but tied to theories and contexts in those areas. For the sciences, you can support your points with facts and research.

Generally, as you begin college or university, early essay assignments will require details that are a mixture of your own thoughts and ideas derived from other sources. Key points in judging your support are logical derivation, fairness, focus and specificity, and credibility.

When evaluating your own ideas and responses, ask yourself the following:

- Are my ideas based on reasoning, or am I just stating an opinion that I cannot back up logically?
- Do my ideas and details show bias or unfair judgments? Could I defend them on any basis other than emotion or liking or disliking them?
- Are any of my details just generalities, unfocused statements that do not add to my argument?
- How do I know my points and details are true? Why should readers find them credible?

When you choose facts or information not based on your own experience, you have several types of information to choose from, some of which are more useful than others:

- **Common Knowledge**

  In some cases, this is information generally known in various communities; i.e., to Canadians, the prime minister's name. In college or university what is common knowledge depends on the subject; for example, in a psychology essay you would not have to define *conditioning*. Facts that are common knowledge are sometimes useful, but by their nature, they are less interesting to readers. Moreover, the goal of postsecondary writing is to explore what is not common knowledge.

- **Anecdotal Knowledge (Hearsay)**

  This is information derived neither from personal experience nor from documented research; for example, *Childcare facilities on this campus are excellent, according to most students.* This type of information is useless as support, as it leaves readers wondering how credible it can be.

- **Expert Evidence**

  This term covers published information from reputable sources. It must be relevant to your topic to be of any value. Facts and statistics belong to this category, and so must be credited to their source. Research is fundamental to postsecondary information in all subjects.

In general, where any supporting point or detail is concerned, the crucial question appears above: "How do I know this is true? Why should my readers believe it?" If you can only answer, "Because I just know," or "Because it's how I feel," you will not be credible to your readers. Good support is based on your own direct experience (if it is suitable), on clear logic, and, if appropriate, on accurate research.

You will learn more about creating effective support for each method of essay development in Part Two.

● ● ● ● **ACTIVITY**

Read the following brief paragraph. What types of supporting-evidence details do you find here? Each one contains one of the detail types listed below and is numbered. In the blank space beside each number, mark the letter for the type of detail-information it presents.

a. Unsupportable personal opinion
b. Personal statements based on bias, emotional response
c. Common knowledge
d. Hearsay/anecdotal evidence
e. Expert evidence, correctly cited
f. Unsupported fact
g. Unfocused generalization

> Success is something most people never attain.(1) _____ It is an illusion that everyone should stop chasing.(2) _____ The price of success is dedication and hard work.(3) _____ In fact, some say that successful folks never notice that they are working; their work is their life.(4) _____ Jim Pattison, for example, the Vancouver-based entrepreneur, is said never to stop working. (5) _____ His pleasure is expanding his business empire, buying another team or TV station.(6) _____ People like that are unfair examples to the average person, though, because not everyone can work that hard.(7) _____ Many do not have the physical energy and the will power.(8) _____ And most people do not have the luxury of working for their own businesses; they have to work for others.(9) _____ Therefore, it is hard to agree with Thoreau, who said, "We were born to succeed, not to fail."(10) _____

Making Sure You Have Enough Supporting Details

Readers cannot "see what you see" in your mind, so your words do the work of showing your thoughts to them. This is where providing *enough* specifics is essential. When you offer enough details to properly clarify a supporting point, you show your readers what makes that point true for you.

If your supporting points are not adequately developed, that is, if there are not enough details to illustrate or prove the point of a paragraph, then you are forcing your reader to figure out why your point is valid. That is not the reader's job; it is your job as a writer. You could not, for instance, write a paragraph about the importance of a good resumé and provide only one reason why, even if it took you five sentences to write up that reason. Without additional support, your paragraph is underdeveloped and readers will not accept your point or your knowledge of it.

Students may try to disguise unsupported paragraphs through repetition and generalities. Do not fall into this "wordiness trap." Be prepared to do the hard work needed to ensure that each paragraph has solid support.

• • • • ACTIVITY

Take a few minutes to write a paragraph in the third-person point of view supporting the point "managing time is a student's biggest problem." Afterward, form small groups, and read your paragraphs aloud. The paragraphs people enjoy most are sure to be those with plenty of specific details.

When writing in the "invisible" third-person point of view, close attention to specific details is even more essential. There is no distracting *I* or *me* to take readers' or listeners' attention away from what you are saying and how well you are saying it.

Here once again is the essay-writing checklist; notice that you have, even without writing a first draft, just about completed the second step. Good writing is the result of planning every time.

Four Steps for Effective Essay Writing

1. **Discover your point, and advance a clear thesis statement.**
2. **Support your thesis with specific evidence.**
3. **Organize and connect your specific evidence.**
4. **Revise, edit, and proofread your essay.**

ORGANIZE YOUR SUPPORT

Organizing information makes it easier to understand and easier to remember. If you choose a clear, recognizable principle of organization, you will find it easier to judge and revise details. Order your points so that they follow logically from your thesis, and serve your purpose and topic, making it easier for readers to follow your argument. When you choose appropriate transitions or signal words to emphasize your order, you help your reader discover relationships that connect things, and, as you will see in Chapter 4, make them seem more coherent.

Time order, emphatic order, and **spatial order** are three common principles of organization for an essay's supporting points.

1. **Time** or **chronological order** means that points and details are ordered as they occur in time. *First* this is done; *next* this; *then* this; *after* that, this; and so on. You will often use time order for setting out a sequence of events, explaining how to do something, or narrating an anecdote.

Here is a brief outline of an essay in this book in which time order is used. This is an example of the process method of development, explaining how to do something or how something is done. The expanded thesis lists its supporting points in time order and the topic-sentence points follow this order, previewing the essay's process for readers.

Thesis: However, for success in exercise, you should follow a simple plan consisting of arranging the time, making preparations, and warming up properly.

1. To begin with, set aside a regular hour for exercise.

2. Next, prepare for your exercise session.

3. Finally, do a series of warm-up activities.

Which words and phrases in the topic sentences above indicate that the writer will use time order? How do these lead the reader along?

2. **Emphatic order** emphasizes the most interesting or important detail by using "least to most" sequences in the arrangement of supporting points. Place the points in least to most important order, or in least powerful to most powerful order—save the best til last. Variations on this include most-familiar-to-least-familiar, simplest-to-most-complex, order of frequency, and order of familiarity. Final positions are the most emphatic because the reader is most likely to remember the last thing he or she reads. *Finally, last of all,* and *most important* are typical words or phrases showing emphasis. Here is a brief outline of an essay that uses emphatic order:

Thesis: Celebrities lead very stressful lives.

1. For one thing, celebrities don't have the privacy an ordinary person does.

2. As well, celebrities are under constant pressure.

3. Celebrities also live with anxiety because they are only as good as their last success.

4. Most important, celebrities must deal with the stress of being in constant danger.

Which words or phrases in the topic sentences above help to show emphatic order?

● ● ● ● **ACTIVITY**

Writers often combine two orders in an essay because their topic and viewpoint suit the combination. Read the essay "Movie Night in the Bush" in Chapter 10. Which principle of organization or combination of principles has the writer chosen? Why, based on the subject of the essay, might the writer have chosen this order or combination of orders? How does the writer indicate the order(s)?

3. **Spatial order** means that you create a pattern in space for the reader to follow. You arrange items according to their physical position or relationships. If you describe a room, you could start at the doorway, then go around the four walls, ending back at the door. To emphasize spatial order, use positional transitions or signal words that lead and place the reader, such as *to the right, starting at . . . ,* or *under. . . .* You will find spatial order essential for descriptions; you

may apply this principle to examples as well, leading readers along a route; or you could classify items by physical placement; i.e., *southern B.C. is home to temperate rainforest . . . the northern part is mainly boreal forest.* Showing yet another use of spatial order, here is a brief outline of a process essay explaining how to reach Toronto's High Park on foot:

Thesis: The joy of finding a forest at the end of an afternoon city walk is worth the effort.

Right from your start at the corner of Bloor and Ossington, you see interesting stores and restaurants.

Then as you continue west and south on Dufferin, you find a cool green rest-stop: Dufferin Grove Park.

On the march west again from Dufferin and Bloor, you will want to walk briskly through the dry rundown stretch of Bloor west of Lansdowne.

Finally, walking downhill, you reach the edge of the forest at Keele and Bloor.

Which words or phrases in the topic sentences above help to show spatial order and guide readers through the walk?

In Chapter 4, you will learn more about transitions ("signal words") used to clarify and guide your reader's progress through your supporting points, details, and sentences.

REVIEW ACTIVITIES

Review Activity: Relating the Parts of an Essay to Each Other

Each group below contains one topic, one thesis statement, and two supporting sentences. In the space provided, label each item as follows:

T—topic
TH—thesis statement
S—supporting sentence

Group 1

a. TV forces politicians to focus more on appearance than substance.

b. Television is having an increasingly strong impact on the way Canadian elections are conducted.

c. The time and expense involved in creating commercials for parties and leaders might be better used in serving the public.

d. Television

e. Television can destroy politicians' reputations as it exposes them to viewers.

Group 2

a. Canadian colleges are more affordable than most universities.

b. There are several advantages to attending a college rather than a university.

c. Colleges

d. Canadian colleges typically offer more career-oriented programs and more internship opportunities than do universities.

Group 3

a. Medicine

b. Antibiotics have enabled doctors to control many diseases that were once fatal.

c. Organ transplants have prolonged the lives of thousands of people.

d. Advances in modern medicine have had great success in helping people.

Review Activity: Outlining

Your ability to distinguish between supporting points and details that fit under those points is important to thesis and outline development. In each of the four lists below, supporting points and details are mixed together. Put the items into logical order by filling in the outline that follows each list.

1. *Thesis:* Downtown high schools have multiple problem areas.

Drugs	a. _____
Leaky ceilings	(1) _____
Students	(2) _____
Unwilling to help after class	b. _____
Few after-school programs	(1) _____
Doors locked at 4:30 p.m.	(2) _____
Buildings	c. _____
Poorly equipped gyms	(1) _____
Much too strict	(2) _____
No morning or afternoon community involvement	d. _____
Cliques	(1) _____
Teachers	(2) _____

2. *Thesis:* Starting fitness programs early in life is a wise move.

Make new friends	a. _____
Reduce mental stress	(1) _____
Social benefits	(2) _____
Lifelong good habit	b. _____
Improves self-image	(1) _____
Mental benefits	(2) _____
Tones muscles	c. _____
Meet interesting instructors	(1) _____
Physical benefits	(2) _____

Review Activity: Adding Specific Details

In the following essay, specific details and sub-details are needed to explain the ideas in the supporting paragraphs. Add a sentence or two of clear, convincing details for each supporting point.

Introduction

Retail Therapy

Apparently, humans have managed to create a new disorder. It's a behavioural problem that can do some real damage. However, unlike other self-damaging behaviours such as excessive tanning or smoking, this one is not likely to put sufferers in the hospital. Instead, this disorder sends them to the store. "Oniomania" is the technical term for what they are suffering from, and it has nothing to do with onions. People know it better as compulsive shopping disorder (CSD) or shopaholism. Sufferers shop to keep up with "the Joneses," to lower anxiety, and to put excitement into their "boring" lives.

First Supporting Paragraph

One of the first reasons people shop compulsively is to keep up with real or imaginary peers. Perhaps low self-esteem drives this competitive shopping.

_____

In addition, filling the shopping cart does not fill up the holes in someone's self-esteem.

_____

Mostly, compulsive shopping results in an even lower sense of worth when the shopper faces bills he or she cannot pay.

_____

Second Supporting Paragraph

More often than they mention the need to "keep up," shopaholics say that shopping lowers anxiety.

_____

They very frequently say a sense of relief, a relaxed "floating feeling" comes over them when they start shopping.

_____

But over time, relief gives way to even more anxiety resulting from bills they cannot pay.

_____

Third Supporting Paragraph

Most often, though, the blanket response to questions about excessive shopping is that it relieves boredom.

_____

As well, shoppers eagerly turn to all forms of advertising and promotion, saying these beat boredom by helping them to anticipate new things to shop for.

_____

Finally, the sheer simplicity of consuming—go to a store or go online; see something, and buy it—makes shopping an easy diversion to turn to whenever time moves too slowly.

_____

Conclusion

Whether CSD is really a new disorder by itself, or just a new response to low self-esteem, anxiety, or boredom, it has become such a widespread problem that organizations like Shopaholics Anonymous have come into being. Shopaholism, in fact, affects more than just those afflicted and their families; growing levels of credit-card debt raise interest rates for everyone.

Review Activity: Developing Adequate Support

The following body paragraphs were taken from student essays. Two of the paragraphs provide sufficient details to support their topic sentences convincingly. Write _AD_ for _adequate development_ beside those paragraphs.

Three paragraphs use vague, wordy, general, or irrelevant sentences instead of real supporting details. Write _U_ for _underdeveloped_ beside those paragraphs.

_____ 1. People can be cruel to pets simply by being thoughtless. They don't think about a pet's needs or simply ignore those needs. It never occurs to them that their pet can be experiencing a great deal of discomfort as a result of their failure to be sensitive. The cruelty is a result of the basic lack of attention and concern—qualities that should be there but aren't.

_____ 2. Primetime programming on Canadian television would benefit from some major changes. Some shows should be eliminated completely. In fact, all the boring "made in Canada" shows that no one watches should be cancelled. Commercials, Canadian or American, should be changed so people could watch them without wanting to channel-surf or turn off the TV. Expand good, popular programs so that viewers stay loyal to Canadian programming and interests. The ideal Canadian primetime lineup would be a big improvement over what is now available on the major networks.

_____ 3. A friend's rudeness is much more damaging than a stranger's. When a friend says sharply, "I don't have time to talk to you just now," people feel hurt instead of angry. When a friend shows up late for lunch or a shopping trip, with no good reason, it is easy to feel taken for granted. Worst, though, is when a friend pretends to be listening, but his or her wandering eyes show a lack of attention. Then, anyone feels betrayed. Friends, after all, are supposed to make up for the thoughtless cruelties of strangers.

_____ 4. Sitting in the cockpit of a real plane, one of the school's Cessnas, after weeks of sitting in model cockpits and flight simulators, is an exciting experience. Students feel momentarily confident because everything is familiar; all the controls are exactly where they were in "rehearsals." The familiarity soon joins forces with excitement, though, when the instructor begins to take them step-by-step through the pre-flight checks. The repetition of the pattern of words "fuel gauge" and "altimeter" works like a soothing charm—everything will be fine. It is only when the student aviator knows that the instructor's next words will be "Start it up" that he or she feels a flutter of nervous anticipation. The instructor's voice is confident and normal. The student's stomach tightens. And he or she reaches for the starter, ready to fly . . . or just taxi down the runway.

Review Activity: Evaluating Support

Identify the types of information represented by the following statements. Explain your choices for each.

The *Reform Party of Canada* was a Western-based group that emerged from a coalition of discontented Western interest groups.

English classes are always boring.

After all, people are the same everywhere.

Political leaders make a lot of meaningless statements, even Barack Obama, who said, "I take a lot of tips from Canada."

Shopping malls have replaced village squares, according to some people.

Review Activity: Organizing Through Time, Spatial, or Emphatic Order

Use **time order** to organize the scrambled lists of supporting ideas below. Write *1* beside the supporting idea that should come first in time, *2* beside the idea that logically follows, and *3* beside the idea that comes last in time.

_____	***Thesis:*** Applying for unemployment benefits is often a depressing, frustrating experience.
_____	People arrive at the office feeling downhearted, and the tangle of paperwork they face only adds to their misery.
_____	Long lineups are only the beginning; processing a claim is not straightforward.
_____	There are weeks to wait for that first cheque, even after a claim goes through.

Use **emphatic order,** or order of importance, to organize the following scrambled lists of supporting ideas. For each thesis, write *1* beside the supporting point that is perhaps less important or interesting than the other two, *2* beside the point that appears more important or interesting, and *3* beside the point that should be most emphasized.

_____	***Thesis:*** Part-time jobs can be valuable life experiences for students.
_____	Working with the public teaches young people how to get along with many kinds of people.
_____	Balancing work and school teaches lessons in time management.
_____	Paying for tuition, books, and possibly rent means that part-time work is a necessity for most students.

Use **spatial order,** organizing by location, to organize the following scrambled lists of supporting ideas. For each thesis, put the statements in a logical sequence as dictated by their locations.

_____	***1. Thesis:*** An examination of the building will show why it is condemned.
_____	On the second floor, walls and ceilings are broken down.
_____	Starting in the basement, all evidence points to massive leakage.
_____	Throughout the main floor, all electrical work is substandard.
_____	Under the eaves, families of resident raccoons have caused damage.

CHECKLIST OF LEARNING OUTCOMES FOR CHAPTER 3

Be sure that you have understood and met the learning outcomes for this chapter. Answer the following questions:

✓ Why make an outline so late in the writing process? What are the main values of outlines?

✓ Explain the connection between your thesis and supporting points.

✓ Explain why details for your supporting points must be specific.

✓ Evaluate three types of information not drawn from personal experience.

✓ How do readers respond to insufficient details in an essay's body paragraphs? Why?

✓ Describe the three main ordering principles for essay content.

Drafting and Preparing to Revise: Creating Coherence, Introductions, and Conclusions

LEARNING OUTCOMES

After reading this chapter and working through its activities, you will

- compose your first draft;
- review the four goals or bases for effective writing;
- use various techniques to achieve coherence;

- write engaging introductions that suit your essay's purpose and content;
- write effective conclusions for your essays;
- create attractive and relevant titles.

You have completed the first two steps in writing an effective essay: advancing a thesis and supporting it with specific evidence. Once you have written your first draft, you will learn about the third step for writing effective essays: creating coherence, connecting your essay at all levels. Next, you will learn how to start an essay with an attractive introductory paragraph and how to finish it with a well-rounded concluding paragraph. You will then be prepared for the tasks of revising, editing, and proofreading.

DEVELOPING A FIRST DRAFT FROM AN OUTLINE

Now that you have your detailed outline and prewriting notes in hand and have decided on your principle of organization, you are fully prepared to compose your first draft and concentrate on putting your ideas into paragraphs and sentences.

Even if drafting is part of your prewriting process, this is your first "official" prepared draft.

You are following a goal-directed method of essay writing and right now, your immediate goal is to draft, to get the ideas in your outline down in sentences, following your outline's pattern. Concentrate on the general shape and content of your essay, not on fine details. This draft is meant to be rough; it gives you something to revise.

Try to write in a relaxed frame of mind. Keep your outline open onscreen beside your draft document, or to the side on your desk if you prefer to write by hand. But do not be rigidly shackled to your outline as you proceed—just keep shaping your ideas as you write. Here are some tips to help make writing a first draft easier and more effective:

- Leave as much time as possible between completing your outline and starting your draft. When your mind is relaxed, you will see your ideas more clearly and find connections more quickly.
- If additional thoughts and details come to you as you write, put them in your draft and note them on your outline and your draft.
- If one of your points or details no longer works for you, and you feel blocked as you try to replace that material, just leave a blank space and add a comment like, "Do later," and then keep going to finish your draft.
- Do not worry about spelling, punctuation, or grammar; you will correct these things in a later draft as you edit and proofread.
- Write your thesis at the top of your document, to help keep you focused and stay focused on pursuing your supporting points and details.

THE FIRST DRAFT: JED'S WORK IN PROGRESS

You have seen Jed Gawrys' work before; in Chapter 2, you shadowed his prewriting and discovery draft, and his thesis planning and outlining in Chapter 3. Now here is his first draft:

1   What fans really enjoy about pro sports isn't teamwork or suspense. It's competitiveness and violence. And society applauds these values. We will pay top dollar to see competitiveness, cruelty, and discrimination based on the star system. The key values in professional sports reflect society's acceptance and support of destruction and harm to human life.

2   Competition is what sports are about. Because competition leads to winners and losers. Winning brings in the money and money pays players, coaches, and determines ticket prices. Players are so driven by money that morality and sportsmanship go out the window. Coaches tell players to hurt the opposition in hockey and football. (Put in McMurtry thing.) How different is this from big business? Society praises people who get ahead at any cost and forgets about people who lose jobs when big companies close operations. Politics are no different. So-called moral politicians smear their opponents.

3   Football is built on tackling and maiming opposition players. In the NHL, it's the same. These aren't something added to these games, they're key

parts of them, especially for fans. In the NHL in 2008, there were 664 fights in 1230 games (NHL Fight Stats from NHL site). Society relies on fights and violence, too, because societies and governments are built on making themselves more powerful, no matter who suffers in the process. People who need help don't get it—the sick and the poor—they're powerless. But everybody is distracted by "corporate wars" while governments spend billions on weapons and armed forces. If that money were spent on trying to help people, not trying to "win" power struggles, everyone would win.

4   The third and possibly most devastating aspect of professional sports that is reflected in our society is discrimination. Sports leagues are huge organizations but only a few players have a lot of playing time. Star players are the most skilled and pro sports discriminates against players who aren't as skilled. Being the best, being stars means more than any work ethic another player might have. Society makes people stars just like the movie business. These people are not necessarily good or moral; they just seem good because they are so famous. Actors are paid millions for working a few months a year—Will Smith—BE SPECIFIC AND FIND A SOURCE . . . Everyone admires him but who admires the guy who picks up the garbage twelve months a year? He works harder and does something valuable but people consider him lower-class. City workers like that can work fifty or sixty hours a week for poor wages. Is it because they don't appear successful according to society's standards that we don't value their skills?

5   The main values that we see in sports, like extreme competitiveness, violence and winning at any cost, and discrimination directly reflect society's values. Pro sports may never change but society needs to.

With your first draft complete, you, like Jed, can learn techniques that will prepare you to revise that draft.

EVALUATING YOUR ESSAY: PREPARING TO REVISE

There are four goals or bases on which you and your instructor will evaluate your essays. These bases, as you will see on pages 82 and following, are **unity, support, coherence,** and **effective sentence skills.** If your support flows logically from your thesis, you are on your way to **unity;** as you develop and refine your support so that it is specific, appropriate, and abundant, you are working toward the goal of effective **support.** And now, as you learn how to create **coherence,** you are working to meet the third goal. To achieve coherence, you will organize and connect all three levels of your essay with the use of transitions, transitional sentences, and other transitional structures.

Creating Coherence

Coherence means literally "sticking together." When you create coherence, you show your reading audience a smooth, clear sequence from sentence to sentence, and paragraph to paragraph. When you decided on a principle of organization for your essay, you learned the value of "signal words," or transitions, to guide your readers. You were, in fact, already preparing to make your essay coherent.

Coherence is the product of choices you make in the outlining, drafting, and revising stages of the writing process. First, as you outline and draft, you *organize* your entire essay according to time, emphasis, or spatial placement, as appropriate to your subject and purpose. Second, as you write and revise your rough draft, you *connect* paragraphs and sentences with appropriate methods of transition.

The boxed summary below provides techniques for achieving coherence at the essay level, paragraph level, and sentence level. Refer to these points as you work on your drafts.

---

1. To Create Coherence at the Essay Level

- Write an effective thesis statement with clear, logically derived supporting points.
- Indicate the order for the supporting points of your thesis, and sustain that order through your topic sentences and body paragraphs.

2. To Create Coherence at the Paragraph Level

- Write topic sentences that refer clearly to the thesis-point covered by that paragraph.
- Write topic sentences that cover all details and examples found in each body paragraph.
- Reinforce, with transitional phrases or structures, the order established in your thesis in each body paragraph's topic sentence.
- Use transitions in each body paragraph's topic sentence that remind the reader of the ending of the previous paragraph.
- Use transitional phrases or structures in each body paragraph's closing sentence that connect that paragraph with the one that follows.
- Use concluding or summarizing phrases to signal your concluding paragraph.

3. To Create Coherence at the Sentence Level

- Within each paragraph of your essay, use transitional phrases or devices to show relationships between sentences and to mark changes of direction, meaning, or emphasis.

TRANSITIONS AND TRANSITIONAL SENTENCES

Transitions in General

Transitions have two functions:

1. Transitions signal the direction of a writer's thought.

2. Transitions are links or "bridges" between paragraphs, sentences, and thoughts, like road signs.

Transitions are not "ornaments" or additional words to be plugged in mechanically at certain points in an essay. Transitional words, phrases, and sentences form essential parts of your essay's coherent and logical movement from one idea to the next. Writers often know the direction in which they are proceeding, but the reading audience may not; transitions are essential to a reader's clear understanding of every level of your essay.

Sentence- and Paragraph-Level Transition Words and Phrases

To achieve coherence at the sentence level within your paragraphs, use transitions to guide your readers through the logical pattern behind your arrangement of the sentences. As you have seen in the previous chapter, you will use many of these transitions to begin body paragraphs as well; you will find *time, emphasis,* and *spatial* transitions listed below. All these transitions *show* readers what you mean more accurately.

In the box below are some common transitions, grouped by the type of expression or according to the kind of signal they give to readers. Note that certain words provide more than one kind of signal.

Addition signals: again, besides, for one thing, then, one, first of all, second, the third reason, also, next, another, and, in addition, moreover, furthermore, finally, last of all

Cause or Effect: since, because, therefore, thus, hence, for the reason that, so, accordingly, otherwise, if, then

Conceding or allowing a point: indeed, although, admittedly, it is true that, no doubt, naturally, to be sure, though

Time signals: first, then, next, after, after that, afterward, as, at that time, at the moment, before, currently, presently, earlier, while, meanwhile, soon, now, during, while, eventually, gradually, immediately, finally, in the future, in the past, one day, so far

Emphasis: assuredly, decidedly, more, most, just, better, best, certainly, especially, even, undoubtedly, clearly, mainly, principally, above all, least (most) of all, indeed, of course, in effect

Space signals: above, behind, beyond, beside, next to, across, on one (the other) side, on the opposite side, to (on) the left, to (on) the right, closer in, farther out, above, below, on the top (bottom), near(by), north, south, east, west

Change-of-direction or contrast signals: but, however, instead, nevertheless, yet, in contrast, although, otherwise, still, on the contrary, on the other hand

Illustration signals: for example, for instance, specifically, as an illustration, (in) that way, once, such as, in other words

Conclusion signals: therefore, consequently, thus, then, as a result, in summary, to conclude, last of all, finally

At the sentence-to-sentence level within paragraphs, transitional words and expressions are essential. Your sentences are your most constant points of contact with your readers. So if your writing flows from sentence to sentence, it eases readers' way through your thoughts, and points out when a change of direction, an example, or an ending is coming.

The following activity will give you practice with transitional words and phrases.

● ● ● ● **ACTIVITY**

1. Choose *time* transitions for the blanks in the following selection:

   _____ you've snagged the job of TV sports reporter, you have to begin working on the details of your image. _____, invest in two or three truly loud sports jackets. Look for gigantic plaid patterns in odd colour combinations like purple and green or orange and blue; your role model is Don Cherry. These should become familiar enough to viewers that they will associate that crazy jacket with that dynamic sportscaster. _____, try to cultivate a distinctive voice that will be just annoying enough to be memorable. A nasal whine or a gravelly growl will do it. _____ be sure to speak only in tough, punchy sentences that seem to be punctuated with imaginary exclamation points. _____ , you must share lots of pompous, obnoxious opinions with your viewers. Your tone of voice must convey the hidden message, "I dare anyone to disagree with me."

2. Choose *space* signals and one *emphatic* transition for the following selection:

   The vegetable bin of the refrigerator contained an assortment of weird-looking items. _____ a shrivelled, white-coated lemon was a pair of oranges covered with blue fuzz. _____ the oranges was a bunch of carrots that had begun to sprout points, spikes, knobs, and tendrils. The carrots drooped limply over a bundle of celery. _____ the carrots was a net bag of onions; each onion had sent curling shoots through the net until the whole thing resembled a mass of green spaghetti. _____ item, though, was a head of lettuce that had turned into a pool of brown goo. It had seeped out of its bag and coated the bottom of the bin with a sticky, evil-smelling liquid.

3. Choose *illustration, time, change of direction, causal,* and *conclusion* transitions for the following selection:

   _____ , because data-storage formats have evolved so significantly, maintaining a clean hard drive is easier than ever. _____ computer users, worried about power outage-related file losses, saved 50 to 200 KB of data on flimsy five-inch diskettes. These certainly helped unclog those little 186K hard drives, but they were fragile and prone to damage caused by handling or extreme temperatures. Increasing use of computers in the early 1990s led to improvements, _____ the 3.5-inch hard-case disk. _____ they required the addition of a new drive on home PCs, they were durable and stored nearly ten times more data than a five-inch diskette. As all disks record information magnetically, _____ , their content could still be erased by contact with magnets. The smaller disks still degraded or the information simply disappeared after unpredictable lengths of time. _____, the heavily cased Zip drive delivered over one gigabyte of storage to accommodate larger image and text files, again for the price of a new external drive. Its reign was cut short by the entry of CD technology into the file-storage race; CD and DVD slots and writers became common on new computers. _____, readable-only CDs seal their contents and do not allow re-entry, and while writable CDs can be erased and reused, both versions are easily scratched. _____, the "key" to safe, portable data appeared. The tiny USB key, able to store 32 GB or more of information, stores as much as many computers' hard drives. "Keys" require only standard USB ports, no formatting, and easily store huge MP3, image, video, and text files. _____, now that the hard drive is clean, and the computer is running quickly, just do not lose the keys.

OTHER TRANSITIONAL STRUCTURES FOR SENTENCE- AND PARAGRAPH-LEVEL COHERENCE

In addition to transitional words and expressions, there are three other kinds of connecting words and phrases you can use to tie together the specific evidence in an essay: repeated words, pronouns, and synonyms. Use these to connect one sentence to another, and to make sentences in a paragraph flow more smoothly.

Repeated Words You have probably been taught not to repeat yourself when you write. However, repeating key words helps tie together the flow of thought in an essay. Below, repeated words remind readers of the selection's central idea.

> One reason for studying *psychology* is to help parents deal with children. Perhaps a young daughter refuses to go to bed when parents want her to and bursts into tears at the least mention of "lights out." A little knowledge of *psychology* comes in handy. Offer her a choice of staying up until 7:30 p.m. with her parents or going upstairs and playing until 8:00 p.m. Since she gets to make the choice, she does not feel so powerless and will not resist. *Psychology* is also useful in rewarding a child for a job well done. Instead of telling a ten-year-old son what a good boy he is when he makes his own bed, tell him how neat it looks, how pleasing it is, and how proud of him you are for doing it by himself. The *psychology* books all say that being a good boy is much harder to live up to than doing one job well.

There is no rigid rule about how much repetition is bad, and how much is useful; the suitability of repeated words depends on the context and purpose of the writer. Often, if a term is important to understanding the material, repeating it is effective; it helps your reader home in on what is important, and helps him or her process the information.

You may, if possible, wish to use variations on or repeated parts of a key word, rather than simple repetition. This technique prevents possible monotony. Variations on words are similar to, but not identical to synonyms, another transitional structure. Following is an example:

People have mixed reactions to the amount of money spent on the Canadian space program. Typically, the public tends to think that space exploration and space technology, like the Canadarm, just cost too much. Jerman Mayzelle, an Ottawa federal employee, says, "The Canadian dollars going into space, based on our GNP and economy, are out of line. The money could be better spent elsewhere." However, when an item of space technology is successful, the general public is thought to approve of our country's accomplishments.

Pronouns Pronouns (he, she, it, you, they) are another way to connect ideas. Also, using pronouns in place of other words can help you avoid needless repetition. (Note, however, that pronouns should be used with care to avoid problems such as unclear pronoun reference, as described in Part 4.) Here is a selection that makes use of pronouns to continue the reference to *people:*

Another way for people to economize at an amusement park is to bring their own food. If they pack a nourishing, well-balanced lunch of cold chicken, carrot sticks, and fruit, they will avoid having to pay high prices for hamburgers and hot dogs. They won't eat as many calories. Also, instead of filling up on soft drinks, they should bring a thermos of iced tea. Iced tea is more refreshing than pop, and it is a great deal cheaper. Every dollar that is not spent at a refreshment stand is one that can be spent on another ride.

Pronouns also have a "summing up" function; they connect ideas naturally because pronouns almost always refer you to something you read earlier in a passage. When you read "This is true because . . . ," you automatically think about what *this* could mean. The pronoun *this* causes you to add up, quickly and without thinking, all the ideas that *this* stands for before going on to the *because* part of the sentence.

Synonyms Using synonyms (words alike in meaning) can also help move your readers clearly from one thought to the next. In addition, just as when you use variations on words, when you use synonyms, you increase variety and interest in your text by avoiding needless repetition. To strengthen your vocabulary and widen your knowledge of synonyms, you may use a thesaurus or the "thesaurus" function under "tools" on your word-processing program. A print thesaurus and the thesaurus tool in Word both supply you with lists of *alternate words or phrases* for any word you look up. Alternate words or phrases or synonyms are not exact substitute-words, though. Neither type of thesaurus can understand the shadings of meaning a synonym presents. Only you know the exact meaning you intend. Always have a dictionary at hand when you use either type of thesaurus; check the meaning of any word presented to you as a synonym.

Note the synonyms for *method* in the following selection:

There are several methods of fundraising that work well with small organizations. One technique is to hold an auction, with everyone either contributing an item from home or obtaining a donation from a sympathetic local merchant. Because all the merchandise, including the services of the auctioneer, has been donated, the entire proceeds can be placed in the organization's treasury. A second fundraising procedure is a car wash. Club members and their children get together on a Saturday and wash all the cars in the neighbourhood for a few dollars apiece. A final, time-tested <u>way</u> to raise money is to hold a bake sale, with each family contributing homemade cookies, brownies, layer cakes, or cupcakes. Sold by the piece or by the box, these baked goods will satisfyingly fill both the stomach and the pocketbook.

Parallel Structure Parallel structure is word repetition at a higher level. You create parallel structure with the repetition of phrases, clauses, and sentences. Repeating a phrase or sentence creates a rhythm, similar to that in the chorus of a song. The rhythm of the repeated text tells readers that the ideas in the parallel structures are related. Their minds say, "If that sentence started with 'The pursuit of happiness . . .,' and this one does too, then the ideas in the last parts of both sentences are probably related." As with basic repetition, the overuse of parallel structure can result in monotony. But within a paragraph, where there will be ideas and details related to the topic sentence, parallel structure is appropriate.

The effectiveness of parallel structure is based on how the parallel phrases sound when spoken silently by audiences as they read. Great public speakers have always used parallel structure to add emphasis and coherence to their texts. Martin Luther King Jr's "I Have a Dream" speech is a well-known example:

> I have a dream that one day this nation will rise up and live out the true meaning of its creed: "We hold these truths to be self-evident, that all men are created equal."
>
> I have a dream that one day on the red hills of Georgia, the sons of former slaves and the sons of former slave owners will be able to sit down together at the table of brotherhood.
>
> I have a dream that one day even the state of Mississippi, a state sweltering with the heat of injustice, sweltering with the heat of oppression, will be transformed into an oasis of freedom and justice.
>
> I have a dream that my four little children will one day live in a nation where they will not be judged by the color of their skin but by the content of their character.
>
> I have a *dream* today!

PARAGRAPH-TO-PARAGRAPH TRANSITIONS: TRANSITIONAL SENTENCES

To achieve coherence *between* the paragraphs in your essay, use transitional material at the "entrance" and "exit" points of each paragraph. Your reader will move smoothly from the end of one paragraph to the start of the next.

Following are the specific uses for transitions and transitional sentences at the paragraph level, as indicated in the box on page 57:

- **Topic sentence transitions:** signal and reinforce time sequence, emphatic order, or another order **or** link the paragraph topic with the preceding paragraph's topic.
- **Concluding sentence transitions:** link to the following paragraph's topic **or** suggest a conclusion.

• • • • **ACTIVITY**

Below is a brief sentence outline of an essay. The second and third topic sentences serve as transitional, or linking, sentences. Each reminds you of the point in the preceding paragraph while stating the point to be developed in the current paragraph. In the spaces provided, add the words needed to complete the second and third topic sentences. If possible, try to write a concluding sentence that leads into the paragraph that follows.

Thesis	The most important values parents can teach are the importance of family support, hard work, and a good education.
First Supporting Paragraph	First, good parents show that family members should stick together, especially in times of trouble_____. . . .
Second Supporting Paragraph	In addition to teaching about the importance of_____ parents should emphasize the value of_____. . . .
Third Supporting Paragraph	Along with the value of _____ parents must stress the importance of_____. . . .

Your first draft is complete, and you are prepared to revise it for coherence. Now prepare yourself to create an effective introduction, conclusion, and title.

INTRODUCTIONS, CONCLUSIONS, AND TITLES

Introductory Paragraph

A good introduction welcomes your readers, makes them comfortable with your subject, states your thesis, and leads on to your first body paragraph. While your first paragraph must be unified and coherent, like your other paragraphs, it performs a lot of specialized tasks that body paragraphs do not.

Because you must know what your essay will say, and why and how it will say it, before you try to interest readers, you may find it awkward or wasteful to write a full introduction with your first draft. You will find it easier to return to your opening paragraph when you revise that draft. This is the approach that Jed, the student writing about sports and society, takes, as you will see at the end of this section.

Functions of Your Introduction

1. It attracts the readers' interest, encouraging them to continue reading the essay.

2. It supplies any background information that may be needed to understand the essay.

3. It presents a thesis statement that usually appears near the end of the introductory paragraph.

If you write an extended thesis, your opening paragraph indicates at least a basic plan of development: the supporting points for the thesis are listed in the order in which they will be presented. In many cases, the thesis and plan of development appear in the same sentence, but they need not do so.

Contents of Your Introduction

If your intention is to engage and interest your readers, a blunt statement of your thesis in the first lines of your opening paragraph will not do the job; neither will a dry announcement: "This essay will deal with the destructive effects of casinos on the local economy." Whatever your purpose, you must attract your readers, so open your introductory paragraph with an idea that will *catch their attention,* and *lead* them *into* your essay. An introductory paragraph usually consists of three elements:

1. Attention-getter or lead-in

2. Steps to, or development leading to, thesis (transition from attention-getter to thesis)

3. Thesis

PAT AND YOUR INTRODUCTION

The first chapter introduced you to the PAT formula: *Purpose, Audience, Thesis (or Topic).* Nowhere in your essay is your attention to these elements as important as in your opening. Unless your introduction reveals your *purpose* in an appropriate manner that appeals to your *audience* and prepares them to understand and be interested in your *thesis,* they may not even read your essay. Therefore, consider first which overall approach will best suit your topic (and thesis) and your audience.

General Approaches to Your Introduction

There are three basic approaches to writing an introduction, and there are specific methods based on each approach. Think first in general terms about how you wish to introduce yourself to your readers:

1. Logical Openings

If you are writing an essay that explains or argues a concept that you would like readers to consider within a larger context, introduce your readers to that larger context first. Then move logically through the development section of your introduction by narrowing that general opening context to a more specific level, finally ending with your very specific thesis statement.

This is sometimes called "the funnel opening":

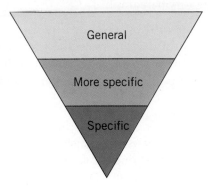

Introduce your audience gradually, in logical and increasingly specific terms, to your thesis. You may also proceed from ideas your audience knows to ideas that are less familiar or unknown to them. Logical openings are suitable for essays on literature, essays in the humanities, and essays in the sciences.

2. Striking or Dramatic Openings

Openings designed to spark your reader's interest start with a very specific idea or technique. Logical approaches are gradual; striking openings, as the name suggests, are direct. Ask a surprising question related to your thesis; relate a short anecdote, or choose an interesting quotation. These are familiar techniques, known to most people from marketing and advertising, but, used well, they are highly effective in provoking readers' interest, or even catching readers a bit off-base. Be careful that there is a clear line of development between your opening strategy and your thesis—a question unrelated to the point of your essay will do nothing but annoy readers. This category of openings works well with persuasive or argumentative essays.

3. Emotional-Appeal Openings

If you choose to open with an appeal to the emotions of readers, open with statements designed to hit a chord of sympathy with them. You may open with a vivid description of some incident; for instance, a traffic accident—such an opening attention-getter speaks to readers' emotions and bypasses logic. These openings must be based on predictable responses so that audiences are likely to share the feeling you evoke. Nonetheless, knowing your audience as well as possible is essential when you choose to appeal to emotion; if your appeal misses or offends, you lose your reader. If used carefully, the appeal to emotions can be appropriate for persuasive essays about social issues, but at a postsecondary level, it is less useful than other types of introductions.

METHODS OF INTRODUCTION

These methods are grouped by the approach they are based on, to help you think about what sort of introduction would be appropriate to your purpose, audience, thesis, and perhaps your tone.

If your purpose is to explain the seriousness of an issue, and you are uncertain how much your audience understands about its gravity or how it relates to them, avoid a general opening and proceed immediately to establish this issue's relevance to readers. Alternatively, if your topic suits a light approach, you could take a humorous tone and begin with an amusing anecdote or question.

Logical Methods

1. ***Begin with a somewhat general statement of your topic, and narrow it down to your thesis statement: a funnel opening.*** General statements ease the reader into your thesis statement by first introducing the topic. However, avoid sweeping statements like "the world these days," or "humanity's problems;" no writer could handle such huge concepts. In the example below, the writer talks generally about diets and then narrows down to comments on a specific diet.

   Bookstore shelves today are crammed with dozens of different diet books. The Canadian public seems willing to try any sort of diet, especially the ones that promise instant, miraculous results. As well, authors are more than willing to invent new fad diets to cash in on this craze. Unfortunately, some of these fad diets are ineffective or even unsafe. One of the worst fad diets is the "Zone Diet." It is expensive, doesn't achieve the results it claims, and is a sure route to poor nutrition.

2. ***Supply background information or context.*** Much of your future career writing and many assignments will be based on subject matter unfamiliar to general readers. Therefore, this introductory approach is relevant and useful. Whenever you write about a subject that is not considered "general knowledge" or "common interest," use this method. If you must explain an accounting method, analyze some technical process, or evaluate a software's operation, always give enough background information to make your thesis and support clear and understandable to your audience.

   MP3 is a three-character code seen everywhere today. But what is an MP3? It is simply a compressed file containing audio data: music, speech, or sound effects. Sounds are compressed from earlier, larger WAV files for quick downloading. MP3 compression matches twelve bytes of a WAV with only a single byte in MP3 format; it removes sounds people's ears cannot usually hear. MP3s are an important part of the downsizing of media since they offer good audio quality, they are divisible into cuts or sections, and they are very portable.

3. ***Begin with familiar, known information or situations, and move to the lesser known or unfamiliar.*** This is sometimes called a "comparison" or analogy introduction because it makes use of the way humans learn about most things: by comparing them to something they already know. This is a form of logic readers understand immediately. Typically, if your thesis or topic is relatively unknown to your readers or is complex, this is a good alternative to the funnel or background context opening.

People call each other all sorts of animal-names. Kittens, dogs, pigs, bunnies, vultures: each of these animals represents some aspect, positive or negative, of humanity. But the animal whose name is an insult everywhere is surprisingly one of the most similar to human beings. The first similarity is that both rats and humans are omnivorous—they eat everything . . .

4. *Explain the importance of your topic to the reader.* If you can convince your readers that the subject applies to them, or is something they should know more about, they will want to keep reading.

Diseases like scarlet fever and whooping cough used to kill more young children than any other illness. Today, however, child mortality due to disease has been almost completely eliminated in first-world countries by medical science. Instead, car accidents are the number one killer of children. Most children fatally injured in car accidents were not protected by car seats, belts, or restraints of any kind. Several steps must be taken to reduce the serious dangers car accidents pose to children.

Striking or Dramatic Approaches

1. *Start with an idea or situation that is the opposite of the one you will develop.* This approach, sometimes called the "contrast" introduction, works because your readers will be surprised, and then intrigued, by the contrast between the opening idea and the thesis that follows it.

Technology is the enemy of art. The keyboard and mouse are no substitutes for the artist's hand and eye. Screens are not galleries. Or, so traditionalists would say. But what about displaying the artist's work, or getting feedback on it? Here, the emergence of online art communities has been a blessing for anyone looking to share their craft and garner critiques from fellow artists. PHP Scripting has created user-friendly interfaces containing easy-to-upload personal galleries, comment features and message boards. Millions of users can submit art pieces every minute for show and/or critique. With sites boasting a wide range of categories including digital art, photography, analog painting, and more, artists are bound to find similar creators in their genre to inspire them and commune with.

2. *Use an incident or brief story.* Stories are naturally interesting. They appeal to a reader's curiosity. In your introduction, an anecdote will grab the reader's attention right away. The story should be brief and should be related to your main idea. The incident in the story can be something that happened to you or something you have heard or read about. Students who must write reports for courses in business and social-services disciplines find anecdotal introductions useful.

On a Friday morning in a large Canadian mall, a woman buys two sweatshirts, jeans, a doormat, baby sleepers, and a leather backpack. Her bill comes to $650.00. She pays cheerfully with a platinum credit card, smiling at the clerk who sports several piercings and a headset. Not a single customer or clerk notices her. Why should they? Well, she is sixty-seven years of age, and except for the baby pajamas, she is shopping for herself at an apparently youth-oriented store. In stores like The Gap, Old Navy, or Roots, where this woman just shopped, demographics should be predictable. However consumer patterns are changing rapidly, and retailers must understand and respond to new age groups, new buying habits, and new merchandise mixes.

3. ***Ask one or more questions.*** You may simply want the reader to think about possible answers, or you may plan to answer the questions yourself later in the paper. Questions provoke responses, and the reader responds by paying attention.

   What is love? How do we know that we are really in love? When we meet that special person, how can we tell that our feelings are genuine and not merely infatuation? If they are genuine, will these feelings last? Love, as we all know, is difficult to define. Yet most people agree that true and lasting love involves far more than mere physical attraction. Love involves mutual respect, the desire to give rather than take, and the feeling of being wholly at ease.

4. ***Use a quotation.*** A quotation can be something you have read in a book or article. It can also be something that you have heard: a popular saying or proverb ("never give advice to a friend"), a current or recent advertising slogan, or a favourite expression used by friends or family. Remember to give the source for your quotation, because you are adding someone else's voice to your own.

   "To figure something out, you've got to be confused." So said K-OS, the dean of Canadian hip-hop artists. The story behind the growth of Canadian hip hop began with some confusing blends of rap and rock. Although Devon and Maestro Fresh Wes were successes in the early 1990s, what broke the music through to mainstream audiences of the time was the unlikely mix of Frankie Fudge's rap breaks on Celine Dion's hit single "Unison." For Canadian rappers, figuring out how to reach their audiences would mean negotiating with various media groups, developing their own music association, and waiting until 2001 for urban music stations to be licensed.

5. ***Use a definition.*** You can use definitions either to confirm your thesis' point or to contrast with it. Definitions are good specific hooks and guide readers straight into your content. But avoid the clichéd, "According to Oxford (Webster, Gage . . .)"; readers can open the dictionary for themselves. If you quote or paraphrase a definition, be sure to cite it correctly. Refer to Part 3 for information on citation.

   In *What Is Liberal Education,* Leo Strauss asserts that "Liberal education is the ladder by which we try to ascend from mass democracy as originally meant" (11). While liberal education may indeed have been used for such a purpose, it has an intrinsic value and should be accessible to all. In a free, democratic society citizens do have a choice. Liberal education gives people the tools to make informed choices.

Emotional-Appeal Approaches

1. *Write a vivid description of an emotionally powerful incident or scenario.* If you are certain of the direct relationship between the scene you describe and your thesis, then you may try this approach. Read Chapter 9 for tips on clear, detailed description. Keep your description to about three sentences, so it does not overshadow your development to your thesis.

   Fruit flies never seem much of a menace in themselves, but when they cluster outside back doors and in alleys in a haze of hot, stomach-turning stench, they seem like messengers of disease and disorder. Much of Canada's largest city is in the grip of a fruit-fly infestation, the result in part of the six-week city workers strike that gave rise to mountains of rotting trash in temporary dump-sites throughout the metropolis.

2. *Make a claim for the sympathy of your readers.* Many successful claims for sympathy are written in a "reportorial" way, as if you are bringing news of your topic to readers without obvious commentary. Following this formula lessens the risk of suffocating or battering readers by trying to force them to feel something.

   There is a man in Nova Scotia who wears his life on his face. His skin is deeply creased, and each of these creases has a story to tell about growing up in the East. He is every man and woman who grew up on hard biscuit and grease, who started smoking too young, who lived in decrepit houses in dying communities. He came down to Toronto for a while to make a better living, but got lonely and drank too much. Now he sits outside the old hotel, waiting for nothing but his welfare cheque. This is the human face of Maritimes' economic failure.

● ● ● ● **ACTIVITY**

In groups or on your own, write introductory paragraphs on any three of the following topics, using a *different* method for each. Remember to include an attention-getter, development, and a thesis. Be sure your method suits your topic.

1. Flu epidemics
2. Daycare problems
3. Student newspapers
4. First-semester challenges
5. Online courses
6. The best things in life . . .

CONCLUDING PARAGRAPH

The concluding paragraph is your chance to remind the reader of your thesis and bring the essay to a satisfactory end.

As you look over your first draft's final paragraph, consider, once again, your purpose, your essay's content, your audience, and also the impression or effect you would like to leave with readers. Do you want readers to smile, to think seriously, or to take some action?

Conclusions should never wander, and they should never introduce new ideas or examples. You are closing off your conversation with your reader, not starting a new one. Conclusions should be proportional to your essay's length and argument. For a short essay, a two-sentence concluding paragraph is probably too brief, but a lengthy ten-sentence concluding paragraph would likely lose readers' attention.

Whichever concluding approach you choose, remind readers of where they began—your thesis statement. They will recognize this return to the beginning as a signal of completion and will appreciate your effort to close the essay in a satisfying way.

Methods of Conclusion

There are two basic methods for concluding your thesis' argument: close the circle after proving your point, or leave an "open door" by challenging or recommending that readers see your point in a larger perspective. There are, in turn, two approaches to using each method.

Closing the Circle

There are two approaches to "closing the door"; each is based on reassuring readers that you have met the challenge that your thesis posed to readers.

1. ***End with a summary and final thought.*** In other words, restate the thesis and supporting points without using the wording you used before. Instead, reinforce how you arrived at your thesis. This should be followed by a final comment that "rounds off" and broadens the scope of the essay. This combination of a summary and a final thought is the most common method of concluding an essay. Here is an example:

   > Catalogue shopping at home, then, has distinct advantages. Such shopping is convenient, saves consumers money, and saves time. It is not surprising that growing numbers of devoted catalogue shoppers are welcoming those full-colour mail brochures that offer everything from turnip seeds to televisions.

2. ***Answer any questions your lead-in or introduction asked.*** Use your thesis to answer a lead-in question you posed; doing so gives readers a sense of closure and reinforces the notion that you have proved your point. Here is a conclusion that Jed Gawrys might have used:

   > What do fans hope to see at an NHL or NFL game? They hope to see brutal competition, fierce fighting, and stars winning out over all. Anything else is not worth the ticket price—the excitement comes from the brutal values that pro sports are built on. Unfortunately, those are the same values that North Americans put into practice every day of their lives.

Opening the Door

There are two approaches to leading your readers back out into a wider context of thinking, as you do when you "open the door" with your conclusion.

1. *Include a thought-provoking question or short series of questions.* A question grabs the reader's attention. It is a direct appeal to your reader to think further about what you have written. It may involve (1) why the subject of your essay is important; (2) what might happen in the future; (3) what should be done about this subject; or (4) which choice should be made. In any case, be sure that the question is closely related to your thesis. Here is an example:

> What, then, happens now in the twenty-first century when most of the population will be over sixty years old? Retirement policies may change dramatically, with the age-sixty-five testimonial dinner and gold watch postponed for five or ten years. Television is already changing as the Metamucil generation replaces the Pepsi generation. Glamorous grey-haired models sell everything from prescription medicine to banking plans. It will be a different world indeed when the young find themselves outnumbered.

2. *End with a prediction or recommendation to act.* Like questions, predictions and recommendations also involve your readers. Recommendations to take some action are also useful for many types of business writing, including cover letters for résumés. A *prediction* states what may happen in the future:

> If people stopped to think before acquiring pets, there would be fewer instances of cruelty to animals. Many times, it is the people who adopt pets without considering the expense and responsibility involved who mistreat and neglect their animals. Pets are living creatures. They do not deserve to be treated as carelessly as one would treat a stuffed toy.

A *recommendation* suggests some action that should be taken about a situation or problem:

> Stereotypes such as the helpless homemaker, harried female executive, and dotty grandma are insulting enough to begin with. In magazine ads or television commercials, they become even more insulting. Such hackneyed caricatures of women are not just the objects of derisive humour; these stereotypes now pitch a range of products to an unsuspecting public. Consumers should boycott companies whose advertising continues to use such stereotypes.

● ● ● ● **ACTIVITY**

In the space provided, note whether each concluding paragraph ends with a summary and final thought (write *S* in the space), a prediction or recommendation (write *P/R*), or a question (write *Q*).

_____ 1. Disappointments are unwelcome but regular visitors to everyone's life. People can feel depressed about them, or they can try to escape from them. The best thing, though, is to accept a disappointment and then try to use it somehow. Step over the unwelcome visitor and then get on with life.

_____ 2. Holidays, it is clear, are often not the fulfilling experiences they are supposed to be. They can, in fact, be very stressful. But would we rather have a holiday-free calendar?

3. People's dreams of stardom, of seeing their names in lights and their pictures on the covers of magazines, are based on illusions. The celebrities whose lives are documented for all to see give up their private lives, endure constant pressure, and are never completely safe. The price of fame is too high, and never worth its cost.

TITLES

TIPS ON TITLES

- Titles are always a few words or a brief phrase, not complete sentences.
- Titles do not substitute for thesis statements; never make readers guess about your point once they begin reading your essay.
- Do not repeat your thesis in your title.
- Compose your title *after* you have written your essay.
- Make your title a short phrase, never a sentence.
- Do not underline the title or put quotation marks around it. You should, though, capitalize all but small connecting words in the title.

A well-written title may take a variety of forms, depending, once again, on an essay's purpose, audience, and tone.

Essays aimed at informing readers often display titles that are highly condensed summaries of their content: *A College Diploma: Your Ticket to Success?*

Academic essays in many disciplines use titles that describe their content succinctly: *Soap Operas and Festivals: A Comparative Analysis.*

You will generally want your title to entice audiences to read your essay. An audience of your peers will be intrigued by a reference in your title to common interests or by a familiar phrase reworked to suit content. Will your instructor? A humorous essay should have a title that fits its tone, suggesting that what follows will entertain its readers.

Titles may be specialized to suit patterns of essay development, covered in Part 2, as well:

- *Exemplification:* Adjustment Issues of Mature Students
- *Process:* How Photosynthesis Works
- *Classification and Division:* Forms of Workplace Discrimination
- *Definition:* What Fitness Means
- *Cause and Effect:* Rage Addiction: Effects on the Family
- *Comparison/Contrast:* Energy Drinks Versus Nutritious Meals
- *Argumentation:* Why English is Such a Challenge

• • • • ACTIVITY

- Skip a space between the title and the first line of the text. (See chapter on Manuscript Form on the OLC *Online LearningCentre* at **www.mcgrawhill. ca/olc/langan.**)

Write an appropriate title for the introductory paragraphs that follow.

1. When people see rock-concert audiences only on television or in newspaper photos, the audiences at these events may all seem to be excited teenagers. However, attending a few rock shows would show people that several kinds of ticket-buyers make up the crowd. At any concert, there are usually the typical fan, the out-of-place person, and the troublemaker.

   Title: _____

2. Are you sitting in a messy room right now? Are piles of papers or heaps of clothes tilting at weird angles and leaning on towers of magazines, boxes, and bags all around you? You are not alone, and you should not feel ashamed. Messes are just the natural overflow of our personalities. Messes say that we are too busy, too interesting to spend time cleaning, organizing, and turning into obsessive organizers. Most of all, a good mess is full of potential treasures. A mess is a safety zone, a sign of an active life, and a source of inspiration.

   Title: _____

REVIEW ACTIVITIES

1. CONNECTING SPECIFIC EVIDENCE

Review Activity: Identifying Transitions

The following items use transitions or connecting words to help tie ideas together. The connecting words you are to identify are set off in italics. In the space, write *T* for *transition*, *RW* for *repeated word*, *S* for *synonym*, or *P* for *pronoun*.

_____ 1. Maurizio wears a puffy, black, quilted down-filled jacket. In this *garment,* he resembles a stack of inflated inner tubes.

_____ 2. Plants like holly and mistletoe are pretty. *They* are also poisonous.

_____ 3. A strip of strong cloth can be used as an emergency fan-belt replacement. *In addition,* a roll of duct tape can be used to patch a leaky hose temporarily.

_____ 4. I'm always losing my soft contact lenses, which resemble little circles of thick Saran wrap. One day, I dropped both of *them* into a cup of hot tea.

_____ 5. The moulded plastic chairs in the classrooms are hard and uncomfortable. When I sit in one of these *chairs,* I feel as if I am sitting in a bucket.

_____ 6. One way to tell if your skin is aging is to pinch a fold of skin on the back of your hand. If *it* doesn't smooth out quickly, your skin is losing its youthful tone.

Review Activity: Transitional Sentences

Below is a brief sentence outline for an essay. The second and third topic sentences serve as transitional, or linking, sentences. Each reminds us of the point in the preceding paragraph and announces the point to be developed in the current paragraph. In the spaces provided, add the words needed to complete the second and third topic sentences.

Thesis	In order to set up a daycare centre in your home, you must make sure your house conforms to provincial and municipal regulations, obtain the necessary legal permits, and advertise your service in the right places.
First Supporting Paragraph	First of all, as a potential operator of a home daycare centre, you must make sure your house will conform to provincial and municipal regulations. . . .
Second Supporting Paragraph	After making certain that _____ you must obtain _____
Third Supporting Paragraph	Finally, once you have the necessary _____ you can begin to _____

2. INTRODUCTIONS AND CONCLUSIONS

Review Activity

In the box below are common kinds of introductions and conclusions. After reading the two pairs of introductory and concluding paragraphs that follow, use the space provided to write the number of the kind of introduction and conclusion used in each case.

Introductions	Conclusions
1. General to narrow	1. Summary and final thought
2. Background information	2. Question(s)
3. Starting with an opposite	3. Prediction or recommendation
4. Stating importance of topic	
5. Incident or story	
6. Question(s)	
7. Quotation	

Pair 1

_____	One March night at 2 a.m., I lay curled up, shivering and coughing in a sleeping bag outside the Air Canada Centre. No, I am not homeless, and I was not alone. I was lying on the cement with at least a few thousand other people in their late teens and early twenties. For the first seven or eight hours, I enjoyed myself, singing and sharing stories and food. But by two o'clock, my throat hurt and I was losing interest in the piece of paper that was my shortcut to stardom. At four o'clock in the morning, I packed up my bags, gave someone my number, and decided I was not going to be the next _Canadian Idol_. Becoming a professional singer has no shortcuts; it means more voice lessons, more auditions, and more experience.
_____	Shows like _Canadian Idol_ encourage people to dream of instant stardom. The reality of learning to be an entertainer is not a matter of a magic moment of discovery; it involves patience, work, and tough skin. No one applauds when I miss notes or lose at an audition; no one cares. People who are stars at their local karaoke place should think twice before they decide they are ready to be an "idol."

Pair 2

_____	What would life be like if we could read each other's minds? Would communications be instantaneous and perfectly clear? These questions will never be answered unless mental telepathy becomes a fact of life. Until then, we will have to make do with less perfect means of communication. Letters, email, telephone calls, and face-to-face conversations do have serious drawbacks.
_____	Letters, email, phone calls, or conversations cannot guarantee perfect communication. With all our sophisticated skills, we human beings often communicate less effectively than howling wolves or chattering monkeys. Even if we were able to read each other's minds, we'd probably still find some way to foul up the message.

CHECKLIST OF LEARNING OUTCOMES FOR CHAPTER 4

To ensure that you have understood and met the learning outcomes for this chapter, answer the following questions:

✓ What is most essential in writing a first draft? Why?

✓ What are the three levels at which an essay must be coherent?

✓ Which techniques are used to achieve coherence at the paragraph and sentence level?

✓ Why do readers need sentence-level coherence?

✓ Where, at a paragraph-to-paragraph level, are transitional words and phrases essential? Why?

✓ What are three approaches to writing introductions?

✓ Which methods of introduction belong to each of the three methods?

✓ What are two approaches to concluding an essay?

✓ Which methods belong to each approach?

✓ What questions would you ask as you revise an introduction? A conclusion?

Online
LearningCentre

For bonus material and additional activities please go to the OLC at www.mcgrawhill.ca/olc/langan

Revising Your Essay: Using the Bases for Effective Writing

LEARNING OUTCOMES

After reading this chapter and working through its activities, you will

- know the importance of three of the four bases as tools for revising as well as writing essays;
- be prepared to revise your essay's content and structure for unity, support, and coherence;
- develop skill in evaluating and revising with techniques based on the bases for effective writing.

The last three chapters have focused on the first three steps for effective essay writing: advancing a thesis, supporting it with specific evidence, and then organizing and connecting this evidence. These are the essential foundations of the content and structure of good essays. You have begun to prepare for revising your first draft, as you learned to create coherence and effective introductions and conclusions.

Now you will learn to revise, part of the fourth step to an effective essay. You will do so by using the bases for effective writing to evaluate your work—the same bases your instructor will use to grade your essays.

REVISING

Revising is as essential as prewriting, outlining, and drafting. Your first draft is your attempt to put your ideas into sentences in the shape of an essay. When you revise, you are evaluating and rewriting as you work on the entire content and structure of your essay. Professional writers say writing *is* revising. In other words, the work of revising, restating, and restructuring is what creates a good piece of writing.

Typically, students confuse revising with editing or proofreading; they look over a first draft, fix a few sentences and some spelling errors, and believe they have revised their essay. This is far from the case. Revising means literally *re-seeing*. Revising consists of three activities:

- Building on existing strengths in your draft;
- Evaluating your draft according to accepted standards for essay writing;
- Rewriting your draft based on your evaluation.

Have you shied away from revising simply because there seemed to be no established pattern to follow? If so, you are like many college and university students who bypass revising because they are not sure how to go about it.

This book offers you an established, effective pattern for revising. In fact, the process you have followed in writing your essay, from refining your thesis statement through rigorous outlining and evaluating of your support, has prepared you for revising. The goals you worked with throughout the writing process are those you will use to guide you during revision. Below you will find some overall tips to help you get started, followed by a checklist for revision.

GENERAL REVISING TIPS

1. First, set your first draft aside for a while. Then, come back to it with a fresh, more objective point of view. Allow yourself at least one day for your revision.

2. Second, work from printed text. You'll be able to see your work more impartially than if you were just looking at your own familiar handwriting.

3. Third, revise on the computer. Put your revisions in a different colour from the text of the draft you are working on. Each time you revise, print a copy on which you can make manual changes.

4. Fourth, read your draft aloud. Hearing how your writing sounds will help you spot problems with meaning and style, and errors and omissions.

5. Finally, as you read your draft aloud, add your thoughts and changes above the lines or in the margins of your paper. Your written comments can serve as a guide when you work on the next draft. When you revise on the computer, create a "notes" section at the end of your document for your comments.

REVISING CHECKLISTS

Go through these checklists each time you revise an essay. Eventually the steps will become automatic.

Overview

General Note-Taking

Read your draft aloud, or have someone read it to you.
Note, on your draft, any sections
    a. that you or your reader found difficult to understand;
    b. where ideas seemed out of order;
    c. where there was a "bump," a place where the text did not flow;
    d. where there appeared to be information missing.

Revising Content

Reviewing Your Purpose, Audience, and Thesis (PAT)

First, go back to your notes about your thesis.

I. Purpose

a. What was your stated purpose when you wrote your thesis?
b. Has it changed in any way? If so, how?
c. If your purpose has not changed, are you satisfied with the way your main points and supporting details fulfill it? If not, what will you change?
d. If your purpose has changed somewhat, how has it changed? How will you change any of your supporting points or details to suit this change?

II. Audience

a. Whom did you decide was your audience when you composed your thesis?
b. Has this changed in any way? If so, who is (are) your audience(s) now?
c. If your audience is still the same, do your thesis, supporting points, and details still seem relevant and interesting to them? Are there changes that would enhance your audience-focus? What are they?
d. If your audience has changed, how will you modify your thesis, supporting points, and details?
e. Although this is an issue of style as well as content, are there any spots where your tone is not appropriate for your audience? Make notes of these so you can make the necessary changes.

Reviewing Your Content: Unity and Support

I. Unity

a. Is my thesis as clearly stated as possible? How could I make it clearer?
b. Is a simple, an extended, or a specialized thesis statement most appropriate? Why, relative to this essay?

c. Is there a direct line of reasoning from my thesis to my supporting points? *or* Are my supporting points relevant to my thesis question?

II. Support

a. Are my supporting points truly distinct and clear?

b. Do my supporting points answer a specific question related to my thesis? What is it?

c. Do my topic sentences follow the order that my thesis presents (if it is an extended thesis)?

d. Does each of my paragraphs open with a topic sentence that presents one of my supporting points?

e. Are the supporting details and sub-details in each body paragraph specific, rather than vague or general? If not, what can I change?

f. Are my supporting details of an appropriate nature for my argument, my audience, and my purpose? If not, what should I change?

g. Do my supporting paragraphs contain unsupportable personal opinions or obvious items of common knowledge?

h. If I have used external research, do I have research notes with essential citation material?

i. Do I have enough details and sub-details to make each of my supporting points clear and credible to readers? If not, where should I add support?

Revising Content and Structure

Coherence

I. Principle of Organization

a. What is my principle of organization for my essay's supporting points?

b. How is this principle appropriate to my thesis?

c. Is my principle of organization emphasized in each of my topic sentences?

d. Does each of my body paragraphs contain transitions or signal-words that reinforce my organizing principle (if appropriate)?

II. Paragraph- and Sentence-Level Coherence

a. Have I used sentence-to-sentence transitions within each body paragraph so that the sentences flow in a logical sequence?

b. Are there places in my paragraphs where synonyms, variations on words, pronouns, or parallel sentence structures might add coherence?

c. Have I used paragraph-to-paragraph transitional sentences at the opening and closing sentences of the body paragraphs, so that there is a sense of continuous flow for readers?

III. Introductions, Titles, and Conclusions

a. Is my introductory approach suitable for my thesis and audience?

b. How well does my method of introduction work as a guide into my essay?

c. Have I developed my introduction sufficiently so that readers are prepared for my thesis near the end of the paragraph?

d. Which form of conclusion did I choose? Why, relative to my thesis and argument?

e. Have I written enough of a conclusion to satisfy readers that my argument has proved my point?

f. Did I introduce any new ideas, contradict my point, or give any examples in my conclusion?

g. What type of title have I chosen? Why, relative to my essay?

REVISING: A STUDENT MODEL

In the last chapter, you read the first draft of Jed Gawrys' essay about sports and society. Now you can follow his progress in revising that draft.

Please note: in this chapter, all of Jed's drafts appear showing sentence and spelling errors that have been corrected in earlier chapters.

Here is his first-draft introduction:

> What fans really enjoy about pro sports isnt teamwork or suspense. Its competitiveness and voilence. And society applauds these values. We will pay top dollar to see competitiveness, cruelty, and discrimnation based on the star system. The key values in professional sports reflect societies acceptance and support of destruction and harm to human life.

Here is his revised introduction again:

> What do fans hope to see at an NHL or NFL game? Attending a game is an intense experience, and what create that intensity? Competition and fights are what gets crowds on their feet. They are also what sells movies, what drives business, and what starts wars. Fans want to see extreme competitivenness, voilence, and discrimnation in favour of stars. Those words describe what's wrong with North American society—sports and society play by the same values.

After reading these, and the revising checklist above for introductions and conclusions, answer the following:

1. In his first draft, what is Jed's thesis statement?

2. How does he state his thesis in his next draft?

3. Compare the development from attention-getter to thesis in the two drafts. How has the second draft changed in this respect?

4. What would you do to further revise his introduction, based on the checklist and your own thoughts? (Read the body of the essay on the following page to help you decide.)

Here is Jed's first-draft conclusion:

> The main values that we see in sports, like extreme competitiveness, voilence and winning at any cost, and discrimnation directly reflect societies values. Pro sports may never change but society needs to.

Here is his revised conclusion again:

> What do fans hope to see at an NHL or NFL game? They hope to see brutal competition, fierce fighting, and stars winning out over all. Anything else is not worth the ticket price—the excitement comes from the brutal values that pro sports are built on. Unfortunately, those are the same values that North Americans put into practice every day of their lives.

After reading these, and the revising checklist on the previous pages for introductions and conclusions, answer the following:

- Compare Jed's restatement of his thesis in the first and second drafts.
- How has he varied the way he states his thesis in each? Which is preferable, and why?
- Do you agree with Jed's chosen form of conclusion? Why or why not?
- Would his revised conclusion satisfy readers that his essay has proved his point? Why or why not? (Read the body paragraphs below to help you decide.)
- Are there any errors such as new ideas or contradictions in Jed's revised conclusion?

REVISING THE BODY OF THE ESSAY

Jed would, in fact, revise his introduction and conclusion yet again. Here are some of the revision notes he made on the first draft of his body paragraphs, before starting the checklist:

> Competition is what sports are about. Because competition leads to winners and losers. I don't know if this sentence adds anything. Winning brings in the money and money pays players, coaches, and determines ticket prices. Players are so driven by money that morality and sportsmanship go out the window. Relate this to competition because that's the point. Coaches tell players to hurt the opposition in hockey and football. Put in McMurtry thing. He's specific about this. Get the page number, too. This really needs an example in here—is there that thing in McM about hockey sticks? How different is this from big business? Society praises people who get ahead at any cost and forgets about people who lose jobs when big companies close operations. Am I losing the thread here? I'm thinking about Walmart and car-factory shutdowns, I guess—I'm not clear enough on what I'm saying here. I can't just cut to the chase without explaining the other half of this point about competition. ADD DETAILS. Politics are no different. So-called moral politicians smear their opponents.

> Football is built on tackling and maming oposition players. NOT A TOPIC SENTENCE—CHANGE IT. The topic is that sports and society accept voilence—I was too specific. In the NHL, it's the same. These aren't something

added to these games, they're key parts of them, especially for fans. In the NHL in 2008, there were 664 fights in 1230 games (NHL Fight Stats from NHL site). *Find the url—you need it for works cited.* Society relies on fights and voilence, too. *That's not clear enough—I want compare the priorities that society has and how sports and society just accept violence and suffering as necessary and society just ignores suffering, too. Im still not clear here.* Because societies and governments are built on making themselves more powerful, no matter who suffers in the process. People who need help don't get it—the sick and the poor—they're powerless. But everybody is distracted by "corporate wars" while governments spend billions on weapons and armed forces. *Too vague—I need something definite. I think there's something in McM about this—look it up and get the page #.* If that money was spent on trying to help people, not trying to "win" power struggles, everyone would win.

The third and possibly most devestating aspect of professional sports that is reflected in our society is discrimnation. Sports leagues are huge organizations but only a few players have a lot of playing time. Star players are the most skilled and pro sports discrimnates against players who aren't as skilled. *You could say that better—some of this doesn't sound too mature either.* Being the best, being stars means more than any work ethic another player might have. *Where's that stuff about the hockey player who was up on a morals charge? It would work here.* Society makes people stars just like the movie business. *What happened to the idea about skills? That's supposed to be what sports and society base prejudices on. This part isn't about fame—Im offtrack again. I've lost my comparison that this is based on. Fix it.* These people are not necessarily good or moral; they just seem good because they are so famous. Actors are paid millions for working a few months a year— Will Smith. BE SPECIFIC AND FIND A SOURCE . . . *This was Forbes online, I think—I can google it.* Everyone admires him but who admires the guy who picks up the garbage twelve months a year? He works harder and does something valuable but people consider him lowclass. City workers like that can work fifty or sixty hours a week for poor wages. Is it because they don't appear successful according to society's standards that we don't value their skills?

• • • ACTIVITY

Jed is concentrating mainly on his supporting points, details, and sub-details here.

Paragraph Content

1. Where in each paragraph does he wish to add details and examples?

2. What forms of supporting details does he use most?

3. Where does he use evidence from outside sources? What are the sources?

4. What information does he remind himself to find?

5. Does he present any statements that are unsupported personal opinion? If so, where?

6. Are there places where Jed sees that his support is too general, where he needs to be more specific? Where should he be more specific and why?

7. Does Jed ever think that he is not following through logically on his topic sentence? If so, where?

8. Where is Jed's support not clear enough? Why do you think so?

Paragraph Structure

1. Where is there no topic sentence? How might a topic sentence for this paragraph read?

2. In which paragraph(s) does Jed think that he is not following through on his method of development, which is to compare sports and society?

3. Where would you add transitional sentences to openings and closings of paragraphs?

4. Choose one paragraph and add sentence-level transitions as appropriate.

Where does Jed make a note to himself about his word choice and tone? Who is his audience and why do you think he makes this note?

Jed continued with his revising. First he followed up on his notes, and in doing so, wrote a second draft. Then, using his second draft, he worked through the revision checklist, ending up with a significantly improved third draft.

Now, you will practise evaluating the work of other student writers, using three of the **four bases**—*unity, support,* and *coherence.* You have encountered these bases before, and have worked through revising with Jed.

REVIEW: FOUR BASES FOR WRITING AND EVALUATING ESSAYS

Four Steps	*Four Bases Defined*
1. Discover your point, and advance a clear thesis statement. →	**Unity:** a single main idea pursued and supported by the points and details of the essay
2. Support your thesis with specific evidence. →	**Support:** specific details and examples to explain each supporting point
3. Organize and connect the specific evidence at essay, paragraph, and sentence levels. →	**Coherence:** clear organization and logical connections between paragraphs, supporting points, and sentences
4. Revise, edit, and proofread your essay. →	**Effective Sentence Skills:** sentence structure, grammar, spelling, and punctuation free of errors

BASE 1: UNITY

● ● ● ● **ACTIVITY**

The following are personal student essays based on the topic "Someone I Remember." Which one makes its point more clearly and effectively, and why?

Essay 1

One Chance

1 Some nights, memory takes over. It is true that some moments do not let go easily and that memory's grip weakens with time, but there are still nights when it fills the room. On such nights, there is no more self, only a shadow out there. And along the narrow passages she comes, down a hot dusty path. Then she waits. She calls out again, about long-lost days she wants to relive.

2 She likes to begin in the same place every time. In 1986 in Pakistan, there was a woman of status, wealth, and intelligence who became a professor of the Arabic language at a university. Few women were professors; fewer still excelled. She used to think she had it all; she shunned those of lower status with the direct, hard tone in her voice. Her sharp edges made students fear her and colleagues leave her to herself. She never relied on anyone, nor did she ever reveal much to anyone. She was a sharp-edged enigma, but a beauty who left a trail of envious whispers behind her.

3 It was not until the day that she fell in love with a colleague that she lost her sense. She had engaged in affairs before, as it pleased her, when it pleased her. But this one was different. He was beautiful. She praised every inch of his perfection in silent poems, and this brought trouble to the narrow rooms in her mind. She lifted her eyes from her books and stared at the clouds, just waiting for it to rain. She loved the rain; it would fill her imagination with desires she wished to fulfill. It was then that she decided that she could not live without him; she wanted him for eternity. She wanted him; love or lust, it did not matter. The rain told her what she wanted and how to get what she deserved. After that, it was just a matter of planning. The smart woman was a good planner; she found opportunities in hallways and moments in lecture halls. She did everything to get closer to him and to pull him closer to her; she knew she could do it. It was just a matter of time. And she was right, as always. He fell under her spell. They soon married and had two children.

4 As time went by, her sharp edges returned. She snapped at her husband and children. He was patient; maybe he thought caring for her would make her soft again. He had his work, his students loved him, and his classes were full of life. But every night there was another fight; sometimes she struck blows to his face that shamed him at the university. The time came when he became ill, though days of tests in a clinic showed nothing more than acute stress. Because he could no longer live under such circumstances, he blamed himself for being a fool and a coward. He kept his feelings to himself—whom could he tell? There were the children and he loved them too much to ruin their lives; he must hide his misery so they could have some happiness. Thus he became the relentless reason behind the madness.

5   Still, not even such love can change fate. Some things are just meant to be. The husband filed for divorce after his children reached their teen years. He could endure the pain no longer; he chose life over slow suicide. Now she spends her life alone on that narrow path, lying to herself with memories of golden days of her life. My last memory of her is her pulling me down a staircase, beating my head on the floor because she knows I can never love her. She is my mother and she taught me to think before I do anything because I can only live life once.

Essay 2

Leaving Rudolph

1   For ten years of my life, the person I considered my best friend was an odd choice on my part. I felt loyal to the boy I first met at our babysitters. We shared Uncle Arjun and Auntie Regannie, who were no relation to either of us. At that time, as we chattered away about *Halloween* movies and Nintendo, it never occurred to me that my new friend had a learning disability. Nathan McCord was like Rudolph the Red-Nosed Reindeer, ostracized for his differences by other children. But I only saw his red light, which, for a while at least, guided my way to empathy.

2   Nathan took the short bus to public school; otherwise, he didn't seem very different from any other kid. He would be hard to pick out of a crowd as the one with a mental speed-bump. He could speak naturally and carry on a conversation like any of the boys in the playground. In fact, despite one obvious problem, a weak left arm that curled up like a chicken wing, he was very athletic, joining the basketball team and even winning a couple of championships. Basketball was a big thing at our school. The kids who played were schoolyard celebrities. Anyone who spent enough time around Nathan, though, eventually picked up on his condition. Simple mathematical equations were as difficult as climbing Everest for him, and spelling any word more complicated than "dog" required vigorous and repeated sounding out of vowels. Nonetheless, outside of class, right until high school, Nathan was my friend, and just another kid most of the time.

3   High school changed him, and me too. We went to different schools. Nathan's face turned into pepperoni pizza and his hair into greasy french fries. I worked part-time at The Gap. Whenever we got together, if my friends saw us, they heckled him, and for a while I was more ashamed of them than of him. My high-school friends played hockey, not basketball. But more and more Nathan was starting to try my patience. He was afraid of this and he didn't like that, for no reason. He feared going downtown, and I found that absurd. He wanted to stay home, with his wheelchair-bound father and drum-playing brother, in a world of his own, made up of wrestling, *Austin Powers* and *Planet of the Apes* movies, and KISS. Eventually, I only saw him at his job at the Paramount Chinook, where he worked as a floor sweeper. Whenever we met, he seemed to disintegrate more and more, his arm eventually looking like a shriveled bean with a *Friday the 13th* tattoo. His valediction came in a message on my

voicemail saying that his father died, and inviting me to go to his wake. I made a painful decision; I couldn't go.

4   I was moving right along now, through the cloudy night where I could only see changes in myself, not in him. I had no idea where to put our childhood friendship in my adult world. I had to let go of Nathan; I had to turn out the lights and let him sweep up after me.

Understanding Unity

Essay 1 is more effective because it is completely unified. All the details in this essay are on target; they support and develop each of its three topic sentences.

Here is an outline of essay 1, showing why it is unified.

Thesis: She calls out again, about long-lost days she wants to relive.

(This is a descriptive essay that also makes use of imaginative elements of narrative method of development. A "ghost" hounds the writer, making her remember some crucial things about her mother.)

Supporting Point 1: She likes to begin in the same place every time.

Supporting Details:

- in 1986 she was a successful professor in Pakistan
- she thought she had it all: (a) shunned people of lower status
- she was hard-edged: (a) students feared her, (b) colleagues left her alone
- never relied on anyone; didn't reveal much to anyone
- some people envied her

Supporting Point 2: It was not until the day that she fell in love with a colleague that she lost her sense.

Supporting Details:

- she became fascinated by a colleague, a man she found beautiful
- she daydreamed of him
- she decided she would have him
- she made herself run into him at the university
- he fell under her spell and they married and had children

Supporting Point 3: As time went by, her sharp edges returned.

Supporting Details:

- she snapped at her husband and children
- every night there was another fight
- she hit her husband's face, leaving marks that made him ashamed at work
- her husband became ill from stress
- he blamed himself for wanting to leave
- he loved the children so much that he hid his misery

On the other hand, essay 2 contains some details irrelevant to its topic sentences. In the opening paragraph, the sentence, "We shared Uncle Arjun and

Auntie Regannie, who were no relation to either of us" does not directly contribute to the writer's introduction of his friend Nathan. In the second supporting paragraph (paragraph 3), the sentence, "My high-school friends played hockey, not basketball" does not relate to its topic sentence: "High school changed him, and me too." Such details should be left out in the interests of unity.

Revising for Unity

● ● ● ● **ACTIVITY**

Go back to essay 2, and cross out the sentences in the first supporting paragraph (paragraph 2), and in the second supporting paragraph (paragraph 3) that are off target and do not help support their topic sentences.

The difference between these two essays illustrates the first important base or goal for revising your essay: **unity.** To achieve unity is to have all the details in your essay related to your thesis and three supporting topic sentences. When you outline, and again when you revise, ask yourself whether each detail and example relates to your thesis and supporting points. If it does not, leave it out.

BASE 2: SUPPORT

● ● ● ● **ACTIVITY**

Both of the following essays are unified. Which one communicates *more* clearly and effectively, and why?

Essay 1

Dealing with Disappointment

1   One way to look at life is as a series of disappointments. Life can certainly appear that way because disappointment crops up in the life of everyone more often, it seems, than satisfaction. How disappointments are handled can have a great bearing on how life is viewed. People can react negatively by sulking or by blaming others, or they can react positively by trying to understand the reasons behind the disappointment.

2   Sulking is one way to deal with disappointment. This "Why does everything always happen to me?" attitude is common because it is an easy attitude to adopt, but it is not very productive. Everyone has had the experience of meeting people who specialize in feeling sorry for themselves. A sulky manner will often discourage others from wanting to lend support, and it prevents the sulker from making positive moves toward self-help. It becomes easier just to sit back and sulk. Unfortunately, feeling sorry for oneself does nothing to lessen the pain of disappointment. It may, in fact, increase the pain. It certainly does not make future disappointments easier to bear.

3   Blaming others is another negative and nonproductive way to cope with disappointment. This all-too-common response of pointing the finger at someone else doesn't help one's situation. This posture will lead only to

anger, resentment, and, therefore, further unhappiness. Disappointment in another's performance does not necessarily indicate that the performer is at fault. Perhaps expectations were too high, or there could have been a misunderstanding as to what the performer actually intended to accomplish.

4   A positive way to handle disappointment is to try to understand the reasons behind the disappointment. An analysis of the causes for disappointment can have an excellent chance of producing desirable results. Often, understanding alone can help alleviate the pain of disappointment and can help prevent future disappointments. Also, it is wise to try to remember that what would be ideal is not necessarily what is reasonable to expect in any given situation. The ability to look disappointment squarely in the face and then go on from there is the first step on the road back.

5   Continuous handling of disappointment in a negative manner can lead to a negative view of life itself. Chances for personal happiness in such a state of being are understandably slim. Learning not to expect perfection in an imperfect world and keeping in mind those times when expectations were actually surpassed are positive steps toward allowing the joys of life to prevail.

Essay 2

Reactions to Disappointment

1   Gertrude Stein said that people have "to learn to do everything, even to die." In life, everyone may face and master many unavoidable adversities; one misery everyone experiences is disappointment. No one gets through life without experiencing many disappointments. Strangely, though, most people seem unprepared for disappointment and react to it in negative ways. They feel depressed or try to escape their troubles instead of using disappointment as an opportunity for growth.

2   One negative reaction to disappointment is depression. A woman trying to win a promotion, for example, works hard for over a year in her department. Halina is so sure she will get the promotion, in fact, that she has already picked out the car she will buy when her salary increase comes through. However, the boss names one of Halina's co-workers to the position. The fact that all the other department employees tell Halina that she is the one who really deserved the promotion doesn't help her deal with the crushing disappointment. Deeply depressed, Halina decides that all her goals are doomed to defeat. She loses her enthusiasm for her job and can barely force herself to show up every day. Halina tells herself that she is a failure and that doing a good job just isn't worth the work.

3   Another negative reaction to disappointment, and one that often follows depression, is the desire to escape. Jamal fails to get into the university his brother is attending—the university that was the focus of all his dreams— and decides to escape his disappointment. Why worry about college at all? Instead, he covers up his real feelings by giving up on his schoolwork and

getting completely involved with friends, parties, and "good times." When Carla doesn't make the college basketball team—something she wanted very badly—she refuses to play sports at all. She decides to hang around with a new set of friends who get high every day; then she won't have to confront her disappointment and learn to live with it.

4   The positive way to react to disappointment is to use it as a chance for growth. This isn't easy, but it's the only useful way to deal with an inevitable part of life. Halina, the woman who wasn't promoted, could have handled her disappointment by looking at other options. If her boss doesn't recognize talent and hard work, perhaps she could transfer to another department. Or she could ask the boss how to improve her performance so that she would be a sure candidate for the next promotion. Jamal, the fellow who didn't get into the college of his choice, should look into other schools. Going to another college may encourage him to be his own person, step out of his brother's shadow, and realize that being turned down by one college isn't a final judgment on his abilities or potential. Rather than escape into drugs, Carla could improve her basketball skills for a year or pick up another sport—like swimming or tennis—that would probably turn out to be more useful to her as an adult.

5   Disappointments are unwelcome but regular visitors to everyone's life. People can feel depressed about them, or they can try to escape from them. The best thing, though, is to accept a disappointment and then try to use it somehow. Step over the unwelcome visitor on the doorstep and get on with life.

Understanding Support

Here, essay 2 is more effective; it offers specific examples of how people deal with disappointment, so we can see for ourselves people's reactions to disappointment.

Essay 1, on the other hand, gives us no *specific* evidence. The writer tells us about sulking, blaming others, and trying to understand the reasons behind a disappointment but never shows us any of these responses in action. In an essay like this one, we would want to see *examples* of how sulking and blaming others are negative responses to disappointment and, similarly, how understanding the reasons behind the disappointment is a positive response.

Revising for Support

● ● ● ● **ACTIVITY**

Create an outline by printing a copy from the OLC. Fill in the outline with the thesis, supporting points, and details for essay 2. Now, as you look over the outline, ask yourself the revising questions for support on page 78.

Next, try filling in an outline for essay 1. Once again, use the revising questions on support to discover where you will need more specific supporting details and/or sub-details.

Revise one of the three supporting paragraphs in "Dealing with Disappointment" by providing specific supporting details, sub-details, and/or examples.

Examining these essays leads to the second base or goal for revising your essay: **support.**

BASE 3: COHERENCE

● ● ● ● **ACTIVITY**

The following essays are based on the topic "Diplomas, Degrees, and Success." Both are unified, and both are supported. Which one communicates *more* clearly and effectively, and why?

Essay 1

Degrees of Success

1   Alina Dacosta started classes at the University of Victoria intending to become a secondary-school math teacher. A few Spanish courses she took as options reinforced the love of the Spanish language and culture she developed during a year studying in Ecuador. She changed her concentration to Spanish and followed what she really cared about. But many of today's students go the other direction; they feel pressed to change programs away from their interests in order to chase high-paying jobs. Should academic and professional programs follow the job market? The fact is, first-year students have several years to finish diplomas and degrees and the jobs that are hot today could cool off in that time.

2   Career experts continue to advise students to go into whatever area most interests them, even if it is a less specialized liberal arts field, such as English or sociology. Students are often wary of such advice, perhaps because of the recent recession or because of parental experiences with or reactions to the recession. In the eighties, any discipline related to computers was the hot ticket. Students shifted programs and majors; new courses were written, and new colleges opened to take advantage of this career and financial bonanza. The future looked rosy. Just before 2000, increasingly sophisticated technology eliminated the need for thousands of computer- and programming-related positions. In spite of the bursting of the computer-studies bubble and the decline in the North American obsession with finance degrees, there remains a general perception increasingly contradicted by employment statistics. Dr. E. Michele Ramsey of Penn State university notes this media reinforcement: "Too often I find that stories about choosing a college diploma or a degree point to what people have in the last few decades considered safe-income programs, such as those on a business or science and technology base and implicitly devalue, without reflection, other degrees as ones that may provoke passion but do not promise career success." (Ramsay) The bias reflected in Dr. Ramsey's statement could continue to affect student choices; it could also further affect the composition of postsecondary institution course

offerings, leaving some faculties and courses to wither and others to expand, based on perceived market trends.

3   Most serious of all, for students themselves, is how a careerist approach to educational choices affects their decision-making at a vulnerable stage in their lives. They deny themselves both productive dreaming that might open them up to other avenues and the freedom to entertain a realistic spectrum of prospects for themselves. Instead of seeing postsecondary education as an extended period of growth and enrichment, they see it as a fast-track to a corner office. North American statistics show that engineers are the highest paid profession at the moment, and because of this, engineering schools have suddenly enjoyed an influx of enrolment (Coburn). The attitude is so widespread that registrars and admissions officers find themselves being asked the same question over and over. One notes, "as a college admissions counselor, I see one common mistake winding its way through the hopes and dreams of many of higher-education aspiring high school seniors. Three guesses what that is: *The desire to land a high-paying job straight out of college*" (Berry 6). With such an end in view, students face a distorted set of binaries: "instant money-makers" or "useless but interesting programs."

4   Decisions are difficult for many students. Some pick a program or degree in a promising field but end up changing their minds, costing them time and money. Elaine Marell, a member of a B.C. university advisory board says, "They may pick that high-salary-prospect program, then when students find out that that's not what they're passionate about, then they switch programs and even faculties, and sometimes have to go back a year to pick up required courses." (Marell 21) Currently, North American graduates with degrees in nursing, health care, accounting, economics, general science and engineering report the most success in finding jobs, according to placement officials (Marciana). One student trying to combine his interests with practical considerations is Tyler Parma, who uses his blog as a forum for broadcast and journalism students. A passionate sports fan, Parma wants to become a TV network sports commentator. He enrolled in the journalism stream of a five-year English and Communications degree program in which students spend one year in hands-on television broadcasting studies at a college connected to his university. He plans to add business courses as a backup because of the competitive field he plans to enter (Benjamin). There has been some renewal in the computer sciences employment markets, in areas such as informatics and software design. Unfortunately some parents pressure their children to obtain a diploma or degree that will get them a job immediately, and admissions officers are at a loss whether or not to advise students whether or not to bow to such pressure. "Before the dip in the economy, they had a little more opportunity to have a year or two where they worked odd jobs, worked part time or took internships that led to other jobs," notes an Alberta college counselor (Rostvecki 6). There is, at least in Canada's economy, evidence of an upswing in most areas.

5   Data indicate that the choice of college or university program can't be so easily distilled into simple binaries such as "study what you love" or "study

what will pay." As Canada's economy becomes more global, changing its employment patterns, those same binaries could become less and less useful as decision-making factors. Taking this fact into account, the calculations of students too closely focused on well-paid positions upon graduation may not necessarily add up to assured financial success.

Essay 2

Your Ticket, Sir or Madame?

1   Anna works at a Shoppers Drug Mart branch on Yonge Street in Toronto. She has a degree in fashion and design and successfully competed in numerous design competitions while at university. She also worked in Canada's fashion industry for five years after graduation, prior to taking up her current position behind a counter. "I'm happier here," is her answer when questioned about her current and less lucrative career choice. Did Anna's degree bring her success? Maybe, but did it bring her happiness as well? In fact, the relationship between a postsecondary degree, success, and happiness is less straightforward than it appears.

2   Initially, students in general enroll in postsecondary education motivated by better chances of career success. Is this success as Oxford defines it: "the accomplishment of an aim or purpose, the attainment of fame, wealth, or social status"? If so, where is happiness? Apparently, it is not on the wish list for students starting college or university. In recent years, though, marketing based on equating success with graduation has driven postsecondary enrolments to record numbers. Humber College in Toronto recently posted significant growth figures, more than 10% over the previous year in 2008, according to *Metro Canada*. Barb Riach, the registrar, remarked that the mix of different credentials offered made it "attractive for students and for parents who want to see lots of opportunity for their children." (Coulton 17) Not just students, but parents as well, it seems, equate higher education with opportunities and success. So is a degree or diploma essential to that first step toward success?

3   Also, more often than not, students buy into the accepted wisdom that graduates are more attractive to prospective employers than those with high-school papers. College or university credentials do, in theory, make a job hunter more attractive on paper. But in today's market, employers want significantly more than just academic or core professional skills. Kate Lorenz of CareerBuilder.com argues, "it's no longer enough to be a functional expert. To complement unique core competencies, there are certain 'soft skills' every company looks for in a potential hire." Soft skills are ". . . a cluster of personal qualities, habits, attitudes and social graces that make someone a good employee and compatible co-worker. Companies value soft skills because research suggests and experience shows that they can be just as important an indicator of job performance as hard skills." Moreover soft skills are inherent in the individual, not learned; they are positivity, flexibility, and the ability to

work under pressure. Most often these skills, not core skills, are the deciding factors when employers sift through heaps of résumés from well qualified candidates.

4   Then, too, many students believe that core skills can only be acquired in an academic setting, an oddly conservative mind-set for young people. In some areas of the job market, these students may confront outsider competition with a distinct edge—candidates, who in fact sidestepped or did not complete relevant diplomas or degrees. One such recent outsider is Juan Carlos Obando, now a fixture in the fashion press, who appeared first in 2008 as a nominee in the fifth annual CFDA/Vogue Fashion Fund competition. The fund is a hotly contended dowry for highly qualified up and coming designers and artisans. Obando differed from his expensively degreed competition in that he was completely self-taught . . . for only three months. An *Elle* magazine feature described the skills and drive that Obando brought to the table: "without having ever taken a sewing class, he bought a vintage Azzedine Alaïa jacket and Gucci pants, ripped them apart, studied the construction, and put them back together again" ("Lone Star" 190). Not only did Obando contend with graduates of Ryerson and Parsons, he did so while maintaining a full-time position as creative director at an advertising agency. The fine arts and fashion degrees may not have given the remaining nominees the edge they needed when confronted with talent and passion.

5   But perhaps the most prevalent reason students give for pursuing diplomas and degrees is that they stand to make more money than their high-school educated peers. They are right. Stats Can's 2006 census states bluntly, "men and women of all ages, full-time full-year earners with a college or university degree earned substantially more than their counterparts who . . . earned a high school diploma" ("Higher education: Gateway to higher incomes"). There is no arguing that a diploma or a degree is a valuable asset, but it is one that students should use to supplement their own inherent talents and interests. Qualifications supplement passion and talent; they do not substitute for these essentials. Over-reliance on degrees, or even multiple qualifications is a mistake. Students should learn to exercise inner traits such as self-knowledge and perseverance to choose and navigate future career paths. The self-aware individual with passion and drive will often achieve success and material gain, with or without academic credentials. Canadian and U.S. media abound with example of success stories of those who combine passion with ability and drive: Jim Carrey, whose lack of academic credentials has not stopped him from managing a successful career to the tune of 20 million per movie, Paul Quarrington, whose unfinished English degree never hampered him from churning out best-selling novels and TV and movie scripts; not to mention Bill Gates, possibly the shrewdest, wealthiest college drop-out in the world.

6   More than any other consideration, it is passion, not luck or certification, that fuels success. Success and happiness do seem to co-exist in the lives of those who follow their passion. By all means get the diploma, get the degree, but try to do what you love as well—passion and drive will follow.

As the Chinese proverb says, "There are many paths to the mountaintop, but the view is the same."

Understanding Coherence

In this case, essay 2 is more effective because the material is clearly organized and logically connected. Using emphatic order, the writer develops four reasons why students work for diplomas or degrees, ending with the most prevalent one: to make more money. The writer includes transitional words as signposts, making movement from one idea to the next easy to follow. Major paragraph-opener transitions include *initially, also, then too,* and *but perhaps the most prevalent* to assert the organizing principle and tie the supporting paragraphs together clearly.

Although essay 1 is unified and supported, the writer does not clearly organize and connect the material. The most important idea (signalled by the phrase, "most serious of all") is discussed in the second supporting paragraph instead of being saved for last. None of the supporting paragraphs organizes its details in a logical fashion. The first supporting paragraph opens with advice for students today, then abruptly shifts to the 1980s, and then back to today, ending up in the future. The second supporting paragraph seems to show a logical sequence of ideas, but then it presents a statistic about engineering graduates that does not relate to that sequence. The third supporting paragraph, like the first, leaps from an opening idea (students changing their minds about programs of study) to an employment statistic, to an example related to the opening idea, then to a detail about yet another area of study and employment. In addition to its disorganized paragraphs, to make things even more trying for readers, essay 1 uses practically no paragraph-to-paragraph or sentence-level transitional devices.

REVIEW ACTIVITIES

Review Activity: Revising Essays for Coherence

1. Using the "Revising Content and Structure" section of the revision checklist on page 78, revise one of the three supporting paragraphs in "Degrees of Success" by providing a clear method of organizing the material and by including transitional words.

2. Choose one of the body paragraphs of "Your Ticket, Sir or Madame?," and identify the sentence-level transitions within it.

These two essays lead to the third base or goal for revising essays: **coherence.** To achieve coherence, all the paragraphs, supporting ideas, and sentences must be clearly organized and connected. As already mentioned, key techniques for achieving coherence in an essay include the use of time order or emphatic order, transitions, and other connecting words.

You are now familiar with three of the bases for revising essays: *unity, support,* and *coherence.* In this section you will expand and strengthen your understanding of these bases as you evaluate and revise essays for each of them.

Review Activity: Revising Essays for Unity

The following essay contains sentences that either do not relate to the thesis of the essay or do not support the topic sentence of the paragraph in which they appear. Cross out the irrelevant sentences, and write the numbers of those sentences in the spaces provided.

Covering the Bases

1   ¹For the past three years, Samantha has played ball with the boys. ²In fact, she plays first base with the York University Men's baseball team. ³The team plays a long schedule and they are serious about the game. ⁴In those respects, they are no different from other university baseball teams. ⁵In one respect, the York Lions are different from every other team in their league in Canada—they are the first to have a female player. ⁶As a fourth-year psychology student, Samantha has had chances to observe male behaviour at first hand. ⁷Some players are tough to convince; others are still occasionally patronizing; fortunately, most just see her as a great first base-player.

2   ⁸At Samantha's debut game, a couple of George Brown Huskies' players were not too ready for a mixed-gender team. ⁹During the warm-up, no one commented or paid any special attention to Samantha, but the game itself was another thing. ¹⁰A fielder sniped, "You mean you're on the starting line, with three guys still on the bench?" ¹¹Samantha let that one roll. ¹²Another asked if she had custom equipment; her answer was not printable. ¹³When she came up to bat, the Huskies pitcher called his outfielders to move in on her. ¹⁴This amused Samantha, who also plays varsity hockey. ¹⁵She works out daily at the university's fitness centre, doing general cardio and specialized weight training. ¹⁶That first game, she confounded the skeptics by hitting a line drive over the left fielder's head.

The number of the irrelevant sentence: _____

3   ¹⁷Later that first season at another conference game, the Carleton team treated Samantha to some patronizing attitude. ¹⁸The Ravens had watched her in batting practice, so they did not try anything as obvious as drawing their outfield in. ¹⁹They could not have avoided hearing about her ability as a player. ²⁰Instead, they tried a more subtle approach, annoying her with fake concern. ²¹For example, one Ravens' player on base during the first inning said to her, "Careful, Hon. When you have your foot on the bag, someone might step on it. I know it's not hockey, but it's a tough game." ²²Samantha takes most ribbing in good spirit; she laughs it off. ²³Anger management is just basic psychology. ²⁴Needless to say, this great all round athlete survived the first season without injury, either to her body or her self-esteem.

The number of the irrelevant sentence: _____

4   ²⁵Happily, most of the university ball teams just accept her, as her Lions' team-mates do. ²⁶They criticize, coach, and curse her out just as they do each other. ²⁷No one questions her batting average; it has been rising every year. ²⁸The York Lions are not amazed when she makes a solid hit or stretches for a wide throw. ²⁹She was in the top three in the Baseball Canada Senior Women's Invitational, and is looking forward to a career in sports psychology. ³⁰If she is taken out of a game for a pinch runner, she takes it in stride; nearly every player is taken out sometimes. ³¹André Lachance, her manager on Baseball Canada's women's national team said, "She's a true leader and a gifted athlete, and she's bound to strengthen the Lions' lineup."

The number of the irrelevant sentence: _____

5   ³²Because of Samantha's education and intuitive reading of people, she feels that the defensive attitudes she encountered in her first year were simply normal human behaviour in an unfamiliar situation, not blatant sexism. ³³Once the other conference teams adjusted to her presence, she was "just one of the guys."

Review Activity: Revising Essays For Support

The following first draft of an essay lacks supporting details at certain key points. Identify the spots where details are needed.

Formula for Happiness

1   ¹Everyone has his or her own formula for happiness. ²As we go through life, we discover the activities that make us feel best. ³I've already discovered three keys for my happiness. ⁴I depend on karate, music, and self-hypnosis.

2   ⁵Karate helps me feel good physically. ⁶Before taking karate lessons, I was tired most of the time, my muscles felt like foam rubber, and I was twenty pounds overweight. ⁷After three months of these lessons, I saw an improvement in my physical condition. ⁸Also, my endurance has increased. ⁹At the end of my workday, I used to drag myself home to eat and watch television all night. ¹⁰Now, I have enough energy to play with my children, shop, or see a movie. ¹¹Karate has made me feel healthy, strong, and happy.

The spot where supporting details are needed occurs after sentence _____.

3   ¹²Singing with a chorus has helped me achieve emotional well-being by expressing my feelings. ¹³In situations where other people would reveal their feelings, I would remain quiet. ¹⁴Since joining the chorus, however, I have an outlet for joy, anger, or sadness. ¹⁵When I sing, I pour my emotions into the music and don't have to feel shy. ¹⁶For this reason, I enjoy singing certain kinds of music the most since they demand real depth of feeling.

The first spot where supporting details are needed occurs after sentence _____.

The second spot occurs after sentence _____.

4   [17]Self-hypnosis gives me peace of mind. [18]This is a total relaxation technique that I learned several years ago. [19]Essentially, I breathe deeply and concentrate on relaxing all my muscles. [20]I then repeat a key suggestion to myself. [21]Through self-hypnosis, I have gained control over several bad habits that have long been haunting me. [22]I have also learned to reduce the stress that goes along with my clerical job. [23]Now, I can handle the boss's demands or unexpected work without feeling tense.

The first spot where supporting details are needed occurs after sentence _____.

The second spot occurs after sentence _____.

5   [24]In short, my physical, emotional, and mental well-being have been greatly increased through karate, music, and self-hypnosis. [25]These activities have become important elements in my formula for happiness.

Review Activity: Revising Voice and Point of View

Revise the essay above so that it is written in third-person point of view. Tip: start by substituting *people* for *I* and *me*, then see what other variations on this substitution you can come up with.

Review Activity: Revising Essays for Coherence

The essay that follows could be revised to improve its coherence. Answer the questions about coherence that come after the essay.

Noise Pollution

1   [1]Natural sounds—waves, wind, bird songs—are so soothing that companies sell CDs of them to anxious people seeking a relaxing atmosphere in their homes or cars. [2]One reason why "environmental sounds" are big business is the fact that ordinary citizens—especially city dwellers—are bombarded by noise pollution. [3]On the way to work, on the job, and on the way home, the typical urban resident must cope with a continuing barrage of unpleasant sounds.

2   [4]The noise level in an office can be unbearable. [5]From nine to five, phones and fax machines ring, modems sound, computer keyboards chatter, intercoms buzz, and copy machines thump back and forth. [6]Every time the receptionists can't find people, they resort to a nerve-shattering public address system. [7]And because the managers worry about the employees' morale, they graciously provide the endless droning of canned music. [8]This effectively eliminates any possibility of a moment of blessed silence.

3   [9]Travelling home from work provides no relief from the noisiness of the office. [10]The ordinary sounds of blaring taxi horns and rumbling buses are occasionally punctuated by the ear-piercing screech of car brakes. [11]Taking a shortcut through the park will bring the weary worker face to face with chanting

religious cults, freelance musicians, screaming children, and barking dogs. [12]None of these sounds can compare with the large radios many park visitors carry. [13]Each radio blasts out something different, from rap to talk radio, at decibel levels so strong that they make eardrums throb in pain. [14]If there are birds singing or there is wind in the trees, the harried commuter will never hear them.

4   [15]Even a trip to work at 6 or 7 a.m. isn't quiet. [16]No matter which route a worker takes, there is bound to be a noisy construction site somewhere along the way. [17]Hard hats will shout from third-storey windows to warn their co-workers below before heaving debris out and sending it crashing to earth. [18]Huge front-end loaders will crunch into these piles of rubble and back up, their warning signals letting out loud, jarring beeps. [19]Air hammers begin an ear-splitting chorus of rat-a-tat-tat sounds guaranteed to shatter sanity as well as concrete. [20]Before reaching the office, the worker is already completely frazzled.

5   [21]Noise pollution is as dangerous as any other kind of pollution. [22]The endless pressure of noise probably triggers countless nervous breakdowns, vicious arguments, and bouts of depression. [23]And imagine the world problems we could solve, if only the noise stopped long enough to let us think.

1. What is the number of the sentence to which the transition word *Also* could be added in paragraph 2? _____

2. In the last sentence of paragraph 2, to what does the pronoun *This* refer?

   _____

3. What is the number of the sentence to which the transition word *But* could be added in paragraph 3? _____

4. What is the number of the sentence to which the transition word *Then* could be added in paragraph 4? _____

5. What is the number of the sentence to which the transition word *Meanwhile* could be added in paragraph 4? _____

6. What word is used as a synonym for *debris* in paragraph 4? _____

7. How many times is the key word *sounds* repeated in the essay?

8. The time order of the three supporting paragraphs is confused. Which supporting paragraph should come first? _____ Second? _____ Third? _____

CHECKLIST OF LEARNING OUTCOMES FOR CHAPTER 5

To ensure that you have understood and met the learning outcomes for this chapter, answer the following questions:

✔ How can you achieve unity in your essays?

✔ How can you make supporting evidence effective?

✔ What three items might you put on a checklist for achieving coherence in your essays?

Editing and Proofreading: The Final Drafts of Your Essay

LEARNING OUTCOMES

After reading this chapter and working through its activities, you will be ready

a. to edit your essay's sentences

- for correct parallel structure;

- for consistent verb tenses;

- for a consistent pronoun point of view;

- for use of specific vocabulary that makes your meaning clear to readers.

b. to proofread your essay for errors in grammar, punctuation, and spelling

- for active, rather than passive verbs;

- for concise, accurate wording;

- for varied sentence structures when needed.

Now your essay is nearly ready to submit to your instructor. Evaluating your work for the first three goals of effective writing, you have revised your first draft so that it is unified, well supported, and coherent. It is time for you to remember your audience once again: how will your reader feel about your well-structured and logical content if it is expressed in ungrammatical sentences and misspelled words?

You will learn to edit and proofread your second draft for the final, fourth base of effective writing: correct sentence skills, accurate word choices, appropriate sentence structure, and correct mechanics.

BASE 4: EDITING YOUR SENTENCES AND WORD CHOICES

Editing means examining your sentences and word choices—your style of writing—with an eye to stating your meaning as clearly and appropriately as possible. When you edit, you increase your focus on *the way* you express yourself.

The following strategies will help you to edit your sentences and word choices effectively.

- Use parallel structure.
- Use a consistent point of view.
- Use specific words.
- Use active verbs.
- Use concise words.
- Vary your sentences.

Use Parallel Structure

Words and phrases in a pair, a series, or a list should appear in the same grammatical structure: parallel structure. By balancing the items in a pair or a series, you will underline the fact that the items are related and make the sentence clearer and easier to read. Notice how the parallel sentences that follow read more smoothly than the non-parallel ones.

Non-parallel (Not Balanced)	*Parallel (Balanced)*
The stock clerk's job includes checking the inventory, initialling the orders, and *to call* the suppliers.	The stock clerk's job includes checking the inventory, initialling the orders, and calling the suppliers. (A balanced series of verb forms—participles or *-ing words—checking, initialling, calling*)
The lab trainer demonstrates equipment and protection procedures; *hands-on instruction is not offered.*	The lab trainer demonstrates equipment and protection procedures; she does not offer hands-on instruction. (Balanced use of the active voice: *The lab trainer demonstrates . . . ; she does not offer . . .*)

After you have revised your content and structure, try to put matching words and ideas into matching structures, as part of your editing activities. Errors in parallel structure often show up in lists of items within sentences.

What Should Be Parallel?

If you are unsure of exactly what a noun, preposition, phrase, or clause is, please turn to the index at the back of the book, or to Part 4. Parallel structure may apply to whole sentences as well as to single words and phrases. Basically, parallel structure is a form of repetition; you repeat a grammatical pattern, whether it is a single noun or a whole sentence. When you write a list or series of items, each item must be of the same type.

1. Nouns in Series

Nouns are words that name objects, beings, or concepts. When you write a sentence containing a list of nouns, make sure that every item on your list actually is a noun, not a phrase or a verb form.

> She had *grace, elegance,* and *she was very charming.*
> (*noun, noun, clause*)
> *Grace, elegance,* and *the appearance of charm* were the hallmarks of the geisha.
> (*noun, noun, phrase*)

Correct each sentence above so that it presents a series of nouns.

2. Adjectives in Series

Adjectives describe nouns and pronouns. When writing a list of adjectives, or descriptive words, do not include a phrase or a clause; stay with adjectives.

> Sierra was *lively, attractive,* and *she had a good personality.*
> (*adjective, adjective, clause*)
> He is *healthy, strong,* and an *athlete.*
> (*adjective, adjective, noun*)

Correct each sentence above so that it presents a series of adjectives.

3. Verb Forms in Series

Infinitives ("to" forms), participles or gerunds ("ing" forms), or verb tenses (present, past, future) must be consistent in a list or series.

> People preferred *to enter* freely, *to stay* a while, and then they *left.*
> (*infinitive or "to" phrase, infinitive phrase, past tense*)
> They made their living *selling cars* and sometimes *they rented parking spaces.*
> (*gerund or "ing" phrase, clause*)

Correct each sentence above so that it presents a consistent series of verb forms.

4. Prepositional Phrases in Series

Prepositions are words indicating position ("to," "from"), and when a preposition precedes a noun or pronoun, it forms a prepositional phrase ("in the house," "in front of the door," "after him"). Do not shift from prepositional phrases to other structures in a list or series.

> The new hybrid car is known *for its fuel economy, for its acceleration,* and *because it is attractive.*
> (*prepositional phrase, prepositional phrase, adverbial clause*)
> He is interested *in physics, in mathematics,* and *knitting.*
> (*prepositional phrase, prepositional phrase, noun*)

Correct each sentence above so that it presents parallel prepositional phrases.

5. Parallel Clauses in Series

Clauses contain subjects, verbs, and predicates or objects. For more on independent and dependent clauses, see Chapter 23. Series inside sentences and bulleted lists presenting clauses should be consistent.

> The jury consisted of *people who earned less than $50,000 a year, who had completed only high school,* and *they lived in downtown areas.*
> (*subordinate clause, subordinate clause, independent clause*)
> Malena's speech contained at least three clichés: *a watched pot never boils, look before you leap,* and *that early birds get the worm.*
> (*independent clause, independent clause, dependent clause*)

Correct each sentence above so that it presents parallel forms of clauses.

6. Parallel Use of Verb Voice

Voice in verbs refers to whether the subject of the verb acts (active voice) or receives the action (passive voice). For more information on passive verbs, see Chapter 26. Verbs in series or in parallel patterns should be in the same voice.

> Birds *swooped* down from the sky, *hovered* over the fields, then all the seed just planted *was eaten* by them.
>
> (*active voice, active voice, passive voice*)
>
> The garden *has been weeded* well, *watered* thoroughly, and *you have planted* it attractively.
>
> (*passive voice, passive voice, active voice*)

Correct each sentence above so that it presents uniform verb voices in its series.

7. Parallel Structure in Comparisons or Contrasts

When one idea is compared or contrasted with another, usually in structures containing *than* or *as,* both ideas should be expressed in the same, or parallel, form.

> Instructors praised her creative writing more for her *energy* than for *how she wrote.*

The ideas on both sides of the comparison or contrast should be expressed in the same way (parallel).

> Instructors praised her creative writing more *for her energy* than *for her writing.*

8. Parallel Structure in Two-Part (Correlative) Constructions

Two-part constructions are marked by the use of expressions like *both . . . and, either . . . or, neither . . . nor,* and *not only . . . but also.* Ideas in both parts of the construction must be parallel.

> The new assistant proved himself not only to be *competent* but also a *person who could be trusted.*

The ideas in both parts of the two-part construction should be expressed in the same way (parallel).

> The new assistant proved himself not only to be *competent* but also *trustworthy.*

● ● ● ● ● **ACTIVITY**

Edit each sentence so that its list or series is in balanced, parallel structure.

1. The novelty store sells hand buzzers, plastic fangs, and insects that are fake.

2. Many people share the same three great fears: being in high places, working with numbers, and speeches.

3. To decide on a career, students should think carefully about their interests, hobbies, and where their skills lie.

4. At the body shop, the car was sanded down to the bare metal, painted with primer, and red enamel was sprayed on.

Maintain Consistency

Consistent Verb Tenses

Do not shift verb tenses unnecessarily. Keep a consistent sense of time in your essay. (For information about verb tenses, refer to Chapter 26 of this book.) If you begin writing an essay in the present tense, do not shift suddenly to the past. If you begin in the past, do not shift, without reason, to the present. Notice the inconsistent verb tenses in the following example:

Kizzy *punched* down the risen yeast dough in the bowl. Then, she *dumps* it onto the floured worktable and *kneaded* it into a smooth, shiny ball.

The verbs must be consistently in the **present tense:**

Kizzy *punches* down the risen yeast dough in the bowl. Then, she *dumps* it onto the floured worktable and *kneads* it into a smooth, shiny ball.

Or the verbs must be consistently in the **past tense:**

Kizzy *punched* down the risen yeast dough in the bowl. Then, she *dumped* it onto the floured worktable and *kneaded* it into a smooth, shiny ball.

TIP: To check the verb tenses in a draft, use the highlighting tool to mark each verb. Then, go back and make each highlighted verb consistent in tense.

● ● ● ● **ACTIVITY**

Make the verbs in each sentence consistent with the first verb used.

1. An aggressive news photographer knocked a reporter to the ground as the stars arrive for the MuchMusic Video awards.

2. The winning wheelchair racer in the marathon slumped back in exhaustion and asks for some ice to soothe his blistered hands.

3. "Martial arts movies are so incredible," said Sean. "They're more than just action; they showed real ethical values."

4. When windstorms struck Vancouver's Stanley Park in 2006, many trees are severely damaged.

Consistent Pronouns

Do not shift your point of view or voice unnecessarily. Be consistent in your use of first-, second-, or third-person pronouns.

	Singular	*Plural*
First-person pronouns	I (my, mine, me)	we (our, us)
Second-person pronouns	you (your)	you (your)
Third-person pronouns	he (his, him) she (her) it (its)	they (their, them)

Note: Any person, place, or thing, as well as any indefinite pronoun such as *one, anyone, someone,* and so on, is a third-person pronoun.

For instance, if you start writing in the first person, *I,* do not jump suddenly to the second person, *you.* Or if you are writing in the third person, *they,* do not shift unexpectedly to *you.* Look at the following examples.

Inconsistent

One of the fringe benefits of my job is that **you** can use a company credit card for gas.(The writer begins with the first-person pronoun *my,* but then shifts to the second-person *you.*)

Though **we** like most of **our** neighbours, there are a few **you** can't get along with. (Again, the writer begins with the first-person pronouns *we* and *our,* but then shifts to the second-person *you.*)

Consistent

One of the fringe benefits of my job is that **I** can use a company credit card for gas.

Though **we** like most of **our** neighbours, there are a few **we** can't get along with.

● ● ● ●   **ACTIVITY**

Cross out inconsistent pronouns in the following sentences, and revise with the correct form of the pronoun above each crossed-out word.

I

Example   When I examined the used car, ~~You~~ could see that one of the front
fenders had been replaced.

1. Many people are ignorant of side effects that diets can have on your health.

2. It is expensive for us to take public transportation to work every day, but what choice do you have if you can't afford a car?

3. During the border crisis, each country refused to change their aggressive stance.

4. One of the things I love about my new apartment is that you can own a pet.

Use Specific Words 1

To be an effective writer, you must use specific rather than general words. Specific words create pictures in the reader's mind. They help capture interest and make your meaning clear.

● ● ● ● **ACTIVITY**

Revise the following sentences, changing the vague, indefinite words into sharp, specific ones.

> *Example*   Several of our appliances broke down at the same time.
> *Our washer, refrigerator, and television broke down at the same time.*

1. *Salty snacks* are my diet downfall.

2. I swept aside the *things* on my desk in order to spread out the road map.

3. Our neighbour's family room has *a lot of electronic equipment.*

4. *Several sections* of the newspaper were missing.

Use Specific Words 2

Again, changing vague, indefinite writing into lively, image-filled writing captures your reader's interest and makes your meaning clear. This is especially important in descriptive writing (see Chapter 9).

Compare the following sentences:

General

> She walked down the street.
> Animals came into the space.
> The man signed the paper.

Specific

> Anne wandered slowly along Rogers Lane.
> Hungry lions padded silently into the sawdust-covered arena.
> The biology teacher hastily scribbled his name on the course withdrawal slip.

The specific sentences create clear pictures in our minds. The details show us exactly what has happened. Here are four ways to make your sentences specific.

1. Use exact names.

   > *He* sold his *bike.*
   > *Vince* sold his *Honda.*

2. Use lively verbs.

   > The flag *moved* in the breeze.
   > The flag *fluttered* in the breeze.

3. Use adjectives before nouns.

   > A man strained to lift the crate.
   > A *heavyset,* perspiring man strained to lift the *heavy wooden* crate.

4. Use adjectives that relate to the senses—sight, hearing, taste, touch, smell.

> That woman jogs three kilometres a day.
> That *fragile-looking, grey-haired* woman jogs three kilometres a day. (*sight*)
>
> A whistle told the crowd that there were two minutes left to play.
> A *piercing* whistle told the *cheering* crowd that there were two minutes left to play. (*hearing*)
>
> When he returned, all he found in the refrigerator was bread and milk.
> When he returned, all he found in the refrigerator was *stale* bread and *sour* milk. (*taste*)
>
> Neil stroked the kitten's fur until he felt its tiny claws on his hand.
> Neil stroked the kitten's *velvety* fur until he felt its tiny, *needle-sharp* claws on his hand. (*touch*)
>
> Sonia placed a sachet in her bureau drawer.
> Sonia placed a *lilac-scented* sachet in her bureau drawer. (*smell*)

● ● ● ACTIVITY

Using the methods described above, rewrite each of the following sentences, adding specific details.

Example   The person got off the bus.
The teenage boy bounded down the steps of the shiny yellow school bus.

1. The car would not start.

2. The test was difficult.

3. The boy was tired.

4. My room needs cleaning.

Use Active Verbs

When the subject of a sentence performs the action of the verb, the verb is in the *active voice*. When the subject of a sentence receives the action of a verb, the verb is in the *passive voice*.

The passive form of a verb consists of a form of the verb *to be* (*am, is, are, was, were*) and the past participle of the main verb (which is usually the same as its past tense form). In general, active verbs are more effective than passive ones. Active verbs give your writing a simpler and more vigorous style.

Passive	*Active*
The computer was *turned on* by Aaron.	Aaron *turned on* the computer.
The car's air conditioner *was fixed* by the mechanic.	The mechanic *fixed* the car's air conditioner.

Using the active voice communicates directly to readers. Notice how much simpler the active-voice sentences above are to understand. Grammatically, these sentences are more straightforward.

Using the passive voice involves using a "by" structure to indicate a sentence's subject, the agent or "doer." Because of this, passive voice places less emphasis on the subject; the subject, in fact, will not appear first in the sentence. The emphasis is on the object that receives the verb's action: here, the computer and the air conditioner.

Choosing a verb voice means considering where you wish to place emphasis for your reading audience. If your intention, as it should be, generally is to make your points clearly, active verbs are your choice. However, there are writing occasions when the passive voice is suitable:

- When you wish to emphasize the thing or person acted upon.

    Your behaviour will be reviewed by the disciplinary committee.

- When you wish to de-emphasize the subject of a sentence, or when the subject is not known.

    The hit-and-run driver was eventually stopped by police after a wild chase.

ACTIVITY

Rewrite the following sentences, changing verbs from the passive to the active voice and making any other word changes necessary.

Example   Fruits and vegetables are painted often by artists.
Artists often paint fruits and vegetables.

1. Many unhealthy foods are included in the typical Canadian diet.

2. The family picnic was invaded by hundreds of biting ants.

3. Antibiotics are used by doctors to treat many infections.

4. The fatal traffic accident was caused by a drunk driver.

Use Concise Words

Using more words than necessary to express a meaning—"wordiness"—is often a sign of lazy or careless writing. Your readers may resent the extra time and energy they must spend when you have not done the work needed to make your writing direct, clear, and concise.

Here are some examples of wordy sentences:

In this paper, I am planning to describe the hobby that I enjoy of collecting old comic books.
In Ben's opinion, he thinks that digital television will change and alter our lives in the future.
The officer apprehended the intoxicated operator of the vehicle.

Omitting needless words improves these sentences:

I enjoy collecting old comic books.
Ben thinks that digital television will change our lives.
The officer arrested the drunk driver.

Following is a list of some wordy expressions that could be reduced to single words.

Wordy Form	Short Form
at the present time	now
in the event that	if
in the near future	soon
due to the fact that	because
for the reason that	because
is able to	can

ACTIVITY

Revise the following sentences, omitting needless words.

1. In conclusion, I would like to end my essay by summarizing each of the major points that were covered within my paper.

2. Controlling the quality and level of the television shows that children watch is a continuing challenge to parents that they must meet on a daily basis.

3. In general, I am the sort of person who tends to be shy, especially in large crowds or with strangers I don't know well.

Vary Your Sentences

One part of effective writing involves varying the kinds of sentences you write. If every sentence follows the same pattern, writing may become monotonous to read.

While your main goal is always to write clear, straightforward sentences, you may occasionally wish to

- Combine two related ideas into one sentence;
- Emphasize some idea within a sentence more than another idea;
- Open with a word or phrase that emphasizes the meaning of the sentence;
- Create series of words instead of short, choppy sentences.

Note: In the section on parallel structure, you encountered the words *phrase* and *clause*. To clarify and review:

- *A phrase* is a sequence of words intended to be meaningful, but, because it may lack a subject or a verb, it is not a sentence; for example, *sitting alone, my over-whelming impression, in the daytime.*

- *A clause* is a sequence of words containing a subject and a verb; *independent clauses* are complete sentences—they can stand alone or be parts of sentences; *dependent clauses* contain subjects and verbs but they cannot stand alone; for example, *when the dawn broke, after the end of the war, unless you act on my suggestion.*

Use Compound Sentences

When you add a second complete thought (independent clause) to a simple sentence, the result is a *compound* sentence, which gives equal weight to two closely related ideas. The two complete statements in a compound sentence are usually connected by a comma plus a joining or coordinating word (*and, but, for, or, nor, so, yet*). The technique of showing that ideas have equal importance is called *coordination.* Following are compound sentences, which each contain two ideas that the writer considers equal in importance.

> Sameer worked on the engine for three hours, but the car still wouldn't start.
> Bananas were on sale this week, so I bought a bunch for the children's lunches.
> We laced up our roller skates, and then we moved cautiously onto the rink.

● ● ● **ACTIVITY**

Combine the following pairs of simple sentences to form compound sentences. Use a comma and a logical joining word (*and, but, for, so*) to connect each pair of statements.

> *Example*   The weather was cold and windy.
> Al brought a thick blanket to the football game.
> *The weather was cold and windy, so Al brought a thick blanket to the football game.*

1. My son can't eat peanut butter snacks or sandwiches.
   He is allergic to peanuts.

2. Diego tried to sleep.
   The thought of tomorrow's math exam kept him awake.

3. This coffee bar has its own bakery.
   It has takeout service as well.

4. The cardboard storage boxes were soggy.
   Rainwater had seeped into the basement during the storm.

Use Complex Sentences

When you add a dependent thought (dependent clause) to a simple sentence, the result is a *complex* sentence. You emphasize one idea over another when you create a complex sentence—one idea is subordinated to another. The dependent thought begins with one of the following subordinating words:

after	if, even if	when, whenever
although, though	in order that	where, wherever
as	since	whether
because	that, so that	which, whichever
before	unless	while
even though	until	who
how	what, whatever	whose

Look at the following complex sentence:

Although the exam room was very quiet, I still couldn't concentrate.

The idea that the writer wishes to emphasize here—*I still couldn't concentrate*—is expressed as a complete thought. The less important idea—*Although the exam room was very quiet*—is subordinate to the complete thought. The technique of giving one idea less emphasis than another is called subordination.

Following are other examples of complex sentences. In each case, the part starting with the dependent word is the less emphasized part of the sentence.

Even though I was tired, I stayed up to watch the horror movie.
Before I take a bath, I check for spiders in the tub.
When Ivy feels nervous, she pulls on her earlobe.

• • • •   ACTIVITY

Use appropriate subordinating words to combine the following pairs of simple sentences and form new sentences that contain a dependent thought. Place a comma after a dependent statement when it starts the sentence.

Example   Rita bit into the hard taffy.
She broke a filling.
When Rita bit into the hard taffy, she broke a filling.

1. I had forgotten to lock the front door.
   I had to drive back to the house.

2. The bear turned over the rotten log.
   Fat white grubs crawled in every direction.

3. Kevin had sent away for a set of tools.
   He changed his mind about spending the money.

Begin with a Special Opening Word or Phrase

You can change the sentence patterns and rhythms in your paragraphs by using different openings. Among the special opening words that can be used to start sentences are past participles of verbs (*-ed* words), present participles of verbs (*-ing* words), adverbs (*-ly* words), infinitive forms of verbs (*to* word groups), and prepositional phrases. Here are examples of all five kinds of openers:

Past participle (-*ed*) word:
Concerned about his son's fever, Paul called a doctor.

Present participle (-*ing* word):
Humming softly, Renata browsed through the rack of CDs.

Adverb (-*ly* word):
Hesitantly, Winston approached the instructor's desk.

Infinitive (*to* word group):
To protect her hair, Shastyn uses the lowest setting on her blow dryer.

Prepositional phrase:
During the exam, the exhaust fan hummed loudly. (For information about prepositional phrases, see pages 346–347.)

● ● ● ● **ACTIVITY**

Combine each of the following pairs of simple sentences into one sentence by using the opener shown at the left and omitting repeated words. Use a comma to set off the opener from the rest of the sentence.

Example	-*ing* word	The pelican scooped small fish into its baggy bill. It dipped into the waves.
		Dipping into the waves, the pelican scooped small fish into its baggy bill.

-*ly* word   1. Amber signed the repair contract.
              She was reluctant.

to word group   2. The interns volunteered to work overtime.
                   They wanted to improve their chances of obtaining permanent positions.

prepositional phrase   3. The accused murderer grinned at the witnesses.
                        He did this during the trial.

-*ed* word   4. The vet's office was noisy and confusing.
              It was crowded with nervous pets.

-*ing* word   5. Aakash tried to find something worth watching.
               He flipped from channel to channel.

Place Adjectives or Verbs in a Series

Some parts of a sentence may be placed in a series. Among these parts are adjectives and verbs. Here are examples of both in a series:

Adjectives:
I gently applied a *sticky new* Band-Aid to the *deep, ragged* cut on my finger.

Verbs:
The truck *bounced* off a guardrail, *sideswiped* a tree, and *plunged* down the embankment.

● ● ● ● **ACTIVITY**

Combine the simple sentences into one sentence by using adjectives or verbs in a series and by omitting repeated words. In most cases, use a comma between the adjectives or verbs in a series.

> ***Example***   Scott spun the basketball on one finger.
> He rolled it along his arms.
> He dribbled it between his legs.
> *Scott spun the basketball on one finger, rolled it along his arms, and dribbled it between his legs.*

1. The baby toddled across the rug.
   He picked up a button.
   He put the button in his mouth.

2. Water trickled out of the tap.
   The water was brown.
   The water was foul-tasting.
   The tap was rusty.
   The tap was metal.

3. By 6 a.m. I had read the textbook chapter.
   I had taken notes on it.
   I had studied the notes.
   I had drunk eight cups of coffee.

● ● ● **ACTIVITY**

Following is a draft of a student's paragraph. Edit the paragraph's sentences where needed to demonstrate effective use of

- Parallel structure;
- Consistent verb tense;
- Consistent pronoun point of view or voice;
- Specific words;
- Concise words;
- Active verbs;
- Varied sentence structure.

> Violence in video games has been around since the beginning of video game history. Space Invaders and Pac-Man were the first violent games, even though blood and gore were not parts of the action when you "killed" the "enemy." The game industry and graphics evolved, so video games have become more realistic to look at, faster to respond, and experiencing them is more of a thrill. But the more real the game looked, the more powerfully is presented the message of violence. At this point in time, a child can play a game where they chop up a body into pieces with a rusty sword. And to them that's pure entertainment. Grand Theft Auto is controversial for its brutality because it gave players freedom to do what they want; you are able to grab any weapon, shoot a

huge selection of people in your town, and it lets you escape the police. Many offences around North America have been blamed on this game. The offences were serious. A boy in the United States was hooked on this game and became a very aggressive boy. He was arrested for a little offence that was not major and taken to the police station where two cops were shot by him and he stole their cars soon after that took place. More than a very large percent of teenage boys in America have played the game Grand Theft Auto and are more likely to commit a crime than those who have not played. There are many issues surrounding the fact that violent video games have a psychological effect on children and young people alike.

PROOFREADING: AN INTRODUCTION TO THE FINAL STEP

After editing sentences in your essay so that they flow smoothly and clearly, and bring out your intended meaning most effectively, you must perform one last step before your essay is ready for your audience.

Proofreading means checking for and correcting mistakes in grammar, punctuation, spelling, mechanics, and word use. Even if you write an otherwise effective essay, you will make an unfavourable impression on readers if you present a paper full of mistakes. You cannot hope to achieve the purpose of your essay if someone finds it hard to read.

Because you are most likely starting your semester at this point, you will not have covered the grammatical concerns noted in the list below. Therefore, once you have edited your sentences to your satisfaction, but before you submit your first essay to your instructor, try the following proofreading tips, then ask your instructor about any of the items below that you have not yet studied in class.

Proofreading Tips

1. Have two essential tools on hand: a good dictionary and a grammar handbook. You can use the one in this book in Part 4. Even if you use the spell checker and grammar checker on your word-processing program, you will still need to check spellings and uses of certain phrases.

2. Use a sheet of paper to cover your essay so that you can expose only one sentence at a time. It may help to read each sentence out loud. If it does not read clearly and smoothly, chances are something is wrong.

3. Pay special attention to the kinds of errors you tend to make. For example, if you tend to write run-ons or fragments, be especially on the lookout for those errors.

4. Once you have essays or assignments returned with errors noted, begin an "Errors Log." Make notes of the name of the error, what it is, and how to correct it. Each time you proofread an essay after that, check for the errors listed in your log.

5. Try to work on a word-processed draft, where you will be able to see your writing more objectively than you can on a handwritten page. Use a pen with coloured ink so that your corrections will stand out.

6. Work on one item at a time. Check your spelling, each verb for subject/verb agreement, tense for use and consistency, pronoun reference and agreement, and so on. Finally, check each sentence for correct structure, and then go over punctuation carefully. Use Part 4 of the text and this chapter as references.

Bookmark this list and return to it as you work through the semester. Always ask your instructor about any grammatical problems you encounter.

To proofread an essay, check it against the agreed-upon rules or conventions of written English. Here are the most common of these conventions, followed by the pages in Part 4 of this book where these matters are covered:

1. Write complete sentences rather than fragments. (349–358)

2. Do not write run-ons. (359–368)

3. Use verb forms correctly. (369–374)

4. Make sure that subjects, verbs, and pronouns agree. (375–379)

5. Eliminate faulty modifiers. (399–404)

6. Use pronoun forms correctly. (390–394)

7. Use capital letters where needed. (405–410)

8. Use the following marks of punctuation correctly: apostrophe, quotation marks, comma, semicolon, colon, hyphen, dash, parentheses. (414–435)

9. Eliminate slang and clichés. (443–445)

10. Eliminate careless spelling errors. (79–80)

Both the list of sentence skills on the inside front cover of this book and the correction symbols on the inside back cover also include page references so that you can turn quickly to any skill you want to check.

A FINAL NOTE: When you have proofread and corrected your essay, take the final step and set it up correctly for your reader. For help, see the chapter "Manuscript Form," on the OLC.

A series of editing tests appears on the OLC. You will probably find it most helpful to take these tests after reviewing the sentence skills in Part 4.

REVIEW ACTIVITIES

You now know the fourth step in effective writing: revising content and structure, then editing, and proofreading sentences. This closing section will provide further practice in editing sentences. Work through the following series of review activities:

1. Using parallel structure

2. Using a consistent point of view

3. Using specific words

4. Using active verbs

5. Using concise words

6. Varying your sentences

1. USING PARALLEL STRUCTURE

Review Activity

Cross out the unbalanced part of each sentence. In the space provided, revise the unbalanced part so that it matches the other item or items in the sentence.

Example   Cigarette smoking is expensive, disgusting, and a ~~health risk.~~
Unhealthy

1. A sale on electrical appliances, furniture for the home office, and stereo equipment begins this Friday.

2. To escape the stresses of everyday life, people rely upon watching television, reading books, and the kitchen.

3. The keys to improving grades are to take effective notes in class, to plan study time, and preparing carefully for exams.

4. Qualities that are important in friendship are a sense of humour, being kind, and dependability.

5. My three favourite jobs were veterinary assistant, gardener, and selling toys.

6. Housekeeping shortcuts will help you do a fast job of doing laundry, cleaning rooms, and food on the table.

2. MAINTAINING CONSISTENCY: VERB TENSE AND POINT OF VIEW

Review Activity 1

Change verbs, where needed, in the following selection so that they are consistently in the past tense. Cross out each incorrect verb, and write the correct form above it. You will need to make ten corrections.

My uncle's shopping trip last Thursday was discouraging to him. First of all, he had to drive around for fifteen minutes until he finds a parking space. There was a half-price special on paper products at FoodSaver, and every spot is taken. Then, when he finally got inside, many of the items on his list were not where he expected. For example, the pickles he wanted are not on the same shelf as all the other pickles. Instead, they were in a refrigerated case next to the bacon. And the granola was not on the cereal shelves, but in the health food section. Shopping, therefore, proceeds slowly. About halfway through his list, he knew there would not be time to cook dinner and decides to pick up a barbecued chicken. The chicken, he learned, was available at the end of the aisle he had already passed. So he parks his shopping cart in an aisle, gets the chicken, and came back. After adding half a dozen more items to his cart, he suddenly realizes it contained someone else's food. So he retraced his steps, found his own cart, transfers the groceries, and continued to shop. Later, when he began loading items onto the checkout counter, he notices that the barbecued chicken was missing. He must have left it in the other cart, certainly gone by now. Feeling totally defeated, he returned to the deli counter and says to the clerk, "Give me another chicken. I lost the first one." My uncle told me that when he saw the look on the clerk's face, he felt as if he'd flunked Food Shopping.

Review Activity 2

Cross out inconsistent pronouns in the following sentences, and write the correct form of the pronoun above each crossed-out word.

Example   Many shoppers are staying away from the local music store because
            they
            ~~you~~ can now download songs from the Internet.

1. These days people never seem to get the recognition they deserve, no matter how hard you work.

2. All you could hear was the maddening rattle of the furnace fan, even though I buried my face in the pillow.

3. When we answer the telephone at work, you are supposed to say the company name.

4. Each year I pay more money for my tuition. Despite the cost, however, one must finish school in order to get a better, more meaningful job.

3. USING SPECIFIC WORDS

Review Activity 1

Revise the following sentences, changing vague, indefinite words into sharp, specific ones.

1. When my relationship broke up, I felt *various emotions*.
2. The *food choices* in the cafeteria were unappetizing.
3. *Bugs* invaded our kitchen and pantry this summer.
4. All last week, the weather was *terrible*.

Review Activity 2

Using the methods described on pages 105–106, add specific details to the sentences that follow.

1. The salesperson was obnoxious.
2. The child started to cry.
3. The game was exciting.
4. The lounge area was busy.

4. USING ACTIVE VERBS

Review Activity

Revise the following sentences, changing verbs from the passive to the active voice and making any other word changes necessary.

> ***Example***   Soccer is played by children all over the world.
> *Children all over the world play soccer.*

1. The pizza restaurant was closed by the health inspector.
2. Huge stacks of donated books were sorted by the workers in the library.
3. Gasoline prices will not be increased by suppliers this winter.
4. High-powered lights were used by the crew during filming of the commercial.

5. USING CONCISE WORDS

Review Activity

Revise the following sentences, omitting needless words.

1. I finally made up my mind and decided to look for a new job.
2. Due to the fact that the printer was out of paper, Ayesha went to the store for the purpose of buying some.

3. Marika realized suddenly that her date had stood her up and was not going to show up.

4. The salesperson advised us not to buy the computer at this time because it was going to have a drop in price in the very near future.

6. VARYING YOUR SENTENCES

Review Activity

Combine the sentences in the following paragraph to form four sentences. Omit repeated words. Try to find combinations in each case that flow as smoothly and clearly as possible.

Lena and Miles wanted a vacation. They wanted a vacation that was nice. They wanted one that was quiet. They wanted one that was relaxing. They rented a small cottage on Shuswap Lake. Their first day there was very peaceful. The situation quickly changed. A large family moved into a nearby cottage. They played music at top volume. They raced around in a speedboat with a loud whining engine. Lena and Miles were no longer very relaxed. They packed up their things. They drove off. They returned to their quiet apartment.

CHECKLIST OF LEARNING OUTCOMES FOR CHAPTER 6

To ensure that you have understood and met the learning outcomes for this chapter, answer the following questions:

✓ How does editing differ from revising? How does editing differ from proofreading?

✓ Explain parallel structure.

✓ Why is it important to maintain a consistent pronoun point of view in essays?

✓ Why do readers prefer specific, rather than vague word choices?

✓ What is an active verb, and why are active verb forms preferable?

✓ How do readers benefit from concise wording in essays?

✓ What is the difference between a compound and complex sentence?

Introduction to Essay Development

LEARNING OUTCOMES

After reading this chapter, you will

- identify the main patterns of development for essays;

- know why various patterns are used;

- relate the use of different patterns of essay development to writing assignments.

PATTERNS OF ESSAY DEVELOPMENT

Narration and **description** are basic to all writing. When you recount a series of events, you are creating a narrative line. If you appear as the narrator, you are present as a voice; or, if you are an "invisible" narrator, you are a controlling presence connecting events. In both cases, you create a trail for readers to follow. When you try to show readers how something looks, feels, or works, you are "drawing with words," or using description.

Exposition refers to different patterns of presenting the supporting points in the body of the essay. Patterns of expository development are shown in the box following. Usually, you will find that the topic of the essay and your purpose will determine which expository pattern of development, or combination of patterns, is most appropriate.

- **Illustration by examples:** essays that present specific facts, observations, or scenarios to make your points and details concrete for readers. Each pattern of essay development will make use of examples in this way.

- **Process:** essays that demonstrate or break down a process to instruct or show readers how something works, or how something happens.

- **Cause or Effect:** essays that show or analyze causes and effects to break down and explain either the reasons for (causes) or the consequences (effects) of some situation or issue.

- **Comparison and/or Contrast:** essays that compare or contrast show the similarities and/or differences between two subjects or two aspects of one subject.

- **Definition:** essays that mainly define explore various meanings of a word or concept.

- **Classification and Division:** essays that classify or break a subject down into categories to help readers grasp different aspects of that subject.

Argumentation or **persuasion** naturally occurs in many well-supported essays as the thesis point is carefully explained and defended.

- Essays whose *main* goal is arguing a point use specific tactics either to gain support for a potentially contentious idea or to defend a position about which there might be differences of opinion.

- Essays whose *main* goal is persuasion are intended to alter the thinking of the reading audience, or to move readers' emotions in the direction of the writer's position. Persuasion is meant to lead to action on the reader's part—or at least to an openness to change. Persuasion, unlike argumentation, will rarely openly challenge a reader; instead it will offer a series of appeals, based on knowledge of the audience. Essays that argue or persuade will often make use of several patterns of development as part of making their point.

Facts about Essay Writing and Methods of Development

1. Essays Generally Use Primary and Secondary Patterns of Development

You will practise writing essays that mainly follow a single pattern for supporting your point. However, more often than not, you will also, consciously or unconsciously, use secondary or subordinate methods to explain your points. You will probably use at least an example or two, whether you write about a process or trace the causes of some problem. The essay "Altered States" (pages 152–153) uses *examples* as a main method, but the writer also uses the *cause and effect* pattern to explain the origins of altered states of mind. Most sample essays in the following chapters show primary and secondary patterns of development, and you will often be prompted to identify these so you can understand why their authors might have chosen more than a single pattern to write about their topics.

2. Essays Generally Involve Presenting an Argument

No matter which pattern you choose for your subject, your essay will generally offer some form of argument or persuasion. The overall essay structure of opening with a thesis and then providing support constitutes the basis of an argument.

The writer of "Everyday Common Scents" (page 140) does not merely *describe* a variety of ordinary smells; her descriptive details make an effective *argument* for the importance of paying attention to everyday pleasures. Another writer *contrasts* home-cooked meals with fast-food meals; the contrasts, based on taste, nutrition, and cost, form a *persuasive argument* for his thesis ("What's For Dinner?" pages 197–199). Your essays generally have the overriding purpose of persuading your reader that the argument or point you advance is valid.

BASIC CONSIDERATIONS AS YOU BEGIN AN ESSAY

Before you begin work on any essay, always consider two points basic to all writing tasks:

- The nature and length of the assignment
- Your understanding of your subject

Understanding the Nature and Length of an Assignment

Writing tasks and assignments in Canadian colleges and universities are highly varied. The writing formats assigned to you may include essays, summaries, reports, letters, case studies, and analyses. Essay structures, as set out in this book, will prepare you to manage information appropriately in various types of essays as well as in formats other than the essay.

Whatever the writing task, do not begin an assignment until you know exactly what type of paper the instructor has in mind. Is the assignment mainly a research summary of other people's ideas? Should it be based entirely on your own ideas? Or should it consist of a comparison of your ideas with those of other authorities? If you are not sure what type of assignment you have been given, chances are that other students feel similar confusion. Never hesitate to ask an instructor about an assignment. Finally, find out how long the paper is expected to be. Most instructors indicate the approximate length desired in assignments. Some instructors deduct marks for going significantly over or under length requirements. Knowing the expected length of a paper will help you decide how detailed your treatment of a subject should be and how much time to allot to it.

Knowing Your Subject

Whenever possible, try to write on a subject that interests you. You will then find it easier to put more time and energy into your work. More important, try to write on a subject that you already know something about. If you have no direct experience with the subject, you may still have some indirect experience—knowledge gained from thinking, reading, or talking about the subject as well as from prewriting.

If you are asked to write on a topic about which you have no experience or knowledge, do whatever research is needed to gain background information. "Research Skills," Chapter 18, will show you how to find and use relevant information. Without direct or indirect experience, or the information you gain through research, your writing task may seem overwhelming and you may be unable to provide the specific evidence needed to develop your paper.

CHECKLIST OF LEARNING OUTCOMES FOR CHAPTER 7

To ensure that you have understood and met the learning outcomes for this chapter, answer the following questions:

✓ How do the expository methods of development differ from narration and description?

✓ Why is argumentation or persuasion consistently part of essay writing?

✓ If you are assigned an essay on the subject of "Attendance and Success," which pattern of development would you choose, and why? If your essay shows readers how to install a software package, which pattern would you choose, and why?

Online
LearningCentre

For bonus material and additional activities please go to the OLC at www.mcgrawhill.ca/olc/langan

Narration

LEARNING OUTCOMES

After reading this chapter and working through its writing assignments, you will be ready to write a narrative essay that

- narrates an experience about a specific conflict or change;

- organizes and sequences your supporting material in time order to offer an accurate and coherent narrative;

- shows careful selection of details essential to your point;

- is revised to recreate events as clearly as possible and "show" readers your point;

- concludes by returning to its main point in an interesting manner.

Narrating or telling stories is a basic human activity; we experience things every day and we want to tell others what happened. Just as the great myths and legends did, narrative stories teach humanity's lessons, but narratives also form the basis for career and academic writing forms that serve a variety of purposes.

As a narrative writer, you relate your experience or observations for a purpose. Your purpose and topic in turn will determine how personal or subjective your record of your experience will be. If your connection to and presence in your story are vital to its success, you may write a first-person narrative. But if your goal is to show readers a careful record of events, then you will use narrative to recreate what you observed or experienced and its meaning; you will write a third-person observational narrative, used in case studies and reports. Every profession's writing tasks use narration to record and recreate events and experiences.

Narrative writing has some distinct characteristics; it

- Is told from a particular point of view
- Is written in chronological order
- Makes and supports a point
- Is filled with precise detail
- Uses vivid verbs and modifiers (adjectives and adverbs)
- Uses conflict and sequence as does any story
- May use dialogue

Acquiring skill in narrative writing will bring you immediate benefits. Narration is often part of essays using other patterns of development. In fact, because you describe people, places, objects, and feelings as you narrate, you nearly always use narration and description together. As you proceed through college or university, you will write short narratives or anecdotes that serve as supporting details in many types of essays and reports: examples will sometimes take the form of anecdotes to support your point, or a brief story about a person or event could help to persuade readers of the truth of your thesis.

In this chapter, you will be asked to write a narrative essay that illustrates some point. To prepare for this task, first read the student essays that follow, and then work through the questions accompanying the essays. Both essays use narrative as their main method of developing their points.

STUDENT ESSAYS TO CONSIDER

Accessing a Challenge

1   During my third semester in Social Services, I was an intern at a provincial government agency during their "Accessibility Awareness" campaign. The purpose of the campaign was to make service workers more sensitive to the problems faced by people with various physical challenges. Along with two other students from Fanshawe, I was asked to "adopt a challenge" for a day, doing all my work without one physical ability. Some of the workers, like me, chose to use wheelchairs; others wore sound-blocking earplugs, hobbled around on crutches, or wore eye masks.

2   Just sitting in the wheelchair was instructive. I had never considered before how awkward it would be to use one. As soon as I sat down, my weight made the chair begin to roll. Its wheels were not locked, and I fumbled clumsily to correct that. Another awkward moment occurred when I realized I had no place to put my feet. I fumbled some more to turn the metal footrest into place. I felt psychologically awkward as well, as I took my first uneasy look at what was to be my only source of mobility for several hours. I realized that for many people, "adopting a wheelchair" is not a temporary experiment. That was a sobering thought as I sank back into my seat.

3   Once I sat down, I had to learn how to cope with the wheelchair. I shifted around, trying to find a comfortable position. I thought it might be restful, even kind of nice, to be pushed around for a while. I glanced around to see

who would be pushing me and then realized I would have to navigate the contraption by myself! My palms reddened and my wrist and forearm muscles started to ache as I tugged at the heavy metal wheels. I realized as I veered this way and that that steering and turning were not going to be easy tasks. Trying to make a right-angle turn between aisles of office partitions, I steered straight into a divider and knocked it over. I felt as though everyone was staring at me and commenting on my clumsiness.

4   When I had to actually settle down to work, other problems cropped up, one after another. If someone working in another cubicle called out a question to me, I could not just stand up to see him or her. No matter how I strained to raise myself with my arms, I could not see over the partition. I had to figure out how to turn my wheels in the confined space of my cubicle and then wheel down the aisle between workstations to find whoever asked me the question. Also, those aisles were so narrow that there was no "passing lane" where people could get by me. For instance, a visiting MPP had to squeeze embarrassingly close to me just to move past my wheelchair. This made me feel like a nuisance as well as an impostor and added to my sense of powerlessness. Thanks to a provincial initiative, however, this whole building will soon have full wheelchair accessibility with ramps and arm-level elevator buttons.

5   My wheelchair experiment was soon over. It's true that it made an impression on me. I learned more from my internship than I ever expected to, and I wouldn't dream of parking my car in a wheelchair space. At the same time, I also realize how little I know about working with physically challenged people. A few hours of a "voluntary challenge" gave me only a hint of the challenges, both physical and emotional, that people with any physical limitation must overcome.

Wireless Days

1   Dark already at four o'clock, it is a cold, sleety December afternoon in St John's Newfoundland. Jimmy McKenny, Bill Mahan, Gilles LeFevre, and Ivor Jamieson are huddled, gritting their teeth and shivering for the fourth day in a row. The case of kites, wire, and flattened weather balloons keeps blowing open unless one of them sits on it. From several yards away, at the edge of the cliff by the old hospital, an Italian scientist is shouting for another kite. Not one of these men knows it yet, but the rubber and canvas kite Jimmy is dragging out of the case is going to make history. It will carry aloft the aerial that receives three pips of sound, the first wireless radio signal, from the other side of the Atlantic. Anyone who uses a cell phone or listens to the radio owes something to Jimmy and those men; they are responsible for the birth of wireless communication in Canada.

2   "In December 1901 Marconi assembled his receiver at Signal Hill, St. John's, nearly the closest point to Europe in North America" ("Marconi," *Newfoundland and Labrador Heritage*). At twenty-seven, after building a transmitter in Cornwall, England, Guglielmo Marconi came to the windy hilltop where Jimmy, Bill, Gilles, and Ivor are crouched. Bill Mahan's job is to keep notes, and as Jimmy wrestles with the kite, Bill puts his hand to his brow, trying to wipe his hair out of his eyes. The sleet and the spray from the waves below dampen the notebook pages and his bare fingers are so stiff that he can barely write. Looking up, he sees Signor Marconi shouting again

in his direction, and gesturing at him to come. He scrambles over to grab the kite, but Marconi, his voice nearly swept away in the wind, tells Bill to come now and to bring his notes. Marconi grips Bill's arm, shouting, "We heard it! The signal!" He pushes one earpiece from his headset receiver into Bill's hand, and rips the notebook from Bill. What he records is the result of more than a decade of research. Marconi hears three pips, sent from 1700 miles away, the "sky waves" bouncing back to earth after being sent from Cornwall in the southwest of England. He has proved that wireless telegraphy works.

3   Shortly after six o' clock in the evening near the lakeshore in west Toronto, a couple of friends are setting off to sample some wireless signals. "Hurray up Aileen! We're going to miss the King car," shouts Evelyn Guinane, standing at the corner of Triller Avenue. Their destination is a Victoria Street auditorium for a "Radiophonic Demonstration," the first in a series of 1922 media events. When the two step down from the streetcar at Church Street, huge drops of rain sheet down on them. It is March 22nd and at least eight hundred curious wet folks are spilling over the sidewalk and into Victoria Street. They join the crowd, and as soon as the auditorium's double doors open, Evelyn and Aileen are carried together in the forward rush. Inside, many find seats, but more line up against the walls. Finally, the wine-red curtains draw back, exposing a single oak box at centre stage. A spotlight finds the master of ceremonies, who announces, "Ladies and Gentlemen, the Queen." The seated audience rises. For two moments, the only sound is a distant orchestra playing the opening bars of the national anthem. Then chaos erupts. Five men from the front row rush the stage, shouting, "Where's the band?" A woman's voice shrieks, "There's something wrong here—this is witchcraft!" The orchestra playing "God Save the Queen" is neither a hoax nor sorcery; it is in a studio five kilometres away on Bloor Street.

4   A year or so after those superstitious, suspicious Torontonians experienced Marconi's discovery, the main *Salle* of Bonaventure Station swarms with Easter-time travellers. Red-capped porters push hand-trucks piled with luggage through the crowds, and Julie Lemelin looks about anxiously. "Where is Lucille?" she worries. The sisters are setting out on a four-day cross-Canada rail trip on the Canadian National Railway, and they have especially chosen the new CNR line because of its "listening cars" (Vipond 124). Julie and Lucille will sit along the walls of parlour cars with other travellers, wearing black metal headsets plugged into cables running above their heads. As they leave Montreal, they hear the smooth tones of the announcer, "Good afternoon, ladies and gentlemen, *mesdames et messieurs* . . ." For twenty minutes they listen to a program of light opera and waltzes. Then the signal fades. A railway official enters the car to announce that they will next enjoy a travelogue about the Thousand Islands when the train enters the Kingston broadcast and telegraph tower's area. Near Toronto, they will hear a news broadcast from NBC in New York, news that anyone lucky enough to have a radio receiver in the area will also hear. And so it will go, all the way to Vancouver, music and information available whenever the trains are close enough to radio signals. The sisters are listening to the first national radio network in North America, CNR Radio, which will eventually become the CBC.

5   Now it is a hot, humid late morning in July on Parliament Hill in Ottawa. The Union Jack waves feebly in atop raw, spindly pinewood towers planted as bases for speakers in the grass of the park. Luke and Eva Golan, with their

children Basil and Antony have staked their blanketed spot in the midst of sweaty, excited families and couples, forty thousand people waiting to celebrate Canada's Diamond Jubilee in 1927. Atop the Peace Tower, a radio technician is perched with his microphones, waiting to catch the peal of the noon bells as Canada turns fifty. Everyone wants to hear those bells; they have been silent for eleven years, since Parliament burned down ("On this Day–July 1, 1927"). The hillside crowd cheers as they hear them. On the CNR listening car, as it winds round the mountain track into Banff, travellers smile at each other and applaud as they hear the pealing. In Rio de Janeiro, and in London, millions hear Ottawa's bells, and during the hours of wireless broadcast that follow, those millions will be connected to Canada for the first time.

6   Hardik rides the bus to the University of Manitoba campus with his Bluetooth in his ear, listening to a podcast of a physics lecture. He is only one of millions of Canadians who are still receiving signals courtesy of Signor Marconi, signals he was the first to catch on that wind-whipped late December afternoon. The early days of wireless broadcasting in Canada are full of events that brought people together to hear from others many kilometres away. The "sky waves" still bounce across a vast nation, descending to land in ever-smaller receivers, but always linking us with tight, invisible bonds.

A list of sources used by Warren, the author of "Wireless Days," is available on the OLC. There you will see his sources noted as an MLA-style Works Cited list.

■ Questions

About Unity

1. Which essay lacks an opening thesis statement? How could its author have stated his or her point in a thesis?

2. Which sentence in paragraph 4 of "Accessing a Challenge" should be omitted in the interests of paragraph unity?

3. Which sentence in paragraph 2 of "Wireless Days" should be omitted in the interests of paragraph unity?

About Support

4. Blending narration and description: label as *sight, touch, hearing,* or *smell* all the sensory details in the following sentences taken from the essays.
   a. "My palms reddened and my wrist and forearm muscles started to ache as I tugged at the heavy metal wheels."
   b. "No matter how I strained to raise myself with my arms, I could not see over the partition."
   c. "The sleet and the spray from the waves below dampen the notebook pages and his bare fingers are so stiff that he can barely write."

5. Explain how the writer of "Wireless Days" sets up the chronology or time-frame for his essay, paragraph by paragraph.

About Coherence

6. The first stage of the writer's experience in "Accessing a Challenge" might be called *sitting down in the wheelchair*. What are the other two stages of the experience?

7. List three time transitions used in the third paragraph of "Wireless Days."

About Introductions and Conclusions

8. What methods of introduction are used in the first paragraph of "Wireless Days"? Circle the appropriate letters.
   a. Broad, general statement narrowing to a thesis
   b. Idea that is the opposite of the one to be developed
   c. An incident

About the Method of Development

9. Which aspects of "Accessing a Challenge" and "Wireless Days" suggest to readers that these are not fictional stories? What are other differences between the two narrative essays and short stories?

10. Neither essay uses only narration. Referring to pages 119–120, consult with your instructor and explain which other patterns of development you find in these essays.

DEVELOPING A NARRATIVE ESSAY

Writing a Thesis Statement for a Narrative Essay

Narrative essays tend to be about conflict, change, or discovery. Each leads readers to new states of awareness or alters their views of themselves or their lives in some way. Your narrative essay's thesis can be some general truth that the conflict or discovery reveals. The essay illustrates how the writer came to understand the thesis. Whether your narrative essay's thesis explains a change or a human truth, it is the point or "lesson" of the essay.

A thesis for a narrative essay focused on change might be similar to the following:

That turn in the road was a genuine turning-point for Yonggi.

A thesis based on an easily understood human truth could be something like this:

The value of family is, and should be, an unforgettable lesson.

When you work on a thesis statement for a narrative essay, ask yourself, "What specific moment or event changed me?" or "What truth did I learn from that experience?" That moment or event will be your topic and what you learned or the new feelings resulting from that pivotal experience will be the viewpoint that shapes your thesis statement.

Making a Point: Are You Writing a Narrative Essay or a Story?

While some narrative essays have the feel of a story, their structure is that of an essay. When you write a fictional story, you may not reveal a clear point at all; your story's point may be woven throughout it, or in your characters' actions or feelings. But when you write a narrative essay, your job is to make your point in your thesis, then to select events and emotions that will maintain your readers' interest as they see your meaning shown in your supporting details.

- How does Dorota, the author of "Accessing a Challenge," keep your attention on her point throughout the essay?
- Why do you believe she chose the events she did to support her point?
- If Dorota had written about her experience as a fictional short story, how would it differ from her essay?

Ultimately, your narrative essay will persuade your readers of the truth of your thesis "lesson," and help them to feel that they have learned something of value.

What Is Your Purpose and Who is Your Audience?

The main purpose of your narrative essay is to engage readers with a story. Colourful details and interesting events that build up to a point of some kind make narrative essays enjoyable for readers and writers alike.

At one time or another, you have probably listened to someone tell a rambling story that didn't seem to go anywhere. You might have wondered impatiently, "Where is this story going?" or "Is there a point here?" Keep these reactions and questions in mind as you think about your own narrative essay. To satisfy your audience, your story must have a clear overall purpose and point.

Also, your story should deal with an event or a topic that will appeal to your audience. A group of young children, for example, would probably be bored by a narrative essay about your first job interview. They might, however, be very interested if you wrote about the time you were chased by three tiny terriers or stood up to a class bully. Your audience will determine *how* you write your narrative as well.

1. If you write to an audience who knows you about working two part-time jobs:

   Thesis: Working two part-time jobs on top of being a full-time student is just too exhausting.

   I never get home before two a.m. six nights a week. On the bus home, I'm lucky if I don't fall asleep on the person next to me. I have no social life. For me, Saturday and Sunday nights are dates with the computer and my assignments.

2. If you write a narrative for your instructor about this topic:

   Thesis: Because I work two part-time jobs to pay for my education, I am under a great deal of physical and mental strain.

   Because there are only two evenings a week when I am not at work until one in the morning, I have to try to complete all my assignments then. Many times, my head hits the desk before I finish even the first piece of work on my list. If I fall asleep in your class, it is not because I am not interested. In fact, I enjoy English.

3. If you must submit a report as part of a bursary or loan application:

Thesis: Receiving the . . . grant would eliminate the necessity of working twenty-five hours a week on top of studying full-time.

Living alone with no family in this province means that there are no sources of financial support. An older uncle lives in Vancouver, but he is on a pension, so that asking him for any assistance is impossible. Living in downtown Montreal has been an expensive experience. As a result of work-hours required, there is insufficient time for studying and completing assignments.

As you plan your narrative essay, think about how many background details you will need to make your story "come alive" for your audience. If you are sure that your audience knows or shares aspects of the experience you will recount, then you may choose not to include too much background information. If, like Warren Cho, a broadcast journalism student and author of "Wireless Days," you know that readers will need some context to understand and relate to your narrative, then you should supply enough background to help them follow your narrative with understanding and pleasure.

What is Your Point of View in Your Narrative Essay?

Narrative essays recount your experiences or observations. When narratives are based on personal experiences, you will likely use a first-person point of view. You see this type of first-person essay in "Accessing a Challenge." Such essays emphasize the writer's close connection to his or her subject material. The "I" in a first-person narrative essay is *not* the essay's subject, but the "host" presenting a meaningful truth to an invited audience in such a way that the audience experiences it as clearly as possible. The writer's complete involvement in the essay's events is essential to the point. Other types of narrative essay are more effective if the focus is on the events, elements, and/or sequence of the story, *not* on the writer. An "observational narrative" is written in the third-person point of view. The story-report of the CBC's origins, "Wireless Days," invites you to follow the writer at a comfortable distance, looking over his or her shoulder. You learn about the early days of Canadian radio as you would if you were reading a story or watching a TV show or movie. This essay uses narrative as its controlling or primary structure to hold together the various anecdotes in its body paragraphs. The third-person narrative essay does not remind readers of your presence. Writing in this voice, you can emphasize any aspect of the essay that you believe best serves your thesis' point.

- What do you feel that the writer of "Wireless Days" wishes to emphasize? The look and feel of times and places? The events in the storyline? Why?

How Will You Support Your Thesis in a Narrative Essay?

Writing a narrative essay means carefully choosing support: events, anecdotes, scenes, and situations that best support your point.

- Warren, the author of "Wireless Days," has done some research to create the anecdotes in his essay. How does each of the four anecdotes illustrate his point?

To generate support, try asking yourself the journalist's "five *w*'s and an *h*." *Who? What? When? Where? Why?* and *How?* This sort of questioning will yield supporting details and it will often show you a direction for your narrative. If, for example, you are writing about an incident in which you knew you had definitely left childhood behind, and you find that you have the most answers under *who,* you may write a narrative about how the people involved in that incident made you feel.

Next, try to put readers in your place by using strong descriptive words and phrases. The quality of your narrative depends on *specificity,* in your choice of both details and how you describe those details. Think of Bill, the record-keeper in "Wireless Days": readers can almost see him crouching in the cold and damp. Also, note the interesting verbs used in both essays—with narrative writing, accurate, active verbs will add interest and liveliness to your essay.

Finally, consider including some dialogue if you are trying to bring a person or character to life. Speech patterns and turns of phrase show viewers people's feelings, cultural backgrounds, and relationships to the narrator. Dialogue can instantly enliven informative passages, as it does in "Wireless Days." If you choose to employ dialogue, put the dialogue in double quotation marks and, if there are multiple lines of speech, begin a new paragraph with the first line. When another person speaks, begin a new paragraph for that speaker.

A good narrative essay will offer vivid details and active, precise verbs that "sell" your essay's meaning to readers.

ACTIVITY

Choose one effective descriptive phrase and one interesting verb from each of the two student essays. Why is each so effective?

Prewriting: Stage 1

The first stage of prewriting for a narrative essay involves **discovering your story and its meaning.** Freewriting is a particularly helpful technique at this stage. (For more about freewriting, see pages 16–18.) As you consider the story you want to relate, many ideas will crowd into your head. Simply writing them down freely will jog details you may have forgotten and help you decide what the main point of your story really is.

Dorota, the writer of "Accessing a Challenge," spent a half-hour freewriting before she wrote the first draft of her essay. Here is a section of her freewriting:

> My third semester was a co-op in a provincial social services office. I learned more there in one day in a wheelchair than I did in an ordinary week's work. A lot of companies object to spending money on making places accessible, not just for wheelchairs, but having computers set up for people with visual problems and things like that. Everyone should have the opportunity to work. At my office, they had this "Accessiblity Awareness" campaign, and

PART 2   PATTERNS OF ESSAY DEVELOPMENT

at first, I didn't take it too seriously. We were given a handout, and we had to sign up for a "challenge," like wearing an eye-mask or earplugs. I chose to try a wheelchair. For some reason, I thought it would be fun. No way. It was scary and a lot of physical work. I felt really clumsy trying to get it rolling, and my arms ached. Stopping or turning it was worse. And the aisles between office partitions are really narrow. I knocked over one partition . . .

Often the writer's point emerges from freewriting about some memory or feeling, and the writer usually discovers some **conflict** or **change.** The conflict or change may be within you as writer, or it may be between you and some force in the outside world. In either case, the conflict or change is the catalyst that drives the narrator to act. This is the point you wish to illuminate for your readers.

Prewriting: Stage 2

Once you have discovered your story and its meaning, the next stage in prewriting for your narrative essay involves **organizing the events and details.** You will develop that story in chronological order—in time sequence—from what happened first, to what happened next, and so on.

One of the challenges in creating a successful narrative essay is making sure that all the material contributes to your point. You must decide which events, or aspects of the experience, contribute most directly to your main point or to the conflict of feelings you are recreating. Too many details, or unrelated details, sidetrack your reader and weaken your point. Too few details, or details not vividly described in lively words, will leave your narrative "hollow" and fail to create interest among your readers. Accuracy in choice and type of details is essential to good narrative writing.

As Dorota read over her freewriting, she decided that the main point of her narrative essay was her new realization of how difficult it would be to face a constant physical challenge. To support that central point, she needed details to demonstrate the frustrations she felt. She created a trial outline for the first draft of her essay:

Thesis Statement: An accessibility campaign showed me the hardship of spending the day in a wheelchair.

1. Sitting in the wheelchair
   a. Awkward because it rolled
   b. Awkward because the footrest was out of place
   c. Psychologically awkward

2. Moving the wheelchair
   a. I thought someone would push me
   b. It was hard to make the chair move and it hurt my hands
   c. Difficult to steer

3. Ways the wheelchair affected me
   a. Couldn't see
   b. I felt in the way
   c. I felt funny talking to people as they bent down over me

First Draft and Revision

Dorota based her first draft on her trial outline. Here it is:

1   My co-op job for Social Services involved taking on a physical challenge for an "Accessibility Awareness" campaign. Like a few other people I worked with, I chose a wheelchair. Others used earplugs or wore eye masks.

2   It surprised me that I felt nervous about sitting down in my wheelchair. I'm not sure why I felt scared about it. I guess I realized that most people who use wheelchairs don't do it by choice—they have to.

3   When I sat down, I thought that Paula, another co-op student, would push me around. We had talked about her doing that earlier. But she decided instead to "adopt" her own challenge, and she pretended to be blind. I saw her with an eye mask on, trying to fix herself a cup of coffee and knocking it off the table as she stirred it. So I had to figure out how to make the chair move by myself. It wasn't so easy. Pushing the wheels made my hands and arms sore. I also kept bumping into things. I felt really awkward. I even had trouble locking the wheels and finding the footrest.

4   I couldn't see anything above eye level when I sat in the chair. When I tried to get down to work, I could only see inside my cubicle. When somebody asked me a question, or asked me to hand them a file, I couldn't just stand up to see them or reach over with the papers. I kept trying to boost myself up with my arms, but I couldn't see over the top of the partition. So I had to wheel myself out into the aisle every time, and just turning the chair was hard to do. The aisle was too narrow for anyone to get by my chair. The new provincial initiative I was working on will make problems like that better by widening aisles and making office spaces large enough to turn chairs around in. It will be expensive, but it's a worthwhile thing. Another thing I disliked was how I felt when people talked to me. They had to lean down as though I were a kid, and I had to stare up at them as though I were too. One person I talked to who seemed to understand what I was experiencing was Phil Chung, who mentioned that his brother-in-law uses a wheelchair.

Now look at the final draft of her essay on pages 124—125 of this chapter, and answer the following questions about her revised narrative:

- What are the conflicts Dorota feels?
- What are the origins of these conflicts?
- To which events or physical occurrences are these strong feelings connected?
- In Dorota's revised essay, which aspects of her experience are most vividly recreated? How?
- Is Dorota's narrative most effective in the first-person point of view? Why or why not?

WRITING A NARRATIVE ESSAY

■ Writing Assignment 1

Think of an experience in your life that supports one of the following statements. Then, using that statement as your thesis, write a narrative essay about that experience.

- "The chains of habit are too weak to be felt until they are too strong to be broken."—Samuel Johnson
- "Words in mouth, no load upon head."—Jamaican proverb
- "Everyone thinks of changing the world, but no one thinks of changing himself."—Leo Tolstoy
- "Don't grieve. Anything you lose comes round in another form."—Djalâl ad-Dîn Rûmî
- "When you plant lettuce, if it does not grow well, you don't blame the lettuce."—Thich Nhat Hanh
- "Love is so holy, so confusing. It makes a man anxious, tormented."—Gao Xingjian
- "He who awaits much can expect little."—Gabriel Garcia Márquez
- "Stories can conquer fear, you know. They can make the heart bigger."—Ben Okri
- "It is better to walk than curse the road."—Senegalese proverb
- "Silence is an argument carried out by other means."—Ernesto "Che" Guevara
- "Anger is just a cowardly extension of sadness."—Alanis Morissette
- "Man needs his difficulties because they are necessary to enjoy success."—Abdul Kalam
- "We lie loudest when we lie to ourselves."—Eric Hoffer

Prewriting

1. **Do some freewriting** or questioning about the quotation you have chosen. Try to get down as many details as you can think of.

2. This preliminary writing will help you decide whether your topic is promising enough to continue working on. If it is not, choose another quotation. If it is, do three things:

    - Write out your thesis in a single sentence, underlining the emotion, change, or conflict you will focus on. For example:

      "I never felt the chains of my bad habits in high school until <u>I wasted a year of my life.</u>"

    - Think about what creates the source of tension in your narrative. What details can you add that will create enough tension to "hook" readers and keep them interested?

    - Make up a list of all the details involved in the experience. Then, arrange those details in chronological (time) order.

3. Using the list as a guide, prepare an outline showing the major events in your narrative and the supporting details for each stage. Write a first draft based on your outline.

Revising

Once you have a first draft, revise, edit, and proofread your draft, using the four bases for effective essays:

1. **Unity**: Do you state the thesis of your narrative in the introductory paragraph? Any parts of the essay that do not support the thesis should be eliminated or rewritten.

2. **Support**: Do you have enough details? Careful detailing and occasional use of dialogue help make a situation come alive. Try to add more vivid, exact details that will help your readers experience the event as it actually happened.

3. **Coherence**: Use time signals such as *first, then, next, after, while, during,* and *finally* to help connect details as you move from the beginning, to the middle, and to the end of your narrative.

4. **Effective sentence skills**: Refer to the checklist on the inside front cover to edit and proofread your next-to-final draft for sentence-skills mistakes.

Before starting, consider how one student tested whether his plan for his narrative essay was a good one.

- What statement have I chosen as my thesis?
  "The chains of habit are too weak to be felt until they are too strong to be broken."—Samuel Johnson

- Does the incident I have chosen include some kind of conflict, change, or discovery?
  Yes, I am going to write about the day my grade-twelve math teacher told me I had no chance of passing his subject or most of my other subjects. The conflict I felt was between the fantasy I had been living—believing I would pass somehow—and the reality of the habits I'd gotten into: skipping school half the time and wasting whole days sitting in coffee shops with my friends.

- Is the incident limited in time?
  Yes, I'm writing about a twenty-minute conversation.

- Does the incident evoke an emotional response in me?
  Yes, I was ashamed, frightened, and angry at myself.

- Does the incident support the statement I have chosen?
  Yes. I had picked up the "habits" of skipping school and wasting time, so I got used to fooling myself. I was so caught in those "chains" that I wasted a year of school.

■ Writing Assignment 2

In this narrative essay, you will write with a specific purpose and for a specific audience.

Imagine that you are in a town 100 kilometres from home, that your car has broken down several kilometres from a gas station, and that you are not carrying any money.

Option 1: A Personal Narrative

You thought you were going to have a terrible time, but the friendly people who helped you turned your experience into a positive one. It was such a good day, in fact, that you don't want to forget what happened.

Write a narrative of the day's events in your diary so that you can read it ten years from now and remember exactly what happened. Begin with the moment you realized that your car had broken down, and continue until you were safely back at home.

Option 2: An Accurate Objective Narrative

Among the pleasant people who helped you was a police officer who arranged for a tow truck and for emergency repairs to your car. However, she must file a report, which will include your record of events.

Write a third-person narrative report from the point of view of the officer: "The accident occurred at approximately 8:00 p.m. on Thursday, March 15. Two cars were involved . . . ." Describe the situation and all the assistance provided. Consider carefully all the details needed for an accurate record of the event.

Option 3: An Instructive Narrative

Imagine that a friend or relative is an inexperienced and nervous driver. You wish to recreate your experience as a reassuring narrative.

Write a narrative that uses your experience as an instructive series of events to demonstrate that your reader can deal with and even learn from an accident. To discover and state your point clearly, try to visualize someone you know who is nervous about driving, and as you do so, consider the details that would be most reassuring to him or her.

■ Writing Assignment 3

Read the selection "Lamb to the Slaughter" by Roald Dahl on pages 460–467. In Dahl's essay, we learn that Mary Maloney is not as she first appears to be. Note especially the careful descriptions of Mary, descriptions that appear to be contrary to her later behaviour.

After considering Dahl's selection, write a narrative essay about a situation in your life where you met someone who was not as he or she first appeared. Be sure to include sufficient and specific details, as Dahl does, to point out the disparity between who the person first appeared to be and who the person turned out to be. What lesson did you learn from this experience?

CHECKLIST OF LEARNING OUTCOMES FOR CHAPTER 8

To ensure that you have understood and met the learning outcomes for this chapter, answer the following questions after completing any of the chapter writing assignments:

✓ Does your essay's opening paragraph state or clearly imply its point about the emotion or experience you will focus on?

✓ Are your details arranged in time order, with transitional words and phrases to show relationships between paragraphs and events?

✓ Does each detail included in your narrative help to clarify the point in your thesis?

✓ Are your details vivid and accurate enough to recreate your experience for readers?

✓ Do you conclude by returning to your point in an interesting way in your final paragraph?

Description

After reading this chapter and working through its writing assignments, you will be ready to write a descriptive essay that

- offers a dominant impression in the thesis;
- presents a carefully chosen selection of sensory details to reinforce aspects of the dominant impression;
- guides readers with a clear point of view and method of organization;
- concludes with a thought that fixes your dominant impression in the reader's mind.

When you describe objects, places, and people, you are painting or photographing with words. Sometimes your senses and your mind record places, emotions, and people in complex ways that blend feelings with reality. Other times, for other purposes, you try to recreate precisely what you see. In either case, your word pictures must give readers clear, vivid versions of your subjects, using sharp, colourful, and specific details that speak to their senses.

Here is a description with almost no appeal to the senses: "In the window was a fan." In contrast, here is a description rich in sense impressions: "The blades of the rusty window fan clattered and whirled as they blew out a stream of warm, soggy air." Sense impressions in this second example include sight *(rusty window fan, whirled)*, hearing *(clattered)*, and touch *(warm, soggy air)*. The vividness and sharpness provided by the sensory details give you a clear picture of the fan and enable you to share the writer's experience.

Description and narration are uniquely suited to help you express what you see and feel; narration gives your readers a line to follow and description shows readers what you see and experience. Description is also your key tool in explaining what you see in the world. There are two basic forms of description: personal/expressive, and objective, and, as you will see, there are some differences between the purposes and descriptive styles used for each.

You will use descriptive writing skills constantly in academic assignments for which any event, procedure, technology, human behaviour pattern, or strategy must be carefully recreated in words. You will also need the consistent precision and detail selection associated with good descriptive writing for most career writing tasks, such as reports and analyses. Finally, description as a method of development figures prominently as a secondary method in every other method of essay development: consider, for instance, how, in a cause/effect essay, readers will respond to a vivid description of the sluggish, algae-surfaced water of a creek whose pollution is caused by a nearby factory. In the examples below, description is dominant, but other modes blend with it in each case.

In this chapter, you will be asked to describe a person, place, or thing, using words rich in sensory details. To prepare for this task, first read the student essays that follow, and then work through the questions that accompany the essays.

STUDENT ESSAYS TO CONSIDER

The Swimming Pool

1   In small-town BC, there are not that many activities and pastimes available in the summer months, so trips to the pool were a special hot-weather ritual, a pilgrimage with starting points all over town. Hot, freckled kids rankled by shouting and disorderly families; sullen, closed-faced teens stressed just by being who they were, and livewires who had run out of places to cause trouble in, all met at the pool. It was their mystic goal; all roads led there. It was their calm, blue, chlorinated shrine, their echoing shiny-tiled spa where they washed away their jitters.

2   Most summer swimmers claimed that the pool's location was somehow just about twenty minutes from anywhere. If, for instance, someone started from a stuffy, flower-papered living room in a north-end bungalow, walked a block and a half along cracked pavement to the bus stop, deposited a buck and a quarter in the fare box of the downtown bus, she would be at the mall next to the pool in fifteen minutes. Four others, ready to set a record and fresh off the night-shift at the pulp-and-paper mill, whooping and hollering and hopped up on coffee and Red Bull, did a little speeding and slid into the mall lot in twelve flat. Their truck needed an oil-change, but they made it. Someone else caught a ten-minute ride up from the family trailer on the southeast side and was already waiting in the lobby. Inside, it is opening time now, and they all join the noon-time line-up of chattering, jumpy bag-clutching kids and wall-gazing teenagers, waiting to pay and get in.

3   Once in, they face a short separation when they meet the fork in the hot little hall. They must face old Smiley Joe who presides over his television and

the separation of the sexes. They divide into streams, into the transitional change-rooms, where they disappear, eager to shed their skins along with their sweaty T-shirts.

4   Then out they flow again, new souls every one, out of the boy- and girl-doors. Out into the chlorine haze and the skylight glow, where they are all together again. They chatter and their talk rings like singing in the echoing aqua space where no voice is ever alone for long. As they talk, they move out in groups around the rim of the pool, free to look shyly at each other in their new guises. This is a free zone. For seconds, they all seem to pause, then a sport sprints to the diving board, enjoys the rubbery spring as he bounces, and initiates the action with his dive.

5   The kids at the shallow end are the first in; in wiggly puddles of five or six, they are eager to splash each other and bounce up and down. Teenage girls perch along the edge of the pool in batches, too, but they don't splash or bounce—they talk, stretch, and maybe delicately flex a pointed toe into the water until they are ready. Watch the soloists now; these are the models of efficiency. Cutting their way down the lanes, they are already halfway through a lap, focused as knives slicing the bottom of the pool. Territories must be established; boundaries set—for a moment. Sensing a challenge, as always, the older boys breach every liquid border, cannonballing in and cross-hatching the lanes like torpedoes. Now and then the serene back-floaters cut in, unaware of lanes or lines. And the children expand their space, calling "Marco, Polo," and branch out, at least as far as the lifeguard will let them. It is all wonderful, lazy confusion.

6   And no one notices as the afternoon passes.

7   The closing siren screams over the P.A., hounding each of them out of the pool. Cowed or unwilling, the older ones straight-arm themselves out of the water; the children, more pliant and used to obeying, have beaten them to the change-rooms. They all have to leave. The shrine is closed for the day.

Everyday Common Scents

1   Scents go straight to the brain where they wake up memories and feelings. A whiff of some scent wanders idly up the nostrils, then races off to work in the mind's twisty passages. The mind is a busier place than anyone knows. People usually consider only the extremes of the scent scale: a wonderful perfume or a really evil stench. But it's the ordinary aromas of everyday places that bring back fragile memories of long ago and forgotten feelings about the recent past.

2   Offices used to have distinct smells, for instance. Workplaces today just smell like whatever is whooshing through the ventilation system but not the places where yesterday's fathers went every day. Those pale green or grey offices of the 1940s and '50s with their dark wood moldings had a whole menu of smells. There were layers of aromas that surely seeped into the people who toiled there—tired cigarette smoke, prickly twinges of hot wiring, the carbon-y traces of typewriter and elevator oil, and the odd light waft of piney aftershave. This mixture filled the buses too every day, fifty years ago.

3   Elementary schools, on the other hand, probably still smell the way they always did. The chattering hallways are full of the warm familiar smell of kids' hair and breath, soft and kind to the nose as a pet's fur. In winter, the hot breath of school furnaces ripens half-sour aromas of damp boots, sodden snowsuits, and sweet blackening bananas hiding in lockers. All seasons bring hints of that mysterious, minty, poisonous-looking green sweeping powder, and for some reason, canned vegetable soup. These days, however, classrooms may be missing one traditional ingredient in the "school aroma" recipe: the flat, nose-choking dusty smell of chalk; it's been replaced by the solvent stink of whiteboard marker.

4   Take a trip to the corner convenience store. Inhaling brings back dreamy scents and memories—the soapy, powdery smells of baby-pink bubblegum squares, the heavy smell of chocolate, and even the strangely medicinal breath of the ice-cream cooler. Adults' and children's noses alike twitch at the chemical hint of printer's ink from tied bundles of magazines and comics waiting to be shelved, but only the grown-ups remember the coarse stink of sulphur rising every May from flame-red tissue paper packs of firecrackers. Corner stores have always smelled like excitement and dreams to children, and to most adults, too, if they admit it.

5   So every day's scents are a feast for the mind and memory. The past and present jostle for attention right under our noses. Maybe it's time to wake up and inhale the aromas of the coffee, the dog, the classroom, and that fresh basket of clean laundry waiting on the stairs.

■ Questions

About Unity

1. In which supporting paragraph of "Everyday Common Scents" does the topic sentence appear at the paragraph's end rather than the beginning?

2. Which sentence in paragraph 2 of "Everyday Common Scents" should be eliminated in the interests of paragraph unity?

3. Which sentence from paragraph 2 of "The Swimming Pool" should be omitted in the interests of paragraph unity?

4. What is the dominant impression created by the writer of "The Swimming Pool"?

About Support

5. How many separate groups of people are described in paragraph 5 of "The Swimming Pool"? Which descriptions do you find most effective? Why?

6. Label as *sight, touch, hearing,* or *smell* all the sensory details in the following sentences taken from the two essays.
   a. "The chattering hallways are full of the warm familiar smell of kids' hair and breath, soft and kind to the nose as a pet's fur."
   b. "In winter, the hot breath of school furnaces ripens half-sour aromas of damp boots, sodden snowsuits, and sweet blackening bananas hiding in lockers."

c. "Sensing a challenge, as always, the older boys breach every liquid border, cannonballing in and cross-hatching the lanes like torpedoes."

7. What are three descriptive details in paragraph 3 of "Everyday Common Scents" that reinforce the idea expressed in the topic sentence that school smells do not change?

About Coherence

8. Which method of organization does paragraph 2 of "The Swimming Pool" use?
   a. Time order
   b. Emphatic order

   Does this order add to the effectiveness of the writer's overall description of the pool? How?

9. The last paragraph of "Everyday Common Scents" begins with a word that serves as which type of signal?
   a. Time
   b. Addition
   c. Contrast
   d. Illustration

About Introductions and Conclusions

10. Which of the following best describes the introduction to "Everyday Common Scents"?
    a. Idea that is the opposite of the one to be developed
    b. Explanation of the importance of the topic
    c. Broad, general statement narrowing to a thesis
    d. Anecdote

11. Which method of conclusion and which approach does the writer of "Everyday Common Scents" use?

About the Method of Development

12. In which sentences in the first paragraph of "The Swimming Pool" do you find the writer's dominant impression of his subject?

13. Which other patterns of development do you find in "The Swimming Pool"? In "Everyday Common Scents"?

DEVELOPING A DESCRIPTIVE ESSAY

Writing a Thesis Statement for a Descriptive Essay

Descriptive essays need an organizing principle, a focus for the writer's choice of details. This focus is called a dominant impression.

When you work on a thesis statement for a descriptive essay based on something you have experienced, ask yourself, "What do I feel (or think of) when I see (my topic) in my mind?" or "What words come to mind when I think about (my topic)?" In a personal/expressive descriptive essay, your point is the dominant impression you have of the person, place, or thing you will write about. Your thesis statement, then, should clearly express that dominant impression.

A thesis for a descriptive essay about a motorcycle trip could be something like this:

> The trip that was such a thrilling idea was, in reality, gruelling days of bone-chilling wind and stinging rain.

Descriptive essays or reports for more objective writing situations—descriptions of places, people or animals, processes, or situations—call for a slight variation in their thesis statements. If you write scientific or objective descriptions, for example, your dominant impression will be a kind of "preview statement," an overview of the subject of your description. Here is a thesis by Rebecca Tahir, an environmental geography student. She is writing a description of land-types on the north shore of Lake Erie:

> Eight main areas represent important communities on Pelee and Middle Islands; the community types range from forests and savannas to alvars and wetlands.

In which ways does Rebecca's thesis resemble and differ from that of an expressive description?

What Is Your Purpose and Who Is Your Audience?

The main purpose of your descriptive essay is to make your audience see, hear, taste, smell, or feel what you are writing about. Vivid details and accurate, lively verbs, as with narrative essays, are keys to descriptive essays, enabling your audience to picture and experience what you describe.

Whether you are assigned an expressive descriptive essay or a more objective one, when selecting your topic, consider how much your audience already knows about it. If your topic is a familiar one, you can assume your audience already understands the general idea. However, if you are presenting something new or unfamiliar to your readers—perhaps a description of one of your relatives or a chemical reaction arising from some process—provide enough background information to create a "frame" for your word picture. You should also consider whether your audience will know the meanings of any specialized vocabulary you will use.

- How does the author of "The Swimming Pool" set a specific scene about a specific pool for her readers?

Depending on the nature of your descriptive essay, you will want to consider your word-choices. If your essay is personal and evocative, you will choose descriptive adjectives and phrases and lively verbs to bring your subject to life. If your purpose is to create an accurate, objective view of a place or situation, then you will aim for precise words that capture and identify aspects of your subject in such a way that your reader will see them as clearly as possible. You will choose adjectives based on their accuracy rather than on the reaction they will provoke from readers.

Also, consider the dominant impression you want to convey to your audience. For instance, if you choose, as your topic, a park you used to visit as a child, decide if your objective is to make your audience see the park as a pleasant and familiar place or a run-down and depressing one. The dominant impression you choose will determine the kinds of supporting details and examples to include.

What Is Your Point of View in Your Descriptive Essay?

Descriptive essays present vivid and accurate word pictures of their subjects. Therefore, your presence as a writer is always at least secondary, if not invisible. Your point of view is less defined, and should generally be even less evident than it is with narrative writing because the purpose of descriptive writing is to show readers impressions and details. For this reason, choose third-person voice in considering voice or pronoun point of view in descriptive writing.

Some informal or journalistic descriptive essays follow a pattern in which the writer begins with his or her relationship to a person, place, or object, then moves on to describe objects and situations as clearly as possible while minimizing his or her presence. The writer's presence as "I" often distracts readers from the impact of the descriptive details.

- Who do you think the writer of "The Swimming Pool" is? How is he or she connected to his or her subject? How do you know, from the essay?

How Will You Support Your Thesis in a Descriptive Essay?

When you write an expressive or personal descriptive essay in which you want to share your impressions of a place or person, your aim is to evoke in readers not just an image of the place or person, but of your feelings or experience of it as well. To do so, you use descriptive words and phrases that appeal to your readers' senses. Here is how Luisa DaSilva writes about a portrait of her mother:

> The blouse is made of heavy, eggshell-coloured satin and reflects the light in its folds and hollows. It has a turned-down cowl collar and fine stitchwork on the shoulders and below the collar. The tiny rows of gathered stitchwork look hand done. The skirt, which covers my mother's calves, is straight and made of light wool or flannel. My mother is wearing silver drop earrings. They are about two inches long and roughly shield-shaped.

When you are assigned a more objective descriptive essay, share or reproduce your image of the object, person, or place described as accurately as possible and aim for precision in your descriptions. The aim is not to evoke an emotional response in readers. Here is a section of Rebecca's objective description of the islands off the Lake Erie shore:

> Prairie and dwarf flowering shrub species as well as lichen occur in small open areas where limestone-based soil is lowest and bedrock is exposed. Savanna that remains is dominated by White Oak and Chinquapin Oak, with some Blue Ash. It is bordered by relatively undisturbed dry-soil Ash woodland with some immature White Ash and Sugar Maple in abandoned pasture land.

Much descriptive writing is a mixture of expressive and objective description. In expressive descriptive essays, a degree of accuracy and precision is needed to assist readers in seeing what the writer intends them to see.

- Re-read "Everyday Common Scents" and "The Swimming Pool." Where do you find expressive details? Where do you find more objective details?

Prewriting

Melanie Oliveira, author of "The Swimming Pool," was given writing assignment 1, below. She tried to think of the place that brought back the most memories. "I'm only in first year," she said, "so all I had to do was think back to last summer. I grew up in a fairly small town in B.C.—there were only three high schools. Funny thing, though, everybody from all three schools went to the pool—it's where all the kids went. It was a sort of 'kids' world.' And it felt like our special place. We started going there as soon as we were allowed to ride the bus alone, and just kept going back every year. I miss it, just thinking about it—I wonder if I can bring back how it felt to go there."

Here is part of Melanie's freewriting:

Every summer, there is an unofficial "kids' world" in my town—it's a cool, wet world where everybody meets. Everybody including people I never saw at other times of the year, people from the other high schools, got together there at the municipal pool. There were even guys who worked up at the lumber camps there. People stayed in their groups in a way, but everybody kind of remembered or was familiar with the crowd. I took the same bus every day—I started going on my own when I was ten. We lined up and went in for the whole day, every day. No matter how hot it was, it was cool and blue in there.

First Draft and Revision

In her next class, Melanie went over her freewriting with her instructor.

"I like the whole idea you have here about a special 'kids' world.' And you have something good there with the idea of an annual ritual for kids from all over town, too. So, would you say you're going to write an expressive description of the pool?"

"It has to be, doesn't it?" Melanie said. "Because I want to get across how unique the experience of going there is, as well as what the pool is like."

"Right. So in your draft, work on giving readers some objective details about both the place and your experience, and let's see how it works," her instructor said.

Here is Melanie's first draft:

A trip to the pool in my town was a hot-weather ritual for kids from all over. It was the cure for every problem in everyone's life, our goal and our special place.

A lot of the people who came to the pool were strangers to each other the rest of the year. But everybody had a story about how they got there and how long it took them. We told each other those stories in line, waiting to get into the pool. For me it was usually a hot walk along the sidewalk, then a fifteen-minute bus ride to the mall near the pool. Even the guys who worked up at the lumber camps came roaring down in their trucks after the early shift.

I really remember Smiley who sat at a little desk in the hall outside the change-rooms watching TV all day. He used to keep an eye on the people in the line-ups and make sure everybody behaved and no one went into the wrong change-room. He knew everybody's name. Once we changed, we felt like new people—we weren't the same kids who were on the buses or in the family van—we were the citizens of kids' world.

And our world is blue and smells like chlorine. There's no bright sunlight, just the glow coming through the skylight and the echoes of voices bouncing off the tile walls. Kids find their regular groups—there are the little ones bouncing around at the shallow end with the guard, and their voices sound like bird-calls. Lots of kids start out sitting on the edges, seeing who's there and checking each other out. Then one guy always seems to dive, bouncing off the board, and that sets everybody in motion.

First in are the wiggly groups of young ones, splashing each other and bouncing up and down. The teenage girls are in batches, too, but they don't splash or bounce. They just talk, stretch, and flex their toes into the water. Then the show-offs and the soloists show up. They cut their way down the lanes, doing laps, like knives slicing the bottom of the pool. All the groups set their boundaries, at least for a moment. But the older boys break everybody's borderlines, cannonballing and swimming in and out of the lanes like torpedoes. And the children expand their space, calling "Marco, Polo," and go at least as far as the lifeguard will let them.

And so every afternoon passes, until the closing siren screams over the P.A. Everybody out of the pool now, because the shrine is closed for the day.

When she revised and edited her first draft, Melanie worked on finding interesting and colourful verbs. In the finished version of her essay find three examples of verbs that create vivid impressions on you as a reader.

As she revised her draft, Melanie eliminated inconsistent pronoun voices, to make her essay consistently third-person. Find three examples in her first draft, above, where she has used first-person voice.

WRITING A DESCRIPTIVE ESSAY

■ Writing Assignment 1

Write an essay about a particular place that you can observe carefully or that you already know well. Choose a store you know well, a room you have lived in for some time, or a room in the college or university you attend.

Prewriting

1. **Point of View:** Your main focus is on describing a particular location and creating a "word picture" in which you are the "photographer" rather than a participant, so using the third-person approach will keep readers' attention on your subject.

2. **Dominant Impression:** Write a short single sentence in which you name the place or object you want to describe and the dominant impression you have

about that place or object. The dominant impression is your organizing principle. Any details you include in later drafts should agree with or support this dominant impression. Don't worry if your sentence doesn't seem quite right as a thesis; you can refine it later. Here are some examples of such sentences:

The study area was noisy.	The restaurant was noisy.
The bus terminal was frightening.	The variety store was a wild jumble.

3. **Details:** Once you have written your sentence about the dominant impression, make a list of as many details as you can that support that general impression. Here, for example, is the list made by Darren, the writer of "Everyday Common Scents":

Office ventilation air	Caretakers and green sweeping powder
Old cigarette smoke	Old black bananas—smell too sweet
Overheated wiring smell	Chalk smell—sneezing?
Small machine oil—grandfather	Bubblegum—pink, powdery pieces
Hot school hallways	Freezers had a smell, odd
Wet boots—mildew smell?	Firecrackers—mom remembers

Use as many sensory details as possible in describing a scene. Remember that it is through the richness of your sensory details that the reader will gain a picture of the scene.

4. **Organization and Outline:** When you are creating an outline, decide which method of organization is most appropriate for your subject. Use any of the following or one that is unique to your subject.

Physical order—Move from left to right, move from far to near, or follow some other consistent order.
Size—Begin with large features or objects and work down to smaller ones.
Importance—Move from least dominant or important to most dominant or important (or vice versa).

Using your outline, proceed to the first draft of your essay.

Revising

After you have completed the first draft of your essay, set it aside for a while. When you review the draft, try to do so as critically as you would if it were not your own work. Ask yourself these questions:

- Does my essay have a thesis that clearly states my dominant impression?
- Have I chosen an appropriate voice or pronoun point of view? Is my connection to what I am describing important enough to justify my presence in the essay?
- Have I provided rich, specific details that appeal to a variety of senses (sight, hearing, smell, taste, touch)? Do all of my details relate to my dominant impression?
- Is there any irrelevant material that should be eliminated or rewritten?
- Have I organized my essay in some logical manner—physical order, size, importance—or in some other way that is appropriate to my subject?

- Have I used transition words to help readers follow my train of thought and my organization?
- Do I have a concluding paragraph that provides a summary, a final thought, or both?

Continue to revise your essay until you can answer "yes" to each question. Then, be sure to check the next-to-final draft for the sentence skills listed on the inside front cover.

■ Writing Assignment 2

Write an essay about a family portrait. (The picture may be of an individual or a group.)

1. Decide how you will organize your essay. Your decision will depend on what seems appropriate for the photograph. Two possibilities follow:

   - Your first supporting paragraph might describe the subjects' faces, the second, their clothing and jewellery, and the third, the story behind the picture.
   - Your first supporting paragraph might describe the people in the photograph (and how they look), the second, the relationships among the people (and what they are doing in the photo), and the third, the story behind the picture (time, place, occasion, other circumstances).

2. Make an outline for your essay, based on the organization you have chosen.

3. Use your outline to make a list of details that support each of your main points.

4. Use your outline and its list of details to write your first draft.

5. Refer to the guidelines for revising your descriptive essay provided on page 147.

■ Writing Assignment 3

Read the selection "Headlands" on pages 485. Then, write an essay describing a location that you find (or have found) inspirational. For the author, the beach is keenly familiar.

In your introductory paragraph, explain where the place is and your connection with it. Explain what aspects of the location are appealing, pleasant, and/or otherwise familiar, and why. Be sure to state in the thesis your dominant impression of this place. Use any order in your supporting paragraphs that you feel is appropriate. Generally, a spatial method of organization will be best, but you could also go from the least familiar aspect of the location to its most familiar aspect, based on your emotional responses to the place. Use vivid images and sensory details, as Bennett does in his selection, to show readers exactly why you feel as you do about your choice of location.

CHECKLIST OF LEARNING OUTCOMES FOR CHAPTER 9

To ensure that you have understood and met the learning outcomes for this chapter, answer the following questions after completing any of its writing assignments:

✓ Have I created a clear, dominant impression of my subject in the thesis?

✓ Have I used vivid sensory details to illustrate each aspect of the dominant impression?

✓ Does the essay sustain one point of view and one clear method of organization?

✓ Does the final paragraph contain ideas that reinforce the dominant impression in the reader's mind?

PART 2
PATTERNS OF ESSAY DEVELOPMENT

CHAPTER 10

Illustration by Examples

After reading this chapter and working through its writing assignments, you will be ready to write an essay that

- uses distinct, relevant examples to support your thesis;

- uses specific supporting details to clarify those examples;

- uses enough supporting details to clarify and illustrate those examples;

- ends with a conclusion that reinforces how the examples explain the thesis.

Essays that illustrate their point with examples move your readers from the slightly general position of your thesis to clear examples that demonstrate specific particular aspects of its meaning in your support. Each time you illustrate your ideas with clear examples, you increase the likelihood that your audience will see for themselves the truth of your statement. Illustrating a point with examples is especially useful for convincing doubtful readers of a writer's point. Consider an essay showing that dyslexic students are often more intelligent than the average. A well-chosen series of illustrative examples will likely open readers' minds to the truth of such a point, sometimes simply because they may never have given it much thought. Examples convince and persuade because of their appropriateness, clarity, and quantity.

Note the specific examples that follow the general conversational statement below:

Statement	**Specific Examples**
The first day of classes was frustrating.	My marketing class was cancelled. Then, I couldn't find the Mac lab. The lines at the bookstore were so long that I went home without buying my textbooks.

Each of these specific statements adds credibility and strength to the general attitude expressed by the term *frustrating*. Examples are particulars: facts, anecdotes, statistics, and descriptions that stick in readers' minds. These specific examples create and maintain interest in your general ideas.

Learning to provide specific, relevant examples in your writing has distinct benefits for your future career. Case studies, proposals, academic writing, and many types of reports are extensively supported by examples that show a precedent, similar results, or illustrative material to help readers understand the main point. Well-chosen and appropriate examples always make abstract or general ideas concrete and understandable—people remember specifics, not vague generalities.

Every method of development makes use of examples; they clarify arguments, explain steps in a procedure, elaborate on components of a category, and strengthen an argument.

In this chapter, you will be asked to provide a series of examples to support the thesis of your essay. First, read the student essays that follow, and then work through the questions that accompany the essays. Both essays use examples to develop their points.

STUDENT ESSAYS TO CONSIDER

Movie Night in the Bush

1   Today, neighbourhood movie theatres are only memories and multiplex cinemas sell fewer tickets than ever. People watch movies at home on DVDs or computers, or squint at tiny images on iPods or cell phones. Does anyone still relax with an audience in the dark in front of a huge screen, enjoying "a night at the movies"? Well, from May until October, as many as fifty thousand people do—in a "fiveplex" in a house on a tree-covered hillside in the tiny village of Kinmount, Ontario. If the element of surprise is half the battle in attracting people, the Highland Cinemas offer more surprises than most movie houses.

2   First, no one ever forgets just finding the cottage-country movie theatre for the first time. "It's just on the left as you drive out of town; you can't miss it," goes the standard answer to a visitor's question. Hidden among trees and bush, perched atop a hill just past a lumber store at the village limits, people can and do miss it all the time, as they zip along Highway 121. At first glance, Keith Stata's theatre looks like a two-storey wood-panelled house. Only its small marquee, partly hidden by leafy branches, suggests that this is not just an oversized cottage or country home. Kinmount's population is less than four hundred people, not enough to support a movie house of any kind. But those who climb Mr. Stata's winding driveway are in for unexpected treats.

3   Once visitors open the large glass double doors, they leave the bush behind to discover more surprises—a nest of well-equipped and fantastically decorated facilities. Since 1979, the owner has expanded from one basement 35 mm projection room to five air-conditioned theatres presenting a menu of current movies. The screening rooms range in size from eighty seats up to nearly three hundred, all with multi-channel sound systems, and several featuring raked-floor stadium seating. As soon as visitors enter any one of the theatres, they are surrounded by detailed décor—anything from Art Deco wall paintings to mannequins in 1970s garb to gilded cherubs and velvet curtains ("Stata's Dream" 5). In fact, the movie-going experience is so complete that people sometimes forget they are in the middle of the woods; that is, until the occasional bat swoops through.

4   The most surprising aspect of the movie capital of the Kawarthas is not the bat or the décor, though. It is what consumes every inch of the lobby: Canada's largest movie memorabilia museum. Walls are papered floor to ceiling with posters and lobby cards from Hollywood and Europe. Keith Stata particularly enjoys showing off his collection of film projectors to interested visitors; he bought them up as neighbourhood theatres folded, and now owns over four hundred, some from the early 1900s. Visitors occasionally bump into one of the 110 mannequins on display. Each is dressed in a movie costume. "Going to the movies used to be an event. That's what we've tried to recreate here," says Stata (Avery). And, judging from the thousands of ordinary filmgoers and obsessed movie buffs he attracts each year, he has succeeded.

5   Even though summer lineups mean fighting off mosquitoes and the occasional bear lured by the scent of popcorn, the Highland Cinemas are probably the most successful multiplex in Canada. As the owner says, in Kinmount, you remember not only the movie but the movie theatre!

Altered States

1   Most Canadians are not alcoholics. Most do not cruise seedy city streets looking to score crack cocaine or heroin. Relatively few try to con their doctors into prescribing unneeded mood-altering medications. And yet, many Canadians are travelling through life with their minds slightly out of kilter. In its attempt to cope with modern life, the human mind seems to have developed some defence strategies. Confronted with inventions like the television, the shopping mall, and the Internet, the mind will slip—all by itself—into an altered state.

2   Never in the history of humanity have people been expected to sit passively for hours, staring at moving pictures emanating from an electronic box. Since too much exposure to flickering images of "reality-show" contestants, detectives, and talk-show hosts can be dangerous to human sanity, the mind automatically goes into a TV-hypnosis state. The eyes see the sitcom or the dog-food commercial, but the mind goes into a holding pattern. None of the televised images or sounds actually enters the brain. This is why, when questioned, people cannot remember commercials they have seen five seconds before or why the TV cops are chasing a certain suspect. In this hypnotic, trance-like state, the mind resembles an armoured armadillo. It rolls up in self-defence, letting the stream of televised information pass by harmlessly.

3   If a TV watcher arises from the couch and goes to a shopping mall, he or she will again cope by slipping into an altered state. In the mall, the mind is bombarded with the sights, smells, and sounds of dozens of stores, restaurants, and movie theatres competing for the mind's attention. There are hundreds of questions to be answered: Should I start with the upper or lower mall level? Which stores should I look in? Should I bother with the sweater sale at the Bay? Should I eat fried chicken or try the healthier-sounding pita wrap? Where is my car parked? To combat this mental overload, the mind goes into a state resembling the whiteout experienced by mountain climbers trapped in a blinding snowstorm. Suddenly, everything looks the same. The shopper is unsure where to go next and cannot remember what he or she came for in the first place. The mind enters this state deliberately, so the shopper has no choice but to leave. Some kids can be in a shopping mall for hours, but they are the exceptions to the rule.

4   No part of everyday life, however, so quickly triggers the mind's protective shutdown mode as cruising the Internet. A computer user sits down with the intention of briefly checking e-mail or looking up a fact for a research paper. But once tapped into the immense storehouse of information, entertainment, and seemingly intimate personal connections that the Internet offers, the user loses all sense of time and priorities. Prospects flood the mind: Should I explore real estate prices in Vancouver? Subscribe to a mailing list? Chat with a lonely stranger in Kamloops? With a mind dazed with information overload, the user numbly hits one key after another, leaping from topic to topic, from distraction to distraction. Hours fly by as he or she sits hunched over the terminal, unable to account for the time that has passed.

5   Therefore, the next time you see TV viewers, shoppers, or Internet users with eyes as glazed and empty as polished doorknobs, you'll know these people are in a protective altered state. Be gentle with them. They are merely trying to cope with the mind-numbing inventions of modern life.

■ Questions

About Unity

1. Which sentence in paragraph 3 of "Altered States" should be omitted in the interests of paragraph unity?

2. Which sentence in paragraph 2 of "Movie Night in the Bush" should be omitted in the interests of paragraph unity?

About Support

3. Which sentence in paragraph 4 of "Movie Night in the Bush" needs to be followed by more supporting details?

4. Where in "Movie Night in the Bush" do you find facts used as examples? Where do you find descriptions of items used as examples?

5. What three pieces of evidence does the writer of "Altered States" offer to support the statement that the Internet is an "immense storehouse of information, entertainment, and seemingly intimate personal connections"?

About Coherence

6. In paragraph 3 of "Movie Night in the Bush," which three time signals does the author begin sentences with?

7. Which sentence in "Altered States" indicates that the author has used emphatic order, saving his most important point for last?

About Introductions and Conclusions

8. Which essay uses an extended thesis, indicating, in its introduction, the essay's plan of development?

9. Which of the following best describes the concluding paragraph of "Altered States"?
   a. A prediction
   b. A summary with a recommendation
   c. A reference to the point made in the introduction
   d. Thought-provoking questions

About the Method of Development

10. What is the first supporting example for the thesis of "Movie Night in the Bush"? How does the writer's choice of supporting details illustrate and clarify this example?

11. What other purpose might the writer of "Altered States" have, other than to make his thesis clear with illustrative examples?

DEVELOPING AN ESSAY THAT ILLUSTRATES BY EXAMPLES

Writing a Thesis Statement for an Essay that Illustrates by Examples

As you work on a thesis statement for an essay that illustrates your point by examples, ask yourself, "What do the examples I came up with in my prewriting add up to?" If you feel like you have a strong thesis, double-check to see if your examples truly say why it is so. If not, revise your thesis statement. There should be a clear and logical relationship between the point in your thesis and the examples that you will subsequently present.

An extended thesis for an essay that illustrates its point by examples could be something like this:

The *HMCS Scotian* recruitment ceremony, with its marching bands, spectacular stage lighting, and lines of highly decorated officers seemed more like a show than a military procedure.

Note also the thesis statement in "Movie Night in the Bush": "If the element of surprise is half the battle in attracting people, the Highland Cinemas offer more surprises than most movie houses."

- What three examples support the essay's thesis?
- Is this a simple thesis statement or an extended one? Is this an effective choice for this essay? Why or why not?

What Is Your Purpose and Who Is Your Audience?

The main purpose of an essay that uses examples is to convince readers by supporting its thesis with directly relevant illustrations. If, for instance, you decide to write an essay that asserts that online chatrooms are dangerous for children, you could illustrate your point by citing several examples of documented cases in which children were harmed by contacts made through chatting. At all times, your examples must connect clearly to your main point so that readers will see the truth of your assertion.

- What examples does the writer of "Altered States" use to support and illustrate his thesis' point?
- Based on his choices, who would his audiences be? Why would these examples reach these reading audiences?

Examples are highly audience-sensitive. Keep in mind two factors related to your audience's needs when you write an essay that illustrates by examples. First, evaluate how much your audience may already know about your topic and whether you need to provide background information. Next, consider the evidence that supports your point, the kinds of examples that would be most appropriate for your audience. For example, for a group already opposed to children chatting online, it may be sufficient to use some fairly common examples. However, if your audience is undecided about the dangers to children of chatrooms, you might need more specific, more persuasive examples. If, on the other hand, your audience is composed of social workers or behavioural scientists, you would require the objective facts and statistics that only research can supply.

What Is Your Point of View in Your Examples Essay?

Essays that support their point with examples focus on the quality, specific nature, and relevance of those examples. Your presence as a writer, as *I*, may compete with your illustrative examples and supporting details for your reader's attention. By connecting yourself to your illustrating examples, you may be adding information that is not relevant to your reader's desire to understand your point, taking away from the overall effectiveness of your work. Both student essays in this chapter are written in the third-person "invisible" voice for just this reason. Remember, for an essay that illustrates your thesis with examples, it's the quality of your examples, not your connection to the reader that is important.

Read the prewriting samples shown below for "Altered States."

- Where has the author used first-person point of view throughout the essay?

Now, read the final draft above.

- What is the effect on you as a reader of the removal of the author's first-person presence?

How Can You Create Effective Supporting Examples for Your Thesis?

As you have seen in Chapter 3, forms of support for your thesis vary considerably in quality and in their suitability for different types of essays. Examples in essays have four main essential functions, no matter which pattern of development you have chosen.

- Examples clarify your ideas and concepts by showing readers different aspects of those ideas.
- Examples illustrate your points by presenting specific instances, facts, or anecdotes that expand the general meaning of the point out into particulars.
- Examples engage and maintain readers' interest as they pursue the ways by which you demonstrate your thinking.
- Examples sometimes persuade your readers simply because of how many of them you provide; essays that illustrate by examples sometimes prove that "more is better."
- Finally, depending on your purpose as a writer, examples persuade readers with vibrant descriptions, intriguing anecdotes, or objective evidence.

Examples may be derived from your own thinking, observations, common knowledge, or experience. They may be anecdotes, explanations, or descriptions of places or objects. You may use such examples for analyses of characters, explanations of procedures or viewpoints, or any number of personal essay-types.

- How many examples of each type listed above do you find in "Altered States"?

Research provides the objective facts, historical precedents, and statistics that constitute examples suitable for essays destined for technical, academic, or scientific audiences. Although "Movie Night in the Bush" is written for a general adult audience, it provides more objective than personally derived examples. Why do you think the writer made this choice?

You may illustrate your supporting points with either a group of related examples or a single extended example. Anecdotal examples tend to be used singly, while descriptions and explanations are often used in series.

Finally, in some instances, your examples may be similar to objectively real ones, but are the products of your imagination. These are hypothetical examples, such as those in "Altered States." Such examples could be, and are likely to be, true. Their usefulness depends on the purpose and audience for an essay.

- List some of the hypothetical examples used in "Altered States." Why are these suitable for this essay?

Prewriting, Creating a First Draft, and Revising

When Tony, the student author of "Altered States," was considering a topic for his essay based on examples, he noticed how one roommate acted while he was online. Tony said, "He sat down to e-mail his brother, and three hours later he was still there, jumping from site to site. His eyes were glassy, and he seemed to be in another reality. It reminded me of how I feel when I go to a mall. I began to think about how our minds adjust to challenges that our grandparents didn't know anything about. I added "watching television" as the third category, and I had a pretty good idea of what my essay would be about."

Tony needed to do some more work to generate supporting details, so he used diagramming:

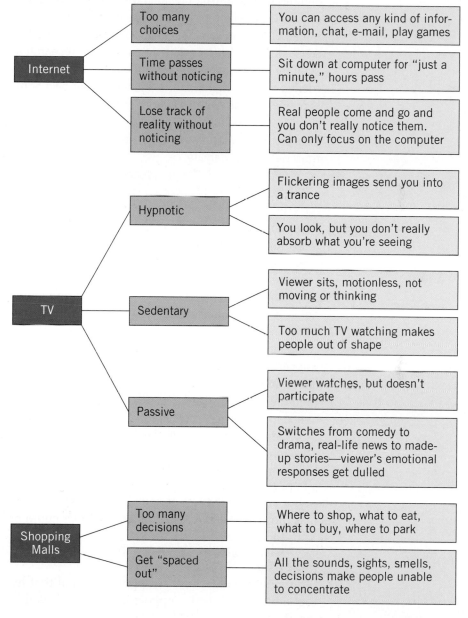

Now Tony saw his thesis: people's minds go into an "altered state" when they watch TV, go to shopping malls, or go online. He then turned his diagram information into an outline, which he used to produce his first draft.

Here is Tony's first draft. Read it, and then answer the questions that follow by comparing his first draft to his revised draft on pages 152—153.

Altered States

1   Modern life makes demands on the human mind that no other period in history has made. As society becomes more and more complex, the mind has developed some defence mechanisms. Confronted with inventions like the Internet, television, and the shopping mall, the mind will slip—all by itself—into an altered state.

2   Take the Internet, for example. A computer user sits down to check his e-mail or look up something. But once tapped into the Internet, you lose all sense of time. You can chat with strangers, research any topic, play a game, or shop for any product. Some people begin to think of the online world and online friends as more real than the people in their own homes. While my roommate is online, he can even have brief conversations with people who come into our room, yet not be able to remember the conversations later. He sits there in a daze from information overload. He seems numb as he hits key after key, going from website to website.

3   Then there's TV. Our grandparents could not have imagined the idea of sitting passively for hours, staring at moving pictures emanating from a box. It's not a normal state of affairs, so the mind goes into something like a hypnotic trance. You see the sitcom or the dogfood commercial, but your mind goes into a holding pattern. You don't really absorb the pictures or sounds. Five minutes after I watch a show, I can't remember commercials I've seen or why the TV cops are chasing a certain suspect.

4   If the TV watcher arises from the couch and journeys into the real world, he often goes to the shopping mall. Here, the mind is bombarded with the sights, smells, and sounds of dozens of stores, restaurants, and movie theatres competing for its attention. Dazed shoppers begin to feel like mountain climbers trapped in a blinding snowstorm. Suddenly, everything looks the same. My father is the worst of all when it comes to shopping in an altered state. He comes back from the mall looking like he's been through a war. After about fifteen minutes of shopping, he can't concentrate enough to know what he's looking for.

5   Internet surfers, TV viewers, and shoppers all have one thing in common. They're just trying to cope with the mind-numbing inventions of modern life. Hopefully some day we'll turn away from such inventions and return to a simpler and more healthy way of life.

- Where are the examples of inconsistent pronoun point of view that Tony corrected for his final draft?
- In which paragraphs did Tony expand his support? What details did he add to these paragraphs?
- Where did Tony remove a supporting detail that he considered too personal, too subjective to truly support his thesis? Was this change effective in your view?
- Where did Tony revise his essay substantially by reordering his support? Why did he do so?
- What change did he make to his final paragraph? Why?

WRITING AN ESSAY THAT ILLUSTRATES BY EXAMPLES

■ Writing Assignment 1

Write an essay that develops one of the following statements or a statement of your own and support your point with examples. Write your essay using the third-person approach.

- The best things in life are definitely not free.
- Living with a roommate teaches people valuable life lessons.
- There is more joy in simple pleasures than in life's great events.
- Technology is no longer our servant, but our master.

Be sure to choose examples that actually support your thesis. They should be relevant facts, statistics, personal experiences, anecdotes, or incidents you have heard or read about. Focus on why and how each example clarifies your supporting points, and your focus will naturally move toward the third-person approach.

Prewriting

1. In addition to thinking about three or more *main* examples to illustrate why each of the best things in life you have chosen is not free, you should provide several *specific* details to explain or illustrate each supporting point for your thesis. You could begin by asking yourself questions like the following:

   - What is it about this "best thing" that should make it free?
   - Why is this one of the "best things" in life?
   - What are the costs of each "best thing"? Is each costly only in terms of money, or is each costly in terms of time, effort, or other considerations?

2. Use the details and examples generated by your questioning to prepare an outline and then a first draft.

Revising

After you have completed the first draft of your essay, set it aside for a while. When you review it, try to do so as critically as you would if it were not your own work. Ask yourself these questions:

- Do I have a clearly stated thesis?
- Have I provided three or more distinct, relevant main examples to support my thesis?
- Have I provided enough specific details of appropriate kinds to support each of the main supporting points/examples?
- Have I used transitions, including transitions between paragraphs, to help readers follow my train of thought?
- Do I have a concluding paragraph that provides a summary, a final thought, or both?

Continue to revise your essay until you can answer "yes" to each question. Then, be sure to check the next-to-final draft for the sentence skills listed on the inside front cover.

■ Writing Assignment 2

In this essay, in which you illustrate your thesis by examples, you will write with a **specific purpose** and for a **specific audience.**

Imagine that you have completed a year of college or university and have agreed to take part in your school's summer orientation program for incoming students. You will be meeting with a small group of new students to help them get ready for post-secondary life.

Prepare a brief presentation to the new students in which you make the point that they must be ready to take on more responsibility than they may have had to do in high school. Use clear examples to illustrate this point. You might want to focus on three of the following areas: instructors, class attendance, time management, class note-taking, textbook study, establishing regular times and places for study, and getting help when needed. You could also focus on just one area and then develop three or more main examples that pertain to that area.

■ Writing Assignment 3

Read the selection titled "The Nobel Lecture" by Kofi Annan on pages 469–473. Then write a third-person voice essay that supports its thesis with examples. Your essay will imagine a Nobel Peace Prize lecture in 2050.

As you consider your thesis, imagine how the world will appear in four decades. Then focus on the challenges and difficulties faced by the world. Which of these issues would be of primary concern for the United Nations and be appropriate content for a Nobel Peace Prize lecture?

CHECKLIST OF LEARNING OUTCOMES FOR CHAPTER 10

To ensure that you have understood and met the learning outcomes for this chapter, answer the following questions after completing any of its writing assignments:

✓ Are there distinct and relevant examples to support my thesis?

✓ Are there enough details and minor examples to make each main example clear?

✓ Does my conclusion reinforce what my examples have shown?

Online
*Learning*Centre

Process

LEARNING OUTCOMES

After reading this chapter and working through its writing assignments, you will be ready to write a process essay that

- begins with a clear statement of the topic and purpose of the process to be followed;

- if it is prescriptive, tells readers exactly what they will need in terms of information, time, space, and equipment to complete the process successfully;

- if it is descriptive, explains to readers how something happens;

- offers complete, carefully sequenced steps and explanations for each stage of the process;

- uses transitions to indicate the order of the steps and connect ideas;

- ends with an appropriate choice of concluding strategy.

Every day you carry out activities by following a series of steps in a definite order. You are following processes. With familiar, automatic processes, such as making coffee, you are not really aware of the sequence of steps you follow. If, on the other hand, someone asks you for directions, or if you are trying to learn how something works from one of your textbooks, you are very aware that there is a whole series of steps involved in the process of giving information or learning something new.

Your process essay *teaches* your readers something that you have to offer. Process writing is unique among methods of essay development and remarkable for its general usefulness. No other pattern of development supports its thesis with steps and no other pattern succeeds or fails based on whether or not its readers can perform or intelligently follow its process.

There are two forms of process writing: *prescriptive,* or "how to do something," which presents the stages and steps in a procedure, and *descriptive,* or "how it happens," which explains the steps in the way something occurs. Prescriptive process aims to help your reader to act, to do something. You write prescriptive process whenever you text friends with directions to a place where you will meet; you write descriptive process when you explain how you managed to become so physically fit. As you work on writing effective process essays, you develop your analytical skills: you break down, or analyze the sequence of steps in a procedure and decide on the overall stages into which you will group these steps.

In your academic and professional career, you will frequently use the skills and methods involved in process writing. You will be asked to follow, evaluate, or give instructions, in person and in print. You could be asked to describe technical procedures or steps in a marketing campaign or some other project. You use textbooks that show you how to perform tasks and explain how things work or how they happened. You will also write essays and reports showing how to perform various tasks and you will explain how stories, plans, and procedures work. Whether your process writing involves *prescribing* or *describing,* you establish the goal, analyze the steps in reaching that goal, and conclude by reiterating the value of following the process.

As you are about to discover, process as a method of development may be your primary pattern, but you will usually blend it with other patterns. You will make use of narrative skills in creating a careful time sequence for ordering steps or if you include brief anecdotal support; you will use descriptive skills in creating word-pictures of objects, actions, and locations; you will use definitions to explain any special terms; and you will use examples to clarify instructions or the results of following those instructions.

In this chapter, you will be asked to write a process essay—one that explains clearly how to do or make something, or one that explains how something happens. To prepare for this task, first read the student essays that follow, and then work through the questions that accompany the essays.

STUDENT ESSAYS TO CONSIDER

Successful Exercise

1   Regular exercise is like the weather—people talk about it, but they tend not to do anything about it! Exercise classes on television, exercise programs on DVDs and podcasts, as well as instructions in books, magazines, and pamphlets now make it easy to have a personal, low-cost exercise program without leaving home. However, for success in exercise, you should follow a simple plan consisting of arranging the time, making preparations, and following the sequence with care.

2   Everyone has an excuse: a heavy schedule at work or school, being rushed in the morning and exhausted at night, too many responsibilities. However, one solution is simply to get up half an hour earlier in the morning. Look at it this way: if you are already getting up too early, what's an extra half-hour?

Of course, that time could be cut to fifteen minutes earlier if you could lay out your clothes, set the breakfast table, fill the coffee-maker, and gather your books and materials for the next day before you go to bed.

3   Next, prepare for your exercise session. To begin with, get yourself ready by not eating or drinking anything before exercising. Why risk an upset stomach? Then, dress comfortably in something that allows you to move freely. Since you'll be in your own home, there's no need to invest in a high-fashion outfit. In fact, trendy, expensive workout clothes can defeat your purpose. Dress for comfort in easy, familiar clothes—do everything to put yourself at ease. Wear, for example, a soft and friendly worn T-shirt and elastic-waisted shorts. A loose, easy-fitting bathing suit is great in summer, and, in winter, a set of cozy long underwear is warm and stretchy. If your hair tends to flop in your eyes, pin it back or wear a headband or scarf. Keeping a set of clothes aside just for your morning exercises helps you turn this activity into a ritual, or even a necessity that you might look forward to.

4   Prepare the exercise area, too. Choose a room with enough floor-space to allow you to stretch and move around freely. Turn off the phone and lock the door, if possible, to prevent interruptions. Will you be using the living room? Then move the coffee table and other pieces of furniture out of the way, so you will not bruise yourself on any hard, pointed corners. If there is no carpet, put down a throw rug, bath mat, or inexpensive yoga mat for floor-based activities. And don't forget to bring in your water-bottle and a towel.

5   Now that you are ready to go, use common sense in getting started. Common sense isn't so common, as anyone who reads the newspaper and watches the world can tell you. You do not need to do each movement the full number of times at first, but you should *try* each one. After five or six sessions, you should be able to do each one the full number of times. Try to move in a smooth, rhythmic way; doing so will help prevent injuries and pulled muscles. Extend your arm as if you are inviting a partner to join you; reach your pointed toes to the ceiling with each leg-raise. Pretend you're a dancer, and make each move graceful, even if it's just climbing up off the floor.

6   Finally, once you have completed the last set of your last exercise, do some slow, loose stretches and lie down for a few minutes on your mat. By giving yourself five minutes to relax and cool off, you reward yourself; you say to yourself, "I've earned this." Reinforce these good feelings with a long hot shower. Congratulations! You have prepared yourself mentally and physically for a great day.

7   Establishing an exercise program isn't difficult, but it can't be achieved by reading about it, talking about it, or watching models exercise on television. To begin with, you're going to have to get up off that couch and do something about it. Otherwise, as the expression goes, "If you don't use it, you'll lose it."

How Search Engines Work

1   Search engines are everyone's best online friend, but how well do users know how their friends work? Why do searches sometimes yield nothing useful, and other times produce pages of hits? A general look at how search engines operate may help users to understand why searches go right and wrong, and how to improve those quests for information.

2   To begin with, search engines do not simply passively log, then place documents in a closed "library." They continuously use automated softwares called spiders or bots that scan the Web and build up and revise their indexes. As spiders or bots scan, they retrieve online documents, then analyze them for possible relevance to the engine's requirements. Collected data from all selected sites is added to an engine's index base. Searchers' queries send commands to check every webpage in the index at that moment. For example, a search for "hound dog" asks the engine to find any and all sites containing the words "hound" and/or "dog." The sites judged as the best are then, in a few seconds, returned to the user as hits or results, usually ranked in order of priority from best to worst.

3   Now, how does the search engine rank those results? Once the search terms are entered, the engine's software evaluates each document in the engine's index. It judges relevance based on the position and frequency of occurrence of the key words. For instance, if "hound" and/or "dog" appear in a site's title, headers, and opening paragraphs, that site is given a priority position in the results. If the words occur repeatedly within the site as well, it will be ranked even higher. Website designers simplify indexing and searching by identifying a site's key words with special html coding called meta tags. Spammers meta-tag misleading words to lure searchers to their sites. Search engine rankings do not, however, guarantee relevance or consistency; a website for "Hound Dog Drill Bits" would probably be quite highly rated, especially if the brand name was used repeatedly, and yesterday's top-ranked site could be displaced or disappear overnight as the busy spiders and bots refresh engines' indexes.

4   Ultimately, though, even though search engines are not perfect, they are better friends when users try to speak their language by using advanced search techniques. These include options for searching for groups of words, linking words, and excluding words that could hinder the search. "Boolean operators" are the logic-based terms AND, OR, NOT, and the "proximal locators" NEAR and FOLLOWED BY. "Hound" AND "dog" tells the search engine to retrieve only documents containing both terms; using OR specifies that at least one of the terms must appear. NOT included in a word-string can eliminate irrelevant sites; for example, someone looking up dog breeds might type in "hound AND dog NOT elvis presley." NEAR used between search words tells the engine that "hound" should be within a certain number of words of "dog," and "hound" FOLLOWED BY "dog" means the words must appear in that order. Search engines that allow users to search for phrases work this way, or require the phrase to be placed within quotation marks, "hound dog." Advanced searches allow users to speak a language that engines understand, so they generally yield more focused results.

5   Search engines are not the total answer for every researcher, but they are instant-acting assets for curious minds. With just a little knowledge of how their engine-friend works, searchers are more likely to find rewarding and relevant information. If not, it's because search engine technology has not quite reached the point where humans and computers can read each other's minds.

■ Questions

About Unity

1. Which supporting paragraph of "Successful Exercise" lacks a topic sentence? Write the paragraph number and a topic sentence that expresses its main point.

2. Which sentences from paragraph 5 of "Successful Exercise" should be omitted in the interests of paragraph unity?

3. Which sentence in paragraph 3 of "How Search Engines Work" should be omitted in the interests of paragraph unity?

About Support

4. Which sentence in paragraph 4 of "Successful Exercise" needs to be followed by more supporting details?

5. Primary and secondary patterns of development: How does the author of "Successful Exercise" use description to expand on her advice to "dress for comfort" in paragraph 3?

6. Primary and secondary methods of development: In "How Search Engines Work," how many examples are used in paragraphs 2, 3, and 4? Describe in a few words what each example is about.

About Coherence

7. Indicate the three time-transition words used in paragraph 3 of "Successful Exercise."

8. In "How Search Engines Work," which time-transition phrase is used in the topic sentence of paragraph 2? In the topic sentence of paragraph 3?

About Introductions and Conclusions

9. Which best describes the introduction of "How Search Engines Work"?
   a. Broad, general statements narrowing to a thesis
   b. Explanation of the importance of the topic
   c. Anecdote
   d. Question

10. Which method of conclusion is used in "Successful Exercise"?
   a. Summary
   b. Thought-provoking question
   c. Prediction
   d. Recommendation

About the Method of Development

11. In each essay above, how many stages have the writers divided their processes into? How many steps are included in each stage for each of the essays?

DEVELOPING A PROCESS ESSAY

Writing a Thesis Statement for a Process Essay

Process essays tell readers how to do something or how something happens. When you write a process essay, you focus on two concerns: what your audience already knows about the essay's topic, and how to supply just enough information so that readers understand each step in the process. Because process essays suit a wide range of topics, the requirements for their thesis statements will vary according to the topic.

Here is a step-by-step approach to creating an effective process-essay thesis statement:

1. Your process essay's ideal thesis statement must present at least (a) a clear statement or definition of your topic and (b) the reason for, or purpose of, the process you will write about.

(a)   (b)   (c)

   Learning to relax is a skill people should master for the sake of their general health.

2. You should generally (c) state to readers the importance of the process you are presenting.

3. Frequently, you may include who the intended audience is, if it is significant to the success or failure of a prescriptive process or the understanding of a descriptive process.

4. You may want to specify the level of the knowledge needed for your audience to understand or complete the process; i.e., Those who are able to perform basic tasks on a sewing machine can easily learn to replace a zipper.

5. For an extended thesis statement, include a brief description of the stages involved in the process, as in "Successful Exercise."

Not every process essay's thesis will include all five of the elements above, but it must include the subject and the reason or purpose for following or understanding the process.

Writing your process-essay thesis statement could be a response to the following questions: *What?* [topic], *To* or *for whom?* [audience], and *Why?* [importance or value].

Your thesis for a prescriptive "how to" process essay could be something like this:

Tired of takeout? Following these fairly easy steps will make the most helpless student a decent "survival cook."

Anyone can plant a small container garden, and just about everyone will enjoy watching their flowers and plants grow day by day.

Your thesis for a descriptive process essay might be similar to the following:

> Learning how plant fertilizers work can make even a beginner's thumb "green" and increase the eco-friendliness of a home.
>
> Volunteering at a local community centre or hospital brings unexpected benefits for students.

What Is Your Purpose and Who Is Your Audience?

The main purpose for a process essay is to inform your audience by presenting or explaining the steps involved in a particular action or procedure. The following questions will help you decide how to achieve your purpose:

- Which type of process paper will you write: descriptive or prescriptive?
- What do you want your audience to know?

If you write a prescriptive process essay, you will speak directly to your readers, telling them how to do something. Do you want to explain how to make the ultimate chocolate-chip cookie? Your process essay will include directions telling your audience exactly what to do, which ingredients and equipment are required, and how to use them.

If you write a descriptive process essay, you will, as an invisible presence, share your knowledge of how something occurs. Do you want your audience to know the steps involved in digesting a chocolate-chip cookie? You will explain the events that happen in the body as it turns food into energy. In this instance, you will not be giving instructions or "prescribing" how to digest; you will give information or describe how digestion occurs.

Your primary purpose is to inform, but you will discover secondary purposes as you prewrite and draft your essay. If you are writing about something you enjoy, you will want readers to appreciate the value, difficulty, or pleasure involved in your process. For instance, you may have spent years learning how to bake desserts, and you know that most readers will be unfamiliar with the skills and work involved. As you write about baking chocolate-chip cookies, one of your purposes will be to help readers to appreciate the care you take in your work and the value of a well-made cookie, so that your audience "sees" and values your effort and its results.

- How does the writer of "Successful Exercise" indicate to readers the value of following her process?

Sometimes you may find the process method useful for persuading readers: if you wish to show that campus emergency procedures are insufficient, then you could use the descriptive process to explain to readers how the procedures work, and where they fall short. This type of persuasive-explanatory look at a multi-stage process is used for many professional and academic writing situations.

Now, who is your audience? As a process writer, you are responsible for helping your readers to act or to understand.

- There are usually two general audiences for process writing: (a) those who may know nothing of the process or (b) those who wish to improve the way they perform or understand the process.

Does your audience know little or nothing about baking? Think about special words used in recipes: you will probably need to explain terms like *fold in,* or *cream the butter or shortening.* Remember to explain seemingly "common-knowledge" actions such as which rack to place the baking sheets on in the oven.

Do your readers have some general cooking experience, but want to know more or improve their baking? Think about specialized information such as the use of a specific type of chocolate or the reason for using one type of fat rather than another.

Although audiences usually consist of a mix of these types of readers, you can refine your audience focus. At the moment, you are likely writing for your instructor, a specified group of adults, and/or your peers. Visualize your audience as clearly as possible. And before submitting your essay, always read it aloud to someone who does not know how to do your process or does not already know how your process works. Make careful note of anything your listener does not understand and make the appropriate changes.

What Is Your Point of View in Your Process Essay?

Address your readers directly in a prescriptive process essay. Speak to your reading audience as *you,* as you would in a letter. Prescriptive process essays are unique among essay types in their use of second-person voice or point of view, as in "Successful Exercise." You will use a mixture of two types of sentences when you address readers. When you give instructions or advice, you will, like Melissa, use imperative ("giving orders") sentences; she advises readers, "prepare for your exercise session," and "use common sense." When you explain something to your readers, you use declarative ("making a statement") sentences, as Melissa does here: "Since you'll be in your own home, there's no need to invest in a high-fashion outfit." Be careful to keep your pronoun point of view consistency in writing a prescriptive process. Do not allow "I" or "we" to slip in; your focus is entirely on showing your readers how to do something.

When you write descriptive process essays, such as "How Search Engines Work," you explain in detail how something happens. You do not address readers directly; you provide them with information. You are not giving instructions, so you do not use imperative sentences; you write only in declarative ("making a statement") sentences. In the descriptive process, you as the writer are a background presence; you do not want to intrude on your reader's understanding of your careful explanation. Therefore, you write in the third-person voice, as the author does in "How Search Engines Work."

How Will You Support Your Thesis in a Process Essay?

Your thesis states that you will show readers how to do something, or how something happens with the steps in the process that your essay covers. Those steps are your supporting points. But you are writing an essay, so those steps need to be organized into groupings, or paragraphs. You have two tasks, therefore: to decide how many steps are needed and to group those steps into an appropriate number of body paragraphs.

Begin by working out the steps in your process: How will you work out how many steps to present to your readers? First, analyze your process to decide how many steps are involved. Revise your list until you are satisfied that a reader could follow or understand it.

Because all process writing is organized in time order, you should examine your list to see where breaks in the sequence might occur.

- See Melissa's prewriting for "Successful Exercise" on page 171 for examples to help you with this task.

Your supporting details for each step will depend on the nature of your process. Your readers may need to know how a step is performed or how it occurs: paragraph 2 of "How Search Engines Work" explains how engines retrieve information. Do your readers need to know why a step is important or why it occurs at a specific point? If you are explaining why cooks must mix butter and sugars together for such a long time and you wish to emphasize the importance of this, then you need to describe how the cookie texture is affected by the suspension of sugar crystals in softened butter.

Related to this is an issue that you as a writer are responsible for: warning readers of potential problems and setbacks, and of how to avoid them. The success of your essay depends on your reader's ability to perform or understand your process; if you omit necessary cautionary advice, you may sabotage the reader.

- Where do you find such cautionary advice in "Successful Exercise"?

Next, work at dividing your series of steps into larger stages of your process: There is no "magic number" of steps that make up a stage; your knowledge of the process and of how much explanation each step requires will help you decide. For example, if you write about baking chocolate-chip cookies, your first stage could be "Assembling your ingredients and equipment," and your second stage "Mixing and combining dry and wet ingredients," and so on. Each stage will contain several steps and necessary explanations.

In terms of your essay's structure, each stage will become one of your body paragraphs; there is no "magic number" of stages or body paragraphs.

- How many stages appear in "Successful Exercise"?
- How many stages appear in "How Search Engines Work"? Why are the steps in each stage grouped together in each essay?
- Finally, how will you guide your readers so they understand when to do things or when things happen?

Transitional words and phrases are especially important in process writing. Your readers must grasp and follow the sequence of your stages and steps if your essay is to be effective.

Guide your audience at every point by emphasizing sequence (first, next, then, finally), numerical order (first, second), and consequence (then, as a result). Review pages 56—61 in Part 1 on the use of transitions.

Acknowledging possible setbacks and showing how to prevent or fix them is reassuring to readers.

Remember also to make use of other methods of development, as needed, in your body paragraphs; if providing an example will help your reader to grasp how or why a step is performed or occurs, then do as the author of "How Search Engines Work" does in paragraph 3. If describing aspects of an instruction will make it clearer to readers, then do as Melissa does in her third paragraph. And it is always very important to include definitions for any words, phrases, or concepts your readers may not understand—one misunderstanding can stop your audience from following your process.

- Where do you find an example of a definition in "How Search Engines Work"?

How Can I Work Out the Steps and Stages in a Process?

Here is one student's prewriting work on her topic, "Dealing with an Unsatisfied Customer." After reading carefully through the steps in her process, fill in the blanks, showing which steps belong in which stage or paragraph in her essay.

ROUGH THESIS: This is how an unhappy customer should be dealt with so that other customers do not become involved and so that the customer feels that he or she has been treated fairly.

1. Introduce yourself courteously and ask for the customer's name.

2. Encourage the customer to step away from other people in the store so that he or she can explain the situation to you.

3. Use a calm and reassuring tone of voice, and suggest that you have lots of time to listen to the customer's problems.

4. Sit down with the customer, if possible, and find a notepad and pen to record the details of the situation.

5. Gently ask the customer to relate the details of the problem in the order in which the events occurred.

6. List these details and ask for clarification as you do so; never challenge the customer as he or she speaks to you.

7. If the customer is justified in any part of his or her complaint, and the product is unsatisfactory, make the adjustment calmly and quietly.

8. If the product is simply not what the customer wanted, and he or she has the receipt from its purchase, offer a refund or replacement, according to company policy.

9. If the customer has no receipt and is still displeased, state the company's policy for this situation, and offer to call your supervisor or manager to provide any additional assistance.

Stage 1 TOPIC SENTENCE: Introduce yourself to the customer; treat him or her calmly and courteously.

Items _____through _____

Stage 2 TOPIC SENTENCE: Carefully note all details of the customer's situation.

Items _____through _____

Stage 3 TOPIC SENTENCE: Provide any adjustments you can, or ask for management assistance.

Items _____ through _____

Prewriting

Melissa, the author of "Successful Exercise," was thinking about possible topics for a process essay. The audience for the essay was to be other students in the class, so she wondered about topics they could relate to. Her instructor's advice was, "Write about a process that's fairly straightforward. Explaining something complex means writing a lot of background information for readers—think of the poor student who tried to explain assembling a car engine."

As her English professor continued talking, he repeated the phrase "step by step," and Melissa started thinking about things she usually did step by step. Driving to school? Too many people would try that one. "Well, what do I do regularly that other people don't do? What am I any good at?" Then it came to her—working out! "Well, I'm a fitness instructor, but I always exercise at home every morning. And I'm always telling customers who are beginners how to do it, anyway."

Melissa started by making a list of what she ordinarily tells her customers at the gym when they ask what they need to buy or do to exercise at home. Then, before her next class, when her prewriting and list of general stages was due, Melissa worked on numbering the steps in her list. She wanted to put them into an order that made sense, then take out any that weren't really necessary:

~~Exercise at the same time every day—it'll become a habit~~

9 Don't try movements that are too demanding for your fitness level

5 Never eat or drink before working out

2 Follow a plan, but follow it!

7 Turn off the ringer on the phone and lock the door ~~the kids will manage~~

8 Move the coffee tables and chairs out of the way

11 Just try basic stretches and movements at first No jerky movements Maybe this is 12?

12 Don't do anything that hurts—start with gradual tries at a movement

13 Give yourself cool-off time

3 Making time isn't so hard—20 minutes is fine to start with

4 Set your morning stuff up ahead of time

2? Get up a little earlier or make time when you get home, but don't work out before bed

? Turn the heat up a bit—it's easier on your muscles. Cut down on coffee and pop—drink more water and green tea

6 Fancy workout clothes aren't necessary

1 Buy some magazines, get a DVD, or go online for the right kind of exercises for you

10? Don't work with weights, no matter how light, if you aren't trained

Melissa was still unsure about some items on her list, but thought she could at least group her steps and tips into four or five stages to begin with. The stages she decided on were (1) making time, (2) preparing for each session, (3) preparing the space, (4) getting started properly, and (5) unwinding and relaxing afterward.

First Draft and Revision

After some preparation, Melissa wrote her first draft:

1　　People can come up with all kinds of reasons not to exercise regularly at home. Today, it's easy to keep up a fitness program. There are so many magazines, DVDs, and books full of tips and good information. To help you succeed at exercising every day, I've developed a basic plan for you to follow.

2　　Most people say they have no extra time. They may go to the gym, but they say that between school and other responsibilities, there's no time left to do a daily workout at home. And it's really necessary to maintain stamina and overall fitness. Get up just a bit earlier, set up your coffee maker and all your morning stuff, and you'll be surprised how much you can get done before you leave for your first classes. But don't schedule exercise time before going to bed.

3　　Next, you need to prepare for your exercise session. Don't eat or drink anything, even a cup of coffee, before you start, or you could get cramps or an upset stomach. Wear anything comfortable. Save the fancy workout clothes for the gym. Pull your hair back or put it in a ponytail—you don't want it in your eyes. No interruptions!

4　　Turn off the ringer on the phone and lock the door. Shove the coffee table out of the way and move the chairs so you don't hurt yourself when you move. Then get out the basic materials you'll need to exercise on, like a mat.

5　　Use common sense when you're starting out. Don't use weights if you're not trained to do so. Just try each of the basic movements you've chosen a few times at first. Don't keep going if an exercise or movement hurts. After several sessions, you should be able to do each exercise the full number of times. Move as smoothly as you can. Jerky motions will hurt muscles and joints. After you've finished, give yourself five minutes cool-off time. Now, take a hot shower and enjoy all that extra energy.

6　　Now I've shown you how to get started on maintaining fitness at home. You just have to stop talking and do something about it.

When she finished her draft, Melissa put it aside for a few days. When she reread it after looking at her class notes, she was able to make some critical changes. Here are her comments:

I think I've got the main ideas here, and four stages, but it still needs more, and it's not too smooth, either. For instance, that first paragraph should probably at least say *what* my basic plan consists of. There's an "I" in there, too. That has to come out. Paragraph 2 seems all right, but I could be a little more specific about what to do ahead. And why did I mention not exercising at night, if this is about doing it in the morning? The third paragraph needs some more support, especially about what kind of clothes to wear; I just told people what not to wear. The last stage is almost right, but I didn't use any transitions. In fact, I need to separate unwinding after exercising from getting started—those are two different things. I need to make this less bumpy, and give it a better concluding wrap up, and take the "I" out, too.

With her self-critique in mind, Melissa revised her draft, producing the version of "Successful Exercise" that appears on pages 162—163.

WRITING A PROCESS ESSAY

■ Writing Assignment 1

Choose a topic from the list below to use as the basis for a "prescriptive" (or "how to") process essay.

- How to break a bad habit
- How to survive a Canadian winter
- How to find an internship (co-op position, summer job)
- How to manage your money while in college or university
- How to fall out of love
- How to make hot and sour soup, oatmeal cookies, rotis, or some other dish

Prewriting

1. Freewrite for ten minutes on the topic you have chosen. Don't worry about spelling, grammar, or organization. Concentrate mainly on the steps involved in the process. Then ask yourself if there is enough material available to you to support a process essay. If so, keep following the steps below. If not, choose another topic, and freewrite about it for ten minutes.

2. Develop a single clear sentence that will serve as your thesis. Your thesis can either (a) state your opinion about this process ("Falling out of love is a hard skill to learn, but a skill that pays off in emotional health") or (b) say it is important that your readers know about this process.

3. Develop your trial thesis statement. *What,* precisely, is your subject/process? *To or for whom* is your process intended? *Why* should your audience follow or know about your process? What will the reward, *value,* or outcome of this process be for them? Do your readers need to know the *level of difficulty* involved?

4. Before you begin explaining your process, think again about your audience. Do they need some background information to follow the steps in your process? If you are explaining how to do something technical or some activity with its own vocabulary, do you need to provide definitions?

5. Make a list of all the steps that you are describing.

6. Number your items in time order; delete items that do not fit the list; add others you can think of.

7. Decide how the items on the list can be grouped into a minimum of three steps.

8. Use your list to prepare an outline for your essay.

Concluding the Process

Which of the following concepts used to complete a process essay might be appropriate for your subject?

- Restating the stages and intended result of the process
- Confirming with the reader that the process is complete and/or successful
- Reassuring the reader of the value in following the steps and of the importance of the process
- Encouraging the reader to try your process
- Offering or repeating any necessary cautions, restrictions, or warnings needed at any stage of the process

Revising

Since the goal of all process writing is to show, using easy-to-follow steps, how to do something (or how something is done), the best way to "test" your draft is to have someone else read it.

Exchange essays with a fellow student, and ask yourselves these questions after reading:

1. Does the writer describe the steps in a clear, logical way? Is there any essential information missing?

2. Has the writer used transitions such as *first, next, also, then, after, now, during,* and *finally* to make the essay flow smoothly and to guide the reader carefully from one step to another?

3. Does the concluding paragraph provide a summary that restates the stages and intended result of the process, a final thought that encourages the reader to try the process, or any of the other recommended conclusion techniques for process essays?

4. Have any sentence-skills errors that you noticed in the essay while reading been noted for correction?

Continue to revise your essay until you can answer "yes" to each question. Then, be sure to proofread the next-to-final draft for the sentence skills listed on the inside front cover.

■ Writing Assignment 2

In this process essay, you will write with a **specific purpose** and for a **specific audience.**

Imagine that your campus newspaper has asked you to write an article to help prepare first-semester students for the challenges of academic life. Write an informal but helpful essay, drawing from your own experience, in which you describe the steps involved in successfully meeting the challenges of a first semester.

■ Writing Assignment 3

Read the selection titled "How to Make It in College, Now That You're Here" on pages 510–515. Then, write a process essay with the thesis, "Here are the tips that will help a student succeed in _____ " (name a course in which you are now enrolled or one that you have taken in the past).

To get started, think of the advice you would like to have had *before* you took that particular course: What would you have wanted to know about the professor? The assignments? The exams? Policies about attendance, lateness, and so on? Pick three to five tips that you believe would be most helpful to other students, and discuss each one in a separate supporting paragraph. Model your introduction after the one in "How to Make It in College" by telling your readers that, on the basis of your own experience, you are going to pass on the secrets for succeeding in this course.

Below are four sample topic sentences for "How to Succeed in Communications 101."

First topic sentence: First of all, a student who wants a good grade in Communications 101 should be prepared for a surprise quiz at every class.

Second topic sentence: In addition, students should speak up during class discussion because Professor Knox adds "participation" into final grades.

Third topic sentence: Next, students must be prepared for several research projects on media and mass communications.

Fourth topic sentence: Most important, students should start early on essays and turn them in on time.

PART 2 PATTERNS OF ESSAY DEVELOPMENT

CHECKLIST OF LEARNING OUTCOMES FOR CHAPTER 11

To ensure that you have understood and met the learning outcomes for this chapter, answer the following questions upon completing any of its writing assignments:

✓ Does my thesis statement contain at least the two items essential for a process thesis?

✓ Have I supplied enough background information to make my process understandable to readers? Is there any special or technical vocabulary that should be explained?

✓ Have I mentioned any equipment or supplies that are needed as well as problems that might be encountered?

✓ Are the main stages and steps in exactly the right order to complete the process?

✓ Are there enough transitions to make the steps in the process clear?

✓ Is each step explained clearly enough with examples, descriptions, and definitions where appropriate?

✓ Have I finished with an effective and appropriate method of conclusion?

Online **Learning**Centre

For bonus material and additional activities please go to the OLC at **www.mcgrawhill.ca/olc/langan**

Cause and Effect

LEARNING OUTCOMES

After reading this chapter and working through its writing assignments, you will be ready to write a cause or effect essay that

- Offers a thesis statement giving your viewpoint on your topic and indicating whether you will examine causes or effects;

- Uses true and logical causes or effects as supporting points to prove your thesis;

- Presents its main supporting points in order of importance;

- Explains the main supporting points with several specific details;

- Concludes with a reassurance that its thesis point is effectively supported.

Why are action movies so popular? What are the consequences of too much pollution? Cause or effect essays spring from questions like these. Like others, you are always seeking to understand the reasons or causes for things as well as their consequences or effects. Therefore, the cause and effect method of development is one your readers will instinctively relate to.

Cause or effect essays involve analysis as you try to examine either the causes or effects of some situation or event. This analysis is not always easy, so cause or effect essays require special attention at the prewriting and planning stages. You will work to avoid the logical errors noted in the sections that follow; generalizations and overly simple views of causes or effects irritate the same readers who may be initially drawn to your essay.

Your ability to carry out an analysis of causes and effects will often be required in academic writing tasks such as explaining why a technical procedure has been developed or what its effects may be, or in examining the effects of military action in some part of the world. Similarly, in career writing tasks, you may be required to explain why a product doesn't sell or what the effects are of either a technical process or business decision.

Although you may develop an essay using cause or effect almost entirely as a primary method, you will also make use of other methods of development in your supporting paragraphs. You will likely use examples, at least as supporting details. Moreover, you will find the cause or effect pattern very useful as a secondary pattern of development. Process essays in particular benefit when you present the *reasons why* (causes) something happens and/or the *results* or *consequences* (effects) of performing an action correctly or incorrectly. Finally, you may already have written a narrative about a meaningful or significant event, and you probably referred to either its causes or the effects.

In this chapter, you will be asked to write an essay about causes or effects. To prepare for this task, first read the student essays that follow, and then work through the questions that accompany the essays.

STUDENT ESSAYS TO CONSIDER

New Country, New Person

1   The "foreign student" sitting quietly in a classroom is doing more than just taking careful notes or daydreaming. He or she is more likely worrying, planning, or just feeling really lonely. Living far away from home can be a new beginning, but it does have major consequences. Foreign students learn some life-changing lessons.

2   For most students, the first major consequence of moving is finding out how it is to live away from their families and homes. No more of the comforts of home that are so easy to take for granted: there is no mother cooking meals or tidying up, no sisters or brothers to talk to or tease, and no familiar room and belongings to return to after classes. Being a foreign student means living in a residence, a room, or an apartment. With no one to take care of them, students must learn basic survival skills fast, perhaps shopping for food and cooking for the first time. Figuring out new and often unfamiliar ingredients is difficult; so is constantly translating instructions and recipes. After preparing a dish that probably does not taste very good, cleaning up the mess is another new and tiring job. Paying bills, rent, and tuition fees means learning to handle money responsibly. Learning to live independently is a day-to-day challenge.

3   Students sometimes look up the new city where their college or university is located on Google, or buy a guidebook before leaving home. But when they arrive, they still find themselves in a completely new environment where they have to get around every day. If the student is lucky enough to have a car, he or she may have the time to just get lost a few times, see where streets lead, and find a way back home. Most are not so fortunate, so they must quickly learn about bus and subway routes, and even how much taxis cost. Learning to find their way to class is just the first step, though, because students immediately

have to figure out how long trips to school will take so they can plan their time. These experiences use up time and energy that students would rather use for schoolwork or making friends, but they are valuable lessons in planning.

4   Finally, foreign students often feel lonely and isolated. They are lucky if family or friends live in their new city, but usually they spend a lot of time alone. They sit alone on the bus, in class, and at meals. Most who live by themselves try to start meeting people and making friends as soon as possible, by joining student or faith-based groups, usually groups where others speak the same first language. Socializing takes a lot more courage and effort than seeing old friends at home did, but putting up with feeling unsure can be endured, if it means finding a new acquaintance or two. Otherwise, the foreign student is always just "the quiet one" in classes. New friends are so important; they help when students just need someone to talk to, or when they face problems with school or money. But most of all, making new friends means new experiences, and living a new life with others.

5   Leaving home and going to another country bring changes and experiences that cannot be compared to anything else in life. It is a new start, where students learn how to be independent, to navigate new places, manage their time, and meet new people. It is difficult to manage without family and friends in another country, but "foreign students" learn how to live and also how to appreciate what they left behind.

Choking the Lungs of the World

1   In less than a century, over two billion gallons of crude oil have been extracted from the Oriente, Ecuador's Amazon basin. As a result of sloppy and damaging oil-drilling methods, the delicate environment of Ecuador has been seriously compromised. Billions of gallons of untreated toxic wastes, gas, and oil have been released into the land, air, and water. The effects have been dire, killing native plants and animals and destroying the living conditions of native peoples in one of the world's most diverse tropical rainforests.

2   Ecuador is defined as a petrostate, meaning that it derives its main national revenue from petroleum sales abroad. While overall the nation's economy has benefited from Texaco's 1967 discovery of oil at the headwaters of the Amazon (*The Center for Economic and Social Rights* [CESR], 1994), the environmental cost of the three-stage process involved in exploration, production, and transportation has been high. Exploring for oil involves trail-cutting through rainforests and use of explosives, both of which kill or drive away wildlife and lead to massive erosion and also water pollution from drilling waste. The next stages, oil production or refining and transportation, mean more water pollution and pipeline spills, at an average rate of 1000 gallons per week (*CESR,* 1994, p.13). Moreover, petroleum pollution is not limited to land and water; Ecuador burns off massive amounts of gas and burns waste oil, releasing huge quantities of methane, carbon dioxide, sulphur dioxide, and other airborne pollutants (Steyn, 2003).

3   In the first place, it is impossible to overstate the severity of the consequences of this pollution for the plant-life of such an ecologically sensitive area. The Amazon rainforest, referred to as the "Lungs of the World,"

is "home to 20% of the Earth's animal and plant species. The Amazon stores 70 billion tons of carbon in its biomass, which helps combat global warming" (Sullivan, 2009). At this point, even a slight climate change to Ecuador would reverse any positive effects of the Kyoto Accord. The Oriente, moment by moment, is losing the carbon-absorbing power provided by the quantity of its tree- and plant-growth, its biomass. The extent of the damage caused by the clearing and cutting of oil-exploration teams can only be understood by comparing the variety in replacement plant-growth with that of the original forest. The term "biodiversity" is useful here: it refers to measuring the number of different species within a given group. In a single hectare of Amazonian original rainforest there are nearly three-quarters the number of different species of trees as there are in all of Canada. Compare this to the second-growth forests that grow in the broken and polluted soil left by oil extraction: only ten percent of the species reappear (Currie-Alder, 2004). The rest are lost.

4 As if doing permanent damage to the forest canopy is not enough, petroleum extraction activities are particularly harmful to wildlife. Habitats are invaded and destroyed by the establishment of base-camps and heliports, the construction of cross-country pipelines, and the development of extensive road systems. These tear up forests and wetlands, expose and pave the earth, and perhaps worst of all, pollute the ground and ground-water channels running beneath. Add to this the constant oil spills and flushing of refineries during oil production, ongoing disasters that poison rivers and lakes and their inhabitants: "Fish have died from water pollution and the game the tribes once hunted have retreated deeper into the jungle as a result of the deforestation" *(Oil Production Cases* 2010*)*. Not only have forest animals been forced away from their natural areas, but they often do not fully re-adjust to new environments, leading to dwindling survival rates. The Oriente, "the richest biotic zone on earth" (*CESR,* 1994, p. 16), no longer shelters the 2700 species recorded as recently as 20 years ago, when it was home to 18 percent of the world's bird species alone (Parker & Smulders, 2008). Today over ten percent of the indigenous species are severely threatened: that is a very high rate of decline.

5 Although rapid declines in biodiversity have received some global attention, repercussions that receive the least notice are the displacement of and loss of human rights for the native people of the Amazon basin. An action by the Ecuadorian government in the 1970s, aimed at protecting petroleum resources from neighbouring countries, encouraged farmers from economically depressed parts of the country to develop land made accessible by oil-industry roads (Steyn, 2003). In moving into the Oriente, the poor farmers displaced upwards of 45 percent of Ecuador's indigenous people. Those who were shuffled away and evicted had lived off the land for thousands of years, fishing, hunting, and food-gathering: living in harmony with their environment. On the other hand, once they arrived, the farmers continued the work of deforestation and levelling that the oil companies had begun, but ironically, the resulting soil erosion negatively affected their crops. But it was not just the farmers who suffered; seismic explosions for ongoing oil drilling led to levels of noise pollution and vibration that scared off game and made hunting increasingly difficult for the

remaining native people. Forced to the edge of their territory, starved, and suffering increasingly from health problems, Ecuador's indigenous people seem to be no one's concern. The policies of a government they barely know, geared to support an industry for whose product they have no use, are costing them their rights and often their lives.

6   Ecuador is a petrostate whose citizens' identity has come to be shaped by the resource they extract via a process that results in great costs to the environment and to animal and human life. International awareness of these issues has raised the question of who will be responsible for these consequences of petroleum extraction, but worldwide reliance on oil and the "out of sight, out of mind" factor often leave that question hanging in the increasingly polluted air.

A Note About Research, References, and Essay Structure

Camilo, author of "Choking the Lungs of the World," is a journalism student. Because Camilo's instructors in his English and journalism courses emphasize the importance of research and reliable sources, he chose to work with research right from the start of the semester. To find appropriate support for his thesis, he spent time reading through articles on his university library's databases and on various Web sites. He made careful research notes and used APA-style citation, as you see here. For more information on research and APA style, see chapters 18 and 19 in Part 3.

In Part 2, you see only the in-text citations in the student essays; here, these cue readers to the References page at the end of Camilo's essay. To see a sample APA References page, refer to Chapter 19. To see samples of References page items, see Chapter 18.

You also see a structural technique in this paper suitable for essays where readers need significant background information to follow the essay. Immediately after the opening paragraph, Camilo includes a paragraph of background context for the essay. Cause- or effect-analysis essays of this type, similar to reviews (another form of analysis) and research papers, benefit from this kind of two-paragraph opening that prepares readers for what is to come. For further examples, see the research papers in Chapter 20.

■ Questions

About Unity

1. Which supporting paragraph in "New Country, New Person" lacks a topic sentence? Which supporting paragraph in "Choking the Lungs of the World" lacks a topic sentence? Identify that paragraph in each essay and write a possible topic sentence for each one.

2. Rewrite the thesis statement of "New Country, New Person" so that it is an extended thesis. Refer back to page 27 for information and to see an example of an extended thesis statement; such statements present the thesis' viewpoint as well as the writer's supporting points.

About Support

3. In paragraph 3 of "Choking the Lungs of the World," the author supports the point of "the severity of the consequences of this pollution for the plant-life" with how many of the following?

   a. Statistics and objective facts
   b. An explanation
   c. A quotation from an authority
   d. Examples
   e. Definitions

   From paragraph 3, give one example of each form of support that you find.

4. In "New Country, New Person," how many examples does Jing, its student author, give to support the topic sentence of paragraph 2?

5. After which sentence in paragraph 2 of "New Country, New Person" should more supporting details be added?

About Coherence

6. Paragraph 4 of "Choking the Lungs of the World" includes two main transition words or phrases. Identify those words or phrases, and explain their function within the paragraph.

7. What are the two transition words or phrases in "New Country, New Person" that signal two major points of support for the thesis?

About Introductions and Conclusions

8. What facts did you learn from the second paragraph of "Choking the Lungs of the World" that helped you to understand specific aspects of the essay?

9. Which of the following methods is used in the conclusion of "New Country, New Person"?

   a. Summary and a final thought
   b. Thought-provoking question
   c. Recommendation

About the Method of Development

10. Which words in the thesis statements of both essays indicate whether each one is a cause or an effect essay?

DEVELOPING A CAUSE OR EFFECT ESSAY

How Can You Avoid Logical Errors in Cause or Effect Essays?

At the prewriting stage, cause or effect essays require an extra step in their preparation. You *analyze* before you write them; you *break apart* some situation or event, and you *examine* its causes or effects. Causes must be true causes, and effects must truly be effects.

- A cause is an action or situation that provokes some result or effect—it is a stimulus.
- An effect is the result of some cause, stimulus, or event—it is an outcome.

Therefore, performing a "logic check" on supporting points for a "cause" or "effect" thesis is necessary before drafting. Try the following criteria for a "logic check."

1. **"Time–sequence" logical errors:** A cause is not necessarily a cause because it happens before an effect: if a dog crosses the road before your car stalls, it is not the cause of the stalling. Similarly, anything that simply happens after another event is not necessarily an effect. Establish a logical causal connection between the prior, or causal event, and the following, or consequential, events.

2. **Logical forms of causes and multiple causes:** There are three main types of causal relationships: necessary, sufficient, and contributory. A *necessary cause* is one that must be present for an effect to occur. Nothing will happen *unless* the cause happens. For example, you must take the courses in your program to achieve the result of your diploma or degree: the courses are *necessary* for obtaining that certificate. A *sufficient cause* is one that is *enough* to make something happen. For example, not taking several courses will result in your not receiving your diploma or degree; that is *sufficient* to cause you not to receive your diploma or degree. To put it another way, a number's being divisible by 4 is sufficient (but not necessary) for its being even, but being divisible by 2 is both sufficient and necessary. Finally, a *contributory cause* is one that helps produce an effect but cannot do so by itself; for example, running a red light can help cause an accident, but other factors/causes must also be present as contributing causes, for example, pedestrians and other cars. Sufficient and contributory causes are often analyzed in "causes" essays.

3. **Chains of effects:** As you prewrite, consider that effects occur differently: some effects occur all at once, others in a sequence. Be specific and trace your cause or effect chains carefully. For an "effects" essay where this is the case, put your effects in order of importance, as Camilo does in "Choking the Lungs of the World." Other times, you will want to show effects happening in a sequence. One effect may lead to another; they follow logically, in a domino effect; therefore, they should be structured in chronological or time order, as Jing did in "New Country, New Person."

   Note: Do not confuse *effect* with *affect*. An *effect,* as above, is a result or consequence of some cause—an action or event: "Meeting her father had a dramatic effect on him." *Effect,* used this way, is a noun, a word for a thing, person, or place. To *affect* is to have an influence on: "He was greatly affected by the meeting with his father." *Affect,* used this way, is a verb, an action word. Do not confuse these words or use them interchangeably. See pages 436–442 for more information on these words.

Writing a Thesis Statement for a Cause or Effect Essay

Essays that deal with causes set out the reasons why some debatable or interesting situation exists. When you write a "cause" thesis statement, you will usually give a brief description of the effect, then provide an argument for the rightness of the causes you offer. To be sure that such a thesis truly involves causes, test it by writing your topic and viewpoint, followed by *because:* for example, Students from Japan would find Canadian students lazy (the effect) because . . . . (the causes).

Complete the following "cause" thesis statements:

- Air pollution has three major causes: _____
- Four important factors leading to student stress are _____

Essays that discuss effects set out the results of a similarly debatable situation or circumstance. Your thesis statements will reverse the procedure for writing a thesis for a causes essay by briefly describing or discussing the cause, then presenting an argument for the rightness of effects you offer. To be sure that such a thesis truly supplies effects, test it by writing it this way: Lower standards in high school caused these results (the effects):. . . .

Complete the following "effect" thesis statements:

- _____are often the physical effects of anger management problems.
- Increases in tuition fees have led to _____

In both cases, remember to suggest or state directly whether your essay will deal with causes or effects.

What Is Your Purpose and Who Is Your Audience?

Your primary purpose for a cause or effect essay will be to inform as you explain the causes of a particular situation, the effects of a situation, or, rarely, a combination of both. Jing's essay is mainly aimed at informing readers about how some newly-arrived students in colleges and universities feel. His secondary purpose is expressive; he wants to share his experiences with readers.

You can certainly use cause or effect essays for argumentation or persuasion. Camilo's essay is a clear example of the effectiveness of this pattern of development for arguing a position. Much journalism, in fact, is based on just such a blend; check the news and you will see articles explaining and evaluating causes or effects to promote a point about some situation.

Whether you choose causes or effects will depend on the topic you choose and your specific secondary purposes. If, for example, your primary purpose is to inform and your secondary purpose is to explain why you chose your program of studies, your essay would focus on the causes for that decision. However, if your secondary purpose is to write a personal expressive essay about the impact a special person has had on your life, your essay would focus mainly on the effects of knowing that person. Your audience will want to understand clearly, from your first paragraph, which of these options you are pursuing.

As with all essays, try to pick a topic that will appeal to your audience. An essay on the negative effects of steroids on professional athletes may be especially interesting to an audience of sports fans. On the other hand, this topic might not be as appealing to people who are neutral about, or dislike, sports. Also, consider, as Camilo did, whether your audience requires any background information on the topic. Finally, in addition to selecting a meaningful topic, be sure to make the relevance of your main point clear so that your audience will readily understand the importance of the causes or effects you are explaining.

What Is Your Point of View in a Cause or Effect Essay?

Cause or effect essays are rooted in logic. Therefore, these essays *examine* logical relationships between ideas or events and are analytical by nature. Writing a cause or effect essay will require preparation and skill. You must demonstrate the ability to present your facts clearly, focusing on presenting a logical sequence of supporting points and carefully explained details.

Ideally, therefore, cause or effect essays deflect attention away from the writer's personal opinion and presence; they are written in the third-person voice. The intrusion of "I" can weaken readers' confidence in the truth of the essay's point and in the validity of specified causes or effects. The first-person voice can make it seem that the writer is attempting to justify his or her own views rather than demonstrating the logical truth of the essay's point. For example, a thesis could state, "I believe Canadian gun-control laws should be strengthened." But this first-person thesis actually limits the meaning of the sentence to the writer alone; it does not suggest an analytical examination of either causes or effects related to the statement. If, on the other hand, the thesis begins, "Canadian gun-control laws should be strengthened because . . .," then it is more forceful. A third-person point of view does not limit itself simply to what the writer believes; instead, it hints that support will be objective and logical. The purpose of a cause or effect essay is to convince readers with logic to accept the causes or effects as plausible.

How Will You Support Your Causes or Effects Essay?

First, from your prewriting on, take care to separate causes from effects. Ask yourself, as the student writer below did, which category your points and details truly belong to.

- Out of all the points and details in Jing's lists on the following pages, which are causes and which are effects?

Next, check your prewriting and first draft carefully for (a) generalizations, and (b) logical errors, as listed above.

Then take advantage of any secondary pattern of development that will clarify or argue your thesis and supporting points. Readers expect clear explanations of each cause or effect: examples and explanations are natural choices for supporting details; look at Jing's prewriting on the next page to see how he has used examples to clarify and expand on his points. Narrative anecdotes often involve and touch the emotions of readers; if you are writing about the effects of living on welfare, including a word-sketch of a person surviving on welfare will probably work better than a dry list of potential effects. Careful description will help to convince readers of the rightness of your position: describing the chilly temperature and clutter in the welfare recipient's rooms would be a good choice for the student noted above. Even process analysis is useful if you wish to enumerate the steps by which some effect came about.

- Where in Camilo's essay do you find evidence of step-by-step or process treatment of supporting details?

Finally, consider which forms of supporting details will best serve your thesis: will you use personal, subjective opinions or experiences, as Jing did, or will those survive logical scrutiny? Or will you use objective facts and authoritative information derived from research, as Camilo did?

Prewriting

Jing, the author of "New Country, New Person," was assigned a cause or effect essay. Because he had come to Toronto from Hong Kong a year ago, he spent a few minutes thinking about *why* he had wanted to attend school so far from home:

- wanted to get out on my own—my whole family always in the same business
- I inherited a bit of money from my grandfather
- just seemed too easy, nothing was my own, and nothing new
- looking after myself is tough
- now I feel like a different person, not the "second son"
- my cousin went to university in Vancouver and is really doing well
- it was so hard at first and sometimes I miss everybody

The next day, when he went back to his notes, he noticed that in his list of points he was starting to include ideas that were *results,* or *consequences,* of coming to school on his own in Canada, such as having to take care of himself and missing his family. He explained, "I started at Ryerson when I'd only been in Canada for a month, so the first semester was really difficult. I didn't know anyone in Toronto, really, except for some friends of my uncle, and they lived in Markham, north of the city. I guess I was kind of spoiled and trying to live on my own made me grow up in a hurry."

Thinking more about the experiences that had resulted from leaving Hong Kong led Jing to make a second list of ideas for an essay about the effects of his decision.

Now he needed to find three categories or groupings for the consequences of moving. First, he tried:

1. Missing home
2. Living in a new city
3. Being lonely

Concerned that "missing home" and "being lonely" were too similar, he looked at his list again, and the word "independent" in the first item caught his eye. He missed home, but having to do everything for himself was really the first consequence of being on his own. Next, he noticed that he had items about finding his way around Toronto, and he remembered talking about getting lost and taking the wrong bus with other students. "Learning to get around" was probably more specifically a consequence than just "living" in a new city. Finally, he realized that his overspending was probably not a consequence that related well to any of his groupings, nor were his issues with speaking English, so he crossed out those possibilities. He revised his groups to the following:

1. Learning to be independent

2. Trying to get around in a new city

3. Being lonely and finding new friends

Here is Jing's second list, where he tried placing the list items in the three groups above:

1 Being independent is good, but it's a lot of work

3 Had to figure out how to meet people

1 I hated going back to my empty room every night

2 The TTC is okay, but sometimes I was late to early classes—had to time bus and subway trips

2 People say HK is hard to get around in, but Toronto was worse at first—I got lost so many times

1? Could talk to people in restaurants in Chinese but too expensive to eat out a lot

1 I can't cook! I miss everything my mother made; I miss HK street food

~~I spent so much at first—had to get a loan from my father—he wasn't happy~~

2 I miss my brothers and Mei—there's nobody home here

3 I was so shy when I joined that design club

~~My spoken English wasn't as good as I thought it was~~

1 Didn't recognize a lot of the food in supermarkets—Asian stores are fine, though

1 Cleaning my room all the time is annoying, so is doing laundry

3 I ate lunch by myself for so long

2 Never had enough time for schoolwork the first semester

3 Found a group of gamers I really like last winter

3 Never talked in classes at first, sat by myself

With some idea now of how he could support his three consequence-points, Jing wrote a trial thesis, "Foreign students learn life-changing lessons," then made an outline for his essay.

First Draft and Revision

With his outline, Jing produced the following as a first draft:

1   Coming to a new country to study, becoming a "foreign student," means more changes than I ever imagined. Moving away from home has had major consequences for me.

2   One result of coming to Canada was learning to be independent. I took all the comforts of home for granted. Now, I had to cook, clean up after myself, and worst of all, I had no one to talk to when I got home after classes. In fact, I hated going home sometimes, and facing my mess. Because I never learned to cook or shop for groceries, I was really confused in supermarkets. I had never seen a lot of the packages and products before, and I had no idea how to prepare most meats and vegetables. Downtown where my apartment is, there are Asian markets, and the food there is familiar, but I still had to learn how to cook it. Night after night, I made awful meals, then spent time cleaning up when I should have been doing homework. And I had real problems handling my money, too.

3   Before I left Hong Kong, I looked up Toronto on Google maps, so I thought I could get around the area where my college is without too many problems. I did not count on using the TTC, though. At first, I sometimes took the wrong streetcar because I didn't think to get a transit map, so I was late to morning classes. I should have bought a street guide sooner than I did because I got lost once just trying to go to a convenience store. Finally, I had to actually sit down and plan how I was going to get to school, time my trips, and work out how long it was going to take if I took different routes. Learning to plan just my trips to school was an important lesson—it helped me to start planning my time better.

4   But the biggest consequence of leaving home was loneliness. Friends of my uncle live in Markham, but I hardly ever saw them because the trip up there took nearly two hours by subway and bus. Most of the time, I was alone. E-mailing and chatting online with family and friends at home helped, but I knew I'd have to start meeting people. After a month of sitting by myself in classes and at lunch, I worked up the courage to join a design club, but for the first while I felt too shy to say much. What really helped was meeting a group of gamers; it was so easy to discuss the games we all play. By the end of first semester, I actually had two new friends.

5   Leaving home and moving across the world to another country is not like any other experience. It's a challenge and a chance to make a new start.

Because he had written only a narrative essay and a process essay so far, Jing talked to his instructor. She said that his draft contained good specific details about his experiences, but suggested that it seemed more like a narrative essay about how he felt when he first arrived in Canada. An "effects" essay, she said, should focus completely on demonstrating how his consequences followed from the "cause" of leaving home to study. It should be a bit less personal, not limited only to Jing's experience, but make its point by showing how the specific consequences arise necessarily from his "cause." She suggested that, for this reason, this essay was the ideal occasion for him to work on writing in the third-person voice.

To clear up his thinking, Jing revised his outline to start with his "cause." That way, when he revised his draft, he would look only at this outline to focus himself on its points and support:

Cause: Leaving home to go to college

Thesis: Coming to another country to study has life-changing consequences

Effect # 1: Learning to be independent
Because of leaving home and family . . .
• No cooked meals, no clean room
• Missing belongings
• Missing family and friends to talk to
• Living in apartment or residence
• Having to cook and shop
• Handling money and budgeting

Effect # 2: Trying to get around in a new city (& manage time)
Because of living someplace new . . .
• Have to learn city streets quickly, getting lost
• Carry a map book all the time
• No car, so need to figure out transit system
• [This means] Hard to get to college on time
• Making "trial runs" to time streetcar & bus trips to school
• Learning to plan time

Effect # 3: Being alone and needing to meet new people
Because of knowing nearly no one . . .
• Sit alone in classes and at lunch
• No one to talk to in evening (same as Effect # 1?)
• [This means] Need to get to know people
• Use a lot of courage, time, & energy to find a group or club
• Have to find common interest with others
• Scared to talk to people at first
• Worrying too much about school & money problems if no friends

Jing now felt ready to tackle writing the third-person final version of "New Country, New Person" that appears on pages 177–178.

WRITING A CAUSE OR EFFECT ESSAY

■ Writing Assignment 1

Choose one of the statements below, and begin by generating three briefly stated causes or effects for it. Be sure that you have three separate and distinct causes or effects.

1. Cuts in funding for education have had damaging effects on Canadian colleges and universities.

2. Many politicians and top executives are the offspring of first-generation Canadian families.

3. Garbage disposal problems in Canadian cities and towns have damaged the environment.

Prewriting

1. Examine the series of causes or effects you created, and formulate a thesis statement. The three causes or effects will function as your main points. Make sure that each of your main points is a *separate* and *distinct* point, not a restatement of one of the other points. Also, make sure that *causes* really cause or create the situation identified in your thesis statement and don't simply "come before" it, and that *effects* actually result from the situation and don't just "occur after" that situation.

2. Prepare an outline for your essay. As you are doing so, decide whether you will support each of your main points with several examples or with one extended example.

3. Write a first draft with an introduction that attracts the reader's interest, gives some background information, and presents a thesis statement and plan of development that clearly indicates whether you are focusing on causes or effects.

Revising

After you have completed the first draft of the essay, set it aside for a while. When you reread what you have written, prepare for revising by asking yourself these questions:

- Does the essay have a clearly stated thesis?
- Have I backed up each main point with effective supporting details? Have I considered other patterns of development for my body paragraphs? Do I have enough detailed support to explain each cause or effect? Do I have a relatively equal amount of support for each main point?
- Have I performed a "logic check" on my causes or effects?

  1. Have I made a "time-sequence" logical error?
  2. Have I considered "multiple causes and chains of effects"?

- Have I used transition words to help readers follow the sequence of my train of thought?
- Does my concluding paragraph wrap up my essay and either strengthen my point or give it wider meaning?

Continue to revise your essay until you can answer "yes" to each question. Then, be sure to check the next-to-final draft for the sentence skills listed on the inside front cover.

■ Writing Assignment 2

Writing for a specific purpose and audience: If students from another country visited your college or university, they would encounter some surprising customs and attitudes. You could feel both proud and perhaps embarrassed by the situations those students would encounter. Write a causes essay explaining your feelings about specific aspects of a Canadian post-secondary student's daily life. Give reasons for your feelings.

1. You will probably have an instant reaction to the question, "Am I more proud of or embarrassed by my everyday academic and lifestyle habits?" Go with that reaction to help you come up with supporting points for the thesis. Generate supporting points and details by making a list called "Reasons I'm proud of Canadian post-secondary life" or "Reasons I'm embarrassed by Canadian post-secondary life."

2. Group some of the items into one category. A list of reasons to be proud of Canadian post-secondary life might include, "We're up to date on technological career training" and "Students in most schools are asked for input about their courses." These could be "Advances in Canadian Colleges and Universities," a main supporting point in your essay.

3. Decide on three or more main supporting points and write an outline that includes those points, details, and examples (one extended example or several shorter ones). Below is a brief outline of one student's thesis and supporting points.

   Point: Canadian colleges and universities have made several important advances in recent years.

   1. Technology is used to prepare students for careers
   2. Academic programs are tuned in to career growth areas, like digital animation and professional writing
   3. Students are consulted about satisfaction with courses each year

Using your outline, write the first draft of your cause essay using third-person point of view. Refer to the guidelines for revising your causes essay provided on page 189.

■ Writing Assignment 3

Read the selection titled "What is Poverty?" by Jo Goodwin Parker on pages 475–478. Consider Goodwin Parker's position that poverty may be near-impossible to rise above, that poverty entraps and imprisons the poor. Do you agree or do you see her attitude as defeatist or passive? What about the poor, the street people, or the unemployed in your area? Are they trapped or unwilling to try? What do the media say?

Do some online research about poverty, or street people, or unemployment where you live. What is your response to the media's and politicians' viewpoints? As noted in Part 3, make careful research notes of your findings so that you are able to correctly quote and paraphrase any relevant ideas. Then, write a causes or effects essay presenting your viewpoint and findings on poverty or street people or unemployment in your city or town. Your thesis could be something like the following:

PART 2
PATTERNS OF ESSAY DEVELOPMENT

- The reasons why children of welfare families do not fare well in school are malnutrition, . . . (causes)

- Shelter closings in downtown Vancouver have driven street people to desperation; closings have made addicts more desperate, sick people more . . . (effects)

CHECKLIST OF LEARNING OUTCOMES FOR CHAPTER 12

To ensure that you have understood and met the learning outcomes for this chapter, answer the following questions after completing any of its writing assignments:

✓ Does the thesis state a clear viewpoint and indicate whether the essay deals with causes or effects?

✓ Is each cause or effect truly a cause or effect? Does each clearly support the point of your thesis?

✓ Are your causes or effects presented in an effective order with appropriate transitions to reinforce meaning and to guide the reader?

✓ Are the supporting points adequately explained and clarified by specific details and examples?

✓ Does the conclusion reinforce the thesis' point?

Online
Learning Centre

For bonus material and additional activities please go to the OLC at **www.mcgrawhill.ca/olc/langan**

Comparison or Contrast

LEARNING OUTCOMES

After reading this chapter and working through its writing assignments, you will be ready to write a comparison or contrast essay that

- compares or contrasts limited aspects of two subjects or two sides of a subject;

- contains in its thesis statement
  (1) both subjects,
  (2) the intention to compare or contrast, and
  (3) a clear point about the comparison or contrast;

- uses either the one-side-at-a-time or the point-by-point method to develop its comparison or contrast;

- carefully compares or contrasts both subjects within one of these structures according to a valid basis for comparing or contrasting;

- concludes by summing up the results gained by comparing or contrasting the two subjects, confirming your viewpoint on these results.

Comparison or contrast writing begins with the way you ordinarily think about things. When you *compare* two things, you show how they are similar; when you *contrast* two things, you show how they are different. You routinely compare or contrast two brand-name products, two jobs, or two solutions to a problem.

Writing about two sides of an issue or about two related topics, however, is more demanding than discussing them. In this respect, examples you see in advertisements or magazine articles are misleading: comparisons or contrasts between particular models from Toyota and Honda set out as bulleted points opposite each other. That seems simple enough; you read both lists, compare or contrast one bulleted item with another, and that's it. Writing essays, though, means setting out, in sentence and paragraph form, not the "bulleted points," but topics and supporting details for each point in such a way that readers can compare or contrast along with you. When you write comparison or contrast essays, you present items or ideas that have a common basis for consideration, then you analyze those items or ideas for appropriate points of comparison or contrast. Similarities or differences, in supporting details, make the comparison or contrast clear to readers.

Comparison essays inform readers of new material by showing similarities between familiar ideas and unfamiliar or seemingly dissimilar concepts. Essays that contrast sometimes persuade by examining the differences between two subjects and making decisions about them. Each must make a point with its comparison or contrast.

Comparison and contrast patterns are used constantly in academic and career writing tasks. You may compare one software package with another; you may compare two playwrights' use of irony; you may contrast the accuracy of two accounting procedures; or your manager may need you to prepare a report comparing the work patterns of two employees. In turn, your textbooks will use comparison and/or contrast to present new material to you and to make points about different concepts, processes, or events.

In this chapter, you will be asked to write a comparison or contrast essay, using one of two methods of body-paragraph development. Each method displays, in different ways, similarities and differences between things or ideas that reflect our natural thinking patterns.

To prepare for this task, first read about the two methods of development you can use in writing this type of essay. Then, read the student essays that follow, and work through the questions that accompany the essays.

METHODS OF DEVELOPMENT

Comparing or contrasting two subjects requires you to do three things during the prewriting stage:

1. Decide on two ideas, people, or items that have a *valid basis for comparison or contrast*. For example, you could compare or contrast a Microsoft operating system with a Macintosh OS. Your basis for comparison or contrast would be *computer operating systems*. In this case, you can compare or contrast one system with the other. On the other hand, if you tried to compare or contrast Firefox with a Macintosh OS, there would be no valid basis for comparing or contrasting the two. You could, however, compare or contrast Firefox with Safari because both are Internet browsers with shared characteristics such as e-mail and Web navigation.

2. Develop a viewpoint about what you are comparing or contrasting. For a successful essay, you must decide what point you wish to make and what you have learned as you focus on similarities or differences. For example, if you are listing points to compare a year you spent in university with the year you are

now spending in college, you may find that there are good points about both experiences. Gradually, you may emerge with a thesis stating that both forms of education have value but in *different* ways.

3. Finally, you should choose one of two methods of development: the *one-side-at-a-time* method or the *point-by-point* method. Each of these methods is illustrated below.

One Side at a Time

The one-side-at-a-time structure may be used either for the supporting paragraphs or for the entire essay. Whether you choose this method for your body paragraphs or for an essay, the one-side-at-a-time method presents all the points for one side, followed by all the points for the other side.

Look at the following supporting paragraph from "Two Mothers," a student essay that follows.

> Moreover, both hard work and acts of caring are second nature to most mothers; these reflect their concern for their children in different ways. Mama's caring nature is seen through the efforts she makes for her children. She helps "raise the money . . . to send (Dee) to Augusta to school," (Walker 271) because that is the only way Dee will have a chance at a better future. Had it not been for Mama's effort, the outward evidence of her caring nature, Dee's future would have been uncertain at best. Conversely, David Sedaris' mother appears to be paralyzed, to lack any ability to show care for her children. She throws her kids out of the house, and listens, apparently heartlessly, to them yelling outside (Sedaris 75). She has, in fact, thrown them out into a snowstorm, and her attitude seems to be summed up in the story's title: "let it snow." Is she concerned at all? Seemingly not; she "refill(s) her goblet" and "pulls the drapes," (75) insulating herself from them. Her indifference or self-centredness shows not just a lack of concern but an inability to care for her children. Walker's Mama is characterized by her caring nature and focus on her children, just as Sedaris' mother's character is characterized by her utter lack of care for David and his sister and her withdrawal away from any relationship with them into alcoholism.

The first half of the paragraph explains one side of the contrast fully: the caring nature of Mama, from Alice Walker's story. The second half of the paragraph deals entirely with the other side of the contrast: the indifference of David Sedaris' mother character. The following outline of the paragraph illustrates the one-side-at-a-time method.

Outline (One Side at a Time)

Topic Sentence: Moreover, both hard work and acts of caring are second nature to most mothers, reflecting their concern for their children in different ways.

1. Mama (Alice Walker)
   a. Raises money to send Dee away to school
   b. Shows she wants a better future for her daughter

2. Unnamed Mother (David Sedaris)

   a. Throws children out of the house alone in a storm
   b. Ignores their requests to come in
   c. Pours herself another drink
   d. Pulls the drapes closed

Note: It is not essential to have exactly the same number of supporting details for each point; in fact, it is preferable not to strain your comparison or contrast by trying to make both sides "equal." Generally, you will find that, as Anya did in "Two Mothers," the points of comparison or contrast even out over the course of three to five body paragraphs.

Point by Point

Now look at the supporting paragraph below, which is taken from the essay "What's for Dinner?"

> Another area where the home-cooked meal shines is nutrition. Fast-food options are often full of empty calories and fat. A fast-food burger, if it is a Big Mac, contains approximately 576 calories, of which 270 come from fat; the fat makes up 46 percent of the burger (*Weightloss for All*). Add fries, and it adds another 610 calories, with 261 of those coming from fat. A quarter-pound burger pan-broiled at home amounts to about 200 calories, and with sides of oven-roasted potatoes and steamed vegetables, will add up to the calorie-count of just the Big Mac alone, and a much lower proportion of fats. A KFC deep-fried, battered chicken breast contains about 450 calories (*Weightloss for All*), and more than half of those are fats. A Swiss Chalet chicken breast is a little better at 300 calories (*Swiss Chalet*), but a chicken breast, with skin, floured, seasoned, and fried at home will add up to only 150 calories, with one-third of those coming from fats. Takeout burger or chicken meals are rarely balanced, either; generally takeout means no vegetables other than potatoes.

In this case, the paragraph contrasts the nutritional value of the same food cooked two different ways point by point. The following outline of the paragraph illustrates the point-by-point method.

Outline (Point by Point)

Another area where the home-cooked meal shines is nutrition.

1. Hamburgers

   a. Big Mac with fries
   b. Home-cooked burger with oven-roasted potatoes and vegetables

2. Chicken

   a. KFC or Swiss Chalet chicken breast
   b. Home-cooked, pan-fried chicken breast

Before you begin writing a comparison or contrast essay, decide whether you are going to use the one-side-at-a-time format or the point-by-point format. Use that format as you create the outline for your essay.

STUDENT ESSAYS TO CONSIDER

Two Mothers

1   Nowhere in the world does an ideal mother exist, as every child and every family have different needs and different expectations of what such a person would be. Literature reflects the endless diversity of mothers, as shown in their words and actions and those of their children. The role of the mother character seems static at first; it does not always hint at the wide spectrum of characteristics a mother in a specific piece may possess. In Alice Walker's short story "Everyday Use" and David Sedaris' essay "Let It Snow," the relationship between mother and child unravels yet again. The mother in each work has the same role to play in the domestic scenario; however, the characters are differentiated by the ways the authors explore their personalities. Mama in "Everyday Use" and Sedaris' unnamed mother in "Let It Snow" are wildly different women in terms of their attitudes toward work, caring, and bonding with their children.

2   Walker shows readers the unselfconscious Mama, a mother who handles the roughest of jobs with her "rough, man-working hands" (Walker 270). A mother's role usually entails taking on more tasks than any other character does; in fact, mothers are pretty much the hardest working people around. The condition of Mama's hands shows the effort she puts into the tasks she performs in and around the family's house, such as in the winter when she "work(s) outside all day, breaking ice" in order to "get water for washing" (Walker 270). She does many brutal outdoor jobs. On the other hand, Sedaris presents a mother in "Let It Snow" who is the opposite of Mama, largely because of "the secret life she (leads)" (Sedaris 75). For instance, instead of cooking, the Sedaris children's mother is "in the kitchen, watching television," (75) numbed by her drinking. Her problem with alcohol hinders her desire or ability to work in and around the house; she lacks the grit and commitment of Mama in Walker's story. Mothers work hard for many reasons and one of those reasons may be because they care so much.

3   Moreover, both hard work and acts of caring are second nature to most mothers; these reflect their concern for their children in different ways. Mama's caring nature is seen through the efforts she makes for her children. She helps "raise the money . . . to send (Dee) to Augusta to school" (Walker 271) because that is the only way Dee will have a chance at a better future. Had it not been for Mama's effort, the outward evidence of her caring nature, Dee's future would have been uncertain at best. Conversely, David Sedaris' mother appears to be paralyzed, to lack any ability to show care for her children. She throws her kids out of the house, and listens, apparently heartlessly, to them yelling outside (Sedaris 75). She has, in fact, thrown them out into a snowstorm, and her attitude seems to be summed up in the story's title: "let it snow." Is she concerned at all? Seemingly not; she "refill(s) her goblet" and "pulls the drapes" (75), insulating herself from them. Most significantly, her indifference or self-centredness shows not just a lack of concern but an inability to care for her children. While Walker's Mama is characterized by her caring

nature and focus on her children, Sedaris' mother-character is characterized by her utter lack of care for David and his sister and her withdrawal away from any relationship with them into alcoholism.

4   A mother's ability to care is a most essential indicator of the depth of her relationship with her children. Such care begins and nourishes the process by which mother and child build lasting bonds. The bonds between Mama and her children and those between Sedaris' possibly intentionally unnamed mother stand in stark contrast. Near the end of Walker's story, Mama and her daughter Maggie take quiet comfort in each other's company, "the two of (them) sat there just enjoying, until it was time to go in the house and go to bed" (Walker 277). The Sedaris children however enjoy no such comfort; they call their mother a "bitch," and feel abandoned outdoors when they go "down the hill and (toboggan) with other children" (Sedaris 75) without her company. They are independent, wayward children. Whether or not their mother feels much of a bond with her offspring the story never reveals, but her actions show no desire for closeness.

5   To conclude, although Mama and Sedaris' mother take on the same role, the difference between the ways they enact it is seen through both authors' portrayal of their traits. Their characters are shown as contrasting through the warmth or the chill of their relationships with their children. Mama may not have much, but she builds a rich bond with both daughters through her hard work and care, while Sedaris' suburban mother has withdrawn from even trying to care for or spend time with her children. In these works, a mother's role does not depict what a mother should do, but rather what mothers in fact do. Just as in the world, no two mothers are the same. For some people, each of these mothers might be ideal, but that all depends on their expectations and the complex interactions between mothers and children.

What's For Dinner?

1   Swiss Chalet, McDonald's, and Tim Hortons tempt hungry Canadians every day with billboards and TV commercials. Hot succulent chicken, fries and a roll, wholesome sandwiches with a doughnut on the side, or the Darth Vader of food, the Big Mac: they are all ready, right now, nearby. How can home cooking compete? Well, on the basis of taste, ease of preparation, nutritional value, and cost, the home-made meal wins every time.

2   Sometimes people are just hungry and in a hurry to eat. A burger, fried chicken, or pizza seem like tasty ideas—at first bite. Let those cool down for a few minutes, though, and the sliver-thin burger leaves a fatty scum in the mouth and the chicken batter tastes like fried socks. Take-out tacos, that smell so appetizing to a famished person's nose, are not just impossible to eat but also nearly inedible when people try to eat them: tacos turn into a mess of cardboard splinters and mystery meat with shreds of rusty lettuce. Not appetizing enough? Try a sub—the mystery meat here is the warm, slightly pickled variety and the tomatoes are suspiciously tough, kind of a vegetable chew-toy . . . but not as much fun. McDonalds would like folks to think "they're lovin' it" (*McDonalds*), but fast food usually disappoints by the third mouthful.

3   There are better-tasting alternatives to any of those cheap and nasty options, meals that are quick and easy to prepare. In half an hour, even inexperienced cooks can sauté a chicken breast, chop, or burger, bake a potato, and make a salad. The meat will be juicy inside and crispy outside; the baked potato will be hot and ready for toppings, and the salad will taste cool and fresh. Each can be seasoned and cooked exactly to taste, not according to a corporate formula. If the palate craves Italian flavour, takeout pizza is not the only option; the crust is usually chewier than the box it came in. Anyone can buy a good crust at the supermarket and dress it up or down to taste with different cheeses, seasonings, and toppings in exactly the desired quantities. A comforting bowl of pasta is as easy as boiling water, then opening a jar of gourmet sauce or just applying oil, garlic, and parmesan cheese. Add raw vegetables and dip, and dinner is complete. Cooking a simple meal is easy and always tastes better than predictable takeout options.

4   Another area where the home-cooked meal shines is nutrition. Fast-food options are often full of empty calories and fat. A fast-food burger, if it is a Big Mac, contains approximately 576 calories, of which 270 come from fat; the fat makes up 46 percent of the burger (*Weightloss for All*). Add fries, and it adds another 610 calories, with 261 of those coming from fat. A quarter-pound burger pan-broiled at home amounts to about 200 calories, and with sides of oven-roasted potatoes and steamed vegetables, will add up to the calorie-count of just the Big Mac alone, and a much lower proportion of fats. A KFC deep-fried, battered chicken breast contains about 450 calories (*Weightloss for All*), and more than half of those are fats. A Swiss Chalet chicken breast is a little better at 300 calories (*Swiss Chalet*), but a chicken breast, with skin, floured, seasoned, and fried at home will add up to only 200 calories, with one-third of those coming from fats. Takeout burger or chicken meals are rarely balanced, either; generally takeout means no vegetables other than potatoes.

5   Finally, home cooking is always less expensive than takeout. Most ingredients for an ordinary dinner add up to about five dollars at the supermarket. In contrast, a quarter chicken takeout dinner for one costs about nine dollars. A chicken breast bought at the supermarket is at most two dollars, a potato thirty cents, and vegetables a dollar or two—the whole meal cooked at home costs about half of the takeout bill. Burgers and fries are cheaper forms of fast food, in general. But a quarter pound of ground beef is perhaps eighty cents at most; add the potato and vegetables, and the home-made burger meal tops out at about $2.50, compared to most burger-and-fries (no veggies) combos, which will be at least $5.00 or more. Even a fully loaded pizza made at home is better value than the delivery model. The supermarket crust, jar of sauce, mozzarella, and even pepperoni may total $7.00, but in most places, a medium or large pizza will be over $10.00, and there will be a delivery charge. Where economy is concerned, do-it-yourself meals are clear winners.

6   Stopping at a drive-through window or picking up the phone is tempting when hunger strikes. But the food never tastes as good as it looks in the menu pictures, and it is nearly never nutritionally balanced. And if the savings that

result from cooking at home are not enough, consider the ritual of making a meal exactly to taste as a soothing end to a busy day.

A Note About Research and References

Both student essays use references to external sources. Anya, the author of "Two Mothers," needed to refer to the works of literature her essay was based on, and Sari, in "What's For Dinner?," wanted objective, reliable facts to support her thesis' argument. In both essays, you see items in parentheses near the ends of sentences. These are in-text citations in the MLA style. In Chapters 18 and 19 of Part 3, you will see that in-text citations are essential parts of the MLA and APA styles of managing reference material.

"Two Mothers" is a literary version of a contrast essay. If your English course concentrates on short stories and essays, then you will likely use the illustration by example, comparison or contrast, and argumentation patterns of development. Your essays will focus on illuminating and arguing a point about a significant issue or concept in readings prescribed for your course.

■ Questions

About Unity

1. Which paragraph in "Two Mothers" contains its topic sentence within the paragraph rather than at its beginning? What is the topic sentence?

2. Which sentence in paragraph 4 of "Two Mothers" should be omitted in the interests of paragraph unity?

3. In which paragraph in "What's for Dinner?" is the topic sentence at the end rather than at the beginning, where it generally belongs in student essays?

About Support

4. In paragraph 3 of "Two Mothers," how many examples does the writer give to support her claim that the children in Sedaris' story do not feel much of a bond with their mother?

5. Which sentence in paragraph 2 of "Two Mothers" should be followed by supporting details?

6. Which sentence in paragraph 4 of "What's for Dinner?" should be followed by supporting details?

About Coherence

7. In paragraph 3 of "Two Mothers," what "change of direction" signal does the author use to indicate she has finished discussing Walker's character and is now going to discuss Sedaris' character?

8. Write the words in the last section of paragraph 3 of "Two Mothers" that indicate the writer has used emphatic order (see Chapter 3) in organizing her supporting points.

About Introductions and Conclusions

9. Which of the following best describes the opening paragraph of "What's for Dinner"?

   a. Broad, general statement narrowing to a thesis
   b. Explanation of the importance of the topic
   c. Beginning with an opposite
   d. Question

10. The conclusion of "Two Mothers" falls into which category?

   a. Some observations and a prediction
   b. Summary and final thought
   c. Question or series of questions

About the Method of Development

11. Trace Sari's contrast structure in paragraphs 3 and 4 of "What's for Dinner?"

DEVELOPING A COMPARISON OR CONTRAST ESSAY

Writing a Thesis Statement for a Comparison or Contrast Essay

In academic, business, or technical writing, comparison and contrast is valuable because it offers readers a new way to see familiar concepts or things. Writing an effective thesis for such an essay requires you to have a purpose for examining and interpreting the results of setting up likenesses and/or differences. That purpose is crucial; it becomes your point, your thesis.

That purpose will usually emerge during prewriting. As you work on your comparison/contrast essay, ask yourself, *What did I learn from this? Why did I compare or contrast these?* or *What important or significant ideas emerged from putting these two ideas together?* Your point is what you learned.

A comparison or contrast thesis does not announce "A and B are very different," or "A and B have important similarities." Neither of these offers a point derived from comparing or contrasting. Instead, an effective thesis offers readers what the writer discovered from setting one thing up against another—that "something new" is the writer's purpose. For example, "A and B's similarities are so pronounced that buyers could easily be fooled . . ."

Therefore, a formula for a comparison/contrast thesis might be

- topic + intention to compare and/or contrast + suggestion or statement of outcome/discovery gained from comparing and/or contrasting

In some cases, it might also be appropriate to mention the basis of comparison and/or contrast (see page 193).

An example of a comparison essay's thesis, following the formula above, would be:

The coverage of the student walk-out in the *Vancouver Sun* and the *Vancouver Province* was so similar that the reporters might have plagiarized each other.

An example of a contrast essay's thesis, following the formula above, would be:

The contrasts between the cooking styles of the two chefs are so pronounced that diners often do not recognize a dish they ordered previously.

- What is the point each author makes with his or her thesis? Explain how each might have arrived at that point.

What Is Your Purpose and Who Is Your Audience?

Whether you choose to compare or contrast two items depends on your primary purpose, that is, the specific point you want to convey to your audience. Often your primary purpose will be to persuade, as in the first example below.

Suppose the main point of your essay is that campus child-care facilities are superior to neighbourhood daycare. To convince your audience of your claim, you might contrast the two items to point out the differences—child-care staffs, all-day proximity to children, daily activities available, security, and price—that make the campus child-care preferable.

If, however, your main point is that Kingston's tap water is just as good as bottled water, you will still be arguing or persuading, but you could equally be informing readers when you compare the two, pointing out and emphasizing the similarities that support your point. For example, Kingston's tap water and bottled water might be equally clean, fresh, and mineral-rich; a small amount of research would give you the facts you need. In this case, you will be using description and objective examples to develop your body paragraphs, to make your support as clear as possible.

Be sure to keep your audience in mind when planning your essay. If you are writing about Macs and PCs for computer studies or technology students, for example, you could assume your audience is familiar with the two systems and with specialized terminology. On the other hand, if your audience is made up of health-care or broadcast students, you could not make such assumptions, and it would be up to you to provide background information and define specialized terms. Focusing on your audience will help you determine the tone of your essay as well. If you are writing for an audience of programmers, it is appropriate to write in an objective, technical tone. However, if you are writing for a more general audience, you should assume a straightforward and helpful formal tone. For more on formal and informal styles, see page 215 in Chapter 14.

What Is Your Point of View in a Comparison or Contrast Essay?

Initially, your main concerns with this method of development are to develop skills required to construct a clear structure for comparing and/or contrasting two items, and to show a point that emerges clearly from such comparing or contrasting.

As with most patterns of essay development, when you select a point of view or voice for a comparison/contrast assignment, consider how essential your connection to the topic is to making the essay's point. The student essays in this chapter both present examples of a third-person point of view: focus and emphasis fall on structural clarity and the quality of factual support. Sari, author of "What's for

PART 2

PATTERNS OF ESSAY DEVELOPMENT

Dinner?," felt that any first-person presence would detract from the impartial support she wished to provide for her thesis. She wanted her essay to be based on specific facts that were as accurate as possible, so she did some online research about the nutritional content in various foods, and then included her sources within the essay. Otherwise, she felt her essay would seem more the product of her own opinions than of objective facts. Similarly, Anya, whose English course emphasizes literature, was anxious to continue to practise what her professor calls "staying behind the curtain" in her contrast essay. She wanted the proof for her thesis to rest clearly on the text-based quality of her supporting points and details. This type of third-person, factually supported comparison or contrast essay is characteristic of professional examples you will find in textbooks and of future academic or career writing tasks.

How Will You Support Your Comparison or Contrast Essay?

Depending on your purpose(s) and audience, your main task in supporting a comparison or contrast thesis is selecting points and details. Notice, for example, that in the section below, Sari rejects the supporting point about the degree of processing involved in fast food and home-cooked food. She does so on the basis that she believes that a general audience will easily grasp her four other supporting points, but might be less receptive to, or interested in, food-processing and its effects on mealtime choices.

Now, consider the possibility that Sari decided to change her primary purpose and write an entirely different essay: a humorous contrast paper strongly in favour of delicious fatty fast foods.

- What could her thesis be for such an essay?
- What would be four good supporting points for this thesis?
- Note at least two probable details for each supporting point.

Approach building your support this way:

1. **Brainstorm for ideas about both sides of your comparison or contrast.** See Sari's and Anya's work in this chapter.

2. **Work out points of comparison or contrast** that apply to both sides. These are your criteria, or your points of judgment.
   - Say that you have chosen to compare massage therapy with acupuncture as treatments for muscle pain. On what bases can you compare these treatments? Cost? Duration of sessions?
   - Come up with four or five appropriate points for comparisons of your own.

3. **Set up your points of comparison or contrast in two columns and continue to work on supporting details.** In Sari's case, based on her purpose, her details are mainly factual. In "Two Mothers," supporting details are taken from the short stories Anya writes about.
   - What are Anya's supporting details on pages 196—197? What type of details are they? How do they relate to her purpose and audience for her essay?

Consider which secondary methods of development will create the most effective supporting details for your points. Examples are not your only choice;

you may use explanations, descriptions, definitions, or even brief anecdotes to make the fine points of a comparison or contrast clearer or sharper for readers.

- Where in "What's for Dinner" do you find examples of description? Are these effective?

4. **Try to come up with relatively balanced numbers of supporting details for each side of your comparison or contrast.** Your supporting points, of course, will be applied equally to both sides, and you will aim to balance your details for each point. But do not strain to create an equivalency or a contrast where none exists, and do not state the obvious just to create a balance between your two subjects or sides.

- How many supporting details appear for each side of the contrast in each body paragraph of "What's for Dinner"?
- How many appear for each character in each body paragraph of "Two Mothers"?

5. **Be sure you have made each supporting detail clear to your readers.** Read your essay to someone else and work on areas where your reader needs further explanation from you.

Prewriting

Sari, a first-year Health Sciences student, is interested in the aspects of her program related to nutrition and wellness. As her friends know all too well, she has very clear opinions about North American food, and fast food in particular.

"I feel as if I get into endless discussions and arguments about what people should eat and why. I even forced a couple of friends to watch *Supersize Me* when they didn't really want to. So when one of the topics listed for this essay was fast food, I jumped right at it. But I didn't want to end up writing a rant based on my feelings alone—I'm a science student and we're taught to rely on facts and specifics, so I thought I would see how well I could back up ideas I had about how easily people fall into the trap of eating fast food."

To generate ideas for her paper, Sari started with a mix of questioning and listing. She wanted to see where her focuses would be.

Trial Thesis: Fast food is never a good choice because . . .

- it's not nutritious
- it's overpriced and tasteless compared to cooking for yourself
- it never ends up being a balanced meal or snack
- it doesn't really taste that good after the first few bites
- it's full of chemicals and preservatives
- it's expensive for what it is

Why isn't it nutritious?

- the fat-to-protein ratio is way out of whack
- burgers, fries, pizzas, even Asian meals in food courts just sit a lot of the time—the nutrients die under the heat lamps

- most of it is over-processed—nobody cooks it in most chains—it comes in bags on trucks and it's reheated

How overpriced is it?

- a quarter-chicken dinner is around $9
- but a chicken breast with the bone in would only cost about $2 max
- add potatoes or some starch and either of those would only cost about 50 cents or less per person—how much does a bun cost?

At this point, Sari saw what she was doing. She was coming up with ideas, but not contrasts. She knew this was to be a comparison or contrast essay, but it was only once she started thinking about the idea of fast food being overpriced that she started contrasting prices.

So she decided to put labels on the types of food she was going to contrast: fast food and home cooking. She then began to prewrite in a different way; she made two columns, using keywords based on possible supporting points she had listed under her trial thesis:

Fast Food	*Home Cooking*
1. Price	1. Price
2. Nutrition	2. Nutrition
3. Taste	3. Taste
4. Amount of processing	4. Amount of processing
5. Time and difficulty	5. Time and difficulty

Working from this rough supporting-point list, Sari made point-form notes of details under each heading. As she did so, she realized that she was not sure of some facts she wanted to include, such as calorie counts, fat percentages, and prices. For example, under *nutrition,* she wanted to include the caloric values for Big Macs and fried chicken, as well as for the ingredients involved. She knew this was a very basic type of research and that a simple check of some Web sites would be sufficient for a short essay. She took the time to record the URLs for each site she used, knowing she could go back for more detailed citation information later. Finally, she decided that, although she was not yet sure of the order of her supporting points, the idea of food processing would probably be too complex to explain and support, particularly for a non-technical audience. Sari thought four supporting points would be enough to carry her thesis.

Now Sari was ready to try a first draft.

First Draft and Revision

1   Everyone is tempted by fast food. We see it everywhere—it's on billboards, it's on TV, radio, and the Internet, and it's in every cafeteria on campus. People

react automatically when they see the logos or hear the theme songs for fast-food chains; they are conditioned to be hungry and buy the products. Why? Well, fast food is ready as soon as someone walks up to a counter; there's no waiting—it's fast. And it must be good because everyone is eating it, right? Wrong. Fast food can not compete with home cooking on any count: taste, waiting or prep time, nutrition, and cost.

2   Sometimes people just want something to eat, fast. The burger, chicken, or pizza seem to be good ideas until they cool down a bit. The burger has no texture and it leaves a fatty taste in the mouth; the chicken batter is no longer crispy or fresh. If someone cooks either of these at home, then they can eat them straight from the stove, and the fresh taste does not change. Another example??? Fast food disappoints eaters quickly; it's the first bite that hooks them.

3   Anyone can come up with alternatives to fast-food options. You don't need to be a cook; burgers, chicken, pizza, and pasta are easy to make. In half an hour, even an inexperienced cook can fry or bake chicken or a burger. If someone wants Italian food, they can buy a crust at the supermarket and dress it with different cheeses, seasonings, and toppings. There's no better or easier comfort food than a bowl of pasta; just boil water, add sauce and cheese. With salad or raw veg and dip, it's a balanced meal.

4   Home cooking beats fast food where nutrition is concerned, too. Fast-food options are often full of empty calories and fat. A fast-food burger, like a Big Mac contains ??? calories (put in the number and the site) and about half of that is fat, which is too high a proportion for healthy eating. If someone adds fries, that's going to be about (?) calories, and a lot of those are coming from fat. Cook a quarter-pound burger at home and it adds up to about 200 calories, add oven-roasted potatoes and steamed vegetables, and it will be about the same as just the Big Mac alone, and a much lower proportion of fats. Chicken is not always low-calorie either. A KFC deep-fried, battered chicken breast contains about (???) calories and half of those are fats. These fast-food meals are not balanced either because there aren't any vegetables other than potatoes.

5   Home cooking is less expensive than takeout. Ingredients for an ordinary dinner add up to about five dollars at the supermarket. A quarter chicken takeout dinner for one costs at least eight or nine dollars. A supermarket chicken breast is around two dollars, a potato thirty cents, and vegetables a dollar or two. A quarter pound of ground beef is less than a dollar; add the potato and vegetables, and the home-made burger meal costs around $3.00 (?), compared to most burger meals, which will be at least ???. Even a pizza made at home is better value. The crust, jar of sauce, mozzarella, and even pepperoni is about six or seven dollars, but in most places, a medium or large pizza will be over ten dollars, and there will be a delivery charge.

6   It's always tempting to stop at a drive-through window or pick up the phone when hunger strikes. But the food never tastes as good, it's not nutritionally balanced, and it costs more than if you cooked it at home.

Sari put the first draft of her essay aside and took it to her English class the next day. Her instructor asked students to work in small groups, reading their drafts aloud and making revision suggestions to one another. Here are the notes Sari made on the basis of her group's comments:

- The first paragraph's too general—use specific brand names and examples—they work better as hooks
- I don't think I'm consistently contrasting details in the paragraphs—I'm not sticking consistently with "one side at a time" or "point by point" inside my paragraphs—par. 3 doesn't have a contrast and par. 4 needs more details after the KFC thing
- Why am I talking about conditioning in the opening?
- My second paragraph needs more examples and the third doesn't have enough details for my first point
- I've got a "we" in the first sentence and a "you" later—this is supposed to be 3rd person
- I need some transitions at the start of paragraphs and to put in my notes and facts from my research

After making these observations about her first draft, Sari wrote a second draft with her citations, and then wrote her third draft, the final version of "What's for Dinner," which appears on pages 197–199.

WRITING A COMPARISON OR CONTRAST ESSAY

■ Writing Assignment 1

Write an essay of comparison or contrast on one of the topics below:

- Two possible career choices
- Two fashion designers
- Two games, sports, or leisure activities
- Two magazines you read regularly
- Two forms of communication (e.g., phone calls and e-mail)
- Two ways of spending (e.g., cash and credit cards)

Prewriting

1. As you select your topic, keep in mind that you won't merely be *describing* the two things you're writing about; you will be *emphasizing* the ways they are different or alike.

2. Make two columns on a sheet of paper—one for each of the subjects you'll write about. In the left-hand column, jot down words or phrases that describe the first of the two. Write anything that comes into your head. Then, go back and write a corresponding word or phrase about the subject in the right-hand column. For example, on the next page is Nazima's list of characteristics about two games she plays. She began brainstorming for words and phrases to describe Scrabble, then wrote a list for volleyball.

Scrabble	**Volleyball**
Quiet	Noisy, talking and yelling
Involves words	Involves ball and a net
Played sitting down	Played standing up, jumping
Involves as few as 2 players	Involves 12 players
Can let mind wander when it's not your turn	Have to stay alert every minute
Mental concentration, not physical	Mental and physical concentration required
Part chance (what letters you get), part strategy and skill	Mostly skill, strategy; little chance
Some see as boring, nerdy game	Seen as glamorous—stars get advertising contracts
Players' size unimportant	Being tall helps

3. Your list of characteristics will help you decide if the two things you are writing about are more alike (in which case you'll write an essay *comparing* them) or different (in which case you'll write an essay *contrasting* them.)

4. Look over your list, and think about how the characteristics you've written down (and others that occur to you) could fit into three or four categories that can serve as your supporting points or "points of comparison or contrast."

5. Decide if you will design your essay with the *one-side-at-a-time* method of development or the *point-by-point* method of development. Be consistent in your use of one method or the other as you prepare an outline.

Nazima decided on three headings under which the two games could be contrasted, and she resolved to use the *point-by-point* method of development.

Fill in the blanks in her outline to indicate the supporting points, or points of contrast, between the two games.

Trial Thesis: Although they are two of my favourite activities, Scrabble and volleyball could hardly be more different.

Point: _____

- Scrabble requires a board and letter tiles
- Volleyball needs a ball and a net
- Scrabble can be played by two people
- Twelve people needed for a volleyball game
- Scrabble can be played anywhere there's room for two people to sit down
- Volleyball needs a large room and high ceilings or an outdoor playing area

Point: _____

- You have to concentrate mentally to play Scrabble
- You need mental and physical concentration to play volleyball

- It doesn't matter what size you are to play Scrabble
- It helps to be tall to play volleyball
- There's some chance involved in Scrabble
- Chance is not a big part of volleyball

Point: _____

- Scrabble players are seen as "eggheads" by the general public
- Star volleyball players are seen as glamorous by public
- Volleyball players get contracts to endorse athletic shoes
- Scrabble players don't endorse anything, even dictionaries
- Volleyball players are admired for the power of their spike
- Scrabble players are admired for the number of unusual two-letter words they know

6. Using your own outline, proceed to write the first draft of your essay.

Revising

As you review the first draft of your essay, ask yourself these questions:

- Have I made it clear in my thesis statement what two things I am writing about, my viewpoint about them, and whether I will compare or contrast them?
- Do my supporting points represent the ways in which I will compare or contrast my two subjects?
- Does each of my supporting paragraphs have a clear topic sentence?
- Have I consistently used either the *one-side-at-a-time* or the *point-by-point* method of development?
- Have I used transition words to help readers follow my train of thought?
- Have I rounded off my essay with a conclusion that confirms what my comparison or contrast has shown?

Continue to revise your essay until you can answer "yes" to each question. Then, be sure to check the next-to-final draft for the sentence skills listed on the inside front cover.

■ Writing Assignment 2

In this comparison or contrast essay, you will write with a **specific purpose** and for a **specific audience.**

Option 1: Your niece or nephew is finishing high school soon and is thinking about getting a job instead of going to college or university. You would prefer to see him or her give college a try. Write him or her a letter in which you contrast the two courses of action. Use the one-side-at-a-time method in making your analysis.

Option 2: Write a letter to your boss in which you compare your abilities with those of the "ideal" candidate for a position to which you would like to be promoted. Use a point-by-point method to discuss each ideal requirement, and then describe how well you measure up to it. Use the requirements of a job you're relatively familiar with or a job you would really like to apply for some day.

■ Writing Assignment 3

Read the selection titled "The Story of Mouseland" by Tommy Douglas on pages 498–500. Pay special attention to how the author compares and contrasts government and cats. Notice how he makes the comparisons and contrasts to describe government more fully. Then, write an essay in which you use a comparison to fully describe three aspects of an activity, place, or person. You may use serious or humorous supporting details.

Following are some suggestions that you might consider for a thesis statement:

Thesis: In a few significant ways,

- going to college or university is like working at a career.
- meditation is like exercise.
- instructors should be like parents.

Feel free to use any other thesis that makes a comparison to fill out a description of an activity, person, or place. (Note that a comparison that points out similarities between things that are otherwise quite different, as in the above examples, is called an *analogy*.)

CHECKLIST OF LEARNING OUTCOMES FOR CHAPTER 13

To ensure that you have understood and met the learning outcomes for this chapter, answer the following questions after completing any of its writing assignments:

✔ Have you chosen two subjects or two sides of one subject that can logically be compared or contrasted?

✔ Does a worthwhile point emerge from the process of comparing or contrasting the two parts of your thesis?

✔ Does your thesis statement state both subjects (or both sides of your subject), whether you will compare or contrast, and the point you will make based on that action?

✔ Have you consistently used the method of development (either the *point-by-point* or

one-side-at-a-time method) most appropriate to your subject(s)?

✔ Have you used a valid basis for comparing or contrasting and presented an equal amount of supporting material for both sides or both subjects?

✔ Does the conclusion sum up the points made during the comparison or contrast and reinforce your thesis point?

Online
LearningCentre

CHAPTER 14

Definition

After reading this chapter and working through its writing assignments, you will be ready to write a definition essay that

- states in its introduction and thesis how the subject is unique;

- uses an appropriate degree of formality or objectivity while developing the definition;

- offers several supporting points to both clarify and limit the definition of the subject;

- concludes with a summary of the subject's definition and its significance.

You often define things informally to explain what you mean by a particular word. You might say, "Bob is really an inconsiderate person." Then you explain *inconsiderate*, saying, "He borrowed my accounting book overnight but didn't return it for a week. And when I got it back, it was covered with coffee stains."

Definition essays continue this process of explaining and clarifying. A definition essay is an extended definition that explains your understanding of a term in a more complete and formal way and makes use of skills from many methods of development: *Narration* may create the line and sequence for your explanation, *description* gives precision and specificity to details, *comparing* or *contrasting* ideas establishes what something is or is not, *dividing* your term into various categories or aspects of its meaning organizes your essay, and *examples* illustrate different aspects of a word or phrase's meaning.

Today, you constantly hear and read about new terms: *visioning,* or *imagineering,* for instance. Accountants use terms like *statistical sampling inventory;*

childcare workers speak of *attention deficits* in children; and technology creates its own vocabulary: consider *data integrity* and *ISP.*

Defining is a fundamental communications skill in career and academic pursuits. Engineers define *stress* differently from psychologists; police and security officers need a clear understanding of *reasonable grounds* for some action they take. Instructions and reports of every kind must make many terms and phrases clear to their readers. Indeed, definitions play a key part in your postsecondary education: you learn by moving from the known to the unknown, and each time you learn something new, you must define it for yourself. Your textbooks consist, in part, of definitions: by learning new terms, you are able to grasp and work with new, larger concepts and frameworks. In academic essays, you will frequently redefine terms relevant to your areas of study so you can apply them to works or ideas you are learning.

In this chapter, you will be asked to write an essay in which you define and illustrate a term. To prepare for this task, first read the student essays that follow, and then work through the questions that accompany the essays.

STUDENT ESSAYS TO CONSIDER

Ladder to the Gods

1   "Liberal Education is the ladder by which we try to ascend from mass democracy to democracy as originally meant" (11), so states Leo Strauss. This functional definition omits two points: a liberal education has its own innate value and it should be accessible to all. In democratic societies, citizens have choices, and a liberal-arts education equips them to make informed choices.

2   To understand Strauss' statement, it is necessary to get a clearer sense of what he means by the word "democracy." Our less-than-perfect societies are what he calls "modern democrac(ies)" (12), where the majority of citizens are neither educated nor virtuous. Contrast this with his idea of a "true democracy," an idealized, unattainable society in which the majority is wise, virtuous, and highly reasonable. The modern democratic majority, on the other hand, also known as mass culture, does not rule. In fact, its apathy allows an elite group to climb a ladder he calls "liberal education." These people ascend to leadership for reasons so mysterious that Strauss cannot explain them: the elite are "groupings of men who for whatever reason are on top or have a fair chance to arrive on top" (11). How do these people rise, and why, then, are they especially eligible for liberal education?

3   Upon examining Strauss' "true" democratic elite, they begin to sound like shadowy imaginary ideals; they learn "perfect gentlemanship," they strive for "human excellence" and embark on a "quest for wisdom" (12). They, in fact, sound like a bunch of wizards or motivational speakers. Their eligibility for their education is never, in fact, explained; they are some sort of worthy aristocracy, apparently. This elite apparently receives education through "intercourse with the greatest minds" which provides them "with experience in things beautiful" (13). It is hard to imagine the curriculum of such wispy generalities. But nonetheless, these are the people who will rule over the rest, the common

apathetic "citizens who read nothing but the sports page and the comic section" (11). If Strauss were correct, why would anyone bother with a liberal-arts education at all? People would prefer to go home and read the comics.

4   But are today's citizens really so delusional or apathetic that they do not know what a democracy is? Common sense dictates that people elect their mortal leaders, not idealized phantoms, in a democracy, but that does not relegate everyone else to the status of lazy illiterates. People know that they can contribute to their democracy. They do so by becoming educated so that they may make informed choices.

5   And what form of education best helps people to become informed citizens? An education consisting of the study of literature, languages, philosophy, history, visual arts, mathematics, and science: a liberal-arts education. The study of these subjects teaches practical life-skills such as careful reading and critical thinking. Contrary to the belief that a liberal education consists of reading musty old pages and parroting them back in essays, the purpose of such an education is educated independent thought, not blind adherence to, or imitation of, the ideas of others. Tradition is not something to worship, but something to question, based on study and reflection. Informed independent thought then characterizes discussions between "ordinary people" during their education, as they refine other vital skills such as effective communication and careful listening. Moreover, discussions of ordinary people with other ordinary people about contemporary issues are thus enriched by a liberal education, which, in this case, fosters interdependency and community, not elitism.

6   If acquiring these skills along with knowledge of the thoughts and actions of past societies is a desirable necessity for ordinary people in a democracy, then Strauss' idea of an elite, liberally educated minority of rulers sounds very anti-democratic indeed. "Liberal," by definition, is unrestricted, generous, radical, abundant, democratic, and progressive. It is not elitist. It does not blindly cling to the unexamined authority of tradition and things past. Instead it presents history and tradition as material to be examined, as maps of the past to be scrutinized for clues about the present. A liberal education serves the citizen of a democratic society; it is a companion on life's journey. Through the analysis of the progress of understanding through the ages, the ordinary person finds a much clearer view of the methods by which society has arrived at its present state.

7   Happily, whether or not ordinary people strive to become rulers, they may all benefit from a liberal education, should they choose to acquire one or not. Not because it will allow them to become an elite group, nor because it allows them to experience "things beautiful." Liberal-arts educations are of benefit because they allow people the freedom to make informed choices. Such study trains people in critical thinking and gives them the tools necessary to allow them to live life to the fullest, to examine everything, the beautiful and the ugly, and, most importantly, to *decide for themselves* which is which.

Student Zombies

1   Schools divide people up into categories. From first grade on up, educators label students "advanced" or "challenged" or "remedial" or

"antisocial." Students pigeonhole their fellow students, too; there's the "brain," the "jock," the "dummy," and the "keener." In most cases, these narrow labels are misleading and inaccurate. But there is one label for a certain type of student that is actually accurate in a frightening way—the "zombie."

2   Zombies are the living dead. Most people haven't known a lot of real zombies personally, but they do know how zombies act. Horror movies offer guidance in this respect. The special effects in horror movies are much better these days. Over the years, movies have shown that zombies clump around graveyards and plod relentlessly down streets, their eyes glued open by makeup artists, in slow-motion pursuit of dinner: the living. Zombie students do just about the same thing. They shuffle around campus, eyes glazed, staring off into space. When they do manage to wander into a classroom, they sit down mechanically and contemplate the ceiling. Zombie students rarely eat, dance, talk, laugh, or toss Frisbees in quadrangles and on lawns. Instead, they vanish when class is dismissed and return only when some mysterious zombie-signal summons them back into a classroom. The signal may not occur for weeks at a time.

3   Zombies are controlled by some mysterious force. According to legend, zombies are corpses that have been brought back to life to do the bidding of some voodoo master. Student zombies, too, seem directed by a strange power. They continue to attend school although they have no apparent desire to do so. They show no interest in course-related issues such as tests, marks, papers, and projects. Yet, some inner force compels them to wander through the halls of higher education.

4   An awful fate awaits all zombies unless something happens to break the spell they have fallen under. In the movies, zombies are often shot, stabbed, drowned, or electrocuted, all to no avail. Finally, the hero or heroine realizes that a counterspell is needed. Once that spell is cast, with the appropriate props of chicken feet, human hair, and bats' eyeballs, the zombie-corpse can return peacefully to its coffin. The only hope for a student zombie to change is for him or her to undergo a similarly traumatic experience. Sometimes the evil spell can be broken by a grade transcript decorated with large red "Fs." At other times, a professor will succeed through a private, intensive exorcism session. In other cases, though, zombies blunder around for years until they are gently persuaded by college or university administration to head for another institution. Then, they enrol someplace else or get a job in the family business.

5   Every student knows that it's not necessary to see *Shaun of the Dead, Pontypool, Zombieland,* or *Twenty-Eight Days* to see zombies in action—or non-action. Forget the campus film series. Just sit in a classroom and wait. Student radar will let you know who you're looking for—those who walk by day; those who stroll in without books or papers of any kind; those who look at no one; and those who sit in the very last row of seats. The ones with MP3 players plugged into their ears don't count as zombies; that's a whole different category of "student." So listen up, *Day of the Living Dead* is showing every day in a classroom near you.

■ Questions

About Unity

1. Which paragraph in "Ladder to the Gods" has a topic sentence buried within the paragraph rather than at the paragraph's beginning?

2. Which sentence in paragraph 2 of "Student Zombies" should be omitted in the interests of paragraph unity?

3. Which sentence in the final paragraph of "Student Zombies" introduces a new topic and should be eliminated?

About Support

4. Which essay develops its definitions through a series of comparisons?

5. Which sentence in paragraph 4 of "Ladder to the Gods" should be followed by supporting details?

6. In which paragraph of "Ladder to the Gods" does the author use the contrast pattern to develop her support?

About Coherence

7. Identify the transitional words and phrases used to open body paragraphs in "Ladder to the Gods." Give reasons why each is used to advance support for the essay's thesis.

8. How many paragraphs in "Student Zombies" open with transitional connectors? Rewrite the opening sentences for the paragraphs with appropriate transitional material.

9. Which sentence in paragraph 2 of "Student Zombies" begins with a change-of-direction transitional word?

About Introductions and Conclusions

10. Which method of introduction is used in the opening paragraph of "Student Zombies"?
    a. Anecdote
    b. Opposite
    c. Quotation
    d. Broad, general statement narrowing to a thesis
    e. Questions

11. Identify the method and approach of the conclusion of "Ladder to the Gods."

About the Method of Development

12. Which other methods of development do you find in "Ladder to the Gods"? Where do you find description in "Student Zombies"?

13. In how many paragraphs does the author of "Ladder to the Gods" define and work with the idea of *democracy*? Trace the meaning of the word as it appears in her essay.

DEVELOPING A DEFINITION ESSAY

Writing a Thesis Statement for a Definition Essay

The thesis statement for a definition essay identifies the subject (term being defined) and provides a brief, general statement of the writer's understanding of that term's meaning. Effective thesis statements, depending on the subject, (1) place a term within a larger category of like things, *or* (2) specify a term's meaning by stating what it is and what it is not, *or* (3) explain the origin of the term.

An example of a definition thesis statement that places its subject (or term) within a larger category of like things follows:

- Anger is an intense emotion.

An example of a definition thesis statement that states what the subject is and what it is not:

- A good friend is honest and caring, never harsh or smothering.

An example of a definition thesis statement that explains the origin of the term/subject:

- Being consistently virtuous requires strength of character; in fact, the Latin root of the word "virtue," *virtus,* meant "strength."

Definition essay thesis statements may also suggest the writer's point of view by suggesting his or her reason for presenting a more detailed definition; i.e., ". . . baseball fans seem to define insanity because they are insanely loyal."

What Is Your Purpose and Who Is Your Audience?

The main purpose of a definition essay is to inform, in other words to explain your understanding of a term or concept. You might define a complex, abstract concept such as *heroism* by giving concrete examples of it, to help readers see what the term connotes to you. Or you might give a new twist to a familiar term such as *homemade* by presenting a series of narratives, anecdotes about homemade things and their qualities. As with many methods of development, your secondary purpose (or primary, perhaps, if you are like one of this chapter's student authors, Kelly) is to persuade your audience that your definition is a legitimate one. "Ladder to the Gods" demonstrates how essential it is to define key terms in academic papers and research papers. Extended definitions are frequently used for argumentation; a writer might define a concept such as *centre of excellence* to argue that some institution is not a centre of excellence. Alternatively, like the author of "Student Zombies," your main purpose could be to entertain readers with a humorous definition.

As always, consider your audience. If you are writing a highly personal definition of a concept like patriotism, an audience will expect a less formal essay. Additionally, an audience of politically minded people reading about patriotism might require different examples from an audience of peers. If you choose to write a slightly more formal definition essay—one that takes a serious tone and deals with a technical or more abstract topic—make sure that you supply enough background information so that a general reader can understand and follow your supporting details.

Essential to both audience and topic considerations is the issue of tone: the style of wording and sentence writing you use, whether formal or informal. In this chapter's student essay-samples are an example of a more formal style in "Ladder to the Gods" and a more informal style in "Student Zombies." In the latter essay, you see examples of informal usage such as the appearance of *you* in the final paragraph, the use of contractions (*it's, haven't*), the use of casual, folksy phrases (*from first grade on up, listen up*), and a higher quantity of shorter sentences than a formal essay might contain. Formal style does not mean stuffy or full of large, pompous words. In fact, it conveys respect for the reader by using clear standard vocabulary, sentences of suitable length, and, frequently, third-person pronoun point of view. It is the style you will use for academic and professional writing.

- Where do you find examples of good, clear formal style in "Ladder to the Gods"?
- In which chapter in Part 2 do you find another student essay that presents effective use of formal style?

What Is Your Point of View in Your Definition Essay?

Definition essays focus on making clear to readers as precisely as possible a writer's ideas about the meaning of some term, concept, or process. Therefore, at a post-secondary level, it is more appropriate for writers to place their emphasis on the topic being defined, on clarifying their ideas, rather than on their connection to the topic. Writing in the third-person point of view or voice is preferable. Although your definition or interpretation of something may derive to a degree from your own experiences, it is not necessary to assert your presence as *I* in your definition or support. Readers will be aware that your definition essay presents your view; they do not need to be reminded of, or distracted by, your first-person presence. Highly personal and effective informal first-person definition essays may inform and amuse readers, but they tend to tell readers more about the writer than about the topic they define.

As preparation for other academic and career writing tasks that clarify the meanings of technical or abstract terms, writing in the third-person, less intrusive voice is more effective.

How Will You Support Your Definition Essay?

When you write an extended definition, you have a number of techniques available to you, such as differentiation, determining boundaries, use of synonyms, and exploring connotations or shades of meanings. This broad menu allows you to select a way of managing the meanings of your topic that will suit your purpose and audience.

Dictionary definitions are useful, though not ideal as opening sentences, because they often display two techniques you may wish to incorporate in writing your own definition. A dictionary definition will usually show a word in its category, or larger group of similar things, then indicate how it differs from those similar items in its category. For instance, democracy will be placed within the category or class of political systems. It can then be differentiated from other such systems by its characteristics: for example, unlike a monarchy, it is either enacted by the people who vote for it themselves, or by a representative they elect—it is not governed by a hereditary ruler determined by bloodline. Differentiating means saying what something is not so as to clarify what it is; i.e., a food sensitivity is not a true food allergy.

You may, as Kelly, the author of "Ladder to the Gods," has done, create a definition by setting out for readers a specific meaning for some term. Set your own boundaries around what that term or concept will mean for your essay; this is sometimes called a stipulative definition because it sets out meanings on which the content of a paper will depend.

Or, you may work through a variety of synonyms (words that mean the same) for your topic. When you do so, you are imitating a typical conversational or teaching pattern: the speaker uses a new word, then gives a number of synonyms so that listeners can home in on words familiar to them. Listeners then connect those to the previously unknown word. For instance, a professor might use a somewhat unfamiliar word like *mendacity*, then offer a list of such words as *deceit, dishonesty, fraudulence,* and *untruthfulness* so that students will connect one or more of those words to the new term.

Keep in mind also that there are very few perfect, exact, unchanging meanings for words. Words mean different things to different people. The literal, basic meaning of a word is called its denotative meaning. A dog, for example, has the denotative meaning "domestic canine." A canine is the class of animal; domestic differentiates dogs from wolves or coyotes. But dog, like many words, has a range of other meanings: these are connotative meanings, which are associated with the term dog. The word dog tends to have some negative connotations, actually: for example, a man who cheats, or ugly, or aggressive. Denotative meanings are objective, emotionally neutral meanings agreed on by most people, whereas connotative meanings are rarely, if ever, neutral—they convey the emotion, background, and attitude of the speaker or writer. Your definition essays will often explore what a word connotes to you; if you were to write about "patriotism," you might begin by presenting your definition of the word, using some of the techniques above.

Definition essays generally make good use of other patterns of development in their body paragraphs. In your essay, you might use examples as support: patriotism means wearing a red maple-leaf pin when you travel, putting out decorations on Canada Day, or supporting Canadian artists and companies. Frequently, depending on the term or concept you are working with, you will use vivid description to bring to life the meaning of a word. As well, you will use some elements of classification and division when you analyze your topic to separate it into component parts according to a common aspect. Or, like the author of "Ladder to the Gods," you might wish to use definition as the basis for an argumentation essay in which patriotism is about becoming politically active and developing intelligent views on Canada's national and international policies.

The key to successful definition, though, is specificity of supporting detail. As you have seen, definitions make ideas specific by setting boundaries around them, then attempting to be as precise as possible in capturing the essence of a term's meaning.

- Where in both student essays do you find particularly effective uses of specifics in the supporting details?

Prewriting

Kelly, the author of "Ladder to the Gods," is a General Arts student who began her degree after completing a Broadcast Journalism diploma. As her essay reveals, she feels very strongly about the practical and intellectual value of the liberal arts curriculum. She was given the opportunity to submit one end-of-semester essay that would fulfill the requirements of both her English and her Philosophy professors, and she decided to try using the definition pattern of development.

Her philosophy class was discussing Leo Strauss, a conservative American philosopher who believed that great thinkers wrote "deliberately . . . so that the average reader will understand it as saying one thing but the few for whom it is intended will grasp its real meaning" (Locke *Front Page*). His concept of the best knowledge being restricted to a special select group offended her so she decided to argue against some of his ideas.

Kelly liked freewriting, so she just started writing to see where her ideas took her. Here is her first go at freewriting:

> Strauss is all about his elite group of people who understand hidden meanings. Who are they? These are the people who apparently rise because they truly understand some kind of superior, mystical "liberal education," one we can't get at a regular university or college. Where do they get their degrees? Not only that, he takes every opportunity to beat up "modern democracy," where apparently we're all drooling and reading comics. Why even have a democracy if it's something that can't ever be achieved? Where do these mysterious phantom leaders come from? Are they elected? If so, we must live in some kind of acceptable democracy—we elect these superior people. Maybe they're all Scientologists . . . But supposedly they're controlling us because we're too lazy to care about anything. And Strauss says they just "arrive on top." This doesn't make sense. I wonder about their so-called liberal arts education. These apparently are the only people worthy of this education. I'm not sure where this is going. And when I look around me, and I remember people I interviewed when I was in journalism, they didn't seem that lazy or uninformed whenever there was an election. Most of them were really opinionated and interested in various issues—who is Strauss to say who's ignorant? For that matter, why shouldn't anyone get the education they want to have? How can people learn to think more clearly without some kind of education? Liberal arts does teach people to think—that's what it's about, after all.

Because her English professor emphasized that argumentative essays (see pages 236—252) could use a variety of patterns of development to assert their thesis, and because Kelly wanted to focus on the concepts of *democracy* and *liberal-arts education,* she decided to use definition as her primary method of development and blend it with other methods to mount her argument.

Looking over her prewriting and thinking about using the definition method of development, Kelly decided to develop ideas and details about her topic by diagramming her thoughts. She wanted to trace a path that she could follow through her essay.

"I thought I wanted to base my essay on three definitions, and I wanted to focus on a simple image to keep my line of thought clear, so I just drew a line of arrow-diagrams," Kelly said. "It helped me clarify the ideas that were all tied up in my prewriting."

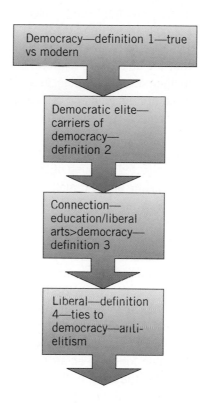

With her prewriting, diagramming, and a rough outline in hand, Kelly decided to work on a first draft.

First Draft and Revision

Here is her first draft:

1 In *What Is Liberal Education,* Leo Strauss says that "Liberal education is the ladder by which we try to ascend from mass democracy to democracy as originally meant." (get page number) Here immediately we see the idea of something finer or better that's been lost.

2   What does Strauss mean by "democracy" here? Well, he uses the term in two different ways: "mass democracy" and "democracy as originally meant." (put in source) Usually he means "mass democracy" is modern democracy and "original" democracy is "true democracy." ( ) Is this double-talk? True democracy is a society in which most people are wise, virtuous, and highly reasonable. And we can never attain this, according to Strauss. Contrast this with modern democracy, apparently not ruled by an educated elite. The majority creates their own governing elite with their apathy and lack of education. This elite group apparently all has liberal-arts education. And apparently they are all virtuous, too.

3   But who is so easily fooled, really? Does anyone not know what a democracy is? People elect leaders—they contribute to their choice of government. They do not vote mindlessly—they are informed by education, which helps them to critically understand media.

4   How do people to become informed citizens? They acquire whatever they are able to of literature, languages, philosophy, history, visual arts, mathematics, and science: a liberal-arts education. They learn life-skills such as careful reading and critical thinking. A liberal education isn't reading musty old pages and parroting them back in essays. It exists to encourage independent thought, not to get people to dumbly follow leaders or just copy ideas from the media. We learn about tradition to think about it and question it. Tradition is the collected thinking of the past (Do I need this definition?) and discussing it and writing about it makes people better communicators and better thinkers. These are also valuable life-skills. When people get together and discuss things, or get together to act for shared ideas, they become communities, communities of thoughtful people.

5   These thoughtful people, with whatever amount of liberal education, don't sound like Strauss' apathetic common people at all. In fact, his elite phantoms who have the finest education don't belong to a democracy at all. They sound selfish, not liberal. "Liberal," by definition, is unrestricted, generous, radical, abundant, democratic, and progressive. It is not elitist. Liberals do not worship the past blindly; they look for maps of the past to examine for clues about the present. By learning to analyze how progress was made in the past, ordinary people, on their own, can understand the societies they live in today.

- After reading this part of Kelly's first draft, compare it to the first two paragraphs of her finished essay on pages 211–212. Where does her thesis appear in her finished essay?
- How has she revised and developed her use of the contrast pattern of development in her final version?
- How has she used quotations to make her details more specific in her finished second paragraph?
- How does she reach her own definition of *democracy?* In which paragraph?
- How many definitions appear in the finished essay versus the first draft?
- What does she add to paragraph 3 in her finished essay? How does this information relate to the paragraphs that precede and follow it?

WRITING A DEFINITION ESSAY

■ Writing Assignment 1

Choose one of the terms below as the subject of a definition essay. Each term refers to a certain kind of person.

Intellectual	Optimist	Spiritualist
Fashionista	Pessimist	Sophisticate
Artist	Team player	Musician
Good neighbour	Nerd	Procrastinator
Busybody	Gourmet	Loner
Athlete	Workaholic	Environmentalist

Prewriting

1. As you work on your opening paragraph, you may want to refer to the dictionary definition of the term. Depending on your term and on your dictionary, you may find an "essential definition," or you may find a range of meanings. If you find several meanings, be sure to use only one. Try not to begin your essay with "According to *Oxford* . . ."

2. Remember that the thesis of a definition essay is actually a more polished version of "what _____ means to me." The thesis presents what *you* think the term actually means, without using the words "I" or "me."

3. As you plan your supporting paragraphs, think of the different parts or qualities of your term. Here is the three-part division of a student thesis and essay about baseball fans:

   They behave insanely, they are insane about trivia, and they are insanely loyal.

4. Support each part of your division with either a series of examples, a single extended example, an explanation, or a quotation. Such supporting details may also "limit" your description by saying what some quality or type of person is *not*.

Revising

Once you have completed the first draft of your essay, review it with these questions in mind:

- Does my thesis statement indicate how I define the term, and does it indicate my plan of development for the essay? Have I introduced my term with enough background to interest my reader?
- Does each of my supporting paragraphs have a clear topic?
- Have I supported each of my topic sentences with a suitable pattern of development for the supporting details?
- Have I rounded off my essay with an appropriate concluding paragraph?

Continue to revise your essay until you can answer "yes" to each question. Then, be sure to check the next-to-final draft for the sentence skills listed on the inside front cover.

■ Writing Assignment 2

In this essay, you will write with a **specific purpose** and for a **specific audience.**

You work in a doctor's office and have been asked to write a brochure that will be placed in the patients' waiting room. The brochure is intended to tell patients what a healthy lifestyle is. Write a definition of a *healthy lifestyle* for your readers, using examples wherever appropriate. Your definition might focus on both mental and physical health and might include eating, sleeping, exercise, and recreational habits.

Alternatively, you might decide to take a playful point of view and write a brochure defining an *unhealthy lifestyle.*

■ Writing Assignment 3

Read the selection titled "Shame" on pages 451–454. Then, write an essay in which you define a term, as Dick Gregory does in "Shame," by using the narration method of development. You can use one of the terms listed in Writing Assignment 1 or think of one of your own. In your introduction, fill in a brief background for your readers—when and where the experience happened. Your thesis should express the idea that because of this experience, you (or the person or people you are writing about) learned the meaning of the word _____ (fill in the term you have chosen). Break the narrative at logical points to create a minimum of three supporting paragraphs. You might first want to look at the examples of narrative essays given on pages 124–127.

CHECKLIST OF LEARNING OUTCOMES FOR CHAPTER 14

To ensure that you have understood and met the learning outcomes for this chapter, answer the following questions upon completing any of its writing assignments:

✓ Does your thesis and/or introductory paragraph locate your subject within its class and state how it is unique?

✓ Does the opening paragraph set the tone and degree of subjectivity or objectivity with which you defined your subject?

✓ Does each supporting point clearly expand on and illustrate your subject, and is the type of support chosen appropriate to your subject?

✓ Does the final paragraph summarize all meanings presented and suggest the significance of your particular definition?

Online LearningCentre

Division and Classification

LEARNING OUTCOMES

After reading this chapter and working through its writing assignments, you will be ready to write a division and classification essay that

- divides its subject into categories according to a logical classifying principle;

- states in its thesis the subject, classifying principle, and category divisions;

- arranges its categories in an order that best supports its thesis statement;

- includes several specific supporting details to explain each category-division or main supporting point;

- presents a concluding paragraph that returns to the subject as a whole and offers final thoughts on your essay's subject categories.

You divide and classify every day. You *divide* when you analyze a novel by breaking it down into parts such as theme, plot, character, and setting; you divide when you break down an event into stages for the purpose of understanding it. When you divide, you move from a large whole concept to a set of limited, concrete categories, as you will see on the following page in "National Treasures." You *classify* when you sort out everything from a pile of socks to a desktop full of documents by placing them into groups of like items, whether those "classification groups" are black ankle socks or document files. When you classify, you move in the opposite direction: you group ideas or objects into progressively more general or even abstract categories. An example of this is the "identity tree": *Kenyo Smythe, 17 Passmore Drive, Abbotsford, British Columbia, Canada, North America, Western Hemisphere, Earth, Solar System.*

Division and classification essays require you to choose a classifying principle that suits your audience and your purpose. For example, writing about contemporary music for fellow students might involve the classifying principle of *tastes* in music and the categories of *R&B, New Folk,* and *Rap.* Writing about new software for a computer animation course would require you to find a classifying principle and categories within the software relevant to that course's content.

Division and classification is an essay-development strategy you will use as both a primary and secondary pattern of development. You may have already used it to set up your definition essay, or you may have divided a seemingly single effect into a set of repercussions in an effects essay.

Division and classification activities will be part of your academic and career writing. Marketing students and professionals sort consumers into groups or categories to facilitate product development and sales decisions. Accounting students may have to sort out different procedures and programs suitable for businesses of various sizes. Your textbooks divide concepts into chapters and headings, and in many subject-areas you must divide a topic into manageable or appropriate categories for writing assignments.

In this chapter, you will be asked to write an essay in which you divide or classify a subject according to a single principle. To prepare for this task, first read the student essays that follow, and then work through the questions that accompany the essays.

STUDENT ESSAYS TO CONSIDER

National Treasures

1   A tourist's-eye view of Canada would include snowy ski hills, sparkling mountain lakes, granite-grey rock shields, night-time city-views, and, of course, evergreen forests. Picturesque as those piney woods might be, they present a misleadingly simple image of the country's vast and varied forestation. Canada is nearly half forest, and home to highly diverse climatic, soil, and water conditions. Because of this diversity, Canada's landscape actually hosts seven different forest regions and numerous sub-regions: fifteen ecozones, each supporting characteristic tree species and forest types. In fact, one of the country's greatest resources and ecological treasures is 417 million hectares of highly diversified forest *(Natural Resources Canada).*

2   Perhaps the picture of Canada as windswept rocky ground and deep evergreen woods has its roots in the vast belt of Boreal forest that stretches from Newfoundland and Labrador west to the Rockies. The forest, appropriately, derives its name from Boreas, ancient Greek god of the north wind and of winter, and Boreal forest defines the very idea of northern woods. Beginning with the northern Taiga woods, it consists mainly of hardy conifers, pines, firs, and spruce that will endure baking hot summers and long, harsh winters. The evergreen darkness, though, is sparked with luminous white birch and the delicate trembling aspen. The forests here are measureless and many have not been surveyed. And closer to the southern prairie borders of the north wind's

woods in Alberta, Saskatchewan, and Manitoba, the warmer climate nurtures soft green willows, alders, and tall grasses. These are trees pushed into service by farmers; they grow along the edges of fields and keep the wind from tearing away the soil they share with crops. And here the Boreal balance is starting to shift away from the dominance of pine, spruce, cedar, and fir.

3   Moving east and south from those prairie woodlots, skirting south of Lake Superior, and finally descending into lower Ontario and Quebec, then all the way to the Maritimes, Boreas' southern boundaries merge with different forest-blends. Here, along the edge of the northern shield, the Boreal balance shifts from the dominance of pine, spruce, cedar, and fir to deciduous varieties that thrive in a more moderate climate. The Great Lakes/St. Lawrence woods are a fairly balanced coniferous-deciduous mix, woods scented with eastern white cedar on hot days, and ablaze with red and gold maples in the fall. Hundred-year oaks live side by side with aspens, birch, ash, and poplar, and forest floors are carpeted with ferns and lichen. In some areas at least, hundreds of years of settlement, agriculture, and industry have altered the growth patterns, and suppressed some varieties ("Mixedwood Plains"). However, for the moment, until cottagers and property developers bulldoze them down, these woods are eastern Canada's treasures, hosting a rich animal and plant ecosystem. The vast Acadian forests of the Maritimes are less damaged at this point; in many areas they continue the Great Lakes-St. Lawrence growth with eastern white pine, red pine, yellow birch, and eastern hemlock. But nearer the Atlantic, they are purely Acadian, covered in thriving red spruce, sugar maple, beech, and yellow birch ("Atlantic Maritime").

4   Not so far east as the Maritimes, but farther south again, the Lake Erie and Lake Ontario shores have yet another treasure-house all their own: the warm-weather Carolinian forest. The climate here is benign enough to foster scented and flowering trees that are more associated with the American mid-south; in fact, geographically, Point Pelee in Lake Erie is farther south than northern California. This forest ignores national borders and treats southern Ontario to a unique mix of deciduous trees with only eastern white pine, tamarack, and red cedar as representative evergreens. Although beech trees and sugar maples dominate wooded areas, there is a group of trees and plants that are found only here in Canada. They include magnolia or tulip trees, cucumber trees, pawpaw, red mulberry, Kentucky coffee trees, sassafras, and black oak; forty percent of Ontario's rare plants grow only in this Carolinian forest ("Carolinian Forest Plants"). Unfortunately, this is also "one of Canada's most threatened habitats" *(Trees of the Carolinian Forest 27)*. Over ninety percent of the original forest has given way to two hundred years of farming, industry, and settlement.

5   Way, way west, on another Boreal border beginning in the Alberta foothills, the Subalpine forest begins, which, in turn, at greater altitudes, gives way to Montane growth. Subalpine is coniferous forest mainly, with slopes showing white spruce, black spruce, alpine fir, lodgepole pine, but also aspen, poplar, and white birch. As wooded areas grow near the treelines, tree-growth gives way to deciduous shrubs like scrub birch and conifers like spruce and fir that

can survive by clinging to the mountainsides of Alberta and interior B.C. The Montane woods at mid-levels in British Columbia are home to industrially valuable trees such as Ponderosa pine and Douglas fir, and here, logging and pulp-and-paper production are jeopardizing Canada's western forest cover and disturbing soil balances. Second-growth planting and planned harvesting may yet redress some of the losses of mountain and valley woods.

6   And finally, where the coastal forests line the Pacific, there is hope. The Montane tree patterns fall away near the ocean to become the deep-green forests of Pacific Maritime growth, the silent, shadowy spruce and pine of Emily Carr's paintings. Here, where totem poles stood, these forest-sentinels guarded their people from the rough sea winds. Here, the climate is moderated and the woods are dense; it is a model for other parts of Canada, a place where harvesting is controlled, and the elders are respected. "This ecozone has the most productive forests and the biggest and oldest trees of Canada" ("Pacific Maritime").

7   From the Taiga and tundra scrub of the north, to Pacific firs, across five time zones to southern sassafras and New Brunswick spruce and sugar maple, Canada has been blessed with a renewable resource, a national treasure. With the threat of global pollution and a thinning ozone layer, surely this rich and diverse blanket of green growth that protects humans, animals, and the soil it grows in ought to be itself protected.

Mall People

1   Just what goes into "having fun"? For many people, "fun" involves getting out of the house, seeing other people, having something interesting to look at, and enjoying a choice of activities, all at a reasonable price. Going out to dinner or to the movies may satisfy some of those desires, but often not all. An attractive alternative does exist in the form of the free-admission shopping mall. Teenagers, couples on dates, and the nuclear family can all be observed having a good time at the mall.

2   Teenagers are drawn to the malls to pass time with pals and be seen by other teens. The guys saunter by in ball caps, T-shirts, and baggy jeans, with headsets on at all times. The girls stumble along in high-heeled shoes and tank tops, with cell phones tucked in the pockets of their track pants or lowrise jeans. Travelling in a gang that resembles a wolf pack, the teenagers make the shopping mall their hunting ground. Mall managers have obviously made a decision to attract all the teenage activity. Their raised voices, loud laughter, and occasional shouted obscenities can be heard from as far as half a mall away. They come to "pick up chicks," to "meet guys," and just to "hang out."

3   Couples find fun of another sort at shopping malls. The young lovers are easy to spot because they walk hand in hand, stopping to sneak a quick kiss after every few steps. They pause at jewellery store windows so they can gaze at diamond engagement rings and gold wedding bands. Then, they wander into lifestyle stores like Crate and Barrel or furniture departments in the large mall stores. Finally, they drift away, their arms wrapped around each other's waists.

4   Mom, Dad, little Jenny, and Fred, Jr., visit the mall on Friday and Saturday evenings for inexpensive recreation. Hearing the music of the antique carousel

housed there, Jenny begs to ride her favourite pony, with its shining golden mane. Shouting, "I'm starving!" Fred, Jr., drags the family towards the food court, where he detects the seductive odour of pizza. Mom walks through a fabric store, running her hand over the soft velvet and slippery silk materials she finds. Meanwhile, Dad has wandered into an electronics store and is admiring the flat-screen TV he'd love to buy someday. The mall provides something special for every member of the family.

5   Sure, some people visit the mall in a brief, businesslike way, just to pick up a specific purchase or two. But many more are shopping for inexpensive recreation. The teenagers, the dating couples, and the nuclear families all find cheap entertainment at the mall.

■   Questions

About Unity

1. In what way do the topic sentences of "National Treasures" resemble those of an objective descriptive essay?

2. Which sentence in paragraph 2 of "Mall People" should be omitted in the interests of paragraph unity?

3. Which sentence in paragraph 2 of "National Treasures" should be omitted in the interests of paragraph unity?

About Support

4. After which sentence in paragraph 3 of "Mall People" are more supporting details needed?

5. After which sentence in paragraph 4 of "National Treasures" are more supporting details needed?

6. "Mall People" develops its support with expressive description. Label as *sight, touch, hearing,* or *smell* all the sensory details in the following sentences:
   a. "Hearing the music of the antique carousel housed there, Jenny begs to ride her favourite pony, with its shining golden mane."
   b. "Shouting, 'I'm starving!' Fred, Jr., drags the family towards the food court, where he detects the seductive odour of pizza."
   c. "Mom walks through a fabric store, running her hand over the soft velvet and slippery silk materials she finds."

About Coherence

7. What are the time transition words used in the second supporting paragraph of "Mall People"?

8. Which topic sentence in "National Treasures" functions as a linking sentence between paragraphs?

9. How does the author of "National Treasures" take the reader across Canada?

About Introductions and Conclusions

10. Identify the method and approach used in the introduction to "National Treasures."

11. What conclusion technique is used in "Mall People"?
    a. Summary
    b. Prediction or recommendation
    c. Question

About the Method of Development

12. What is the classifying principle in "National Treasures"? What are the categories that follow from it?

13. "National Treasures" makes good use of description as a secondary method. Where do you find effective descriptive words and phrases? Why do you find these effective in the context of the essay?

DEVELOPING A DIVISION AND CLASSIFICATION ESSAY

Writing a Thesis Statement for a Division and Classification Essay

The division and classification essay is built upon the classifying principle you choose and the particular divisions or categories you present for your topic. Your thesis statement should, then, present (1) your topic, (2) your classifying principle (or purpose for dividing the topic), and (3) your categories, if appropriate. The "trick" with division-and-classification thesis statements is that with this method of development, the classifying principle and categories you apply to your topic actually represent your viewpoint. This type of thesis statement is another variation of the "topic + viewpoint" formula.

An example of a division and classification thesis statement following this formula:

(1)

(3)   (2)

There are many different brands and models of cell phones, but, based on users' preferences, they all fall into three categories: the functional, the decorative, and the fully loaded.

Here, the writer's viewpoint is expressed by the phrase "users' preferences." She indicates that personal preference is a meaningful and potentially interesting classifying principle for cell phones.

Here is another example that follows the formula:

Not many lighthouses on the Great Lakes are still functional; however, several on the Lake Erie shore, such as the Port Abino lighthouse, are of historical value.

- What is the topic of this thesis statement?
- What is the writer's viewpoint?
- How is his or her viewpoint expressed?

Review the two student essays that appear at the beginning of this chapter.

- What is the thesis of "National Treasures"? What is its classifying principle? How does this principle express the author's viewpoint?
- What is the thesis of "Mall People"? What is its classifying principle? What are the categories that the author has chosen?

What Is Your Purpose and Who Is Your Audience?

In general, you write a division and classification essay to inform your readers of some idea connected to your choice of classifying principle and/or classes. Your secondary or specific purposes related to informing may range over quite a broad spectrum, from serious to comic.

If, like Matt, the author of "National Treasures," you wish to persuade readers by informing, then division and classification may be a good choice of pattern of development. Matt is a forestry student who has studied Canadian ecozones and forest types, so he wishes not only to explain to readers what the main forest zones are, but to indicate where such forests are endangered. He wants his readers to understand the value, diversity, and richness of Canadian woodlands. Thinking of his main audiences as his English professor and his peers, he knew he had a couple of tasks at least: to find a workable way to lead readers across the country's geography, and to explain terms that could be unknown to his readers. For his organizational principle, he remembered the method he had used in writing objective descriptions in English, biology, and chemistry classes—choose a clear starting point and trace a directional path in each paragraph.

- Where do you find examples of definition in "National Treasures"?

Matt thus had two of the ingredients of a successful division and classification essay: a topic that lends itself to being divided and classified, and an appropriate scheme or principle of classification that is relevant and interesting to a potential audience.

- What is Matt's topic and how does he divide it?
- Why is it potentially interesting—or not—to audiences?

Once you have selected your topic and figured out how to divide it, or how to organize its parts into a whole of some kind, you need to provide specific details so that your audience fully understands the categories you have selected. For the example, if you chose to write about clothes and your purposes were informing and entertaining your audiences, you might begin with a classifying principle of fashion. You could then work with four classifications: clothes that are stylish, clothes that have classic style, clothes that are going out of style, and clothes that are so unattractive that they were never in style. You might classify skateboarding shorts as part of the "going out of style" category, while preppy pinstriped shirts might belong in the "clothes that are stylish" group, navy-blue blazers in the classic style group, and Metallica T-shirts in the "never stylish" group. For this essay, these classifications could work for a peer audience in a college or university. But an audience of fashion-conscious young people would probably have very different opinions about what is and is not stylish, as would an audience of investment bankers. For that matter, an audience of style-obsessed, label-conscious "downtown people" would have much more interest in clothing and accessory styles than an audience of academic instructors.

What Is Your Point of View in Your Division and Classification Essay?

As a method of essay development, division and classification is based on analysis, or breaking up a topic or concept into components or categories. The main focus of these essays for readers is the way they present valid and interesting divisions of a topic. Analytical writing, and essay writing in general, is expected to be about more than just the writer's personal opinion or experience. To quote David Rayside's article, "Essay Writing: A Personal View," ". . . most essays are about some phenomenon that you are expected to reflect upon with ideas and evidence and logic that are not just about you."

The division and classification essay in college or university is the product of rigorous thought, and is an essay type where structure and quality of ideas predominate. Therefore, the less intrusive third-person point of view is ideal.

How Will You Support Your Division and Classification Essay?

One important fact about support for division and classification essays is that simply supplying examples does not constitute classifying. When you classify, you first decide on your categories, then provide supporting details.

- What are the classifications in "National Treasures"?
- Choose three categories of forests and list the examples and details that support these classes.

Description is essential to effective support in division and classification essays. At the very least, you must describe the characteristics that members of your classifications possess. To give your essay flavour and accuracy as well as appeal to readers, you will want to use sharp, skillful descriptions.

- Where are two instances of effective description in "Mall People"?

Moreover, definition, process, and cause or effect analysis can all play effective parts in an essay whose primary mode is division and classification. You could use process to outline the steps by which something came to be included in one of your classifications; you could even include an anecdote to illustrate one of your classifications.

- Where in "National Treasures" is definition used, and why?
- Where is effects analysis used in this essay?

Prewriting

Julia liked malls and liked to look at people; she thought her observations about "people at malls" would make a good topic for a division and classification essay.

However, she did not immediately know how she wanted to group those people or what she wanted to say about them, so she began her prewriting by listing her observations about mall shoppers. Here is what she came up with:

- Families with kids
- Lots of snacking
- Crowds around special displays—automobiles, kiddie rides
- Older people walking mall for exercise
- Groups of teenagers
- Women getting made up at makeup counter
- Dating couples
- Blind woman with guide dog
- Lots of people talking and laughing rather than shopping
- Interviewers stopping shoppers to fill out questionnaires
- Kids hanging out, meeting each other

As Julia reviewed her list, she concluded that the three largest groups of "mall people" were families with children, groups of teens, and dating couples. She decided to organize her essay around those three groups and created a trial outline that her essay would follow. Here is Julia's outline:

Thesis: The shopping mall offers inexpensive fun for several groups.

1. Teens
   a. Roam in packs
   b. Dress alike
   c. Meet new people

2. Dating couples
   a. Act romantic
   b. Window shop for future home
   c. Have lovers' quarrels

3. Families
   a. Kids' activities
   b. Cheap food
   c. Adults shop

First Draft and Revision

Julia's list-making and outlining prepared her for writing the first draft of her essay:

1   Malls aren't only places to go shopping. They also offer free or at least cheap fun and activities for lots of people. Teenagers, dating couples, and families all like to visit the mall.

2   Teenagers love to roam the mall in packs, like wolves. They often dress alike, depending on the latest fashion. They're noisy and sometimes rude, and mall

security sometimes kicks them out of the building. Then, they find somewhere else to go, maybe one of the warehouse-sized amusement and video-game arcades that are springing up everywhere. Those places are fun, but they tend to be more expensive than just "hanging out" at the mall. Teens are usually not as interested in shopping at the mall as they are in picking up members of the opposite sex and seeing their friends.

3   Dating couples also enjoy wandering around the mall. They are easy to spot because they walk along holding hands and sometimes kissing. They stare at diamond rings and wedding bands and shop for furniture together. Sometimes, they have spats, and one of them stamps off to sulk on a bench for a while.

4   Little kids and their parents make up a big group of mall-goers. There is something for every member of the family there. There are usually some special displays that interest the kids, and Mom and Dad can always find things they like to window shop for. Another plus for the family is that there is inexpensive food, like burgers and pizza, available at the mall's food court.

After completing her first draft, Julia put it aside. From previous experience, she knew that she was a better critic of her own writing after taking a break from it. Reading over her first draft the next morning, she noticed several places where it could be improved. Here are the observations she made in her writing journal:

- My first paragraph does present a thesis that gives my viewpoint and a reason why I'd divide up people at malls (malls offer inexpensive entertainment), and it tells how I'm going to develop that thesis (by discussing three groups of people). But it isn't very interesting. I think I could do a better job of drawing readers in by describing what is fun about malls.
- Some of the details in the essay aren't necessary; they don't support my main idea. For instance, the points about teens being kicked out of the mall and about dating couples having fights don't have anything to do with the entertainment malls provide. I'll eliminate them.
- Some of my statements that do support the main idea need more support. For example, when I say there are "special displays that interest the kids" in paragraph 4, I should give an example of such a display. I should also back up the idea that many teens dress alike.

With those observations in mind, Julia returned to her essay and revised it, producing the version that appears on page 226.

WRITING A DIVISION AND CLASSIFICATION ESSAY

■ Writing Assignment 1

What follows are an introduction and a thesis statement for a classification essay on academic stress. Using a separate piece of paper, plan and write the supporting paragraphs and a conclusion for the essay.

Post-Secondary Stress

Jack's heart pounds as he casts panicked looks around the classroom. He doesn't recognize the professor, he doesn't know any of the students, and he can't even figure out what the subject is. In front of him is a test. At the last minute, his roommate awakens him. It is only another anxiety dream. The very fact that dreams like Jack's are common suggests that college and university are stressful situations for young people. The causes of this stress can be academic, financial, social, and personal.

Prewriting

1. Freewrite for five minutes apiece on (1) *academic,* (2) *financial,* (3) *social,* and (4) *personal* problems of college and university students.

2. Then, add to the material you have written by asking yourself these questions:
    - What are some examples of academic problems that are stressful for students?
    - What are some examples of financial problems that students must contend with?
    - What are some examples of social problems that students must face?
    - What are some examples of personal problems that create stress in students?

    Write down quickly whatever answers occur to you. As with freewriting, do not worry at this stage about writing correct sentences. Instead, concentrate on getting down as much information as you can think of that supports each of the four supporting points for the thesis.

3. Go through all the material you have accumulated. Perhaps some of the details you have written down may help you think of even better details that would fit. If so, write down these additional details. Then make decisions about the exact information that you will use in each supporting paragraph. Number the details according to the order in which you will present them.

4. Write out the first draft of your essay.

Revising

After you have completed the first draft of the essay (and, ideally, set it aside for a while), you should prepare yourself to rewrite it by asking the following questions:

- Have I included relevant examples for each of the four divisions?
- Have I provided enough details to support each of the four divisions?
- Have I used transition words and sentences to help readers follow my train of thought?
- Does the concluding paragraph round off the essay by returning to the overall subject?

Continue to revise your essay until you can answer "yes" to each question. Then, be sure to check the next-to-final draft for the sentence skills listed on the inside front cover.

■ Writing Assignment 2

In this division and classification essay, you will write with a specific purpose and for a specific audience.

Unsure about your career direction, you have gone to a vocational counselling service. To help you select the type of work for which you are best suited, a counsellor has asked you to write a detailed description of your "ideal job." You will present this description to three other people who are also seeking to make a career choice.

To describe your ideal job, divide "work life" into three or more elements, using one of the following principles of classification:

- Activities done on the job
- Skills used on the job
- Physical environment
- People you work with and under
- Effects of the job on society

In your essay, explain your ideals for each element. If needed, you may have more than three supporting paragraphs. Use specific details and examples where possible to illustrate your points.

■ Writing Assignment 3

Read the selection "Aboriginal Hot and Heavy" by Drew Hayden Taylor on pages 502–503. Hayden Taylor divides and classifies personal grooming along cultural, specifically Aboriginal, principles. Now, writing in the third-person viewpoint, divide and classify an ordinary activity according to some appropriate, interesting, or funny principle. The activity could be one of the following:

- Texting
- Dating
- Studying

Think of a principle of classification for dividing the activity you choose. If you were considering dating, you could imagine several principles of classification such as

- Places where people might look for a date
- Attributes a potential date must possess
- Reasons for refusing a second date

Once you have an appropriate principle of classification, you will find it easy to divide your subject into three groups or divisions.

CHECKLIST OF LEARNING OUTCOMES FOR CHAPTER 15

To ensure that you have understood and met the learning outcomes for this chapter, answer the following questions upon completing any of its writing assignments:

✓ Do the divisions in your essay's subject follow a consistent principle of classification? Is this principle logically related to your purpose in writing about your subject? Does your dividing principle lead to interesting new thoughts about your subject?

✓ Does your thesis statement mention your subject, your principle of classification, and, if appropriate, your categories or classifications?

✓ Do your category/classification paragraphs appear in an order that best supports your thesis?

✓ Is the number of supporting details for each category roughly balanced, and are all details adequately explained?

✓ Does your conclusion remind readers of your thesis and propose final thoughts about the subject's main divisions?

PART 2
PATTERNS OF ESSAY DEVELOPMENT

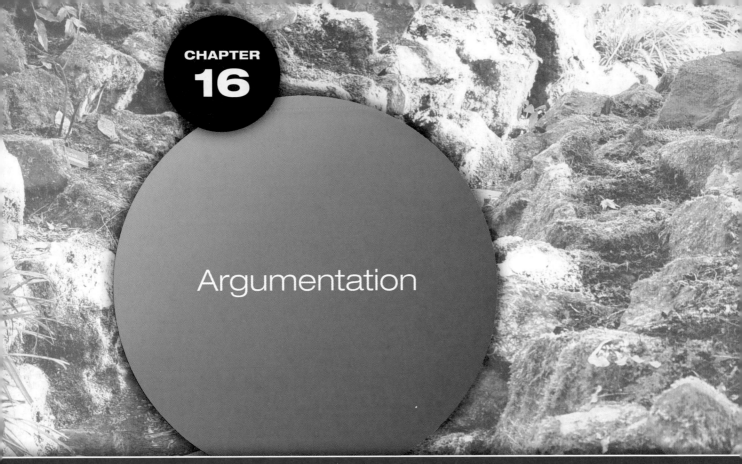

Argumentation

LEARNING OUTCOMES

After reading this chapter and working through its writing assignments, you will be ready to write an argumentation essay that

- begins with a thesis that states a definite point to be argued;

- acknowledges and counters any opposing viewpoints;

- presents, in its supporting points and details, both solid logic and knowledge of the specifics of the subject;

- argues its thesis point objectively and courteously;

- concludes by reinforcing the main argument.

You, and nearly everyone else, possess a natural tendency to question any point of view or opinion: this is the basis for **argumentation** as a method of development. No two minds perceive a person or situation in exactly the same way, so readers nearly always suspend agreement until they are satisfied with the "reasons why."

If you say that student health care available on your campus is inadequate, your listening audience might listen carefully as you state your case, judging whether or not you have solid evidence to support your point. You know that saying, "Well, it's closed half the time, and it just isn't any good" sounds weak and unconvincing, so you try to come up with stronger evidence to back up your statement. Your questioner, unless he or she is a friend, may make you feel uncomfortable, but you may also feel grateful to him or her for helping you to clarify your opinion.

Arguing a point in an essay requires you to do three things: (1) search for logical answers as to why you hold an opinion, (2) examine and weigh the usefulness of the emotions associated with your opinion, and (3) present clear and credible information to support the viewpoint you are arguing. The ability to present sound and compelling arguments is an important skill in everyday life. You can use argumentation to make a point in a discussion, write a proposal for a grant or bursary, or ask an employer for a raise. Becoming skilled in clear, logical reasoning can also help you see through faulty arguments that others may make. You'll become a better critic of advertisements, newspaper articles, political speeches, and persuasive appeals that you see and hear every day.

Argumentation is also crucially important for both academic- and career-related communication tasks. The uses of good argumentation skills are endless. In a business course, you may be asked to defend a particular management style; in a technical program, you may be required to analyze and defend the use of a particular procedure; and as a law student you practise writing briefs to persuade judges of your position. In the workplace, you may write proposals that request funding or new equipment, or you may create advertising copy to promote some product or service.

In this chapter, you will be asked to write an essay in which you defend a position with a series of logical reasons. You have already done this in a general way in the previous chapters of this section by making a point and supporting it. The difference is that argumentation advances a *controversial* point—one that at least some of your readers will not be inclined to accept. To prepare for writing an argument essay, first read about five strategies you can use in advancing an argument. Then read the student essays that follow and work through the questions that accompany the essays.

GENERAL STRATEGIES FOR ARGUMENTATION

Because argumentation normally involves controversy, you have to work carefully to convince readers of the validity of your position. Here are five strategies you can use to persuade readers whose viewpoint may differ from yours.

1. Use Tactful, Courteous Language

To truly persuade readers to accept your viewpoint, it is important not to anger them by referring to them or their opinions in rude or belittling terms. Stay away from sweeping, insulting statements like, "Everybody knows that . . ." or "People with any intelligence agree that. . . ." Also, keep the focus on the issue you are discussing, *not on the people* involved in the debate. The third-person viewpoint is especially useful for maintaining your readers' focus on your ideas and for suggesting some distance between you and your subject. Don't write, "*My opponents* say that orphanages cost less than foster care." Instead, write, "*Supporters of orphanages* say they cost less than foster care." Terms like *my opponents* imply that the argument is between you and the "bad guys"—an attitude that puts more distance between you and anyone who disagrees with you. By contrast, an expression like *supporters of orphanages* suggests that those who don't agree are, nevertheless, reasonable people who are willing to consider differing opinions.

2. Point Out Common Ground

Another way to persuade readers to consider your opinion is to point out common ground or ideas that you share. Find points with which people on all sides of the argument can agree. You may be arguing in favour of longer library hours on your campus. Before going into detail about your proposal, think about your audience; remind readers who could be opposed to increased hours that you and they share ideas, such as enabling working students to use the facilities and helping more students to do better work. Readers will be more receptive to your idea once they have considered the ways in which you and they think alike.

3. Acknowledge Differing Viewpoints

Do not simply ignore points of view that conflict with yours. Acknowledging other viewpoints strengthens your position in several ways. First, it helps you spot flaws in the opposing position as well as in your own argument. Second, and equally important, it gives the impression that you are a reasonable person, willing to see all sides of an issue. Readers are more likely to consider your point of view if you indicate a willingness to consider theirs.

At what point in your essay should you acknowledge opposing arguments? The earlier the better—ideally, in the introduction or second paragraph, depending on the overall length of your essay. By quickly establishing that you recognize the other side's position, you get your readers "on board" with you, ready to hear what you have to say.

One effective technique is to cite the opposing viewpoint in your thesis statement. Do this by dividing your thesis into two parts. In the first part, acknowledge the other side's point of view; in the second, state your opinion, suggesting that yours is the stronger viewpoint. Below, the opposing viewpoint is underlined once; the writer's position is underlined twice:

> Although some students believe that studying another language is a waste of time, two years of second-language study should be required of all postsecondary graduates.

Alternatively, try using one or two sentences (separate from the thesis) in the introduction to acknowledge the alternative position. To see this technique in action, look at the introduction to "Teenagers and Jobs" (pages 240–241): "Many people argue that working can be a valuable experience for the young."

A third technique is to use a paragraph within the body of your essay to summarize opposing opinions in greater detail. To do this successfully, you must research opposing arguments. A fair, well-developed summary of the other side's ideas will help convince readers that you have looked at the issue from all angles before deciding on your position. If you are writing an essay arguing that there should be less foreign ownership of Canadian businesses, do some library or online research to find information on both sides of the issue, paying special attention to materials that argue for your viewpoint. You could also talk to local business owners that support Canadian ownership. You would then be in a good position to write a paragraph summarizing opposing viewpoints (Canadian business owners' fears of competition from U.S. companies, profit cuts caused by currency exchange). Once you demonstrate your understanding of opposing views, you are in a stronger position to present your own views.

4. When Appropriate, Acknowledge the Merits of Differing Viewpoints

Sometimes an opposing argument contains a point whose validity you cannot deny. What should you do then? The strongest strategy is to admit that the point is a good one. You will lose credibility if you argue against something that clearly makes sense. Acknowledge the merit of one aspect of the other argument while making it clear that you still believe your argument. The author of "Teenagers and Jobs" takes this approach when discussing the negative effects on students of working more than fifteen hours per week. She states, "Many people argue that working can be a valuable experience for the young," and admits that the other side has a valid point. But she quickly follows this admission with a statement that makes her own viewpoint clear: "However, working more than fifteen hours a week is harmful to adolescents because it reduces their involvement with school, encourages a materialistic and expensive lifestyle, and increases the chance of having problems with drugs and alcohol." In paragraph three of "The Life and Death of the Mall," the author writes "though there may be no causal relationship. . .," letting readers who might disagree and take a logical tack know that he is proposing a viewpoint of his own.

5. Rebut Differing Viewpoints

Sometimes it may not be enough simply to acknowledge the other points of view and present your own argument. When you are dealing with an issue that your readers feel strongly about, you may need to *rebut* the opposing arguments, to point out the problems with an opposing view.

Imagine that your essay states that your college or university should use money intended to build a campus fitness centre to upgrade the library instead. From reading the school paper, you know that supporters of the centre say it will attract new students. You can rebut that point by citing a study conducted by management showing that most students choose a school because of affordable tuition and because of its academic and professional programs and facilities. Emphasize also that many students, already financially strapped, would have trouble paying charges to use the centre.

A rebuttal can take two forms, similar to the two methods of development used for comparison–contrast essays. You can first mention all the points raised by the other side and then present your counter-argument to each of those points, *or* you can present the first point raised by the opposition, rebut that point, then move on to the second opposing point, rebut that, and so on.

STUDENT ESSAYS TO CONSIDER

Teenagers and Jobs

1   "The lives of teenagers and adults are sometimes not so different." Journalist Kate Filion wrote, "Students juggle jobs and school and leisure time in much the same way their parents juggle careers and families: they make important choices—how often they work, what classes they take, what they spend their money on—with almost no adult input . . . there are no safety nets" ("High School Undercover" 83). Many people argue that working can be a valuable experience for the young. However, working more than fifteen hours a week is harmful to adolescents because it reduces their involvement with school, encourages a materialistic and expensive lifestyle, and increases the chance of having problems with drugs and alcohol.

2   Schoolwork and the benefits of extracurricular activities tend to go by the wayside when adolescents work long hours. As more and more teens have filled the numerous part-time jobs offered by fast-food restaurants and malls, teachers have faced increasing difficulties. They must keep the attention of tired pupils and give homework to students who simply don't have time to do it. In addition, educators have noticed less involvement in the extracurricular activities that many consider a healthy influence on young people. School bands and athletic teams are losing players to work, and sports events are poorly attended by working students. Those teenagers who try to do it all—homework, extracurricular activities, and work—may find themselves exhausted and prone to illness. A recent newspaper story, for example, described a girl who came down with mononucleosis as a result of aiming for good grades, playing on two school athletic teams, and working thirty hours a week.

3   Another drawback of too much work is that it may promote materialism and an unrealistic lifestyle. Some parents claim that working helps teach adolescents the value of a dollar. Undoubtedly, that can be true. It's also true that some teens work to help out with the family budget or to save for college or university. However, surveys have shown that the majority of working teens use their earnings to buy luxuries—video-game systems, clothing, and even cars. These young people, some of whom earn $1000 or more a month, don't worry about spending wisely; they can just about have it all. In many cases, experts point out, they are becoming accustomed to a lifestyle they won't be able to afford several years down the road when they no longer have parents paying for car insurance, food, lodging, and so on. At that point, they'll be hard-pressed to pay for necessities as well as luxuries.

4   Finally, teenagers who work a lot are more likely than others to get involved with alcohol and drugs. Teens who put in long hours may seek a quick release from stress, just like the adults who need to drink a couple of martinis after a hard day at work. Stress is probably greater in our society

today than it has been at any time in the past. Also, teens who have money are more likely to get involved with drugs.

5   Teenagers can enjoy the benefits of work while avoiding its drawbacks by simply limiting their work hours during the school year. As is often the case, a moderate approach will be the most healthy and rewarding.

The Life and Death of the Mall

1   During the late 1940s and early 1950s, mass-produced houses started springing up on the outskirts of major North American cities. The suburb, decried by succeeding generations as the nadir of Western culture, the place where creativity goes to die, epitomized to the postwar generation economy, comfort, and family values. Mass production produced more than just ranch-styles and Cape Cod two-storeys though; industry and retail were ready to supply a generation's demands for bobby sox, poodle skirts, doo-wop and rock n' roll records, and revolutionary new domestic appliances. And just like the millions of once-young men who returned from World War II to life in the suburbs, these products needed a home. They found theirs in the modern equivalent of the marketplace, the mercantile counterpart to the tract house, the shopping mall.

2   Bursting with consumer goods, the indoor shopping mall stands as a lead-based-paint-covered testimony to the North American Dream and capitalism's promise of perennial prosperity. Champions of western democracy during the Cold War could have cited shopping malls as concrete proof of the superiority of the North American way of life: there were no shopping malls in Leningrad. Essentially this was Richard Nixon's retort to Soviet chief Nikita Kruschev in the 1959 Kitchen Debate. Their encounter, recorded for colour television, took its name from its location: the kitchen of a model dream house built for the American National Exhibition in Moscow *(Kitchen Debate)*. Supposedly typical of what any hard-working blue-collar citizen could aspire to own, the house was stocked with consumer goods unimaginable to Soviet comrades still reeling from the privations of WW II. Nixon flaunted the power of the U.S. economy by spotlighting its products for sale: lawnmowers, appliances, make-up, and Pepsi-Cola.

3   Though there may be no direct causal relation between the two developments, it seems fitting that the power of the shopping mall rose with that of the Cold War, then began gradually to fail, along with communism. Perhaps with the disintegration of the Soviet Union and the East's wholehearted embrace of consumerism, the West does not get the same selfish ideological joy from its consumer goods. It would, however, be premature to bury the mall quite yet because infusions of long-standing capitalist trends are keeping it alive. For example, consider mystery merchandise: the increasing distance between manufacture and consumption necessary for mass production and distribution has become an abyss at the mall. Just try to make out most products' place of origin. And consider that "time is money." The capitalist faith in progress, based on a linear, forward-moving notion of time makes time valuable. And in few places is this more evident than in mall marketing; mall-shopping helps people manage their time efficiently and live more progressively by bringing everything together in one place.

4   Anyone who falls into rapture at the thought of a GAP or Hollister season-end sale or whose heart skips a beat at the thought of an H & M opening

will find nirvana at the West Edmonton Mall. WEM is theme park, zoo, hotel, casino, golf course, movie theatre complex, ice rink, and of course, shopping mall—a cornucopia of western capitalist decadence. Canadians are lucky to host a paragon of mallness in its last blaze of glory. WEM is a cultural phenomenon: as travel agents say, it's possible to spend weeks in Edmonton, and, except for the drives to and from the airport, never see Edmonton. An entirely contrived experience, WEM satisfies the contemporary desire for consistent and frequent gratification without exertion or risk. Visitors can feel the thrill of being tossed to and fro in the wave pool, knowing all along that the possibility of drowning is as negligible as that of getting a sunburn; they can observe wild animals without ever considering the unnaturalness of the setting or of the animals' quality of life. Most of all, they can spend their imaginary credit-based money on things they do not need, unconcerned about where these came from or where they will go when they get bored of them. Perhaps a historian in the year 2260 will examine earth's culture in search of a structural emblem to represent the material dissipation and spiritual emptiness of 2011; he or she need look no farther than West Edmonton Mall.

5   If the highest imaginable expression of essential mallness was actually realized with WEM, can any further evolution be possible? Could a mall transcend reality, be apotheosized into the virtual, a cybermall? This is precisely what has happened—the mall moved to the Internet. And very rapidly, West Edmonton Mall to the contrary, the traditional mall is becoming irrelevant, and downtown as well as on the edges of cities, there are growing numbers of large vacant boxes, "dead malls" (*Dead Malls*). Dead malls are so prolific that they have their own cult followings and websites. Who could suppress a postmodern chuckle at the thought of returning obsolete consumer goods purchased a few short years ago to the same place from which they were bought, the now-dead mall in its new role as landfill-to-be? Perhaps, bloated with consumer guilt, North Americans should appease their consciences by transporting their dead malls intact to less shopping-privileged parts of the world. Salvation through shopping.

6   In the demolition of the mall, clouded with current environmental concerns, it is possible to see with flawless hindsight the shortsightedness and bankruptcy of classical economics. Capitalism measures as growth not just the construction and functioning of the mall, but also the destruction and replacement of it. To realize the promise of perennial prosperity, continual growth is required. This growth leads to perpetual and superfluous production. By building in intentional obsolescence in material terms and marketing it culturally through the relentless metamorphosis of fashion, consumers are driven to match the never-satisfied pace of the market. Everything goes along swimmingly until some consumer watchdog killjoy points out that this process presupposes infinite resources. And so capitalism ceaselessly devours itself while externalizing the true cost of growth in the form of exploiting the environment. Early free-market advocates promised that its rising tide would lift all ships; they never could have imagined that global warming caused by capitalist progress would make the metaphor real.

7   Perhaps, before malls cycle completely out of existence, one or two should be preserved as cultural monuments. For just as the Parthenon and Notre Dame speak of the values and aspirations of past cultures, so too will temples of capitalism speak to future cultures. As Colosseum and Pantheon

in one, malls have been the temples in which consumers enjoyed the games, enacted their rituals, observed the holy duty to spend, and made their sacrifices to preserve the sanctity of the lie that marched under the banner of Progress and the North American Dream.

■ Questions

About Unity

1. In which paragraph of "The Life and Death of the Mall" is the topic sentence buried within the paragraph instead of appearing in its opening?

2. Which sentence in paragraph 5 of "The Life and Death of the Mall" should be omitted in the interests of paragraph unity?

3. Which sentence in paragraph 4 of "Teenagers and Jobs" should be omitted in the interests of paragraph unity?

About Support

4. Which sentence in paragraph 4 of "Teenagers and Jobs" needs to be followed by more supporting details?

5. Which supporting paragraph in "Teenagers and Jobs" raises an opposing idea and then argues against that idea? What transition word is used to signal the author's change of direction?

6. Which paragraph of "The Life and Death of the Mall" makes use of a single extended example as its support?

About Coherence

7. Which two paragraphs of "Teenagers and Jobs" begin with an addition transition? What are those words?

8. Between which two paragraphs in "The Life and Death of the Mall" are transitional structures used?

About Introductions and Conclusions

9. Which two methods of introduction are used in "Teenagers and Jobs"?
   a. Broad, general statement narrowing to a thesis
   b. Idea that is the opposite of the one to be developed
   c. Quotation
   d. Anecdote
   e. Questions

10. Both essays end with the same type of conclusion. Which method do they use?
   a. Summary only
   b. Summary and recommendation
   c. Prediction

DEVELOPING AN ARGUMENTATION ESSAY

Writing a Thesis Statement for an Argumentation Essay

Persuading your audience of your viewpoint about a certain controversial subject is your primary objective in the argumentation essay, and never is the direct and clear statement of a viewpoint more important than in the thesis statement of this type of essay.

When writing your thesis statement, be direct and unambiguous about your position. If possible, avoid the use of conditional verb forms that soften your position, as in "Volunteer work might help some students to gain experience." You may wish to refer to the main supporting points of your argument in the thesis. This will clearly indicate to readers the direction of your argument.

An example of an argumentation thesis statement follows:

- Colleges and universities must set an example, where recycling is concerned.

An example of an extended argumentation thesis statement follows:

- Lack of family or peer support, financial pressures, and health problems make students drop out of college and university.

How Will You Argue? Or Will You Persuade?

Although nearly every essay you write during the semester will contain elements of persuasion or argumentation, there are sometimes distinct qualities and considerations related to writing whose primary purpose is to argue or persuade. Although persuasion is generally associated with appeals to emotion or human values, and argumentation with logic and reason, there is actually little distinction between the two. Traditionally, three ways of appealing to, or persuading audiences, have been described as *pathos,* the appeal to readers' emotion; *logos,* the appeal to readers' logic; and *ethos,* the appeal based on the character and/or knowledge of the writer. Depending on your purpose and your audience, you can vary the balance between emotional, logical, or knowledge- or values-based support in your essay.

Find two student-example essays in other chapters in Part 2 in which you find effective argumentation. What are the primary and secondary methods of development used in these essays? Why do these essays function effectively as argumentation?

How does the writer of each of the essays you chose convince you of the rightness of his or her point? To what degree does he or she appeal to your emotion, your logic, or to your sense of his or her character and knowledge? Where do you find examples of these appeals?

What Is Your Purpose and Who Is Your Audience?

The main purpose of your argumentation essay is to convince your audience that your particular view or opinion on a controversial issue is correct. In addition, you may, at times, have a second purpose: to persuade your audience to take some sort of action.

To convince your readers in an argumentation essay, it is important to provide them with a clear main point and plenty of evidence to back it up. Say that you want to argue that public schools should require students to wear uniforms. In this case, you might do some research to gather as much evidence as possible to support your point. For instance, you might check to see if uniforms are cheaper than the alternative. Perhaps you could find out if schools with uniforms have a lower incidence of violent behaviour than those without them or if students' academic performance improves when school uniforms are adopted. As you search for evidence, make sure that it clearly links to your topic and supports the main point you are trying to get across to your audience.

Next, you will want to refine your purpose in terms of the overall effect you wish to achieve. Do you want your readers to take action? Then you will have to motivate them to do so. Do you want to inform your readers, to show them why your viewpoint is a valid one? Then you will have to present appropriate, convincing support that allows readers to feel that they might reach your conclusion on their own. Or do you just want to break down your readers' probable resistance to your ideas or viewpoint? Here you will not try to convince your readers; you will instead work to show the positive aspects of your position so they will view it in a more balanced way.

Knowing your audience is important to all essays, but it is critical to the success of your argumentation essay. The following questions will help you sharpen your persuading and arguing skills:

- If your reading audience is the hostile group described last in the preceding paragraph, what is your best position as a writer?
- Which of the classic appeals to readers will you use? Why?
- What types of support will you use?
- Will your support be factual and backed up with research, appealing to readers' logic and their sense of you as a person of knowledge and good values? Why or why not?
- Will your support be filled with vivid, touching descriptions, and human-interest anecdotes? Why or why not?
- What can you assume about your audience?
- How much should you make reference to "their side" of the argument? Why?

How much you counter possible objections depends on how much your readers are likely to disagree with you; if they are neutral or undecided, consider what they already know and how they are likely to feel about the main point of your argument. This type of reader might simply not know enough about your issue or position to hold an opinion, so one strategy would be to provide reliable, frequently objective support with few emotionally based details so you can present yourself as a reliable, informative source.

For the undecided audience, ask yourself the questions above once again. Then answer the following questions:

- What opinion does your audience hold about school uniforms?
- What might your readers' objections be to your argument?
- Why would people not support your main point?
- What, if anything, are the merits of the opposing point of view?

To get inside the head of your reader you might even want to interview a few people you are sure will disagree with you. By becoming aware of the points of view your audience might have, you will know how to proceed in researching and presenting your rebuttal to their arguments. By directly addressing potential opposition, you add credibility to your argument, giving your audience confidence that you are reliable because you have explored alternative views.

Finally, if you believe readers are already on your side, you will be able to use supporting points and details based on shared values and beliefs. You will present your argument logically, and offer sound reasons for your position, so as not to weaken the trust that readers who agree with you wish to place in you. To return to the example about school uniforms, if your audience consists of parents concerned about school discipline and slipping grades, you will be able to strongly reinforce your support in these areas with both objective and possibly anecdotal evidence.

What Is Your Point of View in Your Argumentation Essay?

If argumentation or persuasion is not carefully tailored to reading audiences, they may abandon the effort of even reading something that is irrelevant, unsuited, or unrelated to their interests or background. If your purpose is to convince readers of the rightness of your viewpoint, that does not mean you should "lecture" them. Such an approach, writing as *I,* would put off readers, for various reasons.

First, an effective argument is often supported with a blend of logic (*logos*) and points related to readers' probable values (*ethos*), rather than with subjective, personally derived reasons. Readers confronted with the argument, "I believe failing students hurts their chances of ever succeeding. . . ." usually suspect the writer speaks from personal interest, if not an agenda. Instead, the same opinion, stated more neutrally as "Failing students damages their self-esteem and desire to learn . . .," suggests that the writer will reveal some impartial evidence to back up the points. Effective persuasive writers keep their presence in the background and rely on their ideas. They are informed about the topic and willing to give a logical, well-detailed argument to back it up.

It is vitally important for your readers not to feel "pressured," "crowded," or manipulated by your presence. In a well-supported third-person essay, even skeptical readers may be at least willing to entertain the views in the paper. In a first-person, completely subjective argumentation essay, even readers who somewhat agree with its point will likely be dubious and unconvinced by its content. If an essay's writer seems to derive thesis and support only from personal experience or opinions, then the basis for credibility (leaving aside persuasion of the audience) is extremely narrow. One person's experience does not make a thing true. Empathy might be possible for a few readers, but not much else.

How Will You Support Your Argumentation Essay?

The general categories of support for an argumentation essay are based on the traditional appeals to readers discussed earlier: (1) logical support (*logos*) based on objective facts, statistics, and examples drawn from recognized and credible sources; (2) support based on appeals to readers' values (*ethos*), and presumed shared values and knowledge with the writer; and (3) support based on appeals to readers' beliefs, emotions, and attitudes (*pathos*).

With the possible exception, as noted above, of arguments aimed at wholly hostile audiences, your essay's support will be derived in varying balances from any of these categories, depending on your purpose. Evidence for logical support may be derived from research, interviews, statistics, and, occasionally, personal observations; as wide a range of sources as possible is desirable for you to present yourself in a fair and reliable position. In general, it is safe to say that logical support should predominate and that emotional appeals, when used, should be subtle. Be careful with heartwrenching anecdotes; readers easily feel manipulated. Use common or shared values only when you write for an audience you know agrees with you.

- Where in "The Life and Death of the Mall" do you find evidence of logically derived support?
- Do you find supporting points or details aimed at shared beliefs, emotions, or attitudes? Where?

When you wish to persuade readers by appealing to their emotions, attitudes, or beliefs, you should be certain first of all that your audience will be receptive to such evidence. Using this type of support in arguments presented to hostile audiences or to those about whom you know little or nothing is risky at best. Once you lose a reader by assuming he or she shares your attitude toward, say, homosexual marriage, you are not likely to get him or her back.

In terms of the patterns you use to support your argument, you have at your disposal the entire list of methods of development in Part 2. Specific examples, as you have read, are essential to solid support; generalizations lose audiences almost instantly.

- How many examples do you find in the details in paragraph 4 of "The Life and Death of a Mall"?

Definitions eliminate the risk of potential misunderstandings by readers, so are frequently used as secondary development patterns.

- Where in either student essay might a definition have clarified some aspect of the support?

Narratives in the form of anecdotes and description are invaluable to many argumentation essays. A student writing about the desirability of school uniforms could certainly describe a casually clad, disorderly group of students, then combine contrast with description to portray a disciplined, neat group of uniformed students. Cause and effect and division and classification analysis are also excellent paragraph-development methods for clarifying complex-seeming issues.

- Where do you find a student essay that uses cause and effect for argumentative purposes? What sort of appeals does the writer use in the essay's support?

Prewriting

Before choosing a topic for her essay, Anna, the writer of "Teenagers and Jobs," asked herself what controversial subject she was qualified to argue for or against. She wanted to select something she cared about. As someone who had been active in her high-school community—working on the newspaper, playing basketball, and singing in a chorus—Anna first thought about "student apathy." She had never understood students ignoring opportunities available to them in school. Then she considered individual students she knew and their reasons for not getting more involved in school and extracurricular activities, and she changed her opinion. "I realized that 'apathy' was not really the problem," she explained. "Many of them worked so much that they literally didn't have time for school life."

After focusing her thesis on the idea of "teenagers and work," Anna made a list of what she perceived as the bad points of students working too much:

- No time for sports and other activities
- Students leave right after school—can't stay for clubs, practices
- Don't have time to attend games, other school functions
- Students sleep in class and skip homework
- Stress, extra money contribute to drug and alcohol use
- Teachers frustrated trying to teach tired students
- Ability to buy luxuries makes teens materialistic, unrealistic about lifestyle
- Some drop out of school to work full-time
- Students miss the fun of being young, developing talents and social abilities
- Students burn out, even get sick

Anna reviewed her list of points and identified three main points to develop in her essay. Realizing that some other items she had listed were related ideas that could be useful as support for her main topics, she marked those with the number of the main idea they supported in parentheses.

1—No time for real involvement in school and school activities
(1) Students leave right after school—can't stay for clubs, practices
(1) Don't have time to attend games, other school functions Students sleep in class and skip homework

2—Stress, extra money contribute to drug and alcohol use
(1) Teachers frustrated trying to teach tired students

3—Having extra money makes teens materialistic

(3) Some get so greedy for money they drop out of school to work full-time Students miss the fun of being young, developing talents and social abilities Students burn out, even get sick

(2) Hanging around older co-workers can contribute to drug, alcohol use

(3) Buying luxuries gives teens unrealistic idea of standard of living

First Draft and Revision

Referring to her list, Anna wrote the following first draft of her essay:

1   Many people think that working is a valuable experience for young people. However, when teenagers have jobs, they are too likely to neglect their schoolwork, become overly materialistic, and get into trouble with drugs and alcohol.

2   Schoolwork and the benefits of extracurricular activities tend to go by the wayside when adolescents work long hours. As more and more teens have taken jobs, teachers have faced increasing difficulties. They must keep the attention of tired pupils and give homework to students who simply don't have time to do it. In addition, educators have noticed less involvement in extracurricular activities. School bands and athletic teams are losing players to work, and sports events are poorly attended by working students. Those teens who try to do it all—homework, extracurricular activities, and work—may find themselves exhausted and burned out.

3   Another drawback of too much work is that it may promote materialism and an unrealistic lifestyle. Most working teens use their earnings to buy luxuries. These young people don't worry about spending wisely; they can just about have it all. They are becoming accustomed to a lifestyle they won't be able to afford several years down the road when they have to support themselves.

4   Finally, teenagers who work are more likely than others to get involved with alcohol and drugs. Teens who put in long hours may seek a quick release from stress, just like the adults who need to drink a couple of martinis after a hard day at work. Also, teens who have money are more likely to get involved with drugs.

5   In short, teens and work just don't mix.

What recommendations might Anna's instructor have made after looking over this first draft? Here are her first general comment and her first comment about argumentation. Now add at least three further comments each of a general and argumentation-specific type, tied to Anna's first draft:

Anna—Good beginning. Your thesis may be overstated, but each of your main topics is on the right track. Here are some points to consider:

- *Working a <u>limited</u> number of hours a week might be a good experience.*
- *About writing an argumentation essay specifically: <u>What evidence</u> is there that working teens use drugs and alcohol more than others?*

After considering her instructor's comments, Anna wrote the draft of "Teenagers and Jobs" that appears on pages 240—241.

WRITING AN ARGUMENTATION ESSAY

■ Writing Assignment 1

Write an essay in which you argue *for* or *against* any one of the options below. Support and defend your argument by drawing on your reasoning ability and general experience.

Option 1: Because fast food is available in college and university cafeterias, and because it is so familiar and widely advertised, students choose it more often than other options. In fact, other options, if they are available at all, are usually displayed unappealingly. Colleges and universities should drop the fast-food franchises and feed the student body as well as the student mind.

Option 2: By the time many students reach high school, they have learned the basics in most subjects. Some still have much to gain from the courses that high schools offer, but others might be better off spending the next four years in other ways. For their benefit, high school attendance should be voluntary.

Option 3: Many of today's young people are mainly concerned with prestigious careers, making money, and owning things. It seems that we no longer teach the benefits of spending time and money to help the community, the country, or the world. Most students, in fact, only pay "lip service" to fulfilling any community service requirements in high schools. Canada can lead the way by requiring young people to spend a year working in some kind of community service.

Prewriting

1. As you write your opening paragraph, acknowledge the opposing point of view.

2. Make a list of the thoughts that support your argument. Write down everything that occurs to you. Then identify your strongest points and begin your outline. Are there thoughts in your list that can be used as supporting details for your main supporting points?

3. Plan your supporting paragraphs. Keep in mind that you are writing for an audience of people who, initially, will not all agree with you. It isn't enough to state your opinion. Show *why* you feel as you do, persuading your audience that your point of view is a valid one.

4. Your concluding paragraph is your final chance to persuade your readers to accept your argument. Consider ending with a prediction of what will happen if your point of view does not prevail. Will an existing situation grow worse? Will a new problem arise?

Revising

After you have completed the first draft of the essay, set it aside for a while. When you review it, try to do so as critically as you would if it were not your own work. Ask yourself these questions:

- Have I provided persuasive details to support my argument?
- Have I acknowledged the opposing point of view, showing that I am a reasonable person, willing to consider other arguments?

- Is my language tactful and courteous, or does it insult anyone who does not agree with me?
- Have I used transition words to help readers follow my train of thought?
- Does my final supporting paragraph include a strong argument for my position?
- Does my concluding paragraph summarize my argument or add a final persuasive touch?

Continue to revise your essay until you can answer "yes" to each question. Then, make sure you check the next-to-final draft for the sentence skills listed on the inside front cover.

■ Writing Assignment 2

In this argument essay, you will write with a specific purpose and for a specific audience.

Option 1: You would like to live in a big city, but your parent or partner refuses to budge from the suburbs. Write him or her a letter in which you argue for the advantages of city life. Be sure to acknowledge and rebut the other person's objections to city life. Use specific examples wherever possible.

Option 2: Find a newspaper editorial with which you either strongly agree or disagree. Write a letter to the editor in which you state why you agree or disagree with the position taken by the paper in that editorial. Provide several short paragraphs of supporting evidence for your position. Then, send your letter to the newspaper. When you turn in a copy of your letter to your instructor, also turn in the editorial to which you are responding.

■ Writing Assignment 3

Read the selection "Just a Little Drop of Water" by Eve Tulbert on pages 490–496. As Tulbert opens her argument, notice how she poses the question of water being a source of income or a human right.

Write a third-person persuasive or argumentation essay in which you argue for or against a concept currently in contention in Canada: separate courses of study, and even different marking systems, for different racial and ethnic groups. Is there a justification for offering a different curriculum to African-Canadian students, to Native Canadian students, to Asian-Canadian students, or to any other distinct group? Or does doing so further splinter Canadian society? Present your reasons in order of increasing importance, and develop each paragraph's point with plenty of supporting details derived from your own thinking or research.

CHECKLIST OF LEARNING OUTCOMES FOR CHAPTER 16

To ensure that you have understood and met the learning outcomes for this chapter, answer the following questions upon completing any of its writing assignments:

✓ Does your opening paragraph provide appropriate background for your thesis? Does the thesis clearly state the point your essay will argue?

✓ Does your essay acknowledge and counter any opposing views?

✓ Does each supporting point and detail clearly support your thesis viewpoint and add to the strength of your argument?

✓ Have you maintained both an objective approach and a courteous tone in presenting your argument?

✓ Does your concluding statement reinforce your argument?

Writing a Summary

LEARNING OUTCOMES

After reading this chapter and working through its activities, you will

- identify the essential characteristics of a summary and understand how it differs from an essay;

- analyze a piece of material for its essential content;

- paraphrase another writer's words correctly;

- create a list of the main ideas and support in an original source;

- revise and tighten drafts of a summary by using three methods;

- create an effective summary that presents the main ideas in the same order and proportion as the original.

Summaries are among the most often–used writing formats. You have probably read hundreds of summaries—on search-engine pages, on the backs of DVD and video-game covers, in the openings of chapters in your textbooks, or perhaps on database indexes of articles. A summary delivers a condensed version of the content of some original work, so is an efficient and useful way to present information, highly valuable in a time when the quantity of information available is expanding so quickly.

You will write academic summaries as separate writing assignments and as components of research papers. In this chapter, you will learn how to create an effective summary, and in Chapter 19, you will learn how to apply the principles and techniques of summarizing to writing a research paper. You will also find that writing concise, accurate summaries is an invaluable career skill. You may be required to summarize technical data, minutes of meetings, reports, media presentations, or interviews. Summaries are integral to academic, business, social and human services, and technical communications.

WHAT IS A SUMMARY?

In a summary, you reduce material in an original work to its main points and key supporting details. The three key activities essential to creating an effective summary are *concentrating, reducing,* and *rewording or paraphrasing* an original piece of written work. Each activity characterizes the summary as a form. Summaries may be as short as a single sentence (a précis or nutshell statement), but often they range from 25 percent to 30 percent of the length of the original document.

A summary is not . . .

A summary is **not an essay.** A summary does not present or support your point of view on the original material. It reproduces, in reduced form and in third-person voice, the viewpoint and support of the original text.

A summary is **not an outline.** It is written in sentence and paragraph form so that readers understand the general ideas of the original text, as well as their relationships, in an easy-to-follow form.

A summary is **not simply a paraphrase.** A paraphrase is a complete restatement of a quantity of text, and is about the same length as the original. A summary consists of paraphrases, but is a concentrated and reduced version of the original.

Summarizing is **not note-taking.** Summarizing is a multi-step process that exposes the main ideas in a piece of text, then reduces the word count, and reassembles those main ideas into an original piece of work.

A summary is . . .

A summary is a **concentrated version of the original material.** It presents the main ideas of the original in your own words. A summary does not use the wording of the original source and rarely uses quotations from that source.

A summary presents **the ideas of the original in the same order** and **preserves the sense and flavour of that material.** Its length depends on the requirements of the situation or assignment.

A summary is **a reduced, reworded version of some original text.** Paraphrasing the original is a necessary step in writing a summary. Reduction and concentration of the original into its main ideas are also necessary steps.

Summarizing is **a recognized writing format.** Note-taking is simply listing key points from a text, lecture, or presentation. Creating a summary requires drafting the main ideas back into sentences and revising until a concise, clear paragraph (or more) emerges.

HOW TO SUMMARIZE

Writing a summary brings together reading, study, and writing skills.

- You will *concentrate* or condense the original, so you must preview, read, evaluate, organize, and outline the assigned material.
- You will *reduce* the original text, so you must analyze it carefully, to clearly identify the main points, supporting points, and any repetitious or unneeded material.
- You will reword or *paraphrase* the original text, so you must understand the meanings of all its words, phrases, and sentences in context so that you can correctly restate all its key ideas.

Summarizing can really help you to practise focused reading, "getting inside" material. A summary is *concentrated;* every word and phrase you rewrite in your own words must restate essential ideas of the original, so you must know that content thoroughly. Summarizing is a skill; it does not "come naturally" to many people, but if you learn (1) to read the original carefully, (2) to analyze and outline its main ideas, and (3) to express those main ideas in your own words, you will be prepared to face most summarizing challenges.

Summarizing *takes time.* Be prepared to set aside time to read shorter printed pieces several times, to "re-scan" a book you have already read, or to download and print out parts of a Web site whose content you may be summarizing.

HOW TO SUMMARIZE AN ARTICLE OR SHORT PRINT ITEM

Step 1: Preview and Review the Source Material

If you are summarizing an article or a shorter printed piece on any subject, begin by photocopying it (or downloading and printing it) so that you can highlight important points, strike through repetitive phrases or examples, and note the main ideas right on the original.

Take a few minutes to preview the work. You can preview an article in a magazine or journal by taking a quick look at the following:

1. *Title* The title often summarizes what the article is about. Think about the title and how it may condense the meaning of an article. Sometimes a title may be attention-grabbing but so vague that it may not be very helpful (for example, the title of the *Saturday Night* magazine article reprinted in this chapter, "The New, Old Jamaica," which could refer to any number of ideas related to Jamaica).

2. *Subtitle* The subtitle (if given), the caption, or any other words in large print under or next to the title often provide a quick insight into the meaning of an article. An example of useful subtitle information appears in an article in *The Kitchener/Waterloo Record* from November 2002. The article's title is "A Good Old-Fashioned Wholesaler." The title alone does not seem relevant to a

business student looking up articles about independent retail on EBSCOhost. However, the article's subtitle, "Personal Contacts Help Supplier Sell to Small, Independent Retailers," clearly reveals the gist of the article.

3. *First and last several paragraphs* In the first paragraphs, the author may introduce the subject and state the purpose of the article. In the last several paragraphs, the author may present conclusions or a summary. Opening and closing paragraphs are points of *maximum attention* for readers as they seek information. Journalists and Web site creators know this and structure their content accordingly. Previews or summaries can give you an overview of what the entire article is about.

4. *Headings, subheadings, special typography, and graphics* Note any headings or subheadings that appear in the article. They often provide clues to the article's main points and give an immediate indication of what each section is about. Look carefully at any pictures, charts, or diagrams that accompany the article. Page space in a magazine or journal is limited, and such visual aids are generally used to illustrate important points in the article. Note any words or phrases set off in *italic type* or **boldface print;** note also bulleted lists or boxed sections of material. Such ideas have probably been emphasized because they are important points in the article.

Read the article once through for a general sense of its meaning. Do not slow down or turn back and reread. Then, *read the article a second time to note its main ideas.* Check or highlight main points and key supporting details. Pay special attention to all the items noted in the preview. Also, look for definitions, examples, and enumerations (lists of items), as these often indicate key ideas. Identify important points by turning any headings into questions and then reading to find the answers to the questions.

Finally, *reread your checked or highlighted sections.* Go back and reread more carefully the areas you have identified as most important. Also, focus on other key points you may have missed in your first reading.

For information on summarizing a book, film, or TV show, go to the OLC at www. mcgrawhill.ca/olc/langan.

Step 2: List the Main Ideas, Write a First Draft, and Revise Your Summary

Before you begin your summary, list all the main ideas in your source material. Number these ideas, and leave space after each numbered item to fill in the supporting details. Leave some time, if possible, before reviewing and editing your list. Check your list of ideas and support against your original material. Look for omissions, for possible repetition in either the original or in your list, as well as for duplications of ideas in examples, quotations, or explanations. A piece of supporting information may be repeated for emphasis, or it may be duplicated in dialogue.

With your edited list, you can prepare the first draft of your summary, keeping these points in mind:

1. Identify, at the start of the summary, the title and author of the work. For example, "in Samra Habib's article, 'The New, Old Jamaica' she writes. . . ."

2. Write your draft in the third person. Never use *I* or *we;* when you summarize, you are invisible as a writer. You are restating the original work in reduced form. You add nothing at all. Your summary contains no commentary or views of your own. Do not change a single idea that appears in the original.

3. Express the main points and key supporting details in your own words. Your task is to put the original entirely into your own words, then reduce it. Do not imitate the style of the original.

4. Limit the use of quotations. You should quote from the material only to illustrate key points. A one-paragraph summary should not contain more than one quoted sentence.

5. Preserve the balance and proportion of the original work. If the original text devoted 70 percent of its space to one idea and only 30 percent to another, your summary should reflect that.

Step 3: Prepare for Your Second Draft

Ideally, first drafts are a bit long. It is better to include a few too many details than to omit necessary information. Prepare your second draft by following these tips:

1. Check again for the required word count or length. Use the word count on your word-processing software to check your document, or simply count each word, including *a* and *the.*

2. Review your summary to reduce *wordy phrases* such as "because of the fact that . . ." (just use "because"), "in order to . . ." (just use "to").

3. Note each major idea and its support as it appears on your revised list, and note each in your draft. See if each idea can be rephrased more concisely.

4. Write a final draft of your summary.

HOW TO PARAPHRASE

Paraphrasing—putting another person's ideas into your own words—is a key skill for effective summaries and research papers. When you paraphrase, you do more than change a word or two. You must express the other writer's material *completely* in your own words. To summarize you must paraphrase, and because paraphrasing is key to writing effective research essays, you will learn more about this essential skill in the following chapter.

When summarizing written text, first paraphrase the original source to express its main ideas, then concentrate those ideas to express them as concisely as possible. Paraphrasing correctly begins with understanding the exact meaning of the words and phrases you restate. Any time you are not sure of a meaning, look it up in a dictionary. If your original material contains technical or specialized vocabulary, learn what the terms mean so that you paraphrase them accurately. In summaries, it is preferable to put any specialized terms into wording appropriate for a general audience.

Keep in mind that paraphrasing *re-expresses* the ideas of another writer. Never simply replace a few words with synonyms while retaining the original author's sentence structure; this is plagiarism. For additional information on paraphrasing and plagiarism, see pages 278–280. The following are examples, based on the summary example in this chapter, of incorrect and correct paraphrasing.

Original Source:

"The mento sound is a concoction of calypso beats, Latin American musical influences and hints of American big band, with a three-three-two rhythm."

Incorrect Paraphrasing or Plagiarism:

The mento sound mixes calypso beats, Latin American music, and bits of American big band, with an irregular rhythm.

In the example above, the writer has only changed the original's wording in three places: "mixes" for "a concoction of," "bits" for "hints," and "an irregular" for "a three-three-two." These substitutions leave the attempt at paraphrasing too close to the original; this is plagiarism. The sentence structure of the original text is unchanged, indicating that the writer has not fully re-expressed the ideas as his or her own. The examples below show preferable paraphrasings of the original sentence:

Correct Paraphrasing:

Traces of calypso, Latin American, swing styles, and an irregular rhythm characterize the mento sound (2).
Mento sounds like a mix of Jamaican, Latin, and big band music, with a rhythm of its own (2).

In both examples above, the writer has retained the meaning of the original source while using completely different sentence structure and greater conciseness. The parentheses show the paragraph in the original, which is the source of the paraphrase. Within a summary, you will not show in-text paragraph citations, but as stand-alone paraphrases, these identify their source.

Using Cue Words and Phrases: Restating your Original Correctly

When you summarize, you will need to refer to the writer of the original document. When you wish to show your author's ownership of an idea, use verbs such as "she/he writes," "states," "describes," or "discusses." These are neutral words that simply attribute (show ownership of) the ideas of the author you are restating.

Do not indicate your opinion of the author's ideas with the use of cue words that show how you feel about the ideas you are summarizing. Do not comment on or distort the author's views: simply restate them as clearly as possible and use an appropriate cue word or phrase to set up such statements.

Finally, be sure to correctly source every idea from your original. If, for example, the author of your document is quoting or paraphrasing another source, specify this. Otherwise, you are distorting your author's ideas.

Here is a statement from an article from CBC News online, "Canada's Shame," written by Dan Bjarnason, followed by a distorted summary-paraphrase, a correct paraphrase, and a correct summary-paraphrase. Bjarnason quotes other sources in his article, including Scott Murray, a literacy researcher for Statistics Canada.

Original Source:

"Murray's study shows that among heavy-truck drivers in Alberta, for example, the lower their literacy level, the higher the probability that they experience an accident or spillage. These are real effects—driving big rigs off the road into a ditch."

Inaccurate Summary-Paraphrase, Missing In-text Citation:

In Alberta, less literate truck drivers have more accidents.

Accurate Paraphrase with In-Text Citation:

Murray states that, in Alberta, rig and transport drivers who are less literate are more likely to have more, and more serious, accidents, such as steering their huge trucks onto the shoulders of roads or into gulleys ("Canada's Shame").

Accurate Summary with In-Text Citation:

Scott Murray's research into Canadian illiteracy states that less literate Alberta rig drivers tend to have more serious accidents ("Canada's Shame").

● ● ● ● **ACTIVITY**

List as many cue words as possible that mean the same as "writes" or "states." Now trade lists with a partner and rate each other's list for neutrality. Use a scale of 1 to 10: 10 for a word as neutral as "states," and 1 for a word such as "complains," that expresses your attitude or emotional response.

WRITING A SUMMARY

Mark Fernandez, a broadcasting student, was asked to find and summarize a program-related article from a general-interest Canadian magazine. Because he was interested in Caribbean music, especially reggae and ska, Mark looked for articles about music genres. He scanned some of the Canadian magazine listings in his library databases, then noticed cases of several years' issues of *Saturday Night* in the library's periodicals display. Flipping through a few issues led him to an article about mento, a type of Jamaican music that was new to him.

His assignment required him to choose an article of a length that could be accurately summarized in one paragraph of two to three hundred words. Here is the full text of the article he decided to summarize:

The New, Old Jamaica

1   Every decade has its musical genre revivals. In the '70s, Sha Na Na brought back the bop; the '80s had a '60s psychedelic flashback; and swing and oldstyle Cuban ensembles filled dance floors once again in the '90s. Now, North American clubland speakers are throbbing with the sounds of old Jamaica. Mento, a unique Jamaican folk music popular in the 1950s, is finally getting the international attention it deserves.

2   Mento has its roots in music performed with homemade instruments in 19th-century Jamaica; it was extremely popular until the 1960s, when it morphed into ska, reggae, and dance hall. The mento sound is a concoction of calypso beats, Latin American musical influences and hints of American big band, with a three-three-two rhythm. As for the name, *mento* may be derived from the Spanish word *mentar,* which means "to mention" (Spain occupied Jamaica from 1494 to 1655). Another theory is that mento is an African word that describes a lewd dance. Lyrical themes, often humorous commentaries on social situations and celebration of sexuality set mento apart from reggae, whose slower rhythms and more political lyrics grew out of the '60s struggle for civil rights. By the time Jamaica began to record and export its culture to the world, mento had already been eclipsed by reggae and ska. So, unlike artists such as Bob Marley and Prince Buster, mento musicians have been largely unknown beyond the island, until recently.

3   The surprising resurgence of mento is a welcome development for DJs and record collectors who have loved it for years. Particularly bedazzled is DJ Rocky, a regular fixture of the Toronto reggae and ska scene who spins records at the Cloak and Dagger pub on College Street. Rocky says he's intrigued by the growing number of downtown Toronto venues that, in the past two years, have started to play vintage Jamaican music. Until recently, this music was heard exclusively in areas where a significant proportion of Jamaican-Canadians reside. Even more surprising, Rocky recounts, is that during recent gigs in Germany and Japan he played to crowds of smitten fans devoted to vintage Jamaican music who, although they didn't speak English, were able to converse in Jamaican patois, which they'd picked up from the music.

4   A measure of the revival of mento is the belated international recognition of seasoned mento artist Stanley Beckford, known in France as *L'Ambassadeur de Mento.* In 2002, Beckford released his first solo album, *Stanley Beckford Plays Mento* (Universal), after years of playing in various Jamaican mento groups. Last year, he played to thousands of fans at festivals around Europe.

5   Internationally, there is renewed interest in mento greats such as the Jolly Boys and ska legend Laurel Aitken. And mento compilation CDs, such as *Boogu Yagga Gal* (Heritage Music) and *Mento Madness* (V2), have recently been released.

6   DJ Iron Will, who spins with Rocky at the Cloak and Dagger, says he's used to people popping into the pub while he's spinning and asking him what kind of music he's playing. "The music really challenges people, because they've never heard it before; it definitely piques their interest."

Samra Habib

Previewing and Reviewing the Article

Mark read through Samra Habib's article quickly. Debating where to begin summarizing, he looked at the title, "The New, Old Jamaica." It seemed too general to suggest much except the idea that something old, related to Jamaica, was being revived, and there was no subtitle to help him out.

He photocopied the article, noting the month and year of the *Saturday Night* issue where it appeared. He then read the article twice more and numbered the article's paragraphs. Mark focused on the opening and closing paragraphs, looking for the most important ideas, and highlighted them. Here are his point-form notes:

Paragraph 1

- Every decade music genres re-appear
- Examples? 70s Rock & Roll; 80s, 60s music
- Clubs are now reviving mento
- Mento is 1950s Jamaican folk music

Last Paragraph

- Example? Toronto DJ says people are curious about mento
- Mento catches people's attention because they haven't heard it before

Mark then reviewed the article to reassure himself that there were enough interesting ideas for a good one-paragraph summary. The original was just over six hundred words long, and he believed he could reduce it to about one-third of its length. To do so, he highlighted the main points and support in the body of the article. This would help him with the next important stage—listing the main ideas.

Listing the Main Ideas and Writing a First Draft

After he highlighted the article's main points and supporting details, Mark came up with the following list:

Paragraph 1

- Every decade music genres re-appear
- Examples? 70s Rock & Roll; 80s, 60s music
- Clubs are now reviving mento
- Mento is 1950s Jamaican folk music

Paragraph 2

- Mento started in 19th century, with homemade instruments
- Popular pre-1960s—developed into ska, reggae, dance hall
- Sound mix of calypso beats, Latin, swing, and 3-3-2 rhythm
- Word "mento"? Spanish mentar = "to mention"
- Jamaica was Spanish—1494–1655
- Mento might be African word for a sexy dance
- Lyrics can be funny—about society and sex

- Not like reggae—slower, more political (60s)
- Ska and reggae popular types of Jamaican music
- Mento artists not known outside Jamaica until now

Paragraph 3

- DJs and record collectors always liked mento
- Toronto DJ Rocky says older Jamaican sounds popular in clubs
- Used to only be played in Jamaican areas
- Germany and Japan—fans of older Jamaican genres
- Non-English speakers and patois—learned it from the music

Paragraph 4

- Evident that mento is revived
- Major mento star—Stanley Beckford, famous in France
- 2002, S.B. released solo album after playing in groups
- S.B. played festivals in 2003 in Europe

Paragraph 5

- New interest in mento artists worldwide
- Jolly Boys and ska artist Laurel Aitken—new CD examples?

Last Paragraph

- Example? Toronto DJ says people are curious about mento
- Mento catches people's attention because they haven't heard it before

● ● ● ● ACTIVITY

Mark's instructor gave his students a useful tip for preparing a first draft of a summary. He asked students to write a one-sentence summary of each paragraph in their original articles, once they had written their point-form lists of main ideas.

- Read through "The New, Old Jamaica" and write your own one-sentence summary of each of the author's paragraphs.

The following day, Mark revised his list, comparing it to the original article. He was not sure, especially in the article's second and third paragraphs, which points were main ones and which were support. Here is a section of his revised list in which he has crossed out unnecessary points, and indicated main points with an *M* and supporting points with an *S*. He has also made notes to himself on some points.

Paragraph 2

- Mento started in 19th century, with homemade instruments *M*
- Popular pre-1960s—developed into ska, reggae, dance hall *M*
- Sound mix of calypso beats, Latin, swing, and 3-3-2 rhythm *S*
- Word "mento"? Spanish *mentar* = "to mention" *S*
- ~~Jamaica was Spanish—1494–1655~~ *S*
- ~~Mento might be African word for a sexy dance~~ *S*—don't need—lots of definition facts already

- Lyrics can be funny—about society and sex **M**
- Not like reggae—slower, more political (60s) **S**
- Ska and reggae popular types of Jamaican music **S**
- Mento artists not known outside Jamaica until now **S**

Paragraph 3

- DJs and record collectors always liked mento **S**
- Toronto DJ Rocky says older Jamaican sounds popular in clubs **M**
- Used to only be played in Jamaican areas **S**
- Germany and Japan—fans of older Jamaican genres **S**
- ~~Non-English speakers and patois—learned it from the music~~ **S**

After revising his list, Mark was more confident about writing the first draft of his summary, which follows:

> In Samra Habib's article "The New, Old Jamaica," she discusses the revival of an older Jamaican music genre. Revivals of genres are nothing new; Rock and Roll, for example, made a comeback in the 1970s. But in North American clubs, the mento genre is popular for the first time. Mento began in the 19th century as a kind of folk music, sung and played by musicians who made their own instruments. It was very popular in Jamaica until the 1960s, when ska and reggae took over as the main genres. Mento, whose name may come from Spanish or may be of African origin, sounds like a mix of calypso beats, Latin, and swing, with a rhythm all its own. Unlike reggae, which tends to be slower and politically oriented in its lyrics, mento's lyrics are often funny; they tend to be about society and sex. Until recently, mento was mostly unknown outside Jamaica because when Jamaican music reached world popularity, ska and reggae were what people heard. Only DJs and record collectors were mento fans. Now, though, as Toronto's DJ Rocky says, mento, once popular only among Jamaican-Canadians, is getting some play in clubs. It is also developing a global following, with fans in France, Germany, and Japan. Further signs of mento's revival are long-time mento artist Stanley Beckford's first solo CD, his appearance at European festivals, new appreciation of other mento performers, and new mento compilation CDs. Mento is an old genre that's attracting people's interest just because it's new to them (255).

Tightening Up a First-Draft Summary

Re-examining his original article and listing its ideas reassured Mark that he had not eliminated too much of the original in his draft. The word-count tool showed 255 words, about 20 per cent higher than his goal, so he used three methods to tighten his next draft:

1. He edited wordy phrases.

2. He removed repetitions.

3. He condensed related ideas into single phrases or sentences.

In the section of his revision work shown below, Mark notes wordy passages with a **W** and repetitions with an **R**.

Note: Write summaries in the present tense. When you restate someone else's material, it is seen as occurring in the "written present" and for the first time for readers of your summary.

In Samra Habib's article "The New, Old Jamaica," ~~discusses the revival of an older~~ *W* Jamaican music genre. Revivals of genres are nothing new; ~~Rock and Roll, for example, made a comeback in the 1970s.~~ *R* But in North American clubs, the mento genre *W* is popular for the first time. Mento began in the 19th century ~~as a kind of~~ *W* folk music, ~~sung and played by~~ *R* musicians who made their own instruments. ~~It was very popular~~ *W* in Jamaica until the 1960s, when ska and reggae took over as the main genres. Mento, ~~whose name may come from~~ *W* Spanish or ~~may be of~~ *W* African origin, sounds like a mix of calypso beats, Latin, and swing, with a rhythm all its own. Unlike reggae, ~~which tends to be~~ *W* slower and politically oriented in its *W* lyrics, mento's lyrics are often funny; ~~they tend to be~~ *W* about society and sex. Until recently, mento was mostly unknown outside Jamaica because when Jamaican music reached world popularity, ~~ska and reggae were what people heard.~~ *R*

Mark now worked on each sentence individually, rephrasing wordy sections, removing repetitions, and joining similar ideas into single phrases and sentences. Here is his final draft:

In her article "The New, Old Jamaica," Samira Habib covers a newcomer to a familiar media phenomenon—music genre revivals. The newcomer is mento, a Jamaican music genre popular in North American clubs and globally, for the first time. Mento started as a 19th century Jamaican style of folk music, played on homemade instruments. Its popularity continued until the 1960s and the appearance of ska and reggae. Mento's name may be Spanish or African, and its sound is a mix of calypso beats, Latin, and swing. Its rhythm is lively compared to reggae's beat, and its lyrics, less political than reggae's, look humorously at sex and society. Because ska and reggae dominated when Jamaican music hit world popularity, mento endured only among Jamaican fans, DJs, and record collectors. Now, trendy Toronto club people, along with fans in France, Germany, and Japan, have caught onto mento. The worldwide revival of mento has occasioned new interest in notable mento performers, festival appearances by artists, and new mento CDs. Mento is an old genre that catches people's ears because it's a new sound to anyone outside Jamaica (184).

Mark's final word-count was 184 words. The process of listing his article's main ideas and support ensured the quality of his summary's content, and his revisions produced a tightly worded and effective summary.

SUMMARY CHECKLIST

Does your summary

- Keep the basic proportion of ideas of your original?
- Include all main ideas?

- Include only essential supporting points? Eliminate repetitive support?
- Maintain the same order presented in the original document?
- Add nothing to the original document?
- Use appropriate cue phrases, if needed?
- Use only your own words (paraphrases), except where a quotation might be unavoidable?
- Display the word count required by your assignment?

● ● ● ACTIVITY

Write a one- or two-paragraph summary of an article from a Canadian magazine. Your summary should be roughly one-third the length of the original. Follow the steps and advice presented in this chapter. The article's content should relate to your main area of study. For information on how to find magazine articles and journals about a specific subject, refer to the next chapter, "Research Skills."

CHECKLIST OF LEARNING OUTCOMES FOR CHAPTER 17

To ensure that you have understood and met the learning outcomes for this chapter, answer the following questions:

✓ What is a summary, and how does a summary differ from an essay?

✓ What are four parts of an article that you can preview for information about its content?

✓ What is paraphrasing, and what must you do to avoid plagiarism when you paraphrase?

✓ How does listing an original source's main ideas and support help you create a good summary?

✓ What are three methods for revising and tightening drafts of a summary?

✓ What are two requirements for the content of an effective summary?

PART 3 SPECIAL SKILLS AND RESEARCH

Online **Learning**Centre

For bonus material and additional activities please go to the OLC at www.mcgrawhill.ca/olc/langan

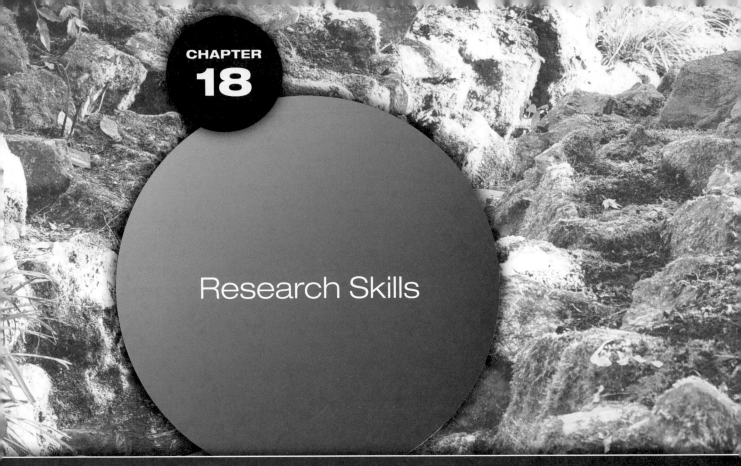

Research Skills

LEARNING OUTCOMES

After reading this chapter and working through its activities, you will

- explain why research is a process;
- identify the goals of academic research;
- identify and explain the two main tasks in creating an academic research paper;
- be prepared to follow the steps for conducting effective research;
- prepare suitable time-plans for research assignments;

- discern how and when to explore a research subject;
- establish a topic-focus and create a trial outline;
- use sources of information effectively;
- evaluate information for quality and usefulness;
- identify the functions of research material in a research assignment.

For some assignments so far you have been your own main source of information; in other assignments, you may have done varying amounts of research to give depth and accuracy to support your points. As you have seen in Part Two, research forms an important part of postsecondary essays and assignments. In most of your courses, you will be routinely required to supplement and extend your own views with material from other sources.

Your first goal when conducting academic research is to explore a topic to the degree of depth appropriate to the assigned task. As you do so, you reach the next goal: learning the conventions, technical or special terminology, and areas of information related to your subject area. This is "learning to speak the language" of your discipline or subject-area. Ultimately, your goal will be to add to the current knowledge-base in the subject-area by presenting your own thesis and supporting ideas and integrating them with the ideas from reliable resources.

These are significant goals, and to reach them, all researchers must begin at the beginning by clearly understanding what is needed for each task and assignment. To assist you, this chapter presents the process, purposes, and methods of conducting college- or university-level research. The next chapter, "Writing and Documenting a Research Paper," follows directly from this chapter to help you assemble and document an effective research paper.

THE RESEARCH PROCESS: AN OVERVIEW

Conducting effective research may be *the* essential skill you can acquire as part of your college or university education. Research is actually one of the most enjoyable aspects of education. Advancement in all areas of knowledge relies on your acquisition and intelligent use of research. In learning to participate in the research process, you join experts and scholars in exploring and expanding the knowledge-base of all subjects. As you polish and widen your research skills, you are also learning techniques for handling and crediting information that you will use and modify throughout your academic and professional career.

No one is born knowing how to conduct or use research, but everyone can learn the process and the skills.

Facts About the Research Process

1. Conducting research means following a set of steps; it is a process that begins by understanding the task involved and concludes with an assignment that meets the requirements of that task.

2. The research process can be learned, just like any other set of skills and techniques.

3. The research process, once learned, is a basic pattern that can be adapted to all subjects and situations.

4. Successfully pursuing the steps of the research process *takes time* and *requires dedication and care;* there are no shortcuts.

THE DISCOVERY STAGE: PREPARING FOR RESEARCH

What Are Your Tasks When Writing Research Essays?

Traditionally, research essays or papers have been longer printed works that demonstrated a writer's insight into, and responses to, material compiled on a specialized topic. Today, your research assignment may appear in online form, as a multimedia creation, as a presentation with text support, or as a familiar print essay. Whichever form your research assignment takes, it will follow a specific pattern of construction that imposes two main tasks on you as a writer:

1. **Investigation: Discovering** your own thoughts about your subject and appropriate secondary support for your ideas.

2. **Synthesis: Blending** your own points with support from research sources to create a clear and correctly documented paper.

Notice that *you* are the key to, and the creator of your research essay. You will begin by **discovering** your own responses to your subject. As you did with other essays, you will create a thesis statement and supporting points.

Depending on how often you have incorporated research into your essays so far, your new challenges will include undertaking the research process in a focused and structured way, selecting solid and appropriate resource material, and **blending** your research with your own ideas clearly and correctly. Think of your research paper as a "prepared conversation," a dialogue between you and authorities in your topic area. You set the structure and drive the conversation, and you decide which "outside" voices and ideas best serve the point of your thesis.

Discovery (investigation) and **blending** (synthesis) are your two overall tasks as you create your research essay. They represent the key stages that all writers work through. In this chapter, you will learn the steps to follow during the *discovery* stage of the research process; the following chapter addresses the *blending* of your own ideas with your research findings for an effective research paper.

Below are the steps that will guide you through the discovery stage of the research process. First, though, be sure to allow yourself enough time: research assignments often have three-week to one-month deadlines. These do not represent a lot of time: you will need to take the list below and make a rough time-plan that you can update and modify* as you go along. Be aware that you will need to allot time for the construction and drafting of your essay as well.

These steps comprise a complete and proven strategy for tackling any research task. Work one step at a time and allow yourself enough time to complete each one. Each time you work through the research process, you will find your investigations less demanding and more rewarding.

The Discovery Stage: Steps for Effective Research

1. Understand all aspects of your assignment. Ask questions and plan your time.

2. Explore your subject to develop ideas and a viewpoint.

---

*Once past this step, the discovery stage, like the writing process, may be iterative or wayward, meaning it may turn back on itself. For example, as you are examining articles from an academic database, you may wish to revise supporting points in your trial outline.

3. Establish your topic focus.

4. Create a trial outline.

5. Decide on your research strategies and make research notes.

6. Find information, using the library and the Internet.

7. Evaluate and select appropriate information.

8. Take time to absorb findings. Begin research notes.

STEP 1: UNDERSTAND ALL ASPECTS OF YOUR ASSIGNMENT

What Are the Specifics of Your Research Assignment?

Academic subjects offer various types of research assignments. There will be very notable differences in assignment goals, handling of source-material, and overall format. Some subjects (psychology, media studies, and scientific/technical disciplines) assign research surveys. These are *not* research essays. Instead, student survey writers examine the resources available for a given topic and impartially note their quality and depth. Most subjects assign research essays, and these follow basic essay structural patterns with some variations. In a research essay, you present a thesis, and integrate research findings with your own views.

While the research process for the survey and the essay will be similar, the techniques for completing each will be very different. A student who does not take the time to understand the differences between a research survey and a research essay cannot do a good job with either one. Because the research essay is common to nearly every subject, this chapter and the next cover its creation in detail.

Therefore, begin by finding out what form of research assignment is expected, and how to manage your resources. If you make errors due to overlooking or not requesting information when you receive an assignment, you may go farther and farther in the wrong direction, wasting time and marks.

1. Ask Questions

Each time you receive a research assignment in any subject, begin a list of questions for your instructor. Use a notebook or bring your laptop when you meet with your instructor. You will need to write the details of your professor's answers and to add more questions as you go along. Speak to or email your instructor any time you are uncertain.

In the box that follows, you will find questions asked by researchers, students, and professionals alike. These may help prompt discussions with your instructor.

> ### *Typical General Research Questions*
>
> 1. What forms of information will be suitable for this task? (i.e., general background information, news/journalism, statistics)
> 2. How much of which types of information will be needed?
> 3. Where will I find appropriate resources?
> 4. How soon will I need main research to be completed?
> 5. Is current or up-to-date information needed here?
> 6. What is the required format or structure for the assignment? Is this an essay, a report, a research summary, an annotated bibliography, or some other format?
> 7. Based on the above, how is research to be used in the assignment?
> 8. How is the research assignment evaluated?
> 9. Which citation method is required?
> 10. Where should I go for help with citation?

This chapter and the next will cover the answers to many of these questions. Please keep in mind, though, your instructor's specific requirements for any given assignment.

2. Manage and Plan Your Time

Your second task is to set up your rough time plan. Allow for your research (*discovering*) and essay creation (*blending*) and drafting. You may, like the student whose schedule is below, set up one time plan for research and another for drafting the essay. Just establish the habit, set aside enough time, and then follow your plan each time you receive such an assignment. If you are unsure about how much time to allow for research or assignment completion, ask your professor and your library technicians.

If, for example, your research essay is due in four to five weeks, you could set up a schedule as follows. Naturally, you will be working around classes, other assignments, and other obligations, so try to be realistic. One student's plan below indicates "days missing" between items—days when her class-load makes research difficult. Keep adjusting your time plan as needed, whenever you make changes.

> ### *Discovery Research Plan*
>
> ESSAY DUE: May 5
> DATE TODAY: March 28
> 1. Explore subject—3 days [Mar. 29–31]
> 2. Establish topic focus—2 days [Apr. 2–3]
> 3. Create trial outline—2 days [Apr. 5–6]

4. Discover what I need from research—2–3 days [Apr. 8–10]

5. Find information in library and on Internet—4 days? [Apr. 11–14]

6. Evaluate and select appropriate information—3 days [Apr. 16–18]

7. Take time to absorb findings. Begin research notes—3 days [Apr. 20–22]

In the previous section, a typical research question appears: *How soon will you need your research information?* Creating a time plan can give you at least an approximate idea. This student will need to have her resources chosen by April 18th. Later, she will probably adjust this schedule as she goes along, and will add her plans for drafting her essay that is due on May 5th, but she now has a general idea of how to space out her tasks.

STEP 2: EXPLORE YOUR SUBJECT

Research essays are usually based on multifaceted, controversial, or topical subjects to expand students' knowledge of important areas of course content. Depending on your instructor's preference, you may be assigned a tidy, pre-narrowed topic, or a list of general subjects. Research papers are longer than standard essays, and the subjects involved are more complex, so before you narrow or define your topic within the subject area, you must first choose and then explore your subject.

As you would do for an essay, choose a subject that interests you. You will be spending a lot of time with aspects of this subject, and enthusiasm will help to fuel your research.

- If your subject is new or unknown to you …

If you know almost nothing about your subject, or if it is an extremely broad one, you will find it difficult to proceed to the next step of narrowing a topic. Brainstorming for an outline of your own thoughts on that subject will be equally difficult. Therefore, budget more, rather than less time to investigate your subject. Begin by reading some *secondary sources* (books, articles, and Web sites about the subject): you will gain introductory knowledge, an awareness of any specialized terminologies in that subject area, and understanding of some subtopics or divisions within the subject. Now is the time to try general reference sources such as encyclopedias and handbooks or guides to your subject area. (For further information on these resources, see pages 280–283.) Some exploratory reading will help you define your topic and develop your own viewpoint or thesis.

- If your subject is a familiar one …

If, on the other hand, your subject is a topic you know something about, or is a *primary source* (a story, article, or text you know from class), it is better to proceed to the next step. Work out your own topic, ideas, thesis, and rough outline before examining secondary sources. Your preliminary thinking will be clearer when uncluttered by ideas derived from external sources. Moreover, until you have worked out a thesis and support, you will not know which of your ideas will benefit from secondary-source-derived information.

Research Tip: Primary and Secondary Sources

There are two broad categories of information available to you: primary and secondary sources.

- **Primary sources are original,** first-hand sources that are the subject itself or inform you directly about the subject. Primary sources *do not* comment on, explain, or analyze the subject. Primary sources are often eyewitness records of an event, situation, or process, or original works of art or literature. A primary source could be a story or article you are writing about for a research paper, a fact-finding interview with a person on the subject of your research, or an event or experiment you are observing as the basis of your paper. These are all direct sources of information.

- **Secondary sources are works** in any medium that refer to, comment on, or analyze your subject area. They are second-hand information—material that has been published on the subject of your research. In other words, secondary sources are the viewpoints of others. Included among secondary sources are encyclopedia articles; reference books; journal, newspaper, magazine, and even blog articles; TV programs; and Web sites.

STEP 3: ESTABLISH YOUR TOPIC FOCUS

Once you have selected and explored a subject, it is time to work out a focus-area within that subject. College and university research papers explore limited topics; they examine a single aspect of a subject in depth. The general background information you read while exploring your subject is therefore not suitable for a research essay. The information you will seek, once you have narrowed your topic and made a rough outline, will be specific and clearly tied to your essay's points and support.

The length of the essay required by your instructor will be one determinant of how narrow your topic and thesis should be: the briefer the essay, the narrower the topic. For example, if the subject is *the halo effect,* a short seven-hundred-word essay could likely cover in five or six paragraphs the topic of its effect in one situation (classrooms) with one type of people (popular students). This short essay using research, in structural terms, would resemble "Choking the Lungs of the World" in Chapter 12 or "What's for Dinner" in Chapter 13. On the other hand, if the required essay length is two to three thousand words, that essay could examine the positive and negative values of the effect as it applies to a range of media and sports figures.

Your task is to discover a topic, then to establish a viewpoint of your own on that topic. Your research paper presents *your viewpoint* on one single aspect (a topic) of some subject. Your support for your viewpoint derives from your own thoughts as well. What you create with a research essay is a dialogue—you propose your thesis and support, then present others' ideas to agree with, oppose, extend, and augment your own voice.

Your goal in narrowing your topic is to discover one aspect that interests you and that provides a potentially rewarding area for research. One way to narrow your topic, which will ultimately help you create a trial thesis, is to ask yourself a series of *research questions.*

Ask Yourself Research Questions

- *What* do I want to discover about _____?
- *Who* are the relevant people (or characters) I should find out about?
- *When* do things occur in _____?
- *Where* does/do happen _____?
- *Why* or *how* does/do _____ occur, or *why* is/are _____ so _____?

Having answered one or more of these questions, you may be prepared to state the focus of your research. Your trial thesis may be as simple as, "Five events led to _____." It is a guide to help you move on to a trial outline. Moreover, you may, as with any prewriting, change your trial thesis as you go on.

An interesting way to explore a range of aspects connected to your topic is to try a directory search with a good search engine such as Google (http://google.ca), or Google Scholar (http://scholar.google.ca). Type in a keyword or phrase related to your topic. Depending on your keyword(s), Google sites offer you several avenues for finding various facets and subcategories of your subject. When you first use Google Scholar, read "About Google Scholar" and "Google Scholar Help," as this engine delivers only scholarly, higher-level results from specialized sources. If you input some very popular keywords or abstract terms such as "wisdom," the search engine automatically returns a "searches related to …" section at the bottom of the screen. Generally, though, just select the "more" option at the top of the screen where Google presents its search options, including "Images," "Groups," and "News." On the "more" screen, you will see a variety of icons with links such as *Catalogs, Answers, Special Searches.* Choose *Directory,* and put in your keyword or phrase. You will then see a *Directory* screen dedicated to your keyword. By examining some of the sites in the directory area, you will find numerous specific aspects of your topic.

Another excellent way to explore varied aspects of your topic is to use your campus or public library's online catalogue. Search for books and magazines by subject. (For more information about library catalogues, see pages 280–281.) Subject headings will give you helpful ideas about how to limit your topic. Titles of books and magazine articles can also suggest different directions to pursue in narrowing your topic. To follow one student's progress in researching and writing a research essay, go to the OLC.

PART 3

SPECIAL SKILLS AND RESEARCH

STEP 4: CREATE A TRIAL OUTLINE

With a trial thesis, you can begin a trial outline to shape your research. Do not expect to work out a final thesis of your limited topic quickly. The time you spend discovering a single line of argument that interests you helps you discover what to look for during your research and what your ultimate thesis statement should be.

Below is a diagram of a partial trial outline. Create a word-processed version of this diagram or download and print a copy from the OLC, and save it as a blank outline that you can copy and paste into new outline documents. Continue to revise your outline, saving different versions with appropriate names (V1, V2). As you work out your first trial outline, you will have blanks in your support. You may even have more blanks than supporting points or details; those are ideal places to do some research. Do not be too critical of yourself; your daydreaming and intuitive sense of why you think your trial thesis is valid will provide some surprisingly strong ideas.

Trial Outline Diagram

Paragraph I: Thesis Statement/Or do I need a first set-up paragraph for my thesis?

Plan of Development: Supporting Points

A. _____

B. _____

C. _____

D. _____

E. _____

Paragraph II: Supporting Point A

Details:

1. _____

2. _____

3. _____

Paragraph III: Supporting Point B

Details:

1. _____

2. _____

3. _____

Paragraph IV: Supporting Point C

Details:

1. _____

2. _____

3. _____

Paragraph V: Supporting Point D

A Note about Research Essay Length

If you turn to the model research papers in Chapter 20, you will notice that they, like nearly all research papers, are significantly longer than typical essay assignments.

The basic essay model you learned in Parts 1 and 2 is a convenient one for routine assignments. Its structure is the model for many longer pieces of writing such as research papers and some reports. As you will see in the next chapter, this format can be expanded at any point in its structure: if background introductory material is needed to set up or explain the thesis, then a first paragraph appears before the second or thesis paragraph. As well, each supporting point for the thesis will occupy at least one body paragraph, and some supporting points may in fact require more than one body paragraph.

The blank template diagram can be expanded to reflect changes in essay content development.

Note: Writing a research paper always begins with your own ideas and trial outline to guide you. It does *not* entail simply finding information and piecing it together as a patchwork of others' ideas.

STEP 5: DECIDE ON RESEARCH STRATEGIES AND MAKE RESEARCH NOTES

Your instructor may specify the types of research material required for your assignment. Even so, discovering precisely what information you will need from resources can be a challenge. Examine your outline with the following questions in mind:

- What, in general, do I need to know more about so I can add supporting details?
- Who are the major authorities or sources of information in my topic area?
- Where do I need more facts to expand my support and fill in my blanks?
- What kinds of information—facts, statistics, details, quotations, technical data—are relevant to this course or subject-area and will make parts of my research paper stronger?
- Where can I find some reliable information in the areas I've noted above?

As you look for potential sources of information, begin with general sources, as you did when working on narrowing your research topic. From now on, use your thesis and trial outline as guides; you may even want to start your thinking by looking up and noting definitions of all the key words in your thesis.

Your purpose in examining general research sources will be a bit different now. You are looking for specific secondary sources. Return to the reference section of your campus or public library and ask the library staff for help finding indexes of publications in your topic area and guides to publications as well. These will guide you to specific reference sources. Ask about journals and periodicals, too; these will be available online or bound. Check textbooks on your topic area as well; textbooks will usually include bibliographies (lists of works used or referred to) relevant to your research. Next, try Internet search engines and directories (see pages 283–284) to get a general idea of the range and quality of information available to you.

As you scan titles and summaries of publications and Web sites, start your research notes and be prepared to take both care and time to do so, as shown on the next page.

Making Research Notes

Begin and maintain your research notes correctly. Doing so will help you avoid having to re-find sources later, and will help you avoid plagiarism.

There are two steps in research note-taking:

1. Record your source material as
   - Quotations: the exact words of another writer, enclosed by double quotation marks; or
   - Paraphrases: complete restatements of another writer's words in your own words and sentences; or
   - Summaries: condensed versions of another writer's ideas in your own words.
2. Then add all required citation information for each research note.

For each item of research you record, you will note specific citation and location information: the author, title of the work, and other essential items. As you do so, you are also preparing the material for your Works Cited or References list. To find the complete list of required citation information required, see below.

Choose one method for setting up your revised research notes, and use it consistently. You could begin a notebook or computer document called "Research Notes," in which you record the answers you give to the questions above as well as documentation information for each item. Maintaining your notes as a computer document allows you to insert ideas exactly where they should go and update or expand your notes cleanly. Using a notebook has the advantage of portability—as does a notebook computer. Many researchers use file or index cards; in whatever form you keep your notes, remember to date each entry. Keep a copy of your trial outline with the notes, so you can refer to it when you are in the library or online.

Begin each research note with a phrase or keyword that refers to the point or idea that the note applies to.

For each research note, you will then need to record

- The complete name(s) of the author(s) of the work
- The complete names of editors, if appropriate
- The complete title of the work (book, journal, magazine, newspaper, government document, Web site)
- The complete name of the chapter or section of a book or Web site, if applicable
- The page numbers you have referred to or quoted from or paraphrased from
- The publisher of the work
- The city of publication
- The year the work was published (and the edition, if applicable)
- The page numbers where you found your information: both individual page numbers and the range of pages you read or checked through
- Locating information (call numbers for library books).

For **journal, magazine, and newspaper articles,** you will also need

- The complete name of the article and section in which your material appears
- The volume, number, and date of the journal in which the article appears
- The page numbers on which the article appears.

For **a Web site,** you will also need

- The date of creation and dates of revision listed for the Web site or of the section of the site you refer to
- Locating information: the URL of the Web site
- The date or dates on which you accessed the Web site.

Make sure that your final research notes are complete, with indications of when you are quoting, paraphrasing, or summarizing another author's ideas. In a research paper, you must document all information that is not common knowledge or a matter of historical record. For example, Stephen Harper's birth date is an established fact and does not need documenting. As you read several sources on a subject, you will develop a sense of what authors regard as generally shared or common information about a subject and what is more specialized information that must be documented. If you do not document and show the source of specialized information about a subject, you are plagiarizing, in effect stealing someone else's work.

By keeping complete and correct research notes, you will find that inserting your source material into drafts of your paper will be much easier, as will creating the Works Cited (MLA) or References (APA) section that appears at the end of your research paper.

Research Tips

As you make research notes, make notes to yourself about how the ideas you find relate to your outline's thesis and probable supporting points. Doing so will be of great help when you come to blend or synthesize others' ideas with your own in the body of your essay. Always set off your own notes to yourself and your thoughts in another colour to keep them visually separated and distinct from others' ideas.

As you proceed with making notes, you will find that certain ideas and key words connected to your topic and thesis crop up over and over again. You will want to note these repeated occurrences of ideas and key words: this is called *cross-referencing*. One way to simplify this process visually is to go through your notes and make lists by key word or idea on which you list the authors' names of those who mention the words and ideas. As you go along in your academic career, you will want to use Word's cross-referencing feature (under *Insert*) or a database program such as *Endnotes*.

Although you may find research note-taking time-consuming at first, you will quickly grow accustomed to the process. It is a skill and a habit that will benefit you throughout your academic and career life. Conducting research is a fascinating and enriching experience—there is no quick approach to it, especially not one that involves stealing information and other people's hard work. That is plagiarism.

Plagiarism

Plagiarism is defined as using and presenting, knowingly or unknowingly, someone else's ideas, words, technical data, or images as your own. You will suffer the same consequences for intentionally plagiarizing work as you will for unintentionally plagiarizing; *there is no "I didn't know" escape hatch.* All colleges and universities teach and reinforce the use of recognized documentation. They also reinforce the penalties for plagiarism: records on students' transcripts, failure, and possible expulsion.

Plagiarism does not depend on the *quantity of borrowed material;* it is *not* a matter of degree. The same rules for use of resources apply to all subjects and programs; there is no subject or course wherein students may "borrow" text, images, coding, scientific information, or any other material without proper documentation. Any uncredited borrowing, even a few words, without credit information is as much plagiarism as an entire paper not of your own creation: theft is theft.

- **Avoid "unconscious plagiarism."**

As you start college or university, you may not be aware of how easy it is to "unconsciously plagiarize" material. Learn how to quote, paraphrase, and cite correctly. Know that your writing style is as personal as your fingerprint. To any instructor who has seen a paragraph of yours even once or twice, phrases in another person's style are immediately detectable. There are many "giveaways" in basic aspects of your sentence-structure and word-choices that will be readily evident to your professors.

If, because of earlier educational or cultural training, a student unconsciously and unknowingly copies words or phrases, then explaining the situation immediately to the instructor is the best course of action. If, on the other hand, a student knowingly decides to use someone else's work, then he or she has made a conscious decision to defraud the instructor. This dishonesty is outright plagiarism; the student risks failure and expulsion.

- **Plagiarism is not simply copying another person's words.**

Plagiarism is not confined to stealing text and misrepresenting sources of ideas in research papers. Every day students buy essays, photograph tests with cell phones, have friends do assignments, and copy and paste text and images from online sources. Growing use of the Internet and file-sharing have given rise among students to a more lenient view of ownership of intellectual or artistic property. Students tend to feel that if no one gets caught, then there is no crime. This attitude reflects impatience and greed; the academic and professional world that awaits these students will not tolerate theft or abuse of intellectual property.

Artists, musicians, designers, writers, and research scientists work extremely hard; their work is their intellectual property. Why is it acceptable to steal their work simply because you can? The educational community does not tolerate theft or fraud—these are taken seriously, and result in disgrace and heavy penalties. Colleges, universities, and businesses operate within legal frameworks in which the theft of ideas is illegal.

- **Plagiarism is easier to catch every year.**

Students who plagiarize seem blissfully unaware that methods for its detection grow more sophisticated each year. Technology is a double-edged weapon—more research information is available online, but tracing the sources of such information is easier and faster than ever. Purchased essays are traceable, no matter what claims essay vendors make. Colleges and universities use such applications as turnitin.com and safeassign.com. Dealing with plagiarism costs you in the long run because time spent tracing sources is time instructors could better spend on course development or careful marking.

What Constitutes Plagiarism?

You may be surprised to discover the range of activities that constitute plagiarism. Make yourself aware of all possible forms of plagiarism noted in your college's or university's policy regarding academic honesty, plagiarism, and penalties. Remember, pleading ignorance will not excuse you from being charged.

Following is a partial list of actions that constitute plagiarism:

- Turning in an assignment or essay bought from any source
- Submitting any published material in any subject or course as the student's work; for example, but not limited to, lab reports, class assignments, html coding, images from any source
- Submitting any copied and pasted material from any online source as the student's own work
- Making use of the exact words from any source other than the student him- or herself without the use of quotation marks and without giving proper credit to the author
- Submitting a pattern or sequence of ideas or setting out someone else's work even if either of these is expressed in the student's own words, without giving appropriate acknowledgment
- Attending classes or a course for another student
- Paying another student to write a paper and submitting it as one's own
- Doing assignments of any type for another student
- Working as a group on an assignment when it is not permitted
- Taking assignments from other students and submitting them as one's own
- Listing false or unused items in a bibliography, works cited, or references list

How to Avoid Plagiarizing

While the knowledge and skills you are learning at college and university are built on centuries of using the knowledge and skills of others, they are set on a clear and honest foundation of honouring their sources. You must adopt a willing and open attitude toward acquiring and mastering research skills—a halfway or careless approach to the use of research is halfway or more to plagiarism. Here are some basic practical tips:

- Never buy any academic material of any kind online or from another student.
- If you are in doubt about whether or not to put exact words from any source in quotation marks, use quotation marks and the correct citation (see Chapter). Err on the side of caution rather than carelessness.
- Never figure that "a few words don't matter." Plagiarism is not measured by volume or quantity of words stolen; five words are just as much theft as fifty.
- Do not slightly change an author's wording to make it fit your own ideas or to pass it off as a paraphrase. Learn how to paraphrase correctly, in the following chapter.
- If you are afraid that a research assignment in any subject is too difficult for you, or if you know you do not have enough time to complete it, speak to your instructor and explain your situation. You will likely receive some assistance or possibly an extension. Either one of those is preferable to the *0* and note on your transcript you could receive for a purchased or plagiarized assignment.

Mastering research skills and techniques reflects your ethics and values as a person. When you document your research correctly, you set up a trust, a contract among you, your readers, and the sources of your information, a guarantee that all parties respect each other and give due credit when needed. In the following chapter, you will find examples of correct and incorrect uses of quotations and paraphrases.

STEP 6: FIND INFORMATION USING THE LIBRARY AND THE INTERNET

Library Resources

Your campus or local library contains many resources for your research in the forms of printed and computerized material. This material is stored systematically.

Discover how your library's storage systems work; this is essential to finding useful information. Learn what is available from your library's cataloguing system and technological resources; it makes starting your research much easier.

Also, do not forget librarians and help desk staff. They are information experts and are there to help you.

Library Catalogues

The library catalogue is your first key to available information. The catalogue is usually an online listing of two types of holdings: those in your library and those available on loan from affiliated library collections.

- **Library collections** consist of information in a variety of media: books, periodicals, encyclopedias, films, CDs, and so on.
- **Campus libraries' online resources** are usually part of the college or university Web site and use a system like BIBCAT, which allows you to look up all kinds of reference materials in different media.

- **Electronic book access** means that your library has electronic publication services that gather and provide the full texts of books, journals, and the latest publications from sources in business and technology. E-books are great up-to-date resources in subject-areas where timeliness is important.
- **Library databases** are special tools containing carefully selected information related to programs offered by your college or university. The catalogue and databases will be accessible to you on any of the terminals in your library.

Research Tip: Learn the Value of Author, Title, and Subject Searches

Most library catalogues allow you to search by author, title, or subject, or by keywords. Author and title screens display useful information, including call numbers to help you locate items, and current availability status. For these searches, you will need to know the authors and/or titles of items you seek.

Most often, searching initially by *subject* will be most productive.

The *subject* section of the catalogue performs three valuable functions:

1. It will give you a list of books, articles, and other publications on a given topic.
2. It will often provide related topics that may yield information on your subject.
3. It will suggest more limited topics, helping you to further narrow your topic.

As you look at *subject* section screens, you see books, the traditional source of information, listed. You also see listings for other sources, such as articles from special-interest and professional journals, and periodicals. Libraries and resource centres have bound volumes and computerized versions of journals and periodicals. Do not forget that, as a student, you have access to a wide range of material on these databases—much of this information is specialized and not available from search engines and ordinary online sites.

Books

Books have traditionally been the most trusted starting point for research, and in some subject areas, this is still the case. Books are time-consuming to write and publish, and therefore are good resources when you seek reputable information that is not necessarily time-sensitive. Books often cover a topic more deeply and from more viewpoints than periodical articles or Web sites. Books and periodical articles usually offer comparable levels of expertise and knowledge on the parts of their authors. However, it takes time to locate the right books and to read them. To locate books you find in the library catalogue, ask a librarian to explain the call-number system by which your library arranges books on the shelves. Once you find the book you seek, try the following tips to help you judge the usefulness of a particular book:

- Look at the front and back pages and cover text on the book. Check the date of publication, and look for information on the author's credentials.
- Check the table of contents for material related to your topic. If many chapters relate to your topic, the book may be a good resource.
- Look through the back index of the book for words and phrases related to your topic. If there are many pages pertaining to those words and phrases, consider using the book.
- Scan the introduction or preface for the author's statement of intentions, viewpoint, and a summary of the book's content.
- Look for a bibliography to find related books on the same subject.

Examine at least two books on your topic so that you can practise thinking critically; weigh one author's views against another's and against your own ideas.

Periodicals

Periodicals (magazines, journals, and newspapers), as research tools, may be new to you, but they are essential sources of specific, focused, current information that is up to date with professional standards in your program. To use periodical articles, you must learn to locate them and then judge their content for quality and currency.

Periodical Indexes

If this is your first experience with using periodicals for research, ask a librarian to help you find out which periodicals your library carries, how these are indexed, and how to access the articles contained in the indexes. There are both printed and online indexes of every kind of periodical, from daily newspapers to highly specialized professional and scientific journals.

Librarians can direct you to the large bound indexes of various periodicals and help you to use them. The *Readers' Guide to Periodical Literature* and the *Canadian Periodical Index* are good places to begin; these are printed each year as new books and articles are listed by author and subject with cross-references to related articles. The *Canadian Periodical Index* or *CPI* lists articles from Canadian specialized and academic publications as well as popular magazines. Other bound volumes of more specialized periodical indexes will be shelved near these volumes, so check for any related to your topic or subject area.

The *CPI.Q* (the *Canadian Periodical Index* search service), and other periodical indexes are also available on library online databases and on CDs in most libraries. You may find these versions easier to use. Search by subject or author, as you would with the library catalogue.

Once you have found articles whose titles sound promising, or whose listings offer summaries relevant to your topic, you must locate the full text of the article itself. If your library stocks a periodical, simply ask the librarian to help you locate the issue you need. If you are using an online index, you may also be able to access the full-text version of the article onscreen. Alternatively, your library may offer database help with finding such articles. The following section of this chapter covers research databases, which can be real assets for college research.

Research Databases and Online Search Services

It is essential to learn how to use the electronic research databases and online search services available through your school's library site. Academic research tasks require specialized or scholarly information you will not find online at general access sites or through search engines. In fact, over 70 percent of this high-quality information exists only on what is called the "invisible Web"—pages protected by firewalls and inaccessible to search engines. Colleges and universities purchase library portals and databases to give you entry to these essential online resources, which are available in three forms:

- Controlled Web sites to which your college or university has purchased access rights
- Online databases to which your college or university provides access
- CD ROM databases owned by your school's library.

Databases include *Lexis Nexis, Proquest,* and *ERIC* (Education Resources Information Centre), and *Project MUSE.* EBSCOhost and PowerWeb house online computer search services. *Dialog* and *CPI.Q* give you access to thousands of magazine articles listed by subject. Listings have summaries or abstracts and sometimes whole articles. Using the EBSCOhost service, you can perform keyword searches through hundreds of periodicals for articles on your topic. You can then email the results of your searches, including summaries or full texts of articles, to yourself at home or print them in the library. Some databases also allow you to open a folder wherein you can collect articles that you find; if this is possible, you will see a "folder" icon on the screen. Finally, your user ID and password or other student code gives you access to database publications ranging from trade and technological publications to encyclopedias and online collections.

Internet Resources

Doing research on the Internet allows you to work almost anywhere, but requires special skills because of its limitless nature. Your campus library's contents are selected to be of interest and use to the student body, but the Internet's vast contents have no such limits. If you learn some basic guidelines for sorting through its mix of commercial and non-commercial material, you will work online more effectively. The following is a general introduction to online research.

Search Engines

A search engine performs like a computerized "card catalogue" for the Internet. Search engines use automated software called bots, spiders, or crawlers that "crawl" through the Internet seeking content when you type in keywords. Directory engines are specialized; they contain information assembled and categorized by people who collect that material from various databases. About.com and

Looksmart are directory engines that display categories for your topic. Google can perform directory searches as well. If you are still working on your focus, or wish to confine your search to a specific area, you will find a directory search useful. Several engines today combine robot and directory functions. Metasearch engines like Google search other engines as well as their own databases, then compile the results. Google (and some other engines) can also search for results in newsgroups and different media, returning findings as text files, image files, and sound files.

There are three important reasons to allow yourself some time to work with search engines. First, even if you have narrowed your research topic, you will need time for trials with your search words. Next, you need time to sift through and scan the sites and links your searches bring up. Finally, you need time to read screens and decide which sites and which passages will be most useful. Outlining and discovering directions for your paper before going online pays off here because you will spot relevant material more quickly.

Finally, online research, for all its apparent ease, involves several pitfalls, the main one being the unreliability of many sites and Web pages. Learning to evaluate online information takes time and practice. Later in this chapter you will find guidelines for judging online resources, but if your campus library offers an online research tutorial, take it as soon as possible.

Research Tip: Increase Your Keyword Power

Entering keywords tells a search engine's database what to look for. Use words from your subject area or discipline, try synonyms, and try placing your words in order of importance. Allow time for some trial and error; no one is an expert at choosing exactly "the right keywords."

Learning to increase the power of your search words and phrases by using search engines' help pages; combining words with Boolean operators such as "and," and "not"; using plus and minus symbols; and trying subsearches are skills that maximize the effectiveness of your online research time. Here are some general guidelines to help you search effectively:

- Search engines are generally *case insensitive;* it does not matter if you capitalize a name. On occasion, though, you may wish to check a search engine's "search help" page for information about using capitals.
- Check your search engine's instructions for information for adding "operators" or "codes" such as + or *and* to link or alter the meanings of groups of keywords.
- Check your search engine's instructions for defining word groups to be taken together or *strings,* such as *liquid crystal display.*
- If you are researching only aspects of a topic that relate to Canada, choose the "Canadian sites only" option on Google and add the word *Canada* or *Canadian* to limit your search.

Try placing your keywords in order of their importance, with the most important idea first. Some engines "weight" a search by the order of the words.

STEP 7: EVALUATE AND SELECT APPROPRIATE INFORMATION

Begin with these general guidelines to help you evaluate your research information.

What kind of information are you searching for?

Information that

(a) is clearly relevant to points and details in your trial outline;

(b) is clearly understandable to you;

(c) you can paraphrase or reasonably incorporate;

(d) comes from reputable, reliable sources.

Why are you performing this research?

To find information that

(a) supports the views that you hold;

(b) expands on and strengthens points you make;

(c) lends authority to your viewpoints.

What you seek are resources whose content is closely tied to your topic and to the supporting points in your trial outline.

For each reference listing, write complete reference notes. You should have more items than you need because you will eliminate some during the step of evaluating each source of information for its quality and relevance.

With your notes at hand, review your assignment's requirements for clues as to how many sources will be appropriate. Reference specialists recommend a variety of secondary sources. As mentioned, books tend to offer careful scholarship and a range of viewpoints; periodical articles offer specific explorations of single viewpoints and timeliness; and Web sites vary widely in quality of information. If your paper should be fairly brief, select only the best pieces of information from your list; if a minimum or specified number of sources is stipulated, then use that as a guideline. In any case, research should support and extend your own ideas; it is *not* the backbone of your paper.

Evaluating Any Source of Information

Deciding how useful your sources are and how much of each to use are skills you will refine throughout your academic program, but the following specific guidelines will help you evaluate sources. Three criteria will be of particular importance as you examine any source of information: *relevance* to your topic, *reliability* of content, and *timeliness* of its information.

Relevance

- Use sources that are more, rather than less, devoted to your topic. If a source's main focus is your topic-area, its information will be less superficial and more specialized.
- Check that a source's treatment of topic-related information is suited to your understanding and needs. Is it too technical or too general?
- Consider, with a periodical source, the type of publication. Is it a general-interest magazine or specialized journal? Journals offer superior research and content quality compared to general-interest magazines and newspapers.

- Rank the source in terms of its importance to your paper's focus to make your final selection easier.

Reliability

- If possible, use sources whose authors are recognized in the field. Look for the author's biography, or ask your instructor or a librarian for help.
- Check for authors who have published other material in your topic area and whose books and articles contain bibliographies and reference lists.
- Learn all you can about the author's overall view of or bias on your topic. Check biographical material, the introduction or preface to the work, or other writers' views of the author.
- Check for references within the source to other material and authors on the subject. If these are not named, the information may be one-sided or biased.
- Look for well-supported arguments, clear logic, and solid proof for points made in your source.
- Always verify important pieces of information in at least three sources. If some information reappears frequently, then it is probably reliable.

Timeliness

- Check for recent publication dates of books and periodical articles.
- On Web sites, look for the most recent updating. This information often appears on the homepage or final page of a site.

Evaluating Internet Sources

Choosing information sources online is a special challenge because the Internet, by design, is unregulated. The additional criteria listed below for judging online resources will help you evaluate your own choices.

- **Author's Reliability:** Always check for any possible information about the author of a site. Does he or she list any credentials? Has the author published other material on the topic? Web site authors should include email contact information.
- **Affiliations and Sponsors:** Is the site affiliated with any known organization? If so, is the organization likely to provide unbiased information? Does the site have affiliations with commercial groups? If so, does this affect the quality of the information on the site? Is the site sponsored by a corporation or special-interest group? If so, will its content reflect this?
- **Objectivity and Completeness:** Read the entire site carefully before deciding to use pieces of information from it. Ask yourself if the author presents all content objectively. Are all sides of any topic stated before the author argues his or her own views? Does the author produce solid support for his or her views?
- **Nature of Links Provided:** What kinds of links are provided on the site? Do they demonstrate serious research or interests? Are they wide-ranging in content? Are they commercial or non-commercial?

- **Organization of Information:** How well is the site's information organized? Is there a site map or index to help you locate information on your topic?
- **Date:** Is the information up to date? Check near the opening or on the last page of the site for copyright, publication, or revision dates. If the site contains articles by a number of writers, check for the dates of these. Knowing such dates will help you decide whether the material is current enough for your needs. Check that the links on a Web site are active and reliable.

Tips for Evaluating Research Findings

When you are trying to decide how valuable some source of information is, consider the following questions:

- **Focus:** How focused is this material on my subject area and topic? Is the information I need a small part of the material or its main content?

- **Depth of Information:** How deeply does this material treat my area of interest? Does it offer a good quantity of information that is new to me?

- **Currency of Information:** How recently was this material published? For this course and for my topic, how important is recent information?

- **Quality of Information:** Is this material at a level of expertise that my instructor expects for this assignment? Is the author a reputable source or a specialist in this field?

STEP 8: ABSORB YOUR RESEARCH FINDINGS AND TAKE NOTES

Set some time aside to consider the sources you have selected. Read carefully each book section, article, and Web page in your research notes. Look for more cross-references and for similarities and differences among your sources. Digest and absorb ideas while you read.

Do not try to review your reference choices in one sitting. Your understanding of material deepens as you take time to read, make connections, and find new ideas of your own.

Keep your trial outline nearby and extra paper for notes of ideas and connections as well as their sources. Continue to refer to your outline to maintain your focus and to help you make decisions on what to record for which part of your outline.

As you make your notes, think about *why* you are doing so. Information from other sources has three functions:

1. **To expand on facts** with examples, statistics, or data that clarify and strengthen your points and ideas

2. **To present another explanation or view** of some point that strengthens your points and ideas

3. **To support with some recognized authority** a point or claim you make

Taking notes should, therefore, extend and support your own ideas rather than replace them. In the next chapter, you will learn how to blend your notes with your own ideas and to give credit for the information you incorporate—both critical aspects of writing an effective research paper.

CHECKLIST OF LEARNING OUTCOMES FOR CHAPTER 18

To ensure that you have understood and met the learning outcomes for this chapter, answer the following questions:

✓ Describe why research may accurately be called a process.

✓ What are the general goals for academic-level research?

✓ What, specifically, are the two main tasks involved in creating an academic research paper? Explain the key words for each goal in your own words.

✓ What steps do you need to follow to conduct effective research?

✓ Why is it essential to prepare a time-plan for research assignments?

✓ Under what circumstances would you do some research *before* narrowing a topic for a research essay?

✓ How would you go about limiting a research topic?

✓ What are the main sources of information available to you for research assignments?

✓ What are the three criteria for evaluating the quality of a source?

✓ Explain the three functions of secondary sources in a research paper.

Writing and Documenting a Research Paper

After reading this chapter and working through its activities, you will

- identify the steps for creating effective research papers;
- revise your trial outline and write an appropriate thesis statement;
- prepare and use quotations, paraphrases, and summaries appropriately and correctly;
- use MLA or APA style, as required, in research assignments;
- assemble, write, and revise your drafts to create an effective research paper.

The first task involved in writing a research essay is, first, the *discovery* of your own ideas about your topic and, second, finding research material to extend, support, or lend authority to your ideas. This chapter addresses the second task: *blending* your ideas with support from outside sources, guiding you through assembling and writing an effective research paper.

Blending your own ideas with your research findings requires you

- to have a firm enough sense of the quality of your own points and support that you do not substitute ideas from other sources simply because they seem preferable or impressive;
- to be familiar enough with the content of your research sources to select relevant material of appropriate length;

- to combine your words with paraphrases, quotations, and summaries of the words of others so that you write smooth sentences that integrate your material from research sources correctly into your text;
- to give credit to your sources each time you use them as quotations, paraphrases, or summaries, using an appropriate style of MLA or APA style for in-text and end-of-paper citation (titled Works Cited for MLA- and References for APA-style citations.

Assemble your paper one step at a time, following the steps in the box below, and you will acquire a solid working strategy for all research assignments.

Five Steps for Preparing a Research Paper

1. Revise your trial outline.
2. Write your first draft.
3. Revise your first draft to insert, integrate, and cite your reference materials. Now you have your second draft ready.
4. As you revise and edit your second draft, work on documenting your research and preparing a Works Cited (MLA) or References (APA) list.
5. Write your final draft.

STEP 1: REVISE YOUR TRIAL OUTLINE

Now that you have read and made notes on sources relating to your topic and support, revise your outline to create a clear, detailed guide as you blend your own ideas with appropriate research. First, though, consider your trial thesis statement and the purpose of your paper.

- All research papers have two main purposes—to inform or to persuade.

Recall the research questions (page 273) that were part of the research process. Do you wish to answer a *what* or *who* question? In that case, your purpose may be to inform—to supply a well-detailed, logical answer to your research question. Was a *why* or *how* question most useful to you? You may then want to persuade your reader. Use the question found most relevant, along with your assignment's requirements, to help you decide on your purpose. Clarifying your purpose helps you reformulate your trial thesis into a stronger thesis statement that guides your choices of supporting details. Once you have revised your thesis to your satisfaction, review your supporting points. Make sure that each one is truly distinct from the others and clearly proves, supports, and clarifies one aspect of your thesis.

Set up your revised outline document by copying and pasting your trial outline into a new document. Add your revised thesis and your supporting points, leaving blank spaces under each supporting heading so that later you can note supporting details as well as the quotations and paraphrases from your research. Instructors may require an outline to be handed in along with a research paper, so revising your outline like this will be well worth the effort.

The diagram below shows how to modify a research paper outline so that you can add quotations and paraphrases from your research sources in the appropriate places.

Revised Outline Diagram

Paragraph I: Background material to set up context for thesis statement

Paragraph II: Thesis Statement

Plan of Development: Supporting Points

A. _____

B. _____

C. _____

D. _____

E. _____

Paragraph III: Supporting Point A

My details:

1. _____

2. _____

3. _____ Add quotation from _____ (page #)

Paragraph IV: Supporting Point B

My details:

1. _____

2. _____ Add paraphrase from _____ (page #)

3. _____

Paragraph V: Supporting Point C

My details:

1. _____ Add quotation from _____ (page #)

2. _____

3. _____

Paragraph VI: Supporting Point D

As noted in the previous chapter, research papers, even the shorter examples in Part 2, will nearly always be more than five paragraphs long. Moreover, as you saw on pages 178–180 in Part 2, research essays, including the MLA and APA models in Chapter 20, often require two introductory paragraphs, depending on the quantity of background information an audience may need. The number of body paragraphs is usually determined by the number of supporting points but, with longer research essays, you will sometimes find that some of your supporting points may need to be divided into subtopics, each with its own paragraph, as is the case in paragraphs 4 and 5 of the MLA model research paper in Chapter 20.

The boxed outline above also includes the page numbers for the quotations and paraphrases to be included. Transfer the author's name and the page number information from your research notes each time you incorporate material from a research source. The next section of this chapter will show you how to prepare your research notes correctly, using accurate and properly credited quotations, paraphrases, and summaries.

Note: Research essays are nearly always written in the third person. The emphasis in a research paper is on your ideas, your proof, and the quality of your research rather than on your personal response. Using "I" or phrases like "in my opinion" could distract readers from the content and argument in your paper and should be avoided. Let your facts speak for themselves.

Quotations, Paraphrases, and Summaries: How and When to Use Them

Once you have finished your revised outline, you have some decisions to make about how to use the material in your research notes. When will you quote an author, and why is it important to keep his or her own words? When should you put an author's ideas into your own words, or paraphrase them? What should you do with a long passage in one of your sources that seems useful and relevant, but is just too long to work into your essay? Learning the material below will help you each time you have a research assignment in any of your courses.

Quotations

What Is a Quotation?

Each time you use the exact words of another writer, you must identify these words as a *direct quotation*—with double quotation marks. Quoting means using phrases or sentences word for word, with punctuation exactly as it appears in the original. Follow each quotation with an in-text citation in MLA (pages 303–306) or APA style (pages 313–318), depending on your course and subject.

Here is an example of a direct quotation in MLA style:

"Conversely, the category of boredom implies a set of expectations of the external world that apparently did not afflict our remote predecessors" (Meyer Spacks 11).

Here is the same quotation in APA style:

"Conversely, the category of boredom implies a set of expectations of the external world that apparently did not afflict our remote predecessors" (Meyer Spacks, 1996, p. 11).

You will see the full citation for this book as it would appear in a Works Cited (MLA) or References (APA) page in step 4 on page 302.

The in-text citation, comprising the parentheses containing the author's name, year of publication (APA only), and page number at the end of the quotation, indicates the author and exact location in the source in which the words quoted appear, pointing the reader to the source as it is listed in the Works Cited (MLA) or References list (APA) at the end of the paper.

How Do You Quote Correctly?

Quoting an author's exact words follows patterns based on MLA or APA conventions. Following are rules to cover various situations when you wish to use a quotation:

1. **When you wish to make any change to the wording in a quotation** to make its meaning clearer or to help it work with your sentence structure, do so by using square brackets, not parentheses.

    MLA style: "[a]s service providers hired to solve others' problems, designers often lose these disagreements" (White 125).
    APA style: "[a]s service providers hired to solve others' problems, designers often lose these disagreements" (White, 2002, p. 125).

    Note that the lower-case letter *a* in brackets above shows that the word has been changed from a capital *a* by the student. The upper-case *a* in the original source indicated the beginning of a sentence. Here the student will be integrating this quotation into a sentence of her own, so the lower-case letter is appropriate. Note also that the same convention, the use of brackets to indicate a change of letter or phrasing, is common to both MLA and APA styles.

2. **When you wish to omit words from a quotation,** you may do so, as long as you do not change its meaning. To show omission, use an *ellipsis*, three dots, in both MLA and APA styles.

    Here is an example in MLA style of a direct quotation with the missing words in the first sentence and at the end of the quotation replaced by ellipses:

    "One of the oldest examples of the exploitation of emptiness is the scholar's margin . . . reserved for note-taking. It also makes facing pages look more connected . . ." (White 129).

    MLA style uses the final ellipses; APA does not. Here is an example, in APA style, of the same direct quotation with missing words replaced by an ellipsis.

    "One of the oldest examples of the exploitation of emptiness is the scholar's margin . . . reserved for note-taking. It also makes facing pages look more connected" (White, 2002, p. 129); here, White traces . . .

    Note that in APA style, ellipses are not used at the beginnings or endings of quotations. In the example above, the student continues her sentence from the word *connected,* after the in-text citation. If, in either style, your quotation includes an omission at the end of a sentence, followed by the next sentence in the quoted material, use four dots in a row.

    MLA style: "One of the oldest examples of the exploitation of emptiness is the scholar's margin. . . . It also makes facing pages look more connected. . . ." (White 129).
    APA style: "One of the oldest examples of the exploitation of emptiness is the scholar's margin. . . . It also makes facing pages look more connected. . . ." (White, 2002, p. 129).

3. **When a quotation appears within your quotation,** use single quotation marks for the material quoted from another source within your quotation.

    MLA style: "Good readability makes the page look comfortable to read. Poor readability makes pages look dull or busy. Richard Lewis, an expert on annual reports, says, 'Make exciting design. Dullness and mediocrity are curses of the annual report'" (White 9).

APA style: "Good readability makes the page look comfortable to read. Poor readability makes pages look dull or busy. Richard Lewis, an expert on annual reports, says, 'Make exciting design. Dullness and mediocrity are curses of the annual report'" (White, 2002, p. 9).

Note, first, that this rule applies in the same way to both MLA and APA styles. Next, note that at the end of the internal and main quotations, the single quotation mark ends the internal quotation and the double quotation marks end the main quotation.

When Should You Use a Quotation?

Quotations are accepted and expected in formal research and academic writing, but as supplementary material only; they do not make up most of the body of the work.

Following are some ground rules to help you decide when to quote, rather than paraphrase:

- Use quotations sparingly, only when they truly extend, explain, or lend authority to your own points.
- Use quotations when the exact words of your source material are crucial to understanding the context of your assignment.
- Use quotations when the source and/or the author is such a recognized authority in your topic that quoting lends credibility to your argument or support.
- Use quotations when your source material contains specialized, technical, or extremely effective wording or phrasing that would be unsuitable to paraphrase.

Unless the use of a quotation meets one or more of the above criteria, paraphrase or summarize instead. In a short (i.e., 1000 words) research paper, five brief quotations (i.e., fewer than four lines each) would be sufficient. Papers created out of chunks of quotations strung together are annoying and confusing to read; the effect is like overhearing a babble of voices, and the writer's intention is lost in them.

When you wish to use a longer quotation of more than four lines of text, do so cautiously and correctly. In short papers, such long quotations give the impression of "filling space" to replace your own thoughts. There are distinct rules for including longer quotations.

To insert a long quotation using MLA style, set it up as follows:

From the Greeks, this revised alphabet passed to the rest of Western Europe through the Romans and, along the way, underwent several modifications to fit the requirements of spoken languages encountered. As a result, we talk about the Roman alphabet as the writing system used for English. Another line of development took the same basic Greek writing system into Eastern Europe, where Slavic languages were spoken. (Yule 24)

To insert a long quotation (more than 40 words) using APA style, set it up as follows:

From the Greeks, this revised alphabet passed to the rest of Western Europe through the Romans and, along the way, underwent several modifications to fit the requirements of spoken languages encountered. As a result, we talk about the Roman alphabet as the writing system used for English. Another line of development took the same basic Greek writing system into Eastern Europe, where Slavic languages were spoken. (Yule, 2006, p. 24)

In both MLA and APA styles, long quotations are set off from the body of your text on a new line, not enclosed by quotation marks, and indented for their full length from the left margin. A long quotation concludes with final punctuation. In both styles, the in-text citation appears in parentheses after the quotation's final punctuation.

Note the longer quotation used on page 2 of the MLA model paper in the next chapter (page 330). Its content includes factual and numerically exact support, which is best stated directly. Do not paraphrase where exactness is essential (i.e., for statistics, technical data, or complex numerical information).

Variations in in-text citation contents and methods of integrating quotations, paraphrases, and summaries appropriately are covered in step 3.

Paraphrases

What Is a Paraphrase?

Paraphrasing is the key research-writing skill you need to acquire: you will be restating authors' words in every type of research assignment in every subject you study. As discussed in Chapter 17, paraphrasing involves putting the words of another writer completely into (a) your own words, (b) your own style, and (c) your own sentence structures. A paraphrase, like a quotation, must be accompanied by an in-text citation, showing the source from which its ideas are drawn.

How Do You Paraphrase Correctly?

Correct paraphrasing means putting another writer's words completely into your own words, then giving credit to the original source. Here are tips to guide you with restating other authors' words, a checklist to use each time you paraphrase another writer's words:

- Do not use synonyms—retain the phrasing and sentence structure of the original.
- Do not imitate or follow the sentence structure of the original.
- Do not change the sentence structure but use the same words.
- Do insert in-text citations for any paraphrased material.
- Do, if you use a paraphrase/quotation mix, use quotation marks around any quoted words or phrases taken directly from the passage you are paraphrasing.
- Do not change the meaning of a passage that you paraphrase.
- Do not add to the meaning or ideas found in your source material.

The following examples show how to paraphrase correctly and avoid plagiarism. Here, a student wishes to use the ideas in a passage from page 36 of *A History of Reading* by Alberto Manguel.

Original Source

"By the time the first scribe scratched and uttered the first letters, the human body was already capable of the acts of writing and reading that still lay in the future; that is to say, the body was able to store, recall, and decipher all manner of sensations, including the arbitrary signs of written language yet to be invented."

Example of Plagiarism

As soon as people had figured out alphabets, the human body was already capable of writing and reading letters. The body could store, recall, and decipher feelings and letters that had yet to be invented.

If the student writes the sentences immediately above without crediting the source, he or she is plagiarizing. The student has borrowed Manguel's wording without acknowledging him as the author. Even though the student has shortened and changed the general form of the passage, significant sections of the phrasing belong to the original.

Example of Acceptable Use of Paraphrasing

Alberto Manguel suggests in *A History of Reading* that once people had figured out alphabets, the human body was ready to read and write letters. He contends that the body could store, recall, and decipher feelings and letters that had yet to be invented (36).

Here the student has indicated the source of the ideas (Alberto Manguel) and used correct MLA style by inserting the page reference in parentheses at the end of the sentence. A better method of writing a paraphrase that uses some of the exact wording of an original source is to put that wording in quotation marks.

Example of Good Use of Paraphrasing (Paraphrase/Quotation Mix)

MLA style: Alberto Manguel suggests in *A History of Reading* that once people had figured out alphabets, the human body was ready to read and write letters. He contends that the body could "store, recall, and decipher" feelings and letters that had "yet to be invented" (36).

APA style: Alberto Manguel (1996) suggests in *A History of Reading* that once people had figured out alphabets, the human body was ready to read and write letters. He contends that the body could "store, recall, and decipher" feelings and letters that had "yet to be invented" (p. 36).

When Should You Paraphrase?

Paraphrasing is essential to the process of *blending*—synthesizing your research with your own ideas on your topic. Well-written paraphrases make reading your paper a smooth process for readers because paraphrases do not interrupt the flow of your words as much as quotations. Writing good paraphrases reflects well on you; it demonstrates your understanding of your research sources and your ability to use these intelligently.

Good paraphrases

- shorten lengthy passages;
- eliminate or explain unnecessary technical language;
- make the ideas in the source-material clear in the context of your paper;
- may be better than wordy, bulky, or awkwardly written quotations of source material.

Methods of integrating paraphrases appropriately are covered in step 3 (page 298).

Summaries

Should you wish to summarize material for a research paper, follow the guidelines in Chapter 17. A summary in a research essay might consist of only a few sentences; in fact, on most occasions, this type of summary will usually consist of only the main points in the original. As with quoting and paraphrasing, it is essential to properly acknowledge your original source with an in-text citation when summarizing.

When Should You Summarize?

You may want to summarize the main points in a passage of source material in several instances in your research paper. Some subjects and disciplines, especially in the sciences, require that a summary or abstract of the essay's content appear before the essay itself. An APA research essay will contain just such a summary or abstract. See the APA-style student research essay in Chapter 20, pages 338—343, for an example of such a summary.

No matter what subject or course you write a research essay for, summarized sections of source material are very useful for presenting context or background information to set up a section of your essay's argument. You may also include a summary of a writer's viewpoint in comparisons or contrasts within your essay; you can offset your own points and details against those in the summary. Alternatively, a summary could be very useful in explaining the causes or effects of some situation or process: summaries are briefer than paraphrases so they are convenient additions to your thesis.

STEP 2: WRITE YOUR FIRST DRAFT

Begin by reviewing your research notes. Then, using your revised outline as a guide, you are ready to write the first draft of your research paper. Concentrate on writing clear sentences that get your ideas across. At points where you wish to insert support from your research, make a note to yourself right in your draft (perhaps in another colour to highlight the information) of what you would like to add.

Generally, it is preferable to simply start writing your draft. Do not stop to introduce and document your quotations, paraphrases, or summaries. Simply write in reminders of where your research insertions should go.

As you work on your draft, think of where you can enhance your thesis by using some of the following methods of development:

- Will your readers need definitions of some of the words, phrases, or concepts associated with your topic area?
- Will a comparison or contrast of one of your supporting points or details help to clarify the way you are developing your ideas?
- Should one or more ideas be divided into categories or classifications so that you can explain them more clearly?

- Does your thesis and support require some analysis and discussion of the causes and/or effects of situations, conditions, or concepts within your essay?
- Will breaking down some scenario or condition into its stages or steps make your point clearer?

Make notes to yourself in your draft of any areas where using a specific method of development would deepen or clarify your support. You will want to use another colour of print or pen to do so, so that you can easily separate these notes from your notes about where to insert research material.

Put your draft away for a day at least. Then, read it aloud to yourself or someone else, noting any weak spots, repetitions, or logic problems. When you have done so, you are ready to work with the material in your research notes.

STEP 3: REVISE YOUR FIRST DRAFT TO INTEGRATE AND CITE YOUR REFERENCE MATERIALS

Revise your first draft in four stages:

1. Prepare the paraphrases, summaries, and quotations from your sources. Arrange your research notes in the order in which you will use them. Be careful to check that your quoted material is exactly as in the original sources. This is the time to pay close attention to any notations you have made concerning each paraphrase, summary, or quotation's relationship to your overall purpose, thesis, and individual items of support.

2. Integrate your paraphrases, quotations, and summaries smoothly into the flow of your sentences and place your citations correctly. Follow the instructions in this chapter very carefully. Citing your sources correctly shows your readers that you recognize that they need to see certain signals to know when you are borrowing ideas. Trust between writer and reader, and between instructor and student, is thus maintained, and you as the writer are seen as trustworthy and careful.

3. Read your essay aloud and start your revision by correcting any repetitious or weak spots in your content, using any notes you have made when reading your essay aloud.

4. Next, focus on revising your essay to clearly express your meaning, following the same methods you learned in Chapter 5. Edit your sentences for clarity and variety of structure. Then proofread your paper for sentence skills and mechanical errors, referring to Part 4 of this book and to your dictionary for help.

Finally, move on to step 4. Using the sections that follow, or a reference guide to MLA or APA style (whichever you use), check each in-text citation. Then you are ready to create your Works Cited (MLA) or References (APA) list.

Integrating Material from Another Source

To integrate a piece of research material into the overall flow of your paper, write clear sentences into which you can smoothly fit the idea that you wish to support with a quotation, paraphrase, or summary. Your source material must be understandable in the context of your paper. Create a background for the ideas you are supporting so that your quoted or paraphrased material (a) makes sense to readers and (b) adds to the quality of your own thoughts.

You may integrate your material by identifying the author and the title of his or her work, either (1) before (introducing), (2) in the midst of (embedding), or (3) immediately after (tagging) that material. Finally, complete the context for your quotation or paraphrase by explaining it further, adding your own ideas to it, or arguing against it.

To integrate a direct quotation according to MLA and APA style in any of the three positions described above, follow one of the methods shown in the examples below. Then, consult the more complete list of examples of in-text citations in the MLA and APA lists in step 4 following this section.

Identify Your Source before Your Quotation or Paraphrase

When you preface a quotation or paraphrase with your own introductory statement, you are *introducing* your own context, controlling, in a sense, how the reader will understand it. Here the student shows, through her choice of words (her introductory verb or cue word *argues*) and positioning of her quotation, that she is presenting one view of a situation (Thompson's), and that she does not necessarily agree with this view (Thompson *argues*). She has set up a context wherein she may refute or argue against her source, or add more material to support Thompson's view.

Integrating a Quotation with Your Own Introduction

MLA style: E.A. Thompson, in *The Huns,* argues that Rome did not fall because of the force of one powerful leader: "There is not much evidence to show that Attila was a genius. It is only in terms of the development of their society that we can explain why the Huns attacked Rome at all . . ." (46).

APA style: E.A. Thompson (1999), in *The Huns,* argues that Rome did not fall because of the force of one powerful leader: "There is not much evidence to show that Attila was a genius. It is only in terms of the development of their society that we can explain why the Huns attacked Rome at all" (p. 46).

This student will then go on to explain why she agrees or disagrees with Thompson's point, thus completing the context for the quotation with her own ideas.

Note here the use of the colon after the independent clause that precedes the quotation. When you use a colon to set up or introduce a quotation, your introductory clause must be a complete thought, not a fragment of a phrase such as "He writes:".

Incorrect introductory use of a colon

E.A. Thompson argues: "There is not much evidence to show that Attila was a genius" (46).

Integrating a Paraphrase with Your Own Introduction

When you integrate or work a paraphrase into your essay, you follow the same citation pattern as you would for a quotation. Here, if you are like the student author above, you will indicate your control of the paraphrased material by preceding it with your own introductory clause and cue word or verb. Remember, when you paraphrase, you restate each of the author's ideas in the order in which they appear in the original, and change the wording, the phrasing, and the sentence structure into your own.

> **MLA style:** E.A. Thompson, in *The Huns,* argues that history does not support the theory that Attila single-handedly brought about the downfall of Rome. In Thompson's view, the leader of the Huns was no diamond-in-the-rough, intellectually gifted barbarian leader. The nature of the Huns' culture and society is the most likely cause of their invasion of Rome (46).

> **APA style:** E.A. Thompson (1999), in *The Huns,* argues that history does not support the theory that Attila single-handedly brought about the downfall of Rome. In Thompson's view, the leader of the Huns was no diamond-in-the-rough, intellectually gifted barbarian leader. The nature of the Huns' culture and society is the most likely cause of their invasion of Rome (p. 46).

Identify Your Source in the Midst of Your Quotation or Paraphrase

When you begin with part of your quoted or paraphrased material, identify your source, and complete your quotation or paraphrase, you are *embedding* your source within their ideas. By doing so, you have placed your emphasis on your source material, making your reader wait to see your response to it.

Integrating a Quotation by Embedding the Source

> **MLA style:** "Filmmaking began in America as the work of what we like to call rugged individualists," asserts Kolker, "despite the fact that Edison was a company that created many things besides film" (110).

> **APA style:** "Filmmaking began in America as the work of what we like to call rugged individualists," asserts Kolker (2006), "despite the fact that Edison was a company that created many things besides film" (p. 110).

Integrating a Paraphrase by Embedding the Source

> **MLA style:** American movie-makers were, initially at least, hardy independent operators, asserts Kolker, even Edison, for whom movies were only one of hundreds of enterprises (110).

> **APA style:** American movie-makers were, initially at least, hardy independent operators, asserts Kolker (2006)—even Edison, for whom movies were only one of hundreds of enterprises (p. 110).

Identify Your Source Following Your Quotation or Paraphrase

When you follow your quoted or paraphrased material with the identification and citation of your source, you strongly emphasize your source's ideas. You do, however, set up the expectation in your readers that you will assert your own position regarding, or in response to, these ideas in the sentence that follows your integrated source material. When you *tag* your quotation or paraphrase with the author's name, you are setting up that material for your agreement, expansion, or rebuttal. Tagging is not simply a neutral method of integrating source material; it makes readers anticipate what you have to say about that material.

Integrating a Quotation by Following It with Its Source

MLA style: "Indian pop music is called 'cine music' or 'film music' because almost all of the songs come from hit movies in Hindi, Tamil, or other regional languages. Virtually all movies are musicals . . .," points out Titon in *Worlds of Music* (150).

Notice in the MLA example above that the quotation flows grammatically into the end of the sentence, following the comma after the ellipsis. You must ensure that the end of your quoted (or paraphrased) material works smoothly with your tag information.

APA style: "Indian pop music is called 'cine music' or 'film music' because almost all of the songs come from hit movies in Hindi, Tamil, or other regional languages. Virtually all movies are musicals" points out Titon (2001) in *Worlds of Music* (p. 150).

Note once again that APA style does not conclude a quotation with an ellipsis. Note also in both examples that when there is quoted material within a quotation, single quotation marks are used for the internally quoted material.

Integrating a Paraphrase by Following It with Its Source

MLA style: "Cine music" and "film music" are synonyms for Indian popular music. Popular cinema in much of India means movie musicals in Hindi or Tamil, among other languages. These musicals provide the charts with nearly all pop-music hits, points out Titon in *Worlds of Music* (150).

APA style: "Cine music" and "film music" are synonyms for Indian popular music. Popular cinema in much of India means movie musicals in Hindi or Tamil, among other languages. These musicals provide the charts with nearly all pop-music hits, points out Titon (2001) in *Worlds of Music* (p.150).

Having set up another writer's position and ideas, this student would then explain the relationship of this paraphrase to the point he or she is making to ensure that the purpose of the paraphrase is clear to readers.

Integrate short summaries of passages in the same ways as you would paraphrases or quotations.

Signal Words for Integrating Source Material

An effective research essay should consistently indicate the direction of your thesis and support. Successfully integrating source material should continue this process. You can show the purpose of any integrated source material by choosing a verb that indicates your position on the stated author's words, and by using words and phrases that "cue" or "signal" to the audience how the quoted or paraphrased material relates to the surrounding context of your essay.

Signal words are verbs that guide readers into your source material while reminding them of your viewpoint and argument and are always in the present tense; i.e., a writer *states,* or *maintains.*

- **If you agree with your source,** use verbs such as *reveals, states, holds (that), points out, notes,* or *asserts.*
- **If your position relative to your source is neutral,** use verbs such as *states, asserts, believes,* or *observes.* In this case, you may simply be supplying source material to explain or add to a point.
- **If you are arguing against your source,** consider verbs such as *argues, contends, maintains, objects, proposes,* or *opposes.*

STEP 4: DOCUMENT YOUR RESEARCH AND PREPARE A "WORKS CITED" OR "REFERENCES" LIST

Two of the most often used styles of documentation and citation are MLA, or Modern Language Association style, used for English and humanities subjects, and APA, or American Psychological Association style, used for social sciences subjects. Always ask your instructor which style he or she would like you to follow. This book uses MLA style (the documentation style of the *MLA Handbook for Writers of Research Papers,* 7th edition) and presents information about MLA citation first; coverage of some aspects of APA style (the documentation style of the *Publication Manual of the American Psychological Association,* 6th edition) is also offered in this section.

Whether you follow the MLA or APA style of documentation, make sure you only include works that you have actually consulted and for which you have accurate research notes.

The following sections are not intended as comprehensive listings for all possible citation situations. You are strongly advised to consult your college or university library Web site for documentation information, or to ask your instructor or a librarian for a complete source of information on either MLA or APA styles of documentation.

MLA-Style Documentation

MLA citation appears in two locations in your research paper: as an **in-text citation,** in the identification of author and page number within the text of your paper, and in the **Works Cited** list at the end of your paper.

As of April 2009, several changes have been made to MLA formatting and citation rules:

- Titles of published works, such as books, magazines, journals, newspapers, movies, and CDs, are now italicized, rather than underlined.
- All entries in the Works Cited list, whether print or electronic, must now include, at the end of the citation, the medium in which they are published; for example, *Print, Web, DVD.*

- Citations for Web sites no longer include URLs unless it is impossible to find the source otherwise.
- For sources with no publisher, date of publication, or page-numbering, MLA style is to write *n. p.* for sources without name or place of publication, *n.d.* for sources with no publication date, and *n. pag.* for sources with no page numbers.

MLA In-text Citation

In-text citations, as you have seen them at several points in this book, are the signals you place directly in the text of your paper to acknowledge information from any source you quote or paraphrase. In MLA style, in-text citations point readers to specific sources on the MLA Works Cited page.

The citation material appears in parentheses directly after the end of a quotation, but before the period at the end of the sentence: Boggs and Petrie write, "A tight or extreme close-up brings us so close to the object or interest (an actor's face, for example) that we cannot look elsewhere" (136). Here, the period from the quoted sentence is not retained; instead, the quoted sentence ends with only quotation marks. Similarly, with paraphrased or summarized material, the in-text citation (parenthetical citation) appears immediately after the content that is paraphrased or summarized.

MLA In-text Citation for Books in Print Form

1. **If you are using a source for the first time in your essay,** introduce or integrate the quoted, paraphrased, or summarized material from that source with its author's full name and the title of his or her work. Follow your source material immediately with the page number on which your material appears in parentheses.

   In *Grid Systems,* Kimberley Elam reminds readers that "An awareness of the law of thirds enables the designer to focus attention where it will most naturally occur and to control compositional space" (13).

   Here is the Works Cited entry to which this citation refers:

   Elam, Kimberley. *Grid Systems.* New York: Princeton Architectural Press, 2004. Print.

2. **Each time after the first instance that you use the same source,** you are free, in your integrating material, to use either the author's last name or the source's title. Both items are not necessary.

   "Elements do not need to land directly on the intersecting point," points out Elam, "as close proximity draws attention to them" (13).

3. **If, on subsequent uses of a source** in a quotation, paraphrase, or summary, you do not use the author's or the work's name in your integrating material, place the author's name in parentheses with the page number.

   Rectangular elements in composition may be rotated either clockwise or counter clockwise. The complexity and interest of compositions using rotational patterns is significantly greater because of two-directional negative space (Elam 79).

4. **If you place a series or succession of quotations, paraphrases, or summaries by the same author** in your essay, your author's name appears only in the first in a succession of cited passages. Subsequent citations show only relevant page numbers.

5. **If you place a quotation, paraphrase, or summary by one or more other authors** anywhere within your series or succession of citations from a single author, the last name and page number for each author must appear each time within the parentheses.

6. **If you cite more than one work by a single author,** include a shortened version of each title as you cite each of them in your parenthetical citations. You need to distinguish between two or more books as they will appear in your Works Cited list. For example, if you are quoting from two different books by Margaret Atwood for an English research essay, your first citation, referring to her book *The Year of the Flood,* if you have not already introduced Atwood's name, would be (Atwood, *Year* 47). Your second citation, referring to another of her novels, *Morning in the Burned House,* assuming you have mentioned Atwood's name, would be (*Morning* 128). The comma in parentheses only appears after the author's name, when it is necessary to include it.

   Here are the Works Cited entries to which these citations refer, as they would appear in order:

   Atwood, Margaret. *Morning in the Burned House.* Toronto: McClelland & Stewart, 2009. Print.
   ___. *The Year of the Flood.* Toronto: McClelland & Stewart, 2009. Print.

   Notice that the books are listed in alphabetical order (ignoring *a, an,* and *the*), and that instead of the author's name in the second case, three hyphens and a period appear. This is discussed further, under "Books."

7. **If you cite a book with two or three authors,** list the authors' last names as they appear on the title page of the book. When you identify the authors in your essay, list them all, whether in your integrating phrase or in your in-text citation:

   Thompson, Gorbatsevich, and Evans argue against increased provincial interference in municipal school boards (224).
   The authors contend that "adding to an already top-heavy bureaucracy could only be counter-productive" (Thompson, Gorbatsevich, and Evans 224).

   For books with more than three authors, you will generally include the first author's name, followed by the phrase *et al.,* meaning *and others.*

8. **If you use information that is quoted within another source,** use the phrase "qtd. in," followed by the last name of the author of the work wherein you found the quotation.

   Ridley Scott describes the visual density of the set design in *Blade Runner* as his attempt to "build layers of texture, so that visual information is imparted in every square inch of screen" (qtd. in Boggs and Petrie 109).

9. **If you cite a print work where an organization or committee is the author,** then use the organization's name as the author; i.e., (Modern Language Association). Abbreviate the name if it is long.

MLA In-text Citation for Other Print Sources

1. **If you cite a journal or magazine article from a print source,** follow the basic author/title rules above.

   Hutchinson writes in "Faster, Higher, Sneakier," "For our elite athletes, the money has translated into better coaching, more training camps, extra massages, and, just as crucial, access to a shadowy cadre of scientists" (24). In "Faster, Higher, Sneakier," the author examines the current "win-at-any-price" attitude as it manifests itself in the treatment of Olympic athletes and the shadier aspects of sports medicine (Hutchinson 24).

   Here is the Works Cited entry for the article to which the citations above refer:
   Hutchinson, Alex. "Faster, Higher, Sneakier." *The Walrus.* January/February 2010: 24–27. Print.

2. **If you cite the print version of a magazine or newspaper article with no known author,** include a shortened version of the name of the article, in quotation marks, in the in-text citation, along with the page number(s).
   Pension payments do not always travel with their owners, especially if those pensioners emigrate to other countries ("UK Pension" 31).

   Here is the Works Cited entry for the article to which the citation above refers:

   "Should you move your UK pension to Canada?" *Muchmor Canada Magazine.* Winter 2009: 29–33. Print.

MLA In-text Citation for Non-print Sources

1. **Magazine, journal, and newsprint articles from a library database**
   Place the name of the author of the article in parentheses, along with a page number, if available.

   "One reason we do not see blue oceans more often in print is that the unrelenting pressure of the academic reward structure places a higher value on mere publication than superlative publication" (Straub iv).

   Here is the Works Cited entry for the article noted above:

   Straub, Detmar. "Creating Blue Oceans of Thought Via Highly Citable Articles." *MIS Quarterly* 33.4 (2009): iii–vii. *Academic Search Premier.* Web. 12 May 2010.

2. **Article from a Web site**
   Place the author's last name in parentheses. If the site has no author, place the name of the article, in double quotation marks, in the parentheses. No page or paragraph number is required. URLs are not used for in-text citations.
   "Less known is the fact that the Ontario Provincial Police is responsible for law enforcement on over 110,000 square kilometers of provincial waterways" ("Underwater Search and Recovery Unit").

Works Cited List

You have seen several Works Cited entries in the section above. These are included to show the relationship of in-text citations to the corresponding entries in the list of Works Cited at the end of your essay. You are creating this list so that your readers can trace your in-text citations.

To set up your Works Cited list, refer to the model entries on pages 307–312, and follow the steps below. Keep in mind that the model entries do not show all possible sources. If you are uncertain of how to document some source, remember to check your campus library's Web site under "MLA Citation" or to ask a reference librarian.

1. The Works Cited page is a separate sheet, placed after the last page of your essay.

2. This page will have 2.54-cm (one-inch) margins, and the same last-name and page-number header as the rest of the pages of your essay. (See Chapter 20 for MLA essay formatting rules.)

3. Centre the title *Works Cited* in regular typeface at the top of your page. Do not use italics, quotation marks, bolding, or underlining for this title.

4. Double-space before the first entry.

5. Begin each entry at the left margin. When the entry runs more than one line of text, indent each additional line by five spaces, or use the indent tab on your keyboard.

6. Double-space your entire list, including the lines within entries.

7. Do not number entries.

8. Organize your list alphabetically by the authors' last names. If no author is given, the entry is alphabetized by title, ignoring *A, An,* and *The.*

9. Follow capitalizing for words that are used in your sources.

10. Italicize titles of larger or complete works, such as books, journals, magazines, newspapers, Web sites, movies, television shows, works of art, and computer software.

11. Place in double quotation marks the titles of articles, chapters in books, poems, short stories, songs, episodes from television shows or webcasts, and speeches.

12. At the end of each citation, put in the format or medium of the source, such as *Print, Web, Radio, DVD,* or *PDF.*

13. In publication information, use abbreviations for publishers' names and months of the year; i.e., *Farrar* instead of *Farrar Straus and Giroux; Oct.* instead of *October.*

14. When listing numbers of pages used at the end of a book entry, use only numbers. Do not use p., pp., or page(s).

Model Entries for a List of Works Cited

Use these entries as guides as you prepare your list of reference sources. Capitalize words in titles exactly as they appear in the works themselves, and use the exact punctuation marks you see between items for each type of entry you list. You will now use the information you listed for each source when you revised your reference notes.

Books

Book by One Author

Author's Last name, First name. *Title.*
↓   ↓

Hoffert, Paul. *All Together Now.* Toronto: Stoddart, 2000. Print.
↗   ↗   ↑   ↑
City of publication: Publisher, Year of publication. Medium of publication.

Notice that author's names are reversed, with the last name first, and separated from the first name or initials by a comma. After the title (underlined), record the publication information—the city, name of the publisher, and the year of publication. These appear at the front of any book, often on the reverse side of the title page.

If a book's full title (as on the title page inside the book) includes a subtitle, include it by placing a colon after the main title and then copying the subtitle, word for word, as in the example below:

> Meyer Spacks, Patricia. *Boredom: The Literary History of a State of Mind.* 1st ed. Chicago: University of Chicago Press, 1996. 11. Print.

Notice that the second line of the entry is indented by five spaces.

Two or More Entries by the Same Author

> Nuland, Sherwin B. *The Mysteries Within: A Surgeon Reflects on Medical Myths.* New York: Simon & Schuster, 2000. Print.
>
> ___. *The Soul of Medicine.* New York: Kaplan, 2009. Print.

Here, a second book by Sherwin B. Nuland is cited. With two or more books by the same author, do not repeat the author's name. Instead, begin with a line of three hyphens or dashes followed by a period. Arrange works by the same author in alphabetical order.

Book by Two or More Authors

> Kalman, Harold, Ron Phillips, and Robin Ward. *Exploring Vancouver: The Essential Architectural Guide.* Vancouver: UBC Press, 1993. Print.

Give all the authors' names, but reverse only the first name. For a book with more than three authors, either list all authors' names in the order in which they are printed on the book's title page, or list only the first author's name, followed by a comma and the phrase *et al.*

Organization, Corporation, or Group as Author

> Council for Ecumenical Study. *High-Church Influence in Victorian London.* London: Faber, 2003. Print.

Book Prepared by an Editor

> Nolan, Tom. Ed. *Strangers in Town: Three Newly Discovered Mysteries by Ross Macdonald.* New York: Crippen & Landru, 2001. Print.

Book with an Author and an Editor

> Schweitzer, Albert. *Albert Schweitzer: A Biography*. Ed. James Brabazon. Syracuse: Syracuse UP, 2000. Print.

Book by Unknown or Anonymous Author

> *The Canadian Encyclopedia.* 2nd ed. Toronto: McClelland & Stewart, 1988. Print.

If you use one volume of a multivolume work, such as an encyclopedia, then you should indicate the volume used as below:

> Martin, Brendt. *Encyclopedia of Music.* Vol. 2. New York: Greenwood, 1998. Print.

Second or Later Edition of a Book

> Myers, David G. *Social Psychology.* 6th ed. New York: McGraw-Hill, 1999. Print.

Selection from an Edited Book or Anthology

> Lear, Edward. "The Owl and the Pussy-Cat." *Classics of Children's Literature.* Eds. John W. Griffith and Charles H. Frey. 3rd ed. New York: Macmillan Publishing Company, 1992. 190–91. Print.

This entry contains the inclusive page numbers for the item used in the anthology. Citations should list the pages actually used in your essay as the final item, followed by a period.

The editor of the collection or anthology's name appears after the title of the work, preceded by *Ed.,* the abbreviation of the word *Editor.*

Chapter or Section in a Book by One Author

> Secunda, Victoria. "A New Sense of Family." *Losing Your Parents, Finding Yourself: The Defining Turning Point of Adult Life.* New York: Hyperion, 2000. 242–56. Print.

In the entry above, the numbers after the year of publication are the consecutive page numbers of the chapter of the book cited.

Periodicals: Journals and Magazines in Print Form

Article in a Magazine Published Monthly

Author's Last name, First name. *Title of Magazine* Medium of publication.

Callwood, June. "A Date with AIDS." *Saturday Night* March 1995: 52–53. Print.

"Title of Article" Month and year of issue: pages.

After the title of the magazine, the month and year of the issue is listed, followed by a colon, then the pages on which the article appears, then the medium.

Article in a Magazine Published Weekly

> Chin, Paula. "You Were a Good Man, Charlie Brown." *People* 28 Feb. 2000: 52–59. Print.

For an article from a magazine published every week or every two weeks, put in the complete date (starting with the day and abbreviating the month, except for May, June, and July) and the page numbers on which the article appears.

Article in a Scholarly Journal from Bound Volume

> Maynard, Charles. "Coding Correlations." *Computers and the Humanities* 33 (1999): 675–690. Print.

This example shows an entry from a bound version of a scholarly journal. The *33* after the title of the journal is the annual volume number for the year 1999. Notice also that the year of publication is placed within parentheses for such journal articles.

Article in a Scholarly Journal Where the Issue Number is Available

> Lisander, Mary. "ROI in a Declining Economy," *Journal of Canadian Marketing.* 15.4 (2001): 81–89. Print.

In these cases, record the volume number (15), then the issue number (4), separated by a period.

Newspaper Article with Author

> Goddard, Peter. "The New Crime Photography." *Toronto Star* 17 Jan. 2004: J1+. Print.

When citing newspaper articles, omit *The,* if it is part of the newspaper's name. To show continuation pages, add a + sign to the first page of an article (6+, 23+), because newspaper articles are often not printed on consecutive pages, and be sure to include any letter designation used to indicate the section of the newspaper that the article appears in, such as "B4 + ."

If no author is listed for a newspaper article, whether in print or online, begin the entry with the name of the article. If a newspaper has a common name, such as *The Observer,* that does not contain the name of the city where it is published, insert the name of its city of origin in square brackets and regular font after the newspaper's title: *The Gazette* [Kingston].

Editorial

> "Trade Wars Laughable." Editorial. *The Winnipeg Free Press* 15 Mar. 1995: A10. Print.

Editorials are often unsigned, so no author's name appears in this entry. Indicate the nature of the article by adding the word *Editorial* in regular type after the article's title.

Government Publication

> Canada. National Student Load Service Centre. *Budget 2004: The Importance of Learning.* Ottawa: Social Development Canada, 2002. Print.

With government publications, place either the name of the government or agency first, or the author's name. If the name of the government is placed first, then, after the title of the document, place the writer's name preceded with *By,* or the editor's name preceded with *Ed.,* or a compiler's name preceded by *Comp.*

Published Interview

> Frum, Linda. "Peter Bergen Talks to Linda Frum." *Maclean's* 30 Jan. 2006: 10–11. Print.

Sources in Other Media

MLA refers to all electronic resources as *Web Publications.* Therefore, the word *web* is used in place of *print* in Works Cited entries. As noted above, MLA no longer requires a site's URL to be included in an entry. *Radio, television,* and *online posting* are some of the designations for media of publication used in citations.

Article from a Web Site

If no author name is listed, begin with the title of the article.

"Title of Article." *Title of Site.* Sponsoring Institution. Last update of site/
Date of publication

"Texas Blues." *The Blues Source. Blues Source Magazine.* 15 June 2003.
Web. 27 April 2010.

Medium of publication Access date

One section of this Web site is cited as a reference, the article, "Texas Blues." Its title is placed in quotation marks, and because the author is not listed on the site, the listing begins with the title. The name of its sponsoring institution is a magazine, so it appears in italics; sponsoring institutions such as corporations and universities appear in regular font.

When you cite a complete Web site, include the title of the site in italics, the name of the editor (if any), the electronic publishing information (version, if available), the date of publication or last update of site, and the name of the sponsoring institution.

Online Book (Ebook)

> Seton, Ernest Thompson. *The Arctic Prairies: A Canoe-Journey of 2,000 Miles in Search of the Caribou.* New York: C. Scribner's Sons, 1911. *Project Gutenberg.* Web. 8 May 2010.

An online book is cited like a print book, adding the title of the database or project, date of original or print publication, sponsoring organization (Project Gutenberg, in the example above), and date accessed.

Magazine Article from Online Version of Print Magazine

> Ehrenreich, Barbara. "Will Women Still Need Men?" *Time Online.* 21 Feb. 2000. Web. 15 April 2011.

Article from an Online Scholarly Journal

Dean, Francis X., and Martita Philman. "Educational Success for Children in Public Care: Advice from High Achievers." *Child and Group Social Work* 9.1 (2002): 121–30. Web. 15 Oct. 2010.

Online Source in a Reference Database

"Heredity." *Encyclopædia Britannica Online.* Encyclopaedia Britannica, Sept. 1999. Web. 2 Mar. 2009.

Article from a Database

Lavallee, David. "The Digest." *Journal of Sport and Exercise Psychology* 27.4 (2005): 521–27. *Academic Search Premier.* Web. 8 Jan. 2009.

With articles accessed through library databases such as *EBSCO, InfoTrac,* or *Lexis-Nexis,* follow article citation page-number notation with the name of the online service used.

E-mail Message

Baer, Max. "Re: Submitting Design Proposal." Message to Harold Ziegler. 11 May 2008. Email.

Listserv, Discussion Group, or Blog Posting

Hanlan Merv. "Re: Espagnol or Sauce Brune: Any Difference?" Online posting. *ClassicCooks.* Cooks Board, 29 Sept. 2008. Web. 5 Apr. 2009.

Television Program

"Salmon Farming." *The Nature of Things.* Narr. David Suzuki. CBC. 21 Nov. 1993. Television.

Notice here that the episode of the TV show is cited in quotation marks, and the title of the series to which the episode belongs is in italics. Items such as narrator or director are optional, but the name of the network presenting the program and the date of broadcast must be included.

Film

Titanic. Dir. James Cameron. Paramount Pictures, 1997. Film.

Not a Love Story: A Film about Pornography. Dir. Bonnie Sher Klein. National Film Board of Canada, 1986. Film.

When citing films, include at a minimum the title of the film, the director's name (Dir.), the distributor, and the year of release. Additionally, if you have a reason to emphasize performers or others involved in the film's production, place their names immediately after the director's name, preceded by an abbreviated form of their title (Perf., Cine.).

For additional information on citing films, see section 5.7.3 of the *MLA Handbook.*

DVD or Videocassette

> *Rashomon.* Dir. Akira Kurosawa. 1950. Criterion, 2003. DVD.

Cite the DVD or videotape version of a film just as you would a film, but include the film's release year and the release year of the DVD after the distributor's name.

CD or Sound Recording

> Gray, Macy. *The Trouble with Being Myself.* Epic, 2003. CD.

> Bach, Johann Sebastian. *The Well-Tempered Clavier.* Perf. Angela Hewitt. Hyperion, 2009. CD.

Citations of CDs usually begin with the performing artist's name. You may also list a sound recording by its composer (Comp.) or performer (Perf.), whichever will make the CD the simplest to locate. In other cases, as with films, list the composer and performer information after the title. Note the medium (CD, Audiocassette, LP) at the end of the citation. MP3s are considered digital audiofiles, and their citation information appears below.

If you are citing one song on a CD, then put its title in quotation marks before the italicized title of the CD.

Digital Files (PDFs, MP3s, JPEGs)

Identify what you are citing; for example, a piece of music, an image, or a Microsoft Word document. Give the author's name as usual, the title, the date of creation, and the medium of publication.

> Rossini, Gioacchino. *Chrysanthemums.* Naxos. 2002. MP3.

Note: For a practice activity on MLA Works Cited lists, go to the OLC.

APA-style Documentation

Like MLA style, APA style (the documentation style of the *Publication Manual of the American Psychological Association*) requires that you use in-text citation of sources for each paraphrase, quotation, or summary, as well as a list of sources at the end of the research paper. The information below is from the 6th edition of the *APA Manual.* Introductory coverage of some aspects of APA style follows; as always, for more information, check your campus's library Web site, or consult your instructor or a librarian.

MLA and APA styles also differ in a number of specific areas. One significant difference concerns the importance of dates of publication in the social sciences. Therefore, in APA style, the date is always included in in-text citations.

There are a few other rules that apply to essays and documents formatted in APA style:

- Capitalize all words that are four letters or more in the titles of sources you refer to in your essay. Short words that are verbs, nouns, pronouns, adjectives, and adverbs are capitalized: e.g., *Seeing in Old Ways, Everything Is Different in Heaven.*
- This can be a bit confusing at first, because in your References list, only the first word of a title will be capitalized: *Seeing in old ways.*

- In APA style, as opposed to MLA, capitalize both words in a hyphenated compound word: *In-Text Citation.*
- APA documentation requires you to capitalize the first word after a dash or colon: "Redesigning the Self: A Look at Sean Combs."

In-Text Citation

Whether you are introducing a paraphrase or quotation, or placing the documentation within parentheses at the end of borrowed material, APA style requires you to include both the author's name and the date of publication; this is called the "author/date" method. You have already seen some APA examples, along with MLA-style examples, in the section "Integrating Material from Another Source." Below you will find a few further examples of integrating source material into sentences in "author/date" APA style; these introduce the APA methods for in-text citation. APA style requires that you use the present tense: "states," (or "has stated" in the present-perfect tense) in your introductory signal words and phrases. Signal words and phrases include the verbs that express your viewpoint of a given author's statement, relative to your essay's thesis.

Integrating a Paraphrase into a Sentence

Developments in satellite carrier digital transmission have sped up the progress of convergence among different media, according to Miller's 2003 article.

If you do not mention the author's name or date at the beginning or end of a sentence containing a paraphrase, then these items must be included in parentheses at an appropriate place in the sentence, as in the following example:

As noted in a recent article (Miller, 2003), developments in satellite carrier digital transmission have sped up the progress of convergence among different media.

Both citations above refer to a listing of Miller's article in the References list at the end of a paper that uses APA style.

Integrating a Quotation into a Sentence

More students than ever are "suffering financially through years, even decades of their careers because of enormous loans incurred to pay tuition fees" (LaRose, 2002, p. 310).

In the example above, the student is quoting a specific sentence from the source. In APA style, the number of the page on which the quoted material appears is placed after the complete work's publication date and is preceded by the abbreviation *p.* for *page.* Other abbreviations used in such APA parenthetical citations include *pp.* for *pages, chap.* for *chapter,* and *sec.* for *section.*

Placing In-Text Citation in a Block Quotation

In an APA-style research paper, as noted in the preceding section on using quotations, a quotation longer than 40 words is set in a block that begins on a new line separate from the last line of the body of the essay. The quoted material is not placed in quotation marks and it is indented five spaces from the normal left margin of the essay. The block quotation is double spaced, and the in-text citation appears after the final punctuation of the quotation.

> From the Greeks, this revised alphabet passed to the rest of Western Europe through the Romans and, along the way, underwent several modifications to fit the requirements of spoken languages encountered. As a result, we talk about the Roman alphabet as the writing system used for English. Another line of development took the same basic Greek writing system into Eastern Europe, where Slavic languages were spoken. (Yule, 2006, p. 24)

APA In-Text Citation for Books in Print Form

1. **If you are citing an entire book by one author as the source of your information,** place the author's last name, a comma, and the year of the book's publication in parentheses at the end of that sentence.

   Marino's argument concerning urban redevelopment receives serious criticism from more mainstream groups of architects and developers (Smith, 2006).

2. **If you are citing a specific page within a book by a single author,** place *p.* plus the page number (or *pp.* for a sequence of pages) after the year of publication and a comma within the parentheses.

   Photosynthesis is the start of the journey of energy and the basic materials of life from plant to animal to animal to decomposer (Watson, 2009, p. 12).

3. **If you are citing a work with two authors,** place an ampersand between the names of the authors in the parenthetical citation. You must name both authors in your parenthetical citation each time you cite those authors:

   (Rimes & Blackwell, 2002, p. 60).

   You must also name both authors in signal phrases, but here, in the text of your essay, use *and* between the names, not an ampersand.

4. **If you are citing a work with three to five authors,** list the name of every author, up to five names.

   Changes in patient behaviour are rapid and long lasting during intensive therapies (Annis, McLellan, Stuart, & Main, 2001, Chapter 6).

   Here, a chapter, rather than a particular page is cited, so *chap.* is used to refer to the source. Every time you cite multiple authors after the initial citation, use only the first author's last name followed by *et al.* in the signal phrase or in the parentheses: (Annis et al., 2001)

5. **If you cite the same source twice or more in the same paragraph,** you may omit the year from the signal phrase or the parenthetical information. For example, using the in-text citations, the first citation would read: (Smith et al., 2002, p. 22), and later citations would read: (Smith et al., p. 23).

6. **If you cite a source by an unknown author,** place the title of the source in the signal phrase or a shortened version of the title (its first two words) in

the parenthetical citation. For a citation from page 152 of a book called *Latin Grammar: An Intensive Course,* published in 2003, the in-text citation would be (*Latin Grammar,* 2003, p. 152).

In APA format, titles of books and reports are italicized, and titles of chapters and sections appear in double quotation marks.

7. **If you cite an organization as author of any publication,** use the full name of the group in the signal phrase and in the parenthetical citation.

   Management of malaria has shown great improvement due to faster delivery of malaria nets and treatments to afflicted areas (World Health Organization, 2009).

   If the organization or group has a brief, well-known acronym, such as WHO for the World Health Organization, the abbreviation or acronym may be used in all citations after the first instance.

8. **If you cite more than one work by a single author,** include in your parenthetical citation the author's last name and the year of publication for each work.

9. **If you cite multiple works published the same year,** add *a, b, c,* and so on after the year. By doing so, you enable readers to distinguish between the books or other works as they will appear in your References list.

   For example, if you are quoting from two different books by Michael Mann for a sociology essay, if you have not previously introduced Mann's name, your first citation, referring to his book *The Dark Side of Democracy: Explaining Ethnic Cleansing,* published in 2004, would be (Mann, 2004). Your second citation, referring to his book *Incoherent Empire,* published in 2005, would be (Mann, 2005). APA, even for direct quotations, does not always specify including page numbers; however, it is best to check with your instructor before omitting them from in-text citations.

   Here are the References list entries to which these citations refer:
   Mann, Michael. (2004). *The dark side of democracy: Explaining ethnic cleansing.* London, England: Cambridge University Press.
   Mann, Michael. (2005). *Incoherent empire.* London, England: Verso Books.

   Notice that the books are listed in order of year of publication, and that the author's name appears in each entry.

10. **If you use information that is quoted within another source,** use, in the parenthetical citation, the phrase *as cited in . . .,* followed by the last name of the author of the work wherein you found the quotation. Always name the first source in your signal phrase.

    Melandro states that . . . (as cited in Alexander, 2005, p. 95).

APA In-Text Citation: Articles from Periodicals, Journals, and Other Print Sources

In general, the rules that apply to citations from books apply as well to citations from other print sources. The author/date information is always crucial.

1. **If you cite a journal or magazine article from a print source,** follow the basic author/date rules. **If you are citing the entire work,** supply author and date of publication:

   The rules of the game, apparently, have changed radically in the past ten years (Jones, 2003).

   If you are citing a specific page, include the page number in the parenthetical citation:

   Joannes' studies (2007, p. 26) have shown that quantifiable improvements in yield occur . . .

2. **If you cite the print version of an article with no author given,** list the first two or three words of the title of the article (leaving out any initial *a, an,* or the, with its capitalization as it appears in the source. Put the title in quotation marks, if it refers to an article, chapter of, or selection from a book. Italicize the title if it refers to a periodical or report. Follow with the date of publication in the parentheses.

   Statistics published over a decade ago on climate change . . . ("Climate and Weather," 1997).

3. **If you cite any type of printed personal communication, such as a letter, interview, or email,** give the name of the person you communicated with, the phrase *personal communication,* and the full date of the communication. In APA style, items of personal communication are not included in the References list.

   The survey results received were insufficient to include in a report (D. Ibare-Keith, personal communication, May 13, 2009).

APA In-Text Citation for Electronic Sources

APA mainly follows the same author/date conventions for electronic sources as it does for print sources. There are, however, a few exceptions worth noting.

1. **If you are referring to an entire Web site, rather than a specific page from a site,** you place the site's URL in parentheses at the end of the final sentence referencing the site.

   As an introduction to museology, the International Council of Museums Web site is useful; it offers an array of links to museums, codes of ethics documents, and archival information (http://www.icom.org/).

   An entire Web site does not appear as an entry in the References list; it is only shown in the text of the essay.

2. **If you are citing an individually authored Web site,** treat it as you would a print document: cite author and most recent revision date.

   Recent interviews with epidemiologists confirm . . . (Landis, 2010).

3. **If you are citing a specific page within a Web site with no author,** put the site's title and date of publication or most recent revision in the parentheses.

Red tide along the Gulf Coast of Florida continues to cause food sensitivities in those who have previously not reacted adversely to certain shellfish (*Tidelands Research,* 2008).

In this case, the full entry for the site, including the article or page referenced, will appear in the References list.

4. **If you are citing an article from a Web site that has no author,** place the title of the article, in double quotation marks, in parentheses, along with the most recent publication date for the site or article.

   On the Election Guide Web site, one article shows that Belgium appears to have a similar type of government to that of the U.K., a constitutional monarchy ("Country Profile: Belgium," 2008).

5. **If you are citing an online article where there is no author and no date given,** place the title of the article in your introductory signal phrase in the author position, then use the abbreviation *n.d.,* for *no date,* in the parentheses. Or, if you do not place the title in the signal phrase, use the title's first or second words, followed by n.d. in parentheses.

   "Improving medical charting skills involves helping nursing staff to recognize common documentation errors related to patient injury" ("Nursing Documentation Skills," n.d.).

6. **If you cite an online article where no form of page numbers appears,** check for numbered paragraphs.

   Smyth's coverage of the increases in the size and number of fandoms with a decade-long increase in internet use . . . (para. 7).

   Either use the abbreviation *para.* as above, or the paragraph symbol: ¶. If there is no paragraph numbering, but there are sections or headings, put the title of the heading or section in the parentheses and count the paragraphs after the heading until you reach the one containing your source material.

   Studies of fan behaviour are still relatively recent entries in academic publishing (Smyth, Respectability, para. 7).

   Only include page numbers in your citation if you are referring to an article available as PDF files or html files with page numbers embedded in the coding. Page numbers that appear after an article is printed cannot be used.

References List

The APA-style References list is the equivalent of an MLA Works Cited list. To set up your References list, refer to the model entries on pages 320–322, and follow the steps below. Pay particular attention to the capitalizing rules in the APA system.

Keep in mind that the model entries do not show all possible sources. You will probably find a section devoted to APA documentation on your campus library's Web site; printed style sheets may also be available. Your library will have a copy of the 6th edition of the *Publication Manual,* but if you are uncertain of any aspect of APA style, ask your instructor or a librarian for assistance.

1. The References list appears on separate sheets of paper, placed after the last page of your essay.

2. APA requires a one-inch margin on all sides of the page. This page will have one-inch margins, and the same short-title and page-number header in the upper right corner as the rest of the pages of your essay. (See Chapter 20 for APA essay formatting rules.)

3. Centre the title *References,* in regular typeface with normal capitalization, at the top of your page. Do not use italics, quotation marks, bolding, or underlining for this title.

4. Double-space before the first entry.

5. Begin each entry at the left margin. When the entry runs more than one line of text, indent each additional line by five spaces or hanging indent, or use the indent tab on your keyboard.

6. Double-space your entire list, including the lines within entries.

7. Do not number entries.

8. When creating entries, place authors' last names first, then, after a comma, the first name or first name and initial(s). For every author of any work, use the last name and initials for all the authors, unless there are more than six authors. If there are seven or more authors for a source, include the first six authors, followed by *et al.* after the sixth author's name. Use commas after authors' names and after an ampersand.

9. Organize your list alphabetically by the authors' last names. List works with multiple authors by the last name of the first author as it appears on the book's title page. If no author is given for a work, the entry is alphabetized by title, ignoring *A, An,* and *The.*

10. When there is more than one work by an author, list each in order of year of publication, beginning with the earliest published work.

11. Capitalize only the first words in the titles and subtitles of major works (book, article in magazine, film, Web page). Capitalize the first word after a colon or a hyphen in such titles, and capitalize proper nouns. Do not capitalize the first letter in the second word of a hyphenated combination; i.e., *In-text.*

12. For journal articles, use only initial capitals for titles.

13. Italicize titles of larger or complete works, such as books, journals, magazines, newspapers, Web sites, movies, television shows, works of art, and computer software.

14. Do not use double quotation marks around the titles of journal and magazine articles, chapters in books, essays in anthologies and collections, articles from Web sites, or episodes from television shows. Use regular roman font, following the capitalization rules above.

15. Single-space after final punctuation in a listing.

16. When listing online sources, include the source's URL. When listing sources with a DOI (digital object identifier), include those.

17. When you list an American city as a place of publication, include (after a comma) the US postal abbreviation for its state; i.e., MA for Massachusetts. Do the same for Canadian cities and provinces, and for global capitals, list their country in full, after a comma (London, England).

Reminders: In addition to the importance of dates in APA, another notable difference between MLA and APA styles of documentation lies in the formatting of titles. In an MLA-style Works Cited list, a major published work's title (book, magazine, journal, newspaper, film, TV show, and so on) is capitalized, as it appears in the source, and italicized (i.e., *The Common Writer*). In an APA-style References list, only the first word of the title is capitalized (i.e., *The common writer*). In MLA citation, the titles of articles, chapters in books, essays, poems, songs, and other short selections published in larger works are placed in double quotation marks. In APA style, the titles of magazine articles, book chapters, essays, and other short items are shown in plain font with no quotation marks. Only journal articles appear with their main words capitalized.

Model Entries for an APA References List

Use these entries as guides as you prepare your APA-style list of reference sources. Be very careful to use capitals and lower-case letters in titles exactly as the models below present them. Use the exact punctuation marks you see between items for each type of entry you list.

Books in Print

Book by One Author

Author's last name, Initials.   (Year of publication)   *Title: Subtitle.*

Stanley, R. (2003). *Making sense of movies: Filmmaking in the Hollywood style.* New York, NY: McGraw-Hill.

Hanging indent,   City and state (province or country) of publication: Publisher
5 spaces

Book by Two or More Authors

Marriott, L., & Lennard, P. (1997). *Heralding the new age.* Vancouver, BC: Raincoast Press.

Two or More Books by the Same Author (published the same year)

McLuhan, M. (1970a). *Culture is our business.* New York, NY: McGraw-Hill.
McLuhan, M. (1970b). *From cliche to archetype.* New York, NY: Viking Press.

Books with More than Seven Authors

Brown, D., Harper, H., Friel, M., Ingham, M., Otter, G., Raskin, J., Daley, A., (2008). *Basic writing skills.* Toronto, ON: McGraw-Hill.

Second or Later Edition of a Book

> Garofalo, R. (2003). *Rockin' out: Popular music in American culture* (2nd ed.).
> New York, NY: Pearson.

Revised Edition of a Book

> Coleman, Loren. (2001). *Mysterious America: The revised edition* (Rev. ed.).
> New York, NY: Paraview Press.

Book with an Editor or Editors

> Cawkwell, T., & Smith, J.M. (Eds.). (1972). *The world encyclopedia of film.*
> New York, NY: A & W Visual Library.

Book with Unknown Author

> *The Merriam-Webster dictionary.* (2005). Springfield, MA: Merriam-Webster.

Organization or Group as Author

> Canadian Diabetes Association. (2005). *Living with diabetes.* Toronto, ON:
> Digitach.

Book by Unknown Author

> *Study of waste retrieval.* (2005). Windsor, ON: Urban Press.

One Volume from a Multivolume Series

> Fredrickson, B. (1997). *Jungian studies* (Vol. 3). Chicago, IL: Northeastern
> Press.

Chapter from a Book

> Wellinski, J. (2000). Variable audience demographics. In *Media patterns* (pp.
> 134–156). Toronto, ON: Sigma.

Print Articles in Periodicals

Article by a Single Author in a Magazine

(Year of publication, Month).

Author's Last name, For weekly publication,

Initials. (Year of publication, Month and Day).

Silberman, S. (2001, December). The geek syndrome. *Wired, 9*(12), 174–183.

Title of article. *Title of Magazine, Volume*(Issue), pages.

After the year of publication, insert the month for magazines published monthly or month and day for magazines published weekly. The volume number is included as well, as it is for scholarly journals.

Article by Two Authors

> Thysman, M., & Smythe, L. (1998). Browning's puzzle. *Poetry,* 387–411.

Here, there is no volume or issue number to include.

Article with an Unknown Author

> Evolutionary ecology. (2005, April). [Editorial]. *Canadian Science, 23,* 10.

Article in a Reference Book or Entry in an Encyclopedia

> Guignon, C. B. (1998). Existentialism. In E. Craig (Ed.), *Routledge encyclopedia of philosophy* (Vol. 3, pp. 493-502). London, England: Routledge.

If no author is known, the citation begins with the article title.

Article in a Newspaper

> Gilbert, P. (2004, February 8). Snow removal financing issues. *The Toronto Star,* pp. B1, B6.

Editorial

> Marbert, P. (2005, November 8). Social services let-down. [Editorial]. *Saskatoon Star Phoenix,* p. A11+.

Article in Government Document

> Foreign Affairs Canada. (2005). *Foreign policy and EU representation. Ottawa.*

Article in a Scholarly Journal with Continuous Paging through the Volume

> Limb, G. E., & Hodge, D. R. (2008). Developing spiritual competency with Native Americans: Promoting wellness through balance and harmony. *Families in society, 89,* 615–622.

In APA style, the title of the article does not appear in quotation marks and only the first word of the title is capitalized. As well, the title and volume number of the journal are both italicized. Note as well that in entries for journal articles, page numbers appear without the *p.* or *pp.* designation.

Article in a Scholarly Journal with Paging by Issue

> Devine, P. G., & Sherman, S. J. (1992). Intuitive versus rational judgment and the role of stereotyping in the human condition: Kirk or Spock? *Psychological Inquiry, 3*(2), 153–159.

Sources in Electronic Media

The DOI System

With the 6th edition of the *Publication Manual,* the APA presents the addition to journal documentation of the DOI or digital object identifier. The DOI is a unique number assigned to an article that may be in print or online; it is a reliable and consistent way of accessing digital information, in general, more reliable than a URL. Library databases relevant to disciplines that use APA, among them PsycARTICLES and PsycINFO, list a Digital Object Identifier (DOI) for individual articles.

When you search through your library's databases, you will see in an article's record the phrase *Digital Object Identifier,* followed by a series of digits and periods. In References lists, include the DOI at the end of your APA citation, preceded by *doi:* in regular font. Do not place a period after the digits in the DOI, as this can change the meaning of the identifier.

Here are two article citations from the section above, shown with their DOIs.

Limb, G. E., & Hodge, D. R. (2008). Developing spiritual competency with Native Americans: Promoting wellness through balance and harmony. Families in society, *89,* 615-622. doi:10.1606/1044– 3894.3816

Devine, P. G., & Sherman, S. J. (1992). Intuitive versus rational judgment and the role of stereotyping in the human condition: Kirk or Spock? *Psychological Inquiry, 3*(2), 153–159. doi:10.1207/ s15327965pli0302_13

Article from a Web site

Author's last   (Year of
name, initials.   publication, month).   Title of article.   *Title of site.*
↓   ↓   ↓   ↓

Ioannou, S. (2004, May). Essay tips for student writers. *Canadian Student Writing Resources.* Retrieved January 10, 2005, from http://www3.sympatico.ca/susanio/WWCcomp.html.

↑
URL   Date retrieved

Notice, first, the APA citations for material retrieved from the Internet do include the URL. Next, note that the article on this Web site appears first, with no quotation marks and only the first word of its title capitalized. The date that the student accessed the information is preceded by the word *Retrieved,* and the word *from* precedes the URL.

Article in an Online Encyclopedia, No Known Author

Boss brass. (2009). In H. Kallmann & G. Potvin (Eds.), *Encyclopedia of music in Canada.* Retrieved May 28, 2010, from http://www. thecanadianencyclopedia.com/index.cfm?PgNm=TCE&Params=U1A RTU0000367

Article from an Online Database (No DOI)

Melino, L. (2003). New treatments for dysgraphia. *Journal of Research Psychology, 15,* 210–228. Retrieved May 12, 2006, from Proquest database.

Article from an Online Database with DOI

Sagarin, B. J., & Lawler-Sagarin, K. A. (2005). Critically evaluating competing theories: An exercise based on the Kitty Genovese murder. *Teaching of Psychology, 32*(3), 167–169. doi:10.1207/s15328023top3203_8

Article in an Online Scholarly Journal with Paging by Issue (No DOI)

> Barry, J. M. (2004). The site of origin of the 1918 influenza pandemic and its public health implications [Commentary]. *Journal of Translational Medicine, 2*(3), 1-4. Retrieved November 18, 2009, from http://www.translational-medicine.com/content/2/1/3

Article in an Online Scholarly Journal with DOI

> Zhao, S., Grasmuck, S., & Martin, J. (2008). Identity construction on Facebook: Digital empowerment in anchored relationships. *Computers in Human Behavior, 24*(5), 1816–1836. doi:10.1016/j.chb.2008.02.012

Article in an Online Newspaper

> Bradsher, K. (2005, November 3). Poverty and superstition hinder drive to block bird flu at source. *New York Times.* Retrieved November 3, 2009, from http://www.nytimes.com/2005/11/03/international/asia/03bird.html?th&emc=th

Blog Post

> McAdoo, T. (2009, September 10). Use of First Person in APA Style [Web log message]. Retrieved from http://blog.apastyle.org/.

E-mails, Interviews, and Personal Communications

In APA style, no personal communication (emails, interviews, conversations) is included in the References list, but, as noted previously, they can be cited parenthetically in an essay's main text: (E. Robbins, personal communication, January 4, 2009).

Electronic Mailing List Posting

> SaFeddern, T. (2004, May 10). Summary: EBN (nursing) resources [Electronic mailing list message]. Retrieved from Nursing & Allied Health Resources Section of the Medical Library Association (NAHRS), http://listserv.kent.edu/cgi-bin/wa.exe?LIST=NAHRS

Sources in Other Media

Television Program

> Waldman R. (Writer). (2006). Darkness calls [Television series episode].
> D. Chase (Producer), *The sopranos.* New York: HBO.

Film

> Jackson, P. (Director). (2001). *The lord of the rings: The fellowship of the ring* [Motion picture]. United States: New Line Productions, Inc.

Music CD

> Waits, T. (1980). Ruby's arms. On *Heartattack and vine* [CD]. New York: Elektra.

Note: For practice activities on APA-style Work Cited lists go to the OLC.

STEP 5: WRITE YOUR FINAL DRAFT

Having written your second draft, complete with documentation, you are now ready to work on your final draft. As you write your third draft, trace your argument carefully, looking for potential errors, weak spots, or lack of support. Check for points that require further explanation, and for concepts that might benefit from definition or clarification. When revising for content, refer again to the revision instructions in Part 1 of this book, and use the checklist on the inside front cover to be sure that your paper meets the four bases for effective writing: *unity, support, coherence,* and *effective sentence skills.* Do a final proofreading, then leave yourself enough time to rewrite anything that seems unclear and to check your documentation of quotations, paraphrases, or summarized material.

As you begin revising, create a formal version of an outline, if one is required by your instructor. Generally, either a *topic outline* or a *sentence outline* will be required. A topic outline contains your thesis plus phrases stating your supporting points and subtopics. Roman numerals are used for first-level headings (main supporting points), capital letters for second-level headings (subtopics of supporting points), and numbers for third-level headings (details supporting subtopics). This type of outline differs from a *working outline* diagram as you have seen elsewhere in this book; it is a formalized, hierarchical display of the arrangement of your points and support. A sentence outline may follow the same pattern but will contain complete sentences.

Preparing and revising a third draft of your research paper is the minimum requirement, as far as drafting and revising are concerned, because research papers usually have a significant mark value. Instructors may make significant deductions for documentation, language, usage, and mechanical errors. Be especially careful when proofreading your revision. Correct sentence skills and mechanical errors and use your dictionary as well as your computer's spell checker to catch spelling errors.

Always leave yourself at least one or two days between revising and editing your second draft and the writing and careful proofreading of your final draft. You will see your content with a clearer eye, and you may spot errors that previously eluded you.

You now have the fundamentals for conducting research, assembling a paper, and documenting your sources. In the chapter that follows, you will find one model research paper in the MLA style, and one research essay in the APA style, showing how all the steps in the research process come together in the final draft of a paper.

CHECKLIST OF LEARNING OUTCOMES FOR CHAPTER 19

To ensure that you have understood and met the learning outcomes for this chapter, answer the following questions:

✓ What are the steps involved in writing an effective research paper?

✓ What is your first task when you revise your trial outline? What are the two general purposes of research papers?

✓ When should you use quotations? When should you paraphrase material? What is one essential feature of a good summary?

✓ What are citation styles, and what does correct documentation tell readers?

✓ Why is a second, or a third, revision essential for research papers?

PART 3
SPECIAL SKILLS AND RESEARCH

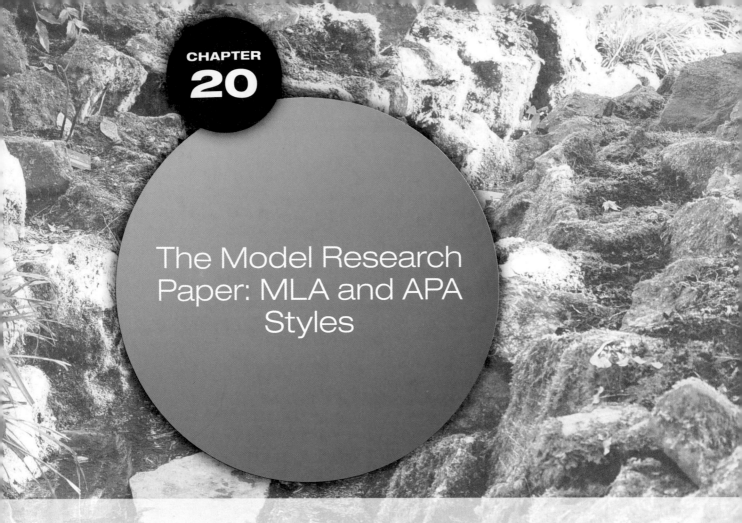

The Model Research Paper: MLA and APA Styles

In this chapter you will find examples of an MLA-style and an APA-style research paper, and before each essay, a section on how to set up each type of research essay and notes drawing your attention to the relevant aspects of each style of essay documentation.

THE MLA-STYLE RESEARCH PAPER: THE FORMAT

Currently MLA-style research essays do not require a separate title page. If your instructor requires a title page, start on line 21 in centred alignment. Put your essay's title on line 21, then, as indicated below, double-space each line of text, starting with the word *by*.

General Requirements

To begin at the absolute beginning, research essays, like any other essay, are word-processed on 8.5 × 11 paper. Double-space the entire essay and use 12-point type, preferably in a clear, legible font such as Times New Roman, in which the roman (plain) font is easy to distinguish from the italic font.

Set margins to one inch all around, and indent each paragraph with the tab key. Now is a good time to learn to follow the MLA rule of leaving only one space after a period or other punctuation at the end of a sentence.

Set up a header to appear in the top right-hand corner of each page. The header should be one half-inch from the top edge of the page and is set flush right against the margin. In the header, include your last name, a space, and the page number.

The First Page of Your Essay

Begin, for your first page only, on the upper-left margin of the page, with your full name. Down one (double-spaced) line, the name of your instructor; down one more (double-spaced) line, the name of your course; down a fourth (double-spaced) line, the date, written as day, month, year.

Now, double-space and centre your title. As with all your essay titles, type it with regular capitalization (on the main words, not on articles), in plain font, not bolded, not underlined, and not in quotation marks.

Double-space again, indent, and you are ready to type the first line of your essay.

THE MLA-STYLE RESEARCH PAPER: A MODEL

Model First Page with a Top Heading

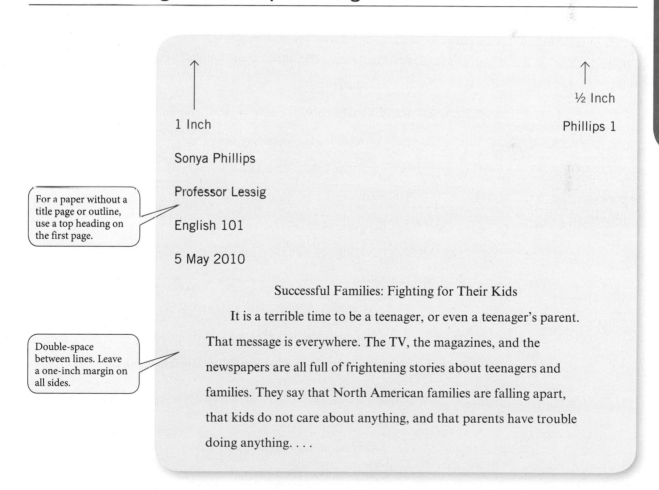

↑
1 Inch

↑
½ Inch

Phillips 1

Sonya Phillips

Professor Lessig

English 101

5 May 2010

For a paper without a title page or outline, use a top heading on the first page.

Double-space between lines. Leave a one-inch margin on all sides.

Successful Families: Fighting for Their Kids

It is a terrible time to be a teenager, or even a teenager's parent. That message is everywhere. The TV, the magazines, and the newspapers are all full of frightening stories about teenagers and families. They say that North American families are falling apart, that kids do not care about anything, and that parents have trouble doing anything. . . .

Model Outline Page

After the title page, the header will number all pages in the upper-right corner a half-inch from the top. Place your name before the page number. Use small roman numerals on outline pages. Use arabic numbers on pages following the outline.

The Word *Outline* (without underlining, italics, or quotation marks) is centred one inch from the top. Double-space between lines. Leave a one-inch margin on all sides.

Phillips i

Outline

Thesis: Although these are difficult times to be raising teenagers, successful families are finding ways to cope with the challenges.

I. Meeting the challenge of spending quality time together

    A. Barriers to spending quality time

        1. Increased working hours

        2. Rising divorce rates

        3. Women in workforce

    B. Danger of lack of quality time

    C. Ways found to spend time together

        1. Working less and scaling back lifestyle

        2. Home schooling allows some families to spend more time together

II. Meeting the challenge of creating sense of community

    A. Lack of traditional community ties

    B. Ways found to create sense of community

        1. Intentional communities

        2. Religious ties

III. Meeting the challenge of limiting the negative impact of media and technology

    A. Negative impact of media and technology

        1. Creation of environment without protection

        2. Flood of uncontrolled, inappropriate information

    B. Ways of controlling media and technology

        1. Banning TV

        2. Using technology in beneficial ways

Model Research Paper

This is the first page of an essay where the instructor has required a title page.

Double-space between lines of the text. Leave a one-inch margin all around the page. Your name and the page number appear as a header half an inch from the top right-hand corner of the page.

Common knowledge is not documented.

A typical first-time citation, or integrated citation, consists of the author's last name or (if no author is provided) the title of the source and a page number. The Works Cited provides full information about the source.

Extended thesis, followed by plan of development.

Successful Families: Fighting for Their Kids

It is a terrible time to be a teenager, or even a teenager's parent. That message is everywhere. The TV, the magazines, and the newspapers are all full of frightening stories about teenagers and families. They say that North American families are falling apart, that kids do not care about anything, and that parents have trouble doing anything about it. Bookstores are full of scary-sounding titles like these: *Teenage Wasteland, Cold New World, A Tribe Apart,* and *Teen Torment.* These books describe teenage problems that include apathy, violence, suicide, sexual abuse, depression, loss of values, poor mental health, teen crime, gang involvement, and drug and alcohol addiction.

Naturally, caring parents are worried by all this. According to a 2004 Ipsos-Reid poll sponsored by *The Globe and Mail,* less than half of Canadian parents feel they are doing a better job of raising their teenagers than their parents did ("Parents"). But leaving aside globally popular Canadian shows like *DeGrassi: The Next Generation,* most popular TV shows do not give a realistic view of North American teens, so these frightening books and depressing statistics do not provide a complete picture of what is going on in families today. The fact is that *not* all teens and families are lost and without values. While they struggle with problems in our culture like everyone else, successful families, especially families from Canada's diverse newer cultures, are doing what they have always done: finding ways to protect and nurture their children. They are fighting the battle for their families in three ways: by fighting against the loss of quality family time, by fighting against the loss of community, and by fighting against the influence of the media and technology.

Phillips 2

It is true that these days, parents face more challenges than ever before when it comes to finding quality time to spend with their children. Economist Edward Wolff explains the loss of time:

> Over a thirty-year time span, parental time has declined 13 percent. The time parents have available for their children has been squeezed by the rapid shift of mothers into the paid labour force, by escalating divorce rates and the subsequent abandonment of children by their fathers, and by an increase in the number of hours required on the job. The average worker is now at work 163 hours a year more than in 1969, which adds up to an extra month of work annually. (qtd. in Hewlett and West 48)

As a result, more children are at home alone than ever before. And this situation does leave children vulnerable to getting in trouble.

Numerous studies show that children who are home alone after school are twice as likely to experiment with drugs and alcohol than children who have a parent (or another adult) home in the after-school hours.

Yet, creative parents still come up with ways to be there for their kids. For some, it has been a matter of cutting back on working hours and living more simply. For example, in her book *The Shelter of Each Other*, Mary Pipher tells the story of a couple with three-year-old twin boys. Eduardo worked sixty-hour weeks at a factory. Sabrina supervised checkers at a K-Mart, cared for the boys, and tried to watch over her mother, who had cancer. Money was tight, especially since daycare was expensive, and the parents felt they had to keep the twins stylishly dressed and supplied with new toys. The parents were stressed over money problems, their lack of time together, and especially having so little time with their boys. It bothered them that the twins had begun to cry when their parents picked them up at daycare, as if they would rather stay with the daycare workers. Finally, Sabrina and Eduardo made a difficult decision. Sabrina quit her job, and the couple invited her mother (whose illness was in remission) to live with them. With the three adults pooling their resources, Sabrina and Eduardo found that they could manage without Sabrina's salary. The family no longer ate out, and they gave up their cable TV. Their sons loved having their grandmother in the house. Sabrina was able to begin doing relaxed, fun projects with the boys. They planted a garden and built a sandbox together. Sabrina observed, "I learned I could get off the merry-go-round" (195). Other parents have "gotten off the merry-go-round" by working at home, even if it means less money than they had previously. "[H]eading home is a real possibility for those parents who can master the new home-office technology. . . . If enough people can manage to do this, the neighbourhoods might once again come alive for workers and their children" (Louv 285).

Some parents even home-school their children as a way to be sure they have plenty of time together. Home schooling used to be thought of as a choice made only by very religious people or back-to-nature radicals. In Canada, home schooling is sometimes now called home-based learning, or HBL. HBL, or "deschooling" or "unschooling," is so popular that provincial governments have issued guidelines for parents, and the HBL central organization sponsors an extensive Web site full of resources including online courses and information for parents *(Canadian Home-Based Learning)*. Home-based learning is seen by its adherents as a superior form of education. Some Canadian universities even have admissions officers whose job it is to review applications from home-schooled students. Parents who home-school have different

Annotations (left margin):

Only the page number is needed as the author has already been named in the text.

Quotation marks acknowledge the phrase is copied from previous citation.

The capital letter in brackets shows the word was capitalized by the student but did not begin the sentence in the original source.

The ellipses show that material from the original source has been omitted.

Author and page number with no comma.

reasons for doing so, but, according to a cover story in *Newsweek,* "Some . . . are looking for a way to reclaim family closeness in an increasingly fast-paced society. . . . Still others worry about unsavoury influences in school—drugs, alcohol, sex, violence" (Kantrowitz and Wingert 66). Home schooling is no guarantee that a child will resist those temptations, but some families do believe it is a great way to promote family closeness. One fifteen-year-old, home-schooled since kindergarten, explained why he liked the way he had been raised and educated. He ended by saying, "Another way I'm different is that I love my family. One guy asked me if I'd been brainwashed. I think it's spooky that liking my family is considered crazy" (Pipher 103).

Quitting their jobs or teaching children at home are things that many parents cannot do. However, other parents find a second way to nurture their children through building community ties. They help their children develop a healthy sense of belonging by creating links with positive, constructive people and activities. In the past, community was not so hard to find. In *The Way We Really Are,* author Stephanie Coontz writes, "Right up through the 1940s, ties of work, friendship, neighborhood, ethnicity, extended kin, and voluntary organizations were as important a source of identity for most Americans, and sometimes a more important source of obligation, than marriage and the nuclear family" (37). Even when today's parents were teenagers, neighbourhoods were places where children and teens felt a sense of belonging and responsibility. Today, in many parts of Canada, parents miss what one study calls "the centrality of family." This centrality meant that "family time was an extremely important aspect of their lives and their leisure . . . that family comes first" (Tirone). Webs of relatives gave children and teens a sense of belonging and provided parents with a sense of

> Ellipses show where the student has omitted material from the original source. The quoted material is not capitalized because the student has integrated it into a sentence with an introductory phrase.

Phillips 5

security. Today's parents fear their children may grow up isolated and dependent on media products for companionship and guidance.

One way that some families are trying to build old-fashioned community is through "intentional community" or "cohousing." Begun in Denmark in 1972, the cohousing movement is modelled after the traditional village. It brings together a number of families who live in separate houses but share some common space. For instance, families might share central meeting rooms, dining areas, gardens, daycare, workshops, or office space. They might own tools and lawn mowers together rather than each household having its own. The point is that they treat their neighbours as extended family, not as strangers. *The Canadian Cohousing Network* states on its site that "Cohousing provides personal privacy combined with the benefits of living in a community where people know and interact with their neighbours" ("Cohousing"). More than twenty such communities currently exist in Canada.

Other families turn to religion as a source of community. Michael and Diane Medved, authors of *Saving Childhood,* are raising their family in a religious Jewish home. Their children attend Jewish schools, go to synagogue, and follow religious customs. They frequently visit, eat, play with, and are cared for by neighbouring Jewish families. The Medveds believe their family is stronger because of their belief "in planting roots—in your home, in your family, in your community. That involves making a commitment, making an investment both physically and emotionally, in your surroundings" (Medved and Medved 200). Other religious traditions offer a similar sense of community, purpose, and belonging for a family. Marcus and Tracy Glover are members of the Nation of Islam. They credit the Nation with making their marriage and family strong and breaking a three-generation cycle of single motherhood (Hewlett and West 201–202).

Citation for an online source: no page number is given because the online document does not provide it.

Quoted material extends from one page to another, so both page numbers are given.

PART 3
SPECIAL SKILLS AND RESEARCH

A final way that families are fighting to protect their children is by controlling the impact of the media and technology. Authors Hewlett and West and Pipher use similar words to describe the effect of this impact. As they describe growing up today, Hewlett and West write about children living "without a skin" (xiii), and Pipher writes about "houses without walls" (12). The authors mean that unlike in the old days, when children were protected from the outside world while they were in the home, there is little such protection today. Even in their own living rooms, children only have to turn on a TV, radio, or computer to be hit with a flood of violence and sick humour. Children are growing up watching reality TV, full of programs that celebrate materialism, vulgarity, and winning at any cost. Sadly, many parents seem to have given up even trying to protect their growing kids against this onslaught. Canadian parents are blessed with children's programming that has been shown all over the world, but Canadian children prefer soaps, music videos, wrestling, and Home Shopping. Canadian parents are like the mother quoted in *USA Today* as saying, "How can I fight five hundred channels on TV?" (Donahue D1).

Fortunately, other parents are still insisting on control over the information and entertainment that comes into their homes. Some limit their children to public TV stations like Ontario's TVO; others subscribe to *The TV Project,* an online educational organization that helps parents "understand how television affects their families and community and propose alternatives that foster positive emotional, cognitive, and spiritual development within families and communities" *(The TV Project)*. Others ban TV entirely from their homes. More try to find a way to use TV, the Internet, and other consumer electronics as useful tools but not allow them to dominate their homes. One American family, the Millers, who home-school

Phillips 7

their children, described to Mary Pipher their attitude towards TV. They had not owned a TV for years but purchased one to watch the Olympics. The set is stored in a closet unless a program is on that the family agrees is worthwhile. Some programs the family has enjoyed together include the World Cup soccer games, the TV drama *Sarah Plain and Tall,* and an educational TV course in sign language. Pipher was impressed by the Miller children, and she thought their limited exposure to TV was one reason why. In her words,

> Calm, happy children and relaxed, confident parents are so rare today. Probably most notable were the long attention spans of the children and their willingness to sit and listen to the grown-ups talk. The family had a manageable amount of information to deal with. They weren't stressed by more information than they could assimilate. The kids weren't overstimulated and edgy. Nor were they sexualized in the way most kids now are. (107)

Pipher's words describe children raised by parents who will not give in to the idea that their children are lost. Such parents structure ways to be present in the home, build family ties to a community, and control the impact of the media and technology in their homes. Through their efforts, they succeed in raising nurtured, grounded, successful children. Such parents acknowledge the challenges of raising kids in today's Canada, but they are up to the job.

> The conclusion provides a summary and restates the thesis.

Works Cited

> Works Cited list is double-spaced. Titles of books, magazines, and the like are italicized.

"A Lot Easier Said Than Done: Parents Talk About Raising Children in Today's America." *Public Agenda.* Oct. 2002. Web. 9 Mar. 2010.

Canadian Home-Based Learning Resource Page. 2001. Web. 12 Mar. 2010.

PART 3
SPECIAL SKILLS AND RESEARCH

Phillips 8

Coontz, Stephanie. *The Way We Really Are.* New York: Basic Books, 1997. Print.

Donahue, Deirdre. "Struggling to Raise Good Kids in Toxic Times." *USA Today* 1 Oct. 1998: D1–D2. Print.

Hewlett, Sylvia Ann, and Cornel West. *The War Against Parents.* Boston, New York: Houghton Mifflin, 1998. Print.

The Intentional Communities Home Page. Fellowship of Intentional Communities. Web. 8 Mar. 2010.

Kantrowitz, Barbara, and Pat Wingert. "Learning at Home: Does It Pass the Test?" *Newsweek* 5 Oct. 1998: 64–70. Print.

Louv, Richard. *Childhood's Future.* Boston: Houghton Mifflin, 1990. Print.

Medved, Michael, and Diane Medved. *Saving Childhood.* New York: HarperCollins/Zondervan, 1998. Print.

"Parents on Parenting: Part IV." *Ipsos News Center.* April 2004. Web. 10 Mar. 2010.

Pipher, Mary. *The Shelter of Each Other.* New York: Putnam, 1996. Print.

The Television Project Home Page. The Television Project. Web. 8 Mar. 2010.

Tirone, Susan. "Leisure and Centrality of Family." *Journal of Leisurability* 24.3 (1997). *ProQuest.* Web. 10 Mar. 2010.

"What is Cohousing?" *The Canadian Cohousing Network.* Winter 2007. Web. 10 Mar. 2010.

> Include the date you accessed a Web source—in this case, March 10, 2010.

THE APA-STYLE RESEARCH PAPER: THE FORMAT

Unlike MLA-style papers, research essays in APA format must have title pages. The APA paper has four parts: title page, abstract, body, and references. While APA does require an abstract for all research essays, check for your instructor's preference in this respect. Instructors may not ask for an abstract for a brief two- or three-page essay in APA style, but always confirm such arrangements with your own instructor.

General Requirements

An APA-style research essay, like any other essay, is word-processed on 8.5 × 11 paper, and the entire essay is double spaced. Times New Roman in 12-point size is preferred, as is placing one space after final sentence punctuation.

Before starting on a near-to-final draft, set your margins to one inch all around, and set up a header, or running head, that is your title (or a shorter version of it), to appear flush left, in the top left-hand corner of each page, including your title page. For the title page only, begin with the words, *Running head,* followed by a colon, then your title or abbreviation in full caps. On every other page, only your title and page number will appear. Place page numbering flush right in the running head, and allow your title page to be page one. Use normal capitalization for your title or abbreviated title. The two-part running head does not appear on your title page.

The Title Page

Begin your title page by placing your essay's title (in regular capitalizing, with only the main words capitalized) in centred alignment on the top half of the page. The title page is double spaced. In APA style, titles must be brief, preferably no more than twelve words long, so that a title occupies, at most, only two lines on your title page. Type your title in upper- and lowercase letters centred in the upper half of the page. Next, include your name, with your middle initial, and on the next line, the name of your college or university.

The Abstract

The first page of your essay is the abstract; as you have learned, an abstract is a summary. In the APA-style paper, an abstract is a one-paragraph (150–200 words) summation of the main points of your paper. Your summary will, at a minimum, state the topic of your research, your paper's intention, your main points, and conclusion.

Because the abstract is actually page two of your essay, your running head (without the words *running head*) will appear at the top, and you will title this page *Abstract,* in centred alignment at the top of the page. This title appears in regular font, with no italics, no bolding, no full caps, no underlining, and no quotation marks.

The abstract paragraph does not begin with an indentation; it begins flush left with the margin.

The Body

Now you are ready to begin typing the draft of your essay. Centre your title at the top of the first page after the abstract (page 3), and type it with regular capitalization, with no bolding, no underlining, no italics, and no quotation marks. Indent your first paragraph and all subsequent paragraphs, and pay attention to in-text citation, referring back to the previous chapter as needed.

The References

Follow the instructions on pages 319–324 for setting up and creating entries for your references page.

The research essay that follows is the work of Mark Moreira, a student in a first-year "Writing for the Sciences" course.

PART 3
SPECIAL SKILLS AND RESEARCH

THE APA-STYLE RESEARCH PAPER: A MODEL

Model Title Page

On title page only, the words "Running head" appear before the text of the running head. For all pages following only the text of the running head itself appears at the top of each page, with the page number.

Running head: SPECIALIZATION AND SURVIVAL 1

Specialization and Survival: Dinosaurs and Gigantism

Mark Moreira

Simon Fraser University

Model Abstract Page

"Abstract" is centred as a title.

There is no indent for the first line of the paragraph that contains the abstract. This rule applies only to the Abstract page.

Abstracts should contain 150–250 words. Any abbreviations or acronyms used in the essay should be defined in the abstract.

The running head is the essay's full title or a short version of it. The running head is printed in full caps, and is flush with the left margin.

Titles summarize the essay's general idea, then name the specific aspects to be covered.

Titles are centred on the page in 12-point Times New Roman. Titles are not bolded, underlined, or italicized. They follow standard capitalization.

Writer's name and educational institution are double-spaced and centred under title.

SPECIALIZATION AND SURVIVAL: DINOSAURS AND GIGANTISM   2

Abstract

Dinosaurs dominated the earth's terrain from 250 million years ago to 65 million years ago, during the Mesozoic Era (Macleod et al., 1997). Of these, the largest, and the largest of all land animals, was the sauropod (Senter, 2007). Why this creature grew to extraordinary sizes is likely due to its unique biology and anatomical specializations (Sander and Clauss, 2008). Physical specializations that enabled them to grow to their gargantuan size included methods of digestion, diffused lung structure, and elongated necks (Wedel 2003; Sander and Clauss, 2008). Scientists also hypothesize that a variable basal metabolicate rate (BMR) and efficient production of numerous and fast-growing offspring (Sander and Clauss, 2008) contributed to the thriving and surviving of these giant creatures. This paper will examine the sauropod, focusing on its size and possible causes for the extreme growth of these mega-herbivores.

Model Research Page

Specialization and Survival:

Dinosaurs and Gigantism

Dinosaurs, especially the largest among them, the sauropods, must have been highly efficient animals. They thrived for over one hundred million years from the Late Triassic to the end of the Cretaceous, when they were more than likely wiped out by the Chixulub meteorite impact (Sander and Clauss, 2008, p. 203). Fossilized remains are found worldwide, spread through North America, Africa, Europe, and Asia (Curry Rogers & Wilson, 2005; Thilborn, 2004). Size is the singular characteristic of the sauropod. From fossils, scientists have been able to approximate that sauropod mass more than likely exceeded seventy metric tonnes in some cases—these creatures were considerably larger than today's largest land animal, the elephant, which has a mass of approximately ten metric tonnes (Sander & Clauss, 2008; Curry Rogers & Wilson, 2005). Their linear dimensions were just as impressive; it is believed that sauropods were up to forty metres long and seventeen meters tall. Dinosaur anatomy of the sauropod variety included an exceedingly long neck and tail, as well as a bulky torso, all supported by four pillar-like legs (Sander & Clauss, 2008, p. 206). Senter (2007) documented neck lengths found among various species of sauropods as reaching over nine metres in length; with comparable tail lengths, these were massive and elongated creatures.

The evolution of those irregularly long necks is a well-researched aspect of the mega-herbivores (Curry Rogers & Wilson, 2005; Clauss, Schwarm, Ortmann, Streich, & Hummel, 2007; Senter, 2007; Sander & Clauss, 2008; Wedel, 2003). To understand why and how their necks developed this way, scientists turn to other related physical traits. Their small heads and highly specialized respiratory systems are two additional, equally important characteristics that help explain why sauropods developed such long necks.

Title of paper is centred, not bolded.

The first paragraph here sets up the context and precise background information needed for the essay's content.

In-text citations include author's names(s) and year of publication.

If there are three to five authors for an article, place all authors' names in the first citation; after that, use only the first author's name and the phrase *et al*.

The thesis or statement of the problem to be addressed appears in the second paragraph.

PART 3
SPECIAL SKILLS AND RESEARCH

The relatively small, light head was critical for the development of the long neck. Like a bowling ball on a finger, a long neck would not support a large, heavy skull. One reason for the lightness of this dinosaur's cranium is the general lack of any major dental development—the sauropods were not chewers. Sander and Clauss (2008) report that, unlike modern herbivores such as cows, sauropods did not chew their food at all, and therefore had no use for large, heavy teeth or massive jaws. This fact has even more implications for gigantism: it allowed for the evolution of a long neck, and also contributed to the sheer mass of this saurian's torso (Sander & Clauss, 2008). The dinosaur's digestive tract did all the work of digesting its food; there was no breaking down of the leaves and branches they ate by biting, grinding, or chemicals in the mouth. Long digestive times were needed, as was a long digestive tract (Clauss et al., 2007). This extended alimentary canal was one of the main reasons for this dinosaur's massive torso. As with cows and ruminants, a raw plant diet does require a larger gut capacity, an extended digestive tract, and increased digestion time (Hummel et al., 2008; Clauss et al., 2007). Thus the knowledge of dinosaur dentition, as well as the relationship between body mass and digestion time is critical to understanding saurian gigantism.

Due to their long necks and massive size, sauropods would have had difficulty breathing, had their respiratory systems been one-piece, nose-to-lungs operations, as they are with modern humans. If a dinosaur were to attempt to move air along the great distance from mouth to lungs, it would have been similar to trying to breathe through a hose. Instead, sauropods developed a specialized, spread-out, heterogeneous respiratory system (Sander & Clauss, 2008). Similar to modern birds, where a lung-and-air-sac respiratory system overcomes such problems (Wedel, 2003), the sauropods of the Mesozoic era utilized air sacs in their neck vertebrae, ribs, and abdomen to control breathing (Bakker, 1972; Curry Rogers & Wilson, 2005; Sander & Clauss, 2008; Wedel, 2003). Sauropod air sacs had two main purposes: first, they ventilated the lungs by ensuring that air only flowed in one direction through the long neck at any given time. Second, using air sacs created increased surface area for gas exchange, and in turn, more efficient oxygen exchange with the blood (Bakker, 1972). Efficient oxygen exchange, the process of oxygenating the blood, was crucial for the massive sauropods during the Mesozoic era, as the atmospheric oxygen levels were less than today's levels (Berner & VandenBrooks, 2007). Using such a diversified respiratory system allowed for the development of long dinosaur necks without resultant oxygen deprivation.

Although sauropods did reach gigantic sizes, it is not likely that they were born that way. Sauropod mothers are believed to have laid many eggs at once, a fairly primitive form of reproduction, but one that increases the odds of survival (Sander & Clauss, 2008). Once the eggs hatched, the newborn sauropds weighed only ten kilograms, meaning that there would have been significant growth from infancy to adulthood. Scientists now believe that growth among these creatures was not constant throughout life, but was much more rapid during infancy, slowing over the thirty years it would take the dinosaur to reach adulthood (Sander & Clauss, 2008; Curry Rogers & Wilson, 2005). A variable metabolic rate, or BMR, was responsible for this. BMR is defined as the amount of energy used by an organism in a resting state, relative to its mass. Among other things such as heat production and food energy needed, BMR can also be related to growth (Bakker, 1972; Seebacher, 2003). Infant sauropods likely had a considerably higher BMR than adults (Sander & Clauss, 2008). The higher BMR in young dinosaurs would allow for the rapid

> In-text citations for multiple articles consulted for any statement show the authors listed alphabetically by last name.

growth that would slow gradually during the decades needed to reach maturity. Sander and Clauss (2008) also noted that without this gradual slowing in metabolic rate, the massive adult dinosaur would have had difficulty managing the resulting high body-temperatures and huge food requirements that accompany a high BMR. The idea of variable metabolic and growth rates throughout their lives helps explain how sauropods could grow to such huge sizes without severe consequences.

Mesozoic sauropods had several defining characteristics as creatures, as well as causes for their extreme growth. Their massive body dimensions were largely a result of specialized anatomical and biological specializations. Their long necks could develop because of their light skulls containing no heavy grinding teeth. Because of not chewing their food, they developed a long digestive tract and, in turn, a large, bulky torso to contain it. Their long necks caused further specialization—their heterogeneous, dispersed respiratory system that used air sacs thoughout the neck and body to ensure efficient oxygen exchange. During their life-spans, their variable metabolic rates allowed for rapid growth in infancy and a natural slowdown of BMR during adulthood, protecting them from problems that could have arisen from massive size and high metabolism. All their physical specializations allowed these dinosaurs to grow to their massive adult size and become the largest organisms ever to walk on earth.

The conclusion restates the problem addressed by the paper, and returns to the more general context of the paper's opening paragraph.

SPECIALIZATION AND SURVIVAL   7

References

Bakker, R.T. (1972). Anatomical and ecological evidence of endothermy in dinosaurs. *Nature,* (238), 81–85.

Berner, R. A. & VandenBrooks, J.M., (2007). Oxygen and evolution. *Science,* (316), 557–558.

Clauss, M., Schwarm, A., Ortmann, S., Streich, W.J., & Hummel, J. (2007). A case of non-scaling in mammalian physiology body size, digestive capacity, food intake, and ingesta passage in mammalian herbivores. *Comparative Biochemistry and Physiology Part A, 148*(2), 249–265.

Curry Rogers, K.A., & Wilson, J.A. (Eds.). (2005). *The sauropods: evolution and paleobiology.* London: University of California Press.

Hummel, J., Gee, C.T., Südekum, K., Sander, P.M., Nogge, G., & Clauss, M. (2008). In vitro digestibility of fern and gymnosperm foliage implications for sauropod feeding ecology and diet selection. *Proceedings of the Royal Society B, 275*(1638), 1015–1021. doi:10.1098/rspb.2007.1728/rspb.2007.1728

MacLeod, N., Rawson, P.F., Forey, P.L., Banner, F.T., Boudagher-Fadel, M.K., Brown, P.R., . . . Young, J.R. (1997). The cretaceous-tertiary biotic transition. *Journal of the Geological Society, 154*(2), 1015–1021. doi: 10.1144/gsjgs.154.2.0265

Sander, P.M., Clauss, M. (2008). Sauropod gigantism. *Science 322* (5899), 200–201. doi: 10.1126/science.1160904

Seebacher, F. (2003). Dinosaur body temperatures: the occurrence of endothermy and ectothermy. *Paleobiology, 29*(1), 105–122.

Senter, P. (2007). Necks for sexual selection as an explanation for dinosaur neck elongation. *Journal of Zoology, 271,* 45–53.

Thilborn, T. (2004). Extramorphological features of sauropod dinosaur tracks in the Uhangri Formation, Korea. *Ichnos, 11*(3–4), 295–298.

Wedel, M.J. (2003). Vertebral pneumaticity, air sacs, and the physiology of sauropod dinosaurs. *Paleobiology, 29*(2), 243–255.

> The References list is a separate page, with the title *References* appearing centred at the top. The running head continues on this page.
>
> All entries are double-spaced, and listed (with no numbering) in alphabetical order by authors' last names.

PART 3
SPECIAL SKILLS AND RESEARCH

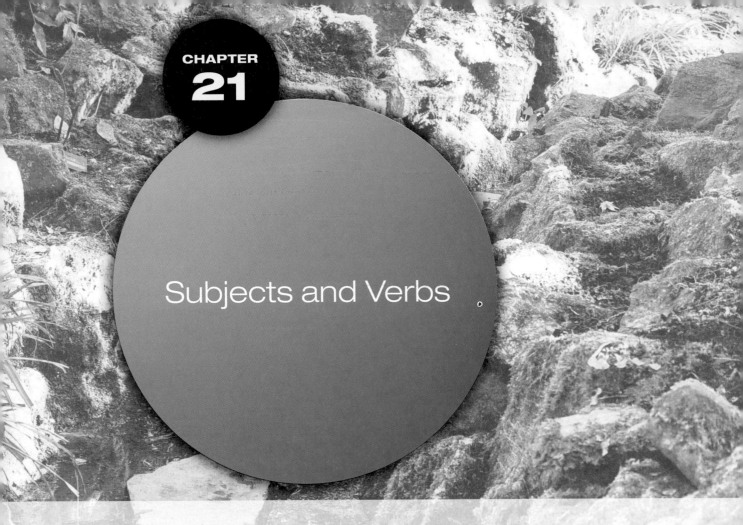

Subjects and Verbs

PRE-TEST

Test your knowledge of subjects and verbs in the following five sentences. Draw one line under the subject and two lines under the verb.

1. At the end of each day, the nurse writes his report.
2. Ashley takes night classes at Lambton College.
3. Emilio teaches his client new stretching exercises.
4. The baby giggled while her mother massaged her small toes.
5. Anna's insomnia was cured with regular acupuncture visits.

Subjects and verbs are the basic building blocks of English sentences. Understanding them is an important first step toward mastering sentence skills.

Every sentence has a subject and a verb. *Who* or *what* the sentence speaks about is called the *subject;* what the sentence says about the subject is called the *verb.* In the following sentences, the subject is underlined once and the verb twice:

The patient cries for help.
Many therapists attended the conference.
That lecture hall is new.
The technologist fixed the computer.

A SIMPLE WAY TO FIND A SUBJECT

Tip: Think of the subject of a sentence as the "actor" or the "doer" of an action. For example, in the sentence "Ruth enjoys playing soccer on the weekend," "Ruth" is the actor of the action "enjoys."

To find a subject, ask *whom* or *what* the sentence is about. As shown below, your answer is the subject.

> *Whom* is the first sentence *about?* The patient.
> *What* is the second sentence *about?* Many therapists.
> *Whom* is the third sentence *about?* That lecture hall.
> *What* is the fourth sentence *about?* The technologist.

A SIMPLE WAY TO FIND A VERB

To find a verb, ask what the sentence says *about* the subject. As shown below, your answer is the verb.

> What does the first sentence *say about* the patient? He or she cries.
> What does the second sentence *say about* the therapists? They attended.
> What does the third sentence *say about* the lecture hall? It is new.
> What does the fourth sentence *say about* the technologist? He or she fixed the computer.

A second way to find the verb is to put *I, you, he, she, it,* or *they* in front of the word you think is a verb. If the result makes sense, you have a verb. For example, you could put *he* in front of *cries* in the first sentence above, and the result, *he cries,* would make sense. Therefore, you know that *cries* is a verb. You could use the same test with the other three verbs as well.

Finally, it helps to remember that most verbs show action. In the sentences already considered, the three action verbs are *cries, attended,* and *visited.* Certain other verbs, known as *linking verbs,* do not show action. They do, however, give information about the subject. In "That clinic is new," the linking verb *(is)* joins the subject *(clinic)* with a word that identifies or describes it *(new).* Other common linking verbs include *feel, appear, look, become,* and *seem.*

● ● ● ● ● ACTIVITY

In each of the following sentences, draw one line under the subject and two lines under the verb.

1. Daily massage eases my baby's tension and fussiness.

2. Acupuncture reduces the pain of my headaches.

3. Chin graduated with honours from the Business Executive program at Sir Sandford Fleming College.

4. The clinic offers many workshops to rehabilitate patients on their road to recovery.

5. The police car raced along the freeway at a frightening speed.

6. Marta's Web site confuses me.

PART 4
HANDBOOK OF SENTENCE SKILLS

7. On St. Patrick's Day, our neighbourhood bar serves green beer.

8. My nine-year-old brother learned cursive writing in his grade 3 class.

9. More men want to become educational assistants.

10. The inexperienced paramedic shrank from touching the patient's raw, burned skin.

MORE ABOUT SUBJECTS AND VERBS

Tip: Subjects and verbs are *never* in prepositional phrases.

1. A sentence may have more than one verb, more than one subject, or several subjects and verbs.

    The law student coughed and sneezed.
    Broken glass and empty cans littered the college parking lot.
    Juliet, Ming, and Andrew met after math class and headed downtown.

2. The subject of a sentence never appears within a *prepositional phrase*. A prepositional phrase is simply a group of words that begins with a preposition. Following is a list of common prepositions:

about	before	by	inside	over
above	behind	during	into	through
across	below	except	like	to
among	beneath	for	of	toward
around	beside	from	off	under
at	between	in	on(to)	with

Tip: The word *preposition* contains the word *position*. Many prepositions begin a phrase showing the position of something or someone relative to something else or someone else: for example, "The printer is *beside* the computer."

Crossing out prepositional phrases will help you find the subject or subjects of a sentence.

At the end of the day, Dale types his class notes on a laptop.
On the fourth floor of the residence at Sheridan College, students studied diligently.
A ray of bright sunlight filled the Registrar's Office of Camosun College in Victoria, British Columbia.
On the last day of his ethics exam, Chang celebrated with his friends until well after midnight.
At night, my grandmother knits in the lounge at the retirement home.

3. Many verb forms consist of more than one word. Here, for example, are some of the many forms of the verb *work:*

work	worked	should work
works	were working	will be working
does work	have worked	can work
is working	had worked	could be working
are working	had been working	must have worked

4. Words like *not, just, never, only,* and *always* are not part of the verb, although they may appear within the verb.

   The new manual confused only the first-year paramedic students.
   Raine has just finished her firefighter diploma program.
   The orientation session at New Brunswick Community College will not run for two days this year.

5. No verb preceded by *to* is ever the main verb of a sentence.

   On Tuesday afternoons, my physiotherapist has decided to work from home.
   My roommate Natasha wants to be a police officer in Calgary, Alberta.

6. No *-ing* word by itself is ever the verb of a sentence. (It may be part of the verb, but it must have a helping verb in front of it.)

   The interns working the night shift this weekend. (not a sentence because the verb is not complete)
   The interns are working the night shift this weekend. (a sentence)

● ● ● ● **ACTIVITY**

Draw a single line under subjects and a double line under verbs. Crossing out prepositional phrases may help you to find the subjects.

1. On a busy street in downtown Winnipeg, the accident victim complained of dizziness.

2. The graduates of the esthetician program stood outside in the hot sun.

3. The young man talked about his childhood on the counsellor's couch.

4. On the weekends, my brother worked with an occupational therapist to reach his desired goals.

5. A newspaper advertisement about a part-time social worker attracted my attention.

6. Two of the oldest banks in Kamloops are being torn down.

7. Antonio enjoys his work rehabilitating people with head injuries.

8. In the summer, my roommate wants to volunteer at a hospital in Guatemala.

9. The pen fell from the student's hand and landed on the floor.

10. The scar in the hollow of Brian's throat is the result of an emergency operation to clear his windpipe.

● ● ● ● **POST-TEST**

Draw a single line under subjects and a double line under verbs. Crossing out prepositional phrases may help you to find the subjects.

1. Before the accounting test, Lidia and Cory ran to the coffee shop on the second floor.

2. In North America, "scrubs" has replaced the traditional nurse uniform.

PART 4

HANDBOOK OF SENTENCE SKILLS

3. Waiting in the long ticket line, Matt shifted his weight from one foot to another.

4. The youths completed 100 hours of community service work.

5. The mail carrier abruptly halted her Jeep and backed up toward the mailbox.

6. I am impressed with my father's knowledge of computers.

7. Many people complain about the rising costs in the Canadian health-care system.

8. The rewards of being a police officer far outweigh the challenges.

9. In October, the Global Environmental Convention takes place in St. John's, Newfoundland.

10. The students in the residence lounge looked tired and solemn.

Fragments

PRE-TEST

Test your knowledge of fragments by trying to correct the following incomplete sentences:

1. Studying in the comfort of my own home.

2. Jeremy has switched programs. Because he has decided to become a social service worker.

3. Proofreading essays for spelling mistakes is a difficult task. Especially when your paper has lots of homonyms.

4. Werner often procrastinates when he should be studying. To prepare for final exams.

5. The debating team beginning its first round of speeches.

Every sentence must have a subject and a verb and must express a complete thought. A word group that lacks a subject or a verb and that does not express a complete thought is a *fragment.* Following are the most common types of fragments that people write:

1. Dependent-word fragments

2. *-ing* and *to* fragments

3. Added-detail fragments

4. Missing-subject fragments

Once you understand the specific kind or kinds of fragments that you may write, you should be able to eliminate them from your writing. The following pages explain all four fragment types.

DEPENDENT-WORD FRAGMENTS

Some word groups that begin with a dependent word are fragments. Below is a list of common dependent words. Whenever you start a sentence with one of these words, you must be careful that a fragment does not result.

after	if, even if	when, whenever
although, though	in order that	where, wherever
as	since	whether
because	that, so that	which, whichever
before	unless	while
even though	until	who
how	what, whatever	whose

In the example below, the word group beginning with the dependent word *after* is a fragment:

> After I cashed my paycheque. I treated myself to dinner.

A *dependent statement*—one starting with a dependent word like *after*—cannot stand alone. It depends on another statement to complete the thought. *After I cashed my paycheque* is a dependent statement. It leaves us hanging. We expect in the same sentence to find out *what happened after* the writer cashed the cheque. When a writer does not follow through and complete a thought, a fragment results.

To correct the fragment, simply follow through and complete the thought:

> After I cashed my paycheque, I treated myself to dinner.

Remember, then, that *dependent statements by themselves are fragments.* They must be attached to a statement that makes sense standing alone.

Here are two other examples of dependent-word fragments:

> I won't leave the house. Until I hear from you.
> Rick finally picked up his socks. That he had thrown on the floor days ago.

Until I hear from you is a fragment; it does not make sense standing by itself. We want to know in the same statement *what cannot happen* until I hear from you. The writer must complete the thought. Likewise, *That he had thrown on the floor days ago* is not in itself a complete thought. We want to know in the same statement what *that* refers to.

Tip: Read these sentences out loud to find the fragments. Are you left hanging? Do you sense a lack of completion? If so, then you've probably found a fragment.

How to Correct Dependent-Word Fragments

In most cases you can correct a dependent-word fragment by attaching it to the sentence that comes after it or the sentence that comes before it:

> After I cashed my paycheque, I treated myself to dinner.
> (The fragment has been attached to the sentence that comes after it.)

> I won't leave the house until I hear from you.
> (The fragment has been attached to the sentence that comes before it.)

> Rick finally picked up his socks that he had thrown on the floor days ago.
> (The fragment has been attached to the sentence that comes before it.)

Another way of correcting a dependent-word fragment is simply to eliminate the dependent word by rewriting the sentence.

> I cashed my paycheque and then treated myself to dinner.
> I will wait to hear from you.
> He had thrown them on the floor days ago.

Tip: Dependent-word fragments are often the most common among student writers. Be extra careful when starting sentences with such words as *after, when, while, since,* etc.

Notes

1. Use a comma if a dependent-word group comes at the *beginning* of a sentence (see above):

> After I cashed my paycheque, I treated myself to dinner.

However, do not generally use a comma if the dependent word group comes at the end of a sentence:

> I won't leave the house until I hear from you.
> Rick finally picked up the socks that he had thrown on the floor days ago.

2. Sometimes the dependent words *who, that, which,* or *where* appear not at the very start but *near* the start of a word group. A fragment often results:

> I drove slowly past the old brick house. The place where I grew up.

The place where I grew up is not in itself a complete thought. We want to know in the same statement *where the place was* that the writer grew up. The fragment can be corrected by attaching it to the sentence that comes before it:

> I drove slowly past the old brick house, the place where I grew up.

• • • • • **ACTIVITY 1**

Turn each of the dependent-word groups into a sentence by adding a complete thought. Use a comma after the dependent-word group if a dependent word starts the sentence. Note the examples.

Examples Although I felt miserable

Although I felt miserable, I tried to smile for the photographer.

The student who found my i-clicker

The student who found my i-clicker returned it the next day.

PART 4

HANDBOOK OF SENTENCE SKILLS

1. If I don't get a raise soon

2. After the mid-term exam

3. When I heard the news of the power failure downtown

4. Because my grades improved since last semester

5. The restaurant that we tried down the street

• • • • ACTIVITY 2

Underline the dependent-word fragment in each selection. Then, rewrite the selections, correcting each fragment by attaching it to the sentence that comes before or the sentence that comes after—whichever sounds more natural. Use a comma after the dependent-word group if it starts the sentence.

1. When I graduate. I will get a job. That may not exist today.

2. Since Kim was not read to as a child. She has a difficult time keeping up with her course readings. As a result, she has vowed to read every day to her own children.

3. Many students enjoy group-work activities. Because the time goes by faster. More active learning also takes place.

4. Whenever he has time. Dimitri likes to paint outdoors. He finds it relaxing and therapeutic.

5. Before I turn on the microwave to cook something. I have to turn off the overhead light in the kitchen. Otherwise the circuits overload.

-*ING* AND *TO* FRAGMENTS

When an *-ing* word appears at or near the start of a word group, a fragment may result. Such fragments often lack a subject and part of the verb. *Doing, walking,* and other such verb forms ending in *ing* are *verbals, not complete verbs;* these words alone cannot be the "true verb" in a sentence. *To do, to receive,* and other *to* forms of verbs are *infinitive forms of verbs, not personal finite forms of verbs;* these must be "limited," or "made finite," as in *we do,* or *they received,* or used in combination with "true verbs."

Underline the word groups in the selections below that contain *-ing* words. Each is a fragment.

1. Ellen walked all over the neighbourhood yesterday. Trying to find her dog Bo. Several people claimed they had seen him only hours before.

2. We sat back to watch the movie. Not expecting anything special. To our surprise, we clapped, cheered, and cried for the next two hours.

3. I called to cancel my train ride home. It being the day before my psychology midterm. I knew my parents would understand.

People sometimes write *-ing* fragments because they think the subject in one sentence will work for the next word group as well. Thus, in the first selection, they think the subject *Ellen* in the opening sentence will also serve as the subject for *Trying to find her dog Bo*. But the subject must actually be *in* the sentence.

How to Correct *-ing* Fragments

1. Attach the fragment to the sentence that comes before or the sentence that comes after it, whichever makes sense. Item 1 could read, "Ellen walked all over the neighbourhood yesterday trying to find her dog Bo."

2. Add a subject and change the *-ing* verb to the "true" form of the verb. Selection 2 could read, "We didn't expect anything special."

3. Change *being* to the "true" form of the verb *be (am, are, is, was, were)*. Selection 3 could read, "It was the day before my psychology midterm."

How to Correct *to* Fragments

When *to* appears at or near the start of a word group, a fragment sometimes results:

> At the Chinese restaurant, Tim used chopsticks. To impress his date. He spent one hour eating a small bowl of rice.

The second word group is a fragment and can be corrected by adding it to the preceding sentence. The *infinitive* verb form *to impress* has been made part of the "true verb" *used:*

> At the Chinese restaurant, Tim used chopsticks to impress his date.

● ● ● ● **ACTIVITY 1**

Underline the *-ing* fragment in each of the selections that follow. Then, make it a sentence by rewriting it, using the method described in parentheses.

Example   Rushing home from work. Stan was excited about his new promotion. He has now made the leap from police officer to sergeant.
(Add the fragment to the sentence that comes after it.)

Rushing home from work. Stan was excited about his new promotion.

1. Preparing for my PowerPoint presentation for two days. I was proud of my efforts. Everyone in the room clapped at the end of my talk.
(Add the fragment to the preceding sentence.)

2. Fire trucks raced wildly through the streets, their sirens blaring. Coming to a stop at my house. I was only burning a pile of leaves.
(Correct the fragment by adding to it a subject and by changing the verbal to a "true verb" form.)

3. My phone doesn't ring. Instead, a light on it blinks. The reason for this added feature being that I am partially deaf.
(Correct the fragment by changing the verbal to a "true verb" form.)

• • • • **ACTIVITY 2**

Underline the *-ing* or *to* fragment in each selection. Then rewrite each selection, correcting the fragment by using one of the methods described on the previous page.

1. Taking French immersion in high school. Shelley felt lucky. She was able to converse with ease on her vacation in France.

2. Leif bought a new laptop for college. To make note-taking easier and faster in class. As a result, his grades are strong.

3. Staring at the clock on the far wall and shifting from foot to foot. I nervously began my speech. I was afraid to look at any of the people in the room.

4. Thinking about the upcoming Thanksgiving weekend at home. Winston found it hard to concentrate at his desk. He was looking forward to seeing his old friends again.

5. To find the only available public transportation around here. You have to walk two blocks out of your way. The endless sidewalk construction continuing throughout the season.

ADDED-DETAIL FRAGMENTS

Added-detail fragments lack a subject and a verb. They often begin with one of the following words:

also	especially	except	for example	like	including	such as

Underline the one added-detail fragment in each of the selections that follow:

1. Before a race, I eat starchy food. Such as bread and pasta. The carbohydrates provide quick energy.

2. Bob is taking a night course in auto mechanics. Also, one in plumbing. He wants to save money on household repairs.

3. My son keeps several pets in his room. Including hamsters, mice, and gerbils.

People often write added-detail fragments for much the same reason they write *-ing* fragments. They think the subject and verb in one sentence will serve for the next word group. But the subject and verb must be in *each* word group.

How to Correct Added-Detail Fragments

1. Attach the fragment to the complete thought that precedes it. Item 1 could read, "Before a race, I eat starchy foods such as bread and pasta."

2. Add a subject and a verb to the fragment to make it a complete sentence. Selection 2 could read, "Bob is taking a night course in auto mechanics. Also, he is taking one in plumbing."

3. Insert the fragment within the preceding sentence. Item 3 could read, "My son keeps several pets, including hamsters, mice, and gerbils, in his room."

· · · · **ACTIVITY 1**

Underline the added-detail fragment in each of the selections below. Then, make it a sentence by rewriting it, using the method described in parentheses.

Example   My sister likes watching daytime television shows. Especially quiz shows and soap operas. She doesn't mind commercials.
(Add the fragment to the preceding sentence.)

My sister likes watching daytime television shows, especially quiz shows
and soap operas.

1. Lois works evenings in a video store. She enjoys the fringe benefits. For example, seeing the new movies first.
(Correct the fragment by adding a subject and verb to the fragment.)

2. Bonnie's hands are sore after practising massage techniques in lab. And her fingertips sometimes feel numb. Like pins and needles.
(Add the fragment to the preceding sentence.)

3. Electronic devices keep getting smaller. Such as video cameras and cell phones. Some are so tiny they look like toys.
(Correct the fragment by inserting it into the preceding sentence.)

· · · · **ACTIVITY 2**

Underline the added-detail fragment in each selection. Then, rewrite to correct the fragment. Use one of the three methods described above.

1. Left-handed students face problems. For example, right-handed desks that make writing almost impossible. Spiral notebooks can also be uncomfortable to use.

2. Nanette always wears her lucky clothes during exam week. Such as a blouse printed with four-leaf clovers. She also carries a rhinestone horseshoe.

3. Hundreds of moths were fluttering around the stadium lights. Like large flecks of snow in a blizzard. The thirty-degree weather, though, made this form of precipitation unlikely.

4. Luc buys and sells paper collectors' items. For instance, vintage comic books, trading cards, and movie posters. He sets up a display at local flea markets and fall fairs.

5. I wonder now why I had to learn certain subjects. Such as geometry. No one has ever asked me about the hypotenuse of a triangle.

MISSING-SUBJECT FRAGMENTS

In each item below, underline the word group in which the subject is missing:

1. Alicia loved getting wedding presents. But hated writing the thank-you notes.

2. Mike has orange pop and potato chips for breakfast. Then, eats more junk food, like root beer, chocolate bars, and cookies, for lunch.

How to Correct Missing-Subject Fragments

1. Attach the fragment to the preceding sentence. Item 1 could read, "Alice loved getting her wedding presents but hated writing the thank-you notes."

2. Add a subject (which can often be a pronoun standing for the subject in the preceding sentence). Selection 2 could read, "Then, he eats more junk food, like root beer, chocolate bars, and cookies, for lunch."

● ● ● ● **ACTIVITY**

Underline the missing-subject fragment in each selection. Then rewrite that part of the selection needed to correct the fragment. Use one of the two methods described above.

1. Every other day, Karen runs three kilometres. Then, does 50 sit-ups. She hasn't lost weight, but she is more muscular.

2. I like all kinds of fresh pizza. But refuse, under any conditions, to eat frozen pizza. The sauce on them is always dried out, and the crust tastes like leather.

3. Many people are allergic to seafood. Their mouths swell up and they choke when they eat it by mistake. And can even have trouble breathing or need to go to the emergency ward.

4. The Nurses' Association meets once a month. The members discuss patient rules and protocol. And even hygiene concerns and vaccinations.

5. Last semester, I took six courses. And worked part-time in a discount drug store, snoozing during some of the late shifts. Now that the term is all over, I don't know how I did it.

A Review: How to Check for Sentence Fragments

1. Read your paper aloud from the *last* sentence to the *first*. You will be better able to see and hear whether each word group you read is a complete thought.

2. Ask yourself of any word group you think is a fragment: Does this contain a subject and a verb and express a complete thought?

3. More specifically, be on the lookout for the most common fragments:

   - Dependent-word fragments (starting with words like *after, because, since, when,* and *before*)

   - *-ing* and *to* fragments (*-ing* or *to* at or near the start of a word group)

   - Added-detail fragments (starting with words like *for example, such as, also,* and *especially*)

   - Missing-subject fragments (a verb is present but not the subject)

• • • • POST-TEST 1

Each word group in the following student paragraph is numbered. In the space provided, write *C* if a word group is a complete sentence; write *F* if it is a fragment. You will find eight fragments in the paragraph.

_____	1
_____	2
_____	3
_____	4
_____	5
_____	6
_____	7
_____	8
_____	9
_____	10
_____	11
_____	12
_____	13
_____	14
_____	15
_____	16
_____	17
_____	18
_____	19
_____	20

¹I'm starting to think that there is no safe place left. ²To ride a bicycle. ³When I try to ride on the highway, in order to go to school. ⁴I feel like a rabbit being pursued by predators. ⁵Drivers whip past me at high speeds. ⁶And try to see how close they can get to my bike without actually killing me. ⁷When they pull onto the shoulder of the road or make a right turn. ⁸Drivers completely ignore my vehicle. ⁹On city streets, I feel more like a cockroach than a rabbit. ¹⁰Drivers in the city despise bicycles. ¹¹Regardless of an approaching bike rider. ¹²Doors of parked cars will unexpectedly open into the street. ¹³Frustrated drivers who are stuck in traffic will make nasty comments.

¹⁴Or shout out obscene propositions. ¹⁵Even pedestrians in the city show their disregard for me. ¹⁶While jaywalking across the street. ¹⁷The pedestrian will treat me, a law-abiding bicyclist, to a withering look of disdain. ¹⁸Pedestrians may even cross my path deliberately. ¹⁹As if to prove their higher position in the pecking order of the city streets. ²⁰Today, bicycling can be hazardous to the rider's health.

Now (on separate paper) correct the fragments you have found. Attach the fragments to sentences that come before or after them, or make whatever other change is needed to turn each fragment into a sentence.

• • • • POST-TEST 2

Underline the two fragments in each item below. Then, make whatever changes are needed to turn the fragments into sentences.

Example   Sharon was going to charge her new suit (b)<u>But then decided to pay cash instead.</u> She remembered her new Year's resolution. (t)<u>To cut down on her use of credit cards.</u>

1. We both began to tire. As we passed the halfway mark in the race. But whenever I heard Reggie's footsteps behind me. I pumped my legs faster.

2. I have many assignments to complete. Such as a journal entry and a progress report. My fear is that I will run out of time. With three children to care for at home.

3. My children joke that we celebrate "Hanumas." With our Jewish neighbours. We share Hanukkah and Christmas activities. Including making potato pancakes at their house and decorating our tree.

4. Punching all the buttons on his radio in sequence. Phil kept looking for a good song. He was in the mood to cruise down the highway. And sing at the top of his voice.

5. I noticed two cartons of cigarettes. Sticking up out of my neighbour's garbage bag. I realized he had made up his mind. To give up smoking for the fifth time this year.

6. I've decided to leave home. And rent an apartment. By being away from home and on my own. I will get along better with my parents.

7. The alley behind our house was flat. Except for a wide groove in the centre. We used to sail paper boats down the groove. Whenever it rained hard enough to create a "river" there.

8. Don passed the computer school's aptitude test. Which qualifies him for nine months of training. Don kidded that anyone could be accepted. If he or she had four thousand dollars.

● ● ● ● **POST-TEST 3**

Turn each of the following word groups into a complete sentence.

Examples With trembling hands

With trembling hands, I headed for the front of the classroom.

As the race wore on

Some runners dropped out as the race wore on.

1. After the lecture

2. Such as editing for spelling and grammar

3. During the mystery movie

4. But soon grew frustrated

5. Nico, who works at his uncle's restaurant

6. To get to class on time

7. People lining up for the flu shot

8. Hurrying to get dressed

9. On the day of the open house

10. Losing my temper

Run-Ons

PRE-TEST

Test your knowledge of run-ons. Decide whether each of the following sentences is a fused sentence or a comma splice.

1. Paola wants to be a library technician, she enjoys helping people find information.

2. The computer email system in a Winnipeg company failed someone had hacked into it overnight.

3. My personal training sessions are an investment in my health, I now have more energy.

4. Brittany enjoys reading in the morning, her husband prefers reading in the evening.

5. Christopher does not enjoy working in an office he prefers working outdoors.

WHAT ARE RUN-ONS?

Tip: One of the best ways to catch a run-on is by reading your work out loud. As you read, look for the subject and the verb.

A *run-on* is two complete thoughts that are run together with no adequate sign given to mark the break between them.*

Some run-ons have no punctuation at all to mark the break between the thoughts. Such run-ons are known as *fused sentences:* they are fused, or joined together, as if they were only one thought.

Fused Sentences

Competition in the workforce is prevalent a diploma can increase job security.
Facebook is a popular social network people from around the globe use it to keep in touch with relatives.

In other run-ons, known as *comma splices,* a comma is used to connect, or "splice" together, the two complete thoughts. However, a comma alone is *not enough* to connect two complete thoughts. Some stronger connection than a comma alone is needed.

Comma Splices

Competition in the workforce is prevalent, a diploma can increase job security.
Facebook is a popular social network, people from around the globe use it to keep in touch with relatives.

Comma splices are the most common kind of run-on. Students sense that some kind of connection is needed between two thoughts, so they often put a comma at the dividing point. Again, however, the comma alone is not sufficient. A comma is simply a punctuation pause-mark, which cannot join ideas. A stronger, clearer mark is needed between the two complete thoughts.

Words that Can Lead to Run-Ons: People often write run-ons when the second complete thought begins with one of the following words:

I	we	there	now
you	they	this	the
he, she, it	that	next	

Remember to be on the alert for run-ons whenever you use one of these words in your writing.

---

*Note: Some instructors refer to each complete thought in a run-on as an *independent clause.* A *clause* is simply a group of words having a subject and a verb. A clause may be *independent* (expressing a complete thought and able to stand alone) or *dependent* (not expressing a complete thought and not able to stand alone). Using this terminology, we would say that a run-on is two independent clauses run together with no adequate sign given to mark the break between them.

How to Correct Run-Ons

Here are three common methods of correcting a run-on:

1. Use a period and a capital letter to break the two complete thoughts into separate sentences:

   Competition in the workforce is prevalent. A diploma can increase job security.
   Facebook is a popular social network. People from around the globe use it to keep in touch with relatives.

Tip: Please note that the word *for* means "because" and even though it is included in this list of joining words, it is less common in daily usage. Instead, writers simply use *because*.

2. Use a comma plus a joining word *(and, but, for, or, nor, so, yet)* to connect the two complete thoughts:

   Competition in the workforce is prevalent, so a diploma can increase job security.
   Facebook is a popular social network, and people from around the globe use it to keep in touch with relatives.

3. Use a semicolon to connect the two complete thoughts:

   Competition in the workforce is prevalent; a diploma can increase job security.
   Facebook is a popular social network; people from around the globe use it to keep in touch with relatives.

Tip: Use the semicolon to connect sentences that are similar and relatively short. The semi-colon is a useful punctuation mark but should be used sparingly.

A semicolon is a form of "punctuation glue." It can join two independent parts of a sentence without a joining word.

A fourth method of correcting a run-on is to use *subordination*. The following activities will give you practice in the first three methods. Subordination is described on pages 109–110 and on page 366.

Method 1: Period and a Capital Letter

One way of correcting a run-on is to use a period and a capital letter between the two complete thoughts. Use this method especially if the thoughts are not closely related or if another method would make the sentence too long.

● ● ● ● ACTIVITY

In each of the following run-ons, locate the point at which one complete thought ends and another begins. Each is a *fused sentence*—that is, each consists of two sentences fused, or joined together, with no punctuation at all between them. Reading each sentence aloud will help you "hear" where a major break or split between the thoughts occurs. At that point, your voice will probably drop and pause.

Correct the run-on by putting a period at the end of the first thought and a capital letter at the start of the next thought.

Example Nik's watch is no longer working. (H)e accidentally dropped it in the lake.

1. The men at the door claimed to have paving material left over from another job they wanted to pave our driveway for a "bargain price."

2. It is hard to remember a time when email didn't exist it has become an essential part of our personal and professional lives.

3. Linh, a legal assistant who speaks Vietnamese, helps other people from her country write wills she assists others by going with them when they have to appear in court.

4. A five-year-old child knows over 6000 words he or she has also learned more than 1000 rules of grammar.

5. Sarah considers herself lucky to have met her husband online she now owns a successful online dating company to help others find love.

6. Coco likes to shop on eBay she has found many good bargains for children's clothing.

7. In their workplace communications course at Niagara College some students create brochures on Word templates others design their own newsletters.

8. On Valentine's Day, patients receive a red rose at the Cape Breton Regional Hospital this act of kindness boosts their spirit.

Method 2: Comma and a Joining Word

Another way of correcting a run-on is to use a comma plus a joining word to connect the two complete thoughts. Joining words (also called *conjunctions*) include *and, but, or, nor, so,* and *yet.* Here is what the three most common joining words mean:

> ***and***   in addition
>
> Blane works full-time as a massage therapist, and he takes evening classes.
> (Blane works full-time as a massage therapist; *in addition,* he takes evening classes.)
>
> ***but***   however, on the other hand
>
> I turned to the want ads, but I knew my dream job wouldn't be listed.
> (I turned to the want ads; *however,* I knew my dream job wouldn't be listed.)
>
> ***so***   as a result, therefore
>
> Maria spends all her spare time emailing her friend in Calgary, so her grades have started to fall.
> (Maria spends all her spare time emailing her friend in Calgary; *as a result,* her grades have started to fall.)

Tip: FANBOYS *(for, and, nor, but, or, yet, so)* is an easy way to remember these joining words.

• • • • ACTIVITY 1

Insert the joining word *(and, but, so)* that logically connects the two thoughts in each sentence.

1. Elaine woke up to discover her computer had crashed, _____ luckily many of her files were retrieved.

2. The library had just closed, _____ I couldn't get any of the reserved books.

3. The professor's lecture at Algonquin College was full of multimedia, _____ it made for an exciting and meaningful class.

4. Although my baby enjoys having baths, she is scared of running water, _____ she likes having her hair washed even less.

5. Estella thought the virus had infected her entire hard drive, _____ it only affected a few of her files.

6. My ten-year-old sister receives daily insulin shots, _____ she was diagnosed with diabetes last year.

7. I like my psychology course, _____ the workload is time-consuming.

8. The classroom was eerily quiet, _____ the only sound was the clicking noise of fingers on keyboards.

● ● ● ● ● **ACTIVITY 2**

Add a complete and closely related thought to go with each of the following statements. Use a comma plus the joining word in parentheses when you write the second thought.

Example   I had a pounding headache, (so) <u>so I decided to leave school early.</u>

1. The corner store is convenient, (but)

2. Gloria could not decide whether to attend night class, (or)

3. Aisha studied for an hour before dinner, (and)

4. Paul can't retrieve his email, (so)

5. I needed a haircut, (but)

● ● ● ● ● **ACTIVITY 3**

Correct each run-on with either (1) a period and a capital letter or (2) a comma and a logical joining word. Do not use the same method of correction for every sentence.

Some of the run-ons are *fused sentences* (there is no punctuation between the two complete thoughts), and some are *comma splices* (there is only a comma between the two complete thoughts).

Example   There was a strange odour in the house, (so) Chin called the gas company immediately.

1. Devon quickly sent an email while eating the baby watched with interest.

2. The professor likes to receive her students' essays online a great deal of paper is saved.

3. Our environmental studies class is working on a weather project with students from Russia we communicate by computer almost every day.

4. The bristles of the paintbrushes were very stiff, soaking them in turpentine made them soft again.

5. Throughout the day, Jordynn logs her patients' progress on a chart, she always remembers to include precise detail.

6. Mario got a can of pop from the refrigerator he walked outside to sit on the porch steps.

7. Lin wants to become a dental hygienist there are many job opportunities in dentistry.

8. Rose borrows CDs from the library to listen to on the way to work, some are music and some are recordings of best-selling books.

Method 3: Semicolon

A third method of correcting a run-on is to use a *semicolon* to mark the break between two thoughts. A semicolon (;) looks like a period above a comma. It signals more of a pause than a comma alone but not quite the full pause of a period. When it is used to correct run-ons, the semicolon can be used alone or with a transitional word.

Semicolon Alone: Here are some earlier sentences that were connected with a comma plus a joining word. Now, they are connected by a semicolon alone. Notice that the semicolon alone—unlike the comma alone—can be used to connect the two complete thoughts in each sentence:

> The professor's lecture at Algonquin College was full of multimedia; it made for an exciting and meaningful class.

> Estella thought the virus had infected her entire hard drive; it only affected a few of her files.

> My ten-year-old sister receives daily insulin shots; she was diagnosed with diabetes last year.

> Maria spends all her spare time emailing her friend in Calgary; her grades have started to fall.

Using semicolons can also add to sentence variety.

● ● ● ● ACTIVITY

Insert a semicolon where the break occurs between the two complete thoughts in each of the following sentences.

Example The plumber gave me an estimate of $150; I decided to repair the tap myself.

1. Rob couldn't find his forensics textbook he was at a loss.

2. The battery light started to flicker on Rob's laptop he quickly plugged it in to save his work.

3. The Great Wall of China is immense it's the only architectural structure visible from the moon.

4. When Cheyenne kept squinting at the blackboard in class, she realized the problem she needed a new pair of eyeglasses.

5. When Samuel first entered the virtual world of Second Life, he was amazed the three-dimensional characters looked so real.

6. In the neonatal unit of the Vancouver General Hospital, loud noises could be heard throughout the halls newborn babies were crying.

Semicolon with a Transitional Word: A semicolon can be used with a transitional word and a comma to join two complete thoughts. Here are some examples:

Larry believes in being prepared for emergencies; therefore, he stockpiles canned goods in his basement.

I tried to cash my paycheque; however, I had forgotten to bring my identification.

Ahmed finds shopping online is addictive; consequently, he is wary of giving credit card numbers to dubious Canadian Web sites.

Most people agree that drinking and driving is dangerous; however, some believe that texting and driving is riskier.

A short nap at the end of the day relaxes me; in addition, it gives me energy to finish my homework.

Peter downloaded his favourite songs onto his iPod; meanwhile, his cat stretched out on the floor.

Following is a list of common transitional words (also known as *adverbial conjunctions*), with brief meanings.

Transitional Word	*Meaning*
however	but
nevertheless	however
on the other hand	however
instead	as a substitute
meanwhile	in the intervening time
otherwise	under other conditions
indeed	in fact
in addition	also, and
also	in addition
moreover	in addition
furthermore	in addition
as a result	thus, therefore
thus	as a result
consequently	as a result
therefore	as a result

• • • • **ACTIVITY**

For each sentence, choose a logical transitional word from the box on the previous page, and write it in the space provided. Use a semicolon *before* the connector and a comma *after* it.

Example I dread going to parties; however, my husband loves meeting new people.

1. Jasmine suffers from migraine headaches _____ her doctor has advised her to avoid caffeine and alcohol.

2. Ray's apartment is always neat and clean _____ the interior of his car looks like the aftermath of a tornado.

3. I try to attend all my math classes _____ I'll get too far behind to pass the weekly quizzes.

4. B.J. was singing Nelly Furtado tunes in the shower _____ his toast was burning in the kitchen.

5. The reporter was tough and experienced _____ even he was stunned by the tragic events.

A Note on Subordination

A fourth method of joining related thoughts is to use *subordination*. Subordination is a way of showing that one thought in a sentence is not as important as another thought. (Review the description of subordination on pages 109–110.) Below are three earlier sentences, recast so that one idea is subordinated to (made less important than) the other idea. In each case, the subordinate (or less important) thought is underlined. Note that each subordinate clause begins with a dependent word.

Because the library had just closed, I couldn't get any of the reserved books.

When the entrance exam was over, Elena felt confident about her answers.

The computer mouse was named after the small furry animal because the tail comes out the end.

A Review: How to Check for Run-Ons

1. To see if a sentence is a run-on, read it aloud and listen for a break marking two complete thoughts. Your voice will probably drop and pause at the break.

2. To check an entire paper, read it aloud from the last sentence to the first. Doing so will help you hear and see each complete thought.

3. Be on the lookout for words that can lead to run-on sentences:

I	he, she, it	they	this	then	now
you	we	there	that	next	

4. Correct run-ons by using one of the following methods:

- Period and a capital letter
- Comma and a joining word *(and, but, for, or, nor, so, yet)*
- Semicolon alone or with a transitional word
- Subordination

POST-TEST 1

Correct each run-on with either (1) a period and a capital letter or (2) a comma (if needed) and the joining word *and, but, for,* or *so.* Do not use the same method of correction for every sentence.

Some of the run-ons are fused sentences (no punctuation between the two complete thoughts), and some are comma splices (only a comma between the two complete thoughts). One sentence is correct.

1. Our sociology professor lectured last night for three hours, by the end we were tired and hungry.

2. Sheila forgot to write her student number on the test form the computer rejected her answer sheet.

3. Our boss expects us to work four hours without a break he wanders off to a vending machine at least once an hour.

4. The thieves would have stolen my iPhone it was engraved with a special identification number.

5. For the past year, Joshua blogged constantly with his college friends, but now he is addicted to tweeting.

6. Our class wanted to help the Haiti victims we sent a donation to the Red Cross.

7. I bought Wii Fit for my best friend, I visit her house every week to play tennis.

8. Claire wants to study kinesiology at the University of Lethbridge the tuition fees are too high.

POST-TEST 2

Correct each run-on by using (1) a period and a capital letter, (2) a comma and a joining word, or (3) a semicolon. Do not use one method exclusively.

1. Aunt Jeanne wanted to live in a warmer climate for her health she moved to Vancouver.

2. The average Canadian teenager spends 38 hours a week on school work, the average Japanese teenager spends about 60.

3. The real Laura Secord had nothing to do with chocolate, she was a brave woman who ran through the forests of southern Ontario, she relied on the help of Native Canadians to warn British troops of an American attack.

4. Spell check is a blessing for many writers it doesn't catch words that sound alike and look alike.

5. Marek accepted the business award his classmates applauded his hard work.

6. When Charlotte set up her own business on eBay, she was excited her sales soared in the first year.

7. My son uses a calculator for his grade 6 math homework the teacher insists it is not a crutch.

8. The words *month, silver, purple* and *orange* have something in common, no other English words rhyme with them.

• • • • POST-TEST 3

Locate and correct the four run-ons in the passage that follows.

The world of email has changed the way I communicate. Every day at work I send and receive several messages emailing is an efficient way for me to reach my colleagues, supervisors, and clients. With email, I don't necessarily need to rely on voicemail or face-to-face contact for quick, non-urgent answers when I'm not at work, I use my personal email to "chat" with friends and family. The cost is relatively low compared to long distance phone calls. And many of my friends prefer to text rather than pick up the phone. Email does have its drawbacks however some people use it to avoid personal contact. For sensitive issues, whether at work or with friends and family, I always make an effort to meet in person.

• • • • POST-TEST 4

In-class Activity: On your own, write a run-on sentence (either fused or a comma splice). Afterward, trade your paper with a partner. Correct each other's run-on sentence using three of the following methods:

1. Comma and a joining word

2. Period and a capital

3. Semicolon

4. Semicolon with a transitional word

Regular and Irregular Verbs

REGULAR VERBS

A Brief Review of Regular Verbs

Every verb has four principal parts: *present, past, past participle*, and *present participle*. These parts can be used to build all the verb tenses (the times shown by a verb).

Most verbs in English are regular. The past and past participles of a regular verb are formed by adding *-d* or *-ed* to the present. The *past participle* is the form of the verb used with the helping verbs *have, has,* or *had* (or some form of *be* with passive verbs). The *present participle* is formed by adding *-ing* to the present.

Here are the principal parts of some regular verbs:

Present	Past	Past Participle	Present Participle
shout	shouted	shouted	shouting
prepare	prepared	prepared	preparing
surprise	surprised	surprised	surprising
tease	teased	teased	teasing
frighten	frightened	frightened	frightening

A Note about Verb Tenses and Other Languages

English verb tenses can be particularly confusing to students from other language backgrounds. Not all languages express time distinctions through their verbs in the same ways that English does. Some language groups may have only three tense-forms; others may have tenses English does not use. Because of the structural differences between Asian languages and English, ESL students from Asian cultures may find English verb tenses confusing. Asian languages do not alter verb forms to indicate changes in time; instead a "time marker" word is used, and the verb's form does not change. For these students, extra patience and practice with English verb tenses are required, but with continued attention to verb tenses, students can master their use.

Present-Tense Endings: The verb ending *-s* or *-es* is needed with a regular verb in the present tense when the subject is *he, she, it,* or any *one person* or *thing*. Take care to make the subject *agree* with its verb.

> He reads every night.
> She watches television every night.
> It appears they have little in common.

• • • • ACTIVITY 1

Verbs in the sentences that follow do not agree with their subjects. Cross out each incorrect verb form, and write the correct present tense of the verb in the space provided.

wakes   1. My radio ~~wake~~ me up every morning with soft music.

clown   2. Brian and Risa always ~~clowns~~ around at the start of the class.

watches   3. My wife ~~watch~~ our baby in the morning, and I take over afternoons.

want   4. Many more men ~~wants~~ to go to nursing school next year.

works   5. My brain ~~work~~ much better at night than it does in early morning.

Past-Tense Endings: The verb ending *-d* or *-ed* is needed with a regular verb in the past tense.

> This morning I completed my research paper.
> The recovering hospital patient walked slowly down the corridor.
> Some students hissed when the new assignment was given out.

• • • • ACTIVITY 2

Verbs in the sentences that follow need *-d* or *-ed* endings. Cross out each incorrect verb form, and write the standard form in the space provided.

caved   1. One of my teeth ~~cave~~ in when I bit on the hard pretzel.

complained   2. The accident victim ~~complains~~ of dizziness right before she passed out.

realized   3. We ~~realize~~ a package was missing when we got back from shopping.

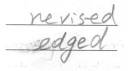

4. Glen ~~revise~~ three pages of his report today.

5. The impatient driver edges her car into the intersection while the light was still red.

IRREGULAR VERBS

Tip: One of the most common errors with irregular verbs is in the following example:

Incorrect:
I have *ate* the apple.

Correct:
I have *eaten* the apple.

Irregular verbs have irregular forms in the past tense and past participle. For example, the past tense of the irregular verb *choose* is *chose;* its past participle is *chosen.*

Almost everyone has some degree of trouble with irregular verbs. When you are unsure about the form of a verb, you can check the list of irregular verbs on this page and the next. (The present participle is not shown on this list because it is formed simply by adding *-ing* to the base form of the verb.) You can also check a dictionary, which gives the principal parts of irregular verbs.

A List of Irregular Verbs

Present	*Past*	*Past Participle*
arise	arose	arisen
awake	awoke *or* awaked	awoken or awaked
be (am, are, is)	was (were)	been
become	became	become
begin	began	begun
bend	bent	bent
bite	bit	bitten
blow	blew	blown
break	broke	broken
bring	brought	brought
build	built	built
burst	burst	burst
buy	bought	bought
catch	caught	caught
choose	chose	chosen
come	came	come
cost	cost	cost
cut	cut	cut
do (does)	did	done
draw	drew	drawn
drink	drank	drunk
drive	drove	driven
eat	ate	eaten
fall	fell	fallen
feed	fed	fed
feel	felt	felt
fight	fought	fought
find	found	found
fly	flew	flown
freeze	froze	frozen
get	got	got *or* gotten
give	gave	given

Present	Past	Past Participle
go (goes)	went	gone
grow	grew	grown
have (has)	had	had
hear	heard	heard
hide	hid	hidden
hold	held	held
hurt	hurt	hurt
keep	kept	kept
know	knew	known
lay	laid	laid
lead	led	led
leave	left	left
lend	lent	lent
let	let	let
lie	lay	lain
light	lit	lit
lose	lost	lost
make	made	made
meet	met	met
pay	paid	paid
ride	rode	ridden
ring	rang	rung
run	ran	run
say	said	said
see	saw	seen
sell	sold	sold
send	sent	sent
shake	shook	shaken
shrink	shrank	shrunk
shut	shut	shut
sing	sang	sung
sit	sat	sat
sleep	slept	slept
speak	spoke	spoken
spend	spent	spent
stand	stood	stood
steal	stole	stolen
stick	stuck	stuck
sting	stung	stung
swear	swore	sworn
swim	swam	swum
take	took	taken
teach	taught	taught
tear	tore	torn
tell	told	told
think	thought	thought
wake	woke *or* waked	woken *or* waked
wear	wore	worn
win	won	won
write	wrote	written

• • •• • ACTIVITY

Cross out the incorrect verb form in each of the following sentences. Then write the correct form of the verb in the space provided.

_____flown_____   ***Example***   After it had ~~flew~~ into the picture window, the dazed bird huddled on the ground.

_____   1. As graduation neared, Michelle worried about the practicality of the program she'd chose.

began   2. Before we could find seats, the theatre darkened and the opening credits ~~begun~~ to roll.

went   3. If Jake ~~had went~~ to the tutor for help, he would have done better on the test.

shrank   4. The inexperienced nurse shrunk from touching the patient's raw, burned skin.

had spoken   5. After Lawrence Hill ~~had speak~~ about his novel *The Book of Negroes,* the audience asked many questions.

forgot   6. Sheila ~~had~~ forget to write her student number on the test form, so the computer rejected her answer sheet.

gone   7. If I had ~~went~~ to work ten minutes earlier, I would have avoided being caught in the gigantic traffic snarl.

written   8. The students would have ~~wrote~~ the exam on Monday, but the teacher changed the date to Thursday.

• • • • • POST-TEST 1

Cross out the incorrect verb form in each sentence. Then, write the correct form in the space provided.

was walking
walked   1. The health inspectors ~~walk~~ into the kitchen as the cook was picking up a hamburger off the floor.

had stolen   2. The thieves ~~would have stole~~ my stereo, but I had had it engraved with a special identification number.

has struggled   3. Canadian actor Keanu Reeves ~~struggled~~ with dyslexia for years and finally overcome the learning disorder.

have   4. Because I ~~has~~ asthma, I carry an inhaler to use when I lose my breath.

are   5. Peter Robinson's crime novels, popular all over the world, ~~is~~ fast-paced and suspenseful.

checked   6. Yesterday I ~~check~~ my bank balance and saw my money was getting low.

have   7. Many childhood diseases ~~has~~ almost vanished in Canada.

tore   8. Trevor ~~teared~~ a page in her dictionary by accident.

• • • • • POST-TEST 2

Write short sentences that use the form requested for the following verbs.

Example   Past of *grow*   *I grew my own tomatoes last year.*

1. Past of *know* _____ I knew that there was _____

2. Present of *take* _____ He takes EAP course this semester

3. Past participle of *give* _____ The instruction is given by the teacher.

4. Past participle of *write* _____ It was written by hand.

5. Past of *do* _____ They didn't go to the restaurant yesterday

6. Past of *talk* _____ I talked my mom on the phone last night.

7. Present of *begin* _____ The movie begins from this Monday

8. Past of *go* _____ I went snowboarding last Saturday

9. Past participle of *see* _____ He has never seen Tokyo Sky tree.

10. Present of *drive* _____ She drives me home every day.

A Note about Nonstandard Forms of Regular Verbs

Many people have grown up in communities where nonstandard forms of regular verbs are used in everyday speech. Instead of saying, for example, "That girl *looks* tired," a person using a community dialect or patois might say, "That girl *look* tired." Community dialects have richness and power but are generally not accepted in academic and professional writing tasks, where standard English verb forms must be used.

Subject–Verb Agreement

PRE-TEST

Test your knowledge of subject–verb agreement by selecting the correct verb in parentheses in the following sentences.

1. Each of the students (is, are) using Twitter in the classroom.

2. Either Tatjana or her friends (is, are) bringing dessert to the baby shower.

×3. My computer professor, as well as my counsellor, (has, have) advised me to switch programs.

4. The social committee (is, are) planning a fundraiser.

5. A pair of kitchen scissors (is, are) in the second drawer.

A verb must agree with its subject in number. A *singular subject* (one person or thing) takes a singular verb. A *plural subject* (more than one person or thing) takes a plural verb. Mistakes in subject–verb agreement are sometimes made in the following situations:

1. When words come between the subject and the verb

2. When a verb comes before the subject

3. With compound subjects

4. With indefinite pronouns

5. With units of time, mass, money, length, and distance

Each of these situations is explained on the following pages.

WORDS BETWEEN SUBJECT AND VERB

Words that come between the subject and the verb do not change subject–verb agreement. Note the following sentence:

The crinkly <u>lines</u> *around Joan's eyes* <u>give</u> her a friendly look.

In this sentence, the subject *(lines)* is plural, so the verb *(give)* is plural. The words that come between the subject and the verb are a prepositional phrase: *around Joan's eyes.* They do not affect subject–verb agreement. (A list of prepositions can be found in the box on page 346.)

To find the subject of certain sentences, cross out prepositional phrases.

The lumpy <u>salt</u> ~~in the shakers~~ <u>needs</u> to be changed.

An old <u>television</u> ~~with a round screen~~ <u>has sat</u> in our basement for years.

• • • • **ACTIVITY**

Underline the subject and lightly cross out any words that come between the subject and the verb. Then double-underline the verb in parentheses that you believe is correct.

1. Some members of the parents' association (want, wants) to ban certain books from the school library.

2. Chung's trench coat, with its big lapels and shoulder flaps, (make, makes) him feel like a tough private eye.

3. One of the culinary courses (involve, involves) field placement.

4. The rising costs of necessities like food and shelter (force, forces) some people to live on the streets.

5. In my opinion, a slice of pepperoni pizza and a good video (make, makes) a great evening.

6. Members of the class (design, designs) their own websites as term work.

VERB BEFORE SUBJECT

A verb agrees with its subject even when the verb comes *before* the subject. Words that may precede the subject (when the verb comes before the subject) include *there, here,* and, in questions, *who, which, what,* and *where.*

Here are some examples of sentences in which the verb appears before the subject:

There <u>are</u> spelling <u>mistakes</u> in my homework.

In the distance <u>was</u> a <u>billow</u> of black smoke.

Here <u>is</u> the <u>newspaper</u>.

Where <u>are</u> the children's <u>coats</u>?

If you are unsure about the subject, ask *who* or *what* of the verb. With the first example above, you might ask, "*What* are in my homework?" The answer, *mistakes,* is the subject.

● ● ● ● **ACTIVITY**

Write the correct form of each verb in the space provided.

1. There __are__ dozens of frenzied shoppers waiting for the store to open. (is, are)

2. Here __are__ the notes from yesterday's computer graphics lecture. (is, are)

3. When __do__ we take our break? (do, does)

4. There __were__ scraps of yellowing paper stuck between the pages of the cookbook. (was, were)

5. At the very bottom of the grocery list __was__ an item that meant a trip all the way back to aisle one. (was, were)

6. Among the students in the class __are__ those who can't keep up with the assignments. (is, are)

COMPOUND SUBJECTS

A compound subject is two subjects separated by the joining word *and.* Subjects joined by *and* generally take a plural verb.

A patchwork <u>quilt</u> and a sleeping <u>bag</u> <u>cover</u> my bed in the winter.

<u>Clark</u> and <u>Lois</u> <u>are</u> a contented couple.

When subjects are joined by *either . . . or, neither . . . nor,* or *not only . . . but also,* the verb agrees with the subject closer to the verb.

Neither the <u>negotiator</u> nor the union <u>leaders</u> <u>want</u> the strike to continue.

The nearer subject, *leaders,* is plural, so the verb is plural.

● ● ● ● **ACTIVITY**

Write the correct form of the verb in the space provided.

1. A crusty baking pan and a greasy plate _____ on the countertop. (sit, sits)

2. Spidery cracks and a layer of dust _____ the ivory keys on the old piano. (cover, covers)

3. Not only the assistant manager but also the support staff _____ that the company is folding. (know, knows)

4. On *The Martha Stewart Show,* home decor and gardening _____ many viewers. (attract, attracts)

5. Neither Tasha nor the rest of the class _____ to work on that project. (want, wants)

6. Either my dog or the squirrels _____ breadcrusts I put out for the birds. (eat, eats)

INDEFINITE PRONOUNS

Tip: Words ending in *–one, –body,* and *–thing* always take singular verbs.

The following words, known as *indefinite pronouns,* always take singular verbs:

(*-one words*)	(*-body words*)	(*-thing words*)	
one	nobody	nothing	each
anyone	anybody	anything	either
everyone	everybody	everything	neither
someone	somebody	something	

Note: *Both* always takes a plural verb.

● ● ● ● ACTIVITY

Write the correct form of the verb in the space provided.

1. Neither of those students _enjoy_ the food in the cafeteria. (enjoy, enjoys)

2. Somebody without much sensitivity always _____ my birthmark. (mention, mentions)

3. The people at the local hardware store _____ friendly advice about home fix-it projects. (give, gives)

4. Everyone _____ the college kite-flying contest in the spring. (enter, enters)

5. One of these earrings constantly _____ off my ear. (fall, falls)

6. Each of the students _____ in careful block letters. (print, prints)

7. Anybody in the groups we saw _____ who should belong to the committee. (decide, decides)

UNITS OF TIME, MASS, MONEY, LENGTH, AND DISTANCE

Units of time, mass, money, length, and distance take singular verbs.

Four hours is a short time to wait for concert tickets.

Ten dollars is a good price for a child's haircut.

● ● ● ● ACTIVITY

Write the correct form of the verb in the space provided.

1. Two weeks' vacation _____ all he wanted. (was, were)

2. Ten pesos _____ not very much. (is, are)

3. In England, five pounds _____ approximately $10 Canadian. (equal, equals)

4. Five centimetres _____ like a small amount, but my hair looks much shorter. (seem, seems)

5. One metre of cloth _____ enough to make a hijab. (is, are)

● ● ● ● POST-TEST 1

In the space provided, write the correct form of the verb.

1. After the restaurant makeover was complete, most of the original appliances _____ donated to the Salvation Army. (was, *were*)

2. Each of their children _____ given a name picked at random from a page of the Bible. (*was*, were)

3. Many of the chapters in the business textbook _____ useful Web sites in the margins. (*include*, includes)

4. Envelopes, file folders, and a telephone book _____ jammed into Ian's kitchen drawers. (is, *are*)

5. Neither of the main dishes at tonight's dinner _____ any meat. (*contains*, contain)

6. Even though the athlete was fit, 50 kilometres _____ like a long distance to run. (seem, *seems*)

7. A metal grab bar bolted onto the tiles _____ it easier for elderly people to get in and out of the bathtub. (*makes*, make)

8. In exchange for a reduced rent, Karla and James _____ the dentist's office beneath their second-floor apartment. (cleans, *clean*)

POST-TEST 2

Cross out the incorrect verb form in each sentence. In addition, underline the subject or subjects that go with the verb. Then write the correct form of the verb.

1. Why ~~is~~ Thomas and his mother baking banana bread so late at night?
   are
2. Seventy hours of work ~~are~~ too exhausting in one week.
   is
3. Hamburgers, hotdogs, and a pot roast ~~was~~ on the menu for the Boy Scouts' camping trip.
   were
4. Here ~~is~~ the low-calorie cola and the double-chocolate cake you ordered.
   are
5. The odour of those perfumed ads ~~interfere~~ with my enjoyment of a magazine.
   interferes
6. One of my roommates ~~are~~ always leaving wet towels on the bathroom floor.
   is
7. A man or woman in his or her forties often ~~begin~~ to think about making a contribution to the world and not just about him- or herself.
   begins
8. Each of the family's ~~donations~~ to the food drive were over fifty dollars.
   donation

POST-TEST 3

Complete each of the following sentences using *is, are, was, were, has,* or *have.* Then underline the subject.

Example For me, popcorn at the movies is *like coffee at breakfast.*

1. The magazines under my roommate's bed were old
2. The student with more experience was chosen the speech contest
3. My colleague and her friend have the same hobbies.
4. Neither of the hockey players is from Russia
5. Twenty dollars _____

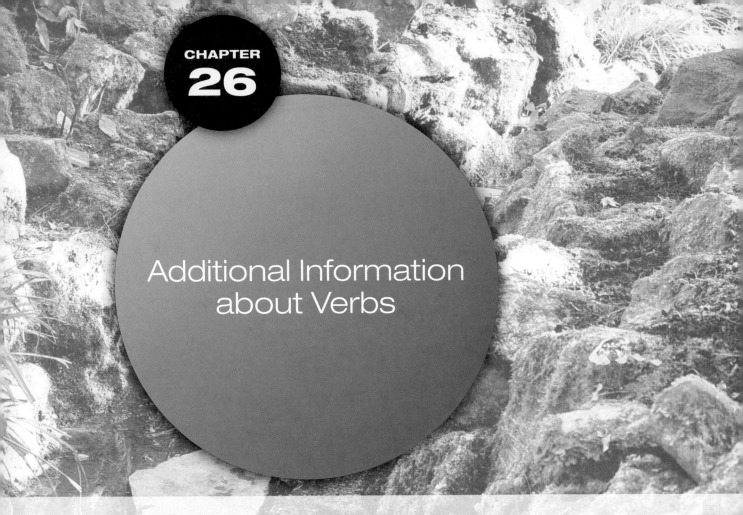

CHAPTER 26

Additional Information about Verbs

The purpose of this special section is to provide additional information about verbs. Some people will find the grammar terms here a helpful reminder of what they learned earlier in school about verbs. The terms will increase their understanding of how verbs function in English. Other people may welcome more detailed information about terms used elsewhere in this book. Remember that the most common mistakes with writing verbs have been treated earlier in this section.

VERB TENSE

Verbs tell us the time of an action. The time that a verb shows is usually called the *tense*. The most common tenses are the simple present, past, and future. In addition, there are nine other tenses that enable us to express more specific ideas about time than we could with the simple tenses alone. Below and on the next page are the 12 verb tenses and examples of each one. Read them over to increase your sense of the many different ways of expressing time in English.

The 12 English Verb Tenses

Tenses	Examples
Simple Tenses	
Present	I *work.* Tony *works.*

Tip: In your writing, choose one verb tense and be consistent. If you're writing in the present tense, for example, stick to the present throughout (unless, of course, you need to shift tenses for logic).

Past	Ellen *worked* on her report.
Future	You *will work* on a new project next week.

Perfect Tenses

Present perfect	We *have hired* two salespeople.
	Patricia *has tried* to form a union for contract workers.

The present perfect most commonly refers to an action that took place in an indefinite past, at a time that is *not* specified.

> We *have applied* for hospitality jobs in Whistler.
>
> Roxa *has found* a managerial position at the Royal Bank in Moncton.

With certain verbs that suggest a prolonged activity, the present perfect can indicate an action that starts in the past and continues until the present.

Past perfect	The businessman was not able to get a hotel room because he *had* not *booked* in advance.
	By September 15, 2009, the CEO at Canadian Tire *had expanded* the number of stores in Saskatoon.

The past perfect tense indicates an action that took place *before* a specified time in the past or *before* another action expressed in the simple past.

Future perfect	Hopefully, the recession *will have receded* by the end of the year.
	I *will have completed* my performance reviews by the end of the year.

The future perfect tense refers to an action taking place *before* a specified future time or another future action.

Progressive (or Continuous) Tenses

Present progressive	I *am working* on my speech for the upcoming conference.
	You *are working* too hard.
	The printer is *not working* properly.
Past progressive	He *was working* at home today.
	The chefs *were working* on their new recipes.
Future progressive	My son *will be working* in our store this summer.

Progressive, or *continuous tenses,* as the word *continuous* suggests, refer to ongoing actions in the present, past, or future.

Present perfect progressive	Milos *has been working* late this week.

(Milos began *working* late earlier this week, and *continues to do so.*)

Past perfect progressive	Until yesterday, I *had been* working nights.

(I *worked* nights for some time in the past, and *continued to do so* until yesterday. The action, while continuous, was *in the past, and is completed.*)

| Future perfect progressive | My mother *will have been working* as a nurse for 45 years by the time she retires. |

(My mother *worked* as a nurse in the past, *continues to do so, and will continue to work as a nurse* in the future, until retirement.)

● ● ● ● **ACTIVITY**

On a separate piece of paper, write 12 sentences using the 12 verb tenses.

HELPING VERBS

There are three common verbs that can either stand alone or combine with (and "help") other verbs. Here are the verbs and their forms:

Tip: Think of helping verbs as "linking" verbs. Here's a sentence with a linking verb:
Molly is happy.
In this sentence, the verb *is* links the word *happy* to the subject *Molly*.

| be (am, are, is, was, were, being, been) | do (does, did) |
| have (has, having, had) | |

Here are examples of the verbs:

Used Alone	*Used as Helping Verbs*
I *was angry* to be laid off work.	I *was growing* angry to be laid off work.
Jill *has* the key to the filing cabinet.	Jill *has forgotten* the key to the filing cabinet.
He *did* well on the training course.	He *did fail* the previous training course.

Modal Auxiliaries

There are nine other helping verbs (traditionally known as *modals,* or *modal auxiliaries*) that are always used in combination with other verbs. Here are the nine modals and sentence examples of each:

can	I *can see* the rainbow.
could	I *could* not *find* a high-paying job.
may	The financial meeting *may be postponed.*
might	Keesha *might resent* your advice.
shall	I *shall see* you tomorrow.
should	He *should get* his car *serviced.*
will	Terry *will want* to see you.
would	They *would* not *understand.*
must	You *must visit* us again.

Note from the examples that these verbs have only one form. They do not, for instance, add an *-s* when used with *he, she, it,* or any one person or thing.

• • • • • **ACTIVITY**

On separate paper, write nine sentences using the nine helping verbs (modals) listed in the box on the previous page.

VERBALS

Verbals are words formed from verbs. Verbals, like verbs, often express action. They can add variety to your sentences and vigour to your writing style. (Verbals, as mentioned in Chapter 22, are not "finite" or "true verbs.") The three kinds of verbals are *infinitives, participles,* and *gerunds.*

Infinitive

An infinitive is *to* plus the base form of the verb.

I have *to practise* many times before making a speech.
Lina hopes *to write* for a newspaper.
I requested my team *to submit* their travel reports.

Participle

A participle is a verb form used as an adjective (a descriptive word). The present participle ends in *-ing*. The past participle ends in *-ed* or has an irregular ending.

Hearing the news that she was fired, the *crying* woman wiped her eyes.
The *astounded* man stared at his *winning* lottery ticket.
After *interviewing* the first candidate, Muhammad made a phone call.

Gerund

A gerund is the *-ing* form of a verb used as a noun.

Exercising helps relieve stress from work.
Eating junk food makes me feel sluggish during the day.
While *doodling* in his notebook, Jordan lost track of the discussion.

• • • • • **ACTIVITY**

On separate paper, write three sentences using infinitives, three sentences using participles, and three sentences using gerunds.

ACTIVE AND PASSIVE VERBS

When the subject of a sentence *performs the action* of a verb, the verb is in the *active voice.* When the subject of a sentence *receives the action* of a verb, the verb is in the *passive voice.*

The passive form of a verb consists of a form of the verb *be* plus the *past participle of the main verb*. Look at the active and passive forms of the verbs below:

Active Voice	*Passive Voice*
Iva *proofread* the PowerPoint slides.	The PowerPoint slides *were proofread* by Iva.
(The subject, *Iva*, is the doer of the action.)	(The subject, *PowerPoint slides*, does not act. Instead, it receives the action of proofreading.)
Marco *delivered* the paycheques.	The paycheques *were delivered* by Marco.
(The subject, *Marco*, is the doer of the action.)	(The subject, the *paycheques*, does not act. Instead, it receives the action of delivering.)

In general, active verbs are more effective than passive ones. Active verbs give your writing a simpler and more vigorous style. At times, however, the passive form of verbs is appropriate when the performer of the action is unknown or is less important than the receiver of the action. For example:

The performance reports *were reviewed* yesterday.
(The performer of the action is unknown.)

Alan *was hurt* by your thoughtless remark.
(The receiver of the action, Alan, is being emphasized.)

ACTIVITY

Change the following sentences from the passive to the active voice. Note that you may have to add a subject in some cases.

Examples The suspect was detained by a police officer.
> *The police officer detained the suspect.*
The annual conference was cancelled.
> *The president of Sears cancelled the annual conference.*
(Here a subject had to be added.)

1. The interview was led by a panel of executives.

2. Karl's travel expense forms were signed by the head nurse.

3. The income tax returns were reviewed by the accountant.

4. The supermarket shelves were restocked after the truckers' strike.

5. The teenagers were appalled by the working conditions in the sweatshops of Malaysia.

Pronoun Agreement and Reference

● ● ● ● ● ● **PRE-TEST**

Test your knowledge of pronoun use in the following sentences. Can you spot the unclear or vague pronoun references?

1. A student has their own writing style.

2. A college education prepares someone for their future career choice.

3. Everyone wants to get the best job they can.

4. When Patti's mother told her she was having an operation, she was obviously upset.

5. If anyone has a question, they may ask at the end of the presentation.

Pronouns are words that take the place of *nouns* (persons, places, or things), short-cuts that keep you from unnecessarily repeating words when you write. Here are some examples of pronouns:

Eddie left *his* camera on the bus. (*His* is a pronoun that takes the place of *Eddie's.*)
Elena drank the coffee even though *it* was cold. (*It* replaces *coffee.*)
As I turned the newspaper's damp pages, *they* disintegrated in my hands.
(*They* is a pronoun that takes the place of *pages.*)

This section presents rules that will help you avoid two common mistakes people make with pronouns. Here are the rules:

1. A pronoun must agree in number with the word or words it replaces.

2. A pronoun must refer clearly to the word it replaces.

PRONOUN AGREEMENT

A pronoun must agree in number with the word or words it replaces. If the word a pronoun refers to is singular, the pronoun must be singular; if that word is plural, the pronoun must be plural. (Note that the word a pronoun refers to is known as the *antecedent,* or "before-goer." The antecedent is the pronoun's point of reference in the sentence.)

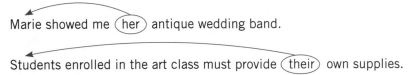

Marie showed me (her) antique wedding band.

Students enrolled in the art class must provide (their) own supplies.

In the first example, the pronoun *her* refers to the singular word *Marie;* in the second example, the pronoun *their* refers to the plural word *Students.*

• • • • ACTIVITY

Write the appropriate pronoun *(their, they, them, it)* in the blank space in each of the following sentences.

Example   I opened the wet umbrella and put *it* in the bathtub to dry.

1. Kasey and Bruce left for the movies earlier than usual because _____ knew the theatre would be packed.

2. The clothes were still damp, but I decided to fold _____ anyway.

3. Young adults often face a difficult transition period when _____ leave home for the first time.

4. Paul's grandparents renewed _____ marriage vows at a huge fiftieth wedding anniversary celebration.

5. The car's steering wheel began to pull to one side, and then _____ started to shimmy.

Indefinite Pronouns

The following words are always singular:

(*-one words*)	(*-body words*)	
one	nobody	each
anyone	anybody	either
everyone	everybody	neither
someone	somebody	

Tip: To avoid sexist pronoun reference, use *his or her, him or her, he or she* where applicable. An even easier option is to use the plural form in your writing.

Incorrect:
The student is writing his test.

Better:
The student is writing his or her test.

Best:
The students are writing their test.

If a pronoun in a sentence refers to one of these singular words (also known as *indefinite pronouns*), the pronoun should be *singular*.

Somebody left (her) backpack on the chair.

One of the servers just called and said (he) would be an hour late.

Everyone in the club must pay (his) dues next week.

Each circled *pronoun* is *singular* because it refers to an *indefinite pronoun*.

Note: There are two important points to remember about indefinite pronouns:

1. In the last example, if everyone in the club was a woman, the pronoun would be *her*. If the club had women and men, the pronouns would be *his or her*:

   Everyone in the club must pay his or her dues next week.

   Some writers follow the traditional practice of using *his* to refer to both women and men. Most writers now use *his or her* to avoid an implied sexual bias. To avoid using *his* or the somewhat awkward *his or her,* a sentence can often be rewritten in the plural:

   Club members must pay their dues next week.

2. In informal spoken English, *plural* pronouns are often used with the indefinite pronouns. We would probably not say this:

   Everybody has *his or her* own opinion about the election.

   Instead, we are likely to say this:

   Everybody has *their* own opinion about the election.

   Here are other examples:

   Everyone in the choir must buy *their* robes.
   Everybody in the line has *their* ticket ready.
   No one in the class remembered to bring *their* books.

   In such cases, the indefinite pronouns are clearly plural in meaning. Also, the use of such plurals helps people to avoid the awkward *his or her.* In time, the plural pronoun may be accepted in formal speech or writing.

● ● ● ● **ACTIVITY**

Underline the correct pronoun.

1. Neither of the potential buyers had really made up (her, their) mind.

2. Not one of the new cashiers knows what (he, they) should be doing.

3. Each of these computers has (its, their) drawbacks.

PART 4
HANDBOOK OF SENTENCE SKILLS

4. Anyone trying to proofread (his or her, their) research papers should use the instructor's checklist.

5. If anybody calls when I'm out, tell (him, them) I'll return in an hour.

PRONOUN REFERENCE

A sentence may be confusing and unclear if a pronoun appears to refer to more than one word or does not refer to any specific word. *Pronouns must have a clear point of reference, or antecedent.* Look at this sentence:

Miriam was annoyed when they failed her car for a faulty turn signal.

Who failed her car? There is no specific word to which *they* refers. Be clear:

Miriam was annoyed when the safety inspectors failed her car for a faulty turn signal.

Here are sentences with other faulty pronoun references. Read the explanations of why they are faulty and look carefully at how they are corrected.

Faulty	*Clear*
Peter told Vijay that he cheated on the exam.	Peter told Vijay, "I cheated on the exam."
(Who cheated on the exam: Peter or Vijay? Be clear about your *pronoun reference*.)	
Mia is really a shy person, but she keeps it hidden.	Mia is really a shy person, but she keeps her shyness hidden.
(There is no specific word, or *antecedent*, that *it* refers to. The adjective *shy* must be changed to a noun.)	
Rosa attributed her success in business to her parents' support, which was generous.	Generously, Rosa attributed her success in business to her parents' support. *Or:* Rosa attributed her success in business to her parents' generous support.
(Does *which* mean that Rosa's action was generous or that her parents' *support* was generous?)	

● ● ● ACTIVITY

Rewrite each of the following sentences to make the vague pronoun reference clear. Add, change, or omit words as necessary.

Example   Susan and her mother wondered if she had been working out long enough to enter a competition.
Susan's mother wondered if Susan had been working out long enough to enter a competition.

1. Cameron spent all morning birdwatching but didn't see a single one.
2. The supervisors told the nurses that they would receive a pay raise.
3. Ruth told Annette that her homesickness was affecting her study habits.
4. Kyle took the radio out of his police car and fixed it.
5. Pete visited the tutoring centre because they could help him with his economics course.

POST-TEST 1

Underline the correct word in parentheses.

1. Each of the little girls may choose one prize for (her, their) own.
2. I asked at the computer shop how quickly (they, the shop employees) could fix my laptop.
3. The coaches told each member of the varsity basketball team that (his or her, their) position was the most important one in the game.
4. Marianna tried to take notes during the class, but she didn't really understand (it, the subject.)
5. When someone is late for class, (they, he or she) should quietly enter through the back door of the classroom.

POST-TEST 2

Cross out the pronoun error in each sentence below, and write the correction in the space provided at the left. Then, circle the letter that correctly describes the type of error that was made.

Example

____*his (or her)*____   Anyone without a ticket will lose ~~their~~ place in the line.

    Mistake in: a. pronoun reference (b.) pronoun agreement

_____   1. Could someone volunteer their services to clean up after the fraternity party?
    Mistake in: a. pronoun reference b. pronoun agreement

_____   2. The referee watched the junior hockey game closely to make sure they didn't hurt each other during checking.
    Mistake in: a. pronoun reference b. pronoun agreement

_____   3. If job hunters want to make a good impression at an interview, he should be sure to arrive on time.
    Mistake in: a. pronoun reference b. pronoun agreement

_____   4. Neither of those women appreciated their parents' sacrifices.
    Mistake in: a. pronoun reference b. pronoun agreement

_____   5. There wasn't much to do on Friday nights after they closed the only movie theatre in the northern Manitoba town.
    Mistake in: a. pronoun reference b. pronoun agreement

For bonus material and additional activities please go to the OLC at www.mcgrawhill.ca/olc/langan

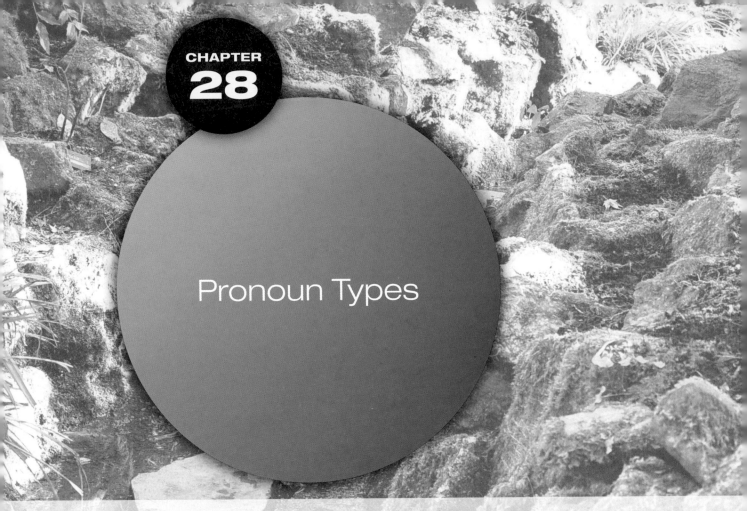

Pronoun Types

This section describes some common types of pronouns: *subject* and *object pronouns, possessive pronouns,* and *demonstrative pronouns.*

PRE-TEST

Tip: Pronouns are words that take the place of nouns. Instead of writing *Bob* throughout an essay, you would naturally alternate with *he, his,* and *him.* Pronouns add variety to your writing.

Read the following sentences and try to spot the confusion in pronoun use. How would you correct the following pronoun errors?

1. Marc is taller than me.

2. That there briefcase belongs to the entrepreneur.

3. My father and me enjoy watching the Toronto Blue Jays.

4. Are the tickets to *West Side Story* yours'?

5. Her and Natalie are best friends.

SUBJECT AND OBJECT PRONOUNS

Pronouns change their form depending upon the place they occupy in a sentence. The following box contains a list of subject and object pronouns.

Subject Pronouns	Object Pronouns
I	me
you	you (no change)
he	him
she	her
it	it (no change)
we	us
they	them

Subject Pronouns

Subject pronouns are subjects of verbs.

He is leaving home for college. (*He* is the subject of the verb *is leaving*.)
They are moving into our old apartment. (*They* is the subject of the verb *are moving*.)
We physiotherapists should have a say in the decision. (*We* is the subject of the verb *should have*.)

Several rules for using subject pronouns—and several kinds of mistakes that people sometimes make with subject pronouns—are explained below.

Rule 1: Use a subject pronoun in spots where you have a compound (more than one) subject.

Incorrect	*Correct*
My brother and *me* are enrolled at Queen's University.	My brother and *I* are enrolled at Queen's University.
Him and *me* meet every Wednesday night for a game of basketball	*He* and *I* meet every Wednesday night for a game of basketball.

Hint for Rule 1: If you are not sure which pronoun to use, try each pronoun by itself in the sentence. The correct pronoun will be the one that sounds right. For example, "Him knows the lyrics to all their songs" does not sound right. "He knows the lyrics to all their songs" does.

Rule 2: Use a subject pronoun after forms of the verb *be*. Forms of *be* include *am, are, is, was, were, has been, have been,* and others.

It was *I* who left the light on.
It may be *they* in that car.
It is *he*.

The sentences above may sound strange and stilted to you because they are seldom used in conversation. When we speak with one another, forms such as "It was me," "It may be them," and "It is him" are widely accepted. In formal writing, however, the grammatically correct forms are still required.

Hint for Rule 2: You can avoid having to use the subject pronoun form after *be* by simply rewording a sentence. Here is how the preceding examples could be reworded:

> I was the one who left the light on.
> They may be in that car.
> He is here.

Rule 3: Use subject pronouns after *than* or *as*. The subject pronoun is used because a verb is understood after the pronoun.

> You play better than I (play). (The verb *play* is understood after *I*.)
> Jenny is as bored as I (am). (The verb *am* is understood after *I*.)
> We don't need the money as much as they (do). (The verb *do* is understood after *they*.)

Hint for Rule 3: Avoid mistakes by mentally adding the "missing" verb at the end of the sentence.

Object Pronouns

Object pronouns (*me, him, her, us, them*) are the objects of verbs or prepositions. (*Prepositions* are connecting words like *for, at, about, to, before, by, with,* and *of.* See also page 346.)

> Tamara helped *me.* (*Me* is the object of the verb *helped.*)
> We took *them* to the college. (*Them* is the object of the verb *took.*)
> Leave the children with *us.* (*Us* is the object of the preposition *with.*)
> I got in line behind *him.* (*Him* is the object of the preposition *behind.*)

People are sometimes uncertain about which pronoun to use when two objects follow the verb.

Incorrect	*Correct*
I gave a gift to Arundhati and *she.*	I gave a gift to Arundhati and *her.*
She came to the movie with Kara and *I.*	She came to the movie with Kara and *me.*

Hint: If you are not sure which pronoun to use, try each pronoun by itself in the sentence. The correct pronoun will be the one that sounds right. For example, "I gave a gift to she" does not sound right; "I gave a gift to her" does.

● ● ● ● **ACTIVITY**

Underline the correct subject or object pronoun in each of the following sentences. Then, show whether your answer is a subject or object pronoun by circling the *S* or *O* in the margin. The first one is done for you as an example.

S   Ⓞ   1. The textbooks my parents purchased for Victor and (I, me) are very expensive.

S   O   2. No one has a quicker temper than (she, her).

S   O   3. Your grades prove that you worked harder than (they, them).

S   O   4. (We, Us) runners train indoors when the weather turns cold.

S	O	5. (She, Her) and Betty applied for a bursary.
S	O	6. Chris and (he, him) are the most energetic kids in grade one.
S	O	7. Arguing over clothes is a favourite pastime for my sister and (I, me).
S	O	8. The head of the ticket committee asked Sam and (I, me) to help with sales.

POSSESSIVE PRONOUNS

Here is a list of possessive pronouns:

my, mine	our, ours
your, yours	your, yours
his	their, theirs
her, hers	
its	

Possessive pronouns show ownership or possession.

George revved up *his* motorcycle and blasted off.
The keys are *mine.*

Note: A possessive pronoun *never* uses an apostrophe. (See also page 417.)

Incorrect	*Correct*
That coat is hers'.	That coat is hers.
The card table is theirs'.	The card table is theirs.

● ● ● ● ACTIVITY

Cross out the incorrect pronoun form in each of the sentences below. Write the correct form in the space at the left.

Example   *hers* Those gloves are ~~hers'~~.

_____ 1. The computer stores information on its' hard drive.

_____ 2. Are those seats theirs'?

_____ 3. I knew the sweater was hers' when I saw the Humber College monogram.

_____ 4. They gave us their telephone number, and we gave them our's.

_____ 5. My grammar book has an index but yours' is missing.

DEMONSTRATIVE PRONOUNS

Demonstrative pronouns point to or single out a person or thing. There are four demonstrative pronouns:

this	those
that	those

This is my house right in front of us.
Those are your books on the shelf over there.

Generally speaking, *this* and *these* refer to things close at hand; *that* and *those* refer to things farther away. The four pronouns are commonly used in the role of demonstrative adjectives as well.

These magazine articles are useful for my research paper.
Are *those* articles any good?
That one is the most credible.
The writing is good in *this* one.

Note: Do not use *them, this here, that there, these here,* or *those there* to point out. Use only *this, that, these,* or *those.*

● ● ● ● ● ACTIVITY

Cross out the incorrect form of the demonstrative pronoun, and write the correct form in the space provided.

Example   *Those* ~~Them~~ tires look worn.

_____   1. This here map is out of date.

_____   2. Leave them keys out on the coffee table.

_____   3. I've seen them girls somewhere before.

_____   4. Jack entered that there dog in an obedience contest.

_____   5. Where are them new knives?

● ● ● ● POST-TEST

Underline the correct pronoun in the parentheses.

1. If the contract negotiations are left up to (they, them), we'll have to accept the results.

2. (Them, Those) student crafts have won several awards.

3. Our grandmother told David and (I, me) to leave our muddy shoes outside on the porch.

4. The judge decided that the fault was (theirs', theirs) and ordered them to pay the damages.

5. The black-masked raccoon stared at Rudy and (I, me) for an instant and then ran quickly away.

6. When the reports were handed back to Lynn and (I, me) the professor congratulated us on our high grades.

7. (This here, This) is our new educational assistant.

8. This test without a name must be (hers, her's); I recognize the handwriting.

Adjectives and Adverbs

ADJECTIVES

What Are Adjectives?

Adjectives describe nouns (names of persons, places, or things) or pronouns.

> He is a *diligent* counsellor. (The adjective *diligent* describes the noun *counsellor.*)
> He is also *intelligent.* (The adjective *intelligent* describes the pronoun *he.*)
> Seamus writes an *investigative* report. (The adjective *investigative* describes the noun *report.*)
> It is *detailed.* (The adjective *detailed* describes the pronoun *it.*)

Adjectives usually come before the word they describe (as in *diligent* counsellor and *investigative* report). They also come after forms of the verb *be* (*is, are, was, were,* and so on) and verbs such as *look, appear, seem, become, sound, taste,* and *smell.*

> Your passport is *lost.* (The adjective *lost* describes your passport.)
> The border crossing is *busy.* (The adjective *busy* describes the border.)
> The lawyers were *impatient.* (The adjective *impatient* describes the lawyers.)
> That 911 call was *urgent.* (The adjective *urgent* describes the 911 call.)

Using Adjectives to Compare

For all one-syllable adjectives and some two-syllable adjectives, add *-er* when comparing two things and *-est* when comparing three or more things.

Andrew's beard is *longer* than mine, but Lee's is the *longest.*

Meg may be the *quieter* of the two sisters; however, that's not saying much since they're the *loudest* girls in school.

For some two-syllable adjectives and all longer adjectives, add *more* when comparing two things and *most* when comparing three or more things.

Kiefer Sutherland is *more famous* than his siblings; however, his father, Donald Sutherland, is still the *most famous* member of the family.

The red letters on the sign are *more noticeable* than the black ones, but the Day-Glo letters are the *most noticeable.*

You can usually tell when to use *more* and *most* by the sound of a word. For example, you can probably tell by its sound that "carefuller" would be too awkward to say and that *more careful* is thus correct. In addition, there are many words for which both *-er* or *-est* and *more* or *most* are equally correct. For instance, either "a more fair rule" or "a fairer rule" is correct.

To form negative comparisons, use *less* and *least.*

During my officer training, I was *less fearful* than some of my colleagues.

When the detective came to our house to speak to my parents, I offered her the *most comfortable* chair in the house.

Points to Remember about Comparing

Point 1: Use only one form of comparison at a time. In other words, do not use both an *-er* ending and *more* or both an *-est* ending and *most:*

Incorrect	*Correct*
My suitcase is always *more heavier* than my father's.	My suitcase is always *heavier* than my father's.
Kingston Penitentiary is the *most cleanest* prison I've ever seen.	Kingston Penitentiary is the *cleanest* prison I've ever seen.

Point 2: Learn the irregular forms of the words shown below.

	Comparative *(for comparing things)*	*Superlative* *(for comparing three or more things)*
bad	worse	worst
good, well	better	best
little (in amount)	less	least
much, many	more	most

Do not use both *more* and an irregular comparative or *most* and an irregular superlative.

Incorrect	*Correct*
Pulling over to text a message is *more better* than texting and driving.	Pulling over to text a message is *better* than texting and driving.
Last night, I got the *most worst* snack attack I ever had.	Last night, I got the *worst* snack attack I ever had.

● ● ● ● **ACTIVITY**

Add to each sentence the correct form of the adjective in parentheses.

Examples The *worst* part of my counselling job is conveying bad news to families. (bad)

The *most wonderful* part of fundraising is giving back to the community. (wonderful)

1. The _____ law clerk I ever had was trustworthy and sincere. (good)

2. Aunt Sonja is the _____ of the three sisters. (young)

3. A rain that freezes is _____ than a snowstorm. (bad)

4. That's the _____ CSI episode I've ever seen. (frightening)

5. Being painfully shy has made Leon the _____ friendly person I know. (little)

ADVERBS

What Are Adverbs?

Adverbs describe verbs, adjectives, or other adverbs. They usually end in *-ly*.

The father *gently* hugged the sick child. (The adverb *gently* describes the verb *hugged*.)

The jury member was temporarily tongue-tied. (The adverb *temporarily* describes the adjective *tongue-tied*.)

The lecturer spoke so *terribly* fast that I had trouble taking notes. (The adverb *terribly* describes the adverb *fast*.)

A Common Mistake with Adverbs and Adjectives

People often mistakenly use an adjective instead of an adverb after a verb.

Incorrect	*Correct*
Lola needs a haircut *bad*.	Lola needs a haircut *badly*.
I laugh too *loud* when I'm embarrassed.	I laugh too *loudly* when I'm embarrassed.
You might have won the race if you hadn't run so *slow* at the beginning.	You might have won the race if you hadn't run so *slowly* at the beginning.

● ● ● ● **ACTIVITY**

Underline the adjective or adverb needed. (Remember that adjectives describe nouns, and adverbs describe verbs or other adverbs.)

1. As Mac danced, his earring bounced (rapid, rapidly).

2. The crooks were (foolish, foolishly) to think they could outsmart the CIA.

3. The shock of the accident caused me to hiccup (continuous, continuously) for 15 minutes.

4. The detective opened the door (careful, carefully).

5. All she heard when she answered the phone was (heavy, heavily) breathing.

Well and Good

Two words that are often confused are *good* and *well*. *Good* is an adjective that describes nouns. *Well* is usually an adverb that describes verbs.

• • • • ACTIVITY

Tip: Most sources recommend using *well* in reference to your health. So if someone asks you how you are feeling, it's appropriate to say, "I am well." Otherwise, if no one is asking specifically about your health, it is acceptable to say, "I am good."

Write *good* or *well* in each of the sentences that follow.

1. If you girls do a _____ job of cleaning the garage, I'll take you for some ice cream.

2. If I organize the office records too _____ , my bosses may not need me any more.

3. When Jim got AIDS, he discovered who his _____ friends really were.

4. Just because brothers and sisters fight when they're young doesn't mean they won't get along _____ as adults.

• • • • REVIEW TEST 1

Underline the correct word in the parentheses.

1. The server poured (littler, less) coffee into my cup than into yours.

2. When the firefighters arrived at the burning house, the flames had grown (more worse, worse).

3. The movie is so interesting that the three hours pass (quick, quickly).

4. The talented boy sang as (confident, confidently) as a seasoned performer.

5. Our band played so (good, well) that a local firm hired us for its annual dinner.

6. Tri Lee is always (truthful, truthfully), even when it might be better to tell a white lie.

7. The driver stopped the bus (sudden, suddenly) and yelled, "Everybody out!"

8. Vertical stripes make you look (more thin, thinner) than horizontal ones.

• • • • REVIEW TEST 2

Write a sentence that uses each of the following adjectives and adverbs correctly.

1. careless

2. angrily

3. well

4. most relaxing

5. best

For bonus material and additional activities please go to the OLC at **www.mcgrawhill.ca/olc/langan**

30

Misplaced Modifiers

CHAPTER 30

Misplaced Modifiers

PRE-TEST

The following sentences contain misplaced modifiers. Try to determine the confusion and humour in each. How could each of these sentences be reworded?

1. Curtis asked me to play tennis on the telephone.
2. College instructors who care often about their jobs can make a difference in the classroom.
3. The school was located beside a river which was made of yellow brick.
4. Frances wrote an email to her friend that was short.
5. I nearly earned $1000 last summer.

Misplaced modifiers are words that, because of awkward placement, do not describe the words the writer intended them to describe. This often results in the meaning of a sentence being confused. To avoid this, place words as close as possible to what they describe.

Misplaced Words	*Correctly Placed Words*
Kevin couldn't drive to work in his small sports car *with a broken leg.* (The sports car had a broken leg?)	With a broken leg, Kevin couldn't drive to work in his small sports car. (The words describing Kevin are now placed next to *Kevin.*)

399

Tip: Look at how the placement of the word *just* changes the meaning in the following sentences:

Sue was **just** chosen to organize the contest.

Just Sue was chosen to organize the contest.

Sue was chosen **just** to organize the contest.

The toaster was sold to us by a charming salesperson *with a money-back guarantee.*
(The salesperson had a money-back guarantee?)

He *nearly* brushed his teeth for 20 minutes every night.
(He came close to brushing his teeth, but in fact did not brush them at all?)

The toaster with a money-back guarantee was sold to us by a charming salesperson.
(The words describing the toaster are now placed next to it.)

He brushed his teeth for nearly 20 minutes every night.
(The meaning—that he brushed his teeth for a long time—is now clear.)

● ● ● ● **ACTIVITY**

Underline the misplaced word or words in each sentence. Then rewrite the sentence, placing related words together to make the meaning clear.

Examples Frozen shrimp lay in the steel pans that were thawing rapidly.
Frozen shrimp that were thawing rapidly lay in the steel pans.

The speaker discussed the problem of crowded prisons at the college.
At the college, the speaker discussed the problem of crowded prisons.

1. The patient talked about his childhood on the psychiatrist's couch.

2. The crowd watched the tennis players with swivelling heads.

3. Damian put four hamburger patties on the counter which he was cooking for dinner.

4. Lucy carefully hung the new suit that he would wear to his first job interview in the bedroom closet.

5. Alexandra ripped the shirt on a car door that he made in sewing class.

6. The latest *Twilight* movie has almost opened in 200 theatres across the country.

7. The newscaster spoke softly into a microphone wearing a bullet-proof vest.

8. The tenants left town in a dilapidated old car owing two months' rent.

● ● ● ● **POST-TEST 1**

Write *MM* for *misplaced modifier* or *C* for *correct* in the space provided for each sentence.

_____   1. I nearly napped for 20 minutes during the biology lecture.

_____   2. I napped for nearly 20 minutes during the biology lecture.

_____   3. Ryan paused as the girl he had been following stopped at a shop window.

_____   4. Ryan paused as the girl stopped at a shop window he had been following.

_____   5. Marta dropped out of school after taking ten courses on Friday.

_____   6. On Friday, Marta dropped out of school after taking ten courses.

_____   7. Under his shirt, the player wore a good luck charm which resembled a tiny elephant.

_____   8. The player wore a good luck charm under his shirt which resembled a tiny elephant.

● ● ● ● ● **POST-TEST 2**

Make the changes needed to correct the misplaced modifier in each sentence.

1. Margaret Atwood wrote that someone was as innocent as a bathtub full of bullets in a poem.

2. I almost filled an entire notebook with biology lab drawings.

3. The apprentice watched the master carpenter expertly fit the door with envious eyes.

4. The photographer pointed the camera at the shy deer equipped with a special night-vision scope.

5. The students on the bus stared at the ceiling or read newspapers with tired faces.

CHAPTER
31

Dangling Modifiers

● ● ●
● **PRE-TEST**

The following sentences contain dangling modifiers. Try to determine the confusion and humour in each. How could each of these sentences be reworded?

1. Racing down the street, the thunderstorm frightened the young child.
2. While playing my Nintendo, the cat jumped on my lap.
3. At the age of five, my grandfather taught me how to make cookies.
4. Writing legibly, the letter was completed in one hour.
5. Hiking in the Rocky Mountains, the Pacific Ocean was a beautiful sight.

A modifier that opens a sentence must be followed immediately by the word it is meant to describe. Otherwise, the modifier is said to be dangling, and the sentence takes on an unintended meaning. Note, for example, the following sentence:

While reading the newspaper, my dog sat with me on the front steps.

In this sentence, the unintended meaning is that the *dog* was reading the paper. What the writer meant, of course, was that *he* (or *she*), the writer, was reading the paper. The writer should have written this:

While reading the newspaper, *I* sat with my dog on the front steps.

The dangling modifier could also be corrected by placing the subject within the opening word group:

While *I* was reading the newspaper, my dog sat with me on the front steps.

Here are other sentences with dangling modifiers. Read the explanations of why they are dangling, and look carefully at the ways they are corrected.

Dangling	*Correct*
Shaving in front of the steamy mirror, the razor nicked Sean's chin. (*Who* was shaving in front of the mirror? The answer is not *razor,* but *Sean.* The subject *Sean* must be added.)	Shaving in front of the steamy mirror, *Sean* nicked his chin with the razor. *Or:* When *Sean* was shaving in front of the steamy mirror, he nicked his chin with the razor.
While stir-frying vegetables, hot oil splashed my arm. (*Who* is stir-frying vegetables? The answer is not *hot oil,* as it unintentionally seems to be, but *I.* The subject *I* must be added.)	While *I* was stir-frying vegetables, hot oil splashed my arm. *Or:* While stir-frying vegetables, *I* was splashed by hot oil.
Taking the exam, the room was so stuffy that Keesha nearly fainted. (*Who* took the exam? The answer is not *the room,* but *Keesha.* The subject *Keesha* must be added.)	Taking the exam, *Keesha* found the room so stuffy that she almost fainted. *Or:* When *Keesha* took the exam, the room was so stuffy that she almost fainted.
To impress the interviewer, punctuality is essential. (*Who* is to impress the interviewer? The answer is not *punctuality,* but *you.* The subject *you* must be added.)	To impress the interviewer, *you* must be punctual. *Or:* For *you* to impress the interviewer, punctuality is essential.

The preceding examples make clear two ways of correcting a dangling modifier. Decide on a logical subject, and do one of the following:

1. Place the subject *within* the opening word group:

   When *Sean* was shaving in front of the steamy mirror, he nicked his chin.

Note: In some cases an appropriate subordinating word such as *when* must be added, and the verb may have to be changed slightly as well.

2. Place the subject right *after* the opening word group:

   Shaving in front of the steamy mirror, *Sean* nicked his chin.

• • • • ACTIVITY

Ask *Who?* of the opening words in each sentence. The subject that answers the question should be nearby in the sentence. If it is not, provide the logical subject by using either method of correction described above.

Example   While pitching his tent, a snake bit Steve on the ankle.
              While Steve was pitching his tent, a snake bit him on the ankle.
     Or: While pitching his tent, Steve was bitten on the ankle by a snake.

1. Dancing on their hind legs, the audience cheered wildly as the elephants paraded by.

2. Last seen wearing dark glasses and a blond wig, the police spokesperson said the suspect was still being sought.

3. Pouring out the cereal, a coupon fell into my bowl of milk.

4. Escorted by dozens of police motorcycles, I knew the limousine carried someone important.

5. Tired and exasperated, the fight we had was inevitable.

6. Packed tightly in a tiny can, Farida had difficulty removing the anchovies.

7. Kicked carelessly under the bed, Lisa finally found her sneakers.

8. Working at the photocopy machine, the morning dragged on.

POST-TEST 1

Write *DM* for *dangling modifier* or *C* for *correct* in the space provided for each sentence.

_____   1. While riding the bicycle, a vicious-looking Rottweiler snapped at Tim's ankles.

_____   2. While Tim was riding the bicycle, a vicious-looking Rottweiler snapped at his ankles.

_____   3. Afraid to look his father in the eye, Scott kept his head bowed.

_____   4. Afraid to look his father in the eye, Scott's head remained bowed.

_____   5. Boring and silly, I turned the TV show off.

_____   6. I turned off the boring and silly TV show.

_____   7. Munching leaves from a tall tree, the giraffe fascinated the children.

_____   8. Munching leaves from a tall tree, the children were fascinated by the giraffe.

POST-TEST 2

Make the changes needed to correct the dangling modifier in each sentence.

1. Not having had much sleep, my concentration during class was weak.

2. Joined at the hip, a team of surgeons successfully separated the Siamese twins.

3. Wading by the lakeshore, a water snake brushed past my leg.

4. While being restrained by court officials, the judge sentenced the kidnapper.

5. In a sentimental frame of mind, Céline Dion's song brought tears to Beth's eyes.

POST-TEST 3

Complete the following sentences. In each case, a logical subject should follow the opening words.

Example Looking through the door's peephole, *I couldn't see who rang the doorbell.*

1. Noticing the light turn yellow, _____

2. Being fragile, _____

3. While washing the car, _____

4. Although very expensive, _____

5. Driving by the movie theatre, _____

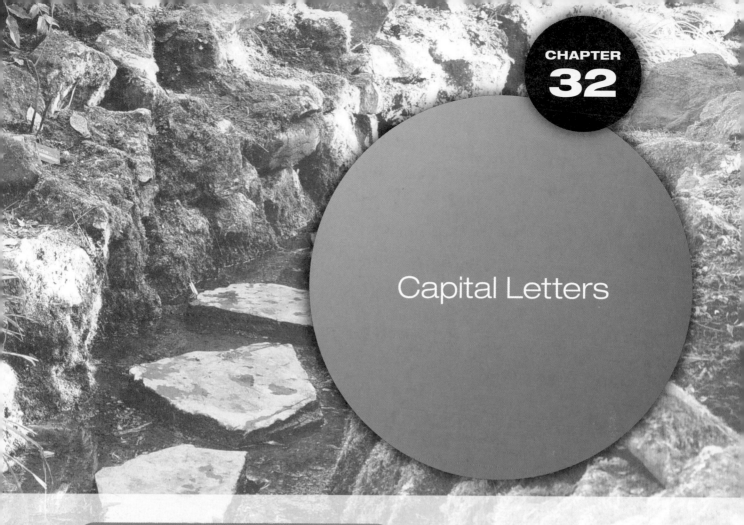

Capital Letters

MAIN USES OF CAPITAL LETTERS

Capital letters are used with

Tip: Think of capital letters for specific people, places, or things, and lower-case letters for general usage.

e.g., The **p**resident of a college versus **P**resident **J**oe **H**olmes.

1. first word in a sentence or direct quotation;

2. names of persons and the word *I*;

3. names of particular places;

4. names of days of the week, months, and holidays;

5. names of commercial products;

6. titles of books, magazines, newspapers, articles, stories, poems, films, television shows, songs, papers that you write, and the like;

7. names of companies, associations, unions, clubs, religious and political groups, and other organizations.

Each use is illustrated on the pages that follow.

First Word in a Sentence or Direct Quotation

The corner grocery was robbed last night.
The doctor said, "Please roll up your sleeve."
"If you feel lonely," said Teri, "call us. We'll be over in no time."

Note: In the third example on the previous page, *If* and *We'll* are capitalized because they start new sentences. But *call* is not capitalized because it is part of the first sentence.

Names of Persons and the Word *I*

Last night, I saw a movie starring Keanu Reeves and Sandra Bullock.

Names of Particular Places

Although James dropped out of Port Charles High School, he eventually earned his degree and got a job with Atlas Realty Company.

But: Use small letters if the specific name of a place is not given.

Although Bill dropped out of high school, he eventually earned his degree and got a job with a real estate company.

Names of Days of the Week, Months, and Holidays

On the last Friday afternoon in June, the day before Canada Day, my boss is having a barbecue for all the employees.

But: Use small letters for the seasons—summer, fall, winter, spring.

Most people feel more energetic in the spring and fall.

Names of Commercial Products

My little sister knows all the words to the jingles for Maple Leaf hot dogs, Tim Hortons doughnuts, Meow Mix cat food, and Swiss Chalet chicken.

But: Use small letters for the *type* of product (hot dogs, doughnuts, cat food, and so on).

Titles of Books, Magazines, Newspapers, Articles, Stories, Poems, Films, Television Shows, Songs, Papers that You Write, and the Like

We read the book *The Cellist of Sarajevo* for our cultural studies class.
In the doctor's waiting room, I watched *Canada AM,* read an article in *Maclean's,* and leafed through the *Winnipeg Free Press.*

Names of Companies, Associations, Unions, Clubs, Religious and Political Groups, and Other Organizations

Joe Duffy is a Roman Catholic, but his wife is Baptist.
The Hilldale Square Dancers' Club has won many competitions.
Brian, a member of the Canadian Auto Workers union and the Knights of Columbus, works for Ford Motor Company of Canada, Inc.

• • • • **ACTIVITY**

Underline the words that need capitals in the following sentences. Then, rewrite the capitalized form of each word.

Example In our resource management class, each student must write a report on an article in the magazine *canadian geographic.*

<u>   *Canadian*   </u>   <u>   *Geographic*   </u>

1. Alexander's collection of beatles souvenirs includes a pair of tickets from their last concert at maple leaf gardens.

2. Yumi read in *chatelaine* magazine that nelly furtado grew up in vancouver.

3. When i have a cold, I use vicks vaporub and chew halls cough drops.

4. Since no man volunteered for the job, the boy scouts in dauphin, manitoba, have a woman pack leader.

5. A nature trail for the blind in point pelee, ontario, has signs written in braille that encourage visitors to smell and touch the plants.

6. My father is a confirmed Edmonton oilers fan, though he lives in saskatoon.

7. Nicole bought a pepsi to wash down her falafel.

8. Vince listened to a Barenaked ladies CD called *barenaked ladies are men* while Donna read an article in *canadian house and home* entitled "All the Trimmings."

OTHER USES OF CAPITAL LETTERS

Capital letters are also used with

1. names that show family relationships;

2. titles of persons when used with their names;

3. specific school courses;

4. languages;

5. geographic locations;

6. historical periods and events;

7. races, nations, and nationalities;

8. opening and closing of a letter.

Each use is illustrated on the pages that follow.

Names that Show Family Relationships

All his life, Father has been addicted to gadgets.
I browsed through Grandmother's collection of old photographs.
Aunt Florence and Uncle Cory bought a mobile home.

But: Do not capitalize words like *mother, father, grandmother, grandfather, uncle, aunt,* and so on when they are preceded by a possessive word (*my, your, his, her, our, their*).

All his life, my father has been addicted to gadgets.
I browsed through my grandmother's collection of old photographs.
My aunt and uncle bought a cabin near Tracadie.

Titles of Persons When Used with Their Names

I contributed to Premier Wall's campaign fund.
Is Dr. Connor on vacation?
Professor Li announced that there would be no tests in the course.

But: Use small letters when titles appear by themselves, without specific names.

I contributed to my premier's campaign fund.
Is the doctor on vacation?
The professor announced that there would be no tests in the course.

Specific School Courses

The college offers evening sections of Introductory Psychology I, Abnormal Psychology, Psychology and Statistics, and Educational Psychology.

But: Use small letters for general subject areas.

The college offers evening sections of many psychology courses.

Languages

My grandfather's Polish accent makes his English difficult to understand.

Geographic Locations

He grew up in the Maritimes but moved to the West to look for a better job.

But: Use small letters in directions.

Head west for five blocks and then turn east on Queen Street.

Historical Periods and Events

During the Middle Ages, the Black Death killed over one-quarter of Europe's population.

Races, Nations, and Nationalities

The survey asked if the head of our household was Caucasian, Asian, or Native Canadian.

Tanya has lived on armed forces bases in Germany, Italy, and Spain.
Denise's beautiful features reflect her Chinese and Filipino parentage.

Opening and Closing of a Letter

Dear Sir: Sincerely yours,
Dear Ms. Henderson: Truly yours,

Note: Capitalize only the first word in a closing.

• • • • **ACTIVITY**

Underline the words that need capitals in the following sentences. Then rewrite
the capitalized forms of the words.

1. During world war II, some canadians were afraid that the japanese would
   invade British Columbia.

2. On their job site in korea, the french, swiss, and chinese co-workers used English to communicate.

3. When uncle harvey got the bill from his doctor, he called the ontario Medical
   Association to complain.

4. Dr. Freeling of the business department is offering a new course called introduction to word processing.

5. The new restaurant featuring vietnamese cuisine has just opened on the south
   side of the city.

UNNECESSARY USE OF CAPITALS

• • • • **ACTIVITY**

Many errors in capitalization are caused by using capitals where they are not
needed. Underline the incorrectly capitalized letters in the following sentences,
and rewrite the correct forms.

1. Kim Campbell—the first female prime Minister—also had the shortest tenure
   in office.

2. For her fortieth birthday, my Aunt bought herself a red Smart car.

3. Canadians were delighted when the Toronto Blue Jays were the first Canadian
   Baseball team to win the World Series.

4. In his Book titled *Offbeat Museums,* Saul Rubin tells about various Unusual
   Museums, such as, Believe it or not, the Barbed Wire Museum.

5. Einstein's theory of relativity, which he developed when he was only 26,
   led to the invention of the Electron Microscope, television, and the Atomic
   bomb.

● ● ● ● **REVIEW TEST 1**

Add capitals where needed in the following sentences.

Example   In an injured tone, Jay demanded, "(W)~~w~~hy wasn't (U)~~u~~ncle lou invited to the party?"

1. To keep warm, a homeless old man sits on a steam vent near the bay store on main street.

2. Silent movie stars of the twenties, like charlie chaplin and mary pickford, earned more than a million tax-free dollars a year.

3. Unique in Canada to the carolinian zone of southwestern ontario are such plants as the green dragon Lily and sassafras trees.

4. When Jean chrétien was first in ottawa, his idols were Wilfrid laurier and Louis st. laurent.

5. In an old movie, an attractive young lady invites groucho marx to join her.

6. "why?" asks groucho. "are you coming apart?"

7. I was halfway to the wash & dry Laundromat on elm street when i realized that my box of sunlight detergent was still at home on the kitchen counter.

8. Although I know that mother loves holidays, even I was surprised when she announced a party in february to celebrate wiarton Willie and groundhog day.

● ● ● ● **REVIEW TEST 2**

On a separate piece of paper, write

1. seven sentences demonstrating the seven main uses of capital letters;

2. eight sentences demonstrating the eight other uses of capital letters.

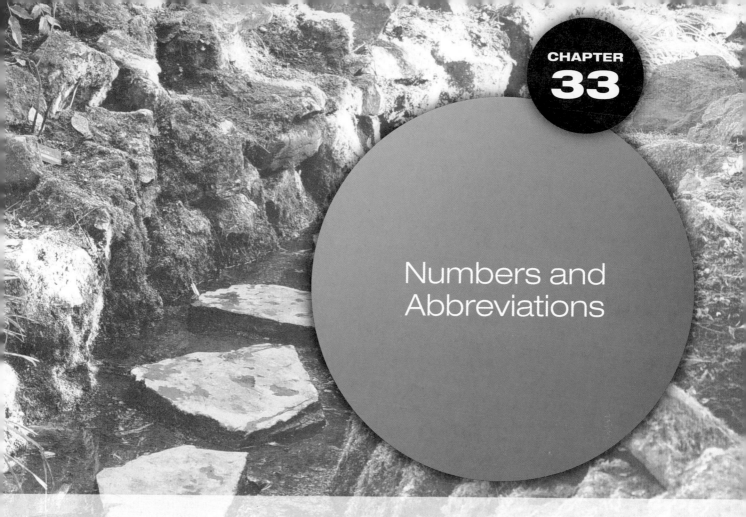

Numbers and Abbreviations

NUMBERS

Tip: In general, numbers smaller than ten should be spelled out.

Here are three helpful rules for using numbers:

Rule 1: Spell out numbers that are made up of no more than two words. Otherwise, use the numbers themselves.

> In Jody's kitchen is her collection of seventy-two cookbooks.
> Jody has a file of 350 recipes.

> It will take about two weeks to fix the computer database.
> Since a number of people use the database, the company will lose over 150 work days.

> Only nine students have signed up for the field trip.
> Nearly 250 students came to the lecture.

Rule 2: Be consistent when you use a series of numbers. If some numbers in a sentence or paragraph require more than two words, then use numbers in every case involving the same category of items.

> After the storm, maintenance workers unclogged 46 drains, removed 123 broken tree limbs, and rescued 3 kittens that were stuck in a drain pipe.

411

Rule 3: Use numbers to show dates, times, addresses, percentages, and parts of a book.

> The burglary was committed on October 30, 2008, but not discovered until January 2, 2009.
> Before I went to bed, I set my alarm for 6:45 a.m.

But: Spell out numbers before *o'clock*. For example: I didn't get out of bed until seven o'clock.

> The library is located at 45 West 52d Street.
> When you take the skin off a piece of chicken, you remove about 40 percent of the fat.
> The name of the murderer is revealed in Chapter 8 on page 236.

● ● ● ● **ACTIVITY**

Cross out the mistakes in numbers, and rewrite the sentence.

1. The Labour Day Parade will begin at three-thirty in front of the newspaper building at one-oh-six Main Street.

2. It took 4 hours to proofread all 75 pages of the manuscript.

3. We expect to have fifty percent of the work completed by March tenth.

ABBREVIATIONS

Using abbreviations can save you time when you take notes. In formal writing, however, you should avoid most abbreviations. Listed below are some of the few abbreviations that are considered acceptable in compositions. Note that a period is used after most abbreviations.

1. *Mr., Mrs., Ms., Jr., Sr., Dr.* when used with proper names:
   Mrs. Levesque   Dr. DaSilva   Howard Kelley, Jr.

2. Time references:
   A.M. or a.m.   P.M. or p.m.   B.C., A.D.

3. Initials in a person's name:
   Pierre E. Trudeau   John F. Kennedy   Philip C. Hoffman

4. Organizations, technical words, and company names known primarily by their initials:
   IBM   UNICEF   CBC   NHL   NDP   AIDS   CAT scan

● ● ● ● **ACTIVITY**

Cross out the words that should not be abbreviated, and rewrite them.

1. Between mid-Oct. and the beginning of Jan., I typically gain about three kgs.

2. I had such a bad headache this aftern. that I called my doc. for an appt.

3. I stopped at the p.o. at about twenty min. past ten and bought five dol. worth of stamps.

• • • •   **REVIEW TEST**

Cross out the mistakes in numbers and abbreviations, and rewrite them.

1. Sanjay was shocked when he transferred from a small h.s. to one with over 5000 students.

2. Grandpa lived to be ninety-nine despite smoking 2 doz. cheap cigars per mo.

3. Although the 2 girls are twins, they have different birthdays: one was born just before midnight on Feb. twenty-fifth, and the other a few minutes later after midnight.

4. In their first week of Fr. class, students learned to count from 1 to twenty-one and studied Chapter One in their textbook.

5. When I cleaned out the junk drawer in the kitch., I found twelve rubber bands, thirty-seven paper clips, and 3 used-up batteries.

Apostrophe

● **PRE-TEST**

Test your skill in apostrophe use by making corrections in the following sentences. Some sentences need apostrophes, while in others the apostrophe should be omitted.

1. Andrew Lloyd Webbers famous 1986 musical is *Phantom of the Opera*.

2. These two tickets to see the Vancouver Canucks are yours'. This one is mine.

3. My friend James hit single stayed in the top-ten list for five weeks.

4. I babysat the children with my brother-in-laws girlfriend.

5. The ballet company made its' decision to end the Canadian tour early.

The two main uses of the apostrophe are

1. to show the omission of one or more letters in a contraction;

2. to show ownership or possession.

Each use is explained on the pages that follow.

APOSTROPHE IN CONTRACTIONS

A *contraction* is formed when *two words* are combined *into one* to make one word. An apostrophe is used to show where letters are omitted in forming the contraction. Here are two contractions:

> have + not = haven't (the *o* in *not* has been omitted)
> I + will = I'll (the *wi* in *will* has been omitted)

Following are some other common contractions:

I + am = I'm	it + is = it's
I + have = I've	it + has = it's
I + had = I'd	is + not = isn't
who + is = who's	could + not = couldn't
do + not = don't	I + would = I'd
did + not = didn't	they + are = they're

Tip: Its vs. it's is many writers' worst enemy. The best way to avoid an error is to spell out the contraction it's as it is in formal writing.

And remember: there is no such word as its' in the English language.

Note: *Will* + *not* has an unusual contraction: *won't*.

● ● ● ● **ACTIVITY**

Write the contractions for the words in parentheses. One is done for you.

1. (Are not) _Aren't_ the reserve books in the library kept at the circulation desk?

2. If (they are) _____ coming over, (I had) _____ better cook more pasta.

3. (I am) _____ the kind of student (who is) _____ extremely nervous before tests.

4. (We are) _____ hoping to find out (who is) _____ responsible for this error; (it is) _____ important to us to keep our customers happy.

5. I (can not) _____ attend the music recital because (there is) _____ a conflict in my schedule.

Note: Even though contractions are common in everyday speech and in written dialogue, it is often best to avoid them in formal writing.

APOSTROPHE TO SHOW OWNERSHIP OR POSSESSION

To show ownership or possession, use such words as *belongs to, possessed by, owned by,* or (most commonly) *of.*

> the car that *belongs to* Santo
> the DVD player *owned by* the school
> the gentleness *of* my father

But the apostrophe plus *s* (if the word does not end in *s*) is often the quickest and easiest way to show possession. Thus, we can say

> Santo's car
> the school's DVD player
> my father's gentleness

Points to Remember

1. The 's goes with the owner or possessor (in the examples given, *Santo, the school, my father*). What follows is the person or thing possessed (in the examples given, *the umbrella, the DVD player, gentleness*).

2. When showing singular possession, place an apostrophe before the *s*.

   Santo's car   not   *Santos'* car (The car belongs to Santo (singular: one person)

       ↗   ↗

   Yes   No

   When showing plural possession, place an apostrophe after the *s*. (But if the word is plural without an *s*, this rule does not apply.)

   The patients' flowers—The flowers belong to the patients (plural: there is more than one patient)

   The children's toys—The toys belong to the children and since the word *children* is plural without an *s*, this is an exception to the rule.

3. Be careful not to confuse *it's* and *its*. The word *it's* is a contraction for *it is* or *it has*.

   It's a beautiful day.

   It's been a wonderful convocation.

The word *its* shows possession or ownership.

   The cat caught its tail.

   Put the garbage in its proper place.

Please note: the word its' does not exist.

• • • • ACTIVITY 1

Rewrite the *italicized* part of each of the sentences below, using the 's to show possession. Remember that the 's goes with the owner or possessor.

Example   *The wing of the bluejay* was broken.
              <u>The bluejay's wing was broken.</u>

1. *The annoying voice of the comedian* irritated me, so I changed the TV channel.

2. *The performance of the goalie* is inconsistent.

3. *The thin hand belonging to the old lady* felt as dry as parchment.

4. In *the window of the art gallery* are two landscape oil paintings of Prince Edward Island.

5. While performing a stunt, dirt flew into *the face of Brad Pitt*.

6. *The new denim shirt belonging to Josh* was as scratchy as sandpaper.

7. *The boots belonging to Rachel* are drying outside in the sun.

8. *The paintings owned by Norval Morrisseau* are rich in Aboriginal culture and symbolism.

• • • • ACTIVITY 2

Add 's to each of the following words to make them the possessors or owners of something. Then, write sentences using the words. The first one is done for you.

1. rock star *rock star's* _____
   The rock star's limousine pulled up to the curb.

2. Javier _____

3. counsellors _____

4. patient _____

Apostrophe versus Possessive Pronouns

Do not use an apostrophe with possessive pronouns. They already show owner-ship. Possessive pronouns include *his, hers, its, yours, ours,* and *theirs.*

Incorrect	*Correct*
The sun warped his' vinyl albums.	The sun warped his vinyl albums.
The Alex Colville painting is theirs'.	The Alex Colville painting is theirs.
The decision is yours'.	The decision is yours.
The plaid suitcase is ours'.	The plaid suitcase is ours.
I saw *Jersey Boys* during its' initial run.	I saw *Jersey Boys* during its initial run.

Apostrophe versus Simple Plurals

When you want to make a word plural, just add an *s* at the end of the word. Do *not* add an apostrophe. For example, the plural of the word *movie* is *movies,* not *movie's* or *movies.'* Look at this sentence:

Nikolas coveted his roommate's collection of vinyl albums and compact discs.

The words *albums* and *discs* are simple plurals, meaning more than one album, more than one disc. The plural is shown by adding *s* only. On the other hand, the *'s* after *roommate* shows possession—the roommate owns the albums and discs.

• • • • ACTIVITY

Insert an apostrophe where needed to show possession in the following sentences. Write *plural* above words where the *s* ending simply means more than one thing.

Example   Arlene's tinted contact lenses *(plural)* protect her eyes *(plural)* from glare.

1. After dancing for four hours, Jonas leg developed a cramp.

2. Vivians decision to study computer science is based on predictions of good opportunities for women in that field.

3. The fires extreme heat had melted the telephones in the office and welded the metal chairs into a twisted heap.

4. At the doctors request, Troy pulled up his shirt and revealed the zipper-like scars from his operation.

5. Of all the peoples names in all the worlds countries, the most common is Muhammad.

6. At the end of the day, Carmens shirt and pants smelled like gasoline, and her fingernails were rimmed with grease.

7. The childrens shouts of delight grew louder as the clown performed his jug-gling act.

8. Tinas camping handbook suggests that we bring water purification tablets and nylon ropes.

Apostrophe with Words Ending in *-s*

Plurals that end in *-s* show possession simply by adding the apostrophe rather than an apostrophe plus *s*.

the Thompsons' porch
the players' victory
her parents' motor home
the Barenaked Ladies' last album
the soldiers' hats

● ● ● ● ACTIVITY

Add an apostrophe where needed.

1. The dancers costumes on *So You Think You Can Dance* were bright and colourful.

2. The Murrays phone bills are often over $100 a month.

3. Users of wheelchairs cannot get up the steep steps at the entrances to many buildings.

4. The twins habit of dressing alike was started by their parents when the twins were children.

5. The screaming fans rushed out to the entrance of the theatre to get the performers autographs.

● ● ● ● POST-TEST

In each sentence, underline the two words that need apostrophes. Then write the words correctly in the spaces provided.

_____   1. The sagging sofas stuffing was coming out in places, and one of the chairs legs was broken.

_____   2. A shaky rope ladder led from the barns wooden floor to the haylofts dusty shadows.

_____   3. The paperback books glaring purple and orange cover was designed to attract a hurrying customers eye.

_____   4. Alicias essay was due in a matter of hours, but she suffered a writers block that emptied her brain.

_____   5. While she waited in her boss office, Marlas nervous fingers shredded a styrofoam coffee cup into a pile of jagged white flakes.

_____   6. Ivan could not remember whether he had left his wallet in his cars glove compartment or at his friends house.

_____   7. Members of the parents association constructed a maze made of old tires for the childrens playground.

_____   8. The cats great green eyes grew even wider as the curious dogs sniffing nose came too close to her.

For bonus material and additional activities please go to the OLC at **www.mcgrawhill.ca/olc/langan**

Quotation Marks

The two main uses of quotation marks are

1. to set off the exact words of a speaker or writer;

2. to set off the titles of short works.

Each use is explained on the following pages.

QUOTATION MARKS TO SET OFF THE WORDS OF A SPEAKER OR WRITER

Tip: Quotation marks always come in pairs. Therefore, don't forget to open your quotation at the beginning *and* close the quotation at the end of the quoted material.

Use quotation marks to show the exact words of a speaker or writer.

"I feel as though I've been here before," Angie murmured to her husband.
(Quotation marks set off the exact words that Angie spoke to her husband.)

Al Gore wrote, "I encourage people to make environmentally conscious choices because we all have to solve this climate crisis."
(Quotation marks set off the exact words that Al Gore spoke.)

"Did you know," said the nutrition expert, "that it's healthier to be a few kilos overweight?"
(Two pairs of quotation marks are used to enclose the nutrition expert's exact words.)

> The biology professor said, "Ants are a lot like human beings. They farm their own food and raise smaller insects as livestock. And, like humans, ants send armies to war."

Note: The end quotation marks do not come until the end of the biology professor's speech. Place quotation marks before the first quoted word and after the last quoted word. As long as no interruption occurs in the speech, do not use quotation marks for each new sentence.

In the four examples above and on the previous page, notice that a comma sets off the quoted part from the rest of the sentence. Also, observe that commas and periods at the end of a quotation always go *inside* quotation marks.

● ● ● ● **ACTIVITY 1**

Tip: Capitalize the first letter of a direct quote when the quoted material is a complete sentence. Otherwise, do not use a capital letter when the quoted material is a fragment or only a piece of the original material's complete sentence.

Place quotation marks around the exact words of a speaker or writer in the sentences that follow.

1. Several people have been credited with saying, Homelessness is a growing concern in Canada.

2. Beata asked, Do you give a discount to senior citizens?

3. This hamburger is raw! cried Phillip.

4. The bumper sticker on the rear of the battered old car read, Don't laugh—it's paid for.

5. I know why Robin Hood robbed only the rich, said the comedian. The poor don't have any money.

6. These CDs, proclaimed the television announcer, are not sold in any store.

7. When chefs go to great lengths, the woman at the weight-loss centre said, I go to great widths.

8. On a tombstone in a Saskatchewan cemetery are the words, Here lies an atheist, all dressed up and no place to go.

● ● ● ● **ACTIVITY 2**

1. Write a sentence in which you quote a favourite expression of someone you know. In the same sentence, identify the person's relationship to you.

Example   My grandfather loves to say, "It can't be as bad as all that."

2. Write a quotation that contains the words *Paulo asked Teresa*. Write a second quotation that includes the words *Teresa replied*.

3. Quote an interesting sentence or two from a book or magazine. In the same sentence, identify the title and author of the work.

Example   In The Dilbert Desk Calendar by Scott Adams, cartoon character Dilbert says, "I can please only one person per day. Today isn't your day, and tomorrow isn't looking good either."

Indirect Quotations

An indirect quotation is a rewording of someone else's comments rather than a word-for-word direct quotation. The word *that* often signals an indirect quotation.

Direct Quotation	*Indirect Quotation*
The nurse said, "some babies cannot tolerate cows' milk." (The nurse's exact spoken words are given, so quotation marks are used.)	The nurse said that some babies cannot tolerate cows' milk. (We learn the nurse's words indirectly, so no quotation marks are used.)
Vicky's note to Dan read, "I'll be home by 7:30." (The exact words that Vicky wrote in the note are given, so quotation marks are used.)	Vicky left a note for Dan that said she would be home by 7:30. (We learn Vicky's words indirectly, so no quotation marks are used.)

● ● ● ● **ACTIVITY**

Rewrite the following sentences, changing words as necessary to convert the sentences into direct quotations. The first one has been done for you as an example.

1. Ted asked Maria if she wanted to see his new Lexus hybrid.
   Ted asked Maria, "Do you want to see my new Lexus hybrid?"

2. Sonya said that her uncle will plant a vegetable garden this spring.

3. Angelo said that his children will be most affected by global warming.

4. My boss told me that I could make mistakes as long as I didn't repeat them.

5. The instructor announced that Thursday's test had been cancelled.

QUOTATION MARKS TO SET OFF THE TITLES OF SHORT WORKS

Titles of short works are usually set off by quotation marks, while titles of long works are underlined or italicized. Use quotation marks to set off titles of such short works as articles in newspapers or magazines, chapters in a book, short stories, poems, and songs. You should underline or italicize titles of books, newspapers, magazines, plays, movies, record albums, and television shows depending on the citation system you use. Note the following examples:

Quotation Marks	*Underlined or Italicized*
the essay "The Internet: A Survival Guide"	in the magazine *This Magazine*
the article "Shoppers Tight-Fisted in Sluggish Economy"	in the newspaper *The Globe and Mail*
the online article "The New Canadian Morality"	in the online magazine *Salon.com*

the chapter "Complementary and Alternative Medicine"	in the book *Health, Illness, and Medicine in Canada*
the story "The Progress of Love"	in the book *My Best Stories*
the article "Beginner Guitar Lesson Archive"	on the Web site *About.com: Guitar*
the song "Someone Who Cares"	in the album *Three Days Grace: Life Starts Now*
the episode "Holidaze"	in the television show *Grey's Anatomy*
	in the movie *Slumdog Millionaire*

Note: In printed works, italic type—slanted type that looks *like this*—is used instead of underlining. (See Chapter 19 for more information about the use of italics when using either MLA or APA style in research.)

• • • • ACTIVITY

Use quotation marks or underline as needed.

1. In Peter Robinson's short story Walking the Dog, the main character meets another dog lover, and they share more than the unique qualities in their canines.

2. I bought People magazine to read an article entitled Timeless Movie Couples.

3. We studied the essay titled Generation WWW by Ken Alexander in The Walrus Magazine.

4. Jamila used an article titled No, no, I'm not Ready to Go by Kerry Sulkowicz from Business Week magazine in her research paper about retirement.

5. The movie Casablanca, which starred Humphrey Bogart, was originally cast with Ronald Reagan in the leading role.

6. I like the TV reality show So You Think You Can Dance Canada better than Canadian Idol.

7. When the Twilight Saga New Moon movie premiered, fans lined up for hours to get tickets.

8. On my father's wall is a framed front page of The Vancouver Sun of February 25, 1940—the day he was born.

OTHER USES OF QUOTATION MARKS

Quotation marks are also used as follows:

1. To set off special words or phrases from the rest of a sentence:
   In elementary school, we were taught a little jingle about the "*i* before *e*" spelling rule.
   What is the difference between "it's" and "its"?
   (In this book, *italics* are often used instead of quotation marks to set off words.)

2. To mark off a quotation within a quotation:

The math professor said, "For class on Friday, do the problems at the end of the chapter titled 'Pythagorean Theorem.'"

Brendan remarked, "Did you know that Humphrey Bogart never actually said, 'Play it again, Sam' in the movie *Casablanca?*"

Note: A quotation within a quotation is indicated by *single* quotation marks, as shown above.

REVIEW TEST 1

Insert quotation marks where needed in the sentences that follow.

1. The psychology class read a short story called Silent Snow, Secret Snow, about a young boy who creates his own fantasy world.

2. While filming the movie *Vertigo,* actress Kim Novak was agonizing over how to play a particular scene until director Alfred Hitchcock reminded her, Kim, it's only a movie!

3. I'm against elementary school students using calculators, said Fred. I spent three years learning long division, and so should they.

4. Composer David Foster wrote many hit movie theme songs including Love Theme from St. Elmo's Fire for the movie *St. Elmo's Fire* and I Have Nothing for the movie *The Bodyguard.*

5. When I gagged while taking a foul-tasting medicine, my wife said, Put an ice cube on your tongue first, and then you won't taste it.

6. Jean reported to her business class on an article in *Newsweek* magazine entitled Environmental Economics.

7. When a guest at the wedding was asked what he was giving the couple, he replied, about six months.

8. Barack Obama, the forty-fourth president of the United States, said, Change has come to America.

REVIEW TEST 2

Go through the comics section of a newspaper to find a comic strip that amuses you. Be sure to choose a strip where two or more characters are speaking to each other. Write a full description that will enable people who have not read the comic strip to visualize it clearly and appreciate its humour. Describe the setting and action in each panel, and enclose the words of the speakers in quotation marks.

PART 4 HANDBOOK OF SENTENCE SKILLS

CHAPTER 36

Comma

Tip: The old adage, "When in doubt, leave it out" is still a good tip for writers who overuse the comma. By following these six rules, you will be more confident and correct in your punctuation. You will use a comma *only when you have a reason to do so*, not simply to make your writing look attractive.

● PRE-TEST

Test your knowledge by inserting commas where needed.

1. Martin bought vegetables fruit and whole grains at the farmer's market.

2. In the morning I run a mile or two before breakfast.

3. The Cirque du Soleil troupe originally from Quebec fascinated the audience with its athletic agility.

4. I like to exercise at home so I purchased a stationary bicycle.

5. My sister asked "What time does your aerobics class begin?"

6. September 4 2009 is my first day of classes at LaSalle College Montreal Quebec.

SIX MAIN USES OF THE COMMA

Commas are used mainly

1. to separate items in a series;

2. to set off introductory material;

3. on both sides of words that interrupt the flow of thought in a sentence;

4. between two complete thoughts connected by *and, but, for, or, nor, so, yet*;

5. to set off a direct quotation from the rest of a sentence;

6. for dates, addresses, numbers, and openings and closing of letters.

You may find it helpful to remember that the comma often marks a slight pause or break in a sentence. Read aloud the sentence examples given for each rule, and listen for the minor pauses or breaks that are signalled by commas.

Comma between Items in a Series

Use commas to separate items in a series.

The street vendor sold watches, necklaces, and earrings.
The pitcher adjusted his cap, pawed the ground, and peered over his shoulder.
The exercise instructor told us to inhale, exhale, and relax.
Joe peered into the hot, steaming bowl of chicken noodle soup.

Notes:

1. The final comma in a series (called a serial comma) is optional, but it is often used. *Be consistent* in your use of commas when you list items.

2. A comma is used between two descriptive words in a series only if *and* inserted between the words sounds natural. You could say:

Joe peered into the hot *and* steaming bowl of chicken noodle soup.

Notice, however, in the following sentence that the descriptive words do not sound natural when *and* is inserted between them. In such cases, no comma is used.

The health professional wore a pale green lab coat. (A pale *and* green lab coat does not sound right, so no comma is used.)

● ● ● ● **ACTIVITY**

Place commas between items in a series.

1. The old kitchen cabinets were littered with dead insect crumbs and dust balls.

2. Renovations for the new forensics building involved installing new lights setting up the computers and sanding the floors.

3. The children splashed through the warm deep swirling rainwater that flooded the street.

4. The police officer's warm brown eyes relaxed manner and pleasant smile made him easy to talk to.

5. Training for the Olympics requires perseverance discipline and passion.

Comma after Introductory Material

Use a comma to set off introductory material.

After yoga class, Kami felt energized and fit.
Muttering under his breath, Matthias reviewed the terms he had memorized.
In a wolf pack, the dominant male holds his tail higher than the other pack members.

Although he had been first in the checkout line, Devon let an elderly woman go ahead of him.

Yes, the new culinary instructor has years of experience.

Note: If the introductory material is brief, the comma is sometimes omitted. In the activities here, you should include the comma.

● ● ● ● **ACTIVITY**

Place commas after introductory material.

1. As Chen struggled with the stuck window gusts of cold rain blew in his face.

2. Her heart pounding wildly Jessie opened the letter that would tell her whether or not she had been accepted at college.

3. Along the once-pretty Don River people had dumped old tires and loads of household trash.

4. When the band hadn't taken the stage 45 minutes after the concert was supposed to begin the audience members started shouting and stamping their feet.

5. Setting down a smudged glass of murky water the server tossed Dennis a greasy menu and asked if he'd care to order.

Comma around Words Interrupting the Flow of Thought

Use a comma on both sides of words or phrases that interrupt the flow of thought in a sentence.

The vinyl car seat, sticky from the heat, clung to my skin.
Marty's new computer, which his wife got him as a birthday gift, occupies all of his spare time.
The hallway, dingy and dark, was illuminated by a bare bulb hanging from a wire.

Usually you can "hear" words that interrupt the flow of thought in a sentence by reading it aloud. In cases where you are not sure if certain words are interrupters, remove them from the sentence. If it still makes sense without the words, you know that the words are interrupters and that the information they give is nonessential. *Such nonessential or extra information is set off with commas.*

Note the following sentence:

Joanna Dodd, who goes to aerobics class with me, was in a serious car accident.

Here, the words *who goes to aerobics class with me* are extra information not needed to identify the subject of the sentence, *Joanna Dodd*. Commas go around such nonessential information. Note, on the other hand, the next sentence:

The woman who goes to aerobics class with me was in a serious accident.

Here, the words *who goes to aerobics class with me* supply essential information—information needed for us to identify the woman being spoken of. If the words were removed from the sentence, we would no longer know exactly who was in the accident: "The woman was in a serious accident." Here is another example:

Pillars of the Earth, a novel by Ken Follett, is one of the most gripping novels I've ever read.

Here, the words *a novel by Ken Follett* could be left out, and we would still know the basic meaning of the sentence. Commas are placed around such non-essential material. However, note the following sentence:

Ken Follett's novel *Pillars of the Earth* is one of the most gripping novels I've ever read.

In this case, the title of the novel is essential. Without it, the sentence would read, "Ken Follett's novel is one of the most gripping novels I've ever read." We would not know which of Ken Follett's novels was so gripping. Commas are not used around the title because it provides essential information.

● ● ● ● **ACTIVITY**

Use commas to set off interrupting words.

1. A slight breeze hot and damp ruffled the bedroom curtains.

2. Canadian actor Jim Carrey originally from Newmarket, Ontario now lives in Los Angeles.

3. The spa which is located in the countryside offers special weekend rates.

4. Sarah who is a healthfood nut prefers to eat a diet of vegetables and fish.

5. The fleet of tall ships a majestic sight made its way into Halifax Harbour.

Comma between Two Complete Thoughts

Use a comma between two complete thoughts connected by *and, but, or, nor, so, yet.*

Samantha closed all the windows, but the predicted thunderstorm never arrived.
I like wearing comfortable clothing, so I buy oversized shirts and sweaters.
Peggy doesn't envy the skinny models in magazines, because she is happy with her own healthy-looking body.

Notes:

1. The comma is optional when the complete thoughts are short.

The ferris wheel started and Wilson closed his eyes.
Irene left the lecture hall for her head was pounding.
I made a wrong turn so I doubled back.

2. Be careful not to use a comma to separate two verbs that belong to one subject. The comma is used only in sentences made up of two complete thoughts (two subjects and two verbs). In the sentence below, there is only one subject *(doctor)* and a double verb *(stared* and *lectured)*. No comma is needed.

The doctor stared over his bifocals and lectured me about smoking.

Likewise, the next sentence has only one subject *(Aaron)* and a double verb *(switched* and *tapped)*; therefore, no comma is needed.

Aaron switched the lamp on and off and then tapped it with his fingers.

● ● ● ● **ACTIVITY**

Place a comma before a joining word that connects two complete thoughts (two subjects and two verbs). Remember, do *not* place a comma within a sentence that has only one subject and a double verb. (Some items may be correct as given.)

1. My favourite soap was interrupted for a news bulletin about an ice storm and I poked my head out of the kitchen to listen to the announcement.

2. The puppy was beaten by its former owner and cringes at the sound of a loud voice.

3. The eccentric woman brought all her own clips and rollers to the hairdresser for she was afraid to use the ones there.

4. The tuna sandwich in my lunch is crushed and the cream-filled cupcake is plastered to the bottom of the bag.

5. The property owner promised repeatedly to come and fix the leaking shower, but three months later he hasn't done a thing.

6. Bonita was tired of summer reruns so she visited the town library to pick up some interesting books.

7. You can spend hours driving all over town to look for a particular type of camera or you can telephone a few stores to find it quickly.

8. Many people strolled among the exhibits at the comic book collectors' convention and stopped to look at a rare first edition of *Superman*.

Comma with Direct Quotations

Use a comma to set off a direct quotation from the rest of a sentence.

The tennis coach cried, "Great footwork!"
"Now is the time to yield to temptation," my horoscope read.
"I'm sorry," said the restaurant host. "You'll have to wait."
"For my first writing assignment," said Nathan, "I have to turn in a five-hundred-word description of my favourite person."

Note: Commas and periods at the end of a quotation go inside quotation marks. (See also page 420.)

● ● ● ● **ACTIVITY**

Use commas to set off direct quotations from the rest of the sentence.

1. The coach announced "In order to measure your lung capacity, you're going to attempt to blow up a plastic bag with one breath."

2. "A grapefruit" said the comedian "is a lemon that had a chance and took advantage of it."

3. My father asked "Did you know that the family moving next door has 13 children?"

4. "Be quiet" a man said to the person seated in front of him. "I paid 50 dollars to listen to the guest speaker, not you."

5. The hospitality instructor explained to the students "Gaining experience behind the scenes in a hotel is just as important as learning how to run the front desk."

Comma for Dates, Addresses, Numbers, and Opening and Closing of Letters

Dates

January 30, 2010, is the day I make the last payment on my car.

Addresses

I buy discount children's clothing from Bouncy Baby Wear, Box 900, Vancouver, British Columbia V6H 4Z1.

Note: No comma is used before a postal code.

Numbers

The insurance agent sold me a $50 000 term life insurance policy.

Openings and Closings of Letters

Dear Lysa,   Sincerely yours,
Dear Roberto,   Truly yours,

Note: In formal letters, a colon is used after the opening: Dear Sir: *or* Dear Madam: *or* Dear Allan: *or* Dear Ms. Mohr:.

ACTIVITY

Place commas where needed.

1. The increased interest rates on my credit card have raised my debt to $15 000.

2. The vegetarian lasagna at Centros 45 Richmond Street is the best in town.

3. In 1965 the first Gold's Gym opened its doors in Venice Beach California.

4. The mileage chart indicates Elaine that we'll have to drive 1231 kilometres to get to Red Deer Alberta.

5. The coupon refund address is 2120 Maritime Highway Halifax Nova Scotia B3J 1V2.

POST-TEST 1

Insert commas where needed. On a separate piece of paper, summarize briefly the rule that explains the comma or commas used.

1. "Kleenex tissues" said the history professor "were first used as gas mask filters in World War I."

2. Dee ordered a sundae with three scoops of rocky road ice cream miniature marshmallows and raspberry sauce.

3. While waiting to enter the movie theatre we studied the faces of the people just leaving to see if they had liked the show.

4. I had left my wallet on the store counter but the clerk called me at home to say that it was safe.

5. The city workers carried signs reading "We're overworked and underpaid."

6. The horseback rider who started riding at age 6 won first place in the dressage competition.

7. On June 16 2008 Tiger Woods won the U.S. Open Golf Championship for the third time.

8. The aerobics instructor a former bodybuilder led the class through an exhausting yet satisfying workout.

POST-TEST 2

Insert commas where needed.

1. Before leaving for the gym Nikki added extra socks and a tube of shampoo to the gear in her duffel bag.

2. My father said "Golf isn't for me. I can't afford to buy lots of expensive sticks so that I can lose lots of expensive white balls."

3. Oscar took a time-exposure photo of the busy highway so the cars' tail lights appeared in the developed print as winding red ribbons.

4. The graduating students sweltering in their hot black gowns fanned their faces with commencement programs.

5. After their deaths many people were surprised to learn that both Michael Jackson and Farrah Fawcett passed away on June 25 2009.

6. In August 2005 Hurricane Katrina swept through New Orleans killing hundreds and displacing many families.

7. "When I was little" said Ameena "my brother told me it was illegal to kill praying mantises. I still don't know if that's true or not."

8. On July 1 1867 Upper and Lower Canada united with New Brunswick and Nova Scotia to form the Dominion of Canada.

POST-TEST 3

In the following passage, there are ten missing commas. Add the commas where needed. The types of mistakes to look for are shown in the box below.

> two commas missing between items in a series
> one comma missing after introductory material
> four commas missing around interrupting words
> two commas missing between complete thoughts
> one comma missing with a direct quotation

When I was about ten years old I developed several schemes to avoid eating liver, a food I despise. My first scheme involved my little brother. Timmy too young to realize what a horrible food liver is always ate every bit of his portion. On liver nights, I used to sit next to Tim and slide my slab of meat onto his plate when my parents weren't paying attention. This strategy worked until older and wiser Tim decided to reject his liver along with the rest of us. Another liver-disposal method I used was hiding the meat right on the plate. I'd cut the liver into tiny squares half the size of postage stamps and then I would carefully hide the pieces. I'd put them inside the skin of my baked potato beneath some mashed peas, or under a crumpled paper napkin. This strategy worked perfectly only if my mother didn't look too closely as she scraped the dishes. Once she said to me "Do you know you left a lot of liver on your plate?" My best liver trick was to hide the disgusting stuff on a three-inch-wide wooden ledge that ran under our dining-room table. I'd put little pieces of liver on the ledge when Mom wasn't looking; I would sneak the dried-up scraps into the garbage early the next day. Our dog would sometimes smell the liver try to get at it, and bang his head noisily against the bottom of the table. These strategies seemed like a lot of work but I never hesitated to take whatever steps I could. Anything was better than eating a piece of meat that tasted like old socks soaked in mud.

● ● ● ● **POST-TEST 4**

On a separate piece of paper, write six sentences, illustrating each of the six main comma rules.

Online LearningCentre

Other Punctuation Marks

COLON (:)

Use the colon at the end of a complete statement to introduce a list or an explanation.

1. A list:

   The store will close at noon on the following dates: October 5, December 24, and December 31.

2. An explanation:

   Here's a tip for cleaning a cello: use a soft cloth and apply light pressure.

● ● ● **ACTIVITY**

Place colons where needed in the sentences below.

1. Bring these items to registration a ballpoint pen, your student ID card, and a cheque made out to the college.

2. The road was closed because of an emergency an enormous tree had fallen and blocked both lanes.

SEMICOLON (;)

The main use of the semicolon is to mark a break between two complete thoughts, as explained on pages 364–365. Another use is to mark off items in a series when the items themselves contain commas. Here are some examples:

> Maya's children are named Melantha, which means "black flower"; Yonina, which means "dove"; and Cynthia, which means "moon goddess."
> Juliette's favourite songs are "Minority," by Green Day; "What About Now," by Daughtry; and "Complicated," by Avril Lavigne.

● ● ● ● **ACTIVITY**

Place semicolons where needed in the sentences below.

1. We have learned the anatomy terms for our massage therapy program memorizing the definitions prepares us for our upcoming midterm . . .

2. My sister had a profitable summer: by volunteering at Habitat for Humanity, she earned $325 by teaching the guitar, $85 and by organizing a fundraiser, $110.

3. The children who starred in the play were Kari Rosoff, nine years old Flora Junco, twelve years old and Ezra Johnson, three years old.

DASH (—)

A dash signals a pause longer than a comma but not as long as a period. Use a dash to set off words for dramatic effect:

> I was so exhausted that I fell asleep within seconds—standing up.
> He had many good qualities—sincerity, honesty, and thoughtfulness—yet he had few friends.

Notes:

1. A dash is formed on a keyboard by striking the hyphen twice (- -). In handwriting, a dash is as long as two letters would be.

2. Be careful not to overuse dashes.

3. Colons used to begin lists of items are generally more acceptable in formal writing than dashes.

● ● ● ● **ACTIVITY**

Place dashes where needed in the following sentences.

1. The victim's leg broken in three places lay twisted at an odd angle on the pavement.

2. The wallet was found in a garbage can minus the cash.

3. After nine days of hiking in the wilderness, sleeping under the stars, and communing with nature, I could think of only one thing a hot shower.

PARENTHESES ( )

Parentheses are used to set off extra or incidental information from the rest of a sentence:

> The opera singer owns three pets (one cat and two dogs) and takes them with her to every performance.
> Oprah Winfrey, the talented talk show host (and creator of *O,* the magazine), has decided to end her show in 2011.

Note: Do not use parentheses too often in your writing.

● ● ● ● ACTIVITY

Add parentheses where needed.

1. Though the first *Star Trek* series originally ran for only three seasons 1965–1968, it can still be seen on many stations around the world.

2. Whenever Jack has too much to drink even one drink is sometimes too much, he gets loud and abusive.

3. When I opened the textbook, I discovered that many pages mostly in the first chapter were completely blank.

HYPHEN (-)

1. Use a hyphen with two or more words that act as a single unit describing a noun.

> The light-footed burglar silently slipped open the sliding-glass door.
> While Cold Play's lead singer Chris Martin was interviewed on the late-night talk show, he talked about his love of music as a young boy.
> Sunday dinners are always a treat because my mother-in-law is a top-notch cook.

2. Use a hyphen to divide a word at the end of a line of writing or typing. When you need to divide a word at the end of a line, divide it between syllables. Use your dictionary to be sure of correct syllable divisions.

> Selena's first year at college was a time filled with numerous new pressures and responsibilities.

Notes:

1. Do not divide words of one syllable.

2. Do not divide a word if you can avoid dividing it.

3. Word processing has eliminated the need to divide words at the end of lines. Unless they contain hyphenation dictionaries, software programs will not split your final word on a line; the word will be fitted into the line you are typing or moved to the beginning of the next line.

● ● ● ● **ACTIVITY**

Place hyphens where needed.

1. The blood red moon hanging low on the horizon made a picture perfect atmosphere for Halloween night.

2. My father, who grew up in a poverty stricken household, remembers putting cardboard in his shoes when the soles wore out.

3. The well written article in *The Economist* magazine described the nerve racking experiences of a journalist who infiltrated the mob.

● ● ● ● **REVIEW TEST**

At the appropriate spot, place the punctuation mark shown in the margin.

— 1. A bad case of flu, a burglary, the death of an uncle it was not what you would call a pleasant week.

( ) 2. My grandfather who will be 90 in May says that hard work and a glass of wine every day are the secrets of a long life.

- 3. The passengers in the glass bottomed boat stared at the colourful fish in the water below.

( ) 4. Ellen's birthday December 27 falls so close to Christmas that she gets only one set of presents.

; 5. The dog-show winners included Freckles, a springer spaniel King Leo, a German shepherd and Big Guy, a miniature schnauzer.

- 6. Cold hearted stepmothers are a fixture in many famous fairy tales.

; 7. Some people need absolute quiet in order to study they can't concentrate with the soft sounds of a radio, air conditioner, or television in the background.

: 8. A critic reviewing a bad play wrote, "I saw the play under the worst possible circumstances the curtain was up."

PART 4 HANDBOOK OF SENTENCE SKILLS

Commonly Confused Words

HOMONYMS

The commonly confused words, known as *homonyms,* on the following pages have the same sounds but different meanings and spellings. Complete the activity for each set of words, and check off and study the words that give you trouble.

Tip: Many of us rely on spell-check as a proof-reading tool. However, don't trust your handy spell-checker to correct your homonyms. Spell-check only checks for words that exist; it doesn't check for meaning.

all ready	completely prepared
already	by then; not earlier than

It was *already* six o'clock by the time I sent my email.
My presentation on virtual reality was *all ready,* but the class was cancelled.

Fill in the blanks: Tyrone was _____ to sign up for the course when he discovered that it had _____ closed.

brake	stop
break	come apart; pause; fail to observe

Sarah had to *brake* quickly to avoid hitting the Doritos chip truck.
During a *break* in the kitchen, Marie chatted with the other culinary students.

Fill in the blanks: Avril, a poor driver, _____ at the last minute and usually _____ the speed limit as well.

course	part of a meal; a school subject; direction
coarse	rough

In my communications course, one of the students used *coarse* language and shocked all of us.

Fill in the blanks: Over the _____ of time, jagged, _____ rocks will be polished to smoothness by the pounding waves.

hear   perceive with the ear

here   in this place

I can *hear* the performers so well from *here* that I don't want to change my seat.

Fill in the blanks: The chairperson explained that the meeting was held _____ in the auditorium to enable everyone to _____ the debate.

hole   an empty spot

whole   entire

A *hole* in my knapsack means that my *whole* assignment is now ruined.

Fill in the blanks: The _____ in Jason's arguments wouldn't exist if he put his _____ concentration into his thinking.

its   belonging to it

it's   the shortened form for *it is* or *it has*

The tall giraffe lowered *its* head (the head belonging to the giraffe) to the level of the car window and peered in at us.

It's (it is) too late to sign up for the theatre trip to Toronto.

Fill in the blanks: I decided not to take the course because _____ too easy; _____ content offers no challenge whatever.

knew   past form of know

new   not old

No one *knew* the full extent of the damage from the oil spillage, but now a *new* home must be found for the birds.

Fill in the blanks: Even people who _____ Andrew well didn't recognize him with his _____ beard.

know   to understand

no   a negative

By the time students complete that course, they *know* two computer languages and have *no* trouble writing their own programs.

Fill in the blanks: Dogs and cats usually _____ by the tone of the speaker's voice when they are being told "_____."

passed   went by; succeeded in; handed to

past   a time before the present; by, as in "I drove past the house"

In the *past* year, Yvonne has *passed* all of her Paramedic exams.

Fill in the blanks: Lewis asked for a meeting with his boss to learn why he had been _____ over for promotion twice in the _____ year.

peace   calm

piece   a part

> The police officers tried to maintain *peace* when one of the protestors threw a *piece* of wood at the crowd.

Fill in the blanks: Nicholas felt at _____ when he heard the familiar _____ of music.

plain   simple

plane   aircraft

> The art students were instructed to draw a *plain* illustration of their favourite *plane*.

Fill in the blanks: After unsuccessfully trying to overcome her fear, Alexandra finally admitted the _____ truth: she was terrified of flying in a _____.

principal   main; a person in charge of a school

principle   a law or standard

> If the *principal* ingredient in this stew is octopus, I'll abandon my *principle* of trying everything at least once.

Fill in the blanks: Our _____ insists that all students adhere to the school's _____ regarding dress, tardiness, and smoking.

right   correct; opposite of *left*

write   to put words on paper

> Without the *right* amount of advance planning, it is difficult to *write* a good research paper.

Fill in the blanks: Connie wanted to send for the CDS offered on TV, but she could not _____ fast enough to get all the _____ information down before the commercial ended.

than (thăn)   used in comparisons

then (thĕn)   at that time; next

> My brother is a better writer *than* I; *then* I got a tutor to improve my skills.

Fill in the blanks: When I was in high school, I wanted a racy two-seater convertible more _____ anything else; but _____ my friends pointed out that only one person would be able to ride with me.

their   belonging to them

there   at that place; a neutral word used with verbs like *is, are, was, were, have,* and *had*

they're   the shortened form of *they are*

The tenants *there* are complaining because *they're* being cheated by *their* building owner.

Fill in the blanks: The tomatoes I planted _____ in the back of the garden are finally ripening, but _____ bright red colour will attract hungry raccoons, and I fear _____ going to be eaten.

threw   past form of throw

through   from one side to the other; finished

> As the inexperienced pizza maker *threw* the pie into the air, he punched a hole *through* its thin crust.

Fill in the blanks: As the prime minister moved slowly _____ the cheering crowd, the RCMP officer suddenly _____ himself at a man waving a small metal object.

to   a verb part, as in *to smile;* toward, as in "I'm going *to* heaven"

too   overly, as in "The pizza was *too* hot;" also, as in "The coffee was hot, *too.*"

two   the number 2

> I applied to two colleges. (The first *to* means "toward"; the second *two* refers to the number of colleges.)
> The health food store is *too* far away; I hear that it's expensive, *too.* (The first *too* means "overly;" the second *too* means "also.")

Fill in the blanks: The _____ of them have been dating for a year, but lately they seem _____ be arguing _____ often to pretend nothing is wrong.

wear   to have on

where   in what place

> *Where* I will *wear* a purple feather boa is not the point; I just want to buy it.

Fill in the blanks: _____ were we going the night I refused to _____ a tie?

weather   atmospheric conditions

whether   if it happens that; in case; if

> Although meteorologists are *weather* specialists, even they can't predict *whether* a hurricane will change course.

Fill in the blanks: The gloomy _____ report in the paper this morning ended all discussion of _____ to pack a picnic lunch for later.

whose   belonging to whom

who's   the shortened form for *who is* and *who has*

> "*Who's* the patient *whose* ankle is sprained?" the nurse asked.

Fill in the blanks: _____ the computer salesperson _____ customers are always praising him for his level of expertise?

your   belonging to you

you're   the shortened form of *you are*

When *you're* cooking for a large group, *your* menu must accommodate many palates.

Fill in the blanks: If _____ having trouble installing _____ software, why don't you contact your network specialist?

OTHER WORDS FREQUENTLY CONFUSED

Here is a list of other words that people frequently confuse. Complete the activities for each set of words, and check off and study the words that give you trouble.

a

both *a* and *an* are used before other words to mean "one"

an

generally, you should use *an* before words starting with a vowel (*a, e, i, o, u*):

  an orange   an umbrella   an indication   an ape   an effort

Generally, you should use *a* before words starting with a consonant (all other letters):

  a genius   a movie   a speech   a study   a typewriter

Fill in the blanks: The morning after the party, I had _____ pounding headache and _____ upset stomach.

accept (ăk sĕpt´)   receive; agree to

except (ĕk sĕpt´)   exclude; but

  It was easy to *accept* the book's plot, *except* for one unlikely coincidence at the very end.

Fill in the blanks: Sanka would have _____ the position, _____ that it would add twenty minutes to his daily commute.

advice (ăd vīs´)   a noun meaning "an opinion"

advise (ăd vīz´)   a verb meaning "to counsel, to give advice"

  I have learned not to take my sister's *advice* on straightening out my life.
  A counsellor can *advise* you about the courses you'll need next year.

Fill in the blanks: Ayesha seems so troubled about losing her job that I _____ her to seek the _____ of a professional counsellor.

affect (uh fĕkt´)   a verb meaning "to influence"

effect (ĭ fĕkt´)   a verb meaning "to bring about something;" a noun meaning "result"

  The cost of tuition will *affect* Mark's decision to attend college.
  If we can *effect* a change in George's attitude, he may do better in his courses.
  One *effect* of the strike will be dwindling supplies in the supermarkets.

Fill in the blanks: The _____ of good reading habits directly _____ a student's academic performance.

among   implies three or more

between   implies only two

After the team of surgeons consulted *among* themselves, they decided that the bullet was lodged *between* two of the patient's ribs.

Fill in the blanks: _____ halves, one enthusiastic fan stood up _____ his equally fanatic friends and took off his coat and shirt.

| **beside** | along the side of |
| **besides** | in addition to |

Besides doing daily inventories, I have to stand *beside* the cashier whenever the store gets crowded.

Fill in the blanks: _____ those books on the table, I plan to use these magazines stacked _____ me while doing my research paper.

| **fewer** | used with things that can be counted |
| **less** | refers to amount, value, or degree |

I've taken *fewer* classes this semester, so I hope to have *less* trouble finding time to study.

Fill in the blanks: This beer advertises that it has _____ calories and is _____ filling.

| **former** | refers to the first of two items named |
| **latter** | refers to the second of two items named |

Sue yelled at her sons, Greg and John, when she got home; the *former* had left the refrigerator open and the *latter* had left wet towels all over the bathroom.

Fill in the blanks: Marco collects coupons and parking tickets: the _____ save him money, and the _____ are going to cost him a great deal of money some day.

| **learn** | to gain knowledge |
| **teach** | to give knowledge |

I can't *learn* a new skill unless someone with lots of patience *teaches* me.

Fill in the blanks: Because she is quick to _____ new things, Mandy has offered to _____ me how to play the latest video games.

| **loose** | Not fastened; not tight-fitting |
| **lose** | Misplace; fail to win; no longer have |

In this strong wind, the house may *lose* some of its *loose* roof shingles.

Fill in the blanks: A _____ wire in the television set was causing us to _____ the picture.

| **quiet** (kwi´ĭt) | peaceful |
| **quite** (kwĭt) | entirely; really; rather |

Avivah seems *quiet* and demure, but she has *quite* a temper at times.

Fill in the blanks: Most people think the library is _____ a good place to study, but I find the extreme _____ distracting.

● ● ● ● ACTIVITY

These sentences check your understanding of *its, it's; there, their, they're; to, too, two;* and *your, you're.* Underline the two incorrect spellings in each sentence. Then spell the words correctly in the spaces provided.

_____ 1. "Its not a very good idea," yelled Angela's boss, "to tell you're customer that the striped dress she plans to buy makes her look like a pregnant tiger."

_____ 2. You're long skirt got stuck in the car door, and now its sweeping the highway.

_____ 3. When your young, their is a tendency to confuse a crush with true love.

_____ 4. After too hours of writing, Lin was to tired to write any longer.

_____ 5. It is unusual for a restaurant to lose it's licence, but this one had more mice in its' kitchen than cooks.

_____ 6. The vampires bought a knife sharpener in order too sharpen there teeth.

_____ 7. Your sometimes surprised by who you're friends turn out to be in difficult times.

_____ 8. When the children get to quiet, Clare knows their getting into trouble.

● ● ● ● REVIEW TEST 1

Underline the correct word in the parentheses. Rather than guessing, look back at the explanations of the words when necessary.

1. I (know, no) that several of the tenants have decided (to, too, two) take (their, there, they're) case to court.

2. (whose, who's) the author of that book about the (affects, effects) of eating (to, too, two) much protein?

3. In our supermarket is a counter (where, wear) (your, you're) welcome to sit down and have free coffee and doughnuts.

4. (Its, It's) possible to (loose, lose) friends by constantly giving out unwanted (advice, advise).

5. For a long time, I couldn't (accept, except) the fact that my husband wanted a divorce; (then, than) I decided to stop being angry and get on with my life.

6. I spent the (hole, whole) day browsing (threw, through) the chapters in my business textbook, but I didn't really study them.

7. The newly appointed (principal, principle) is (quite, quiet) familiar with the problems (hear, here) at our school.

8. I found that our cat had (all ready, already) had her kittens (among, between) the weeds (beside, besides) the porch.

● ● ● REVIEW TEST 2

On a separate piece of paper, write short sentences using the ten words shown below.

1. accept	3. you're	5. then	7. their	9. fewer
2. its	4. too	6. loose	8. passed	10. affect

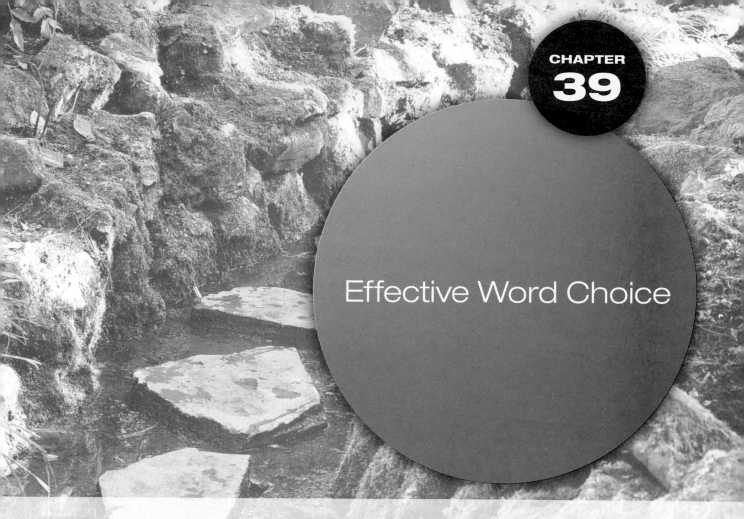

CHAPTER 39

Effective Word Choice

Choose your words carefully when you write. Always take the time to think about your word choices rather than simply using the first word that comes to mind. You need to develop the habit of selecting words that are appropriate and exact for your purposes. Three ways to improve your word choice are by avoiding slang, clichés, and wordiness.

SLANG

We often use *slang* expressions when we talk because they are so vivid and colourful. However, slang is usually out of place in formal writing. Here are some examples of slang expressions:

Someone *ripped off* Ken's new Nike running shoes from his locker.
After the game, we *pigged out* at the restaurant.
Kwame is an *ace* reporter.
The movie really *grossed me out*.

Slang expressions have a number of drawbacks. They go out of date quickly, they become tiresome if used excessively in writing, and they may not communicate clearly to all readers. Also, the use of slang can be an evasion of the specific details that are often needed to make one's meaning clear in writing. For example, in "The movie really grossed me out," the writer has not provided the specific details about the movie necessary for us to clearly understand the statement. Was it the acting, the special effects, or the violent scenes in the movie that the writer found so disgusting? In general, then, you should avoid the use of slang in your writing. If you are in doubt about whether an expression is slang, it may help to check a recently published dictionary.

● ● ● ● ● **ACTIVITY**

Rewrite the following sentences, replacing the italicized slang words with more formal ones.

Example When we told the neighbours to *can the noise,* they *freaked out.*
When we told the neighbours to be quiet, they were upset.

1. When my computer *crashed,* I tried to *keep my cool.*
2. After an *all-nighter,* I fell asleep during the exam.
3. The police chief brought two *big guns* to the press conference.
4. Alex and his friends *chowed down* at the *chintzy* restaurant.

CLICHÉS

A *cliché* is an expression that has been worn out through constant use. Some typical clichés include the following:

short but sweet	last but not least
drop in the bucket	work like a dog
had a hard time of it	all work and no play
word to the wise	it goes without saying
it dawned on me	at a loss for words
sigh of relief	taking a big chance
too little, too late	took a turn for the worse
singing the blues	easier said than done
in the nick of time	on top of the world
too close for comfort	time and time again
saw the light	make ends meet

Clichés are common in speech but make your writing seem tired and stale. Also, they are often an evasion of the specific details that you must provide in your writing. Avoid clichés and try to express your meaning in fresh, original ways.

● ● ● ● ● **ACTIVITY 1**

Underline the cliché in each of the following sentences. Then, substitute specific, fresh words for the trite expression.

Example My boyfriend has stuck with me through thick and thin, through good times and bad times.
My boyfriend has stuck with me through difficult times and all sorts of problems.

1. When all is said and done, more doctors are needed in small cities through-out Canada.

2. When I realized I'd lost my textbook, I knew I was up the creek without a paddle.

3. My suggestion is just a shot in the dark, but it's better than nothing.

4. Nadine got more than she bargained for when she offered to help Larry with his essay.

5. Jacques is pushing his luck by driving a car with bald tires.

6. On a hot, sticky, midsummer day, iced tea or any frosty drink really hits the spot.

7. Lysa, a confident public speaker, was at a loss for words when she was introduced to the Queen of England.

8. Even when we are up to our eyeballs in work, our boss wonders if we have enough to do.

● ● ● ● ACTIVITY 2

Write a short paragraph, describing the kind of day you had. Try to put as many clichés as possible into your writing. For example, "I got up at the crack of dawn, ready to take on the world. I grabbed a bite to eat. . . ." By making yourself aware of clichés in this way, you will lessen the chance that they will appear in your writing.

WORDINESS

Eliminating unnecessary wordiness in your writing results in clear and efficient writing. Avoid the temptation to impress your reader; instead, please your reader by being brief. As much as possible, try to choose simple, one-word substitutes over longer, redundant phrases:

Why say this . . .	When you mean this . . .
A large number of	Many
I personally think	I think
Due to the fact that	Because
In actual fact	In fact
Few and far between	Rare

● ● ● ● ACTIVITY

Underline the wordy phrases in each of the following sentences. Then revise these sentences to make them as concise as possible without losing their meaning.

Example   In my personal opinion, I feel that my essay contains many important ideas and topics that the reader will find very interesting and original.
My essay contains important, interesting, and original ideas for the reader.

1. The meeting began in the morning at 8 a.m. sharp.

2. It has come to my attention that the final conclusion of the novel has yet to be determined.

3. Due to the fact that the winters are so very cold in Canada, many people travel south during the winter months.

4. I personally think that in this day and age new innovations in technology are the way of the future.

5. At the present time, most consumers prefer to buy cars that are black in colour and sleek in appearance.

● ● ● ● **REVIEW TEST**

Certain words are italicized in the following sentences. In the space provided, identify the words as slang *(S)*, cliché *(C)*, or wordy *(W)*. Then replace the words with more effective word choices.

_____ 1. Losing weight is *easier said than done* for someone with a sweet tooth.

_____ 2. *In my view, I feel that* abortion should be outlawed.

_____ 3. Jennifer is so stubborn that talking to her is like *talking to a brick wall.*

_____ 4. Michelle was *blown away* by the Cirque du Soleil show.

_____ 5. The fans, *all fired up* after the game, *peeled out* of the parking lot and honked their horns.

_____ 6. The dress Mary wore was *green in colour* and *a long length.*

_____ 7. That *dude* isn't really a criminal; he's just gotten a *bum rap.*

_____ 8. I failed the test *for the reason that* I was unprepared.

Introduction to the Readings

The reading selections in Part 5 will help you find topics for writing. Each selection deals in some way with interesting, often thought-provoking concerns or experiences of contemporary life. One selection, for example, forces readers to consider poverty at close range, while another explores the burgeoning issue of water privatization and asks if access to water should be a right or a privilege. The varied subjects should inspire lively class discussions as well as serious individual thought. The selections should also provide a continuing source of high-interest material for a wide range of writing assignments.

The selections serve another purpose as well. They will help develop reading skills, which are of direct benefit to you as a writer. Through close reading, you will learn how to recognize the thesis in a selection and to identify and evaluate the supporting material that develops the thesis. In your own writing, you will aim to achieve the same essential structure: an overall thesis with detailed and valid support for that thesis. Close reading will also help you to thoroughly explore a selection and its content. The more you understand what is said in a piece, the more ideas and feelings you may have about writing on an assigned topic or a related topic of your own. A third benefit of close reading is that you will become more aware of authors' stylistic devices—their introductions and conclusions, their ways of presenting and developing a point, their use of transitions, and their choice of language to achieve a particular tone. Recognizing these devices in other people's writing will help you increase your own range of writing techniques.

THE FORMAT OF EACH SELECTION

Each selection begins with a short overview that gives helpful background information and stimulates interest in the piece. The selection is followed by two sets of questions.

- First, there are reading comprehension questions to help you measure your understanding of the material. These questions involve several important reading skills: understanding vocabulary in context, recognizing a subject or topic, determining the thesis or main idea, identifying key supporting points, and making inferences. Answering the questions will enable you and your instructor to quickly check your basic understanding of a selection. More significantly, as you move from one selection to the next, you will sharpen your reading skills as well as your thinking skills—two key factors in making you a better writer.

- Following the comprehension questions are at least seven discussion questions. In addition to dealing with issues of content, these questions focus on matters of structure, style, and tone.

Finally, several writing assignments accompany each selection. The assignments range from narratives to expository and persuasive essays about issues in the world at large. Many assignments provide detailed guidelines on how to proceed, including suggestions for prewriting and appropriate methods of development. When writing your essay responses to the readings, you will have opportunities to apply all the methods of development presented in Part 2 of this book.

HOW TO READ WELL: FOUR GENERAL STEPS

Skillful reading is an important part of becoming a skilful writer. Following is a series of steps that will make you a better reader—of the selections here and in all your own reading.

1. Concentrate as You Read

To improve your concentration, follow these tips:

- First, read in a place where you can be quiet and alone. Don't choose a spot where there is a TV or stereo on or where friends or family are talking nearby. Turn off your MP3 player and take out your earplugs.

- Next, sit in an upright position when you read. If your body is in a completely relaxed position, sprawled across a bed or nestled in an easy chair, your mind is also going to be completely relaxed. The light muscular tension that comes from sitting in an upright chair promotes concentration and keeps your mind ready to work.

- Third, consider using your index finger (or a pen) as a pacer while you read. Lightly underline each line of print with your index finger as you read down a page. Hold your hand slightly above the page, and move your finger at a speed that is a little too fast for comfort. This pacing with your index finger, like sitting upright on a chair, creates a slight physical tension that will keep your body and mind focused and alert.

2. Skim Material before You Read It

In skimming, you spend about two minutes rapidly surveying a selection, looking for important points, and skipping secondary material. Follow this sequence when skimming:

- Begin by reading the overview that precedes the selection.
- Then, study the title of the selection for a few moments. A good title is the shortest possible summary of a selection; it often tells you in a few words—or even a single word—what a selection is about. For example, the title "Shame" suggests that you're going to read about a deeply embarrassing condition or incident in a person's life.
- Next, form a basic question (or questions) out of the title. For instance, for the selection titled "Shame," you might ask, "What exactly is the shame?" "What caused the shame?" "What is the result of the shame?" Forming questions from a title is often a key to locating a writer's thesis, your next concern in skimming.
- Read the first and last couple of paragraphs in the selection. Very often a writer's thesis, *if* it is directly stated, will appear in one of these places and will relate to the title.
- Finally, look quickly at the rest of the selection for other clues to important points. Are there any subheadings that you can relate to the title in some way? Are there any words the author has decided to emphasize by setting them off in *italic* or **boldface** type? Are there any major lists of items signalled by words such as *first, second, also,* and *another?*

3. Read the Selection Straight Through with Pen in Hand

Read the selection without slowing down or turning back; just aim to understand as much as you can the first time through. Place a check or star beside answers to basic questions you formed from the title and beside other ideas that seem important. Number them as *1, 2, 3* . . . List important points. Circle words you don't understand. Put question marks in the margin next to passages that are unclear and that you will want to reread.

4. Work with the Material

Go back and reread passages that were not clear the first time through. Look up words that block your understanding of ideas, and write their meanings in the margin. Also, reread carefully the areas you identified as most important; doing so will enlarge your understanding of the material. Once you have a sense of the whole, prepare a short written outline of the selection by answering the following questions:

- What is the thesis?
- What key points support the thesis?
- What seem to be other important ideas in the selection?

By working with the material in this way, you will significantly increase your understanding of a selection. Effective reading, just like effective writing, does not happen all at once; it must be worked on. Often, you begin with a general impression of what something means, and then, by working at it, move to a deeper level of understanding of the material.

HOW TO ANSWER THE COMPREHENSION QUESTIONS: SPECIFIC HINTS

Several important reading skills are involved in the reading comprehension questions that follow each selection. These skills include the following:

- Understanding vocabulary in context
- Summarizing the selection in a title
- Determining the main idea
- Recognizing key supporting details
- Making inferences

The hints below will help you apply each of these reading skills:

- *Vocabulary in context* To decide on the meaning of an unfamiliar word, consider its context. Ask yourself whether there are any clues in the sentence that suggest what the word means.
- *Subject or title* Remember that the title should accurately describe the entire selection. It should be neither too broad nor too narrow. It should answer the question, "What is this about?" as specifically as possible. Note that you may, at times, find it easier to answer the title question *after* the main-idea question.
- *Main idea* Choose the statement that you think best expresses the main idea—also known as the *main point* or *thesis*—of the entire selection. Remember that the title will often help you focus on the main idea. Then, ask yourself the question, "Does most of the material in the selection support this statement?" If you can answer yes to this question, you have found the thesis.
- *Key details* If you were asked to give a two-minute summary of a selection, the key details are the ones you would include in that summary. To determine the key details, ask yourself the question, "What are the major supporting points for the thesis?"
- *Inferences* Answer these questions by drawing upon the evidence presented in the selection and your own common sense. Ask yourself, "What reasonable judgments can I make on the basis of the information in the selection?"

See the Online Learning Centre for a chart on which you can keep track of your performance as you answer the questions for each selection. The chart will help you identify which reading skills you may need to strengthen.

Looking Inward

SHAME

Dick Gregory

In this selection, Dick Gregory—the comedian and social critic—narrates two painful experiences from his boyhood. Although the incidents show graphically what it can be like to grow up black and poor, the essay also deals with universal emotions: shame, embarrassment, and the burning desire to hold onto one's self-respect.

1   I never learned hate at home, or shame. I had to go to school for that. I was about seven years old when I got my first big lesson. I was in love with a little girl named Helene Tucker, a light-complected little girl with pigtails and nice manners. She was always clean and she was smart in school. I think I went to school then mostly to look at her. I brushed my hair and even got me a little old handkerchief. It was a lady's handkerchief, but I didn't want Helene to see me wipe my nose on my hand. The pipes were frozen again, there was no water in the house, but I washed my socks and shirt every night. I'd get a pot, and go over to Mister Ben's grocery store, and stick my pot down into his soda machine. Scoop out some chopped ice. By evening the ice melted to water for washing. I got sick a lot that winter because the fire would go out at night before the clothes were dry. In the morning I'd put them on, wet or dry, because they were the only clothes I had.

2   Everybody's got a Helene Tucker, a symbol of everything you want. I loved her for her goodness, her cleanness, her popularity. She'd walk down my street and my brothers and sisters would yell, "Here comes Helene," and I'd rub my tennis sneakers on the back of my pants and wish my hair wasn't so nappy and the white folks' shirt fit me better. I'd run out on the street. If I knew my place and didn't come too close, she'd wink at me and say hello. That was a good feeling. Sometimes I'd follow her all the way home, and shovel the snow off her walk and try to make friends with her Momma and her aunts. I'd drop money on her stoop late at night on my way back from shining shoes in the taverns. And she had a daddy, and he had a good job. He was a paper hanger.

3   I guess I would have gotten over Helene by summertime, but something happened in that classroom that made her face hang in front of me for the next twenty-two years. When I played the drums in high school it was for Helene and when I broke track records in college it was for Helene and when I started standing behind microphones and heard applause I wished Helene could hear it, too. It wasn't until I was twenty-nine years old and married and making money that I finally got her out of my system. Helene was sitting in that classroom when I learned to be ashamed of myself.

4   It was on a Thursday. I was sitting in the back of the room, in a seat with a chalk circle drawn around it. The idiot's seat, the troublemaker's seat.

5   The teacher thought I was stupid. Couldn't spell, couldn't read, couldn't do arithmetic. Just stupid. Teachers were never interested in finding out that you couldn't concentrate because you were so hungry, because you hadn't had any breakfast. All you could think about was noontime, would it ever come? Maybe you could sneak into the cloakroom and steal a bite of some kid's lunch out of a coat pocket. A bite of something. Paste. You can't really make a meal of paste, or put it on bread for a sandwich, but sometimes I'd scoop a few spoonfuls out of the big paste jar in the back of the room. Pregnant people get strange tastes. I was pregnant with poverty. Pregnant with dirt and pregnant with smells that made people turn away, pregnant with cold and pregnant with shoes that were never bought for me, pregnant with five other people in my bed and no daddy in the next room, and pregnant with hunger. Paste doesn't taste too bad when you're hungry.

6   The teacher thought I was a troublemaker. All she saw from the front of the room was a little black boy who squirmed in his idiot's seat and made noises and poked the kids around him. I guess she couldn't see a kid who made noises because he wanted someone to know he was there.

7   It was on a Thursday, the day before the negro payday. The eagle always flew on Friday. The teacher was asking each student how much his father would give to the Community Chest. On Friday night, each kid would get the money from his father, and on Monday he would bring it to the school. I decided I was going to buy a daddy right then. I had money in my pocket from shining shoes and selling papers, and whatever Helene Tucker pledged for her daddy I was going to top it. And I'd hand the money right in. I wasn't going to wait until Monday to buy me a daddy.

8   I was shaking, scared to death. The teacher opened her book and started calling out names alphabetically.

9   "Helene Tucker?"

10   "My daddy said he'd give two dollars and fifty cents."

11   "That's very nice, Helene. Very, very nice indeed."

12   That made me feel pretty good. It wouldn't take too much to top that. I had almost three dollars in dimes and quarters in my pocket. I stuck my hand in my

pocket and held onto the money, waiting for her to call my name. But the teacher closed her book after she called everybody else in the class.

13   I stood up and raised my hand.

14   "What is it now?"

15   "You forgot me?"

16   She turned toward the blackboard. "I don't have time to be playing with you, Richard."

17   "My daddy said he'd . . ."

18   "Sit down, Richard, you're disturbing the class."

19   "My daddy said he'd give . . . fifteen dollars."

20   She turned around and looked mad. "We are collecting this money for you and your kind, Richard Gregory. If your daddy can give fifteen dollars you have no business being on relief."

21   "I got it right now, I got it right now, my daddy gave it to me to turn in today, my daddy said . . ."

22   "And furthermore," she said, looking right at me, her nostrils getting big and her lips getting thin and her eyes opening wide, "We know you don't have a daddy."

23   Helene Tucker turned around, her eyes full of tears. She felt sorry for me. Then I couldn't see her too well because I was crying, too.

24   "Sit down, Richard."

25   And I always thought the teacher kind of liked me. She always picked me to wash the blackboard on Friday, after school. That was a big thrill, it made me feel important. If I didn't wash it, come Monday the school might not function right.

26   "Where are you going, Richard!"

27   I walked out of school that day, and for a long time I didn't go back very often. There was shame there.

28   Now there was shame everywhere. It seemed like the whole world had been inside that classroom, everyone had heard what the teacher had said, everyone had turned around and felt sorry for me. There was shame in going to the Worthy Boys Annual Christmas Dinner for you and your kind, because everybody knew what a worthy boy was. Why couldn't they just call it the Boys Annual dinner, why'd they have to give it a name? There was shame in wearing the brown and orange and white plaid mackinaw the welfare gave to three thousand boys. Why'd it have to be the same for everybody so when you walked down the street the people could see you were on relief? It was a nice warm mackinaw and it had a hood, and my Momma beat me and called me a little rat when she found out I stuffed it in the bottom of a pail full of garbage way over on Cottage Street. There was shame in running over to Mister Ben's at the end of the day and asking for his rotten peaches, there was shame in asking Mrs. Simmons for a spoonful of sugar, there was shame in running out to meet the relief truck. I hated that truck, full of food for you and your kind. I ran into the house and hid when it came. And then I started to sneak through alleys, to take the long way home so the people going into White's Eat Shop wouldn't see me. Yeah, the whole world heard the teacher that day, we all know you don't have a daddy.

29   It lasted for a while, this kind of numbness. I spent a lot of time feeling sorry for myself. And then one day I met this wino in a restaurant. I'd been out hustling all day, shining shoes, selling newspapers, and I had googobs of money in my pocket. Bought me a bowl of chili for fifteen cents, and a cheeseburger for fifteen cents, and a Pepsi for five cents, and a piece of chocolate cake for ten cents. That was a good

meal. I was eating when this old wino came in. I love winos because they never hurt anyone but themselves.

30   The old wino sat down at the counter and ordered twenty-six cents worth of food. He ate it like he really enjoyed it. When the owner, Mister Williams, asked him to pay the check, the old wino didn't lie or go through his pocket like he suddenly found a hole.

31   He just said: "Don't have no money."

32   The owner yelled: "Why in hell you come in here and eat my food if you don't have no money? That food cost me money."

33   Mister Williams jumped over the counter and knocked the wino off his stool and beat him over the head with a pop bottle. Then he stepped back and watched the wino bleed. Then he kicked him. And he kicked him again.

34   I looked at the wino with blood all over his face and I went over. "Leave him alone, Mister Williams. I'll pay the twenty-six cents."

35   The wino got up, slowly, pulling himself up to the stool, then up to the counter, holding on for a minute until his legs stopped shaking so bad. He looked at me with pure hate. "Keep your twenty-six cents. You don't have to pay, not now. I just finished paying for it."

36   He started to walk out, and as he passed me, he reached down and touched my shoulder. "Thanks, sonny, but it's too late now. Why didn't you pay it before?"

37   I was pretty sick about that. I waited too long to help another man.

■ Reading Comprehension Questions

1. The word *pregnant* in "pregnant with poverty" (paragraph 5) means
   a. full.
   b. empty.
   c. sick.
   d. satisfied.

2. The word *hustling* in "I'd been out hustling all day" (paragraph 29) means
   a. learning.
   b. stealing.
   c. making friends.
   d. working hard.

3. Which of the following would be a good alternative title for this selection?
   a. Helene Tucker
   b. The Pain of Being Poor
   c. Losing a Father
   d. Mr. Williams and The Wino

4. Which sentence best expresses the main idea of the selection?
   a. Richard felt that being poor was humiliating.
   b. Richard liked Helene Tucker very much.
   c. Richard had to work hard as a child.
   d. The wino refused Richard's money.

5. The teacher disliked Richard because he
   a. was dirty.
   b. liked Helene.

      c. was a troublemaker.

      d. ate paste.

6. *True or false?* Helene Tucker felt sorry for Richard when the teacher embarrassed him.

7. Richard's problems in school were due to his being
    a. hungry.
    b. distracted by Helene.
    c. lonely.
    d. unable to read.

8. The author implies that Richard
    a. was not intelligent.
    b. was proud.
    c. had many friends.
    d. and Helene became friends.

9. The author implies that
    a. Mr. Williams felt sorry for the wino.
    b. Richard's teacher was insensitive.
    c. Richard liked people to feel sorry for him.
    d. Richard's father was dead.

10. The author implies that
    a. the mackinaws were poorly made.
    b. Helene was a sensitive girl.
    c. Helene disliked Richard.
    d. the wino was ashamed of his poverty.

■ Discussion Questions

About Content

1. How might Dick Gregory's teacher have handled the Community Chest incident without making him feel ashamed?
2. What are some of the lessons Gregory learns from the incident involving the wino at the restaurant?
3. Where in "Shame" do we find evidence that Dick Gregory finally does escape from poverty?

About Structure

4. Since Dick Gregory is actually writing about an embarrassing incident in school, why does he devote his first three paragraphs to his feelings about Helene Tucker?
5. What is the connection between the incident involving the wino at the restaurant and the rest of the story?

About Style and Tone

6. In the paragraph beginning, "Now there was shame everywhere," Gregory uses a device called *repetition* when he begins several sentences with the words "There was shame . . . ." What is the effect of this repetition?
7. Why does Gregory use dialogue when he narrates the incidents in the classroom and in the restaurant?

■ Writing Assignments

Assignment 1

Dick Gregory tells us in "Shame" that he was ashamed of his poverty and of being on welfare—to the point that he threw away the warm-hooded mackinaw he had been given simply because it was obvious proof that he and his family were on welfare. Do you think Gregory was justified in feeling so ashamed of his situation? Are other people who are on welfare justified if they feel ashamed? Choose either of the following thesis statements, and develop it in an essay of several paragraphs.

> People on welfare are justified in feeling ashamed.
> People on welfare should not feel ashamed.

Begin by thinking of several reasons to support the statement you have chosen. You might consider any of the following:

- Availability of jobs
- Education or lack of education
- Number of young children at home requiring care
- Illness, physical disability
- Psychological factors (depression, work habits, expectations, mental illness)
- Society's attitude toward people on welfare

Assignment 2

Many people have endured a hurtful or demeaning experience like Dick Gregory's in "Shame," whether it was an event in a classroom, with a group of friends or peers, or in a family situation. Whatever that experience, it is usually embarrassing but educational—it stings, but it teaches.

Write an essay that turns shame or hurt inside out: this essay could be called "The Power of Pain," or something similar. This is an effects essay written in the third-person point of view, for a self-help group, which explains the positive effects or growth that resulted from a shameful or hurtful instance.

Assignment 3

Write an essay about three basic things that people must have in order to feel self-respect. In your thesis statement, name these three necessities, and state that a person must possess them in order to feel self-respect. You could consider any of the following ideas:

- A certain number of material possessions
- A job
- A loving family or a special person
- A clear conscience
- A feeling of belonging
- Freedom from addictions

In your supporting paragraphs, discuss the factors you have chosen, showing specifically why each is so important. In order to avoid falling into the trap of writing generalities, you may want to give examples of people who lack these necessities and show how such people lose self-respect. Your examples may be drawn from personal experience, or they may be hypothetical examples.

MY BODY IS MY OWN BUSINESS

Naheed Mustafa

On many streets in Canada today, women and girls from African and Near or Far Eastern nations wear the traditional long robes of Muslim female dress and the hijab, or head covering, as well. Those accustomed to the feminist thought of the last thirty years see such dress as symbolic of male oppression in Islamic cultures, but Naheed Mustafa presents an opposing argument. Mustafa, educated at the University of Toronto and Ryerson University, is a journalist in her native Pakistan, who chooses to wear the hijab for reasons that are at odds with stereotypes of Muslim belief and behaviour.

1   I often wonder whether people see me as a radical, fundamentalist Muslim terrorist packing an AK-47 assault rifle inside my jean jacket. Or maybe they see me as the poster girl for oppressed womanhood everywhere. I'm not sure which it is.

2   I get the whole gamut of strange looks, stares and covert glances. You see, I wear the *hijab*, a scarf that covers my head, neck and throat. I do this because I am a Muslim woman who believes her body is her own private concern.

3   Young Muslim women are reclaiming the *hijab*, reinterpreting it in light of its original purpose—to give back to women ultimate control of their own bodies.

4   The Koran teaches us that men and women are equal, that individuals should not be judged according to gender, beauty, wealth or privilege. The only thing that makes one person better than another is her or his character.

5   Nonetheless, people have a difficult time relating to me. After all, I'm young, Canadian born and raised, university-educated—why would I do this to myself, they ask.

6   Strangers speak to me in loud, slow English and often appear to be playing charades. They politely inquire how I like living in Canada and whether or not the cold bothers me. If I'm in the right mood, it can be very amusing.

7   But why would I, a woman with all the advantages of a North American upbringing, suddenly, at 21, want to cover myself so that with the *hijab* and the other clothes I choose to wear, only my face and hands show?

8   Because it gives me freedom.

9   Women are taught from early childhood that their worth is proportional to their attractiveness. We feel compelled to pursue abstract notions of beauty, half realizing that such a pursuit is futile.

10   When women reject this form of oppression, they face ridicule and contempt. Whether it's women who refuse to wear makeup or to shave their legs or to expose their bodies, society, both men and women, have trouble dealing with them.

11   In the western world, the *hijab* has come to symbolize either forced silence or radical, unconscionable militancy. Actually, it's neither. It is simply a woman's assertion that judgment of her physical person is to play no role whatsoever in social interaction.

12   Wearing the *hijab* has given me freedom from constant attention to my physical self. Because my appearance is not subjected to public scrutiny, my beauty, or perhaps lack of it, has been removed from the realm of what can legitimately be discussed.

13   No one knows whether my hair looks as if I just stepped out of a salon, whether or not I can pinch an inch, or even if I have unsightly stretch marks. And because no one knows, no one cares.

14   Feeling that one has to meet the impossible male standards of beauty is tiring and often humiliating. I should know, I spent my entire teenage years trying to do it. I was a borderline bulimic and spent a lot of money I didn't have on potions and lotions in hopes of becoming the next Cindy Crawford.

15   The definition of beauty is ever-changing; waifish is good, waifish is bad, athletic is good—sorry, athletic is bad. Narrow hips? Great. Narrow hips? Too bad.

16   Women are not going to achieve equality with the right to bare breasts in public, as some people would like to have you believe. That would only make us party to our own objectification. True equality will be had only when women don't need to display themselves to get attention and won't need to defend their decision to keep their bodies to themselves.

■ Reading Comprehension Questions

1. The word *unconscionable* in "radical, unconscionable militancy" (paragraph 11) means
   a. unbelievable.
   b. unsuitable.
   c. unmanageable.
   d. unthinkable.

2. The word *waifish* in "waifish is good, waifish is bad, athletic is good" (paragraph 15) means
   a. womanly, robust in appearance.
   b. curvaceous, shapely.
   c. sickly.
   d. skinny, neglected-looking.

3. Which of the following would be a good alternative title for this selection?
   a. The Mysterious Eastern Woman
   b. Eastern Privacy and Western Prejudice
   c. Habits and Headgear
   d. My Culture and My Choice of Clothing

4. Which sentence best expresses the main idea of the selection?
   a. Muslim women have the right to dress as they wish.
   b. Women should wear clothing that disguises their bodies to avoid harassment.
   c. Women will be truly free when their appearance is no longer of primary importance.
   d. Every woman has the right to privacy of her person.

5. People don't know what to make of Naheed Mustafa because
   a. she chooses to dress in an outlandish Eastern way.
   b. the *hijab* symbolizes stereotypes of women as victims or Islamic terrorists.
   c. her clothing disguises her true identity.
   d. she is hiding her identity as an educated Canadian under an ethnic costume.

6. *True or false?* Only men have trouble dealing with women who no longer pursue media-dictated ideals of grooming and beauty.

7. The Koran's teaching about the sexes states
   a. that women unintentionally represent temptation to men.
   b. that men and women are judged by their actions.

    c. that no one should be judged by external factors.

    d. that both sexes have the right to privacy.

8. The author implies that

    a. people see her as a militant feminist.

    b. people find stereotyping easier than looking beyond appearances.

    c. people don't want to know her.

    d. her Canadian upbringing and education are disadvantages.

9. The author implies that

    a. women can achieve a degree of personal freedom by clothing choices.

    b. Western women are slow to catch up with Muslim wisdom about dress.

    c. women will never understand what beauty is all about.

    d. women everywhere are totally obsessed by impossible ideas of beauty.

10. Wearing the *hijab* has given the author

    a. a decent anti-fashion statement appropriate to her religion.

    b. a sense of being able to be whoever she truly is by her own standards.

    c. a place to hide from men's expectations of her.

    d. an exotic refuge from the everyday world of Canadian society.

■ Discussion Questions

About Content

1. How does the author feel that people on the street see her? Why does the author feel that way?

2. What are the practical advantages of wearing the *hijab?* What are the ideological reasons for Mustafa's adoption of the garments?

3. What does the author suggest is the basic problem with beauty?

About Structure

4. The clearest statement of the author's thesis is in the last third of the essay. Find the statement and write it down.

5. What is the "change of direction" word in paragraph 11?

About Style and Tone

6. What is your perception of Naheed Mustafa when you read such statements as, "I was a borderline bulimic" who "spent a lot of money I didn't have . . . in hopes of becoming the next Cindy Crawford" and "waifish is good, waifish is bad . . ."?

7. We describe subjects by saying what they are not as well as by saying what they are. In what terms does the author set up her reasons for believing the *hijab* is an ideal form of clothing for her?

8. The author begins her essay with an exaggerated description of one stereotyped image and confesses her defeat at trying to become another stereotyped ideal. Do the examples in the essay give you a clear picture of the "real" person?

■ Writing Assignments

Assignment 1

Naheed Mustafa writes about a personal decision to wear certain clothing, which defines her in one way to observers but means something very different to her as wearer. Our clothing choices *do,* in some ways, define us and communicate information about us to others. The message sent out may not always be the one we intend to communicate. Think about the clothes and accessories you wear to class every day. What is the result of your choice(s) among those who observe you? What do certain garments and jewellery "say" about you, to yourself and to others? Do these messages occasionally conflict?

Write an article for your campus newspaper, defending some choice of personal attire or decoration that may be misinterpreted by others. You could discuss something like a baseball cap, a pierced nostril, a garment representing your ethnic background, or even a certain type of makeup. Use the third-person voice and the cause-effect method of organization to develop your article.

Assignment 2

The image of beauty in any society is constantly changing and subject to the whims of advertising. Nearly our entire consumer economy is based on selling various products to us that will make us more like someone else's ideal of what a beautiful, strong, healthy, or even "good" person is. Should any of us, men or women, model ourselves on TV and magazine concepts of what is attractive?

Write an essay involving one of the following sentences as the basis for your thesis statement, and argue for its validity from your own experience and knowledge.

People are losing their ability to decide what they should look like because of ads showing mostly famished female and six-packed male models.

Ideals of male and female beauty have always evolved from people's dreams and wishes, and portray people's desires to be the best they can be.

Fitness and beauty are not sins.

Assignment 3

What stereotypes, based on aspects of appearance or behaviour, do we carry around with us of various national and cultural groups? Are there any points of truth in these stereotypes? Do such preconceived notions blind us to the characters of people inside the clothing or behind the counter at the store? Think about a specific stereotype based on appearance or on behaviour patterns.

Discuss, in an examples essay, your own reaction to this stereotype. Has your reaction changed as a result of knowing individuals who broke down this stereotype, or is your attitude unchanged?

LAMB TO THE SLAUGHTER

Roald Dahl

In typical Roald Dahl form, this story weaves cleverly through the thoughts and actions of a detective's wife who has just heard some unexpected news. You may find yourself being sympathetic to her situation, but when the police arrive, there may be cause for suspicion. The author paints the setting with masterfully simple words, and allows the reader authentic access into the mind of the protagonist. Despite the dark events, there is much to enjoy about this well-spun tale.

1   The room was warm and clean, the curtains drawn, the two table lamps alight—hers and the one by the empty chair opposite. On the sideboard behind her, two tall glasses, soda water, whiskey. Fresh ice cubes in the Thermos bucket.

2   Mary Maloney was waiting for her husband to come home from work.

3   Now and again she would glance up at the clock, but without anxiety, merely to please herself with the thought that each minute gone by made it nearer the time when he would come. There was a slow smiling air about her, and about everything she did. The drop of a head as she bent over her sewing was curiously tranquil. Her skin—for this was her sixth month with child—had acquired a wonderful translucent quality, the mouth was soft, and the eyes, with their new placid look, seemed larger, darker than before. When the clock said ten minutes to five, she began to listen, and a few moments later, punctually as always, she heard the tires on the gravel outside, and the car door slamming, the footsteps passing the window, the key turning in the lock. She laid aside her sewing, stood up, and went forward to kiss him as he came in.

4   "Hullo darling," she said.

5   "Hullo," he answered.

6   She took his coat and hung it in the closet. Then she walked over and made the drinks, a strongish one for him, a weak one for herself; and soon she was back again in her chair with the sewing, and he in the other, opposite, holding the tall glass with both hands, rocking it so the ice cubes tinkled against the side.

7   For her, this was always a blissful time of day. She knew he didn't want to speak much until the first drink was finished, and she, on her side, was content to sit quietly, enjoying his company after the long hours alone in the house. She loved to luxuriate in the presence of this man, and to feel—almost as a sunbather feels the sun—that warm male glow that came out of him to her when they were alone together. She loved him for the way he sat loosely in a chair, for the way he came in a door, or moved slowly across the room with long strides. She loved the intent, far look in his eyes when they rested on her, the funny shape of the mouth, and especially the way he remained silent about his tiredness, sitting still with himself until the whiskey had taken some of it away.

8   "Tired darling?"

9   "Yes," he said. "I'm tired." And as he spoke, he did an unusual thing. He lifted his glass and drained it in one swallow although there was still half of it, at least half of it left. She wasn't really watching him, but she knew what he had done because she heard the ice cubes falling back against the bottom of the empty glass when he lowered his arm. He paused a moment, leaning forward in the chair, then he got up and went slowly over to fetch himself another.

10   "I'll get it!" she cried, jumping up.

11   "Sit down," he said.

12   When he came back, she noticed that the new drink was dark amber with the quantity of whiskey in it.

13   "Darling, shall I get your slippers?"

14   "No."

15   She watched him as he began to sip the dark yellow drink, and she could see little oily swirls in the liquid because it was so strong.

16   "I think it's a shame," she said, "that when a policeman gets to be as senior as you, they keep him walking about on his feet all day long."

17   He didn't answer, so she bent her head again and went on with her sewing; but each time he lifted the drink to his lips, she heard the ice cubes clinking against the side of the glass.

18   "Darling," she said. "Would you like me to get you some cheese? I haven't made any supper because it's Thursday."

19   "No," he said.

20   "If you're too tired to eat out," she went on, "it's still not too late. There's plenty of meat and stuff in the freezer, and you can have it right here and not even move out of the chair."

21   Her eyes waited on him for an answer, a smile, a little nod, but he made no sign.

22   "Anyway," she went on, "I'll get you some cheese and crackers first."

23   "I don't want it," he said.

24   She moved uneasily in her chair, the large eyes still watching his face. "But you must eat! I'll fix it anyway, and then you can have it or not, as you like."

25   She stood up and placed her sewing on the table by the lamp.

26   "Sit down," he said. "Just for a minute, sit down."

27   It wasn't till then that she began to get frightened.

28   "Go on," he said. "Sit down."

29   She lowered herself back slowly into the chair, watching him all the time with those large, bewildered eyes. He had finished the second drink and was staring down into the glass, frowning.

30   "Listen," he said. "I've got something to tell you."

31   "What is it, darling? What's the matter?"

32   He had now become absolutely motionless, and he kept his head down so that the light from the lamp beside him fell across the upper part of his face, leaving the chin and mouth in shadow. She noticed there was a little muscle moving near the corner of his left eye.

33   "This is going to be a bit of a shock to you, I'm afraid," he said. "But I've thought about it a good deal and I've decided the only thing to do is tell you right away. I hope you won't blame me too much."

34   And he told her. It didn't take long, four or five minutes at most, and she sat very still through it all, watching him with a kind of dazed horror as he went further and further away from her with each word.

35   "So there it is," he added. "And I know it's kind of a bad time to be telling you, but there simply wasn't any other way. Of course I'll give you money and see you're looked after. But there needn't really be any fuss. I hope not anyway. It wouldn't be very good for my job."

36   Her first instinct was not to believe any of it, to reject it all. It occurred to her that perhaps he hadn't even spoken, that she herself had imagined the whole thing. Maybe, if she went about her business and acted as though she hadn't been listening, then later, when she sort of woke up again, she might find none of it had ever happened.

37   "I'll get the supper," she managed to whisper, and this time he didn't stop her.

38   When she walked across the room she couldn't feel her feet touching the floor. She couldn't feel anything at all—except a slight nausea and a desire to vomit. Everything was automatic now—down the steps to the cellar, the light switch, the deep freeze, the hand inside the cabinet taking hold of the first object it met. She lifted it out, and looked at it. It was wrapped in paper, so she took off the paper and looked at it again.

39   A leg of lamb.

40   All right then, they would have lamb for supper. She carried it upstairs, holding the thin bone-end of it with both her hands, and as she went through the living-room, she saw him standing over by the window with his back to her, and she stopped.

41   "For God's sake," he said, hearing her, but not turning round. "Don't make supper for me. I'm going out."

42   At that point, Mary Maloney simply walked up behind him and without any pause she swung the big frozen leg of lamb high in the air and brought it down as hard as she could on the back of his head.

43   She might just as well have hit him with a steel club.

44   She stepped back a pace, waiting, and the funny thing was that he remained standing there for at least four or five seconds, gently swaying. Then he crashed to the carpet.

45   The violence of the crash, the noise, the small table overturning, helped bring her out of the shock. She came out slowly, feeling cold and surprised, and she stood for a while blinking at the body, still holding the ridiculous piece of meat tight with both hands.

46   All right, she told herself. So I've killed him.

47   It was extraordinary, now, how clear her mind became all of a sudden. She began thinking very fast. As the wife of a detective, she knew quite well what the penalty would be. That was fine. It made no difference to her. In fact, it would be a relief. On the other hand, what about the child? What were the laws about murderers with unborn children? Did they kill them both—mother and child? Or did they wait until the tenth month? What did they do?

48   Mary Maloney didn't know. And she certainly wasn't prepared to take a chance.

49   She carried the meat into the kitchen, placed it in a pan, turned the oven on high, and shoved it inside. Then she washed her hands and ran upstairs to the bedroom. She sat down before the mirror, tidied her hair, touched up her lips and face. She tried a smile. It came out rather peculiar. She tried again.

50   "Hullo Sam," she said brightly, aloud.

51   The voice sounded peculiar too.

52   "I want some potatoes please, Sam. Yes, and I think a can of peas."

53   That was better. Both the smile and the voice were coming out better now. She rehearsed it several times more. Then she ran downstairs, took her coat, went out the back door, down the garden, into the street.

54   It wasn't six o'clock yet and the lights were still on in the grocery shop.

55   "Hullo Sam," she said brightly, smiling at the man behind the counter.

56   "Why, good evening, Mrs. Maloney. How're you?"

57   "I want some potatoes please, Sam. Yes, and I think a can of peas."

58   The man turned and reached up behind him on the shelf for the peas.

59   "Patrick's decided he's tired and doesn't want to eat out tonight," she told him. "We usually go out Thursdays, you know, and now he's caught me without any vegetables in the house."

60   "Then how about meat, Mrs. Maloney?"

61   "No, I've got meat, thanks. I got a nice leg of lamb from the freezer."

62   "Oh."

63   "I don't much like cooking it frozen, Sam, but I'm taking a chance on it this time. You think it'll be all right?"

64   "Personally," the grocer said, "I don't believe it makes any difference. You want these Idaho potatoes?"

65   "Oh yes, that'll be fine. Two of those."

66   "Anything else?" The grocer cocked his head on one side, looking at her pleasantly. "How about afterwards? What you going to give him for afterwards?"

67   "Well—what would you suggest, Sam?"

68   The man glanced around his shop. "How about a nice big slice of cheesecake? I know he likes that."

69   "Perfect," she said. "He loves it."

70   And when it was all wrapped and she had paid, she put on her brightest smile and said, "Thank you, Sam. Goodnight."

71   "Goodnight, Mrs. Maloney. And thank you."

72   And now, she told herself as she hurried back, all she was doing now, she was returning home to her husband and he was waiting for his supper; and she must cook it good, and make it as tasty as possible because the poor man was tired; and if, when she entered the house, she happened to find anything unusual, or tragic, or terrible, then naturally it would be a shock and she'd become frantic with grief and horror. Mind you, she wasn't expecting to find anything. She was just going home with the vegetables. Mrs. Patrick Maloney going home with the vegetables on Thursday evening to cook supper for her husband.

73   That's the way, she told herself. Do everything right and natural. Keep things absolutely natural and there'll be no need for any acting at all.

74   Therefore, when she entered the kitchen by the back door, she was humming a little tune to herself and smiling.

75   "Patrick!" she called. "How are you, darling?"

76   She put the parcel down on the table and went through into the living room; and when she saw him lying there on the floor with his legs doubled up and one arm twisted back underneath his body, it really was rather a shock. All the old love and longing for him welled up inside her, and she ran over to him, knelt down beside him, and began to cry her heart out. It was easy. No acting was necessary.

77   A few minutes later she got up and went to the phone. She knew the number of the police station, and when the man at the other end answered, she cried to him, "Quick! Come quick! Patrick's dead!"

78   "Who's speaking?"

79   "Mrs. Maloney. Mrs. Patrick Maloney."

80   "You mean Patrick Maloney's dead?"

81   "I think so," she sobbed. "He's lying on the floor and I think he's dead."

82   "Be right over," the man said.

83   The car came very quickly, and when she opened the front door, two policemen walked in. She knew them both—she knew nearly all the men at that precinct—and she fell right into Jack Noonan's arms, weeping hysterically. He put her gently into a chair, then went over to join the other one, who was called O'Malley, kneeling by the body.

84   "Is he dead?" she cried.

85   "I'm afraid he is. What happened?"

86   Briefly, she told her story about going out to the grocer and coming back to find him on the floor. While she was talking, crying and talking, Noonan discovered a small patch of congealed blood on the dead man's head. He showed it to O'Malley who got up at once and hurried to the phone.

87   Soon, other men began to come into the house. First a doctor, then two detectives, one of whom she knew by name. Later, a police photographer arrived and took pictures, and a man who knew about fingerprints. There was a great deal of whispering and muttering beside the corpse, and the detectives kept asking her a lot of questions. But they always treated her kindly. She told her story again, this time right from the beginning, when Patrick had come in, and she was sewing, and he was tired, so tired he hadn't wanted to go out for supper. She told how she'd put the meat in the oven—"it's there now, cooking"—and how she'd slipped out to the grocer for vegetables, and come back to find him lying on the floor.

88   "Which grocer?" one of the detectives asked.

89   She told him, and he turned and whispered something to the other detective who immediately went outside into the street.

90   In fifteen minutes he was back with a page of notes, and there was more whispering, and through her sobbing she heard a few of the whispered phrases—". . . acted quite normal . . . very cheerful . . . wanted to give him a good supper . . . peas . . . cheesecake . . . impossible that she . . ."

91   After a while, the photographer and the doctor departed and two other men came in and took the corpse away on a stretcher. Then the fingerprint man went away. The two detectives remained, and so did the two policemen. They were exceptionally nice to her, and Jack Noonan asked if she wouldn't rather go somewhere else, to her sister's house perhaps, or to his own wife who would take care of her and put her up for the night.

92   No, she said. She didn't feel she could move even a yard at the moment. Would they mind awfully if she stayed just where she was until she felt better? She didn't feel too good at the moment, she really didn't.

93   Then hadn't she better lie down on the bed? Jack Noonan asked.

94   No, she said. She'd like to stay right where she was, in this chair. A little later, perhaps, when she felt better, she would move.

95   So they left her there while they went about their business, searching the house. Occasionally one of the detectives asked her another question. Sometimes Jack Noonan spoke to her gently as he passed by. Her husband, he told her, had been killed by a blow on the back of the head administered with a heavy blunt instrument, almost certainly a large piece of metal. They were looking for the weapon. The murderer may have taken it with him, but on the other hand he may have thrown it away or hidden it somewhere on the premises.

96   "It's the old story," he said. "Get the weapon, and you've got the man."

97   Later, one of the detectives came up and sat beside her. Did she know, he asked, of anything in the house that could've been used as the weapon? Would she mind having a look around to see if anything was missing—a very big spanner, for example, or a heavy metal vase.

98   They didn't have any heavy metal vases, she said.

99   "Or a big spanner?"

100   She didn't think they had a big spanner, but there might be some things like that in the garage.

101   The search went on. She knew that there were other policemen in the garden all around the house. She could hear their footsteps on the gravel outside, and sometimes she saw a flash of a torch through a chink in the curtains. It began to get late, nearly nine she noticed by the clock on the mantle. The four men searching the rooms seemed to be growing weary, a trifle exasperated.

102   "Jack," she said, the next time Sergeant Noonan went by. "Would you mind giving me a drink?"

103   "Sure I'll give you a drink. You mean this whiskey?"

104   "Yes please. But just a small one. It might make me feel better."

105   He handed her the glass.

106   "Why don't you have one yourself," she said. "You must be awfully tired. Please do. You've been very good to me."

107   "Well," he answered. "It's not strictly allowed, but I might take just a drop to keep me going."

108   One by one the others came in and were persuaded to take a little nip of whiskey. They stood around rather awkwardly with the drinks in their hands, uncomfortable in her presence, trying to say consoling things to her. Sergeant Noonan wandered into the kitchen, came out quickly and said, "Look, Mrs. Maloney. You know that oven of yours is still on, and the meat still inside."

109   "Oh dear me!" she cried. "So it is!"

110   "I better turn it off for you, hadn't I?"

111   "Will you do that, Jack. Thank you so much."

112   When the sergeant returned the second time, she looked at him with her large, dark tearful eyes. "Jack Noonan," she said.

113   "Yes?"

114   "Would you do me a small favor—you and these others?"

115   "We can try, Mrs. Maloney."

116   "Well," she said. "Here you all are, and good friends of dear Patrick's too, and helping to catch the man who killed him. You must be terribly hungry by now because it's long past your suppertime, and I know Patrick would never forgive me, God bless his soul, if I allowed you to remain in his house without offering you decent hospitality. Why don't you eat up that lamb that's in the oven? It'll be cooked just right by now."

117   "Wouldn't dream of it," Sergeant Noonan said.

118   "Please," she begged. "Please eat it. Personally I couldn't touch a thing, certainly not what's been in the house when he was here. But it's all right for you. It'd be a favour to me if you'd eat it up. Then you can go on with your work again afterwards."

119   There was a good deal of hesitating among the four policemen, but they were clearly hungry, and in the end they were persuaded to go into the kitchen and help themselves. The woman stayed where she was, listening to them speaking among themselves, their voices thick and sloppy because their mouths were full of meat.

120   "Have some more, Charlie?"

121   "No. Better not finish it."

122   "She wants us to finish it. She said so. Be doing her a favour."

123   "Okay then. Give me some more."

124   "That's the hell of a big club the guy must've used to hit poor Patrick," one of them was saying. "The doc says his skull was smashed all to pieces just like from a sledgehammer."

125   "That's why it ought to be easy to find."

126   "Exactly what I say."

127   "Whoever done it, they're not going to be carrying a thing like that around with them longer than they need."

128   One of them belched.

129   "Personally, I think it's right here on the premises."

130   "Probably right under our very noses. What you think, Jack?"

131   And in the other room, Mary Maloney began to giggle.

■ Reading Comprehension Questions

1. Which of the following would be a good alternative title for this selection?
   a. No Evidence
   b. The Delicious Murder Weapon
   c. The Detective's Wife
   d. A Trip to the Grocer

2. What is implied in the conversation between Patrick and his wife?
   a. He is too busy at work.
   b. He is going to end their marriage.
   c. She is too attentive.
   d. They want to go out for dinner.

3. The author writes, "She loved to luxuriate in the presence of this man" (paragraph 7). *Luxuriate* means
   a. dance.
   b. relax happily.
   c. make drinks.
   d. read books.

4. The author writes, ". . . punctually as always, she heard the tires on the gravel outside . . ." (paragraph 3). *Punctually* means
   a. in a hurry.
   b. being annoyed.
   c. on time.
   d. to wait.

5. The word *blissful* in the sentence, "For her this was always a blissful time of day" (paragraph 7) means
   a. afternoon.
   b. breezy.
   c. sad and lonely.
   d. perfect happiness.

6. The author implies that
   a. Mary Maloney had been plotting to kill Patrick for some time.
   b. Mary did not mean to kill Patrick.
   c. Mary did not regret killing Patrick.
   d. Mary did not remember killing Patrick.

7. Mary Maloney was pregnant when this story took place. (*True/false*)

8. The author implies that Mary
   a. was surprised when her husband came home.
   b. preferred a disorganized lifestyle.
   c. enjoyed a structured lifestyle.
   d. was surprised by the grocer.

9. The police detectives investigate Mary's story. (*True/false*)

10. Mary and Sam will now be free to have their romantic relationship. (*True/false*)

■ Discussion Questions

About Content

1. In the first four paragraphs of this selection, the author describes, in detail, the mood of the protagonist, Mary Maloney. What particular features does the author include about her, and what effect does that have on the rest of the story?
2. What an author does not say can be as important as what he/she does say. Where in this story can you find an example of that, and what do you imagine was said?
3. The final line states, "And in the other room, Mary Maloney began to giggle." She may be responding to the detective's comment in the previous line; however, she may be responding to something else. Discuss what you think she is giggling about.

About Structure

4. After Mary Maloney is questioned by the police, the detective returns to discuss his findings. The author uses ellipses to convey the detectives' conversation. Why might the author use this form of punctuation? What effect does it have when used in this context?
5. The author uses "artistic license" when constructing sentences. A sentence fragment, or dependent clause, acts like a sentence, but is incomplete. It usually needs a subject, verb, or object. For example, "First a doctor, then two detectives, one of whom she knew by name." This is a sentence fragment. One way to correct it would be to add "came into the room" at the end. Find three other sentence fragments and fix them. Hint: see paragraph 1.

About Style and Tone

6. How well does the style of writing in this selection complement the plot? For example, when Mary Maloney is described to the reader in the first four paragraphs, what might the reader expect to come next? Does this description foretell what is to come, or does it trick the reader into expecting something else? Give examples.
7. The reader is presented with both Mary Maloney's thoughts as well as the narrator's observations. Considering word choice, how do you perceive the character Mary based on what she says about what she has done?
8. Based on the way the characters speak and how the setting is described, when do you think this story takes place? 1900s? 1950s? 2010? What evidence can you find to support your position?

■ Writing Assignments

Assignment 1

Research other short stories by this author. Compile a bibliography of Roald Dahl's other work and identify how many selections are familiar to you. Have any stories been made into films? Identify from this list the author's primary audience. For whom is our story written?

Assignment 2

Write your own story about Mary Maloney one year after this story takes place. How would the characters behave if they reunited for dinner on the anniversary of Patrick's death?

Assignment 3

Retell this same story, but change the point of view. Tell the story from the perspective of detective Noonan. Include information about what detective Noonan might have known about Patrick and retell the events in the same sequence as the original. The story might begin at the police station, instead of the house. Patrick Maloney and Detective Noonan might be having a conversation about Patrick's wife, Patrick's mistress, or the actual father of Mary's unborn child. . . .

THE NOBEL LECTURE

Kofi Annan

This selection is the acceptance speech for the Nobel Peace Prize from former secretary-general of the United Nations, Kofi Annan. In his speech, Annan accepts the award for peace and encourages world leaders to embrace the idea that no one person is more valuable than another. There is considerable wisdom in Annan's words and we would all be a little wiser to heed his cautions and listen to his recommendations. © The Nobel Foundation 2001.

1   Your Majesties, Your Royal Highnesses, Excellencies,
Members of the Norwegian Nobel Committee, Ladies and Gentlemen,

2   Today, in Afghanistan, a girl will be born. Her mother will hold her and feed her, comfort her and care for her—just as any mother would anywhere in the world. In these most basic acts of human nature, humanity knows no divisions. But to be born a girl in today's Afghanistan is to begin life centuries away from the prosperity that one small part of humanity has achieved. It is to live under conditions that many of us in this hall would consider inhuman.

3   I speak of a girl in Afghanistan, but I might equally well have mentioned a baby boy or girl in Sierra Leone. No one today is unaware of this divide between the world's rich and poor. No one today can claim ignorance of the cost that this divide imposes on the poor and dispossessed who are no less deserving of human dignity, fundamental freedoms, security, food and education than any of us. The cost, however, is not borne by them alone. Ultimately, it is borne by all of us—North and South, rich and poor, men and women of all races and religions.

4   Today's real borders are not between nations, but between powerful and powerless, free and fettered, privileged and humiliated. Today, no walls can separate humanitarian or human rights crises in one part of the world from national security crises in another.

5   Scientists tell us that the world of nature is so small and interdependent that a butterfly flapping its wings in the Amazon rainforest can generate a violent storm on the other side of the earth. This principle is known as the "Butterfly Effect." Today, we realize, perhaps more than ever, that the world of human activity also has its own "Butterfly Effect"—for better or for worse.

6   Ladies and Gentlemen,

7   We have entered the third millennium through a gate of fire. If today, after the horror of 11 September, we see better, and we see further—we will realize that humanity is indivisible. New threats make no distinction between races, nations or regions. A new insecurity has entered every mind, regardless of wealth or status.

A deeper awareness of the bonds that bind us all—in pain as in prosperity—has gripped young and old.

8   In the early beginnings of the 21st century—a century already violently disabused of any hopes that progress towards global peace and prosperity is inevitable—this new reality can no longer be ignored. It must be confronted.

9   The 20th century was perhaps the deadliest in human history, devastated by innumerable conflicts, untold suffering, and unimaginable crimes. Time after time, a group or a nation inflicted extreme violence on another, often driven by irrational hatred and suspicion, or unbounded arrogance and thirst for power and resources. In response to these cataclysms, the leaders of the world came together at mid-century to unite the nations as never before.

10   A forum was created—the United Nations—where all nations could join forces to affirm the dignity and worth of every person, and to secure peace and development for all peoples. Here States could unite to strengthen the rule of law, recognize and address the needs of the poor, restrain man's brutality and greed, conserve the resources and beauty of nature, sustain the equal rights of men *and* women, and provide for the safety of future generations.

11   We thus inherit from the 20th century the political, as well as the scientific and technological power, which—if only we have the will to use them—give us the chance to vanquish poverty, ignorance and disease.

12   In the 21st Century I believe the mission of the United Nations will be defined by a new, more profound, awareness of the sanctity and dignity of every human life, regardless of race or religion. This will require us to look beyond the framework of States, and beneath the surface of nations or communities. We must focus, as never before, on improving the conditions of the individual men and women who give the state or nation its richness and character. We must begin with the young Afghan girl, recognizing that saving that one life is to save humanity itself.

13   Over the past five years, I have often recalled that the United Nations' Charter begins with the words: "We the peoples." What is not always recognized is that "we the peoples" are made up of individuals whose claims to the most fundamental rights have too often been sacrificed in the supposed interests of the state or the nation.

14   A genocide begins with the killing of one man—not for what he has done, but because of who he is. A campaign of "ethnic cleansing" begins with one neighbour turning on another. Poverty begins when even one child is denied his or her fundamental right to education. What begins with the failure to uphold the dignity of one life, all too often ends with a calamity for entire nations.

15   In this new century, we must start from the understanding that peace belongs not only to states or peoples, but to each and every member of those communities. The sovereignty of States must no longer be used as a shield for gross violations of human rights. Peace must be made real and tangible in the daily existence of every individual in need. Peace must be sought, above all, because it is the condition for every member of the human family to live a life of dignity and security.

16   The rights of the individual are of no less importance to immigrants and minorities in Europe and the Americas than to women in Afghanistan or children in Africa. They are as fundamental to the poor as to the rich; they are as necessary to the security of the developed world as to that of the developing world.

17   From this vision of the role of the United Nations in the next century flow three key priorities for the future: eradicating poverty, preventing conflict, and promoting democracy. Only in a world that is rid of poverty can all men and women make the

most of their abilities. Only where individual rights are respected can differences be channelled politically and resolved peacefully. Only in a democratic environment, based on respect for diversity and dialogue, can individual self-expression and self-government be secured, and freedom of association be upheld.

18 Throughout my term as Secretary-General, I have sought to place human beings at the centre of everything we do—from conflict prevention to development to human rights. Securing real and lasting improvement in the lives of individual men and women is the measure of all we do at the United Nations.

19 It is in this spirit that I humbly accept the Centennial Nobel Peace Prize. Forty years ago today, the Prize for 1961 was awarded for the first time to a Secretary-General of the United Nations—posthumously, because Dag Hammarskjöld had already given his life for peace in Central Africa. And on the same day, the Prize for 1960 was awarded for the first time to an African—Albert Luthuli, one of the earliest leaders of the struggle against apartheid in South Africa. For me, as a young African beginning his career in the United Nations a few months later, those two men set a standard that I have sought to follow throughout my working life.

20 This award belongs not just to me. I do not stand here alone. On behalf of all my colleagues in every part of the United Nations, in every corner of the globe, who have devoted their lives—and in many instances risked or given their lives in the cause of peace—I thank the Members of the Nobel Committee for this high honour. My own path to service at the United Nations was made possible by the sacrifice and commitment of my family and many friends from all continents—some of whom have passed away—who taught me and guided me. To them, I offer my most profound gratitude.

21 In a world filled with weapons of war and all too often words of war, the Nobel Committee has become a vital agent for peace. Sadly, a prize for peace is a rarity in this world. Most nations have monuments or memorials to war, bronze salutations to heroic battles, archways of triumph. But peace has no parade, no pantheon of victory.

22 What it does have is the Nobel Prize—a statement of hope and courage with unique resonance and authority. Only by understanding and addressing the needs of individuals for peace, for dignity, and for security can we at the United Nations hope to live up to the honour conferred today, and fulfil the vision of our founders. This is the broad mission of peace that United Nations staff members carry out every day in every part of the world.

23 A few of them, women and men, are with us in this hall today. Among them, for instance, are a Military Observer from Senegal who is helping to provide basic security in the Democratic Republic of the Congo; a Civilian Police Adviser from the United States who is helping to improve the rule of law in Kosovo; a UNICEF Child Protection Officer from Ecuador who is helping to secure the rights of Colombia's most vulnerable citizens; and a World Food Programme Officer from China who is helping to feed the people of North Korea.

24 Distinguished guests,

25 The idea that there is one people in possession of the truth, one answer to the world's ills, or one solution to humanity's needs, has done untold harm throughout history—especially in the last century. Today, however, even amidst continuing ethnic conflict around the world, there is a growing understanding that human diversity is both the reality that makes dialogue necessary, and the very basis for that dialogue.

26   We understand, as never before, that each of us is fully worthy of the respect and dignity essential to our common humanity. We recognize that we are the products of many cultures, traditions and memories; that mutual respect allows us to study and learn from other cultures; and that we gain strength by combining the foreign with the familiar.

27   In every great faith and tradition one can find the values of tolerance and mutual understanding. The Qur'an, for example, tells us that "We created you from a single pair of male and female and made you into nations and tribes, that you may know each other." Confucius urged his followers: "When the good way prevails in the state, speak boldly and act boldly. When the state has lost the way, act boldly and speak softly." In the Jewish tradition, the injunction to "love thy neighbour as thyself," is considered to be the very essence of the Torah.

28   This thought is reflected in the Christian Gospel, which also teaches us to love our enemies and pray for those who wish to persecute us. Hindus are taught that "truth is one, the sages give it various names." And in the Buddhist tradition, individuals are urged to act with compassion in every facet of life.

29   Each of us has the right to take pride in our particular faith or heritage. But the notion that what is ours is necessarily in conflict with what is theirs is both false and dangerous. It has resulted in endless enmity and conflict, leading men to commit the greatest of crimes in the name of a higher power.

30   It need not be so. People of different religions and cultures live side by side in almost every part of the world, and most of us have overlapping identities which unite us with very different groups. We *can* love what we are, without hating what—and who—we are *not*. We can thrive in our own tradition, even as we learn from others, and come to respect their teachings.

31   This will not be possible, however, without freedom of religion, of expression, of assembly, and basic equality under the law. Indeed, the lesson of the past century has been that where the dignity of the individual has been trampled or threatened—where citizens have not enjoyed the basic right to choose their government, or the right to change it regularly—conflict has too often followed, with innocent civilians paying the price, in lives cut short and communities destroyed.

32   The obstacles to democracy have little to do with culture or religion, and much more to do with the desire of those in power to maintain their position at any cost. This is neither a new phenomenon nor one confined to any particular part of the world. People of all cultures value their freedom of choice, and feel the need to have a say in decisions affecting their lives.

33   The United Nations, whose membership comprises almost all the States in the world, is founded on the principle of the equal worth of every human being. It is the nearest thing we have to a representative institution that can address the interests of all states, and all peoples. Through this universal, indispensable instrument of human progress, States can serve the interests of their citizens by recognizing common interests and pursuing them in unity. No doubt, that is why the Nobel Committee says that it "wishes, in its centenary year, to proclaim that the only negotiable route to global peace and cooperation goes by way of the United Nations."

34   I believe the Committee also recognized that this era of global challenges leaves no choice but cooperation at the global level. When States undermine the rule of law and violate the rights of their individual citizens, they become a menace not only to their own people, but also to their neighbours, and indeed the world. What

we need today is better governance—legitimate, democratic governance that allows each individual to flourish, and each State to thrive.

35   Your Majesties,

36   Excellencies,

37   Ladies and Gentlemen,

38   You will recall that I began my address with a reference to the girl born in Afghanistan today. Even though her mother will do all in her power to protect and sustain her, there is a one-in-four risk that she will not live to see her fifth birthday. Whether she does is just one test of our common humanity—of our belief in our individual responsibility for our fellow men and women. But it is the only test that matters.

39   Remember this girl and then our larger aims—to fight poverty, prevent conflict, or cure disease—will not seem distant, or impossible. Indeed, those aims will seem very near, and very achievable—as they should. Because beneath the surface of states and nations, ideas and language, lies the fate of individual human beings in need. Answering their needs will be the mission of the United Nations in the century to come.

40   Thank you very much.

■ Reading Comprehension Questions

1. The author states, "Today's real borders are not between nations, but between [the] powerful and [the] powerless . . ." (paragraph 4). (*True/false*)

2. The word *dispossessed,* in the sentence ". . . the cost that this divide imposes on the poor and dispossessed . . . ." (paragraph 3) means
   a. having too much.
   b. deprived of something.
   c. given food and shelter.
   d. remove a ghost.

3. In the sentence ". . . give us a chance to vanquish poverty, ignorance and disease" (paragraph 11), the word *vanquish* means
   a. defeat utterly.
   b. leave alone.
   c. a never-ending battle.
   d. help.

4. For what area of excellence is this Nobel Prize awarded?
   a. writing.
   b. drama.
   c. peace.
   d. public speaking.

5. In the sentence "It has resulted in endless enmity and conflict, leading men to commit the greatest of crimes in the name of a higher power" (paragraph 29), the word *enmity* means
   a. a battlefield.
   b. temporary happiness.
   c. love.
   d. hatred.

6. The word *pantheon* appears in the sentence "But peace has no parade, no pantheon of victory" (paragraph 21), meaning
   a. marching band.
   b. temple or monument.
   c. holiday.
   d. song.

7. The United Nations is founded on which of the following:
   a. The law of religion
   b. The idea that power is more important than people
   c. The principle of the equal worth of every human being
   d. The site of the World Trade Centre

8. If the Centennial Nobel Prize was awarded in 2001, when was the first prize given out?
   a. 1961
   b. 1945
   c. 1941
   d. 1901

9. What form of writing does the start of this lecture take?
   a. Narrative
   b. Argumentative
   c. Compare and contrast
   d. Process

10. In the sentence ". . . a century already violently disabused of any hopes that progress towards global peace and prosperity is inevitable . . ." (paragraph 8), the word *disabused* means
    a. to discuss.
    b. to hold on tightly.
    c. to get rid of a mistaken idea.
    d. to treat nicely.

■ Discussion Questions

About Content

1. Why do you think the author repeatedly returns in this speech to the young girl in Afghanistan? What does he mean when he says, "We must begin with the young Afghan girl, recognizing that saving that one life is to save humanity itself" (paragraph 12)?
2. The author suggests that humanity "gains strength by combining the foreign with the familiar" (paragraph 26). Do you agree? Do you believe that Canada, as a nation, upholds the principles of the UN?

About Structure

3. This selection is delivered in four parts. What are two ways the author separates the sections?
4. The author uses a variety of sentence styles. What is the advantage of using short sentences in a long selection such as this? Why are they used sparingly?

About Style and Tone

5. This is both an acceptance speech as well as a persuasive argument. What style of persuasion does the author use (logical, emotional, analogous, compare and contrast, etc.)?

6. The author addresses members of the audience and states, "The idea that there is one people in possession of the truth, one answer to the world's ills, or one solution to humanity's needs, has done untold harm throughout history . . ." (paragraph 25). Who else might he be addressing? Consider who might disagree with this statement.

7. How would you describe the tone of this selection? The author challenges the world's leaders as well as the world's citizens to realize the cost of injustice. How effective do you consider his argument to be, and what role does his tone play?

■ Writing Assignments

Assignment 1

The author outlines three key priorities for the future (paragraph 18). Find these in the text and explore ways of achieving these key principles. Write suggestions for how you can advocate for them in your own community.

Assignment 2

Canadians have long identified themselves as "peacekeepers." This identity is changing. Research Canada's current role in UN objectives. Write a compare and contrast essay on whether we as Canadians can still call ourselves "peacekeepers."

Assignment 3

The author suggests that "States" (paragraph 33) need to be governed by democratic rule and that, by violating laws against individual citizens, these states are a menace to the global community as well as to their own people. What types of laws are being broken and why? Write a research essay on why some states continue to break these laws, and explain the effect on the global community.

WHAT IS POVERTY?

Jo Goodwin Parker

"What Is Poverty?" is shocking in its directness—the writer glares back, speaks angrily to the reader, demands "listen to me." About its author, Jo Goodwin Parker, virtually nothing is known, except that she first presented this selection as a speech. Imagine yourself in her audience—how would you react to her words, her tone? Is poverty nothing more than an abstract noun to you, a word with no specific meanings? If so, Goodwin Parker offers a wealth of specific and bitterly plain details to help you not just see, but feel.

1   You ask me what is poverty? Listen to me. Here I am, dirty, smelly, and with no "proper" underwear on and with the stench of my rotting teeth near you. I will tell you. Listen to me. Listen without pity. I cannot use your pity. Listen with understanding. Put yourself in my dirty, worn out, ill-fitting shoes, and hear me.

2   Poverty is getting up every morning from a dirt- and illness-stained mattress. The sheets have long since been used for diapers. Poverty is living in a smell that never leaves. This is a smell of urine, sour milk, and spoiling food sometimes joined with the strong smell of long-cooked onions. Onions are cheap. If you have smelled this smell, you did not know how it came. It is the smell of the outdoor privy. It is the smell of young children who cannot walk the long dark way in the night. It is the smell of the mattresses where years of "accidents" have happened. It is the smell of the milk which has gone sour because the refrigerator long has not worked, and it costs money to get it fixed. It is the smell of rotting garbage. I could bury it, but where is the shovel? Shovels cost money.

3   Poverty is being tired. I have always been tired. They told me at the hospital when the last baby came that I had chronic anemia caused from poor diet, a bad case of worms, and that I needed a corrective operation. I listened politely—the poor are always polite. The poor always listen. They don't say that there is no money for iron pills, or better food, or worm medicine. The idea of an operation is frightening and costs so much that, if I had dared, I would have laughed. Who takes care of my children? Recovery from an operation takes a long time. I have three children. When I left them with "granny" the last time I had a job, I came home to find the baby covered with fly specks, and a diaper that had not been changed since I left. When the dried diaper came off, bits of my baby's flesh came with it. My other child was playing with a sharp bit of broken glass, and my oldest was playing alone at the edge of a lake. I made twenty-two dollars a week, and a good nursery school costs twenty dollars a week for three children. I quit my job.

4   Poverty is dirt. You can say in your clean clothes coming from your clean house, "Anybody can be clean." Let me explain about housekeeping with no money. For breakfast I give my children grits with no oleo or cornbread without eggs and oleo. This does not use up many dishes. What dishes there are, I wash in cold water and with no soap. Even the cheapest soap has to be saved for the baby's diapers. Look at my hands, so cracked and red. Once I saved for two months to buy a jar of Vaseline for my hands and the baby's diaper rash. When I had saved enough, I went to buy it and the price had gone up two cents. The baby and I suffered on. I have to decide every day if I can bear to put my cracked sore hands into the cold water and strong soap. But you ask, why not hot water? Fuel costs money. If you have a wood fire it costs money. If you burn electricity, it costs money. Hot water is a luxury. I do not have luxuries. I know you will be surprised when I tell you how young I am, I look so much older. My back has been bent over the wash tubs every day for so long, I cannot remember when I ever did anything else. Every night I wash every stitch my school age child has on and just hope her clothes will be dry by morning.

5   Poverty is staying up all night on cold nights to watch the fire knowing one spark on the newspaper covering the walls means your sleeping child dies in flames. In summer, poverty is watching gnats and flies devour your baby's tears when he cries. The screens are torn and you pay so little rent you know they will never be fixed. Poverty means insects in your food, in your nose, in your eyes, and crawling over you when you sleep. Poverty is hoping it never rains because diapers won't dry when it rains and soon you are using newspapers. Poverty is seeing your children forever with runny noses. Paper handkerchiefs cost money and all your rags you need for other things. Even more costly are antihistamines. Poverty is cooking without food and cleaning without soap.

6   Poverty is asking for help. Have you ever had to ask for help, knowing your children will suffer unless you get it? Think about asking for a loan from a relative, if this is the only way you can imagine asking for help. I will tell you how it feels. You find out where the office is that you are supposed to visit. You circle that block four or five times. Thinking of your children, you go in. Everyone is very busy. Finally, someone comes out and you tell her that you need help. That never is the person you need to see. You go see another person, and after spilling the whole shame of your poverty all over the desk between you, you find that this isn't the right office after all—you must repeat the whole process, and it never is any easier at the next place.

7   You have asked for help, and after all it has a cost. You are again told to wait. You are told why, but you don't really hear because of the red cloud of shame and the rising cloud of despair.

8   Poverty is remembering. It is remembering quitting school in junior high because "nice" children had been so cruel about my clothes and my smell. The attendance officer came. My mother told him I was pregnant. I wasn't, but she thought that I could get a job and help out. I had jobs off and on, but never long enough to learn anything. Mostly I remember being married. I was so young then. I am still young. For a time, we had all the things you have. There was a little house in another town, with hot water and everything. Then my husband lost his job. There was unemployment insurance for a while and what few jobs I could get. Soon, all our nice things were repossessed and we moved back here. I was pregnant then. This house didn't look so bad when we first moved in. Every week it gets worse. Nothing is ever fixed. We now had no money. There were a few odd jobs for my husband, but everything went for food then, as it does now. I don't know how we lived through three years and three babies, but we did. I'll tell you something, after the last baby I destroyed my marriage. It had been a good one, but could you keep on bringing children in this dirt? Did you ever think how much it costs for any kind of birth control? I knew my husband was leaving the day he left, but there were no goodbys between us. I hope he has been able to climb out of this mess somewhere. He never could hope with us to drag him down.

9   That's when I asked for help. When I got it, you know how much it was? It was, and is, seventy-eight dollars a month for the four of us; that is all I ever can get. Now you know why there is no soap, no needles and thread, no hot water, no aspirin, no worm medicine, no hand cream, no shampoo. None of these things forever and ever and ever. So that you can see clearly, I pay twenty dollars a month rent, and most of the rest goes for food. For grits and cornmeal, and rice and milk and beans. I try my best to use only the minimum electricity. If I use more, there is that much less for food.

10   Poverty is looking into a black future. Your children won't play with my boys. They will turn to other boys who steal to get what they want. I can already see them behind the bars of their prison instead of behind the bars of my poverty. Or they will turn to the freedom of alcohol or drugs, and find themselves enslaved. And my daughter? At best, there is for her a life like mine.

11   But you say to me, there are schools. Yes, there are schools. My children have no extra books, no magazines, no extra pencils, or crayons, or paper and most important of all, they do not have health. They have worms, they have infections, they have pinkeye all summer. They do not sleep well on the floor, or with me in my one bed. They do not suffer from hunger, my seventy-eight dollars keeps us alive, but they do

suffer from malnutrition. Oh yes, I do remember what I was taught about health in school. It doesn't do much good. In some places there is a surplus commodities program. Not here. The county said it cost too much. There is a school lunch program. But I have two children who will already be damaged by the time they get to school.

12   But, you say to me, there are health clinics. Yes, there are health clinics and they are in the towns. I live out here eight miles from town. I can walk that far (even if it is sixteen miles both ways), but can my little children? My neighbor will take me when he goes; but he expects to get paid, one way or another. I bet you know my neighbor. He is that large man who spends his time at the gas station, the barbershop, and the corner store complaining about the government spending money on the immoral mothers of illegitimate children.

13   Poverty is an acid that drips on pride until all pride is worn away. Poverty is a chisel that chips on honor until honor is worn away. Some of you say that you would do something in my situation, and maybe you would, for the first week or the first month, but for year after year after year?

14   Even the poor can dream. A dream of a time when there is money. Money for the right kinds of food, for worm medicine, for iron pills, for toothbrushes, for hand cream, for a hammer and nails and a bit of screening, for a shovel, for a bit of paint, for some sheeting, for needles and thread. Money to pay in money for a trip to town. And, oh, money for hot water and money for soap. A dream of when asking for help does not eat away the last bit of pride. When the office you visit is as nice as the offices of other governmental agencies, when there are enough workers to help you quickly, when workers do not quit in defeat and despair. When you have to tell your story to only one person, and that person can send you for other help and you don't have to prove your poverty over and over and over again.

15   I have come out of my despair to tell you this. Remember I did not come from another place or another time. Others like me are all around you. Look at us with an angry heart, anger that will help you help me. Anger that will let you tell of me. The poor are always silent. Can you be silent too?

■ Reading Comprehension Questions

1. The word *oleo* in "I give my children grits with no oleo or cornbread without eggs and oleo" (paragraph 4) means
   a. syrup.
   b. margarine.
   c. butter.
   d. oil.

2. The word *commodities* in "there is a surplus commodities program" (paragraph 11) means
   a. services.
   b. school supplies.
   c. groceries.
   d. goods.

3. Which of the following would be a good alternative title for this selection?
   a. The Poor Cry Out; Do You Hear?
   b. Listen, Learn, and Do Something
   c. The Poor Are the Same Everywhere
   d. The Silence of the Poor

4. Which sentence best expresses the main idea of the selection?
    a. Poverty is so overwhelming that it is impossible to understand.
    b. There is no escape from the sour, grinding world of poverty.
    c. Being poor means losing hope.
    d. Helping the poor means understanding their damaged souls and deadened wills.

5. What were the author's problems after having her last child? What are the reasons she was unable to do anything about each of these problems?

6. The author says "poverty is dirt" because
    a. she has given up on trying to clean her house.
    b. keeping herself, the children, and the house clean is just too much.
    c. every household action must be calculated to cost as little as possible.
    d. hot water and soap cost money she does not have.

7. *True or false?* The author's husband left her because they had too many children too quickly.

8. The author implies that the babysitter she hired
    a. was the only person she tried.
    b. was irresponsible.
    c. was her mother.
    d. was trying to hurt the children.

9. When Goodwin Parker describes her neighbour as "that large man who spends his time . . . complaining about the government spending money on the immoral mothers of illegitimate children," she implies
    a. she is ashamed of having to comply with his method of payment.
    b. that he is an evil hypocrite.
    c. he is a typical church-going, moral person with more opinions than common sense.
    d. he has nothing better to do than complain about government spending.

10. The author implies that poverty
    a. is a cycle that can be broken with help.
    b. destroys its victims.
    c. traps people for generations.
    d. makes education and escape impossible.

■ Discussion Questions

About Content

1. What are the different odours in paragraph 2? What is the cause of each smell and how is each related to poverty?
2. What is the author recalling when she says "poverty is remembering"? What connects these memories?
3. What does the author see as her sons' futures? Why do you think she feels as she does?

About Structure

4. As well as definition as an overall means, Goodwin Parker uses the cause-and-effect method of development within some of her paragraphs. Choose one such paragraph and identify, then explain, its series of causes or events.

5. How often is the "poverty is . . ." paragraph opening used, compared to the total number of paragraphs in the selection? How many paragraphs appear before she first changes her paragraph opening? In the second half of the essay, is there a discernible pattern in the paragraph openings? If so, explain it.

6. In which paragraph does the author repeat this pattern within the paragraph itself? What is the effect of this repetition?

About Style and Tone

7. Who is the audience that Goodwin Parker is addressing? Describe who they might be, and why, based on specifics in the text, you believe as you do.

8. Choose one body paragraph and note the sentence variety within it. How many longer and how many short sentences do you find in the paragraph you choose? Is there a pattern or alternating rhythm of short-to-long sentences? What is the effect of the short sentences? Of the longer sentences?

9. Although the author's style seems plain-spoken, she does use figurative language, such as "red cloud of shame" (paragraph 8). Choose two examples of such figures of speech and discuss their effectiveness related to the selection.

■ Writing Assignments

Assignment 1

Write an essay in the form of a letter to Jo Goodwin Parker. Respond to three points of hers that affect you most (negatively or positively), giving plenty of supporting examples and details; be sure to quote correctly as you write to her.

In this case, because Goodwin Parker's essay is less than formal in style, and because you are writing a letter, you may choose to use first-person viewpoint if doing so will make your responses more vivid to your reader.

Assignment 2

"What is anxiety?" "What is shyness?" Write a definition essay about some challenge or difficulty you face or endure. Support the aspects of your definition with the most specific details possible, as does Goodwin Parker. If appropriate, consider using some cause or effect method of development within a body paragraph or two.

Assignment 3

"I have come out of my despair to tell you this. Remember I did not come from another place or another time." So opens Goodwin Parker's final paragraph, carrying much the same message as media campaigns for various social service organizations. One television awareness campaign shows "the invisible people," the street people and the poor that one group helps.

Consider the concept of "invisible people": the elderly, night-shift workers, anyone whom other groups do not "see." In a division and classification essay, come up with your own three categories of "invisible people." Why are they invisible, and to whom? Why should we be aware of them?

Observing Others

Casey Banas

A teacher pretends to be a student and sits in on several classes. What does she find in the typical class? Boredom. Routine. Apathy. Manipulation. Discouragement. If this depressing list sounds familiar, you will be interested in the following analysis of why classes often seem to be more about killing time than about learning.

1   Ellen Glanz lied to her teacher about why she hadn't done her homework; but, of course, many students have lied to their teachers. The difference is that Ellen Glanz was a twenty-eight-year-old high school social studies teacher who was a student for six months to improve her teaching by gaining a fresh perspective of her school.

2   She found many classes boring, students doing as little as necessary to pass tests and get good grades, students using ruses to avoid assignments, and students manipulating teachers to do the work for them. She concluded that many students are turned off because they have little power and responsibility for their own education.

3   Ellen Glanz found herself doing the same things as the students. There was the day when Ellen wanted to join her husband in helping friends celebrate the purchase of a house, but she had homework for a math class. For the first time, she knew how teenagers feel when they think something is more important than homework.

4   She found a way out and confided: "I considered my options: Confess openly to the teacher, copy someone else's sheet, or make up an excuse." Glanz chose the

third—the one most widely used—and told the teacher that the pages needed to complete the assignment had been ripped from the book. The teacher accepted the story, never checking the book. In class, nobody else did the homework; and student after student mumbled responses when called on.

5   "Finally," Glanz said, "the teacher, thinking that the assignment must have been difficult, went over each question at the board while students copied the problems at their seats. The teacher had 'covered' the material and the students had listened to the explanation. But had anything been learned? I don't think so."

6   Glanz found this kind of thing common. "In many cases," she said, "people simply didn't do the work assignment, but copied from someone else or manipulated the teacher into doing the work for them."

7   "The system encourages incredible passivity," Glanz said. "In most classes one sits and listens. A teacher, whose role is activity, simply cannot understand the passivity of the student's role," she said. "When I taught," Glanz recalled, "my mind was going constantly—figuring out how best to present an idea, thinking about whom to call on, whom to draw out, whom to shut up; how to get students involved, how to make my point clearer, how to respond; when to be funny, when serious. As a student, I experienced little of this. Everything was done to me."

8   Class methods promote the feeling that students have little control over or responsibility for their own education because the agenda is the teacher's, Glanz said. The teacher is convinced the subject matter is worth knowing, but the student may not agree. Many students, Glanz said, are not convinced they need to know what teachers teach; but they believe good grades are needed to get into college.

9   Students, obsessed with getting good grades to help qualify for the college of their choice, believe the primary responsibility for their achievement rests with the teacher, Glanz said. "It was his responsibility to teach well rather than their responsibility to learn carefully."

10   Teachers were regarded by students, Glanz said, not as "people," but as "role-players" who dispensed information needed to pass a test. "I often heard students describing teachers as drips, bores, and numerous varieties of idiots," she said. "Yet I knew that many of the same people had traveled the world over, conducted fascinating experiments or learned three languages, or were accomplished musicians, artists, or athletes."

11   But the sad reality, Glanz said, is the failure of teachers to recognize their tremendous communications gap with students. Some students, she explained, believe that effort has little value. After seeing political corruption they conclude that honesty takes a back seat to getting ahead any way one can, she said. "I sometimes estimated that half to two-thirds of a class cheated on a given test," Glanz said. "Worse, I've encountered students who feel no remorse about cheating but are annoyed that a teacher has confronted them on their actions."

12   Glanz has since returned to teaching at Lincoln-Sudbury. Before her stint as a student, she would worry that perhaps she was demanding too much. "Now I know I should have demanded more," she said. Before, she was quick to accept the excuses of students who came to class unprepared. Now she says, "You are responsible for learning it." But a crackdown is only a small part of the solution.

13   The larger issue, Glanz said, is that educators must recognize that teachers and students, though physically in the same school, are in separate worlds and have an ongoing power struggle. "A first step toward ending this battle is to convince students that what we attempt to teach them is genuinely worth knowing," Glanz

said. "We must be sure, ourselves, that what we are teaching is worth knowing." No longer, she emphasized, do students assume that "teacher knows best."

■ Reading Comprehension Questions

1. The word *ruses* in "students using ruses to avoid assignments" (paragraph 2) means
   a. questions.
   b. sicknesses.
   c. parents.
   d. tricks.

2. The word *agenda* in "the agenda is the teacher's" (paragraph 8) means
   a. program.
   b. boredom.
   c. happiness.
   d. book.

3. Which of the following would be a good alternative title for this selection?
   a. How to Get Good Grades
   b. Why Students Dislike School
   c. Cheating in Our school System
   d. Students Who Manipulate Teachers

4. Which sentence best expresses the main idea of the selection?
   a. Ellen Glanz is a burned-out teacher.
   b. Ellen Glanz lied to her math teacher.
   c. Students need good grades to get into college.
   d. Teachers and students feel differently about schooling.

5. How much of a class, according to Glanz, would often cheat on a test?
   a. One-quarter or less
   b. One-half
   c. One-half to two-thirds
   d. Almost everyone

6. *True or false?* As a result of her experience, Glanz now accepts more of her students' excuses.

7. Glanz found that the school system encourages an incredible amount of
   a. enthusiasm.
   b. passivity.
   c. violence.
   d. creativity.

8. The author implies that
   a. few students cheat on tests.
   b. most students enjoy schoolwork.
   c. classroom teaching methods should be changed.
   d. Glanz had a lazy math teacher.

9. The author implies that
   a. Glanz should not have become a student again.
   b. Glanz is a better teacher than she was before.
   c. Glanz later told her math teacher that she lied.
   d. social studies is an unimportant subject.

10. The author implies that
    a. most students who cheat on tests are caught by their teachers.
    b. most teachers demand too little of their students.
    c. students who get good grades in high school also do so in college.
    d. students never question what teachers say.

■ Discussion Questions

About Content

1. What were Ellen Glanz's main discoveries when she first re-entered high school classes as a student? What did she conclude as a result of these observations?
2. Why, in paragraph 5, did the teacher believe that an assignment must have been too challenging?
3. Why, according to Glanz, is it so difficult for teachers to understand students' passivity? Why, in turn, do students tend to be passive?
4. What could cause a student caught cheating to respond with anger?

About Structure

5. Which method of introduction does Banas use in her essay?
    a. Movement from general to specific
    b. Anecdote
    c. Background information
    d. Questions

   Why do you think she chose this approach?

6. List the time transitions that Banas uses in paragraph 12. How do they help the author make her point?

About Style and Tone

7. Throughout "Why Are Students Turned Off?" Banas shifts between summarizing Ellen Glanz's words and quoting Glanz directly. Find an instance in the essay in which both direct and indirect quotations are used in the same paragraph. What does the author gain or lose from using this technique? (Refer to page 421 for definitions and examples of direct and indirect quotations.)
8. Parallel structures are often used to emphasize similar information. They can create a smooth, readable style. For example, note the series of participles, or -*ing* verb forms, in the following sentence from paragraph 2: "students *doing* as little as necessary to pass tests and get good grades, students *using* ruses to avoid assignments, and students *manipulating* teachers to do the work for them." Find two other uses of parallel structure, one in paragraph 4 and one in paragraph 7.

■ Writing Assignments

Assignment 1

Play the role of student observer in one of your classes. Then, write an essay with *either* of the following thesis statements:

- In class, students are turned off because . . .
- In class, students are active and interested because . . .

In each supporting paragraph, state and explain one reason why that particular class is either boring or interesting. You might want to consider areas such as these:

Instructor: presentation, tone of voice, level of interest and enthusiasm, teaching aids used, ability to handle questions, sense of humour
Students: level of enthusiasm, participation in class, attitude (as shown by body language and other actions)
Other factors: conditions of classroom, length of class period, noise level in classroom

Assignment 2

Glanz says that students like to describe their teachers as "drips, bores, and numerous varieties of idiots." Write a description of one of your instructors, past or present, who either *does* or *does not* fit that description. *Show* in your essay that your instructor was weak, boring, and idiotic *or* dynamic, creative, and bright. In either case, your focus should be on providing specific details that enable your readers to see for themselves that your thesis is valid.

Assignment 3

How does the classroom situation Ellen Glanz describes compare with a classroom situation with which you are familiar—either one from your earlier educational experience or one from the school you presently attend? Write an essay in the third-person voice in which you compare or contrast a class of your experience with those Ellen Glanz describes. Here are some points for comparison or contrast you might wish to include in your essay:

- How interesting the class was/is
- How many of the students did/do their assignments
- What the teaching methods were/are
- How much was/is actually learned
- How active the instructor was/is
- How passive or engaged the students were/are
- What the students thought/think of the instructor

Choose any three of these points for comparison or contrast, or any other three that come to mind. Then, decide which specific method of development you will use: *one side at a time* or *point by point*.

HEADLANDS

Jonathan Bennett

Canadian author Jonathan Bennett spent his youth in Australia combing remote beaches in search of inspiration and insects. The beach serves as a natural metaphor for beginnings and endings, and although this story is set on the other side of the world, see how much of your own experience is captured in this story of recollection and promise.

For James

1   It's still early and the morning sky is empty, neither black nor blue. A small mob of grey kangaroos has come down off the headland. They graze in the light scrub,

moving only a hop or two at a time. In this scrappy light, they are easily mistaken for rocks, or stumps, or shadows. My mug of tea rests on my leg, the concentrated warmth of it calling attention to the outside chill. My bare legs, hanging off the front verandah, move a little involuntarily, twitching to keep warm.

2   In the garage I turn the key in the old, orange Land Rover. My brother instructed me to douse the engine in WD 40. Be nice to her, he joked, and she'll start. Thankfully the old girl does turn over, the clutch having given about half a metre before jamming against the bare metal floor. As I grope at the demands and desires of a 1967 British gearbox, I can almost feel my father sitting beside me, tossing in words of encouragement. The engine roars and the kangaroos bound into the reaches and folds of the headland.

3   I stop at the wharf beside the tea-coloured river and pick out two very large, discarded fish heads from the fishermen's bins. In the half-light of this still morning, I thread a piece of rope through their mouths, aghast, and tie them to the bull bar on the front of the Land Rover. You need these fish heads to stink in order to catch bloodworms, an unsurpassed fish bait. In a few days' time, after having hung in the scorching Australian sun, they will be perfect. It's a simple cycle, rotting fish to catch worms, worms to catch fresh fish. Today, however, the heads are new. Still, I will try.

4   You can imagine Hat Head just from its name. It's a long day's drive north of Sydney, up the murderous Pacific highway. Drive through Taree, Forster and Tuncurry, Port Macquarie and, at Kempsey, you make a right turn and head back for the sea to find this windswept headland, upon which a large hill shaped like a hat—a misshapen Fedora, a punched-out Stetson—juts into the Pacific Ocean. A few hundred people live here year round, the population swelling in the summer with holidaymakers and surfers, fishermen and bush walkers.

5   I drive fast, but stay close to the shore where the sand is firm. In all the times I've returned home to Australia, and have revisited this stretch of coastline, I've never travelled the beach from end to end. No matter how far I go, the beach just seems to continue, to disappear ahead into the haze and wind. Should the orange Land Rover break down, or the tide turn and come in high and sooner than expected, I am a stranded Crusoe: four-wheel drive or not.

6   The sky is lightening now and a few solitary fishermen cast their lines into the surf, reeling in the first dart fish and whiting of the dawn. Seagulls hover out beyond the breakers concentrating on schools of fish that rise and fall in swarm-like formations from the bottom of the ocean as they are chased by larger fish. To my left, sand dunes veined with thin runners of grass and the odd burnt stump of a tree go on forever, disappearing into oblivion, into the haze of scant light and sea spray ahead of me. With my bare feet on the hot metal pedals, I push the Land Rover to go faster. Behind me, my tire tracks recede only to be erased by waves sliding up the beach.

7   The tide is low and I scan the sea, the breakers. I find a deep gully of water between two shallow sand flats where the fish feed. Reversing the Land Rover up the beach into the soft sand, I point its nose down at the sea. If it will not start later, at least I'll have a modest hill to try to jump-start her. I learned these secrets as a boy, by watching my father and my uncle John. I saw first hand what happened to ignorant tourists in lightweight jeeps bogged in fine white sand. We'd have to stop and help dig them out, or winch them free in the worst cases.

8   My fish heads are too new. Standing in the surf up to my knees, I wait as each new wave washes in: when it pauses, caught between advance and retreat, I drag

the fish heads across the sand. I watch for the tiniest indications of blood worms poking their heads up through the sand, smelling what they think is a meal. I swivel my hips, digging down into the sand hoping to feel small, hard shapes on the heels and balls of my feet. Pipies are clam-like bi-valves and I bend to collect them one by one, putting them in a bucket tied to my waist.

9   I smash two pipies together and their shells burst open, exposing blonde flesh and opaque tentacles. The inside of their shells are smooth and opalescent in the new morning light. I drag the fish heads once more across the sand as a wave goes out and, as it does, I see a small break in the diminishing water's film—something interrupting its evenness, like an arrowhead pointing at me. Kneeling beside it, I wait for another wave to come in which washes against me hard, soaking my shorts and most of my T-shirt. The water is cold. I want this bloodworm now.

10   The wave withdraws and I wag the pipi over the area where the bloodworm's head split the rushing water only moments ago. The head emerges again; this time I am close to it and I tempt it with the pipi's flesh. I manoeuvre my fingers in behind its head, ready to pinch and pull in one swift motion. But I must not rush.

11   As children of eight or ten, we would try to catch bloodworms. My uncle John would offer outrageous sums of money—sometimes even five dollars—if we could pull one worm up whole. The chance at these winnings was enough incentive to keep us occupied for hours while he and the other adults fished and wormed. His money could not have been safer.

12   Bloodworms live in the sand and sea and are as thick as a ten-year-old's baby finger. They can be just as long as a boy is tall, a sort of sea-faring millipede, and are difficult to catch because of the innumerable tiny legs that run down either side of their bodies. If all the legs are not going in the same direction then the head will simply rip off. To make matters worse, bloodworms are extremely fast in retreat. I wait for it to twice come to the surface, nibble and recoil, my thumb and forefinger lingering gently around the neck, before I strike.

13   I get the worm first try. I feel it arching, its momentum heading upward and I pull it from beneath the sand with all the precision of a surgeon in mid suture. I fish with it as bait for about an hour, using segments of it at a time. I catch two bream and put them in a bucket of seawater to swim in circles. Not big fish, but with the sand under my feet, the salt in the air, and the horizon before me, I feel elemental. This is why I have travelled up here. Lolling about in the last licks of wave are my two fish heads, bound, dead. After a time, I decide to drive further up the beach, but before I do I upend the bucket in knee-high surf, both fish swimming free.

14   Driving again, I am looking for signs of a sudden tidal shift. Yesterday's paper said it wouldn't happen until late this afternoon, but I drive distracted nonetheless. The beach continues to unfurl ahead of me in slight variations of dune, scrub and surf. A piece of driftwood. A washed-up plastic bag half-filled with sand catches the wind. This is how I remember the drive from my childhood, but now the possibility and concern of being trapped by the tide is no longer my father's, or uncle's worry. I drive on.

15   In the distance a sharp wall of dark rock breaks the horizon as if thrown down by a spiteful God. It punctuates the beach, a piece of geographical exclamation, halting my progress northward, ripping me clear of my thoughts. A sign announces South West Rocks and a turnoff to Trail Bay Gaol.

16   The gaol, constructed of locally quarried pink and grey granite, closed for good in 1903, but was briefly reopened in 1915 to hold World War I internees from

Germany. They were allowed out onto the beach during the day, so the story goes, but locked up at night. I climb up on one of the low walls. Looking out to sea I can't help but scour the distance for a glimpse of Hat Head. All I see is beach and haze.

17   In the lee of the cliffs, I sit on the sand where the internees must have spent their days. I imagine two lovers, freed from nightly lock-up to find each other in broad daylight, their white bodies wading at the shore. In real life, he has made promises to another woman, but shut away up here, he finds himself drawn to this new woman, the curve of her mouth in the morning, the way her hair falls in the bright light.

18   She is younger than he is, I think. She makes her choice and they swim, touching only below the water, swimming deeper into the ocean until neither can stand. Their love is made suspended amongst porpoises, concealed from the island gaolers patrolling the beach.

19   They must have feared the future. Would they know freedom again and, if so, would it kill their love? The sun rises wholly and I am miles from Hat Head. I have travelled to the end of a beach that I had always imagined to be unrelenting.

20   The next few mornings the kangaroos return and I watch them until the light firms and they melt into the landscape of the head. They dissolve one by one, between mouthfuls of tea when I am looking down at a bull ant that is getting too close to my bare leg, or craning my neck to catch a glimpse of a pelican employing an updraft. I fish each dawn, first repeating my worming hunt, then throwing back the catch. I get more adept with each day the fish heads decompose and ripen, until maggots writhe in their eye sockets. Fish eating worms, worms eating fish. Daily too, I press ahead to Trail Bay Goal. The beach, now no longer a fearful passage limited by memory, but the raw atmosphere for my imaginings, the source and cause of those stories still yet to arrive.

■ Reading Comprehension Questions

1. The author uses the word *discarded* in the sentence ". . . two very large, discarded fish heads . . ." (paragraph 3). This word means
   a. put in piles.
   b. thrown away.
   c. without cards.
   d. a type of fish.

2. An alternative title for this selection might be
   a. The Endless Beach.
   b. Breakfast in Australia.
   c. Looking for Hat Head.
   d. Dangerous Tides.

3. In the sentence "I see a small break in the diminishing water's film" (paragraph 9), the term *diminishing* means
   a. shining.
   b. cold.
   c. reducing.
   d. salty.

4. The author chooses the word *manoeuver* in the sentence "I manoeuver my fingers in behind its head, ready to pinch and pull in one swift motion" (paragraph 10). This word means

    a. snap.
    b. toss awkwardly.
    c. move purposefully.
    d. close tightly.

5. In the sentence, "My Uncle John would offer outrageous sums of money—sometimes five dollars—if we could pull one worm up whole" (paragraph 10), the author implies that
    a. the kids were good at getting worms.
    b. Uncle John was rich.
    c. five dollars was a lot of money to the kids.
    d. Uncle John tried to trick the kids.

6. "In the distance a sharp wall of dark rock breaks the horizon as if thrown down by a spiteful God" (paragraph 15). The term *spiteful* in this sentence means
    a. wise.
    b. seeking revenge.
    c. powerful.
    d. seeking comfort.

7. The bloodworm lives inside dead fish heads and comes out when dragged in the sand. (*True/false*)

8. What form of writing does the author use in this selection?
    a. Narrative
    b. Compare and contrast
    c. Argumentative
    d. Process/instructional

9. "Bloodworms . . . are difficult to catch because of the innumerable tiny legs . . ." (paragraph 12). The term *innumerable* in this sentence means
    a. strong for their size.
    b. too many to be counted.
    c. dangerous.
    d. sharp.

10. These trips to the beach inspire the author to write. (*True/false*)

■ Discussion Questions

About Content

1. In the first paragraph the author conveys a sense of stillness. What information is provided to create this effect? Consider word choice and which of our senses the author includes.
2. In paragraphs 5, 7, and 14, the author implies the trip has dangerous elements. What potential dangers are identified?
3. What is the reference to being a "Stranded Crusoe"? What is implied in that image?

About Structure

4. Adjectives are used to describe nouns. In the third paragraph identify which words help to describe the nouns (*river, fish heads, morning, mouths, fish bait, Australian sun,* and *fish.*)

In paragraph 14, the author uses a sentence fragment. Identify the fragment and explain why it is acceptable here.

About Style and Tone

5. The author begins and ends the story with kangaroos off in the distance. What is significant about mentioning kangaroos and how does this help the structure of the story?
6. "This is how I remember the drive from my childhood, but now the possibility and concern of being trapped by the tide is no longer my father's, or uncle's worry. I drive on" (paragraph 14). What is implied in this recollection? What is the mood created by these comments?
7. Along the beach the author finds a jail. This serves as an inspiration for his imagination. What other elements of the setting support the idea of exploring imagination?

■ Writing Assignments

Assignment 1

At the conclusion of this story, the author writes, "The beach, now no longer a fearful passage limited by memory, but the raw atmosphere for my imaginings, the source and cause of those stories still yet to arrive" (paragraph 20). What analogies can be drawn from this selection when considering the beach and the author's inspiration to write? What metaphors arise from this selection? Write an essay detailing the analogies identified in this selection.

Assignment 2

Write your own story about travelling along a beach. Select adjectives to describe your nouns effectively and identify some elements of conflict. Consider also the metaphors that develop when writing about the ocean and the shore as starting or ending points.

Assignment 3

This Canadian author is writing about a time in Australia. Research other Canadian authors whose stories are set outside of Canada. What common features do you recognize in each selection? Among many Canadian authors, you may consider authors such as Yann Martel, Rawi Hage, Camilla Gibb, Timothy Findley, or Carol Shields.

JUST A LITTLE DROP OF WATER: HOW A COMMUNITY-BASED THEATER IN BOLIVIA ADDRESSES THE PROBLEM OF WATER PRIVATIZATION

Eve Tulbert

Have you spent much time thinking about the water you drink? In this selection, Eve Tulbert explores some of the issues of water privatization. You may get thirsty reading about the exploitation of water, but you may also come to realize that for many corporations, the unquenchable quest for profit can be a powerful force.

1   As a community-based artist in the U.S., I haven't thought too much about water. I don't have to. Everyday I can turn on a tap, and fill up a glass with clean, fresh drinking water. All that changed when I came to work with Teatro Trono of Bolivia. I have found that for millions of people all over the world, water is both an everyday dilemma and a political struggle. Private multinational corporations are buying up water contracts all over the Global South. They invest in "blue gold" to turn a profit—at the expense of those who just want a bit of clean water.

2   So, is water a source of income or a human right? Who has a right to control the water? Is it people, or profit, or perhaps *la Pacha Mama,* the mother earth spirit that gave us water in the first place? This is the dramatic question that sparks "La Asamblea de Los Dioses de Agua" (The Meeting of the Water Gods), a community-based performance piece by Teatro Trono.

"We Believe in the Art of the Excluded"

3   Teatro Trono is more than a community theater group. It's a movement. "We want to break the myth that art and beauty are privileges of the rich only," explains Ivan Nogales, the theater's artistic director.

4   Trono was founded ten years ago in the El Alto area of La Paz. They began their work with street kids in the city's detention centers. Their style is physical, vibrant and funny. It comes from a collective directing process in which all of the youth add their ideas to the final product. Their work focuses on the stories of everyday life in one of the poorest areas of Bolivia. Ivan always reminds the youth in his workshops: "Our everyday stories are as amazing as those of great works of literature!"

5   With this philosophy, Trono founded a community arts center in El Alto that teaches theater, circus, dance and visual arts to the children of the barrio. They use play as a way to speak on the social questions that surround them—gender equity, globalization, life in poverty, government corruption and, now, water rights.

6   Like art, "water is not something to gain from. It's a necessity of life," says Nogales. This is the spirit that drives Teatro Trono to question the water policy that surrounds them. As artists confronted by the daily dilemma of water privatization, the group decided to create a mythology of water—a tale in which "water for profit" and "water as spirit of life" come face to face.

At the Miner's Plaza

7   All around the city of El Alto are lively public plazas. On a sunny Sunday morning, people congregate to shop, chat and flirt. But the cast of the Water Gods is all business. From the theater's big truck, bicycles, drums and masks are handed down to the ground below.

8   The youth are busy readying their puppets. Curious children stand in awe. They watch giant colorful figures come to life before them. Luis Vasquez, a 16-year-old actor with Trono, shouts, "Hey where's the bag of nuts and bolts?"

9   "Has anyone seen Saldumi's other arm?" It's hard to keep track of all of the body parts for seven giant water gods—especially when the cast includes 30 actors from eight to 25 years old!

10 Half an hour later, the crowd gathers. Stray dogs settle down in the sun.

11 Women in indigenous dress sell *helados* and *pipocas* to the spectators. The crowd hushes as the music begins. Over a loudspeaker we hear the birdlike trill of a single *quena,* or traditional Bolivian flute.

12   At first we see just a long blue sheet carried in by four young actors. The fabric luffs in the wind as they set it down onto the pavement below. There is a crash of drums and cymbals, and the actors begin to dance and sing. They mime washing clothes, brushing teeth, splashing one another and taking a long cool drink. The actors transform the scene. We are now on the shore of a playful, rushing river.

13   With another drumbeat enters a very comic *empresario*. Vladimir, a young man of 20 years, transforms his body into a hunched and sinister businessman. He points at the river and asks the villagers, "How much is it?" Each one holds out a hand to accept a bit of money from this sinister businessman.

14   The empresario bunches up the river; it is now his own. The crowd of villagers enters again, now to ask him one by one for a drink of water. A girl takes off her golden earrings and hands them over to the empresario. He takes The World's Tiniest Cup out of his pocket and dips it into the river. All of the thirsty actors must share this little drop of water.

Selling the Rain

15   Water is the stuff of life. Like air, sunlight and sustenance, it is one of our most basic human needs. These days, water is also "one of the world's greatest business opportunities." According to a recent report in Fortune magazine, "Water promises to be to the 21st century what oil was to the 20th." "Blue Gold" is a lucrative investment—everybody needs it, and it's impossible to refuse the seller.

16   Fifty-six countries around the globe now have contracts with private, for-profit corporations to run municipal water systems. This growth has been largely due to the policies of the World Bank. The Bank gives developing countries special loans if they privatize more of their national industries. Contracts to run water systems are noncompetitive—they go to just six multinational companies worldwide.

17   This means that for billions of people in the developing world, every time we flush the toilet, brush our teeth or drink a glass of water, a profit goes overseas to Britain, France or to the U.S.

18   In some cases, water privatization leads to devastating effects. In South Africa, when a metered water system broke down, people gathered their water from polluted Lake Emshulatuzi. This led to one of the worst cholera outbreaks in African history. In Argentina, a private company dumps millions of tons of untreated raw sewage into the ocean each year—they're allowed to do so in their government contract.

19   The private companies argue that they can bring better technology and system improvements to third-world water. "We are in the business of being professionals in water and in solving the problems of the electoral bodies who have the responsibility for the water. . . . We bring new technologies to sophisticated demands in terms of water problems—not just access to drinking water, but sophisticated access to drinking water," says Oliver Barbaroux, chief operating officer for Vivendi Water Corp. But can a profit motive ever meet a basic human need?

20   "He's a *maldito* empresario," says Vladimir, talking about the water salesman that he plays in the piece. He hunches his shoulders and sneers as he explains his artistic inspiration. "When I act this role, I think about an old boss that I had when I worked at a restaurant. He would dock our pay; he poured cold water on your head if you weren't working hard enough. This guy only cared about money—that's what made him so mean." Do the multinational corporations do much better?

So What Do the Gods Say?

21   Fourteen-year-old Ximena Flores Vargas is sitting on top of a giant bicycle seat that's been mounted on top of a fruit cart. She's playing Lydia, goddess of amniotic fluid. She's a character like Mother Earth, or Pacha Mama in Bolivian terms. "The first time I got up here, I felt terrified. I thought that I would fall. But now I can concentrate on my role—to be a good goddess who protects the earth!" She waves her arms, and the contraption sways precariously to one side.

22   I ask her what she thinks of the play. "It's about the fight over water," she tells me. "We always get the water dirty. We see it as something to buy."

23   In the world of the play, the villagers and the empresario must face the consequences for polluting and selling the waters. They are transported to a magical place where the Gods of Water tower over them, deciding what to do.

24   They meet an assortment of giant characters: Are, the goddess of reflections; Granizo, the god of ice and hail; Negron, the god of pollution; and Botellon, the god of trapped and bottled water. Different aspects of the nature of water take on different forms with bright costumes, artful masks and towering puppets. The gods decide that humans must face a flood and a drought.

25   "It happens that way," explains Ximena. "Like sometimes it doesn't rain for a long time, and then it floods." Vladimir chimes in, "Just last February, there was a big hail storm in La Paz. There was over a meter of hail. There were deaths, and problems with the water system. It was terrible." In the countryside, the same torrential rains caused the worst crop devastation in years. With not enough to eat, many *campesinos* of the Andean highlands deserted their farms and moved to the city of El Alto.

26   The cities of El Alto and La Paz are built on the Choqueyapu—a convergence of 300 rivers. But you wouldn't know it from walking around here.

27   Ivan's partner Ana tells me, "The rivers are covered over with cement. They run under the city, and they're polluted with garbage, chemicals and dead dogs. These are the same waters that people have to use for their crops and animals downriver in the countryside. It's a shame."

28   With this kind of treatment of water resources, it is easy to believe that flood and drought might be an intentional punishment from a higher power. "Our experience with the water here in Bolivia—it's in our collective consciousness," says Ivan. "There's the privatization issue, but also the droughts, floods, pollution. We've learned that we can't abuse the water without repercussions."

29   This is the driving force behind the Water Gods. The play connects the political and environmental struggle over water to the deeper, underlying forces in the natural world and in Bolivian mythology. Teatro Trono looked deep into its own culture and environment to collectively design the characters. "We were inspired by the indigenous beliefs of Latin America. We did research, we read tales, we visited the Lake (Titicaca). We wanted to know how our ancestors before us thought about this natural resource," explains Doris Mamani, company manager.

30   Members of the company developed puppets to reflect the different forms water can take—ice, rain, polluted waters and the fluids of the human body.

31   Together, and with the help of director Berith Danse and staff from Embassy Theater (based in Holland), they sewed, hammered and welded these Gods of Water into life. As a spectator, one wouldn't guess that the gods were made out of

just nuts and bolts, scrap metal, old bicycle parts and fabric found at a local market. They are, in a word, divine!

32   Luis, an actor and puppeteer, talks about the process. "I constructed Saldumi; it's the tallest one. He's the God of All Waters—salt, mineral and sweet." His friend Caleb adds, "It was a hard process. It took us two months to make the gods. They started to break, and we thought we'd only make it through a few shows, but we learned how to fix them. The rehearsals cost us sweat, and the puppets cost us time and money."

33   For Caleb and Luis, 16- and 17-year-olds, the process of making the gods was both spiritual and educational. "We've forgotten our traditions. We're alienated from our culture. But our gods exist—every year there's a time of rain and a time of sun. This is where our gods come from. We have to learn to honor them again," says Caleb.

34   So, if there truly are spirits of earth and water, then, what would they say to the multinational corporations that are selling the world's water? From her high-up roost, Ximena tells me this: "If Pacha Mama could talk, she would tell us, 'Stop polluting, and stop selling the water,' but she can't talk, so we have to speak for her. That's why we made the play!"

Water Wars Fought in the Streets

35   Out of the hundreds of water-system privatizations across the world, there was just one that didn't go as planned. This was in the Bolivian city of Cochabamba. Just three years ago, people took to the streets to protest the takeover of their local water system by Bechtel, a U.S.-based multinational corporation.

36   In November of 1999, Bechtel signed a 40-year government contract to deliver water to the people of Cochabamba. Three months later, bills had skyrocketed so high that many families could no longer afford the water that they needed.

37   So, they took over the town. "For a month, we lived in the street. We ate in the street. We slept in the street," recounts Felipe Mamani Callejas, a Cochabamba resident. Businesses, schools and offices were all shut down. "The military tried to break our blockade, but we just made it again. I wasn't afraid, because there were so many people behind me."

38   For weeks, the Bolivian military used gas and rubber bullets try to end the blockades. Many Cochabambinos were killed in the confrontation. Protesters played traditional protest music to keep the spirit alive. "We just kept blowing on our instruments so that we wouldn't breathe in the gases. As long as we were play-ing music, the tear gas didn't affect us," says Lenny Olivera of the Coordinadora de la Defensa de Agua.

39   Several weeks later, the government gave in.

40   They cancelled their contract with Bechtel, and turned the control of the water over to the Coordinadora and locally run citizen councils.

41   On the plaza, the huge Water Gods spin in circles, confronting one another and retreating. Their meeting has turned into a war. Loud clashes of cymbals, drums and *rece rece* come from the musicians. The God of Pollution begins to rain acid upon the battlefield. Fire-jugglers and fire-spitters walk among the warring gods, just missing the spectators with their flames.

42   The empresario enters the scene, followed by a woman with the blue river wrapped around her shoulders. She shows the river to the audience in the style

of Vanna White, and carries a "For Sale" sign. Suddenly, there is a din from the other side of the stage. It is the villagers who enter marching and waving imaginary signs. The empresario waves at them, and they fall to the ground with a crash. They rise again, and now the empresario lights an imaginary bomb and throws it to the crowd. They fall once again. But in the end, they rise and march. They are determined to take back their river.

43   The violence in Cochabamba, just like the violence in the play, reflects a deeper truth. There is an inherent violence in taking a life-giving resource from those who need it. To deprive people of water is to deprive them of life. Perhaps that is why people were willing to risk their lives over the Bechtel water contract.

The Ending?

44   In the world of the play, the villagers are victorious. The "river" is spread out again across the plaza. The empresario returns to clean it up, and then everyone takes a good, long drink.

45   The crowd cheers. For many in El Alto, the story of the greedy empresario is all too true. After the performance, children gather to play with the huge puppets, and adults are heard engaging in conversation about water bills and government corruption.

46   But what would it mean if this fantasy ending *was* the real life ending, too?

"The Western model of privatization is wrong development. It's the wrong model. We've bought into some crazy ideas about progress, but there are ways to do it right." Enrique Hidalgo Clares explains his philosophy of "right development" to me as he shows me his work at El Poncho EcoCenter in Bolivia.

47   "We're experimenting with other models. Like here, we collect our rain water from the roofs. We make a simple filter out of carbon to clean the water. For our raw sewage, we send that to this field—that's a bamboo crop. It treats the sewage naturally."

48   At El Poncho, they live in adobe houses, take showers heated by solar power and drink clean water for free. And they do it all with natural materials, no pollution and no profit for a multinational corporation.

49   This kind of "right development" is perhaps what the Water Gods are trying to tell us about. Luis looks up at his towering puppet Saldumi as he talks to me about the play. "Nature is the earth, it's Pacha Mama, it's the whole world. The Gods are very old. People saw their reflections in the water and the rain. They believed that they were in the presence of something magical. The stories of the gods, they can show us the right way to live."

Epilogue

50   "The Meeting of the Water Gods" speaks to a larger question for arts activism.

51   In Bolivia, and in so many places around the world, it is clear to see what happens when multinational corporations and government corruption run rampant.

52   The logic of capitalism measures and prices things that weren't for sale before—trees are felled, water is bottled, elements are mined from deep within mountains. More than that, human lives are measured in hours and wages—here in Bolivia, many people are just earning enough to live. Corporations tell the stories of "efficiency, technology and development" when they describe their work.

53   Arts groups like Teatro Trono remind us of the spiritual value of the natural world that surrounds us. They remind us that some things must not be bought and sold. They teach us that, as artists, we can develop counter-mythologies. We can tell the stories that celebrate the gift of the natural world, and the pricelessness of human life.

54   Learn more about water privatization worldwide at Public Citizen, http://www.citizen.org. Learn more about Teatro Trono by contacting the author: eve.tulbert@gmail.com.

■ Reading Comprehension Questions

1. The term *indigenous* in the sentence "Women in indigenous dress sell *helados* and *pipocas* to the spectators" (paragraph 7) means
   a. hard to swallow.
   b. smart.
   c. native.
   d. colourful.

2. What would be a good alternative title for this selection?
   a. Water Pollution
   b. The Water Gods
   c. Restoring Bolivia
   d. Hope Springs Eternal

3. The term *privatization* in the sentence "In some cases water privatization leads to devastating effects" (paragraph 13) means
   a. to close doors.
   b. to control all of the world's water.
   c. to remove from government ownership.
   d. to pollute.

4. According to this selection, how many countries have private, for-profit corporations running municipal water supplies?
   a. 20
   b. 21
   c. 56
   d. 100

5. The term *lucrative* in the sentence "'Blue Gold' is a lucrative investment—everybody needs it and it's impossible to refuse the seller" (paragraph 11) means
   a. profitable.
   b. natural.
   c. accessible.
   d. dishonest.

6. The author implies that the travelling play is designed to
   a. charge a small fee for entertainment.
   b. keep children out of prison.
   c. educate people in Bolivia about water consumption.
   d. teach the corporations a lesson.

7. The term *convergence* in the sentence ". . . a convergence of 300 rivers" (paragraph 19) means
   a. shaking ground.
   b. coming together.
   c. breaking apart.
   d. polluting.

8. In the sentence "Many Cochabambinos were killed in the confrontation" (paragraph 27), *confrontation* means
   a. burial.
   b. opening doors.
   c. peace talks.
   d. conflict between two groups.

9. The author describes the businessman in the play as "sinister." *Sinister* means
   a. business woman.
   b. "sister" in Spanish.
   c. evil.
   d. drunken.

10. The author implies that for the actors, the benefit of putting on a play goes beyond educating people. It also allows them to
    a. wear costumes.
    b. reconnect with their culture .
    c. get free water.
    d. get interviewed.

■ Discussion Questions

About Content

1. The article discusses how a small town opposed having their water privatized. What was the name of this community and what did they do?
2. Why have so many countries turned their water supply over to for-profit corporations? Why are there so few corporations for so many countries?
3. According to this article, what role does the World Bank play in water privatization?

About Structure

4. The author uses seven headings in this selection. What purpose do these headings serve? Do you find this structure effective?
5. Many news articles take excerpts of text and enlarge them alongside the story. What purpose does this serve? How effective is it in this selection?

About Style and Tone

6. How would you describe the style of this author's writing (argumentative, process oriented, informational, narrative, etc.)? What evidence from the text can you find to support your answer?
7. The author intersperses factual content with reported events. What effect does this have on your understanding of the issues described in this selection?

■ Writing Assignments

Assignment 1

Research how many countries today have privatized their water. Choose one corporation that oversees privatization, and research its literature on the benefits of water privatization.

Assignment 2

The World Bank has been criticized in this article for promoting water privatization. Research one supporter of the World Bank's position and one group opposed to it. Write an essay that compares and contrasts both perspectives.

Assignment 3

The theatre group Teatro Tronto was formed with "street kids in the city's detention centers" (paragraph 2). Using examples from the text, explain what you believe to be the benefit for these children and young adults. Do research to find arts projects in your community. Identify an issue in your community that might be explored and expressed through an arts project. Consider undertaking this project!

THE STORY OF MOUSELAND

As told by Tommy Douglas in 1944

Introduction

1   Tommy Douglas (1904–1986) was one of Canada's best known New Democrats. He was a man of many talents and, being involved in politics since 1936, he is renowned for various reasons. The "Mouseland" story is a small sample of the wit and humour many people knew him for. To see and listen to Tommy Douglas in person was a rare treat. Tommy was a most accomplished orator.

2   Some people saw Tommy Douglas as a true democratic socialist, someone who placed human rights and needs above the mere pursuit of profits and power. Such principles should be implemented at the wish of the majority of the people. A social minded government would plan the economy of the country to allow all people to share in the country's wealth and have equal access to such basic needs as health and education.

3   Others saw Tommy as a great politician whose natural speaking, story telling and debating abilities helped bring social change to the country. Tommy was first elected to the House of Commons in Ottawa in 1936. He later switched to provincial politics and it was during his years as Premier of Saskatchewan that Medicare was first introduced to North America. Prior to Medicare, health care services were only available to those who could pay the price.

4   When the C.C.F. (Co-operative Commonwealth Federation) was renamed the New Democratic Party in 1961, Tommy Douglas was chosen as the Leader of the new party until he resigned in 1971. Tommy Douglas relates his message of social democracy in such a fashion that any audience can understand even the most complicated issue and be well entertained at the same time. To social minded people everywhere, Tommy Douglas remains a constant source of inspiration.

The Story

5   It's the story of a place called Mouseland. Mouseland was a place where all the little mice lived and played, were born and died. And they lived much the same as you and I do.

6   They even had a Parliament. And every four years they had an election. Used to walk to the polls and cast their ballots. Some of them even got a ride to the polls. And got a ride for the next four years afterwards too. Just like you and me. And every time on election day all the little mice used to go to the ballot box and they used to elect a government. A government made up of big, fat, black cats.

7   Now if you think it strange that mice should elect a government made up of cats, you just look at the history of Canada for last 90 years and maybe you'll see that they weren't any stupider than we are.

8   Now I'm not saying anything against the cats. They were nice fellows. They conducted their government with dignity. They passed good laws—that is, laws that were good for cats. But the laws that were good for cats weren't very good for mice. One of the laws said that mouseholes had to be big enough so a cat could get his paw in. Another law said that mice could only travel at certain speeds—so that a cat could get his breakfast without too much effort.

9   All the laws were good laws. For cats. But, oh, they were hard on the mice. And life was getting harder and harder. And when the mice couldn't put up with it any more, they decided something had to be done about it. So they went en masse to the polls. They voted the black cats out. They put in the white cats.

10   Now the white cats had put up a terrific campaign. They said: "All that Mouseland needs is more vision." They said: "The trouble with Mouseland is those round mouseholes we got. If you put us in we'll establish square mouseholes." And they did. And the square mouseholes were twice as big as the round mouseholes, and now the cat could get both his paws in. And life was tougher than ever. And when they couldn't take that anymore, they voted the white cats out and put the black ones in again. Then they went back to the white cats. Then to the black cats. They even tried half black cats and half white cats. And they called that coalition. They even got one government made up of cats with spots on them: they were cats that tried to make a noise like a mouse but ate like a cat.

11   You see, my friends, the trouble wasn't with the colour of the cat. The trouble was that they were cats. And because they were cats, they naturally looked after cats instead of mice.

12   Presently there came along one little mouse who had an idea. My friends, watch out for the little fellow with an idea. And he said to the other mice, "Look fellows, why do we keep on electing a government made up of cats? Why don't we elect a government made up of mice?" "Oh," they said, "he's a Bolshevik. Lock him up!"

13   So they put him in jail.

14   But I want to remind you: that you can lock up a mouse or a man but you can't lock up an idea.

The Moral of the Story

15   "Mouseland" is a political fable, originally told by Clare Gillis, a friend of Tommy Douglas. Tommy used his story many times to show in a humorous way how Canadians fail to recognize that neither the Liberals or Conservatives are truly interested in what matters to ordinary citizens; yet Canadians continue to vote for them.

16   The story cleverly deals with the false assumption by some people that CCF'ers (NDP'ers) are Communists. The ending shows Tommy Douglas has faith that someday socialism, which recognizes human rights and dignity, will win over capitalism and the mere pursuit of wealth and power.

■ Reading Comprehension Questions

1. The word *orator* in the sentence "Tommy was a most accomplished orator" (introduction paragraph 1) means
   a. actor.
   b. public speaker.
   c. New Democrat.
   d. politician.

2. The word *pursuit* in the sentence ". . . the mere pursuit of profits and power . . ." (introduction, paragraph 2), means
   a. dislike.
   b. think.
   c. chase.
   d. reduce.

3. *True or false?* In the sentence "Such principles should be implemented at the wish of the majority of the people" (introduction, paragraph 2), *principles* means administrators of schools.

4. In the same sentence, *implemented* means
   a. carried out.
   b. closed.
   c. fired.
   d. scolded.

5. Which sentence best expresses the main idea of the selection?
   a. Neither Liberals nor Conservatives are interested in what matters to Canadians, but we still vote for them.
   b. People are more like mice than cats.
   c. New Democrats want to be more like the Conservatives and Liberals.
   d. You should not trust cats.

6. The author implies that
   a. cats are misunderstood.
   b. politicians are like big black cats.
   c. New Democrats are a better type of cat.
   d. Canadians are smarter than the mice in his story.

7. The word *campaign* in "Now the white cats put up a terrific campaign" (paragraph 6) means
   a. slogan.
   b. series of events to achieve a goal.
   c. bluff.
   d. jumble of words to confuse people.

8. *True or false?* The author implies that we will always be like mice and politicians will always be like cats.

9. The author implies that
   a. Canadians should not question authority.
   b. politics is bad.
   c. a good idea is greater than just one person.
   d. more people need to go into politics.

10. *True or false?* Mouseland is a fable about politics in Canada.

■ Discussion Questions

About Content

1. Why is this story set in a make-believe place called Mouseland?
2. Why do you think politicians are characterized as cats and people are characterized as mice?
3. Do you believe that you can trust politicians in Canada? Why or why not?

About Structure

4. What form of writing does Douglas use in this selection?
   a. Exposition
   b. Narrative
   c. Informational
   d. Compare and contrast

5. What effect does the writer's use of short, simple sentences have on the reader?

About Style and Tone

6. Who is the audience the author is addressing? Support your answer with evidence from the text.
7. Choose one word to describe the tone of this selection. For example, (funny, angry, sad, clever, light-hearted, playful, mean, deceptive, silly, or others) and explain, with examples from the story, why you believe this to be the tone of the selection.

■ Writing Assignments

Assignment 1

The author uses analogous writing to make his point in this selection. Analogy is an extended metaphor. Watching reality TV is like eating rice cakes. . . . They look like they will fill me, but I always feel empty when they are finished. Consider analogies you know of in your life. For example, going to school is like a box of chocolates—occasionally, some experiences leave a bad taste in your mouth while many others can leave you wanting more. Retell "The Story of Mouseland," but think of a different analogy to explain the same story.

Assignment 2

In Ontario, a Member of Parliament was arrested for going 93 km in a 50-km zone, possessing cocaine, and having an excessive blood alcohol limit. As you probably know, drunk driving and possessing cocaine are criminal offences; however, the Crown attorney said she had no reasonable prospect of conviction and withdrew the charges, leaving the MP to plead guilty to careless driving, pay a $500.00 fine and make a $500.00 charitable donation. How do you see this story relating to "The Story of Mouseland"? Do you agree or disagree that politicians get treated differently than other Canadians? Write a clear thesis statement outlining your position, then write three paragraphs giving examples that support your position.

Assignment 3

How many Canadians do you imagine go out and vote for a new prime minister/political party each election? You may research this through Statistics Canada or other Web sites.

What percentage of voters turned out for the last election? Does this number surprise you? Thinking about "The Story of Mouseland," what reasons might there be for this (many/few) people to vote?

ABORIGINAL HOT AND HEAVY

Drew Hayden Taylor

Drew Hayden Taylor is a comedian, author, and playwright who explores Aboriginal issues with a keen, sometimes piercing sense of humour. This article is about sexuality. Some may find the content too bawdy for their taste. This author takes a liberal approach to Native sexuality and touches on both sobering and humorous issues.

1   Years ago, I had a friend whose life ambition—well, one of them anyways—was to write a book detailing the hundred most beautiful places in the world to make love. Needless to say I was very eager to co-write that book with her but alas both it and the woman disappeared into the mists of what might have happened. Still, I thought it was a very cool idea. And, upon reflection, it still sounds like an interesting concept and I still wonder if such a book would be possible.

2   For obvious reasons, I would attempt to approach the book from an Aboriginal perspective. THE 100 MOST BEAUTIFUL FIRST NATIONS ON WHICH TO MAKE LOVE. I can't really say how popular it would be but it would still be a fun book to put together. I could write about the austere beauty of Saskatchewan's Gordon's Reserve. I could wax poetically on the olichan scented breeze of Hartley Bay or sharing a passionate moment bathed in the lights of Casino Rama. The additional bonus being I could write the whole thing off as business expenses. My accountant would like that.

3   We all know the topic is there, waiting to be explored. But alas, for reasons unknown, Native people don't have a particularly strong reputation for things erotic, which is not only unfortunate, but wrong. I believe this is a gross oversight and something should definitely be done about it. For instance, we have the highest birth rate in the country, so we obviously know a few things about this topic. And it's time to lift that blanket.

4   Historically many of our legends, those particularly involving Nanabush or other Trickster representations, were extremely erotic and graphic. Many were downright bawdy and would put most porn stars to shame. Unfortunately though, during what I refer to as the age of the C.C.E. (Canadian Christian Era), many were outlawed, discouraged, and abandoned as being obscene, leaving many with the impression traditional Native legends were just cute stories for children. Some were. But many weren't.

5   These inaccurate perceptions about the Indigenous hot & heavy need to be addressed, and in this day and age of instant media and communication, the sooner the better. I have a few suggestions on how to better celebrate and procreate (if that's the proper word) a better appreciation of First Nations sexuality.

6   First of all, almost everybody is familiar with the bikini wax known as a "Brazilian", because of those high cut bikini bottoms they like to wear down there. Let's indigenize it and give it a cultural resonance. Instead, get an "Ojibway", which would be in the shape of a dreamcatcher (It's intricate and detailed work but aboriginally well worth it). Or maybe an "Inuit", in the shape of an inukshuk (which traditionally stood as a guidepost for travellers. The metaphor works). Or how about a "Haida", shaped like a salmon (swimming upstream to spawn. Once more, the metaphor fits).

7   What's got me thinking about all this is that, just a few weeks ago, the national media reported that there may soon be a Canadian Adult cable network coming to a television set near you, with at least 50% Canadian content. Pretty soon "paddling your canoe" and "he shoots, he scores" will have a whole new meaning. The Canadianizing of Porn . . . it kind of boggles the mind, doesn't it? Will a 24 replace the popularity of a 69? Maple syrup will supersede whipped cream. And our national symbol of . . . the beaver . . . enough said. Anything is possible.

8   Why should Native people be left behind in this digital revolution? Granted, it's a sticky subject. Many in our community no doubt believe that porn may not be the best way to establish our independence and autonomy. Is the illegal sale of cigarettes a better solution? Nudity vs cancer—I wonder if the Assembly of First Nations needs to have a referendum on this? Or how about the profitable operation of casinos? None of them actually reek of cultural significance. Simply put, vice pays. WE all know that. Native people know that as well as any other culture.

9   This new broadcast tendency also could be a potentially lucrative side business for APTN (the Aboriginal Peoples Television Network). They could start running shows like The Bushcombers or North of 69. Don't get me started on the "Poundmaker" and "Big Bear" mini-series. Once more, anything is possible.

10   I know this is a controversial issue. Anything to do with sex is, especially from such a conservative population as Native people. And Canadians. But I once compiled a book about Native sexuality, called ME SEXY, where I say that often the only impression the dominant culture has about anything to do with Aboriginal sexuality is usually dead hookers, high rates of STD's in First Nations communities, and Residential School sexual abuse.

11   Unfortunately some of that is true, but it's also like saying all White people are Latvian. And believe it or not, we tend to have a little more fun with the topic than the media will have you know.

■ Reading Comprehension Questions

1. The term *ambition* in the sentence "Years ago I had a friend whose life ambition—well one of them anyways . . ." (paragraph 1) means
   a. fear.
   b. goal.
   c. cultural understanding.
   d. regret.

2. The author implies that casinos
   a. should sell cigarettes.
   b. should be more multicultural.
   c. are not culturally symbolic.
   d. are a true symbol of Native culture.

3. The author implies that
   a. Native people do have an erotic history.
   b. Aboriginals always talk about sex.
   c. sex should be easy to talk about.
   d. all White people are Latvian.

4. An alternative title for this selection could be
   a. First Nations Sexuality.
   b. Pornography in Canada.
   c. Canada's Aboriginal Controversy.
   d. The 100 Most Beautiful Places to Make Love.

5. The term *controversial* in the sentence "I know this is a controversial issue" (paragraph 10) means
   a. something illegal.
   b. something immoral.
   c. balanced on both sides.
   d. causing argument or debate.

6. *True or false?* The "Brazilian" is a reference to grooming pubic hair.

7. The author implies that
   a. he would like to write a book about the best places to make love.
   b. he is writing a book on making love.
   c. someone else wrote a book on making love.
   d. it's not a good idea to write a book on making love.

8. The term *referendum* in the sentence "I wonder if the Assembly of First Nations needs to have a referendum on this?" (paragraph 8) means
   a. someone to write a book about it.
   b. a vote by the people.
   c. a vote by the council.
   d. an Aboriginal movie.

9. The author implies that a Canadian adult cable network would need
   a. actors who have acted in Brazilian pornography.
   b. movies made in Canada with adult content.
   c. a special license to show pornography.
   d. to show the world that First Nations people are sexy.

10. The term *autonomy* in the sentence "Many in our community no doubt believe that porn may not be the best way to establish our independence and autonomy" (paragraph 8) means
    a. self-government.
    b. sexual identity.
    c. casino profits.
    d. land claims.

■ Discussion Questions

About Content

1. "Simply put, vice pays" (paragraph 8). How accurate is this statement? Give examples from this text and explain how attempts to be "culturally significant" fail or succeed.
2. The author is brutally frank in his observations and uses edgy humour. Do you think the author is asking for change, or is he making a social commentary on First Nations identity?
3. The author acknowledges that Aboriginals may take offence at being identified with pornography as a means of making money. He compares this to other vices that can be associated with Aboriginals. What are these associations and are they justified criticisms in your opinion?

About Structure

4. How does the author begin this selection (narrative, argumentative, compare and contrast, process)?
5. What is the national news item that the author identifies as compelling him to write this selection?
6. What is the gross oversight in paragraph 3? What reason is given for this in paragraph 4?

About Style and Tone

7. The author makes observations about issues and then includes humorous examples to illustrate his point. Find three examples in the text of when he uses this writing style.
8. In this selection the author includes both humorous and stark, or pointed, observations. What is the effect of this writing style? Are you left laughing, crying, thinking, etc.?

■ Writing Assignments

Assignment 1

Research the Assembly of First Nations' position on the value of casinos for Native communities in Canada. Can you determine how profitable casinos can be? What do casino regulators say about their association with First Nations peoples?

Assignment 2

As late as 1995, a residential school was still operating in Canada. Research one of these schools and determine the reason for operating the school in the first place, then report on the effects on the students who attended residential schools.

Assignment 3

Find a current version of the story of Nanabush, as well as an earlier version. Write a compare and contrast essay outlining the primary differences between the two. Do you agree with the author's observations? Explain your reasons.

Considering Concepts

Joan Dunayer

Dunayer contrasts the glamorous "myth" about alcohol, as presented in advertising and popular culture, with the reality—which is often far less appealing. After reading her essay, you will be more aware of how we are encouraged to think of alcohol as being tied to happiness and success. You may also become a more critical observer of images presented by advertisers.

1   As the only freshman on his high school's varsity wrestling team, Tod was anxious to fit in with his older teammates. One night after a match, he was offered a tequila bottle on the ride home. Tod felt he had to accept, or he would seem like a sissy. He took a swallow, and every time the bottle was passed back to him, he took another swallow. After seven swallows, he passed out. His terrified teammates carried him into his home, and his mother then rushed him to the hospital. After his stomach was pumped, Tod learned that his blood alcohol level had been so high that he was lucky not to be in a coma or dead.

2   Although alcohol sometimes causes rapid poisoning, frequently leads to long-term addiction, and always threatens self-control, our society encourages drinking. Many parents, by their example, give children the impression that alcohol is an essential ingredient of social gatherings. Peer pressure turns bachelor parties, fraternity initiations, and spring-semester beach vacations into competitions in "getting trashed." In soap operas, glamorous characters pour scotch whiskey from

506

crystal decanters as readily as most people turn on the faucet for tap water. In films and rock videos, trend-setters party in nightclubs and bars. And who can recall a televised baseball or basketball game without a beer commercial? By the age of 21, the average North American has seen drinking on TV about 75,000 times. Alcohol ads appear with pounding frequency—in magazines, on billboards, in college newspapers—contributing to a harmful myth about drinking.

3 Part of the myth is that liquor signals professional success. In a slick men's magazine, one full-page ad for scotch whiskey shows two men seated in an elegant restaurant. Both are in their thirties, perfectly groomed, and wearing expensive-looking gray suits. The windows are draped with velvet, the table with spotless white linen. Each place-setting consists of a long-stemmed water goblet, silver utensils, and thick silver plates. On each plate is a half-empty cocktail glass. The two men are grinning and shaking hands, as if they've just concluded a business deal. The caption reads, "The taste of success."

4 Contrary to what the liquor company would have us believe, drinking is more closely related to lack of success than to achievement. Among students, the heaviest drinkers have the lowest grades. In the work force, alcoholics are frequently late or absent, tend to perform poorly, and often get fired. Although alcohol abuse occurs in all economic classes, it remains most severe among the poor.

5 Another part of the alcohol myth is that drinking makes you more attractive to the opposite sex. "Hot, hot, hot," one commercial's soundtrack begins, as the camera scans a crowd of college-age beachgoers. Next it follows the curve of a woman's leg up to her bare hip and lingers there. She is young, beautiful, wearing a bikini. A young guy, carrying an ice chest, positions himself near to where she sits. He is tan, muscular. She doesn't show much interest—until he opens the chest and takes out a beer. Now she smiles over at him. He raises his eyebrows and, invitingly, holds up another can. She joins him. This beer, the song concludes, "Attracts like no other."

6 Beer doesn't make anyone sexier. Like all alcohol, it lowers the levels of male hormones in men and of female hormones in women—even when taken in small amounts. In substantial amounts, alcohol can cause infertility in women and impotence in men. Some alcoholic men even develop enlarged breasts, from their increased female hormones.

7 The alcohol myth also creates the illusion that beer and athletics are a perfect combination. One billboard features three high-action images: a baseball player running at top speed, a surfer riding a wave, and a basketball player leaping to make a dunk shot. A particular light beer, the billboard promises, "won't slow you down."

8 "Slow you down" is exactly what alcohol does. Drinking plays a role in over six million injuries each year—not counting automobile accidents. Even in small amounts, alcohol dulls the brain, reducing muscle coordination and slowing reaction time. It also interferes with the ability to focus the eyes and adjust to a sudden change in brightness—such as the flash of a car's headlights. Drinking and driving, responsible for over half of all automobile deaths, is the leading cause of death among teenagers. Continued alcohol abuse can physically alter the brain, permanently impairing learning and memory. Long-term drinking is related to malnutrition, weakening of the bones, and ulcers. It increases the risk of liver failure, heart disease, and stomach cancer.

9 Finally, according to the myth fostered by the media in our culture, alcohol generates a warm glow of happiness that unifies the family. In one popular film, the only food visible at a wedding reception is an untouched wedding cake, but

beer, whiskey, and vodka flow freely. Most of the guests are drunk. After shouting into the microphone to get everyone's attention, the band leader asks the bride and groom to come forward. They are presented with two wine-filled silver drinking cups branching out from a single stem. "If you can drink your cups without spilling any wine," the band leader tells them, "you will have good luck for the rest of your lives." The couple drain their cups without taking a breath, and the crowd cheers.

10   A marriage, however, is unlikely to be "lucky" if alcohol plays a major role in it. Nearly two-thirds of domestic violence involves drinking. Alcohol abuse by parents is strongly tied to child neglect and juvenile delinquency. Drinking during pregnancy can lead to miscarriage and is a major cause of such birth defects as deformed limbs and mental retardation. Those who depend on alcohol are far from happy: over a fourth of the patients in state and county mental institutions have alcohol problems; more than half of all violent crimes are alcohol-related; the rate of suicide among alcoholics is fifteen times higher than among the general population.

11   Alcohol, some would have us believe, is part of being successful, sexy, healthy, and happy. But those who have suffered from it—directly or indirectly—know otherwise. For alcohol's victims, "Here's to your health" rings with a terrible irony when it is accompanied by the clink of liquor glasses.

■ Reading Comprehension Questions

1. The word *caption* in "The caption reads, 'The taste of success' " (paragraph 3) means
   a. menu.
   b. man.
   c. words accompanying the picture.
   d. contract that seals the business deal.

2. The word *impairing* in "Continued alcohol abuse can physically alter the brain, permanently impairing learning and memory" (paragraph 8) means
   a. postponing.
   b. doubling.
   c. damaging.
   d. teaching.

3. Which one of the following would be a good alternative title for this selection?
   a. The Taste of Success
   b. Alcohol and Your Social Life
   c. Too Much Tequila
   d. Alcohol: Image and Reality

4. Which sentence best expresses the main idea of the selection?
   a. Sports and alcohol don't mix.
   b. The media and our culture promote false images about success and happiness.
   c. The media and our culture promote false beliefs about alcohol.
   d. Liquor companies should not be allowed to use misleading ads about alcohol.

5. According to the selection, drinking can
   a. actually unify a family.
   b. lower hormone levels.

     c. temporarily improve performance in sports.

     d. increase the likelihood of pregnancy.

6. *True or false?* Alcohol abuse is most severe among the middle class.

7. *True or false?* The leading cause of death among teenagers is drinking and driving.

8. From the first paragraph of the essay, we can conclude that
    a. even one encounter with alcohol can actually lead to death.
    b. tequila is the worst type of alcohol to drink.
    c. wrestlers tend to drink more than other athletes.
    d. by the time students reach high school, peer pressure doesn't influence them.

9. *True or false?* The author implies that one or two drinks a day are probably harmless.

10. The author implies that heavy drinking can lead to
    a. poor grades.
    b. getting fired.
    c. heart disease.
    d. all of the above.

■ Discussion Questions

About Content

1. According to Dunayer, how many parts are there to the myth about alcohol? Which part do you consider the most dangerous?

2. Drawing on your own experience, provide examples of ways in which our culture encourages drinking.

About Structure

3. What method does Dunayer use to begin her essay?
    a. Movement from general to specific
    b. An opposite
    c. An incident

4. The body of Dunayer's essay is made up of four pairs of paragraphs (paragraphs 3 and 4, 5 and 6, 7 and 8, 9 and 10) that serve to introduce and develop each of her four main supporting points. What is the pattern by which she divides each point into two paragraphs?

5. Dunayer introduces the first part of the myth about alcohol with the words, "Part of the myth is . . ." (paragraph 3). She then goes on to use an addition transition to introduce each of the three other parts of the myth—in the first sentences of paragraphs 5, 7, and 9. What are those transitions?

6. What method does Dunayer use to conclude her essay?
    a. Prediction or recommendation
    b. Summary and final thought
    c. Thought-provoking question

About Style and Tone

7. Why is the title of the essay appropriate?

■ Writing Assignments

Assignment 1

Describe and analyze several recent advertisements for wine, beer, or liquor on television or radio, in newspapers or magazines, or on billboards. Argue whether the ads are socially responsible or irresponsible in the way that they portray drinking. Your thesis might be something like one of the following examples:

> In three recent ads, ad agencies and liquor companies have acted irresponsibly in their portrayal of alcohol.
> In three recent ads, ad agencies and liquor companies have acted with a measure of responsibility in their portrayal of alcohol.

Alternatively, write about what you consider responsible or irresponsible advertising for some other product or service. Clothing, weight loss, and cosmetics are possibilities to consider.

Assignment 2

Imagine you have a friend, relative, or classmate who drinks a lot. Write a letter to that person, warning him or her about the dangers of alcohol. If appropriate, use information from Dunayer's essay. Since your purpose is to get someone you care about to control or break a dangerous habit, you should make your writing very personal. Don't bother explaining how alcoholism affects people in general. Instead, focus directly on what you see it doing to your reader.

Divide your argument into at least three supporting paragraphs. You might, for instance, talk about how your reader is jeopardizing his or her relationship with three of the following: family, friends, boss and co-workers, teachers and classmates.

Assignment 3

Dunayer describes how alcohol advertisements promote false beliefs, such as the idea that alcohol will make you successful. Imagine that you work for a public service ad agency given the job of presenting the negative side of alcohol. What images would you choose to include in your ads?

Write an informal report to your boss in which you propose, in detail, three anti-alcohol ads. Choose from among the following:

- An ad countering the idea that alcohol leads to success
- An ad countering the idea that alcohol is sexy
- An ad countering the idea that alcohol goes well with athletics
- An ad countering the idea that alcohol makes for happy families

HOW TO MAKE IT IN COLLEGE, NOW THAT YOU'RE HERE

Brian O'Keeney

The author of this selection presents a compact guide to being a successful student. He will show you how to pass tests, how to avoid becoming a student zombie, how to find time to fit in everything you want to do, and how to deal with personal problems while keeping up with your studies. The tips that O'Keeney presents have been culled from his own experience and his candid interviews with fellow students.

1   Today is your first day on campus. You were a high school senior three months ago. Or maybe you've been at home with your children for the last ten years. Or maybe you work full time and you're coming to school to start the process that leads to a better job. Whatever your background is, you're probably not too concerned today with staying in college. After all, you just got over the hurdle (and the paperwork) of applying to this place and organizing your life so that you could attend. And today, you're confused and tired. Everything is a hassle, from finding the classrooms to standing in line at the bookstore. But read my advice anyway. And if you don't read it today, clip and save this article. You might want to look at it a little further down the road.

2   By the way, if this isn't your very first day, don't skip this article. Maybe you haven't been doing as well in your studies as you'd hoped. Or perhaps you've had problems juggling your work schedule, your class schedule, and your social life. If so, read on. You're about to get the inside story on making it in college. On the basis of my own experience as a final-year student, and of dozens of interviews with successful students, I've worked out a no-fail system for coping with college. These are the inside tips every student needs to do well in school. I've put myself in your place, and I'm going to answer the questions that will cross (or have already crossed) your mind during your stay here.

What's the Secret of Getting Good Grades?

3   It all comes down to getting those grades, doesn't it? After all, you came here for some reason, and you're going to need passing grades to get the credits or degree you want. Many of us never did much studying in high school; most of the learning we did took place in the classroom. College, however, is a lot different. You're really on your own when it comes to passing courses. In fact, sometimes you'll feel as if nobody cares if you make it or not. Therefore, you've got to figure out a study system that gets results. Sooner or later, you'll be alone with those books. After that, you'll be sitting in a classroom with an exam sheet on your desk. Whether you stare at that exam with a queasy stomach or whip through it fairly confidently depends on your study techniques. Most of the successful students I talked to agreed that the following eight study tips deliver solid results.

4   *1. Set Up a Study Place.* Those students you see "studying" in the cafeteria or game room aren't learning much. You just can't learn when you're distracted by people and noise. Even the library can be a bad place to study if you constantly find yourself watching the clouds outside or the students walking through the stacks. It takes guts to sit, alone, in a quiet place in order to study. But you have to do it. Find a room at home or a spot in the library that's relatively quiet—and boring. When you sit there, you won't have much to do except study.

5   *2. Get into a Study Frame of Mind.* When you sit down, do it with the attitude that you're going to get this studying done. You're not going to doodle in your notebook or make a list for the supermarket. Decide that you're going to study and learn now, so that you can move on to more interesting things as soon as possible.

6   *3. Give Yourself Rewards.* If you sweat out a block of study time, and do a good job on it, treat yourself. You deserve it. You can "psych" yourself up for studying by promising to reward yourself afterwards. A present for yourself can be anything from a favorite TV show to a relaxing bath to a dish of double chocolate ice cream.

7   *4. Skim the Textbook First.* Lots of students sit down with an assignment like "read chapter five, pages 125–150" and do just that. They turn to page 125 and start to read. After a while, they find that they have no idea what they just read. For the

last ten minutes, they've been thinking about their five-year-old or what they're going to eat for dinner. Eventually, they plod through all the pages but don't remember much afterwards.

8   In order to prevent this problem, skim the textbook chapter first. This means: look at the title, the subtitles, the headings, the pictures, the first and last paragraphs. Try to find out what the person who wrote the book had in mind when he or she organized the chapter. What was important enough to set off as a title or in bold type? After skimming, you should be able to explain to yourself what the main points of the chapter are. Unless you're the kind of person who would step into an empty elevator shaft without looking first, you'll soon discover the value of skimming.

9   *5. Take Notes on What You're Studying.* This sounds like a hassle, but it works. Go back over the material after you've read it, and jot down key words and phrases in the margins. When you review the chapter for a test, you'll have handy little things like "definition of rationalization" or "example of assimilation" in the margins. If the material is especially tough, organize a separate sheet of notes. Write down definitions, examples, lists, and main ideas. The idea is to have a single sheet that boils the entire chapter down to a digestible lump.

10   *6. Review after You've Read and Taken Notes.* Some people swear that talking to yourself works. Tell yourself about the most important points in the chapter. Once you've said them out loud, they seem to stick better in your mind. If you can't talk to yourself about the material after reading it, that's a sure sign you don't really know it.

11   *7. Give Up.* This may sound contradictory, but give up when you've had enough. You should try to make it through at least an hour, though. Ten minutes here and there are useless. When your head starts to pound and your eyes develop spidery red lines, quit. You won't do much learning when you're exhausted.

12   *8. Take a College Skills Course If You Need It.* Don't hesitate or feel embarrassed about enrolling in a study skills course. Many students say they wouldn't have made it without one.

How Can I Keep Up with All My Responsibilities without Going Crazy?

13   You've got a class schedule. You're supposed to study. You've got a family. You've got a husband, wife, boyfriend, girlfriend, child. You've got a job. How are you possibly going to cover all the bases in your life and maintain your sanity? This is one of the toughest problems students face. Even if they start the semester with the best of intentions, they eventually find themselves tearing their hair out trying to do everything they're supposed to do. Believe it or not, though, it is possible to meet all your responsibilities. And you don't have to turn into a hermit or give up your loved ones to do it.

14   The secret here is to organize your time. But don't just sit around half the semester planning to get everything together soon. Before you know it, you'll be confronted with midterms, papers, family, and work all at once. Don't let yourself reach that breaking point. Instead, try these three tactics.

15   *1. Monthly Calendar.* Get one of those calendars with big blocks around the dates. Give yourself an overview of the whole term by marking down the due dates for papers and projects. Circle test and exam days. This way those days don't sneak up on you unexpectedly.

16   *2. Study Schedule.* Sit down during the first few days of this semester and make up a sheet listing the days and hours of the week. Fill in your work and class hours first. Then try to block out some study hours. It's better to study a little every day than to create a huge once-or-twice-a-week marathon session. Schedule study hours for your hardest classes for the times when you feel most energetic. For example, I battled my tax law textbook in the mornings; when I looked at it after 7:00 p.m., I may as well have been reading Chinese. The usual proportion, by the way, is one hour of study time for every class hour.

17   In case you're one of those people who get carried away, remember to leave blocks of free time, too. You won't be any good to yourself or anyone else if you don't relax and pack in the studying once in a while.

18   *3. A "To Do" List.* This is the secret that single-handedly got me through college. Once a week (or every day if you want to), write a list of what you have to do. Write down everything from "write english paper" to "buy cold cuts for lunches." The best thing about a "to do" list is that it seems to tame all those stray "I have to" thoughts that nag at your mind. Just making the list seems to make the tasks "doable." After you finish something on the list, cross it off. Don't be compulsive about finishing everything; you're not superman or wonder woman. Get the important things done first. The secondary things you don't finish can simply be moved to your next "to do" list.

What Can I Do If Personal Problems Get in the Way of My Studies?

19   One student, Roger, told me this story:

Everything was going OK for me until the middle of the spring semester. I went through a terrible time when I broke up with my girlfriend and started seeing her best friend. I was trying to deal with my ex-girlfriend's hurt and anger, my new girlfriend's guilt, and my own worries and anxieties at the same time. In addition to this, my mother was sick and on a medication that made her really irritable. I hated to go home because the atmosphere was so uncomfortable. Soon, I started missing classes because I couldn't deal with the academic pressures as well as my own personal problems. It seemed easier to hang around my girlfriend's apartment than to face all my problems at home and at school.

20   Another student, Marian, told me:

I'd been married for eight years and the relationship wasn't going too well. I saw the handwriting on the wall, and I decided to prepare for the future. I enrolled in college, because I knew I'd need a decent job to support myself. Well, my husband had a fit because I was going to school. We were arguing a lot anyway, and he made it almost impossible for me to study at home. I think he was angry and almost jealous because I was drawing away from him. It got so bad that I thought about quitting college for a while. I wasn't getting any support at home and it was just too hard to go on.

21   Personal troubles like these are overwhelming when you're going through them. School seems like the least important thing in your life. The two students above are perfect examples of this. But if you think about it, quitting or failing school would be the worst thing for these two students. Roger's problems, at least with his girlfriends, would simmer down eventually, and then he'd regret having left school. Marian had to finish college if she wanted to be able to live independently. Sometimes, you've just got to hang tough.

22   But what do you do while you're trying to live through a lousy time? First of all, do something difficult. Ask yourself, honestly, if you're exaggerating small problems as an excuse to avoid classes and studying. It takes strength to admit this, but there's no sense in kidding yourself. If your problems are serious, and real, try to make some human contacts at school. Lots of students hide inside a miserable shell made of their own troubles and feel isolated and lonely. Believe me, there are plenty of students with problems. Not everyone is getting A's and having a fabulous social and home life at the same time. As you go through the term, you'll pick up some vibrations about the students in your classes. Perhaps someone strikes you as a compatible person. Why not speak to that person after class? Share a cup of coffee in the cafeteria or walk to the parking lot together. You're not looking for a best friend or the love of your life. You just want to build a little network of support for yourself. Sharing your difficulties, questions, and complaints with a friendly person on campus can make a world of difference in how you feel.

23   Finally, if your problems are overwhelming, get some professional help. Why do you think colleges spend countless dollars on counseling departments and campus psychiatric services? More than ever, students all over the country are taking advantage of the help offered by support groups and therapy sessions. There's no shame attached to asking for help, either; in fact, almost 40 percent of college students (according to one survey) will use counseling services during their time in school. Just walk into a student centre or counseling office and ask for an appointment. You wouldn't think twice about asking a dentist to help you get rid of your toothache. Counselors are paid—and want—to help you with your problems.

Why Do Some People Make It and Some Drop Out?

24   Anyone who spends at least one semester in college notices that some students give up on their classes. The person who sits behind you in accounting, for example, begins to miss a lot of class meetings and eventually vanishes. Or another student comes to class without the assignment, doodles in his notebook during the lecture, and leaves during the break. What's the difference between students like this and the ones who succeed in school? My survey may be nonscientific, but everyone I asked said the same thing: attitude. A positive attitude is the key to everything else—good study habits, smart time scheduling, and coping with personal difficulties.

25   What does "a positive attitude" mean? Well, for one thing, it means avoiding the zombie syndrome. It means not only showing up for your classes, but also doing something while you're there. Really listen. Take notes. Ask a question if you want to. Don't just walk into a class, put your mind in neutral, and drift away to never-never land.

26   Having a positive attitude goes deeper than this, though. It means being mature about college as an institution. Too many students approach college classes like six-year-olds who expect first grade to be as much fun as Sesame Street. First grade, as we all know, isn't as much fun as Sesame Street. And college classes can sometimes be downright dull and boring. If you let a boring class discourage you so much that you want to leave school, you'll lose in the long run. Look at your priorities. You want a degree, or a certificate, or a career. If you have to, you can make it through a less-than-interesting class in order to achieve what you want. Get whatever you can out of every class. But if you simply can't stand a certain class, be determined to fulfill its requirements and be done with it once and for all.

27   After the initial high of starting school, you have to settle in for the long haul. If you follow the advice here, you'll be prepared to face the academic crunch. You'll also live through the semester without giving up your family, your job, or Monday Night Football. Finally, going to college can be an exciting time. You do learn. And when you learn things, the world becomes a more interesting place.

■ Reading Comprehension Questions

1. The word *queasy* in "with a queasy stomach" (paragraph 3) means
   a. intelligent.
   b. healthy.
   c. full.
   d. nervous.

2. The word *tactics* in "try these three tactics" (paragraph 14) means
   a. proofs.
   b. problems.
   c. methods.
   d. questions.

3. Which of the following would be a good alternative title for this selection?
   a. Your First Day on Campus
   b. Coping with College
   c. How to Budget Your Time
   d. The Benefits of College Skills Courses

4. Which sentence best expresses the main idea of the selection?
   a. In high school, most of us did little homework.
   b. You should give yourself rewards for studying well.
   c. Sometimes personal problems interfere with studying.
   d. You can succeed in college by following certain guidelines.

5. According to the author, "making it" in college means
   a. studying whenever you have any free time.
   b. getting a degree by barely passing your courses.
   c. quitting school until you solve your personal problems.
   d. getting good grades without making your life miserable.

6. If your personal problems seem overwhelming, you should
   a. drop out for a while.
   b. try to ignore them.
   c. tell another student.
   d. seek professional help.

7. Which of the following is *not* described by the author as a means of time control?
   a. Monthly calendar
   b. To-do list
   c. Study schedule
   d. Flexible job hours

8. We might infer that the author
   a. is a writer for the school newspaper.
   b. is president of his or her class.
   c. has taken a study-skills course.
   d. was not a successful student in his or her first year of college.

9. From the selection we can conclude that
   a. college textbooks are very expensive.
   b. it is a good practice to write notes in your textbook.
   c. taking notes on your reading takes too much time.
   d. a student should never mark up an expensive textbook.
10. The author implies that
    a. fewer people than before are attending college.
    b. most students think that college is easy.
    c. most students dislike college.
    d. coping with college is difficult.

■ Discussion Questions

About Content

1. What pitfalls does O'Keeney think are waiting for students just starting college? Are there other pitfalls not mentioned in the article?
2. What is the secret that the author says got him through college? What do you think is the most helpful or important suggestion the author makes in the selection?
3. Do you agree with the author that Roger and Marian should stay in school? Are there any situations in which it would be better for students to quit school or leave temporarily?

About Structure

4. What is the thesis of the selection? In which paragraph is it stated?
5. Why does the article begin with the first day on campus?
6. What method of introduction does the author use in the section on personal problems (starting on page 513)? What is the value of using this method?

About Style and Tone

7. This essay is obviously written for college students. Can you guess where an essay like this one would appear? (**Hint:** Reread the first paragraph.)

■ Writing Assignments

Assignment 1

Write a process essay that explains how to succeed in some other situation—for example, a job, a sport, marriage, child rearing. First, brainstorm the three or four problem areas a newcomer to this experience might encounter. Then, under each area you have listed, jot down some helpful hints and techniques for overcoming these problems. For example, a process essay on "How to Succeed as a Server" might describe the following problem areas in this kind of job:

- Developing a good memory
- Learning to do tasks quickly
- Coping with troublesome customers

Each supporting paragraph in this essay would discuss specific techniques for dealing with these problems. Be sure that the advice you give is detailed and specific enough to really help a person in such a situation.

Assignment 2

Write a letter to Roger or Marian, giving advice on how to deal with his or her personal problem. You could recommend any or all of the following:

- Face the problem realistically. (By doing what?)
- Make other contacts at school. (How? Where?)
- See a counsellor. (Where? What should this person be told?)
- Realize that the problem is not so serious. (Why not?)
- Ignore the problem. (How? By doing what instead?)

In your introductory paragraph, explain why you are writing the letter. Include a thesis statement that says what plan of action you are recommending. Then, in the rest of the letter, explain that plan of action in detail.

Assignment 3

Write a third-person essay contrasting college or university *as students imagine it will be* with college or university *as it is*.

For instance, you may decide to contrast expectations of (1) a residence or rented room, (2) roommates, and (3) night-life, with reality. Alternatively, you could contrast your expectations of (1) fellow students, (2) professors, and (3) postsecondary courses, with reality.

Before making an outline, decide whether you will use the *one-side-at-a-time* or *point-by-point* method of development.

Online **Learning**Centre

Index